The
FABLIAUX

The

FABLIAUX

A NEW VERSE TRANSLATION

Translated by NATHANIEL E. DUBIN

Introduction by R. HOWARD BLOCH

LIVERIGHT PUBLISHING CORPORATION
A Division of W. W. Norton & Company
New York · London

Frontispiece: *The Consummation of Marriage*. Illuminated manuscript page from Aegidi Colonna, *The Trojan War in the Version of Martinus Opifex*, 1445/50, Inv. Hs. 2273, fol. 18. Oesterreichische Nationalbibliothek, Vienna, Austria. Photograph credit: bpk, Berlin / Oesterreichische Nationalbibliothek, Vienna, Austria / Art Resource, NY

Decorative border: Judith Stagnitto Abbate

For information about permission to reproduce selections from this book, write to Permissions, Liveright Publishing Corporation, a division of W. W. Norton & Company, Inc., 500 Fifth Avenue, New York, NY 10110

For information about special discounts for bulk purchases, please contact W. W. Norton Special Sales at specialsales@wwnorton.com or 800-233-4830

Manufacturing by RR Donnelley, Crawfordsville, VA
Book design by Judith Stagnitto Abbate / Abbate Design
Production manager: Anna Oler

Library of Congress Cataloging-in-Publication Data

The fabliaux : a new verse translation / translated by Nathaniel E. Dubin ; introduction by R. Howard Bloch. — First edition
    pages cm
Includes bibliographical references.
Poems in English with parallel Old French text.
ISBN 978-0-87140-357-5 (hardcover)
I. Fabliaux—Translations into English. 2. French poetry—To 1500—Translations into English. 3. Fabliaux. 4. French poetry—To 1500.
I. Dubin, Nathaniel E., translator. II. Bloch, R. Howard.
III. Fabliaux. English.
PQ1319.F25 2013
841'.03'08—dc23

                                        2013002314

Liveright Publishing Corporation
500 Fifth Avenue, New York, N.Y. 10110
www.wwnorton.com

W. W. Norton & Company Ltd.
Castle House, 75/76 Wells Street, London W1T 3QT

1 2 3 4 5 6 7 8 9 0

*F*or my mother, the content of
these tales notwithstanding

CONTENTS

THE FABLIAUX

INTRODUCTION

HE OLD FRENCH comic tale in verse, or fabliau, lies at the origin of European realist literature—part of that "other Middle Ages" opposed to the official culture and high-minded teachings of the Church on matters like money, food, and sex. Scandalous at the time of their creation in the late twelfth century through the early fourteenth, they are still outrageous today. The fabliaux live on in the comic tradition of the West among the tales of Boccaccio, Chaucer, and Lope de Vega, as well as in the German Schwänke and the writings of Rabelais, Molière, and La Fontaine. They are the ancestors of the modern short story, especially of the drôle type, those of Balzac, O. Henry, Mark Twain, or Maupassant. Yet the fabliaux themselves were virtually unknown between the sixteenth-century Renaissance and the rediscovery of the Middle Ages, beginning around 1830 in England, Germany, and France. Even then, they were read by only a handful of antiquarians and scholars.

Not until the present translation has a significant body of the fabliaux been available in a modern anthology—in French, English, or any language—for the general reader. The richness of this collection, which surpasses even the most elaborate medieval manuscript, brings the comic tale to life, after eight hundred years, in a way that it has never lived at any moment in the past. There is, in the pages that follow, a wealth of surprise, enjoyment, and information about one of the great moments of turning in the West, and one of the formative stages in a world still recognizably our own.

To understand just how important the fabliaux are, it is worth reviewing a bit the story of their discovery and the early history of their reception in nineteenth-century France.

Carl von Clausewitz (1780–1831) famously wrote that "war is a continuation of political relations by other means." In the wake of the Napoleonic Wars and the Romantic rejection of the classical past and its stress upon universal man, the awakening nations of Europe turned to the Middle Ages as a way of asserting cultural and territorial claims. Scholarship became "a continuation of war by other means." The Germans discovered their great national epic, *The Niebelungenlied*, at the end of the eighteenth century and used this story of the defeat of the Burgundians by the Huns as a rallying cry after Napoleon vanquished them in 1806. The English discovered *Beowulf* in 1815, the very year the English and the Prussians defeated the French at Waterloo. Never mind that they originally thought it was written in Danish; by 1833, *Beowulf* had been translated into English. That was the year that François Guizot, French minister of public instruction, granted a scholarship of one thousand francs to a young man by the name of Francisque Michel for "a literary voyage to England," with the understanding that Michel was to hunt for Old French manuscripts in English libraries and museums. On July 13, 1835, Michel discovered in Oxford's Bodleian Library what he believed to be the poem sung by Norman knights at the Battle of Hastings (1066), the French conquest of England, a feat of which Napoleon, who died in 1821, had dreamed of repeating as late as 1803. The French had found, at last, their national epic, *The Song of Roland*, a seemingly oral poem written down around the time of the First Crusade (1096), which, in relatively short order, scholars began to compare with Homeric song—a French *Iliad*, no less.

The fabliaux did not fare as well as the epic when it came to making national identity. Though some had been published in the 1750s, and the wicked Diderot had anonymously transformed the tale of "The Knight Who Made Cunts Talk" into a satire of Louis XV in *The Indiscreet Jewels* (*Les Bijoux indiscrets*), the medieval comic tale did not become the subject of scholarly speculation until the middle of the nineteenth century.

The fabliaux depict the enterprising, clever inhabitants of the towns of twelfth- and thirteenth-century northern France, an image of resourcefulness that, at first, appealed to the bourgeois leaders of the industrial and commercial revolution under the Second Empire (1852–1870). Those who would create modern secular France saw in this early version of their bourgeois selves an alternative to aristocratic ladies and knights, kings and courtiers, warrior bishops and pious hermits of the elevated Old French epic and chivalric romance. These literary types belonged to the Old Regime and no longer resonated with the interests and sympathies of a rising middle class. However, scholars soon realized that the outrageously obscene, anticlerical, misogynistic fabliaux, which wildly violate any notion of bourgeois respectability, were an embarrassment, and hardly the stuff of national moral revival. Victor Le Clerc, author of volume 23 of the Benedictine *Literary History of France* (1856), simply refused to speak of the fabliau "The Piece of Shit," in which a peasant woman manages to get her husband to eat a little dropping that she delicately lifts from under her skirt as the couple sits warming themselves around the fire during the long winters of northern France.

By the time of the Franco-Prussian War (1870–

1871), every effort was made to displace the origin of the medieval comic tale as far as possible from France. Gaston Paris, the father of medieval studies, was inspired by the Orientalist theories of German folklorists. He located the origins of the fabliaux in the *Panchatantra*, an ancient Sanskrit collection of animal fables, subsequently translated into Pehlvi, or Middle Persian, from which they were rendered into Syriac, Arabic, Hebrew, and, eventually, into Latin and various vernacular tongues in a long caravan of tales leading from India to France. The first editor of a complete edition in the original language, Anatole de Courde de Montaiglon, writing in the period just after the war with Germany and the beginning of the long wave of anti-Semitism that would culminate at the end of the century in the Dreyfus affair, stresses the semitic roots of the obscene tales in Old French. "The first are the Arabs, but they would not have sufficed. The second and true intermediary is the cosmopolitan people par excellence, the only ones to be so in the Middle Ages, that is the Jews, themselves oriental in spirit and tradition. They alone knew enough Arabic to translate the tales into Latin, the universal tongue by which a tale as well as an idea might enter the European current." De Montaiglon, who confessed to not knowing a single word of Hebrew, considered the Talmud to be a written reservoir of Indian and Persian lore. Both Paris's and de Montaiglon's Orientalist projection of the scandal of the fabliaux outside of France was finally countered by Paris's student Joseph Bédier, who demonstrated in 1893 that only eleven of the one hundred and sixty or so tales show the least bit of resemblance to ancient Eastern sources. But Bédier didn't exactly locate their origin upon native soil. Rather, he opted for the polygenesis of popular tales, part of a universal folklore to be found in Ancient Greece and India as well as in medieval Italy, Germany,

Spain, and France. If everyone is to blame, where, then, is the fault?

Part of a naturalistic sensualism of the High Middle Ages, a celebration of the appetites, the fabliaux make the body speak, and Nathaniel Dubin's translation makes them speak English. These letter-perfect renderings of the original, honed to the highest philological standard, chime marvelously with the light tone and lively pace of the rhymed Old French octosyllabic couplet. This is one of the great translations of medieval literature, which also features the Old French original language, in an edition so heedful of the medieval manuscript tradition that it can also be used reliably by specialists in any field of medieval studies.

Like Seamus Heaney's translation of *Beowulf*, Marie Borroff's *Sir Gawain and the Green Knight*, or Simon Armitage's *Death of King Arthur*, Dubin reproduces the world and the feeling of the medieval tale, and finds linguistically and culturally resonant equivalents for words and things, poetic patterns, and patterns of thought that travel joyfully from the Middle Ages to the present. Thus, in "The Blacksmith of Creil," Dubin captures all the medieval poet's naughty reveling in the apprentice's epically proportioned "well-sharpened tool":

> *that's served to women as a treat,*
> *God's honest truth, one shaped so fair*
> *that Nature must have lavished care*
> *to make it, and surpassed her craft,*
> *around the bottom of the shaft*
> *two palms in length, wide as a fist.*
> *A hole, though shaped like an ellipse,*
> *in which this well-hung stud had placed it*
> *would look as if a compass traced it,*
> *so very round would it become.*
> *About his balls I'll not keep mum,*

> hanging between his ass and pizzle
> like mallets sculpted with a chisel,
> befitting such a master tool.

Dubin's felicitous phrase, which sums up the medieval topos of Natura Creatrix, is an instance of genius in translation: "The blacksmith goes right on repeating / the young man's praises, waxes lyric / in superphallic panegyric. . . ."

Old French had lost tonic word stress by the time the fabliaux were written, yet modern English is highly stressed. Dubin compensates by liberal use of enjambment and slant rhyme. The effect is one of astonishment at the nearly perfect word-for-word, line-by-line renderings, as at the beginning of "The Fisherman of Pont-sur-Seine":

J'oï conter l'autre semaine	*Last week I heard a fisherman*
c'uns peschieres de Pont seur Saine	*who plied his trade at Pont-sur-Seine*
espousa fame baudement;	*married a woman lustily*
assez i prist vin & forment	*with wine and wheat as dowry,*
& .v. vaches & .x. brebis.	*and five milch cows, also ten ewes.*
La meschinete & ses maris	*Each of the married couple views*
s'entramoient de bone amor.	*the other with a tender heart.*

Dubin has a thorough mastery of the rhythms and rhymes of the original, and of the meanings of Old French and English words. The fisherman's wife, who becomes convinced that her husband has been castrated by thieves encountered along the river, sues for divorce, then, in the final division of property, sticks her hand into her husband's pocket, only to discover his body is whole after all: "She calls her servant straightaway: / 'Bring back the animals, I say!' / She calls out loud, 'Bring back the beef! / Return the stock! It's my belief / my husband's meat has been restored / by God, our wonder-working Lord.'" The word *beef, bestes* in Old French, like *meat* in English, is a common euphemism for *penis.* Dubin's translation captures not only the cultural specificity of the word but also the wife's pretentiously prudish avoidance throughout the poem of calling her husband's penis—his "little hanging bit of bowel," his "devilish, dingle-dangle thing"—by its proper name.

In "The Crucified Priest," a sculptor who suspects his wife is unfaithful pretends to leave the house in order to sell at market a crucifix he has just made. No sooner is Roger out the door than the village priest arrives, and Father Coustenz, so named because he is such a constant threat to the sanctity of the household, sits down for a meal with the sculptor's wife as a prelude to more sensual fare. And no sooner have they begun to eat than Roger, who has noticed his wife's elation at his departure, returns to catch the adulterous couple in flagrante delicto. With no exit in sight, the wife advises her lover to slip into Roger's workshop, take off his clothes, and, "standing still, assume a pose among my husband's holy carvings." Roger, meanwhile, pretends to notice nothing, and, after a leisurely dinner, rises from the table, sharpens his carver's knife, and heads to the workshop to complete a bit of unfinished work:

> *The master carver soon caught sight*
> *of the priest with his arms stretched out,*
> *whom he could spot beyond a doubt,*
> *seeing his hanging balls and cock.*
> *"Lady," he says, "I've made a shock-*
> *ing image here by not omitting*
> *those virile members. How unfitting!*
> *I must have had too much to drink.*
> *Some light! I'll fix it in a wink."*

> *The terrified priest never stirred.*
> *The husband, you can take my word,*
> *cut off the prelate's genitalia*
> *and left him nothing, without failure,*
> *to warrant further amputation.*
> *The priest, feeling the laceration,*
> *took to his heels and ran away.*

Captured in flight, Father Coustenz escapes with his life by paying Roger a ransom of fifteen pounds. The moral of the story reflects a tension between the clergy and the relatively new and fragile domestic unit of the nuclear family in the burgeoning urban centers of thirteenth-century France. It bespeaks suspicion of those who heard the confessions of wives in an intimacy more properly reserved for the conjugal bedroom: "This parable has demonstrated, / no matter who is implicated, / in no case should a clergyman / mess with the wife of any man / or hang around her. I allege / he'll leave his balls there as a pledge, / just as the priest, Father Coustenz, / left his three hanging ornaments."

"The Crucified Priest" is typical of the fabliaux. The style and tone are light and lively, the rhymes slightly doggerel—this despite the underlying seriousness of subject and social effect. The anonymous poet or jongleur manages to present an abundance of action and realistic detail with little elaboration or description. The events of "The Crucified Priest" are compressed within the short space of only one hundred lines. The plot, consisting of a single episode and its immediate consequences, is tightly structured around a limited number of characters who, in the absence of real psychological development, are nonetheless a bundle of anxieties and potential delights. The poet presents within the framing symmetry of the duper duped a host of themes characteristic of the genre as a whole: conjugal life as a struggle for mastery; the adulterous triangle consisting of the husband, wife, and her lover, who more often than not is a priest; the creative use of invented stories and disguise; a certain antifeminism; a profit to be derived from thinking quickly on one's feet.

The fabliaux belong to an abundant medieval Latin and vernacular literature intended both to instruct and amuse. Unlike other literary forms of the period—the elevated epic, the courtly romance, and lyric verse, which are meant to inspire noble deeds or lament unhappy love—these often scandalous works are filled with the celebration of bodily appetites: sexual, economic, and gastronomic, and, yes, even a human need for laughter.

Of the one hundred and sixty or so examples of these "comic tales in verse," most are anonymous. Only a few can be attributed to known authors like Jean Bodel, Rutebeuf, or Jean de Condé. To judge by the original language preserved in some forty-three manuscripts, the fabliaux are products of the north and northwest part of France. They portray the goings-on of those who inhabit Picardy, Hainaut, and Normandy, with specific mention of such towns as Cambrai, Abbeville, Compiègne, Arras, Douai, Amiens, and Paris. Urban in outlook, they extol the values of markets and of towns—quick wits, an ability to assess and to anticipate the actions of others, inventiveness when it comes to buying and selling, flexibility, a sense of timing, and persistence.

Though little is known about the medieval audience for the fabliaux, we surmise, from frequent reference to the *jongleur's* having heard his tale elsewhere, that this was an oral form. Like most works composed before the fourteenth century, the fabliaux were intended either to be recited or read aloud. No doubt they were performed publicly at fairs, markets, and in the village square, but there is nothing to deny their performance within the walls of the castle or home. At one time, scholars debated passionately about whether those for whom the fabliaux were created belonged to the upper echelons of society or to the growing class of townspeople gathered in the cities of the north. Most experts now agree that the audience, like that of today's popular literature, was probably mixed and consisted not only of castellans, ladies, and knights living at court but also of that burgeoning group of ordinary townspeople whose habitual life the fabliaux depict.

The fabliaux are a social mirror of their time. This first important expression of European literary realism represents an extremely valuable source of information about daily life in an age from which few documents survive, and those which do survive deal with domains of thought and imagination far removed from everyday experience. Despite the exaggeration, the absurdity, and the scandal of, say, an adulterous priest masquerading as the crucified Christ, the comic tale bears witness to the great urban renaissance of the twelfth century as well as to what went on in the countryside. This world of feudalism in decline, of renewed economic activity, of manufacturing, transportation, and selling of goods, of rampant materialism and social mobility, yields a panoramic image of dispossessed knights and rich peasants, and of the "new men" exercising the new trades connected to the revival of European commerce: salt and spice merchants, bakers, grocers, blacksmiths and artisans, seamstresses, money changers, bookkeepers, carters, wandering students and clerics, as well as the prostitutes, pimps, procuresses, dicers, and thieves who inhabit the demimonde of the brothels and taverns in which so many scenes from the fabliaux take place.

Witness to the rise of a middle class, the comic tale is filled with middlemen and ne'er-do-wells who freeload, like the impoverished antiheroic hero who "had no trade, but used to go / from town to town, where in the castles / of various and sundry vassals / he lodged and ate at their expense"—and who admits to making his living as a professional fornicator: "I am a fucker one can hire, / and I maintain, if you require / my services, I'll service you, / and you'll be thankful for them, too!" The fabliaux are a key to the habits of the common people of the High Middle Ages, to how men and women worked, traveled, ate, bathed, slept, made love, eliminated, wiped their posterior parts, dressed, arranged their hair, made up their faces. They are a virtual catalog not only of the "arts and trades" of medieval France but of the orders of society—ecclesiastical and lay, rural and urban, noble, bourgeois, and peasant. With one notable exception: they contain few examples of the great feudal princes, the barons and dukes who dominate the epic and the romance; and the king of France is completely absent.

The fabliaux provide a unique vision of the emerging domestic unit, its living arrangements, and the means by which those living under the same roof related to one another in what is an embryonic version of the modern nuclear family. Like ancient comedy, the medieval comic tale is the literary form appropriate to the representation of the family, depicting as it does the private life of the thirteenth-century household. These comic tales take us into the living rooms of rich bourgeois. More important, they take us into their bedrooms, where we are treated to a privileged view of medieval erotic life.

The eroticism of the fabliaux is part of a general atmosphere of sensuality, a hedonistic materialism combining appreciation of money and goods, good food and wine, the bath, which often functions as an aphrodisiac, and lovemaking. Indeed, the eroticism of the fabliaux is directly physical, unproblematic, unrepressed, and, against the grain of the Church's official prohibition of sexual pleasure even within marriage, an essential aspect of the healthy satisfaction of human appetites.

The fabliaux display a panoply of erotic activities and delights, of pleasures derived from making love, and even from voyeurism. In "The Mourner Who Got Fucked at the Grave Site," a medieval version of the classical "Widow of Ephesus," the knight who observes his squire making love to the amorous widow "almost faints with pleasure." And the young husband of "The Two Money Changers," by deliberately exposing the body of his mistress to her husband, who is also his best friend, makes it clear that looking can be as important a source of erotic pleasure for the two men as the act itself.

The fabliaux celebrate the body and all its parts. Descriptions of genitalia are as great a source of pleasure as the sexual act itself. "The Ring That Controls Erections" describes a priest whose organ remains—to the wonderment of all—in a state of perpetual tumescence. "Saint Martin's Four Wishes," the story of a peasant who gives the first of four marvelous wishes to the wife who requests that he be covered by pricks, is a virtual paean to the penis: "Then, as soon as the woman spoke, / hundreds of pricks began to poke / out all over. Penises grew / around his nose and his mouth, too. / Some pricks were thick, some oversized, / some long, some short, some circumcised, / curved pricks, straight pricks, pointed and hardy . . . / every bone in the peasant's body / was miraculously endowed / and prickled, fully cocked and proud. . . ."

The fabliaux foreground the female genitalia with a worshipful enthusiasm equal to that for the male. The husband of "Saint Martin's Four Wishes," covered with phalluses, wishes a corresponding fate for his wife, who is immediately covered with as many vaginas as he has pricks: "At once the cunts start to arise. / A pair appears before her eyes, / four on her forehead in a row, / and cunts above, and cunts below, / and cunts behind, and cunts in front, / every variety of cunt— / bent cunts, straight cunts, cunts gray and hoary, / cunts without hair, cunts thick and furry, / and virgin cunts, narrow and tight, / wide, gaping cunts, and cunts made right, / cunts large and small, oval and round, / deep cunts, and cunts raised on a mound, / cunts on her head, cunts on her feet . . . / the peasant's joy is now complete."

Much of the humor of the fabliaux, the comedy of situation, the satire of women, peasants, and priests, the wordplay, and the parody of high literary forms, like the epic catalogs of genitalia, is alien, and even shocking, to the modern sensibility. Yet the medieval comic tale unlocks the world of the body and the senses before the Protestant Reformation, which made later generations sheepish and afraid of the appetites and pleasures, the lusts and thrusts, the passions and peccadilloes of a less repressed time. One can never return, of course, to that happier age before we learned to be ashamed of our desires and fantasies, no matter how absurd, but the tales that Nathaniel Dubin has assembled and translated with such skill and verve are the stuff of pure enjoyment, and a royal road to inhabiting realms and selves distant from our own.

—R. Howard Bloch

TRANSLATOR'S NOTE

I FIRST TURNED my attention to the fabliaux not as a translator, but as a scholar. At the time, I had only a passing acquaintance with the genre, having hitherto focused primarily on those works that burlesque the courtly tradition. As I read more of them, I came to realize the fabliaux differed from short comic romances in more than their focus on priests, peasants, and women. Unlike other forms of medieval narrative, meant to be read aloud, the fabliau authors intended their work for performance. One senses in these texts a storyteller relating to his audience. In fact, the fabliaux contain a fair number of sentences a medieval audience would have found difficult to follow without the gestures and vocal inflections of a performer.

When I turned my hand to translating some of them—I never expected to translate so many (this volume contains only half of those I have done)—I wanted above all to capture the telling. Many of the stories are funny in and of themselves, but even those that are not are told with a verve that provokes laughter. Recent criticism has shown the thematic richness of these texts, and they certainly merit study, but without the wordplay and funny rhymes, they fall flat. In order to give the modern English reader a feeling for these poems, I felt it imperative to respect the integrity of the individual line, to preserve humor and wordplay wherever possible, to give a feeling of performance, and to re-create a reasonable facsimile of the rhythms, all as I understand and hear it. My translation of the exaggeratedly rhetorical opening of the exordium to "The Fucker" (#59) shows how far I will go to achieve this (1–4):

Qui fabloier velt, si fabloit,	*Let fabulists confabulate;*
mais que son dit n'en affebloit	*but tales too fabulous deflate*
por dire chose desresnable.	*a fable's worth and make it feeble.*
L'en puet si bel dire une fable. . . .	*A tale well told can please the people. . . .*

Fortunately, the English language, with its long tradition of humorous verse, is singularly suited to approximate the Old French originals, more so, in fact, than contemporary French.

For one, the syntax of English has a fluidity much like that of Old French, whereas the rigid structure of the Modern French sentence does not. Modern French is a relatively precise language, whereas vagueness does not bother Old French and English speakers.

Old French differs in its tendency to switch between past and present narration for no apparent reason. Rhyme and meter permitting, I follow what is found in the manuscripts, although many readers may find this jarring. Likewise, I have punctuated my English sentences idiosyncratically in an attempt to re-create the breathless, run-on quality of the Old French storytelling.

When it comes to how the languages sound, the phonetic composition of Old French and English is also similar, especially the consonants. That Old and Modern French contrast with English is of no consequence to a translator, but when it comes to verse, rhythm is. Old French accentual patterns resemble French as it is spoken today, with almost no stress accent for individual words, and do not sound at all like English. Their octosyllabic verses are composed of eight syllables, not of four metric feet. I have tried to reproduce this effect by keeping as close to a line-by-line translation as possible, disregarding the number and placement of stresses in each line, and making frequent use of enjambment. I solve the problem of holding to the meter in the same way the fabliau authors did, by doubling a word with a near synonym or adding or omitting fillers. Where the Old French contains an expression that serves no other function than filling up the line, there is no reason to include it if the English line is complete without it, and where the English line is short a few syllables, it does no harm to add a filler the fabliau authors often threw in. (They showed a special fondness for adverbial phrases that mean "quickly" or "suddenly." Their characters seem never to take their time.)

Fabliau diction is not literary. Of course no one spoke in rhymed couplets, but in all other ways the language reflects the everyday speech of the times, so I have translated colloquially to make the voices sound natural. In dialogue, it would not do to translate terms of address literally and have a man call a nun "lady" and his wife "sister." Many Old French words, such as those for town officials, have no exact English equivalent; with others, such as *clerc*, which can refer to any rank in the Church hierarchy, from parish priest to bishop, or may merely designate a student, it is not always possible to tell which one is meant. Proverbs abound in the fabliaux, and these I translate with a semiliteral adaptation instead of looking for an English equivalent. I likewise follow Old French usage for oaths and swearing. These people do not take oaths "on their honor" or swear using sexual terms; they call the saints or take their names in vain. They often have a reason for choosing a particular saint, so I never substitute one saint for another, although I may not know why they chose the one they did. Sexual terms are used only to talk about sex, and in the fabliaux, they talk about it a lot.

Translating the sexual passages did not come easily. In English, we have respectable words and dirty words for every sexual act and organ. With very few exceptions (for example, *urinate* and *piss*), there was only one word in Old French. I therefore had to decide in each case how obscene to make my translation. They did have innocent euphemisms, like *chose* ("thing") or *outil* ("tool") for a man's penis, and also humorous ones, like *pasnais* ("parsnip"), but often the euphemisms are more scabrous than the correct word. The fabliau authors delighted in inventing their own euphemisms and metaphors, and enlarged on them in tasteless detail, like the "instruments" used for bloodletting and the tube of soothing salve in "The Healer" (#44) or the orgasmic vomiting in "The Squirrel" (#60). Also, since in French the word for the male organ has greater shock value than its female counterpart and the reverse is true of English, translating a fabliau inevitably makes it either more or less obscene than the original. Similarly, there are no offensive or titillating terms for the female bosom. Our mores differ, and even the most successful translation cannot elicit an identical reaction from medieval French and English-speaking audiences. But the same is true of the stories themselves. Misogyny, rape, severe beatings, mockery of the disabled, et cetera, did not disturb them as it does us.

Translating wordplay, a basic element of fabliau style, poses a challenge, though not as great a challenge as one might expect. English often enough has an exact or very close equivalent for an Old French pun, especially when the word in question is slang. Take, for example, the last line of "The Girl Who Wanted to Fly" (#27) ("she ended up stuck with a tail") or the extended metaphor for sexual intercourse of a ferret hunting a rabbit (*conin*) in "The Priest and the Woman" (#42). *Conin* is also a diminutive of *con* ("cunt"). In English, we have the words *coney* and *cunny*. Where English offers an opportunity for wordplay that the French does not, in the spirit of the fabliaux, I seize it. Thus, in the same fabliau, "once the priest's sated and he has rung out both his bells." The author's euphemism for orgasm is not a pun in the original. If English cannot pun on the same word as in French, I try to find another word to play with in the same line or a neighboring line and thus clue the reader in on the joke. One can even find an equivalent when the wordplay is a cultural referent. "The Peasant's Fart" (#37) cites a proverb with one word altered: In place of *Trop estraindre fait cheoir*, we find *chiier* ("Clutching too tightly makes you drop something / shit"), which I have rendered as "One lets loose when one grips too tightly." The pun is funnier than the vulgarism. Finally, a few fabliaux are little else than extended wordplay, like "The Two Englishmen and the Lamb," which relies on an English speaker's mispronunciation of *agnel* ("lamb") as *anel* ("donkey colt"). Such texts are untranslatable, and I did not attempt them.

To do the translations, I made my own edition of the texts, using the manuscript transcriptions Willem Noomen provides in his *Nouveau Recueil Complet des Fabliaux* (*NRCF*). Where there is only one manuscript witness or we choose the same base manuscript, the resulting texts will be very close, but never, I think, identical. Noomen's critical editions are superlative—indeed, his notes and the diplomatic transcriptions he provides are essential for any serious study of the fabliaux—but we do not always agree on which readings are erroneous or how to correct them, nor did we use the same criteria in preparing our editions. Noomen seeks to produce as close a text as possible to that of the original author; I looked for the version that pleased me most. The fabliaux changed over time not just because of copyists' errors. Very few fabliau authors were consummate artists like Rutebeuf, Jean Bodel, and Gautier le Leu, and the *jongleurs* who performed these works may well have altered them intentionally. Being professional entertainers, they often had a better grasp of what would please an audience.

Interested scholars may access the rejected readings of my base manuscripts online at http://liverightpub .com/books/fabliaux/rejected. The explanatory notes at the end of this volume serve two purposes: to clarify references which may be unfamiliar to the general reader and to assist students with difficult or especially subtle passages in the Old French.

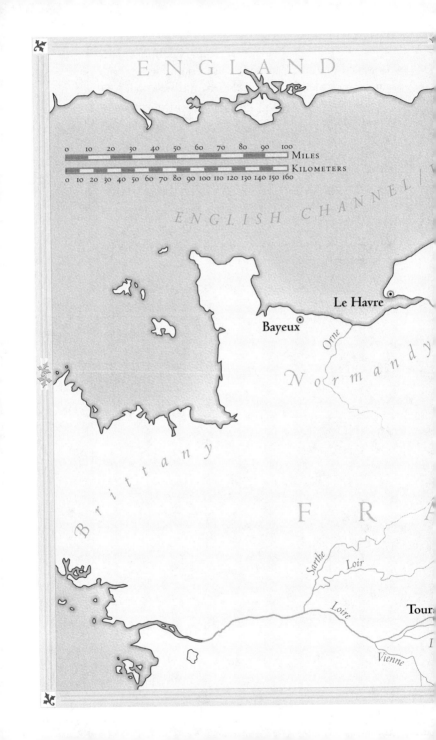

I.

The
SOCIAL FABRIC

NO MEDIEVAL GENRE provides a more exhaustive overview of the society of its times than the fabliaux. Exhaustive, but not accurate. These are not serious sociological studies, but comic tales that present caricatures in impossible situations, a *speculum mundi* that reflects a highly distorted, two-dimensional image.

The first part of this collection brings together texts that give an overview of the world of the fabliaux. We begin with two creation stories and a third fabliau that show how society is organized, followed by a group of tales for each of the three estates—clergy, nobility, the peasants and bourgeoisie—then women, the family unit, and, finally, three set in the afterlife.

The virulent antifeminism of the opening fabliau leaves no doubt how far removed these poems are from the courtly tradition. The next reminds us that God made the world and has ordained a place and purpose for every person in it: priests for praying, knights for defense, the rest of humanity to work, and women to be wives and mothers, subservient to the men who care for them. But it also tells us that if God proposes, man disposes. Almost without exception, the fabliaux present us with lecherous priests, self-serving and none-too-courageous knights, coarse and lazy peasants, and deceitful women.

There is nothing innovative about this point of view. We find the same stereotypes in the works of medieval theologians and moralists. But instead of explicitly condemning the wrongdoers, fabliau authors found this state of affairs amusing. They didn't idealize their world; they accepted it as it was. Such is human nature, and they admired the rapscallion who makes a good job of it. Attempt to rise above your rank and you will fail, but you should nonetheless seize every opportunity to get what you want. Yet there are limits to their daring. When we consider what is missing, for example, even the sexually explicit fabliaux strike us as almost prudish by today's standards. The man is invariably on top but for one comic exception, oral sex is entirely absent, and the rare instances of same-sex relations are all misunderstandings. Their moral stance is thus at once conservative and rebellious. ◆◆◆

1. DU CON QUI FU FAIT
A LA BESCHE

Adans que Nostre Sires fist,
qui puis vers Lui tant se mesfist
qu'il passa son commandement
(se l'Escriture ne nous ment,
5   ce fu par le mors de la pomme) . . .
De la terre forma Dieus l'omme,
puis si en prist une des costes
qu'Il li ot au costé apostes
(onques n'en prist ne plus ne mains),
10   si en fist fame a ses .ii. mains.
Pour ce sueffre fame tant cops
que Nostre Sires le fist d'os.
Qui acoustume fame a batre
.ii. foiz le jor ou .iii. ou .iiii.
15   au premier jor de la semaine,
.x. foiz ou .xii. la quinsaine,
ou ele jeünast ou non,
ele n'en vaudroit se mieus non.
Fame ot biau col & biau viaire;
20   con i oublia Dieus a faire
qu'Il ne s'en estoit donez garde.
      Li maufez i vint & l'esgarde,
.i. petit s'abesse & encline
& vit au tiers neu de l'eschine
25   qu'il n'i avoit c'un seul pertuis;
a Dieu vint & se li dist puis,
« Sire, mal avez esploitié!
A fame faut bien la moitié!
Fetes tost & tornez arriere
30   & metez ou quartier derriere

1. THE CUNT MADE WITH A SPADE

Adam, created by Our Lord,
who afterward defied His word
turning against Him as a rebel
by taking a bite of the apple,
5   if we can trust what scriptures say . . .
God formed man from a lump of clay,
and then He took one of the ribs
He'd placed in his side, and with this,
nor more nor less, with his own two
10   hands He created woman, too.
To suffer blows is woman fated
because from bone she was created
Get your wife used to thrashings, say
two or three or four times a day
15   on the first of the week, or ten
or twelve times every fortnight; then
whether she's fasting or is not,
she'll grow in value quite a lot.
The woman had a lovely neck
20   and face, but God forgot to make
a cunt, so little care He took.
      The Devil came and had a look,
leaned down a bit on an incline
and at the third bump on her spine
25   saw there was only just one hole.
He went to speak to God and told
Him, "Sire, You made an awful gaffe:
The woman's incomplete by half!
So get to work! Make haste, go back to 'er
30   and install in her hinder sector

la chose qui mieus i besoingne,
quar ne vaudroit une eschaloingne
fame s'ele n'avoit tesniere
mise pres de la creponiere.

35 —&, dist Dieus, je n'i puis entendre.
De ce te covient garde prendre. »
Dist deables, « & je comment?
—Je le te di tout vraiement
que tu orendroit le feras,

40 que rien du tien n'i meteras
ne n'en osteras nient du mien. »
Dist le maufez, « Jel ferai bien. »
Dont prist li deables martiaus
& doleoires & cisiaus,

45 besches trenchanz & besaguës
& granz coingnies esmolues,
& regarda selonc son chieus
li quels des feremenz vaut mieus
a l'uevre fere q'ot empris,

50 & dist ja n'i sera repris
que il n'i face une grant roie
car d'autrui cuir, large corroie.
Trestoz les feremenz esgarde
.i. a un, que point ne s'i tarde,

55 & quant il a trestout veü,
si a molt bien aparceü
que la besche est assez trenchant,
s'en puet on fere maintenant
une grande fosse & parfonde.

60 Il dist qu'il n'a si bone el monde,
la besche prent & si s'afiche,
toute enz jusqu'au manche la fiche,
ainsi fist le con a la besche;
vers la fame .i. petit s'abesse,

65 .i. pet li a fet sor la langue.
Por ce a fame tant de jangle,

the thing that is most necessary,
because a woman isn't very
valuable when there's no burrow
placed close by her posterior furrow."
35 "Eh, what?" said God. "I can't see to it.
You'll have to go yourself and do it."
The Devil answered, "I? And how?"
"I'm telling you to do it now,
and I mean what I say. Eschew
40 putting in something made by you
and remove nothing that I've made."
"I'll do just that," the Devil said.
The Devil gathered hammers, adzes,
chisels, mattocks, sharpened axes,
45 cutting tools with double blades,
pruning hooks and trenchant spades,
and gave the tools a close inspection
in order to make his selection
to do the job he undertook,
50 saying that no one will rebuke
him if he makes a spacious trough.
(An ample suit from other's cloth.)
He looked at every implement
one by one, not much time he spent,
55 and when he'd taken time to view
them all, he was convinced he knew
that with the sharp edge of the spade
a great, deep crevice could be made
in scarcely any time at all.
60 He said that there's no better tool
on earth, and takes the spade and pushes
it all in till the handle touches.
Thus with a spade he made the cunt.
He squatted down a bit in front
65 of her and farted on her tongue.
That's why all women, old and young,

por ce borde ele & jangle tant,
& quant li pes li vint devant,
ele le cuida geter hors,
70 mes le pet li remest ou cors
que li deables i lessa
quant sus la fame s'abessa.
Por ce le doit l'en molt soufrir,
de parler ne se puet tenir
75 se n'est par amors ou par don.
          Ja Dieus ne li face pardon
qui d'eles dira fors que bien
ne de lor cons por nule rien,
quar il i a molt bon estruit,
80 mes maint preudomme en sont destruit,
honi en sont & confondu
& lor avoir en ont perdu.

2. DES PUTAINS ET DES LECHEORS

Quant Dieus ot estoré lo monde
si com il est a la reonde
& quanquë il convint dedenz,
.iii. ordres establi de genz
5 & fist el siecle demoranz
clers, [ ] chevaliers [&] laboranz.
Les chevaliers toz asena
as terres, & as clers dona
les aumosnes & les dimages,
10 puis asena les laborages
as laboranz por laborer.
Quant ce ot fet, sanz demorer
d'iluec parti [si] s'en ala.
          Quant Il s'en partoit, veü a

must chatter on and talk such drivel.
Faced with the fart laid by the Devil,
she tried to push it from her mouth,
70   but still today their bodies house
the fart the Devil left inside
when he crouched by the woman's side.
It's something we have to accept:
She won't give up talking except
75   to be nice or to wheedle gifts.

       I pray that God never forgives
whoever seeks to vilify
them or their cunts, no matter why,
for there's fine workmanship in them,
80   but they've destroyed many good men,
who've come to grief and been disgraced
and lost what wealth they once possessed.

2. TROLLOPS AND TROUPERS

When God first made and filled the earth
with people and throughout its girth
all creatures that belong there, then
He set up three orders of men
5   to live on earth by His decree:
the clergy, knights, and peasantry.
Each has his place. He gave the rights
to own and govern to the knights,
and to the clergy tithes and alms,
10   and last of all He gave the farms
to peasants to be sown and tilled,
and thereupon, His task fulfilled,
He left His creatures and withdrew.
       As He was leaving, into view

15 une torbe de tricheors,
 sicom putains & lecheors.
 Poi ot alé quant l'aprochierent,
 a crïer entr'aus commencierent:
 « Estez, Sire! Parlez a nos!
20 Ne nos lessiez! O alez vos?
 De rien ne somes asené,
 si avez as autres doné! »
 Nostre Sire ses esgarda
 quant les oï, si demanda
25 saint [Piere], qui o Lui estoit,
 de cele gent qui la estoit.
 « C'est une gent, fet il, sorfete,
 que Vos avez autresi fete
 com çaus qui de Vos molt se fïent;
30 si huient aprés Vos & crïent
 que lor faciez asenement. »
 Nostre Sires isnelement,
 ançois que riens lor respondist,
 as chevaliers vint, si lor dist:
35 « Vos cui les terres abandoi[n],
 les lecheors vos bail & doin
 que vos d'aus grant cure preigniez
 & qu'entor vos les retaigniez
 que il n'aient de vos soufraite;
40 ne ma parole ne soit fraite,
 mes donez lor a lor demant.
 & a vos, saignor clerc, commant
 les putains molt bien a garder;
 issi le vos voil commander. »
45 Selonc cestui commandement
 ne font il nul trespassement,
 car il les tienent totes chieres,
 si les tienent a beles chieres
 del miaus qu'il ont & del plus bel.

15 there came the profligates in hordes,
    the entertainers and the bawds.
    He'd not gone far when they approached Him,
    began to cry out, and reproached Him:
    "Where are You going, Lord? Do say
20 a word to us! Don't leave us! Stay!
    We're given nothing and are slighted,
    though for the others You've provided."
    Hearing them, our Heavenly Sire
    looked on them and deigned to inquire
25 of Saint Peter, who's standing near,
    about those people over there.
    He answered, "They're a surly race
    also created through Your grace.
    Like those who place their trust in You,
30 they're clamoring that for them, too,
    You see fit to make some provision."
        Our Lord corrected the omission,
    but spoke no word to them; instead
    He went straight to the knights and said,
35 "You lords to whom I gave all lands
    to rule, I now place in your hands
    the entertainers as your charge
    to live among your entourage.
    Be generous and openhanded
40 with them, for I, your God, command it,
    and do not treat them with disdain.
    And you, My clergy, shall maintain
    the harlots under your protection
    in accordance with My direction."
45   In keeping with the Lord's decree,
    the clergy supports harlotry,
    holding these women in esteem
    and making sure they get the cream
    of all of Mother Church's riches.

50 Selonc lou sen de mon fablel,
se vos l'avez bien entendu,
sont tuit li chevalier perdu,
qui les lecheors tienent vis
& d'aus les font sovent eschis.
55 Aler les font sovent deschauz,
mes putains ont peliçons chauz,
dobles mantiaus, dobles sorcoz.
Petit truevent de tiels escoz
li lecheor as chevaliers,
60 & si sont il molt bons parliers;
ne lor donent for viez drapiaus
& petit de lor bons morsiaus,
en gitant com as chiens lor rüent,
mes putains sovent robes müent,
65 avec les clers cochent & lievent,
& sor lor despanses enbrievent.
Li clerc lo font por aus salver,
mes li chevalier sont aver
as lecheors, si se traïssent
70 quant del commandement Dieu issent;
mes ce ne font li clerc noiant:
il sont large & obediant
as putains—l'oevre lo tesmoingne!—
& despendent lor patremoinne
75 & les biens au crucefié.
En tel gent sont il enploié,
des rentes, des dismes, li bien;
a cest conte font li clerc bien
desor toz les autres que font.
80 Se mes fabliaus dit voir, donc sont
par cest commant li clerc sauvé
& li chevalier sont dampné.

50 Contrariwise, my fable teaches,
    if you have understood it well,
    as for the knights, they'll go to Hell.
    They look with scorn on the performers,
    who must live poorer than a dormouse
55 and go about without a pair
    of shoes, while whores get furs to wear
    and well-lined cloaks and fine attire.
    The entertainers for their hire
    get little enough of their lords.
60 For all their fine and noble words,
    they give them only worn-out garments
    and toss them, as they would to varmints,
    of their fine dinners, scraps and messes,
    while harlots often change their dresses,
65 sleep with their priests, and what they're fed
    is counted in the overhead.
    The priests do this for their souls' sake,
    whereas the stingy knights forsake
    the entertainers, and are damned
70 for violating God's command.
    Not so the priestly class, because
    they're generous and serve their whores;
    their actions are my evidence.
    They lay out the inheritance
75 and the wealth of Christ crucified,
    keeping their mistresses supplied
    out of their rents, tithes, and donations,
    and merit our congratulations
    above all others for this act.
80 If what my fable tells is fact,
    the clergy is assured salvation
    and the knights will go to damnation.

5. DES CHEVALIERS, DES CLERS ET DES VILLAINS

Dui chevalier vont chevauchant,
li uns vairon, l'autre bauçant,
& truevent .i. lieu descombré,
d'arbre açaint, de fueille aombré,
5   d'erbes, de floretes vestu.
.I. petit i sont arestu.
Dist l'uns a l'autre: « Dieu merci,
com fet ore biau mengier ci!
Qui averoit vin en bareil,
10   bons pastez & autre appareil,
il i feroit plus delitable
qu'en une sale a haute table. »
Puis si s'en departent atant.
        Dui clerc s'aloient esbatant.
15   Quant le biau lieu ont avisé,
si ont comme clerc devisé,
& dist li uns: « Qui averoit
ici fame qu'il ameroit,
molt feroit biau jouer a li.
20   — Bien averoit le cuer failli,
fet li autres, & recreant
s'il n'en prendoit bien son creant. »
Iluec ne sont plus arestu.
        Dui vilain s'i sont embatu
25   qui reperoient d'un marchié
de vanz & de peles carchié.
Quant ou biau lieu assis se furent
si ont parlé si comme il durent
& dist li uns: « Sire Fouchier,
30   com vez ci biau lieu por chïer.
C'or i chions, or biaus conpere.

3. THE THREE ESTATES

Two knights go riding on their way
on a piebald and dapple gray
and stumble on an open space
among the trees, a shady place
5   decked with flowers and herbs as well.
They stopped and rested there a spell.
One of them said, "By God I swear,
how fine to have a picnic here!
You'd need only a jug of wine and
10   pasties and things on which to dine, and
your feast would be at least as gay as
in a great hall on the high dais."
Then they have to be moving on.
      Two wandering scholars, out for fun,
15   came by and saw the lovely scene.
Speaking as clerics do between
themselves, one said, "Who got to spend
some time here with a lady friend
would spend it with her pleasantly."
20   The other said, "He'd have to be
weak-hearted and easily daunted
not to get everything he wanted."
But they could stay no longer then.
      Two peasants then came barging in.
25   From market they were coming back
with spades and threshers on their backs.
When they had sat down in the pleasance
they started speaking just like peasants:
"Hey, Fouchier, from the looks of it
30   this is the perfect place to shit.
Let's take a dump right now, old pal."

— Soit, fet il, par l'ame mon pere! »
Lors du chïer chascuns s'esforce.

        De cest example en est la force
35   qu'il n'est nul deduit entresait
      fors de chiier que vilains ait,
      & por ce que vilains cunchïent
      toz les biaus lieus, & quant i chïent
      par deduit & par esbanoi
40   je voudroie, foi que je doi
      & aus parrins & aus marrines,
      que vilains chiast des narrines.
      Quoi que je die ne qoi non,
      nus n'est vilains se de cuer non:
45   vilains est qui fet vilonie,
      ja tant n'ert de haute lingnie.
      Dieus vous destort de vilonie
      & gart toute la conpaignie!

**4. LE PRESTRE QUI DIST
      LA PASSION**

      Dire vos vueil une merveille
      a qui nule ne s'apareille
      d'un prestre sot & mal sené
      qui le Venredi aouré
5   ot commencié le Dieu servise.
      Ja furent venu a l'yglise
      la gent, & il fu revestuz,
      mais il ot perdu ses festuz;
      lor le commence a reverser
10   & toz les fielz a retorner,
      mais jusqu'au jor Ascenssïon
      n'i trovast il la Passïon,
      & li vilain molt se hastoient,

"Upon my soul, we may as well."
Then each of them squats down and strains.
    This story patently explains
35   that there's nothing on earth as pleasant
as taking a shit for a peasant,
and therefore a peasant befouls
the fairest spots and moves his bowels
there for delight and recreation,
40   so in light of my obligation
to those good folk, what I propose is
that peasants go shit through their noses.
A peasant, whatever I say,
is one whose heart makes him that way,
45   whose deeds show his vulgarity,
however high his ancestry.
God turn our steps from infamy
and save the present company!

4. HOW THE PRIEST READ THE PASSION STORY

I've something wonderful to tell,
a rarity, a nonpareil,
about a priest, and none too smart.
    It was Good Friday, at the start
5   of God's service, and the priest had
put on his vestments and was clad,
and all the people were in church.
He'd lost his straws and had to search
for his place. He began to look
10   through all the pages in his book,
but he'd have hunted in this fashion
till Doomsday and not found the Passion.
The peasants were all in a hurry

que tot ensanble s'escrioient
15 qu'il les faisoit trop jeüner
quar il estoit tens de disner
s'il eüst le servise fait.
Que vos feroie plus lonc plait?—
tant huchierent & ça & la
20 que li prestres lor commença
& prist a dire isnelepas,
primes en halt & puis en bas,
« *Dixit Dominus Domino meo* »,
mais ge ne vos pui[s] pas en o
25 trover ici conconancie,
si est bien droiz que ge vos die
tot le mielz que ge porrai metre.
  Li prestres a tant lut la letre
sicom aventure le maine
30 qu'a dit vespres du diemaine.
Or sachiez que fort se travaille
que l'offrandë auques li vaille,
lors prist a crier « *Barraban* ».
Uns crierres n'eüst .i. ban
35 si crié com il lor cria!
Chascun de ceus qui oï l'a
bat sa coupe & crie merci.
Ha, Dieus, qui onques ne menti,
qu'i[l] les avoit a droite voie!,
40 & li prestres, qui toute voie
lisoit le cors de son sautier,
reprant hautement a crier
& dit: « *Crucifige eum* »
si que partot l'entendi on,
45 homes & femes, ce me sanble,
& prient Dieu trestuit ensanble
qu'Il les deffende de torment,
mais au clerc ennuia forment

and starting in on grumbling, for he
15 was making them prolong their fast.
It would be dinnertime at last
when the Divine Service was done.
But why should *I* go on and on?
They all sat there and fidgeted,
20 and so here's what the prelate did:
He launched into a reading now,
at first quite loud, then very low,
"Dixit Dominus domino
meo." (As for a rhyme in *-o,*
25 I can't find any, nor make head
or tail of all this. If I said
it as best I can, I'd do better.)
        The priest went following the letter
of his text as blind Fortune led
30 till Sunday vespers had been said.
He wanted, I need hardly state,
to have a full donation plate,
so he cried *"Barrabam!"* aloud.
No town crier has ever crowed
35 a ban with such a booming yell,
and everyone who heard him fell
to beating his breast in contrition.
He had them in a good position,
honest to God, in Whom no guile
40 is found! The priest, who all the while
went reading straight on through his Psalter,
again starts crying helter-skelter,
this time with *"Crucifige eum!"*
The church resounded with his mayhem,
45 and every man and every woman
heard him and prayed to God in common
to save them from eternal torments,
but his clerk is fed up and comments

    & dist au prestre: « *Fac finis.* »
50   & il li dit, « *Non fac*, amis,
    usque as mirabilia. »
    Cil tantost respondu li a
    que longue passïon n'est preuz
    & que ce n'est mie ses preuz
55   de tenir longuement la gent.
    Sitost com ot reçut l'argent
    si fist la Passïon finer.
        Par cest flablel vos vueil monstrer
    que, par la foi que doi saint Pol,
60   ausinc bien chiet il a un fol
    de folie dire & d'outraige
    com il feroit a un bien saige
    d'un grant sens, se il le disoit.
    Fous est qui de ce me mescroit.

𝄢.   LE PRESTRE ET LE LEU

    Un prestre maneit en Chartein,
    s'amoit la fame a .i. vilein.
    Le vilein, qui garde s'en prist,
    en la voie une fosse fist
5   par ou cil seut venir laienz.
    .i. leu vint la nuit & chiet enz
    car la nuit estoit trop oscure.
    Le prestre par mesaventure,
    si com soleit, est revenuz;
10   einz ne sot mot, s'est enz chaüz.
    La dame, cui il anuioit
    du proverre qui tant tarjoit,
    a sa meschine dit: « Cha va
    savoir se cel sire vendra. »

to him, "*Fac finis*. Make an end."
50 The priest replies, "I won't, my friend,
until I reach the miracles."
The clerk immediately tells
him lengthy Passions do not sit
well and he will not benefit
55 by overtaxing his flock's patience,
so when they'd given their donations,
he quickly polished off the Passion.
My fabliau shows in this fashion
that, by the faith I owe Saint Paul,
60 talking nonsense and folderol
equally well exemplifies
a fool, just as someone who's wise
will speak sense when he goes about it,
and no one but a fool would doubt it.

ϟ. THE PRIEST AND THE WOLF

A priest who lived in the Chartrain
loved the wife of another man,
a peasant, but he caught on to't
and dug a pit along the route
5 the priest took when he came their way.
That night a wolf happened to stray
by in the dark and tumbled in,
and the priest likewise, for his sin:
As was his wont, he came a-calling;
10 before he knew it, in he'd fallen.
The wife, annoyed she had to wait
for her priest, who was running late,
called for her maid, whom she directed
to go find out when he's expected.

15 La meschine est par la venue,
    en cele fosse rest cheüe.
    Li vilein par mein se leva,
    vers sa fosse droit en ala.
    Ce qu'il queroit trueve, & jura
20 que chascun son loier avra:
    le leu tua & esbourssa
    le prestre & la garce enchaça.
    A ceus avint grant meschaance
    & au vilein bele chaance:
25 li prestres honte li fesoit,
    li leu ses bestes estrangloit;
    chascun d'eus acheta molt chier,
    cil son deduit, cil son mengier.

6. LE PRESTRE ET ALISON

    Il sont mais tant de menestreus
    que ne sai a dire des quels
    ge sui, par le cors saint Huitace!
        Guillaumes, qui sovent se lasse
5   en rimer & en fabloier,
    en a .i. fait qui molt est chier
    de la fille a une borgoise
    qui meint en la riviere d'Oise,
    si avoit non dame Mahaus;
10 maintes foiz avoit vendu auz
    a sa fenestre & oignons
    & chapeaus bien ouvrez de jons
    qui n'estoient pas de marés.
    Sa fille avoit a non Marés,
15 une pucele qui ert bele.
    .i. jor portoit en ses braz belle

15 On her way the maid passed the pit,
and she as well fell into it.
          The peasant, waking early, thought
he'd go and see what had been caught.
He found his pit full, and he swore
20 that he'd give all of them what-for:
He killed the wolf, gelded the priest,
and told the maid she was dismissed.
On those three grave misfortune fell,
but for the peasant things went well:
25 The wolf who feasted on his flock,
along with the prelate who took
his wife's virtue, paid in full measure,
one for his meal, one for his pleasure.

6. THE PRIEST AND ALISON

by Guillaume le Normand

With all the minstrels found today,
by Saint Eustace, I cannot say
exactly what kind I may be.
          William, who labors tirelessly
5 at putting stories into rhyme,
has made one which is really fine
about a merchant woman's daughter
who lives by the Oise, near the water.
Madame Mahauld, as she was called,
10 from her window for long had sold
garlic and onions, also hats
made out of well-woven reeds that
did not come from swampy terrain.
Marian was (her daughter's name)
15 a virgin girl and beautiful. A
day there was when with *Berula*

& creson cuilli en fontaine;
moilliee en fu de ci en l'aine
par mi la chemise de ling.
20 El ne fu mie de halt ling,
n'estoit fille a baron n'a dame—
ne vos en quier mentir, par m'ame!—
fille estoit a une borgoise.
Ainz nule n'en vi plus cortoise,
25 certes, ne de meillor maniere.
De marcheandise ert maniere
de comin, de poivre & de cire,
mais li chaplelains de Saint Cire
va en la maison molt sovent
30 por le gingenbre c'on i vent,
por citoal & por espice,
por quenele & por recolice,
por l'erbe qui vient d'Alixandre.
Li prestres ot non Alixandre,
35 si fu riches hom a merveille,
mais por Marion sovent veille,
com li vit le sercot porter;
dont ala son cors deporter
au main por le serain du tans;
40 ne cuida pas venir a tens
en la maison ou cele maint—
certes n'a cure c'on l'i maint,
quar molt bien i asenera:
ja mais A.B.C. ne dira,
45 s'il puet, si l'avra convertie.
Ja s'ame a Dieu ne soit vertie
s'il ne fait son pooir sanz faille!
      A tant affubla une faille
por le chaut qu'i fait en esté.
50 Il avoit autre foiz esté
a la maison a la vileine,
qui ne vendoit lange ne leine—

in her arms from the stream, and cress,
she walked home in her linen dress,
all wet to the top of her thighs.
20 Upon my soul, I'll not tell lies:
She wasn't born to noble parents,
no lady's daughter nor a baron's—
a merchant woman was her mother,
but fair and well-bred as no other
25 who's ever come before my eyes.
The nature of her merchandise
was beeswax and pepper and cumin.
The chaplain of Saint-Cyr would come in-
to their abode for ginger very
30 often, and to buy zedoary,
cinnamon, licorice, and spice
she kept in stock as merchandise,
and also for an herb that came
from Alexandria. His name
35 was Alexander, a rich man
who kept his eye on Marian—
he liked the way her tunic fit—
so he'd go walking for a bit
to take the gentle morning air
40 and couldn't come soon enough where
the girl's house was located—he
'd no need of a guide, certainly!
He'll teach her everything, you bet:
Before she's said the alphabet,
45 if he can, he'll have her converted.
Unless all his strength is exerted
to this end, his soul won't see God!
     It's summer and the weather's hot;
he put a light cloth on his head.
50 He'd been to the woman's homestead
quite a few other times before,
who made her living from her store,

molt se garissoit belement;—
& li chapelains arroment
55 avoit la dame saluee,
& el s'estoit en piez levee,
s'a dit, « Sire, bien viegnoiz vos!
Vos demorroiz ci avuec nos
a disner & ferons grant joie,
60 quar vez ci au feu la grasse oie, »
fait ele, qui nul mal n'i tent.
Li chapeleins sa chiere tent
vers la pucele, qu'il esgarde.
Li chapelains estoit nez d'Arde
65 entre Saint Omer & Calais;
a tant s'est asis sor .i. ais
molt pensis (& pas ne fu yvres)
& dit qu'ançois donra .x. livres
qu'il de la pucele ne face
70 sa volenté & face a face,
qui tant ert bele & avenanz
& n'ot mie passez .xii. anz,
cele qui si ert ensaignie,
gorge blanche, soëf norrie,
75 molt estoit bele, simple & saige.
A tant fet on metre les tables
a la maison a la borgoise;
onques n'i ot mengié vendoise
ne poisson a l'eure de lors,
80 fors malarz, faisanz & butors,
dont li osteus fu aesiez,
& li chapelains qui fu liez
& regarde la pucelete
cui primes point la mamelete
85 enmi le piz comme une pomme;
les tables ostent en la somme,
s'ont fait des mengiers lor talenz.
Li chapelains son cuer dedenz

where she sold neither wool nor flax.
The chaplain wasn't at all lax
55   in giving the woman his greeting,
and she rose to her feet on meeting
him and said, "Hearty welcome, sir.
Do stay on awhile with us here
for dinner. We'll have joy and mirth.
60   See the fat goose there on the hearth!"
she says (no evil she intends,
while toward the girl the chaplain bends
a lecherous face to regard her).
The chaplain had been born in Ardres,
65   between Calais and Saint-Omer.
Sitting on a plank for a chair
and lost in thought (he's not a ninny),
he swears that ten pounds of his money
he'd give up sooner than not do
70   with the girl what he wishes to,
face-to-face with her, who was fair
and comely, still in her twelfth year,
her whose behavior was so right,
tenderly cared for, with her white
75   throat, lovely, unaffected, sweet.
        They had the table set to eat
in the good woman's dwelling place.
They didn't make a meal on dace
at that time or have fish at all,
80   but bittern, pheasant, waterfowl,
and all there were well satisfied,
and the contented chaplain eyed
the virgin child, let his glance rest
upon her newly budding breast
85   growing on her chest like an apple.
        At last they take away the table
and have eaten all they desire.
Within the chaplain's heart a fire

ot enbrasé par grant amor;
90   la dame apele par dolçor
(qui avoit non dame Mahaus):
« Dame, fait il, oiez mes maus.
Molt ai esté lonc tens en ire,
or en vueil mon coraige dire,
95   certes, plus ne m'en puis tenir;
des ore m'estuet descovrir.
Marion, vo fille, la bele,
m'a si le cuer soz la mamele
derrompu & trait fors du cors . . .
100   Dame, avroit il mestiers tresors
que j'é? . . . Mais qu'il ne vos ennuit . . .
S'eüsse vo fille une nuit . . .
J'ai meint bon denier monnaé. »
& la dame respont, « Sire, hé!
105   Quidiez vos donc por vostre avoir
issi donques ma fille avoir,
que j'ai touz jors soëf norrie?
Certes ne pris pas une alie
tos voz deniers ne vo tresor.
110   Par les sainz c'on quiert a Gisor,
ge n'ai cure de vostre avoir.
Bien le sachiez, a mon savoir!
Gitez en autre liu voz meins.
— Ma dame, fait li chapelains,
115   por Dieu, aiez de moi merci.
J'aporterai les deniers ci,
s'en prenez a vostre talent. »
& dame Mahauz, cui fu lent
qu'ele ait l'avoir de ses escrins,
120   sa fille qui a blons les crins
li pramet a faire ses bons,
& si vos di que rois ne quons
la peüst avoir a son lit
por faire de li son delit,

had been set blazing by his passion.
90   In an ingratiating fashion
he turns to Mahauld, the girl's mother,
and says, "Lady, hear how I suffer.
I have been vexed for a long time,
but now I mean to speak my mind.
95   Surely, no more can I refrain,
but am compelled to tell you plain
your daughter, Marian the lovely,
has gone and wrenched the heart out of me,
broken inside my breast. I've wealth
100   in plenty. Tell me if that helps . . .
I'm hoping you'll take this aright . . .
Had I your daughter for one night . . .
Of shiny coins I have a stack."
"What, sir?" the woman answers back.
105   "Then do you think your money can
buy you my daughter, Marian,
I've always tenderly cared for?
By both the two saints of Gisors,
I'd say that a sour apple's worth
110   more than the contents of your purse.
Your treasure doesn't interest me,
and that's a fact, undoubtedly.
Put your hands somewhere else instead."
"Dear, good woman," the chaplain said,
115   "have pity on me, for God's sake.
I'll bring the money here. You take
whatever you want of my riches."

        Madame Mahauld, who more than itches
to get at the wealth in his coffers,
120   for the priest's use and pleasure offers
to let him have her blond-haired daughter.
A king or a count would have thought her
a fit companion for his bed
and lovemaking, let it be said,

125 quar de grant beauté plaine fu.
Li prestres se rassiet au fu
entre lui & dame Mahauz,
qui mainte foiz ot vendu auz
& achaté poivre & comin.
130 Pris a congié, prant le chemin
li chapelains a sa maison.
Onques mais ne fu guilez hon
que li prestres fu conchiez!
Toz fu li bainz apareillez
135 que la dame fist aprester:
Damedieus en prist a jurer
& enprés le cors saint Huitasse
le prestre pranra a la nasse
ausin com l'en prant le poisson;
140 lors fait mander Aelison,
une meschinete de vie
qui de cors fu bien eschevie,
a tot le monde communaus.
Oiez que dist dame Mahauz
145 quant ele vit la pecherriz:
coiement en a fait un ris
comme cele qui molt fu saige,
« Aelison, .i. mariaige
t'ai porchacié, par saint Denise:
150 deci a l'aive de Tamise
n'avra feme mielz mariee.
—Avez me voz por ce mandee?
fait Alison. C'est vilenie
de povre meschine de vie
155 gaber qui a petit d'avoir.
—Non faz, se Dieus me doint savoir,
amie, dit dame Mahaus.
Ja de moi ne te venra maus.
Blanc peliçon te frai avoir
160 & bone cote a mon savoir

125   because her beauty was so great.
       The priest sits back down by the grate
       together with Madame Mahauld,
       who had so often bought and sold
       garlic, pepper, and caraway.
130   The chaplain's set out on his way,
       having taken his leave, for home.
       Of all the men who've been tricked, none
       ever fared worse than this priest fared!
       A bath that she ordered prepared
135   before you knew it was made ready,
       and upon Saint Eustace's body
       and by God she begins to swear
       she'll catch the chaplain in her snare
       in the same way you'd catch a fish.
140   Then she has someone go and fetch
       a wanton woman, Alison,
       whose shapely body anyone
       who paid for her could take to bed.
       Now hear what Madame Mahauld said
145   when she saw the loose girl come by,
       quietly laughing on the sly
       as someone clever might have done:
       "Now by Saint Dennis, Alison,
       I've found a husband for you, dear.
150   Between the river Thames and here
       no woman will be better wed."
       "For that you had me come here?" said
       Alison. "How unkind of you
       to make fun of a poor girl who
155   supports herself walking the streets!"
       "I'm not, my dear, so may it please
       the Lord to grant me to be wise.
       You'll have no harm from me," replies
       Mahauld. "You've a white fur to gain,
160   a good coat also—with a train!—

de vert de Doai traïnant.
Fai, si entre en cel baig corant:
senprés te vendrai por pucele. »
Aalison fu molt isnele,
165 s'est asise, si se despoille,
devant la cuve s'*agenoille*
comme cele qui molt fu lie,
lors se deschauce & se deslie
& se plunge comme vendoise.
170 Ez vos la fille a la borgoise
que li prestres avoir quida!
Forment son oirre apareilla
li chapelains en sa maison:
il a mandé un peliçon
175 qui valt .xl. sous de blans
que .i. marcheanz de Mielanz
li vendi qui maint a Provins—
de la cote serai devins:
nueve est de brunete sanguine,—
180 maint chapon & mainte geline
avoit fait a l'ostel porter:
la nuit se vorra deporter
sempres, quant venra a la nuit.
Ne quidiez que il vos anuit
185 li jors qui si enviz trespasse?
Li chapelains n'i fist *espasse*,
ainz a .i. escrin defermé;
sicom Guillaumes a fermé
en parchemin & en romanz,
190 .xv. livres d'esterlins blans
estoit en .i. cuiret cousuz.
Dieus! com il sera deceüz,
que por .i. denier de Senliz
peüst il avoir ses deliz
195 de celui qu'avuec li gerra
sempres quant a l'ostel venra,

I know of, from Douai, and green!
I've poured a fresh bath. Do get in.
I'll soon pass you off as a virgin."
     Alison needed no more urging;
165 she sits down and her clothes she peels
off and down by the bathtub kneels,
and with a joyful, carefree air
takes off her shoes, unbinds her hair,
and, like a fish, jumps in the water.
170 So that's the merchant woman's daughter
the chaplain thinks he will possess!
     Back home, the priest saw to his dress
with gusto, and to what he'd take
with him: He asked for a fur cape
175 worth forty shillings a Provins-
based merchant who was from Milan
had sold to him, and a coat, too.
(A word about the coat: It's new,
bloodred, and made of fine dark cloth.)
180 Many capons and pullets both
he had delivered to the house
that night. He wishes to carouse
just as soon as the night has come.
Do you not find when it drags on
185 that you cannot abide the day?
The chaplain could brook no delay,
but went and opened up a chest
in which, as William tells us next
in French on parchment, was a leather
190 purse where he's sewn up altogether
fifteen pounds sterling currency.
Lord, how bamboozled he will be!
For just a penny from Senlis
he could well have taken his ease
195 with her with whom he will cavort
when he arrives there in a short

ou pres, de tote la nuitiee!
De parisis une poigniee
a traist & mist en s'aumosniere
200 por doner avant & arriere,
dont il fera ses petiz dons.
Dame Mainnaus dit .i. respons
a la pucele de l'ostel:
« Hercelot, fait ele, entent el:
205 va moi tost a maistre Alixandre,
& si li di que ge li mande
que ne face nule atendue. »
Hercelot tot son cuer remue
de la joie du mariaige:
210 « Dame, bien ferai le mesaige,
si m'aïst Dieus, a vostre gré. »
A tant s'en ist par .i. degré
de la maison, qui fu de pierre,
& va jurant Dieus & saint Pierre
215 bon loier en vorra avoir.
« Sire, bon jor puissiez avoir
de par celi qui vos salue,
qui est vostre amie & vo drue,
de par Marion au cors gent. »
220 Une fort corroie d'argent
dona li prestres Hercelot:
« Tien, amie, si n'en di mot.
Encor avras autre loier.
—Mielz me lairoie detranchier,
225 fait Hercelos, que g'en pallasse
ne que vostre amor empirasse.
Par moi est toz li plaiz bastiz. »
Li chapelains a fait .i. ris
quant oï Hercelot paller;
230 a son clerc li a fait doner
.ii. dras de lin fres & noveaus.

time all night long, or just about!
He took a batch of small change out
and stuffed it in his purse, he did,
200   for tips to be distributed
around as the case might demand.
Madame Menhould has a command
for Hercelot, the girl who helps
around the house: "Here's something else
205   for Alexander the priest. Go
at once and say I'd have him know
he shouldn't wait. It's time to start
out." Hercelot replies, her heart
beating for the fun of this union,
210   "Lady, I'll bring your message to him,
so help me God, just as you please."
Then going down the stone steps, she's
out of the house, for, by the Lord
and Saint Peter, a good reward
215   from this, she swears, will come to her.
"I wish a good day to you, sir,
from her who sends greeting to you
and is your friend and lover, too,
the fair and shapely Marian."
220   A sturdy silver belt the man
gave Hercelot as her reward:
"Take this, my friend, but not a word
about all this. There's more to come."
Hercelot answers, "I'll keep mum.
225   Better that I were torn apart
than subvert your love, for my part.
Why, I arranged the whole affair!"
The chaplain gave a laugh to hear
Hercelot say it's all her work,
230   and has her given by his clerk
two fresh and new pieces of linen.

Molt fu li dons Hercelot beaus,
si prist congié, atant s'en torne.
    Li chapelains atant s'*atorne*;
235 a la nuit molt grant joie atent.
Ha! Dieus, comme li viz li tent
plus que roncin qui est en saut!
Il jure Dieus que .i. assaut
fera sempres a la pucele,
240 qui a merveillë estoit bele,
qui de grant beauté pleine fu.
Li prestres molt eschaufez fu
de la fille dame Meinaut;
anvelopé en .i. bliaut
245 avoit la cote & le pliçon,
a tant s'en vait a la meson,
d'esterlins trossez .xv. livres—
certes, tost en sera delivres
se la dame puet de l'ostel.
250 A tant entre enz & ne fait el
comme cil qui grant feste atent.
La dame par la mein le prant,
puis s'assiet lez lui el foier;
la dame fist apareillier,
255 qui molt fu grant com a tel joie.
.II. chapons & une grasse oie
si ot, & malarz & plunjons
& blanc vin qui fu de Soissons,
si s'en burent a granz plentez,
260 & gastieaus rastiz buletez
si mengierent a grant foison.
Aprés mengier dit .i. sarmon
dame Meinaus, qui a parlé:
« Avez vos l'avoir aporté
265 que vos devez doner ma fille?
—Dame, ne sui pas ci por guile.
J'ai les garnemenz aportez,

Happy with all the gifts she's winning,
Hercelot takes her leave and goes.
        The chaplain then gets ready, who's
235 expecting that that night will bring
much joy. His cock is stiffening,
by God, more than a rutting steed!
He swears to God in no time he'd
assail the maiden who was fair
240 and beautiful beyond compare,
magnificent from head to feet.
The priest was totally in heat
for the child of Madame Menhould.
He used a long top shift to fold
245 up the fur cape and coat he carried,
and then off to their house he hurried,
fifteen pounds sterling tied up tight,
of which he'll be relieved, all right,
if Madame Menhould has her way.
250   He enters and acts just as they
do who expect to have a grand
old time. The woman takes his hand
and sits by him close to the fire.
As the occasion did require,
255 she had a lavish banquet laid:
two capons, a fat goose she'd made,
and there were also ducks and loons.
They drank quantities of Soissons
white wine and went on to devour
260 crusty cakes baked of sifted flour
of which there were plenty for each.
Then Madame Menhould makes a speech
and asks him when their dinner's through,
"Say if you've brought the gifts with you
265 for my daughter, as you have promised?"
"I came here meaning to be honest;
I brought all of the finery.

veez les ci. Or esgardez
quar il sont & bel & plaisant!
270 Vos me tenroiz a voir disant
ainz que parte de vo maison.
Foi que ge doi a seint Simon,
ge n'amai onques a trichier. »
Lors rue sor un eschequier
275 .xv. livres d'esterlins blans;
li gorles fu riches & granz
& li avoir fu dedenz mis.

« Hercelot, maintenant as lis!
fait dame Meinauz, alumez!
280 En cele chanbre vos metez.
Faites beaus liz com a un roi. »
Herceloz, qui prant grant conroi
de servir le prestre a son gré
(el avoit monté .i. degré
285 qui de la chose avoit ensoig),
Aelison prist par le poig
d'un coiement liu ou estoit.
La table devant lui estoit
& li boives & li mengiers.
290 « Aelis, tost apareilliez,
s'irois couchier o l'ordené.
Il vos apranra l'ABC
sempres & *Credo in Deum*.
Ne faites noise ne tençon
295 quant vos vorra despuceler.
—Suer, ge ne le puis andurer,
quar ge n'ai mie ce apris.
Tenez ma foi, ge vos plevis,
onques mes cors ne jut a home:
300 ainsi sui pucele come Rome
c'onques pelerins n'i entra

I have it here. Look, and you'll see
what stylish and well-made attire!
270   You won't consider me a liar
when it comes time for me to leave.
Indeed, by Saint Simon, believe
me, I hate selling people short."
He tossed down on a gaming board
275   the fifteen pounds he's brought with him.
The money belt he'd put it in
was large and costly.
                              "Hercelot,
now it's time that all of us got
to bed," Menhould says. "Light a fire
280   there in the room where they'll retire.
Make up a bed fit for a king."
Hercelot, who does everything
she can to help the priest's affairs,
had gone to the top of the stairs
285   (seeing to all the details) and
she took Alison by the hand
where, in a secret place, she stood.
(The table full of drink and food
was in front of him.) "Alison,
290   get yourself ready quickly. Come,
you'll be sharing the prelate's bed.
In the credo and alphabet
he'll give you a fine education.
No noise, now, and no protestation
295   when he takes your virginity."
"It will be harrowing for me;
to me this thing's completely new.
Upon my word, I promise you
I've never known a man. Be sure
300   that I am like Rome, chaste and pure,
where no pilgrim has penetrated

ne mastins par nuit n'abaia;
ainsinc sui veraie pucele! »
En une chanbre qui fu bele
305 mist Herceloz Aelison
par .i. faus huis de la maison,
quar molt [ ] sot bien [le] liu & l'estre;
a tant s'en revint vers le prestre,
si a pris par la mein Maret,
310 en la chanbre arroment la met
si que li prestres la regarde—
Ha! Dieus, com li couchiers li tarde
de la grant joie qui l'atent!—
& Herceloz plus n'i atent,
315 Maret destorne en .i. solier.
Enuit mais porra dosnoier
li prestres a Aelison!
A tant vait seoir au giron
Herceloz lez le chapelain,
320 qui li vendi paille por grain
& changa por le forment l'orge,
& dit Herceloz, « Par seint Jorge,
ge ai couchiee la pucele
soz la cortine qui ventele,
325 molt dolente & molt esploree.
Durement l'ai reconfortee
& li ai prié bonement
qu'ele face vostre talent,
& vos li prametez assez,
330 robes & joaus a plentez,
& ge ai fait molt vostre pont.
—Hercelot, li prestres respont,
ge li donrai a son voloir
de quanque ge porrai avoir.
335 —Vos dites bien, dit Hercelot.
Dit li ai qu'el ne die mot
quant vos seroiz o lui couchiez.

or night dogs bark, unviolated
and virginal and innocent."
        With Alison, Hercelot went
305   into a very lovely room
through a secret door in the home
she knew like the palm of her hand,
then returned to the chaplain and
took Marian's hand speedily
310   and led her, so the priest could see,
to the room. By God, he can't wait
until it's bedtime and he'll sate
himself with the joy he expects!
To a loft Hercelot directs
315   and slyly hurries Marian—
henceforth tonight the chaplain can
go get it on with Alison—
and then Hercelot comes back down
and close beside him takes a seat.
320   She's given him barley for wheat;
in place of corn she's sold him straws.
Hercelot tells him, "By Saint George,
I've put the girl to bed behind
bed curtains flapping in the wind,
325   weeping and grieved beyond endurance.
I've given her what reassurance
I could and urged her that she try her
utmost to fulfill your desire,
and you should likewise promise she
330   will get dresses and jewelry
in plenty. I have served you well."
"Whatever she asks for I will
give her, Hercelot," the priest says,
"of all that I own and possess."
335   "That's spoken well," says Hercelot.
"I also told her she must not
say a word when you lie with her.

Gardez ennuieus n'i soiez,
mais soiez saiges & cortois,
340 que amie avez vos a chois
qui se gist desoz la cortine,
s'est plus blanche que flor d'espine
la pucele qui tant est chiere.
—Tien, Hercelot, ceste aumosniere,
345 fait li prestres. Ci a dedenz
.xx. sous ou plus, par seint Loranz,
s'achate .i. bon pliçon d'aigneaus,
& g'irai faire mes aviaus
a celi qu'ai tant desiree. »
350 A tant a la chanbre boutee
sanz luminaire & sanz chandele;
a tant a sentue la toile
de la grant cortine estendue
la, ou cele gist estendue
355 qui molt hardiement l'atent,
& li prestres plus n'i atent,
les dras leva & dist, « Marie,
dites, en estes vos m'amie,
bele suer, sanz nul contredit? »
360 A tant n'i fait plus de respit,
ainz l'enbraça molt vistement.
Cele soupire durement
& fait par senblant grant martire,
qui bien en sot le maiestire.
365 Ensus de lui est traite & jointe,
& li prestres vers li s'acointe;
une foiz la fout en mains d'eure
que l'en eüst chanté une eure
en cel termine que ge di.
370 « Bele suer, fait li prestres, di,
de ceste chose que te sanble?
Mon cuer & mon avoir ensanble
vos pramet tot & mon voloir.

Now don't be too rough with her, sir;
behave yourself and be polite.
340 Your sweetheart's one of the elite,
who's lying in the curtained bower,
whiter than any hawthorn flower,
precious as any girl on earth."
"Here, Hercelot, accept this purse,"
345 the chaplain tells her, "and its contents—
a pound, if not more, by Saint Lawrence—
and buy a good cloak of lamb's fleece.
I'm going now to take my ease
with her I've so been yearning for."
350   He's pushed open the chamber door;
without a light, without a taper, he
has soon felt his hand brush the drapery,
the curtains which were hung and spread
where she lay stretched out on the bed,
355 ready and waiting for the priest,
who doesn't linger or desist.
He lifted the sheets and asked of her,
"Say, Marian, are you my lover,
you sweet girl, with no opposition?"
360 Then without the slightest transition
he quickly threw his arms around
her. Her sighs make the room resound,
feigning great martyrdom, for she's
much professional expertise.
365 She curled up close to him and drew her-
self on top and the chaplain knew her.
He fucks her even quicker than did
it take him to get a prayer chanted,
as long as it took me to tell.
370   "Say, you sweet girl," the priest says, "well,
what do you think of what we've done?
My heart and everything I own
I mean to give you. Certainly,

Certes, se de moi avez oir,
375 sachiez que bien sera norriz. »
Aalison a fait .i. ris
molt coiement entre ses denz.
Li prestres en ses braz dedenz
quida bien tenir Marion.
380 (Certes non fist, mais Alison—
molt li fu tost li vers changiez!)
Li prestre fu joianz & liez:
de ci au jor que la nuiz fine,
.ix. foiz i fouti la meschine,
385 ne vos en quier mentir de mot.
Or escoutez de Hercelot,
qui en la chanbre fist son lit
la ou cil menoit son delit.
(Li chapelains l'i fist couchier.)
390 Hercelot n'i volt atarder,
qui molt savoit mal & voidie.
Ele s'estoit nue d[r]ecie,
si avoit alumé le fu:
en une couche, qui grant fu,
395 d'estrain de pesaz amassé
a Herceloz le feu bouté,
puis escrie: « Haro! le fu! »
Cil de la vile, qui granz fu,
i acorent tuit abrievé;
400 l'us ont despiecié & coupé
ou laienz grant clarté avoit,
la ou li prestres dosnoioit.
Li maistre bouchiers de la vile
entra laienz, n'i fist devise,
405 le prestre a connu & visé,
a soi l'a maintenant tiré
dedenz la chanbre a une part:
« Ja Damedieus en vos n'ait part,
ne en vos n'en vostre meschine! »

if you conceive a child by me,
375   be sure it will be well looked after."
Alison kept her stifled laughter
between her teeth with modesty.
The priest believed that the one he
held in his arms was Marian.
380   (It wasn't—it was Alison.
The worm had turned before he knew.)
The priest was glad and happy, too:
Till it was day and night had gone
nine times he screwed and pounded on
385   the girl. Truly, I kid you not.
       Now a word about Hercelot,
who'd made her bed up in the chamber
in which he'd exercised his member.
(The priest insisted she sleep there.)
390   Hercelot, who does not much care
to dawdle (she's sly and conniving),
without her clothes on yet, arising,
gets down to work kindling a flame:
inside a mattress on a frame,
395   made out of pea straw that they'd bundled
up, Hercelot her fire kindled,
then cries: "Fire, fire! Raise the alarm!"
The people living in the town,
which was large, came running and tore
400   apart and battered down the door
behind which glowed the conflagration
and where the priest indulged his passion.
The head butcher of the locality
burst in without the least formality,
405   knew who the priest was when he spied
him, and quickly dragged him aside
there in the chamber close up to
him: "May God have no part in you,
neither in you nor in your mistress!"

410 (li bochiers sot bien la covine
       quar bien fu qui conté li a),
       & li chapelain esgarda
       cele qu'il tint par la main nue:
       ce fu Aelison, sa drue!
415 Il quida tenir Marion!
       Li maistres bouchiers d'un baston
       li feri par mi les costez
       & tuit li autre environ lez
       le fierent de poinz & de piez;
420 molt fu batuz et laidengiez,
       et enprés la chape li oste.
       « Nomini dame! Si mal oste,
       fait li prestres, por Dieu, la vie! »
       A tant saut devers la chaucie
425 li chapelains par .i. guichet;
       devers le cul sanble bouquet
       por ce qu'il n'avoit riens vestu.
       Cil de la vile l'ont veü
       que il estoit nuz com .i. dains—
430 certes n'eüst pas en desdaig
       .i. poi de robe sor ses os—
       les cous li parent par le dos,
       par les costez & par les flans
       des bastons, qui furent pesanz,
435 molt fu laidengiez & batuz.
       Il est en maison enbatuz,
       tranblant com une fueille d'arbre.
              Savoir poez [par] ceste fable
       que fist Guillaumes li Normanz,
440 qui dist que cil n'est pas sachanz
       qui de sa maison ist par nuit
       por faire chose qui ennuit
       ne por tolir ne por enbler.
       L'en devroit preudom hennorer
445 la ou il est en totes corz.

410 (The butcher knew about this business
because someone had made him wise
to it.) The chaplain turned his eyes
on her he had in hand, unclad:
Why, it was Alison he'd had!
415 He'd thought that it was Marian!
        With the stick he was carrying
the master butcher struck him in
the ribs, and everyone 'round him
goes pounding on him with their feet 'n'
420 fists. He was cruelly bruised and beaten.
They ripped his cloak off. "God Our Sire,"
the priest exclaims, "out of the fire
and back into the frying pan!"
Then he jumps as fast as he can
425 through a hatchway onto the road.
Seen ass backwards, a little goat
he looked like, having no clothes on.
The townspeople were looking on
and saw him naked as a buck. He
430 would not have scorned to be so lucky
to have a shred of clothes on his
bones! The blows of those heavy sticks
left marks you could see on his back
and ribs and flanks. They beat him black-
435 and-blue and put him through the mill.
He took off for home running, still
trembling like a leaf on a tree.
        This fable clearly lets you see,
which William from Normandy wrote,
440 and tells us the man who goes out
from home at night to rob or thieve
or do anything else to grieve
his neighbor isn't very wise,
whereas, wherever he resides,
445 an honest man deserves praise. Thus,

Se li prestre fu enmorous
si fu laidengiez ne batuz,
& cil ot ses deniers perduz:
il en fouti Aelison,
450 qu'il peüst por .i. esperon
le jor avoir a son bordel.
Il n'i a plus de cest fablel.

🎔. LE PRESTRE CRUCEFIÉ

Un essample voil coumencier
qu'apris de monseignor Rogier,
le franc mestre, le debonaire,
qui bien savoit images fere
5 & bien entaillier crucefis;
il n'en estoit mie aprentis,
ainz entailloit & bel & bien;
& sa fame sor toute rien
avoit aamé un prevoire.
10   Ses sires li a fait a croire
que au marchié voloit aler
& un ymage ou lui porter
dont il avra asez deniers,
& la dame molt volentiers
15 li otroie, s'en fu molt liee,
& il vit sa chiere haitiee,
si se prist a apercevoir
qu'elle le vouloit decevoir
si comme ele a acoutumé.
20 A tant a sor son col levé
un crucefiz par achoison,
si se depart de la maison,
en la vile va, s'i demoure
& atendi jusque a cele ore

as the chaplain was lecherous,
so he was beaten and lambasted
and all the money he spent wasted
on fucking Alison, whom any-
450 one could have had for just a penny,
whenever, in her brothel, though.
There's no more to this fabliau.

7. THE CRUCIFIED PRIEST

A short exemplum about Roger,
the suave, enfranchised master carver,
I now propose to undertake.
He had the skill one needs to make
5 statues and crucifixes; he,
no mere apprentice, artfully
carved sculptures in the finest fashion.
    His wife, carried away by passion,
had taken a priest as her lover.
10 Her husband told her as a cover
he had to go to market, so
he'd bring a statuette in tow
to drop off for a tidy profit,
and she agreed promptly enough—it
15 elated her to see him leave,
and he was not slow to perceive
her joyful look, by which he knew
she had in mind to be untrue,
which was, for her, by now tradition.
20 Then he lifts up into position
a crucifix as a pretext
and steps out of the house, and next
goes into town and cools his heels
and waits around until he feels

25   qu'il sot que il furent ensemble.
    De mautalent & d'ire tremble;
    a son ostel est revenuz,
    par un pertuis les a veüz
    que il seoient au mengier.
30   Il apela, mes a dangier
    li ala l'en son huis ouvrir.
    Li prestres n'ot par ou fuïr:
    « Deus! dist li prestres, que ferai? »
    Dist la dame: « Je vous dirai.
35   Despoilliez vous & si alez
    laiens & si vous estendez
    avec ces autres crucefis. »
    Ou volentiers ou en envis
    le fist li prestres, ce sachiez:
40   tretouz nus s'est *lués* despoilliez,
    emmi les ymages s'estut
    comme s'il fust dolez de fust.
        Quant li preudom ne l'a veü,
    si a tantost aperceü
45   que il est entre ses ymages;
    de ce fist que cortois & sages:
    primes a mengié & beü
    tant comme bon & bel li fu.
    Quant il fu levé du mengier,
50   si coumença a aguisier
    ung sien coutel a une cueuz.
    Li preudom, qui fu fort & preuz,
    a dit: « Dame, tost m'alumez
    une chandelle, & si venez
55   laienz o moi ou ge ai afaire. »
    La dame ne l'osa retraire;
    une chandoille a alumee,
    o son seignor en est alee
    en l'ouvreor inelement,
60   & li sires tout aroument

25   that it's time for their tête-à-tête.

       Shaking from spite and all irate,
he hurries home. When he got back,
he looked in on them through a crack
and saw them sitting down to dine.
30 He called out, but it took some time
before someone let him inside.
The priest had no place he could hide.
He said, "Lord! what shall I do now?"
The lady said, "I'll tell you how.
35 Go in the shop, take off your clothes,
and, standing still, assume a pose
among my husband's holy carvings."
Right willingly, or with misgivings,
the priest obeyed her then and there:
40 Without his clothes, completely bare,
among the images he stood
as if he'd been carved out of wood.
Seeing he isn't in the room,
the good man is led to assume
45 he's hidden with his sculpted figures.
Being intelligent, he figures
that first he'll drink and have a bite
as if he thinks things are all right.

       After his dinner, when he'd done,
50 he went and got a whetting stone
and started sharpening a knife.
The sturdy carver told his wife,
"Now, lady, light a candle quickly
and come into the workshop with me,
55 where I've some business to prepare."
No word of protest did she dare,
but with her husband made her way
directly to his atelier,
holding a candle to give light.
60 The master carver soon caught sight

le prevoire tout estendu
vit, si l'a bien reconeü
a la coille & au vit qui pent.
« Dame, fait il, vilainement
65   ay en cest ymage mespris!
J'estoie yvres, ce vous plevis,
quant telz menbres je y laissé!
Allumez, *si l'*amenderé. »
       Le prestre ne s'osa mouvoir,
70   & ge vous di tretout por voir
que vit & coilles li trencha
que onques riens ne li laissa
que tretout n'ait outre trenchié.
Quant li prestre se sent blecié,
75   si s'en est tost tornés fuiant,
& li preudom tout maintenant
s'est escrïé a molt haut cris:
« Seignor, prenez mon croucefis
qui orendroit m'est eschapé! »
80   A tant a .ii. garçons trouvé
li prestre, portant une *jarle*—
molt li venist mieus estre a Arle,
car il i ot un pautonier
qui en sa main tint un levier,
85   si l'en feri parmi le col
qu'il l'abati en un tai mol,
& quant il l'ot jus abatu,
es lor le preudomme venu,
si le remaine en sa maison.
90   .xv. livres de raençon
li fist inel les pas paier
que onques n'en failli denier.
       Cest essample vous moutre bien
que nul prestre por nule rien
95   ne devroit autrui fame amer
n'a cele venir ni aler,

of the priest with his arms stretched out,
whom he could spot beyond a doubt,
seeing his hanging balls and cock.
"Lady," he says, "I've made a shock-
65 ing image here by not omitting
those virile members. How unfitting!
I must have had too much to drink.
Some light! I'll fix it in a wink."

      The terrified priest never stirred.
70 The husband, you can take my word,
cut off the prelate's genitalia
and left him nothing, without failure,
to warrant further amputation.
The priest, feeling the laceration,
75 took to his heels and ran away.
The worthy man without delay
cried after him with piercing shrieks,
"Good people, catch my crucifix,
which is escaping down the street!"

80   The priest had the bad luck to meet
two fellows carrying a barrel.
He'd have been better off in Arles,
because one rascal in that band
who had a crowbar in his hand
85 swung at his neck with it and struck
him down into a pile of muck.
When he'd been beaten to the ground,
just then the good man came around
and dragged him home, where he was forced
90 to buy his freedom, and it cost
him fifteen pounds. He made him pay
it right then, every last *denier*.

      This parable has demonstrated,
no matter who is implicated,
95 in no case should a clergyman
mess with the wife of any man

qui onques fust en *calengage*,
qu'il n'i laissast la coille en gage
si comme fist prestres Coustanz,
100 qui i laissa les .iii. pendanz.

8. LE PRESTRE QUI OT MERE MALGRÉ SIEN

Icist fableaus, ce est la voire,
si nous raconte d'un provoire
qui avoit une vielle mere
molt felonesse & molt amere:
5   boçue estoit, noire & hideuse
& de toz biens contralïeuse.
Toz li mons l'avoit contre cuer;
li prestres meesme a nul fuer
ne voloit por sa derraison
10   qu'elë entrast en sa maison—
trop ert cuiverte & de put estre.
Or ot une amie le prestre
que il vestoit & bien & bel:
bone cote ot & bon mantel
15   & .ii. peliçons bons & beaus,
l'un d'escureus, l'autre d'aignaus,
si ot riche toissu d'argent.
Assez en parole la gent,
mais la vielle enparole plus
20   de l'amie au prestre que nus,
si a dit a son filz meïsme
que il ne l'aime pas la disme
qu'il fait s'amie, il i pert bien:
a lui ne velt il doner rien,
25   ne bon mantel ne bone cote.

or hang around her. I allege
he'll leave his balls there as a pledge,
just as the priest, Father Coustenz,
100   left his three hanging ornaments.

8. THE PRIEST WHO HAD A
MOTHER FOISTED ON HIM

This fabliau, I tell you true,
tells us a tale of a priest who
had an old beldame for a mother,
a bitter woman and a bother,
5   dark, ugly, hunchbacked, and averse
to all the good things on this earth.
All looked upon her with abhorrence.
The priest found her beyond endurance.
Since all she did was carp and grouse,
10   he wouldn't let her in his house,
she was so loathsome and so dour.
        Now, this priest had a paramour
whom he kept clothed in fine apparel:
two fine fur wraps, the first of squirrel,
15   the other sheepskin, a good cape,
a good overcoat, and to drape
her body in, rich silver fabric.
The parish thinks it's a hot topic,
but the old woman carries on
20   about her more than anyone,
and she says to the priest himself
that he does not love her a twelfth
as much as his wench, that is clear.
Why, he'll give her nothing to wear,
25   neither a mantle nor a coat!

« Taisiez! fet il, vos estes sote!
De quoi me menez vos dangier
se du pain avez a mengier,
de mon potaige & de mes pois?
30 Encor le faz ge sor mon pois,
quar vos m'avez dit mainte honte. »
La vielle dit: « Riens ne vos monte,
quar ge vorrai dorenavant
que vos me teignoiz par couvant
35 *a grant honor* com vostre mere. »
Li prestre a dit, par seint Pere,
jamais du sien ne mengera,
or face au mielz qu'ele porra
ou au pis, tant que il li loist.
40 « Si ferai, mais que bien vos poist,
fait ele, quar ge m'en irai
a l'evesque; le conterai
vostre errement & vostre vie,
com vostre meschine est servie—
45 assez a a mengier & robes,
& moi volez paistre de lobes.
De vostre avoir n'ai nule part. »
      A itant la vielle s'en part
autresi comme forsenee,
50 droit a l'evesque en est alee,
au piez li chiet & si se claime
de son fill, qui noient ne l'aime,
si ne li fait honeur ne bien
ne que il feroit a un chien;
55 de tot en tot a sa meschine,
qu'il aime plus que sa cousine;
cele a des robes a plenté.
Quan la vielle ot tot aconté
a l'evesque ce que lui plot,
60 il li respont a .i. seul mot

"Shut up," he says, "you silly goat!
What right have you to aggravate
me when you have bread on your plate
and I give you my peas and pottage?
30 With bad grace, yes, for in your dotage
you speak to me with such ill will."
The old woman tells him, "Big deal!
From this day forward, I require
that you treat me as I desire:
35 as your mother, with deference."
By Saint Peter, the priest says, hence-
forth she'll not get another bite
from him. Who cares what harm she might
do to him? No, he'll not permit it!
40 "Oh yes, I will, and you'll regret it,"
she says, "for I'll go straightaway
to see the bishop, and I'll lay
bare your behavior and your life,
the way you treat your so-called wife,
45 who gets plenty of food and clothing
while I have to live on your loathing.
Although you're wealthy, I am poor."

     The old woman storms out the door
hysterical and overwrought
50 and goes straight to the bishop's court,
falls at his feet, and states her case:
Her son's behavior's a disgrace,
she gets no more love or respect
than a stray mongrel might expect;
55 his girlfriend's everything to him,
he loves her more than kith or kin;
that one gets dresses by the score.

     Once the old woman's set before
the bishop her long accusation,
60 he says upon consideration

que il fera son fill semondre;
a tant ne li volt plus respondre,
ainz *vieigne* a cort a jor nomé.
La viele l'en a encliné,
65   puis s'en part sanz autre response,
& l'evesque fist la semonse
a son fill que il viegne a cort,
qu'il le vorra tenir si cort
s'il ne fait raison a sa mere.
70   Ge crieng que molt chier le compere.
        Quant li termes & li jors vint
& li esvesques sez plaiz tint,
molt i ot clers & autre gent
& provoires plus de .ii.c.
75   La vielle ne s'est pas tenue;
a l'esvesque en est venue
& li ramentoit sa besoigne.
L'esvesque dit pas ne s'esloigne,
que tantost com son filz venra
80   bien saiche qu'il le soupendra
& toudra tot son benefice.
La vielle, qui fu fole & nice,
quant el ot parler de soupendre,
crient que son filz ne face pendre;
85   lors dist en bas: « Maleüree!
por quoi me sui a lui clamee?
Deable furent a mon naistre
quant mes chiers filz penduz doit estre,
que ge portai dedenz mes flans! »
90   Toz li est esmeüz li sans
& durement fu esbahie;
lors s'apenssa la renoïe[ ]
qu'ele fera l'evesque acroire
c'iert ses filz d'un autre provoire.
95   A tant .i. prestre laienz entre
qui estoit gros par mi le ventre,

he'll have her son appear before
him and till then he'll say no more;
he must come when he's summoned, though.
The old woman left, bowing low,
65 having been promised satisfaction,
and the bishop went and took action,
subpoenaed her son to appear,
intending to make him pay dear
if he won't do right by his parent.
70 He's in for trouble, that's apparent.
The day came which the bishop set
to hear the cases to be pled.
Two hundred folk assemble then,
both commoners and clergymen.
75 The old woman has not stayed home;
before the bishop she has come,
reminding him of her appeal.
The bishop says to wait; he'd deal
with him when he came: he intended
80 to have his benefice suspended
and priestly privilege cut off.
The foolish woman's simple thoughts
fancied he meant hanging and tortures
in punishment for his debauches.
85 Ah, woe is me! Why did I press
these charges? she thought in distress.
By devils was my birth accursed,
when the dear child I bore and nursed
is to be hanged on my account!
90 She flushed, her heart began to pound,
and she was mortally afraid.
The poor wretch got it in her head
to fool the bishop by a con
and call a different priest her son.
95 Another priest arrives at court
just then, a round, potbellied sort

[si ot] le col reont [ ] & gras;
tantost la vielle isnelepas
a l'evesque cria en haut:
100 « Sire, fist el, se Dieus me saut,
c'est mes filz cist gros prestres la! »
Tantost l'esvesque l'apela,
si li dist: « Prestre desvoiez,
dites moi por quoi renoiez
105 vostre mere qui est ici?
Se Dieus ait de m'ame merci,
a poi que ge ne vos soupent!
La bone feme a vos s'atent
que vos *lessiez* povre & frarine,
110 & vos tenez vostre meschine
a bone robe vaire & grise.
Molt est or bien la rente assise
dont estes tenanz & saisiz! »
Li prestres fu toz esbahiz
115 de ce que li esvesques dit:
« Sire, fait il, se Dieus m'aïst,
ge n'oi mere molt a lonc tens,
ne ge ne cuit mie ne pens
que mais ceste vielle veïsse.
120 Bien sachiez ne vos en mentisse,
foi que doi vos, se fust ma mere.
— Quoi? fait l'esvesque. Por seint Pere,
or estes vos trop desloiaus
& trop malvais prestres & faus,
125 qui vostre mere renoiez!
Vos seroiz escommeniez
& soupenduz, ne puet el estre! »
Or ot molt grant paor li prestre
quant il *sot* qu'il ert soupenduz;
130 toz li sans li est esmeüz,
a l'esvesque merci cria

of cleric with a double chin,
and the old woman raised a din
and told the bishop on the spot,
100 "Your Holiness, so help me God,
my son is that fat priest you see!"
He summoned him immediately
and said to him, "Renegade priest,
tell me why you've been such a beast
105 to your old mother, who stands there?
As I trust my soul to God's care,
I'm ready to have you suspended!
This righteous woman, who depended
on your care, you have left to fend
110 for herself, while your lady friend
has costly clothes in which to strut.
To what a worthy use you put
the stipend that I have endowed
you with!" The baffled priest is cowed,
115 hearing the bishop's words, and says,
"So help me God, Your Holiness,
my mother's been dead for some time,
and I do not believe that I'm
acquainted with this one at all.
120 If she were, I'd not have the gall,
believe me, to lie to your face."
"By Saint Peter," the bishop says,
"when was there ever such a hateful,
deceitful priest, and so ungrateful?
125 Your own mother, and you deny her!
You'll be suspended! Do right by her,
or you'll be excommunicated!"
The priest was so intimidated
to hear him threatening suspension,
130 his face flushed a dark purple gentian.
He begged the bishop to relent

& dit que son plaisir fera,
& dit li vesque: « Ge l'otroi.
Or prenez vostre palefroi,
135   si montez vostre mere sus.
Gardez que ge n'en oie plus
parole, plainte ne clameur,
ainz la tenez a grant henor
com vostre mere, qu'il i pere. »
140   Li prestres tantost s'en repere
com li fu donez li congiez;
tart li est qu'il soit esloigniez.
La vielle porte devant soi
sor le col de son palefroi,
145   & maugré sien, ce sai de voir,
li trovera son estovoir.
        Ainz qu'il ait une liue alee,
enmi le fonz d'une valee
le filz a la vielle encontra;
150   cele part el chemin entra,
des noveles le tint molt cort,
& cil li dist que a la cort
devant l'esvesque .i. plait avoit.
Lors regarde, sa mere voit,
155   qui li cligne c'outre passast,
de nule riens ne l'arainast,
& il s'en est outre passez.
L'autre prestre li dit assez:
« Quant venrez a cort, beaus conpaing,
160   Dieus vos i doint autel gaaig
com *j'ai* fait ceste matinee!
Li vesque m'a mere donee,
ou soit a droit ou soit a tort—
ceste vielle hideuse en port,
165   si la me covient maintenir. »
Lors ne se pot mie tenir

and gave assurance that he meant
to do as he was told. "Agreed,"
the bishop says. "Now take your steed
135 and put your mother on its back,
and make sure I hear no more flak,
not one complaint or accusation,
but give her the consideration
a mother's owed, and openly."
140   The priest sets out immediately,
as soon as he's been given leave—
in fact, he cannot wait to leave.
He bears the old woman in front
across the withers of his mount.
145 Against his will, some way or other
he must support her as his mother.
    No more than a league had they gone
when they met the old woman's son
as they were riding through a cwm.
150 He turned aside and went up to 'im
and questioned him on what was doing,
and he replied that he was going
to court at the bishop's subpoena.
He spied his mother. Once he'd seen her,
155 she winked at him to ride on by
without inquiring how or why,
and he continued on his way.
    The other priest had much to say:
"When you come to the bishop's court,
160 may God reward you with the sort
of gift I got this morning, brother!
Our bishop's given me a mother,
and, rightfully or wrongfully,
I'm taking the hag home with me,
165 where I must see to her support."
The old woman's son nearly roared

le filz a la vielle de rire,
si li a dit: « Beaus tres dolz sire,
se vos vostre mere en portez,
170 ja ne vos en desconfortez!
     — Moie? deables! fait li prestre.
Mere au deable puist ele estre,
quar ma mere ne fu el onques! »
Lors li dist l'autre prestre: « Donques,
175 par foi, merveilles me contez!
Qui or vos feroit tels bontez
qu'il por vos la mere peüst
& *tot quant* que li esteüst
tote sa vie li trouvast
180 (mais que la vielle l'otroiast),
que li donrrïez vos, beaus sire? »
Li prestres respont: « Par seint Cire,
cui ge sui hons & chapelains,
ja n'en ere fous ne vileins.
185 Qui de son cors me delivrast
(si que la vielle l'ostroiast),
ge li donrrai .lx. livres!
     — Por tant en seroiz vos delivres,
fait il, se vos les me bailliez.
190   — N'aiez garde que i failliez,
fait il, (se la vielle l'ostroie). »
Cele li dit: « Se Dieus me voie,
& ge l'otroie bonement. »
Lors fiancent le paiement
195 a terme & les deniers a rendre.
Or puet plus asseür despendre
li filz a la vielle sanz faille,
quar cil qui les deniers li baille,
il s'aquita comme loiaus.
200   A icest mot falt li flabeaus.

with laughter upon hearing this:
"Good brother, why take it amiss?
If it's your mother you maintain,
170   you have no just cause to complain."
"Whose? Mine? The devil!" the priest said.
"You mean the devil's dam instead!
This woman's no mother of mine!"
The other said, "Now, that's a fine
175   and wondrous marvel, by the Savior!
If someone would do you the favor
of feeding this mother of yours
and, till she died, from his own stores
supplied her every earthly need
180   (assuming the old girl agreed),
what would you pay him, brother dear?"
The priest replies, "Now, by Saint Cyr,
whom I serve most devotedly,
I'd not be cheap or niggardly!
185   Whoever takes her off my hands
(unless the old girl countermands
it) gets sixty pounds for his trouble."
"Let's have the money on the double,"
he says. "For that I'll set you free!"
190   "Don't go back on our deal," says he,
"and the old girl must give permission."
"I'll go along with your decision,"
she tells them, "as God is my witness."
      The two priests finalize the business
195   and arrange an installment plan.
Now the old woman's real son can
spend lavishly and needn't fret,
because the one who's in his debt
will pay off everything he owes.
200   I've told you enough fabliaux.

9. L'EVESQUE QUI BENEÏ LE CON

Uns evesques jadis estoit
qui molt volantiers s'acointoit
de dames & de damoiseles,
qu'il en trovoit asez de beles
5 & il lor donoit largemant;
por ce faisoient son commant,
car totes beent mais au prandre,
& cil qui ne lor a que tandre
n'en avra jamais bon servise;
10 ceste costume ont aprise.
            Pres de la cité de Baiues,
ice m'est avis a .ii. liues,
ot li evesques un repaire;
riche maison i ot fait faire.
15 Je ne sai la vile nomer.
Sovant s'i aloit deporter
li evesques qant il voloit
por ce que loin de vile estoit.
Uns prestes estut en la vile,
20 qui molt sot d'angin & de guile.
Sa fame avoc lui avoit
li prestes, que il molt amoit
& molt estoit preuz & cortoise,
& a l'evesque molt en poise,
25 si li a par mainte foiz dit
& deveé & contredit
que il l'ostast de sa maison.
Li prestes par bele raison
li dist que sofrir ne s'an puet.
30 « Par noz ordres faire l'estuet,
dit li evesques, araument,

9. THE CUNT BLESSED BY A BISHOP

A bishop lived in days gone by
who very readily would lie
with women, married and unmarried.
Of lovely ones he found his share; he'd
5   give gifts to them generously,
and so they'd do whatever he
asked, for all women long for wealth,
and he who's nothing but himself
to give will never win their favors.
10 (That's one of women's learned behaviors.)
         Close to the city of Bayeux,
I think it was a league or two
away, the bishop had somewhere
to stay, a fine house he'd built there.
15 I don't know the name of the town,
but when he wanted to have fun,
the bishop often went to stay
there, since it was a ways away.
In that same town a priest lived, who
20 was clever and was tricky, too.
A woman lived with him as wife,
the greatest love he had in life,
and worthy and well-bred was she.
This irked the bishop mightily,
25 who, as he very often said
to him, disapproved and forbade
him to keep her under his roof.
In fair words the priest said, in truth,
he could not bear the separation.
30 The bishop says, "No hesitation
will I allow. You must comply

ou autremant je vos desfant
que vos ne bevez ja de vin.
    — Sire, foi que doi saint Martin,
35 fait li prestes, ainz m'an tandrai
de vin si que ja n'en buvrai. »
A tant repaire en sa maison
li prestes & met a raison
sa fame que il a trovee:
40 « Par Deu, fait il, dame Auberee,
or m'est il trop mal avenu,
que l'esvesques m'a desfandu
a boivre vin & deveé.
    — Voire, sire, par les sainz Dé,
45 ja en bevez vos volantiers.
Or est il trop vostre gerriers
qui vin a boivre vos desfant!
Biau sire, son commandemant
covient tenir: ja n'en bevroiz,
50 mais par foi, vos lo humeroiz.
Qant li boivres vos est veez,
li humers vos est commandez,
de par moi, si lo vos enseing. »
    Li prestes n'ot mie en desdaing
55 ce que la dame commanda;
lo boivre laissa, si *huma*
qant lui plot & mestier en ot,
tant que li evesques le sot.
Je ne sai qui l'an encusa:
60 lo provoire tantost manda,
si li desfant que il gardast
que ja mais d'oie ne manjast
tant com sa fame aüst o lui.
« Sire, fait il, a grant enui
65 me torne ce & a contrere
que vos me commandez a faire,
mais tot ce ne vos vaut noiant.

with our will, or otherwise I
forbid you to drink wine again."
The priest says, "I'd sooner abstain
35 from drinking wine for my entire
life, I swear by Saint Martin, sire."

     The priest goes back to where he lives
thereupon and openly grieves
of this to his wife, who awaits
40 him. "By God, Auberée," he states,
now I've been struck by a great mishap!
I may not drink wine, for the bishop
forbids me to, so he's decreed."
"Sir, by God's holy saints, indeed,
45 if he won't let you drink wine, he
must be a hardened enemy
of yours, who drink it with such gusto.
Since he commands it, though, you must, so
you'll drink it no more, by my head,
50 but have to gulp it down instead.
Gulp it down henceforth as commanded
now that your drinking days are ended,
as I advise and tell you plain."
The priest did not at all disdain
55 to act upon her way of thinking.
He took up gulping, gave up drinking,
and when he felt like it, he'd do it,
and went on till the bishop knew it.

     Who turned him in, I've not the least
60 idea, but he summoned the priest
and orders him that he must choose
either never to dine on goose
again or give the woman up.
He says, "Sir, it's a bitter cup
65 I have to drink. What you ordain
certainly goes against the grain,
but it won't do you any good,

Je ne m'an irai pas riant. »
Li prestes plus n'i demora;
70   a sa fame tot raconta
con il a les oës perdues:
l'evesques li a desfandues.
« Dame, fait il, juré li ai
ja mais d'oë ne mangerai.
75   — Voire, fait ele, est il ensi?
Molt vos a ore maubailli,
fait ele, li vilains escharz!
Par foi, vos manjeroiz des jars
a planté, qui que s'an repante,
80   car vos en avez plus de .xxx.
— En non Deu, fait il, jel creant! »

        Ensinc lo refist longuemant
tant qu'a l'esvesque refu dit
& cil li refait contredit
85   que ja mais ne gise sor coute.
« Par foi, ci a parole estote,
fait li prestes, que vos me dites!
Je ne sui reclus ne hermites,
mais des qu'il vos vient a plaisir
90   par quoi je n'i doie gesir,
ensinc lo restuet il a faire. »
A tant se rest mis au repaire;
a sa fame se rest clamez,
& cele dit: « Oïr poëz
95   grant rage & grant forsenerie!
Bien sai que ne vos aime mie
li esvesques ne n'a point chier,
mais tot ce ne li a mestier
ne ne monte .ii. engevins:
100   un lit vos ferai de cousins.
Bien lo ferai soëf & mol.
— Dame, foi que je doi saint Pol,

though I leave in a sorry mood."
The priest then left, no longer waited,
70 went back to his wife and related
how he has lost the taste of goose:
The bishop forbids him its use.
"Lady," he says to her, "I swore
that I would dine on goose no more."
75 "Indeed," she says, "can this be true?
He has dealt wickedly with you,
that cheap, black-hearted churl," she answers.
"In faith, you'll just have to eat ganders
galore, whomever it may hurt. We
80 have here, as you know, more than thirty."
"In the name of God," says he, "I'm
game!"
    So he did for a long time
until someone again disclosed
it to the bishop, who imposed
85 a sanction against feather beds.
"In faith, what you've come up with," says
the priest, "is lunatic and reckless.
Am I a hermit or a recluse?
But since it is your pleasure I
90 am now forbidden thus to lie
me down, then that's what I must do."
Thereupon he went back home to
his wife, laid out what had occurred,
and she says, "Have you ever heard
95 such madness and insanity?
The bishop feels no amity
nor cares much for you, I'll allow you,
but it won't help him. There's more value
in two cents minted in Anjou.
100 I'll lay some cushions out for you
and make a soft and comfy bed."
"As I trust Saint Paul, what you've said

fait li prestes, vos dites bien.
Or ne lo dot je mais de rien
105 puis q'ainsinc m'avez conseillié. »
　　　　Aprés ce n'a gaires targié
li evesques que il ala
en la vile, s'i demora
une semaine tote entierre
110 ainz que il retornast arriere.
Une borjoise en la vile ot
que li esvesques molt amot,
q'a chascune nuit sanz faillir
aloit avoque li gesir
115 (qu'el ne voloit a lui aler
por prometre ou por doner,
tant estoit fiere & orgoillose
envers l'evesque & desdaignose),
tant c'une nuit, si com moi sanble,
120 durent endui gesir ensanble.
Ensinc l'avoient porposé,
mais trestote la verité
en sot li prestes araumant,
qui molt avoit lo cuer dolant
125 de ce que l'evesques li dist
que fame avoc li ne tenist,
si l'an remanbre encore bien,
& dit qu'il ne laira por rien
c'a la borjoise n'aut parler.
130 Maintenant sanz plus arester
s'an va a li, si li a dit:
« Dame, se li cors Deu m'aït,
grant mestier ai de vostre aïe.
Gardez que ne me failliez mie,
135 que ja mais ne vos ameroie.
— Sire, fait ele, se savoie
chose don il vos fust mestier,
jel feroie molt volantiers.

is right and proper," says the priest.
"Since you've advised this, not the least
105 will he perturb me anymore."
    It wasn't all that long before
the bishop made a trip and went
off to the town, and there he spent
an entire week, and only then
110 did he return back home again.
There in the town a woman dwelt
for whom the am'rous bishop felt
great love. Without fail every night
he went to lie down by her side,
115 for she'd not go to him, whatever
pledges he'd make or gifts he'd give her,
she was so very proud and vain
and acted toward him with disdain.
    At length one night, it seems to me,
120 they had agreed that she and he
would bed down and lie with each other,
but the priest was quick to discover
all the details of what they'd plotted,
and, being sad and heavyhearted
125 because the bishop had said to him
that he may not live with a woman
(the memory is with him still),
he affirms not anything will
prevent him from going to speak
130 with the woman. He went to seek
her out and straightaway he said,
"Lady, may God come to my aid,
your assistance would much avail me.
Be careful that you do not fail me
135 or I'll no longer be your friend."
"Sir," she says, "let me understand
how I can be of help to you,
and what I can I'll gladly do.

Or me dites vostre plaisir.
140   — Dame, ne lo vos quier taisir,
fait li prestes. Ne vos anuit,
li esvesques qui doit anuit
o vos gesir en vostre lit
& de vos faire son delit,
145   que l'an lo m'a dit & conté . . .
si me faites tant de bonté,
comme m'amie & ma voisine,
que vos darriere la cortine
me laissiez repondre & tapir.
150   Bien lo vos cuit encor merir
se tant volez faire por moi.
— Par foi, fait ele, jel otroi.
Ce ferai je molt lieemant.
Alez donques delivremant,
155   si vos muciez & reponez.
— Volantiers, qant vos lo volez. »
Lors se muce & atapine
& caiche darrier la cortine
tant que li jorz s'an fu alez.
160   Adonc ne s'est pas obliez
li evesques qui venir dut;
a tot .iiii. serjanz s'esmut,
 a la borjoise vint tot droit,
qui priveemant l'atandoit;
165   n'i ot que li & sa baiasse.
Ne sai que plus vos en contasse
mais que li liz fu atornez,
qui bien estoit encortinez
Dui cerges molt cler i ardoient
170   qui molt tres grant clerté gitoient.
La dame se coucha avant,
& li evesques auraumant
s'i recoucha sanz plus atandre,
& li viz li comance a tandre

What service do you want provided?"
140 "Lady, I've no intent to hide it,"
the priest says. "I mean no offense
by this. The bishop, who intends
to lie in bed tonight with you
and have his pleasure of you, too,
145 as I have heard it said he would. . . .
Do let me, if you'll be so good,
in friendship and neighborliness,
hide and conceal myself someplace
close to your bed, behind the curtain.
150 I'll make it worth your while, I'm certain,
if you will do that much for me."
"In faith," she answers, "I agree.
I'm very glad to do it, so
without further delay now go
155 get out of sight and remain hidden."
"Gladly, since that is what you've bidden."
　　　　He hides himself, concealed behind
the bed curtains, which make a blind
for him, and stays till day has set,
160 when the bishop did not forget
where it was he's supposed to go.
He left with four servants in tow
and went straight without hesitating
to see the woman, who was waiting
165 unobtrusively with her maid.
I can't think what more needs be said,
except the bedding was turned down
with all the curtains tightly drawn
and two glowing candles alight,
170 filling the bedroom with their light.
　　　　The lady was the first to climb
into the bed and, with no time
wasted, the bishop got in with her,
his penis starting to grow stiffer

175 qant il santi la dame nue,
si volt monter sanz atandue,
mais cele li contredit bien
& dit que il n'an fera rien.
« Sire, fait el, ne vos hastez.
180 Se vos volez vos volantez
faire de moi ne de mon con,
i covient que beneïçon
li doigniez & si lo seigniez
ençois que vos i adessez,
185 qu'il ne fu onques ordonez.
La destre main en haut levez,
sel beneïsiez maintenant,
tot autresi hastivemant
comme vos feriez demain
190 la teste au fil a un vilain
se vos li faisiez corone. »
L'evesques ot qu'el li sarmone,
que ja a li n'avra tochié
tant qu'ençois ait son con seignié,
195 si dist: « Dame, foi que vos doi,
quan que vos dites, je l'otroi.
Vos lo volez & jo voil bien.
Por ce n'i perdrai je ja rien. »
Li evesque lo con seigna
200 & puis a dit: « Per onnia,
qan qu'il fait la beneïçon,
dit, secula seculorum »,
& li prestes, qui l'antandi,
maintenant « Aman » respondi,
205 & li evesques, qant il l'ot,
sachiez que grant peor en ot
qant a lo prevoire escoté;
puis a un po en haut parlé:
« Qui es tu qui respondu as?

175 with her unclothed and him beside her.
He cannot wait to mount and ride her,
but she will not allow him to
do anything he wants to do.
"Father," she tells him, "not so fast.
180 If you want to do what you asked
of me, before you turn to messing
with my body and cunt, a blessing
you must pronounce and make as well
the sign of the cross, for I tell
185 you, it's never been consecrated.
Now raise your right hand high," she stated,
"and give your blessing right away,
exactly as another day
you would proceed if it were done
190 on the head of a peasant's son
if he were taking holy orders."
The bishop takes in what she orders:
that lay a hand on her he won't
unless he first has blessed her cunt.
195 He said, "Ma'am, by the faith I owe
you, what you want I will bestow.
You ask for it, and I agree.
The deed entails no loss for me."
        Over her cunt the bishop made
200 the sign of the cross and then said,
"Benedico. Per omnia
in seculorum secula."
As for the priest in hiding, when
he heard him, he chimed in, "Amen,"
205 and as soon as the bishop heard
him—you can be sure he was scared
by the rejoinder the priest made!—
he raised his voice a bit and said,
"Who is it who made that reply?"

210 — Sire, fait il, je sui li laus
cui tu viaus sa fame tolir
si com il te vient a plaisir,
& si m'as lo vin desfandu—
ja mais par moi n'en ert beü.
215 Des hui matin oï retraire
que tu voloies ordres faire;
si i voloie estre, biau sire. »
Li evesques conmance a rire
& dit: « Or m'as tu espié
220 & bien sorpris & engignié!
Or te doin je congié de boivre
& de mangier poucins au poivre
& oës qant tu en voudraus,
& avoc toi ta fame avras.
225 Si garde que mais ne te voie. »
Lors s'an torne cil a grant joie.

10. FREIRE DENISE LE CORDELIER

Li abiz ne fait pas l'ermite.
S'uns hom en hermitage habite,
s'il est de povres draz vestuz,
je ne pris mie .ii. festuz
5 son habit ne sa vesteüre
s'il ne mainne vie ausi pure
coume ses habiz nos demoustre,
mais mainte gens font bele moustre
& mervilleuz semblant qu'il vaillent;
10 il semblent les aubres qui faillent
qui furent trop bel au florir.
Bien dovroient teil gent morir
vilainnement & a grant honte.

210 "Your Grace," he said, "that wretch am I
whose wife you'd take away from him
only because that is your whim;
also the one whom you forbade
to drink wine, and I have obeyed.
215 Today I heard the information
that you'd perform an ordination.
I'd like to witness that, I thought."
The bishop heartily guffawed
and said, "You laid a trap for me
220 and caught me by your trickery.
I henceforth give you my permission
to drink wine and eat peppered chicken
and dine on goose as much as you
would like, and keep your woman, too.
225 Just you keep well out of my sight."
Off goes the priest in great delight.

10. BROTHER DENISE
by Rutebeuf

The monk is not made by his habit.
Whatever cloister he inhabit,
however poor the clothes he wore,
I wouldn't give even a straw
5 for his habit or for his dress
if he led a life any less
pure than his vestments ought to show,
but many people make a show
and great pretense of virtue rare
10 who resemble those trees that bear
no fruit but that were fair of flower.
A wretched, shameful death devour
all people who behave this way!

.i. proverbes dit & raconte
15 que tout n'est pas ors c'on voit luire.
        Por ce m'estuet ainz que je muire
faire .i. flabel d'une aventure
de la plus bele criature
que hom puisse troveir ne querre
20 de Paris juqu'en Aingleterre.
Vous dirai coument il avint.
Grans gentiz homes plus de vint
l'avoient a fame requise,
mais ne voloit en nule guise
25 avoir ordre de mariage,
ainz ot fait de son pucelage
veu a Deu & a Notre Dame.
La pucele fu gentilz fame:
chevaliers ot estei ses peires,
30 meire avoit, mais n'ot suer de frere.
Molt s'entramoient, ce me semble,
la pucele & sa mere ensemble.
Frere meneur laianz hantoient
tuit cil qui par illec passoient.
35 Or avint c'uns en i hanta
qui la damoizele enchanta,
si vos dirai en queil maniere.
        La pucele li fist proiere
que il sa mere requeïst
40 qu'en religion la meïst,
& il li dist: « Ma douce amie,
se meneir voliez la vie
Saint François si com nos faison,
vos ne porriez par raison
45 faillir que vos ne fussi[ez] sainte. »
& cele, qui fu ja atainte
& conquise & mate & vaincue
si tost com ele ot entendue
la raison dou frere meneur,

Hear what the proverb has to say:
15 Not everything that shines is gold.
        For this reason, ere I grow old
and die, I'd pen a fabliau
about the fairest creature. Though
you searched from England far as Paris,
20 you wouldn't find a maiden fair as
she. I'll tell what came to pass.
No less than twenty men had asked,
wellborn and noble, for her hand,
but she neither wished for nor planned
25 a life of conjugality,
for she'd pledged her virginity
to God and the Virgin as well.
She was a noble demoiselle:
Her sire had been a knight, her mother
30 still lived, she'd no sister or brother.
Mother and child, it seems to me,
treasured each other tenderly.
Franciscans would quite often come
by and find shelter in their home.
35 Some twist of destiny once led
a friar there who turned her head.
        I'll tell how he beguiled the virgin.
She begged him to get, with much urging,
her mother's blessing for her daughter's
40 desire to enter holy orders.
"Most sweet and precious child," he answers,
"if you sought to follow Saint Francis
and live his life the way we do,
it only stands to reason you
45 could not fail to become a saint."
The girl, taken in by his feint,
convinced, won over, and ensnared
already, as soon as she heard
the counsel of the Friar Minor,

50　si dist: « Se Dieux me doint honeur,
　　si grant joie avoir ne porroie
　　de nule riens conme j'avroie
　　se de votre ordre pooie estre.
　　A bone heure me fist Dieux neitre
55　si g'i pooie estre rendue. »
　　Quant li freres ot entendue
　　la parole a la damoizele,
　　si li at dit: « Gentilz pucele,
　　si me doint Dieux s'amour avoir,
60　se de voir pooie savoir
　　qu'en nostre ordre entrer vosissiez
　　& que sens fauceir peüssiez
　　gardeir votre virginitei,
　　sachiez de fine veritei
65　qu'en nostre bienfait vos metroie. »
　　& la pucele li otroie
　　qu'el gardera son pucelage
　　trestoz les jors de son eage,
　　& cil maintenant la reçut;
70　par sa guile cele deçut
　　qui a barat n'i entendi:
　　desus s'arme li desfendi
　　que riens son conseil ne deïst,
　　mais si celeement feïst
75　copeir ses beles treces blondes
　　que ja ne le seüst li mondes
　　& feïst faire estauceüre
　　& preïst teile vesteüre
　　com a jone home couvandroit,
80　& qu'en teil guise venist droit
　　en un leu dont il ert custodes.
　　　　　Cil qui estoit plus fel qu'Erodes
　　s'en part atant & li mist terme,
　　& cele a plorei mainte larme
85　quant de li departir le voit.

50   replied, "As God may give me honor,
      if I could be one of your order,
      I cannot think what would afford a
      profounder joy to me on earth.
      The Lord blessed the hour of my birth
55   if I could be a novice there."
      No sooner did the friar hear
      the answer that the maiden gave,
      he said to her, "So may God save
      and grant me His love, if I knew,
60   most noble damsel, it was true
      that it was your desire to serve
      our order and you could preserve
      without guile your virginity,
      then, know it for a certainty,
65   I'd place you in our order now."
      The maiden gives her solemn vow
      that she will guard her maidenhead
      and stay a virgin till she's dead,
      and forthwith the friar received her.
70   His cunning subterfuge deceived her
      from whom his artfulness was hidden.
      Upon her soul she was forbidden
      by him to tell what they'd agreed,
      and likewise he explained she'd need
75   in secret to cut her blond hair,
      careful that no one be aware
      of it, and, tonsured, find a suit
      of clothes tailored and cut to suit
      a young man, and, disguised that way,
80   to come to him without delay
      in a place where he's overseer.
              That second Herod of Judaea
      arranged when they would meet, then left.
      Many a tear the maiden wept
85   to see him go. Though in his preaching

Cil qui la glose li devoit
faire entendre de sa leson,
la mist en male supeçon.
Male mort le preigne & ocie!
90   Cele tint tout a prophecie
quanque cil li a sermonei.
Cele a son cuer a Dieu donei;
cil ra fait dou sien ateil don
qui bien l'en rendra guerredon.
95   Molt par est contrare sa pense
au boen pensei ou cele pense;
molt est lor pensee contraire,
car cele pense a li retraire
& osteir de l'orgueil dou monde,
100   & cil qui en pechié soronde,
qui toz art dou feu de luxure,
a mis sa pensee & sa cure
a la pucele acompaignier
au baig ou il se wet baignier,
105   ou il s'ardra, se Dieux n'en pense,
que ja ne li fera deffence
ne ne li savra contredire
choze que il li welle dire.
A ce va li freres pensant,
110   & ses compains en trespassant,
qui s'esbahit qu'il ne parole,
li a dite ceste parole:
« Ou penseiz vos, Frere Symon?
— Je pens, fait il, a .i. sermon,
115   au meilleur ou je pensasse onques. »
& cil a dit: « Or penseiz donques. »
        Frere Symons ne puet deffence
troveir en son cuer qu'il ne pense
a la pucele, qui demeure,
120   & cele desirre molt l'eure
qu'ele soit ceinte de la corde;

he should have glossed the text he's teaching
with moral precepts and prescription,
he's filled her head with contradiction.
Death cast him in the fiery pit!
90   The girl accepts as Holy Writ
the sermon that he would impart.
To God has she given her heart;
the one he's offered his up to
will give him the reward *he's* due!
95   How very different is his thinking
from the high thoughts that she is thinking!
Their two minds are contrary, for
it's her intention to withdraw
and hide from the world's pridefulness,
100   while he, hemmed in by wickedness
and burning with the fires of lust,
has set his mind and efforts just
on making her accompany
him to bathe in a bath where he
105   will burn up, saving God's protection,
for she'll never raise an objection
nor contradict in any way
whatever he may wish to say.
        While he is thus preoccupied,
110   the confrere walking at his side,
seeing that he says not a word,
asks this question of him, disturbed:
"What are you thinking, Brother Simon?"
He says, "I'm thinking of a sermon,
115   more excellent than any other
I've made." He answers, "Think on, Brother."
Brother Simon cannot dispel
or purge these thoughts, his heart will dwell
on the girl who remains behind,
120   and she has nothing on her mind
except the hour when she will gird

sa leson en son cuer recorde
que li freres li ot donee:
dedens tiers jor s'en est emblee
125 de la mere qui la porta,
qui forment s'en desconforta.
Molt fu a mal aise la mere,
qui ne savoit ou sa fille ere;
grant dolor en son cuer demainne
130 trestoz les jors de la semainne,
en plorant regrete sa fille,
mais cele n'i done une bille,
ainz pense de li esloignier;
ses biaux crins a fait reoignier
135 comme vallez, fu estauciee
& fu de boens houziaus chauciee
& de robe a home vestue
qui estoit par devant fendue,
pointe devant, pointe derriere,
140 & vint en icele meniere
la ou cil li ot terme mis.
Li freres, cui li anemis
contraint & semont & argue,
out grant joie de sa venue;
145 en l'ordre la fist resouvoir—
bien sot ses freres desouvoir—
la robe de l'ordre li done
& li fist faire grant corone,
puis la fist au moutier venir.

150 Bel & bien s'i sot contenir,
& en clostre & dedens moutier,
& ele sot tot son sautier
& fu bien a chanteir aprise;
o les freres chante en l'esglize
155 molt bel & molt cortoisement;
molt se contint honestement.

a friar's belt, his every word
engraved in her heart and her soul.
When three days had gone by, she stole
125 away from the mother who bore
her, leaving her heart grieved and sore,
anguished and sorrowful because
she knew not where her daughter was.
She suffers great distress and fright
130 for days on end without respite,
missing her daughter, bathed in tears,
but the girl neither thinks nor cares
about all that, only of flight.
She's cut her lovely hair short, quite
135 like a boy's, and tonsured her crown,
put a good pair of leggings on
and likewise a tunic and robe, an',
like a man's, the front stayed open,
with stitching in back and in front,
140 and, dressed in this manner, she went
to the location he'd advised.
The friar, whom the Antichrist
holds fast to and bends to his will,
glad she has come, announces she'll
145 be one of their community.
Duping his confreres skillfully,
he dresses her in their apparel
and has her come into the chapel
and clerical estate confers
on her.
150 Seemly her conduct was
in cloister and before the altar:
She knew from end to end her Psalter;
her voice, melodious and fair,
joined in the brothers' songs at prayer,
155 for she'd learned to sing beautifully.
She behaved with great probity.

Or out damoizele Denize
quanqu'ele vot a sa devise;
onques son non ne li muërent,

160   Frere Denize l'apelerent.

       Que vos iroie ge dizant?
Frere Symons fist vers li tant
qu'il fist de li touz ses aviaux
& li aprist ces geux noviaux

165   si que nun ne s'en aparçut;
par sa contenance deçut
touz ses freres. Frere Denize
cortoiz fu & de grant servize.
Frere Denize mout amerent

170   tuit li frere qui laians erent,
mais plus l'amoit Frere Symons;
sovent se metoit es limons
com cil qui n'en ert pas retraiz,
& il s'i amoit mieulz qu'en traiz.

175   Molt ot en li boen limonier;
vie menoit de pautonier
& ot guerpi vie d'apostre
& cele aprist sa pater nostre,
que volentiers la recevoit,

180   parmi le païs la menoit,
n'avoit d'autre conpaignon cure,
tant qu'il avint par aventure
qu'il vindrent chiez .i. chevalier
qui ot boens vins en son celier

185   & volentiers lor en dona;
& la dame s'abandona
a regardeir Frere Denize,
sa chiere & son semblant avise.
Aparceüe c'est la dame

190   que Frere Denize estoit fame;
savoir wet se c'est voirs ou fable.

Everything Miss Denise has wanted
to have has now been fully granted.
They didn't give her a new name:
160 "Brother Denise" the girl became.
What more is there to tell you? Friar
Simon, indeed, did so well by her,
she was converted to his pleasure
and learned an unfamiliar leisure
165 activity, and none perceived
it. His demeanor quite deceived
all their confreres. Brother Denise
was gracious and eager to please.
Brother Denise was held most dear
170 by all the brothers living there,
but no one surpassed Simon's fondness,
who never wearied of the harness:
Between the wagon shafts he'd pull,
and no office pleased him as well.
175 He was an excellent draft horse
and led a life debauched and coarse
and strayed from the apostles' way
and tutored her on how to say
(which she learned gladly) *his* Lord's Prayer.
180 He took her with him everywhere
nor wished for other company,
until it happened he and she
were put up at a knight's abode,
who had his cellar stocked with good
185 wines, which he was most happy sharing
with them. His lady took to staring
at the figure Brother Denise
cuts, mulling over what she sees.
The lady readily detects
190 Brother Denise's rightful sex.
She'll find out if it's truth or fable.

Quant hon ot levee la table,
la dame, qui bien fu aprise,
prist par la main Frere Denize,
195 a son seigneur prist a souzrire,
en sozriant li dist: « Biau sire,
aleiz vos la defors esbatre
& faisons .ii. pars de nos quatre.
Frere Symon o vos meneiz;
200 Frere Denize est aseneiz
de ma confession oïr. »
Lors n'ont talent d'eulz esjoïr
li cordelier; dedens Pontoize
vousissent estre; molt lor poize
205 que la dame de ce parole;
ne lor plot pas ceste parole
car paour ont de parsovance.
Frere Symons *vers* li s'avance,
puis li dit quant de li s'apresse:
210 « Dame, a moi vos ferez confesse,
car ciz freres n'a pas licence
de vos enjoindre penitance. »
& la dame li dit: « Biau sire,
a cestui wel mes pechiez dire
215 & de confession parleir. »
Lors la fait en sa chambre aleir
& puis clot l'uis & bien le ferme,
o li Frere Denize enferme,
puis li a dit: « Ma douce amie,
220 qui vos consilla teil folie
d'entrer en teil religion?
Se me doint Dieus confession,
quant l'arme dou cors partira,
que ja pis ne vos en sera
225 se vos la veritei m'en dites.
Si m'aïst li Sainz Esperites,
bien vos pöez fier en moi. »

When they had risen from the table,
the lady with well-mannered ease
took by the hand Brother Denise
195 and said, giving a gracious smile
to her lord, "Go outside awhile,
my lord, and take your pleasure thus,
and let's pair off, the four of us.
Let Brother Simon go with you.
200 Brother Denise I've chosen to
hear the confession I would make."
These Friars Minor do not take
it as a laughing matter: They'd
sooner be in Pontoise; it weighed
205 heavy on them, what she proposed,
nor did it please them, for it caused
them fear of possible exposure.
Brother Simon moves himself closer
to her and tells her urgently,
210 "Lady, confess your sins to me,
for this man has no competence
in aught concerning penitence."
The lady answers him, "Good Brother,
I'll make confession to no other;
215 this man alone shall know my sin."
She leads her to her chamber then,
closes the door and turns the keys,
and, locked in with Brother Denise,
"My dear young friend," the lady said,
220 "whatever put it in your head
to serve the Church in such a fashion?
May the Lord pardon my transgression,
when your soul takes leave of this earth,
in no way will it be the worse
225 for you if you now tell me truly.
I swear to you upon the Holy
Spirit that you can trust in me."

& cele, qui ot grant esmoi,
au mierllz qu'el puet de ce s'escuze,
230   mais la dame la fist concluze
par les raisons qu'el li sot rendre,
si que plus ne s'i pot deffendre;
a genoillons merci li crie,
jointes mains li requiert & prie
235   qu'el ne li fasse faire honte;
trestot de chief en chief li conte
com il l'a trait d'enchiez *sa mere*
& puis li conta qui ele ere,
si que riens ne li a celei.

240   La dame a le frere apelei,
puis li dist oiant son seigneur
si grant honte c'onques greigneur
ne fu mais a nul home dite:
« Fauz papelars, fauz ypocrite,
245   fause vie meneiz & orde!
Qui vos pendroit a vostre corde,
qui est en tant de leuz nöee,
il avroit fait bone jornee!
Teil gent font bien le siecle pestre
250   qui par defors semblent boen estre
& par dedens sont tuit porri.
La norrice qui vos norri
fist mout mauvaise norreture,
qui si tres bele creature
255   aveiz a si grant honte mise.
Iteiz ordres, par saint Denise,
n'est mie boens ne biaux ne genz!
Vos deffendeiz au jones gens
& les dances & les quaroles,
260   violes, tabours & citoles
& toz deduiz de menestreiz.

The girl, shaken, confusedly
attempts to offer explanation,
230   but no: The lady's refutation
and arguments make such good sense,
they sweep away the girl's defense.
She cries for mercy on her knees,
and with hands clasped she begs and pleads
235   that she not bring her to disgrace.
From beginning to end she says
how he lured her away from home
and mother, and she then made known
her name and laid bare the entire
story.
240   The lady called the friar
and, in her husband's presence, loosed
the most injurious reproof
that has been heaped on any man.
"You hypocrite! You charlatan!
245   What a false, filthy life you lead!
Oh, it would be a blessèd deed
to use the cord that binds your habit
to hang you from the nearest gibbet!
People like you take for a ride
250   the whole world, virtuous outside,
but inside rotten through and through.
The nurse who gave suckle to you
did very wickedly to nurture
a man who such a lovely creature
255   would lead astray so shamefully.
Saint Dennis! this community
is neither noble, fair, nor good!
You tell us that young people should
not be allowed dancing and balls,
260   citterns and tabors and violes
and all delights of minstrelsy.

Or me dites, sire haut reiz,
menoit saint Fransois teile vie?
Bien aveiz honte deservie
265   conme faulz traïstre provei,
& vos aveiz molt bien trovei
qui vos rendra votre deserte. »
Lors a une grante huche overte
por metre le frere dedens,
270   & Freres Symons toz a dens
leiz la dame se crucefie,
& li chevaliers s'umelie,
qui de franchize ot le cuer tendre,
quant celui vit en croix estendre.
275   Suz l'en leva par la main destre;
« Frere, dit il, voleiz vos estre
de cest afaire toz delivres?
Porchaciez tost .iiii c. livres
a marier la damoizele. »
280   Quant li freres oit la novele,
onques n'ot teil joie en sa vie;
lors a sa fiance plevie
au chevalier des deniers rendre.
(Bien les rendra sens gage vendre—
285   auques seit ou il seront pris!)
Atant s'en part, congié a pris
     La dame par sa grant franchise
retint damoizele Denise;
n'onques de riens ne l'esfrea,
290   mais mout doucement li pria
qu'ele fust trestoute seüre
que ja de nule creature
ne sera ces secreiz seüz
ne qu'ele ait a home geü,
295   ainz sera molt bien mariee:
choisisse en toute la contree

You've brought on yourself infamy.
You tell me, Mr. Tonsured Head,
is this the life Saint Francis led?
265 You're a deceitful liar, clearly,
but here's someone who'll make you dearly
pay and make sure you get your due."
        To lock the friar up, she threw
a large storage box open wide.
270 Brother Simon fell at her side
facedown with both his arms stretched out.
The knight takes pity on the lout—
his noble heart's compassionate—
to see him form the Cross, prostrate.
275 With his right hand he lifts the friar
and says, "Brother, do you desire
to save your hide in these dire straits?
Procure four hundred pounds posthaste
so the young lady can be wed."
280 The friar, hearing what he's said,
felt more joy than he'd ever known,
and to the knight he gave his sworn
word that he would pay it in full.
(No need to post collateral.
285 Where he'll get it there's plenty more!)
He takes leave and walks out the door.
        Possessed of noble qualities,
the lady kept young Miss Denise
with her, took care not to alarm
290 her, but adjured her with much charm
that she should reassure herself
that besides them nobody else
would ever know or have a basis
to guess she'd known a man's embraces,
295 but she'd be married nobly and
could choose whomever in the land

celui que mieulz avoir vodroit,
ne mais qu'il soit de son endroit.
Tant fist la dame envers Denize
300 qu'ele l'a en boen penseir mise;
ne la servi mies de lobes!
Une de ses plus beles *robes*
devant son lit li aporta;
a son pooir la conforta
305 con cele qui ne s'en feint mie,
& li a dit: « Ma douce amie,
ceste vestireiz vos demain. »
Ele meïsmes de sa main
la vest ançois qu'ele couchast
310 ne soffrist qu'autres la touchast,
car priveement voloit faire
& cortoisement son afaire,
car sage dame & cortoize ere.
Priveement manda *la* mere
315 Denize par un sien mesage.
Molt ot grant joie en son corage
quant ele ot sa fille veüe
qu'ele cuidoit avoir perdue,
mais la dame li fist acroire
320 & par droite veritei croire
qu'ele ert aus Filles Dieu rendue
& qu'a une autre l'ot tolue
qui laianz le soir l'amena,
qui par pou ne s'en forsena.
325 Que vos iroie je disant
ne lor paroles devisant?—
dou rioteir seroit noianz;
mais tant fu Denize laians
que li denier furent rendu.
330 Aprés n'ont gaires atendu
qu'el fu a son grei assenee;
a un chevalier fu donee

she most desired, provided he,
like her, had a high pedigree.

      The lady's treatment of Denise
300   set her unquiet mind at peace.
Nothing *she* told her was dishonest!
She brought one of her very finest
dresses and placed it on her bed
and, best as she could, comforted
305   her like someone free from deceit
and gently said to her, "My sweet
child, these are the clothes you will wear
tomorrow." She herself took care
before bedtime to try them on,
310   nor would she allow anyone
to touch her, for she wished to do
it modestly and nobly, too,
for she's a well-bred noblewoman.
She sent her courier to summon
315   her mother in strict confidence,
whose heart overflowed with intense
joy as soon as she laid eyes on her,
for she'd thought she'd lost her for sure,
but the lady convinced her to
320   believe and take it to be true
that she'd been living with the order
of the Filles-Dieu, one of whom brought her
there that night, and, to her dismay,
the lady'd taken her away.

325   But why should I go on and on
and tell all that was said and done
again and pointlessly again?
For a time Denise stayed with them
until all her dowry was paid.
330   It wasn't much longer till they'd
had her with her consent betrothed
and married to a knight who'd loved

qui l'avoit autre fois requise.
Or ot non ma dame Denize
335 & fu a mout plus grant honeur
qu'en abit de frere meneur.

11. LE SENTIER BATU

Folie est d'autrui ramprosner
ne gens de chose araisouner
dont il ont anuy & vergoigne—
on porroit de ceste besoigne
5 souvent moustrer p[r]ueve en maint quas.
Mauvés fet juër de voir gas,
car on dist, & c'est chose vraie,
que bonne atent qui bonne paie.
Cui on ramposne ou on ledenge,
10 quant il en voit lieu, il s'en venge,
& tel d'autrui moquier s'atourne
que sus lui meïsme retourne.
Un example vous en dirai
si vrai que ja n'en mentirai,
15 ainsi c'on me conta pour voir.
      Il devoit .i. tournoi avoir
droit entre Perronne & Aties,
et chevaliers en ces parties
sejournoient pour le tournoi.
20 Une fois ierent en dosnoi
entre dames & damoiseles,
de cointes y ot & de beles;
de pluiseurs deduis s'entremistrent
et tant c'une roÿne fistrent
25 pour jouer au roy qui ne ment.
Ele s'en savoit finement

and been her suitor in the past.
She was Madame Denise at last,
335   with more honor accorded her
than when she'd been a Cordelier.

11. THE BEATEN PATH

by Jean de Condé

It's foolish to speak scornfully
and talk of things that patently
will make others feel shamed and slighted.
Many examples can be cited
5   that offer cogent proof of this.
It's wrong to joke about what is
for real. It's said and truly known
that you shall reap as you have sown:
The butt of scorn and calumny
10   will find an opportunity
to strike back. Evil tongues have found
that what goes around comes around.
Here's one example that occurred
that really happened, which I heard,
15   and I won't lie about the case.
      A tournament was to take place
somewhere near Athies and Péronne,
and knights from all around had come
to stay there for the tournament.
20   For dalliance, one day they went
to spend time with some ladies there
who were agreeable and fair.
Among the many games they played,
they made someone their queen to lead
25   them in "The King Who Speaks the Truth."
She played with finesse and could both

entremetre & commander
et de demandes demander,
qu'ele iert bien parlant & faitice,
30 de maniere estoit bele & rice.
Pluseurs demandes demanda
et sa volenté commanda
tant que vint a .i. chevalier
assez courtois & biau parlier
35 qui l'ot amee & qui l'eüst
pris a fame, s'il li pleüst,
mes bien tailliez ne sambloit mie
pour fere ce que plest amie
quant on la tient en ses bras nue,
40 car n'ot pas la barbe crenue,
poi de barbe ot, s'en est eschieus
en tant qu'as fames en maint lieus.
« Sire, ce li dist la roÿne,
dites moi tant de vo couvine
45 s'onques eüstes nul enfant.
— Dame, dist il, point ne m'en vant,
car onques n'en oi nul, ge croy.
— Sire, point ne vous en mescroy,
et si croy que ne sui pas seule,
50 car il pert assez a l'esteule
que bons n'est mie li espis. »
Aprés n'en fu point pris respis,
tantost a .i. autre rala
et d'autre matiere parla.
55   Li pluiseur qui ce escouterent
en sourriant les mos noterent.
Le chevalier qui ce oÿ
de ces mos point ne s'esjoÿ;
esbahis fu & ne dist mot,
60 et quant le geu tant duré ot
que demandé ot tout entour
la roÿne, chascun au tour

issue commands and also question
each one of them at her discretion,
for she spoke well and skillfully
30   and had beauty and artistry.
Of several of them she inquired
something and told what she desired,
until she reached a knight who was
well-spoken and most courteous,
35   who'd been in love with her and would
have married her, too, if he could,
but didn't look like he was made
to do those things that please a maid
when she lies in his arms unclad:
40   In place of a full beard he had
a wisp or two, and frequently
was shy in women's company.
      "Sir, I would like some information
on your family situation:
45   Say if you ever had a child."
"None I can boast about." He smiled.
"I've never sired one, I believe,
my lady." "I don't disbelieve
you, sir, none of us do. With grain,
50   the stubble left behind makes plain
whether the spears were full or not."
She didn't dwell on this, but got
on right away to the next players
and spoke about other affairs.
55   Many of those who listened in
took note of her words with a grin.
The knight to whom the lady said it,
though, was not in the least elated;
he was perturbed, and he kept mum.
60   When the game had gone on for some
time and the queen had gone around
and questioned each one, they were bound

li redemanda, c'est usages.
Son cuer estoit soultis & sages;
65 chascun respondi sagement
son pensser sans atargement.
Quant le tour au chevalier vint,
de la ramprosne li souvint;
volenté ot de revengier,
70 si li a dit sans atargier:
« Dame, respondez moi sanz guille:
a point de poil en vo poinille?
— Par foy, ce dist la damoisele,
vez ci une demande bele
75 et qui bien est assise a point!
Sachiez que il n'en y a point. »
Cil li dist de vouloir entier:
« Bien vous en croy, quar en sentier
qui est batus ne croist point d'erbe! »
80 Cilz qui oïrent cest proverbe
commencierent si grant risee
pour la demande desguisee
que cele en fu forment honteuse,
qui devant estoit couvoiteuse
85 de chose demander & dire
de quoi les autres feïst rire
Or fu son cuer si esperdus
que tout son deduit fu perdus
et li fu sa joie faillie,
90 car devant estoit baude & lie
& molt plaine d'envoisement
Ne se sot plus courtoisement
le chevalier de li vengier:
ne la volt mie ledengier,
95 mes grossement la rencontra
et sa penssee li moustra
si com a lui ot fet la sienne,

by the game's rules to ask in turn. It
went well. She was astute and learned,
65 and answered expeditiously,
speaking her mind judiciously.
When it was the turn of the knight,
he didn't overlook the slight.
Waiting to take revenge and ready,
70 without delay he asked her, "Lady,
say if you have—don't beat around
the bush—hair on your pubic mound."
"Upon my honor, sir," said she,
"now here's a pretty inquiry
75 you're asking me, and apropos!
There isn't, I would have you know."
"I think you're right, because no grass
can grow on a well-trodden path,"
he told her with great satisfaction.
80   Those in the party heard this maxim
and broke into loud laughter for
the message of his metaphor,
which fully embarrassed the queen,
who up until that time had been
85 desirous that her repartee
evoke mirth and hilarity.
Her heart was totally nonplussed
and all the joy she'd had, she lost,
and her good mood faded away,
90 though till then she'd been merry, gay,
overflowing with jollity.
        The knight with greater courtesy
could not have switched places and told
her off, not meaning to insult
95 her, bluntly meeting her halfway
and saying what he had to say,
just as she'd spoken her mind to him,

car il n'est femme terriïenne
qui ja peüst .i. homme amer
100 mes qu'ele l'oïst diffamer
d'estre mauvés ouvrier en lit
de fere l'amoureus delit,
et sus ce point fu ramposnez.
Bien savez le coc chaponnez
105 est as gelines mal venus;
aussi homme qui est tenus
a mal ouvrier est dechaciez
entre fames, bien le saciez,
(ce seront nonnains ou begines)
110 si com chapons entre gelines.
Le chevalier, qui bien savoit
que le cri de tel chose avoit,
pour la ramposne ot cuer dolent,
si ot de soi vengier talent.
115 Il counoissoit, ce puet bien estre,
de cele la maniere & l'estre
ou aucune mescreandise
couru en la marcheandise
qu'i voult fere du marïage,
120 si li descouvri son courage,
et se cele se fust teüe,
ja ne li fust ramenteüe
ceste chose.
                    Vous qui oëz
cestui conte entendre poëz
125 que li voir gas ne valent rien:
poi en voit on avenir bien,
aventure est quant bien en chiet;
on voit souvent qu'il en meschiet,
du bien cheoir sai poi nouvele.
130 Rimé ai de rime nouvele
l'aventure que j'ai contee.
Dieus gart ceulz qui l'ont escoutee!

because in the whole world no woman
can love a man of whom it's said
100 contemptuously that in bed
his performance just doesn't measure
up to what she needs for her pleasure,
and that was how she chose to mock
him. As you know, the caponed cock
105 is ill received by every hen,
and that is how it is with men.
Whoever is reputed so
women will drive away, you know,
like the capon that the hen shuns,
110 as though they were Beguines or nuns.
The knight, who knew his reputation
said he was in this situation,
heartsick that she had mocked him, meant
to pay her back the compliment.
115 It may have well been that he knew
concerning her a thing or two,
or that he harbored some suspicion
that came up when his proposition
of marriage was pending, and he
120 let her know his thoughts openly,
whereas, had she not said a word,
no thought of it would have recurred
to him at all.
                        Good audience,
you grasp the full significance
125 my story holds: To joke about
what's all too real rarely turns out
well. Good may come of it by chance,
but most often it brings mischance.
I seldom find it comes out well.
130 The adventure I had to tell
I've rhymed with rhymes of my invention.
May God save those who've paid attention!

Amen. Ci prent mon conte fin.
Dieus nous doinst a tous bonne fin.

12. LE CHEVALIER A LA
ROBE VERMEILLE

En la conté de Dant Martin
avint entour la seint Martin
le boillant, que gibier aproche,
.i. chevalier qui sanz reproche
5   vesqui el païs son aage.
Molt le tenoient cil a sage
qui de lui estoient acointe.
Une dame mignote & cointe,
fame a .i. riche vavasour,
10   pria cil & requist meint jour
& tant qu'ele devint s'amie.
Entour .ii. liues & demie
avoit entre leur deus ostieus.
Li *amis* a la dame iert tieus
15   qu'il erroit par tote la terre
por honour & por pris conquerre
tant que tuit le tindrent a preu,
& li vavaseur pour son preu
entendoit a autre maniere,
20   qu'il avoit la langue maniere
a beau parler & sagement
& bien savoit .i. jugement
recorder: c'iert touz ses deliz.
        Pour aler as plez a Seint Liz
25   apresta .i. matin son erre,
& la dame manda *bon* erre
son ami par .i. home sage
qui bien sot conter son mesage,

Amen. Thus does my story end.
God bring us all to a good end.

12. THE KNIGHT OF
THE RED ROBE

It happened once that in the region
of Dammartin one summer season
near "hot" Saint Martin's Day, when game
abounds, a knight lived without blame,
5   and had from the day of his birth.
He was esteemed a man of worth
and wisdom by all those who knew
him. A fair lady, gracious, too,
the wife of a rich vavasor,
10   he sought in love, until no more
could she resist, and gave her heart.
Some two and a half leagues apart
their dwellings stood one from the other.
Such a one was the lady's lover
15   as wandered all throughout creation
to win him fame and adulation,
so all thought he ranked with the best,
while the vavasor's interest
inclined in a different direction,
20   for he could use words to perfection
and spoke with skill and with great prudence,
and took delight in jurisprudence
and recollecting court decisions.
      Once to appear at morning sessions
25   he left for Senlis before dawn.
The lady, eager to inform
her love, sent word with a man whose
good sense could best convey the news,

& quant cil oï la novele,
30   robe d'escarlate *vermeile*
a vestue de fres ermine;
comme bachelers s'achemine
qui amours meinent a esfroi.
Montez est sor son palefroi,
35   ses esperons dorez chauciez,
mes por le chaut fu deschauciez,
& prist son esprevier mué
que il meïmes ot mué,
& menoit .ii. chenez petiz,
40   qui estoient tres bien feitiz
por fere as chans saillir l'aloe.
Si com fine amour veut & loe
s'est atornez, d'iluec s'en part,
tant qu'il est venuz cele part
45   ou il cuida trover la dame,
mes n'i trova home ne fame
qui de nis une riens l'aresne.
Son palefroi tantost aresne
& mist son esprevier seoir,
50   vers la chanbre court por veoir
o il cuida trover s'amie,
& cele n'iert pas endormie,
ençois se jesoit tote nue
& si atendoit la venue
55   de son ami, & il vint la
droit au lit ou trovee l'a:
si la vit bele, grase & tendre.
Sanz demorer & sanz atendre
se voloit tot vestu couchier,
60   [& la dame qui molt l'ot chier]
i mist .i. poi de contredit,
debonerement li a dit:
« Amis, bien soiez vos venuz!
Les moi vos coucherez touz nuz

and when he'd heard what the man said,
30 he put on his fine robe of red,
rich, costly wool with ermine fur
to set off down the road to her,
much like a youth who feels Love's force,
up in the saddle of his horse
35 with golden spurs upon his feet.
He wore no leggings for the heat,
and of his sparrow hawk took hold,
tamed by himself, fresh out of molt,
while two young dogs followed in back,
40 endowed with an uncanny knack
for flushing larks out of a field.
        Decked out in fashion, as revealed
to Love's faithful, he rode apace
and came directly to the place
45 where he imagined she'd be found,
but there was nobody around
to give directions or explain.
He tied his horse up by the rein
and set his sparrow hawk to perch,
50 then ran up to her room to search
where he thought she'd be waiting for him,
and found her lying there before him
expecting him, without a thread
of clothing on, awake in bed,
55 and he, her swain, approached the lady
he'd found in bed, waiting and ready.
She seemed so fair and plump and soft,
right then, even before he'd doffed
his clothing, he'd have got in bed,
60 but graciously his mistress said,
who, loving him with great affection,
could well impose a small correction,
"Welcome, my love. I bid you lie
near me quite as unclothed as I,

65 por avoir plus plesant deliz. »
Sor une huche au pié du lit
a cil tote sa robe mise;
ses braies oste, & sa chemise
& ses esperons a ostez,
70 meintenant est el lit entrez.
Ele le prist entre ses braz . . .
d'autre joie, d'autre soulaz,
ne vos quier fere mencïon,
que cil qui ont entencïon
75 doivent bien savoir que ce monte.
Por ce n'en quier fere autre conte,
mes andui firent liéement
tieus deduiz *com funt* li amant.

   En ce qu'il se jurent ensenble,
80 les plez furent, si com moi senble,
contremandé au vavasour.
Ençois qu'il fust prime de jor
fu il a l'ostel revenuz.
« Dont est cil palefroiz venuz?
85 fet il. Cui est cel esprevier? »
Lors vosist cil estre a Pevier
qui dedanz la chanbre enclos iere.
Entre le lit & la mesiere
s'est colez, mes tant fu sorpris
90 qu'il n'a point de sa robe pris
fors ses braies & sa chemise.
Asez a robe sor li mise
la dame: manteaus, peliçons.
Li sires iert en grant friçons
95 du palefroi que il remire;
encor ot au cuer greignor ire
quant il s'en entra en sa chanbre.
Quant voit *la robe* tuit li menbre
li fremisent d'ire & d'angoisse;

65 so we'll enjoy each other best."
    He put his robe down on a chest
    by the bed's foot with all his clothes,
    took off his trousers, shirt, and hose,
    and likewise he took off his spurs
70 and got in bed just as he was,
    and in her arms she clasped him tight. . . .
    To other joy, other delight,
    I've no intention to refer:
    Those who have good sense will infer
75 what's done in such a situation,
    so I'll eschew a full narration
    and just assure you that the two
    did joyously what lovers do.
            While thus the two kept company,
80 the vavasor, it seems to me,
    learned that the hearings were adjourned,
    because of which the man returned
    before morning had even come.
    "Where on earth is this palfrey from,"
85 he said, "and whose hawk can this be?"
    As for the man trapped inside, he
    would sooner have been in Poitiers.
    He slipped behind the bed and lay
    against the wall, but in his haste
90 he left his clothing on the chest
    and only grabbed his shirt and hose.
    The lady piled all sorts of clothes
    on top of him, mantles and furs.
    Her husband, now, already was
95 irate from having seen the horse;
    it only makes his anger worse
    when, entering the lady's chamber,
    he sees the robe. Losing his temper,
    shaking with wrath in every limb,

lors destreint la dame & angoise
       & dit: « Dame, qui est *ceanz*?
       Il a .i. palefroi *laienz*—
       cui est il? Dont vient cele robe? »
       & la dame qui bel le lobe
105   li dist: « Foi que devez seint Pere,
       n'avez vos encontré mon frere,
       qui orendroit de ci s'en part?
       Bien vos a lessié[ ] vostre part
       de ses *joiaus*, ce m'est avis,
110   por tant seulement que je dis
       que tel robe vous serroit bien.
       Onc plus ne li dis nule rien,
       einz despoilla tot meintenant
       cele bele robe avenant
115   & prist la seue a chevauchier.
       Son palefroi qu'il avoit chier,
       & son oisel & ses chenez,
       ses esperons cointes & nez
       freschement dorez vos envoie,
120   a poi que je ne me doloie
       & juroie trop durement,
       mes onques por mon serement
       ne por rien que seüse dire
       ne poi son voleir escondire.
125   Ne vos en chaut, prenez cel don;
       encor en avra guerredon
       se Deus vos done longue vie. »
       & li *vavassors*, qui envie
       avoit du beau *present avoir*,
130   li dist: « Dame, vos dite voir.
       Du palefroi m'est il molt bel,
       & des chenez & de l'oisel,
       mes .i. petit i mespreïtes
       de ce que la robe preïtes,

100 he forces her to answer him.
"Lady, I know someone's inside.
There is a palfrey there outside—
whose is it? And where's that robe from?"
The wily lady with aplomb
105 answers him, "As you trust Saint Pet-
er, my brother, didn't you meet
him? He left just a while ago.
He left you gifts, I'll have you know,
some of the finest things he had,
110 because it happened that I said
how good that robe would look on you,
not one word more. Before I knew
it, he took off the lovely garment
on which I just happened to comment
115 and took his riding cape to wear.
The palfrey which he holds so dear,
his sparrow hawk and his dogs, too,
even his spurs, shiny and new
with gilt, for you he's left behind.
120 I thought I'd go out of my mind
and protested most heartily,
but he would not listen to me.
Neither for oath nor argument
would he abandon his intent.
125 Take what he's left you. Don't be miffed—
in due course you'll repay the gift
if Heaven grants you a long life."
The vavasor answered his wife,
because he wished such fine things were
130 his to keep, "Lady, I concur.
I'm quite delighted that he shared
his palfrey, hunting dogs, and bird,
but you were somewhat in the wrong
to accept that red robe along

135   car ce semble estre coveitise.
      — Non fet, sire, mes grant franchise,
      car on doit bien, par seint Remi,
      prendre .i. beau don de son ami,
      car qui de prendre n'est hardi
140   de doner est acouardi. »
        Atant lesserent la parrolle
      que la dame si beau parrolle
      a son seignor par tel reson
      qu'il n'i set trover acheson
145   por quoi i mete contredit.
      La dame a son seignor a dit:
      « Sire, vos levates matin.
      Foi que devez a seint Martin,
      venez vos delés moi gesir,
150   si vos reposez a loisir.
      L'en apareille le mengier. »
      & cil n'en fist onques dangier;
      maintenant s'est el lit colez;
      si voz di qu'il fu acolez
155   & besiez .ii. tans qu'il ne seut.
      La dame a tastoner l'aqueut
      si soëf que il s'endormi,
      lors bouta du pié son ami,
      & cil tot meintenant se drece,
160   & devers la huche s'adrece
      ou il avoit sa robe mise.
      N'i a pas fete grant devise
      a li servir, ençois s'atourne
      & au plus tost qu'il puet s'en torne,
165   son palefroi prent & si monte.
      De li ne vueil fere lonc conte,
      mes atot son hernois s'en vet
      & le vavasour dormant let,
      qui dormi jusques vers midi,

135   with them. It's pure venality."
     "No higher liberality,
     by Saint Remy, can one extend
     than taking fine gifts from a friend,
     for people who fear to receive
140   are also disinclined to give."
          Thereon they let the matter lie.
     The lady has made use of sly
     argumentation and fair speech,
     nor can the vavasor impeach
145   one word or point out any flaw.
     The lady added one thing more:
     "Sire, you've been up since the wee hours.
     As you trust in Saint Martin's powers,
     come here and lie down next to me
150   for a bit and rest comfortably.
     They're fixing breakfast in the kitchen."
     He didn't put up opposition,
     but quickly slipped into the bed,
     and he was hugged, let it be said,
155   caressed and kissed with twice the warmth.
     She held him softly in her arms
     and stroked him till he fell asleep,
     then signaled her lover to creep
     from undercover with a kick,
160   and he got up and sure was quick
     to grab the robe left on the chest.
     His one concern was getting dressed
     and out and back home on the double,
     and, not taking the time to trouble
165   about her needs, he gets his mount.
     But why prolong what I recount?
     He hurried off with all his gear,
     leaving the husband sleeping there
     quite undisturbed till nearly noon,

170   quant il s'esveilla. Ce vos di
      qu'a la dame n'ennuia point.
              Li vavasor, qui en bon point
      estoit de son riche present,
      a dit c'on li aport avant
175   a vestir sa robe vermeille.
      Uns escuiers li apareille
      une robe vert qu'il avoit,
      & quant li vavasor la voit,
      si li a dit inelepas:
180   « Ceste robe ne veu ge pas;
      einz veil l'autre robe essaier
      dont richement me sot paier
      mes serorges, que je molt pris. »
      Lors fu li vallez entrepris,
185   qui de tot ce riens ne savoit,
      qui tote jor esté avoit
      as chans por les seours garder.
      Lors prist la dame a regarder
      son seignor & si li a dit:
190   « Beau sire, se Deus vos aït,
      or me dites, se vos volez,
      quele robe vos demandez.
      Avez vos dont robe achetee
      ou, se vous l'avez aportee
195   de la ou vos avez esté,
      quele est ele? Est ele a esté?
      — Dame, je vueil ma robe chiere
      qui hui mein sus cele huche iere,
      que vostre frere m'a donee.
200   Bien m'a s'amour abandonee
      & bien doi estre ses acointes,
      quant veut que du sien soie cointes.
      Por ce l'ein ge encore mieus
      qu'il despoilla voiant vos ieus
205   les garnemenz qu'il m'a lessez.

170   when he awoke. However soon,
the lady took it in good stride.

        Her husband, eager and bright-eyed
because of his gifts and their worth,
ordered his servants to bring forth
175   his scarlet robe so he could wear it.
The squire who'd been sent to prepare it
came back with a robe that was green,
and when the vavasor had seen
what he'd been brought, he quickly said,
180   "I want my other robe instead,
not this one, for I want to try
the fit of the rich gift from my
wife's noble brother." When he heard it,
the equerry was disconcerted,
185   had no idea what it all meant,
because his morning had been spent
guarding the reapers and the crops.
The lady turns around and stops,
fixes her husband with a stare.
190   "What's this, husband," she says, "God spare
you? Tell me, if you'll be so kind,
just what robe do you have in mind?
Have you then bought one recently
or brought a robe home from Senlis
195   this morning when you went to court?
What kind is it? Lightweight and short?"
"Lady, I want my very best,
the robe laid out there on that chest
this morning. Your brother bestowed
200   it on me and in that way showed
his love. Our friendship must be close
when he gives me what he loves most,
nor should my love for him be slack.
He took the clothes right off his back
205   and left them for me in your sight."

— Certes, forment vos abesiez,
fet la dame, ce m'est avis.
Bien doit estre chevaliers vis
qui veut estre menestereus:
210 mieus vodroie qu'eüsiez res
sanz eve la teste & le col,
que ja n'i remeinsist chevol!
Ch'apartient a ces jugleours
& a ces bons vïeleours
215 que il aient des chevaliers
les robes, que c'est lor mestiers.
Ce n'apartient pas a vostre oés
d'avoir garnement s'il n'est nués;
Devez vos donc robe baillier
220 se n'est a coustre ou a taillier
& soit fete a vostre mesure?
Se je vos di sens & mesure,
creez moi, si ferez savoir. »
     Lors ne puet il apercevoir
225 que cele robe est devenue;
si cuide bien qu'en sa venue
l'eüst veüe sus la huche.
Meintenant son escuier huche,
mes il furent si enseignié
230 que ja n'i avra gaaignié
a son ués vaillant une poire;
si cuidë il bien & espoire
qu'enseignes vraies en orra,
mes ja par eus rien n'en sara,
235 ençois sera tot bestornez;
tieus les a la dame atornez
que touz les a trez a sa corde:
chascun du tot a li s'acorde.
     Lors ist li sires de sa chanbre
240 & dist: « Dame, dont ne vos menbre?

"You're lowering yourself, all right,
it seems to me," the lady swore,
"for he's a churlish vavasor
who like a minstrel would behave.
210 I'd much prefer to see you shave
with a dry razor, head and neck,
till you were left without a speck
of hair. Fiddlers, perhaps, or clowns
may wear another's hand-me-downs,
215 and may accept (it's their vocation)
the clothes they wear from men of station,
but someone as noble as you
should wear only things that are new.
I ask you, then, should you accept
220 a robe from anyone, except
one cut and tailored to your fit?
I'm telling you what's right and fit,
believe me, so act suitably."
        The vavasor's too blind to see
225 exactly where his robe has gone.
When he came home, he saw it on
the chest—that's what he thinks he saw.
He calls the serving boy once more,
but all by now are in the know,
230 so he will never come to know
a single fact to set him straight.
He thinks, If I investigate,
I'll learn the truth of this affair.
But none will disabuse him there,
235 and he'll be utterly deluded.
All with the lady have colluded;
she leads them all on a short leash,
and all corroborate her speech.
        The husband comes forth from their chamber
240 and says, "Now, wife, don't you remember?

Quant je fui hui mein arivez
.i. palefroi fu ci trovez
& .i. espreviers & .ii. chiens,
& disïez que tot iert miens
245   cel present de par vostre frere.
— Sire, foi que je doi mon pere,
il a bien .ii. mois & demi
ou plus que mon frere ne vi,
& s'il estoit ci orendroit,
250   ne voudroit [il] en nul endroit
qu'en vostre dos fust enbatue
robe que il eüst vestue.
Ce deüst dire .i. fous, uns ivres!
Ja vaut plus de .iiiicc. livres
255   la grant rente que vos avez
& la terre que vos tenez—
querez robe a vostre talent
& parlefroi bel & amblant
& qui voise tost l'anbleüre!
260   De vos ne sai dire mesure,
que vos estes tieus atornez
que touz les ieus avez troublez.
J'ai paour de mauvese encontre
qui vos venist hui mein encontre
265   de fantosme ou de mauvés vent:
vos muëz color si sovent,
que je m'en esbahis trestote.
Ice vos di ge bien sanz doute
que tot le sens avez changié
270   & mauvés songe avez songié.
Criëz a Damle Deu merci
& a mi sire seint Orri
qu'en vostre memoire vos gart!
Il pert bien a vostre regart
275   que vos estes enfantomez.

This morning I was caught off guard
to find a palfrey in our yard,
a sparrow hawk and two dogs, too,
and you said that these were a few
245 of the fine gifts your brother gave me."
"Sire, on my father's soul, God save me,
some two and a half months have passed
since when I saw my brother last,
and, even if he had stopped by,
250 I'm sure I can't imagine why
he'd want to have some robe adorn
your back that he himself had worn.
A fool or drunk might make that claim!
The vast estates under your name
255 and all the income from those grounds
are worth more than four hundred pounds.
Buy your own robe to suit your need
and your own swift and handsome steed
to carry you as suits your station.
260 How can I speak with moderation
when your mind is so turned around,
your sight is troubled and unsound?
I fear today you must have met
with some dread otherworldly threat,
265 some ill wind or some ghostly sprite;
you often flush and then turn white,
so I'm distraught and filled with care.
I tell you, it is all too clear
that your mind's come unhinged, encumbered
270 by evil visions while you slumbered.
Cry God have mercy! Saint Ory
preserve your mind and memory!
Trust in his gracious intercession;
it's plain to see by your expression
275 that by some demon you're possessed.

Par la rien que vos plus amez,
cuidiez vos, au dire voir,
la robe & le cheval avoir?
— Oïl, dame, se Deus me saut.
280 — Deus, dist la dame, vos consaut
& de sa destre mein vos saint!
Car vos vöez a .i. bon seint
& si i portez vostre offrende
que Dieus le memoire vos rende.
285 — Dame, dist il, & je me veu
a Damle Dieu & a seint Leu.
Irai je au baron seint Jame?
— Oïl, sire, ce dist la dame,
com ci a haut pelerinage!
290 Dieus qui vos done tel corage
qu'i vos puist mener & conduire!
Revenés vos en par Estuire
par mon seignor seint Sauveor—
iluec vont li bon pecheor—
295 & devez bien en cele terre
monseignor seint Hernoul reqerre.
Vos deüsiez des l'autre esté
avoir a son mostier esté
o chandele de vostre lonc;
300 por ce que vos n'i fustes onc,
vöez li, sire, a [ ] fere droit.
— Volentiers, ma dame, orendroit
feré, se Deus plest, ceste voie. »
Isi la dame l'en envoie,
305 qui li a fet de voir menchonge
& tot li a torné a songe
ce qu'il a veü a ses ieus,
mes encor esploite ele mieus,
que le fet pelerin a force,
310 & tant se peine & tant s'esforce

I ask, by all that you love best,
whether you, sire, still think it true
that robe and horse belong to you?"
"I do, may God grant me salvation."
280 "God save you from this aberration
and sanctify you with His hand!
Devote yourself to some saint and
make offering to God that He
restore your failing memory."
285 "Lady," he said, "that's what I'll do,
I'll pray to God and to Saint Loup.
Say, should I go to Compostela?"
The lady said, "You would do well. A
great pilgrimage you're undertaking!
290 God strengthen you with courage, making
your feet adhere to the straight track!
Through the Asturias travel back—
stop at Our Holy Savior's shrine,
a pilgrim site for many fine
295 sinners, and don't forget that there's
Saint Arnolphe, who deserves your prayers.
You promised that before last winter
you'd come in person to his minster
and light a candle tall as you,
300 and later you forgot to do
what you had promised. Set it right."
He said he'd leave soon as he might,
God help him, on his pilgrimage.
       The lady bids him bon voyage,
305 having convinced him what his eyes
had seen was all a pack of lies
and made the truth appear a dream.
What's even better, by this scheme
she made the man a penitent.
310 She'd neither let up nor relent

que le fet movoir au tiers jor;
com cele qui het son seignor.

    Cest dit as marïez pramet
que de folie s'entremet
315   qui croit ce que de ses ieus voie,
mes cil qui tient la droite voie
doit bien croirre sanz contredit
tout ce que sa fame li dit.

13. LE SOT CHEVALIER

Puis que je me vuel apoier
a conter ne a fabloier,
je vos doi bien faire savoir,
se Li Leus a tant de savoir
5   c'on doive autorissier ses dis,
d'une aventure qui jadis
avint en la terre d'Ardane
a qatre liues pres d'Andane.
Je vos dirai trestot briément
10 le fin & le commencement.

    En la forest ancïenor
avoit manant .i. vavasor
qui molt estoit bien herbergiés:
d'une part estoit ses vergiés,
15 qui molt ert plains d'arbres eslius—
molt par ert precïeus li lius
qant ce venoit au novel tans;
d'autre part estoit li estans,
plains ert d'oiseaus & de poissons;
20 s'estoit sire des venissons,
s'avoit ses ciens & ses oiseaus;
molt estoit sire & damoiseaus

for three full days till he set out—
she hated having him about.
      This fabliau teaches all men
that they're committing folly when
315   they trust what they've seen with their eyes.
Those who are sensible and wise
won't dream to raise a contradiction
to what their wives say, fact or fiction.

15. THE STUPID KNIGHT

by Gautier le Leu

Since I have chosen the profession
of giving fabliaux expression,
I really ought to let you know
(if old le Leu's so in the know
5   that you can take him at his word)
of an adventure that occurred
some time ago in the Ardennes
just four leagues distant from Andenne.
Without too many words expended
10   I'll tell how it began and ended.
      There in those ancient woods of yore
once dwelt a wealthy vavasor
who comfortably lived off the land:
He had his orchard on one hand
15   with trees of highest quality—
a most delightful place to be
when the season had turned to spring—
and on the other was a spring
where birds abounded, also fish,
20   his forest holdings also rich
in game, and he owned birds and hounds.
He was master and lord of grounds

de tos les biens que tere porte;
ses molins ert devant sa porte.

25 Se il fust sages & senés
en grant anor fust asenés,
mais tant estoit sos par nature
qu'il n'ooit dire creature
qu'il ne redesist maintenant

30 plus de .c. fois en .i. tenant,
car sotie l'ot si deciut,
c'onques n'avoit a feme giut
ne ne savoit que cons estoit.
(Non por uec li vis li estoit.)

35 Por uec qu'il ert de haute gent
& riques d'or fin & d'argent,
li ont si ami feme quisse.
Qant il l'eut esposee & prisse,
il le tint plus d'un an pucele.

40 Molt en pesa le jovencele,
qui vosist ses deduis avoir,
mais cil n'avoit tant de savoir
q'il seüst au con adercier
ne le pucelage percier;

45 non por uec l'avoit il tenue
tamaintes fois en ses bras nue.
Tant estoit cele a plus male a[i]sse
qant ele sentoit le pasnaisse
sor ses cuisses & sor ses hances,

50 qui molt erent söes & blances.
        Qant ne le peut mais consentir
de si faite *chose sentir*,
sa mere mande, & ele i vint.
Or oiés commant l'en avint.

55 Ele li conta tot l'afaire
que ses sire sielt a li faire.
Li dame tres bien s'aparçoit
que li folie le deçoit:

that brought forth every earthly good,
and near his door his grain mill stood.
25 Had he been smart and sound of mind
he'd have been honored by mankind,
but he had such an addled head
that anything somebody said
he would repeat upon the spot
30 over a hundred times nonstop,
his folly so obsessed his brain.
With women he had never lain;
just what cunt was he didn't know.
(The man did have a penis, though.)
35   Because his lineage was old
and he had much silver and gold,
his friends procured for him a wife.
When they began their married life,
he left her virgin one whole year.
40 That put the damsel in despair,
who longed to have gratification.
He never rose to the occasion,
so inexperienced was he,
nor tackled her virginity,
45 yet he had often held her tight
and naked in his arms at night,
and it only increased her ardor
to feel his parsnip growing harder
against her flanks and on her thighs,
50 which were so soft and white and nice.
    When she no more could tolerate
letting things go on at this rate,
she asked her mother to come see 'er.
What happened next you now will hear.
55 She told her of her plight and gave her
a full account of his behavior.
The lady's quick to realize
that simpleness beclouds his eyes.

le chevalier prent par le main,
60 ne sai le nuit ou l'endemain,
si le mena ens en sa canbre,
qui tote estoit ovree a lambre,
puis a ses cuisses descovertes,
aprés a les gambes overtes,
65 se li mostra Dant Conebert,
puis li a dit: « Sire Robert,
veés nule rien en cest val
ne contremont ne contreval?
— Oie, dame, fait il, .ii. traus.
70 — Sire, com fais est li plus haus?
— Il est plus lons qu'il ne soit les.
— & com fais est cil par dalés?
— Dame, plus cors, ce m'est avis.
— Gardés en cel n'adoist vos vis,
75 car il n'est mie a cel ués fais—
qui vit i met, c'est grans mesfais!—
mais on doit el plus lonc boter,
& aprés doit on culeter,
& qant ce vient a deerrains
80 adont doit on serer des rains.
— Dame, fait il, volés je boce
cest trau me vit ens en la boce?
— Nenil, amis, a ceste fois.
Il vos est or mis en defois,
85 mais me fillë en a plus beaus
& plus söes & plus noviaus.
Foutés le plus lonc anquenuit,
comment qu'il vos griet ne anuit.
— Dame, fait il, molt volentiers!
90 Ja n'en ira li traus entiers
que je n'i mete men andolle . . .
& que ferai [j]e de me colle?
— Amis, le plus cort embatés
qant vos au lonc vos conbatés. »

Taking his hand, she led the knight,
60   the next day or that very night
(I'm not sure which), whom she did bring
to her room lined with paneling,
then showed her thighs to the man's view
and, spreading wide apart her two
65   legs, let him see her Lady Jane.
"Sir Robert," she tried to explain,
"do you see something in this cove
either below or up above?"
"Indeed, two holes, lady," he said.
70   "The top one, sir, how is it made?"
"Longer, I'd say, than it is wide."
"And the hole on the bottom side?"
"It's shorter." "Be sure to take care
that your prick doesn't go in there,
75   for it's not made to put pricks in—
to put one there is a grave sin!—
but in the long one, there you may,
and then you ought to bang away
and, when you reach your passion's height,
80   tighten your cheeks with all your might."
"Lady, do you want me to stick
the longer one now with my prick?"
"No. That, my friend, you must not do,
for now it is forbidden you,
85   whereas my daughter has a pair
more pleasing, newer and more fair.
Fuck her long, skinny one tonight,
whatever your qualms or your fright."
"Glad to oblige, lady!" said he.
90   "Her hole will not be safe from me,
for I will poke it with my sausage.
But what do I do with my package?"
"Beat it against the hole that's short
when you besiege the long in sport."

95 Adont li dame se racuevre,
& li chevaliers le canbre uevre,
puis vait a loi de nonsaçant
le cort & le lonc maneçant.
        Le nuit leva uns grans orés,
100 si fais com vos dire m'orés:
qu'el bos esrajoient li arbre,
si caoient les tors de marbre.
A cele eure estoient el bos
de vers cele terre d'Alos
105 .vii. chevalier cortois & sage;
porté avoient un mesage
dont il erent grain & marit.
El bos estoient esmarit;
vers le maison au chevalier
110 vienent fuiant tot estraier.
Li uns s'en est devant tornés
(cil estoit de Sainteron nes);
le pont & le porte trespasse,
qui n'estoit mie povre & basse,
115 ains estoit haute & bien coverte,
& li maisons estoit overte;
laiens vient trestos eslasciés
par l'uis qui ert overs lasciés,
le dame & son segnor salue,
120 puis a se raison despondue,
l'ostel li requiert & demande
avec çaus qui sont en la lande,
& li sires a respondut
tantost com il l'a entendut:
125 « Ja mes osteus n'iert contredis.
Bien soiés [vos] venu tos dis,
vos devant & li autre apriés!
Sont vo conpagnon auques pres?
Alés, si les faites haster. »
130 Puis recommence a rïoter

95　　　The lady then adjusts her clothes.
　　　　The knight opens the door and goes
　　　　threatening, like a simpleton,
　　　　the short hole and the longer one.
　　　　　　　That night an awful storm broke out,
100　　which you will hear me tell about.
　　　　The trees were wildly blown around
　　　　and marble towers hit the ground.
　　　　At that time to the woods had come
　　　　some seven knights who'd set out from
105　　Aalst, able men of high position
　　　　who had been sent out on a mission,
　　　　and, overtaken by the storm,
　　　　they felt distress and feared great harm.
　　　　Toward the foolish knight's abode,
110　　fleeing the storm, they quickly rode.
　　　　One, who had been born in Saint-Trond,
　　　　went on ahead of them alone,
　　　　over the bridge and through the gate,
　　　　which was built high, enclosed and great,
115　　not in the least shoddy or low.
　　　　The castle was unlocked, and so
　　　　the knight went riding straight inside
　　　　through the door, which lay open wide,
　　　　greeted the mistress and the master
120　　and let them know his business after,
　　　　requesting that the knight agree
　　　　to house him and his company.
　　　　The master quickly acquiesced
　　　　on hearing the stranger's request:
125　　"My lodgings I will not withhold.
　　　　I bid you welcome here, all told,
　　　　you first, then the rest of your band.
　　　　Are your companions close at hand?
　　　　Go quickly bid them come along."
130　　Then he begins to carry on

que li plus lons sera foutus
& li plus cors sera batus.
Qant li vallés l'ot & entent
plus n'i areste ne atent;
135   ses conpagnons le reva dire,
trestos dolans & tos plains d'ire:
« Segnor, fait il, jo ai trovet
lasus un erite provet.
Il dist qu'il nos herbergera
140   & aprés nos laidengera,
car il foutera le plus lonc
& si batra le cort selonc. »
La ot un chevalier molt grant
s'ot a non Wales de Dinant:
145   « Segnor, fait il, je sai asés
que je vos ai del lonc passés.
Je n'irai mie a cel erite
qui a tele uevre se delite:
mels ameroie estre tondus
150   que je fusce d'ome foutus! »
Si ot .i. chevalier de Tongres;
cil ot a non Pieres li Hongres.
« Segnor, fait il, je n'irai mie
la deseure par ahatie;
155   je sai bien je sui li plus cors.
Ja n'aroie de vos secors
que je n'i fusce laidengiés
ançois que je fusce vengiés.
Or remanrons andoi ça fors,
160   encor soit li orages fors. »
Li autre crïent a haut ton:
« Segnor, ce ne vaut .i. boton;
nos le ferons tot altrement.
Or nos maintenons sagement:
165   qant nos seromes descendut,
li plus cort voisent estendut

and says the one that's short he'll dun
and fuck the long and skinny one.
            The young knight overhears his threats
and neither hesitates nor waits,
135   but, quite distressed and full of woe,
he goes and lets his comrades know.
"My lords," he said, "the man I asked
to lodge us is a pederast.
He'll give us hospitality,
140   and then he'll treat us shamefully
and fuck the one who's long and thin
and beat the shortest one's brains in."
Among the knights was a tall man
whose name was Walon of Dinant.
145   "My lords," he said, "I know it's true
that I'm the tallest one of you.
I'll not stay with that sodomite
who in such doings takes delight.
I'd sooner be a tonsured friar
150   than submit to a man's desire!"
A knight from Tongres, too, was there,
called the Hungarian, Pierre,
who said, "My lords, I won't agree
to go there out of bravery.
155   I'm much the shortest of the lot.
Were we to go there, you could not
keep him from giving me a whack
before I ever paid him back.
Here shall the two of us remain
160   and weather out the hurricane."
The others cried out to a man,
"That's what I call a worthless plan!
We shall arrange things differently,
better, for sure, and cunningly,
165   for, when we come into his hall,
the shorter ones will stretch out tall

& li plus lonc voisent cranpit
& si siécent tot acropit. »
Ensi l'ont entr'aus creanté.

170   Atant sont en la cort entret,
venu en sont en la maison,
la o li feus ert en saison
car li ivers estoit molt frois.
Lors descendent des palefrois.

175 Ançois que cascuns sa cape oste,
hautement salue sen oste.
Il respont: « Segnor, Deus vos saut! »
A cest mot li maisnie saut,
qui lor corurent as estriers,

180 puis recuellirent lor destriers,
& cil se sont vers le fu trait;
Wales li lons se fist contrait
& Pieres vint sor les ortaus,
si est asis sor .ii. hestaus.

185 Ensi furent par grant dangier
desci q'a l'eure de mangier,
que li mangiers fu atornés
& il fu avant aportés.
Cil corurent metre les tables

190 qui repairoient des estables,
& li baron s'i sont asis.
Wales li lons fu molt pensis.
A premiers orent pois au lart,
aprés ot cascuns .i. marlart,

195 si orent hastes & lardés
& si orent rices pastés,
& si burent a grant desroit
d'un vin d'Ausai molt fort & roit
plainne une bout de .v. sestiers,

200 s'en remest uns bociaus entiers

and the tall go about half-crouched
and, when they sit, hold themselves slouched."
Yes, they said, that's the long and short
of what they'd do.
170   They crossed the court,
approached the house, and entered it.
Inside a welcome fire was lit
because the winter was so frosty.
Then each dismounted from his palfrey
175 and, before each took off his cloak,
gave greeting to their host, who spoke
and said, "My lords, God save you all!"
and all the servants in the hall,
who'd rushed to help them from their steeds,
180 then took their horses by their leads.
The knights approached the glowing grate;
Walon took care not to stand straight
and, walking tippy-toe, Pierre
used table trestles as a chair.
185 So there they sat, anticipating
some awful danger while they're waiting
for dinnertime to come, unnerved.
         At last it's ready to be served.
The servants run and set the tables
190 upon returning from the stables.
The knights sat down to have some food.
Walon was in a pensive mood.
First they brought in bacon with peas,
and then whole mallards, one apiece,
195 then meat on skewers, barded meat,
and excellent pasties to eat.
To quench their thirst, they drank a mass
of strong, robust wine from Alsace,
a whole five-*sestier* keg, and still
200 a smaller cask was left to kill,

que cil avoient aporté
qui molt furent desconforté.
     Qant ont mangiet par grant delit
d'autre part furent fait li lit;
205   la se colcierent li baron.
Entre le dame & son baron
en sont dedens le canbre entré;
ains qu'il aient le suel passé
li chevaliers s'escrie en haut:
210   « En carité, Dame Mehaut,
je me volrai ancui conbatre,
le plus lonc foutre & le cort batre,
se g'i puis adroit asener! »
Wales commence a forsener,
215   qui le nuit cuide fotus estre,
& Pieres, qui gist a senestre,
cuide tres bien qu'il le manace
& qu'il le waite & qu'il le hace,
& cil nes aseüre mie,
220   ains va colcier joste s'amie;
si le commence a descovrir,
puis li fait les ganbes ovrir,
si a une candelle prisse
trestote ardant & tote esprisse,
225   si le regarde entre les ainnes,
qui molt erent söes & sainnes.
Qant il a les .ii. traus trovés
il a parlet com fols provés:
« Ma dolce suer, m'amie ciere,
230   cest grant trau vos fist uns leciere
por les andolles englotir—
je cuit qu'il volra seglotir!
Il sont de molt bele façon;
ce sanle d'uevre de maçon:
235   qant les vos fist vo dame faire,

that they had brought with them that evening.
(They're apprehensive now, and grieving.)
      After they'd dined with great delight,
their beds were made up for the night,
205 and one and all went to retire.
The noble lady and her sire
together to their room withdraw,
but when they've barely reached the door,
the stupid knight exclaims aloud,
210 "I promise you, Lady Mehaud,
my nighttime combat will be strong:
I'll beat the short one, fuck the long,
if I can bring it off aright."
Walon, who's lying on the right,
215 is at his wits' end and despairs,
assuming he'll get fucked, while Pierre's
convinced the threat means that his grim-
intentioned host is stalking him;
nor does *he* set their minds at rest,
220 but lies beside her and undressed
his wife, so that she lies there bare,
then, opening her legs with care,
holding a candle in his hand
that brightly burns and flickers, and
225 between the sweet and soft expanse
where her legs join he casts his glance,
and, when the two holes meet his eyes,
he proves his foolishness and cries,
"My darling wife, my love, my soul,
230 a glutton must have shaped this hole
to gobble sausages galore!
Was that a hiccup that I saw?
They are so comely, I suspect
they're the work of some architect.
235 Your mother made them, it occurs

fist les ille as siens contrefaire.
Li sien me sanlent plus velut
& plus noir & plus cavelut;
cist sont plus bel. Si com moi sanble,
240   por poi qu'il ne tienent ensamble. »
Dont respondi li bele nee:
« Sire, je fui tot ensi nee. »
Atant a le candelle estinte
au mur o il l'avoit atinte,
245   puis a les .ii. traus mesurés.
Il ne fu mie bellurés
qu'il n'ait tant contremont erciet
qu'il a au plus lonc aderciet,
si a tant boté & empoint
250   que li cosse est venue a point
& que li sos fist se besogne,
si com li fabliaus nos tesmogne,
plus de .ii. fois en .i. randon,
car tot li fu mis a bandon,
255   & li harnas & li ostius,
qui molt estoit entalentius.
Li dame li crie mercit:
« Sire, fait ele, soit m'ocit.
Se vos ne m'aportés a boire,
260   ja me verés morir en oire.
La ot ersoir .i. bocel mis,
ne sai s'il est plains o demis,
mais vin i a, de fit le sai,
ne sai de Lezac o d'Ausai—
265   por Deu, beaus sire, aportés m'ent;
n'i metés mie longuement. »
Puis recommence .i. poi a muire;
cil crient que sa molliers ne muire,
molt fu de maltalent espris,
270   en sa main a .i. hanap pris,
desci q'au feu en est venus

to me, by basing them on hers,
though not so dark nor everywhere
so thickly covered up with hair.
These are more fair. I wonder whether
240 they might not almost grow together."
The wellborn beauty let him know:
"Dear husband, I was born just so."
Then he snuffed out the candle, which
he'd placed in the wall in a niche,
245 and tried the two holes out for size.
Unerringly, his proud supplies
he aimed; his uplifted erection
sped in the longer hole's direction
and banged and poked with so much force,
250 his business took its rightful course.
In fact, the numbskull didn't rest,
as our fabliau will attest,
and at least three times at a shot
he gave it everything he's got,
255 his tool and all its fine regalia
so avid he'd no chance of failure.
        The lady begs a truce of him:
"Husband, this thirst will do me in.
If you don't go get me a drink,
260 I'll die before your eyes, I think.
Last night a cask was set aside.
I'm not sure how much is inside,
but I know there's wine for a fact,
Alsace, perhaps, or else Lessac;
265 for God's sake, sire, fetch some for me.
Waste no time; bring it rapidly."
She sets about moaning and sighing;
the knight, afraid his wife is dying,
is all befuddled by his worries,
270 and, reaching for a cup, he hurries
down to the hearth, where the fire glows,

tos despolliés & trestos nus,
puis a pris .i. manefle cort
de qoi li bovier de le cort
275 aparellievent lor atoivre.
(Ce doit on molt bien amentoivre).
Un poi en a le feu overt;
le cul Walon vit descovert,
qui se dormoit tos hasquerés.
280 Li cus ert noirs & masquerés
autresi grans com uns porciaus.
Il cuide ce soit li bociaus
qui la li gist en mi la voie,
mais une cosse le desvoie,
285 qu'il nel set comment deslacier
ne le vin oster ne sacier.
Or entendés del vif maufet!
Il a le manefle escaufet
ausi com li bovier fassoient
290 qant il lor harnas refaisoient,
puis est au vascel aproismiés
u il n'avoit ne vin ne miés,
tant roidement del fer i bote
que li hanas en esclabote
295 del sanc qui de la plaie saut,
& Wales fremist & tressaut,
si s'escria a haute vois:
« Or sus! or sus! car je m'en vois!
Cis erites m'a asalit! »
300 Dont sont si conpagnon salit
qant il oïrent le bescosse,
& li sos a la main escosse
de qoi il tenoit le manefle,
aval le maison le fondefle,
305 si fiert Pieron ens el costet
si c'une piece en a ostet

quite naked, stripped of all his clothes,
and grabs an awl with a short blade,
like those the household's herdsmen made
275 holes with when they would mend their gear.
(Remember what I've told you here.)
          He stirred the fire and in the light
saw Walon's rump loom into sight,
all black and dirty, and so big
280 it looked exactly like a pig
in anguished sleep tossing around.
The knight believes that he has found
the wine cask lying on the floor,
but he is not exactly sure
285 just how to tap the wine inside
and draw some off to give his bride.
Now hear what mischief he committed!
He took the bradawl and he heated
it, much the same as herdsmen who
290 have found some mending job to do,
then went up to the wine cask (he'd
find in it neither wine nor mead!)
and rammed the awl in Walon's crop
so forcefully, it drenched the cup
295 with the blood spurting from the wound.
Walon jumped up, sure he'd been ruined:
"Get up! Get up! I'm out of here!
That pervert there attacked my rear!"
he cried out in a dreadful voice.
300 When his companions heard the noise,
they all jumped up to take a stand,
and the fool swung out with his hand
in which he held the red-hot awl
and sent it hurtling down the hall.
305 It struck Pierre full in the side,
cutting a large chunk from his hide,

que d'autre part en l'asciet busce.
A ces deus en caï li busce,
& il s'en tornent sans congiet;
310 mais il en fuscent bien vengiet
a grant dolor & a grant dame
se ne fust li mere la dame,
qui tot l'afaire lor aconte
& si en fist proier le conte,
315 qui lor fist savoir & entendre
que nus om ne doit sot atendre,
car sovent l'en avient grans maus.
     Li cus Walon en fu vermaus,
& Pieres en eut une trace
320 dont li sans remest en la place,
& li sos eut apris a foutre.
A cest mot est li fabliaus oltre.

14. LE CHEVALIER QUI FESOIT LES CONS PARLER

Fableaus sunt or molt encorsé:
meint denier en ont enboursé
cil qui les content & les portent,
car grant confortement aportent
5 as envoisiez & as oiseus
quant il n'i a gent trop noiseus;
neïs a ceus qui sunt plein d'ire,
quant il oient bons fableaus lire
si lor fet il grant alejance
10 & oublïer duel & pesance
& mavestié & penssement.
Ce dit Garin qui pas ne ment,
qui d'un chevalier nos aconte

which flew across the room and struck
the wall. Those two have rotten luck!
    They left there without more ado
310 and would have taken vengeance, too,
so he'd have paid dear for his acts,
but his wife's mother told the facts
and gave them all a full account
and interceded with the count,
315 who got them all to realize
to heed a fool is most unwise
and often followed by mischance.
    So, Walon had inside his pants
a bright red ass, and Pierre was scarred,
320 and both had bloodied up the yard,
and the dumb knight had learned to screw.
That's my last word; this fable's through.

14. THE KNIGHT WHO MADE CUNTS TALK

by Garin

Fabliaux are now much in demand;
they're a good source of cash in hand
for those who tell and spread them 'round.
In them great comfort's to be found
5 for the fun-loving and the idle,
so long as people aren't too spiteful;
and even those who're filled with woe,
when they hear a good fabliau,
it is a source of great relief
10 and they forget their pain and grief
and their rancor and gloominess.
So Garin, who's no liar, says,
who has a story to recount

une aventure en icest conte
15 qui avoit merveillous eür,
car je vos di tot asseür
que il fesoit le con parler
quant il le voleit apeler.
Le cul qui ert en l'archepel
20 responnoit bien a son apel.
Icest eür li fu donnez
en l'en que il fu adoubez;
si vos dirai con il avint.

    Li chevalier povres devint
25 ainz que il fust de grant aage,
por quant sel tenoit l'en a sage,
mes n'avoit ne vignes ne terres;
en tornoiemenz & en guerres
estoit trestote s'atendance,
30 car bien savoit ferir de lance,
hardiz estoit & conbatanz
& a grant besoinz secoranz.
Adont avint en cel tempoire,
si con lisant truis en l'estoire,
35 que les guerres partout failloient,
nule gent ne se traveilloient,
li tornoi furent desfendu.
Si ot tot le sien despendu
le chevalier en cel termine;
40 ne li remest mantel d'ermine
ne surcot ne chape forree
ne d'autre avoir une denree
qu'il n'eit vendu ou mis en gage,
mes de ce nel ting mie a sage
45 que son hernois a engagé,
si a tot beü & mengé.
A .i. chastel iert sejornant
qui molt ert beaus & despendant

about a knight in this account
15   who had most wonderful good fortune,
for be assured it was his portion
to make cunts speak at his command
whenever he would call them, and
likewise the asshole in its nest
20   had to make answer if addressed.
He got this power in the same
year that he first a knight became.
I'll tell you how it came to be.
      The knight fell into poverty
25   while still quite young. Though people deemed
him worthy to be well esteemed,
he owned no vineyards, took no rents,
but always war and tournaments
preoccupied his mind and will;
30   to wield a lance he had much skill,
and he could fight like one possessed
and, in need, succored the oppressed.
It came to pass that for a spell,
for so I heard the story tell,
35   that suddenly all fighting ended,
no more in war was strength expended,
nor could one hold a tournament.
All that he owned the knight soon spent
at that time and he went flat broke;
40   he pawned his clothes and sold his cloak,
his surcoat, too, and fur-lined cape,
till there was nothing he could scrape
together that was left to pledge.
He did unwisely, I allege,
45   to pawn whatever a knight needs;
with what it paid, he drinks and feeds.
In a citadel he was living
known for its high and easy living,

aussi con or seroit Provins;
50 si bevoit sovent de bons vins.
        Iluec fu lonc tens a sejour
tant que il avint a .i. jour
c'on cria .i. tornoiement
par le païs communement,
55 que tuit i fussent sans essoigne
droit a La Haïë en Toraine;
la devoit estre grant & fiers.
Grant joie en ot li chevaliers;
Hüet, son escuier, apele,
60 si li a dite la novelle
du tornoiement qui la iert.
Ce dit Hüet: « A vos qu'afiert
a parler de tornoiement,
car trestuit vostre garnement
65 sont engagié por la despense?
    — Ha, Hüet, por Deu, car en pense,
fet le chevalier, se tu veus!
Tot dis bien conseillier me seus.
Mieus m'en fust se creü t'eüse!
70 Or pense comment je reüse
mes garnemenz sanz demorance,
& si fei aucune chevance,
la meillor que tu porras fere:
sor toi n'en saroie a chief trere. »
75 Hüet voit que fere l'estuet,
si se chevist au mieus qu'il puet:
le palefroi son seignor vent,
onques ne le fist autrement
& s'en est aquité tres bien,
80 si qu'a paier n'i lessa rien.
Or a les gages en sa mein;
& quant ce vint a l'endemein
andui se sunt mis a la voie,
que nul nes sieut ne ne convoie,

much like Provins—it's a rich town.
He tossed a lot of fine wines down.
       There he had spent a lengthy stay
until it happened on one day
at last a tournament was cried
for all throughout the countryside:
Without fail all the valiant men
should come to La Haie in Touraine,
where it would be held, large and splendid.
The knight was mightily contented,
and called out to his squire, Huet,
and told him what the tidings say.
A tournament! Wonderful news!
"Well," said Huet, "and what's the use?
Why talk about a tournament
when all your knightly trappings went
to pay the food and drink you bought?"
"Huet, by God, give it some thought,
if you are willing," the knight pleaded.
"You've always counseled me when needed.
I'm sorry now I wouldn't hear!
Now think of some way that my gear
right here and now can be redeemed.
Lay the best plan you've ever schemed;
it really doesn't matter what.
Without your help I'm in a spot."
Huet could see what was required
and solved the problem as desired:
His master's palfrey went on sale,
for nothing else was of avail
and for the palfrey he could get
enough to pay off every debt.
Now what was pawned is theirs again.
       Came the next morning, the two men
set out together on their road,
for no one followed them or rode

85 & chevauchent par une lande.
Le chevalier Hüet demande
comment avoit eü ses gages,
& Hüet, qui molt estoit sages
li a dit: « Sire, par ma foi,
90 j'ai vendu vostre palefroi,
car autrement ne poeit estre.
N'en merrez or cheval en destre,
que que vos faciez en avant.
— Combien as tu de remanant,
95 Hüet?, ce dit li chevaliers.
— Par foi, sire, .xii. deniers
avommes sans plus a despendre.
— Dont n'avon nos mestier d'atendre,
fet le chevalier, ce me semble. »
100   Isi s'en vont andui ensemble,
& quant il ont grant voie alee
si entrent en une valee.
Li chevalier erra penssant,
& Hüet chevaucha avant
105 sor son roncin grant aleüre,
tant qu'il trova par aventurre
enmi .i. [pré] une fonteine
qui molt estoit & clere & seine,
si en coroit grant li ruiseaus
110 & entor avoit arbreseaus
vers & foilluz de grant beauté
autresi con el tens d'esté;
li abresel molt bel estoient.
En la fonteine se baignoient
115 .iii. pucelles preuz & senees,
de beauté resembloient fees.
Lor *robe & totes* lor chemises
orent desouz .i. arbre mises,
qui erent batues a or:
120 bien valoient .i. grant tresor,

85 along. They crossed a wood this way.
    The knight inquired of Huet
    how their expenses had been paid,
    and Huet, who was clever, said,
    to him, "My lord, if truth be told,
90 thanks to your palfrey, which I sold
    because it seemed the only course.
    You will not lead a second horse
    with you from now on, come what may."
    "Well, now how much is left, Huet?"
95 his master asked. "Say, is there any?"
    "In truth, my lord," he said, "twelve penny-
    worth and no more to spend, I fear."
    "No point, then, hanging around here,"
    the knight says, "if I'm not mistaken."
100   They go along the road they've taken
    and, when they've gone some distance, then
    they come at last into a glen.
    The knight, who had much on his mind,
    went slowly. Leaving him behind,
105 Huet went quickly riding on
    until by chance he came upon
    a spring that flowed across a green,
    which sparkled bright and very clean.
    The stream is wide, the current rushes,
110 and growing all around are bushes
    all green and leafy, just as pleasing
    as those one sees in summer season,
    such was the beauty of the trees.
    There bathing in the stream he sees
115 three damsels, lovely, noble, wise,
    who looked like fairies to his eyes.
    Their clothing, right down to their shifts,
    they'd hung upon a branch and left,
    garments made all of beaten gold
120 and worth a fortune, truth be told;

si riches ne furent veües.
Quant Hüet vit les fees nues
qui tant avoient les chars blanches,
les cors bien fez, les braz, les hanches,
125   cele part vet a esperon;
ainz ne lor dist ne o ne non,
ençois a lor robes saisies,
ses lessa totes esbahies.
Quant voient que lor robe[ ] enporte,
130   la plus mestre se desconforte,
car molt s'en vet grant aleüre
cil qui de remanoir n'a cure.
Les pucelles molt se dolosent,
crïent & dementent & plorent.
135   Que qu'elles se vont dementant,
ez vos le chevalier venant
qui aprés l'escuier s'en va.
Atant l'une d'elles parla,
si li conta leur mesestance;
140   li chevalier en ot pesance.
Des pucelles ot grant pitié;
lors a le cheval tant cuitié
que Hüet ataint, si li dist:
« Baille ça tost, se Deus t'aïst,
145   les robes, nes enporter mie!
Ce seroit trop grant vilenie
de fere a ces pucelles honte.
— Or tenez d'autre chose conte,
fet Hüet, & ne soiez ivres!
150   Les robes valent bien .c. livres,
car onques plus riches ne vi;
devant .xiiii. anz & demi
ne gaagnerés [ ] autretant,
tant sachiez aler tornoiant!
155   — Par foi, ce dit li chevaliers,
je lor reporteré arriers

never were seen any so rich.
Seeing the maids without a stitch
of clothing on, white skin undraped,
their bodies, arms, and hips well-shaped,
125 Huet spurred on his horse their way;
no word of greeting did he say,
grabbed everything they had to wear,
and left the ladies in despair.
Now when they see their clothing taken
130 the strongest one of them is shaken,
for Huet rides off at top speed
and to the damsels gives no heed.
The maidens do not cease to moan
and yell and rant and weep and groan.
135   While they continue thus to cry,
behold! the knight comes riding by
shortly behind his squire, Huet.
Then one of them spoke up to say
what had occurred and told their plight,
140 which sorely grieved the noble knight
and made him feel great pity for them,
so he spurred his horse on before him,
came to Huet, and called out loud,
"Hand over now, so help you God,
145 those clothes; you'll not carry them off!
To shame these damsels and to scoff
at them would be the height of baseness!"
"Consider rather what the case is,"
Huet replies, "and don't be silly.
150 They're worth a hundred pounds, now really,
for richer garments I've not seen.
That sum within the next fourteen
years and a half you'd never win,
for all the tournaments you're in."
155 "Upon my oath," his master stresses,
"I shall return these ladies' dresses,

lour robes, comment que il praigne.
Je n'ai cure de tel gaaigne
ne ja n'en monteroie en pris.
160   — A bon droit estes vos cheitis »,
fet Hüet par grant mautalent.
Le chevalier les robes prent,
a l'einz qu'il pot vint as pucelles,
qui molt erent plesanz & belles,
165   si lor a lour robes rendues,
& el se sunt tantost vestues
car a chascune estoit molt tart.
Atant le chevalier s'en part,
congié prent & s'en torne arriere.
170   L'une des pucelles premiere
parolle as autres, si leur dit:
« Damoiseles, se Deu m'aït,
cil chevalier est molt courtois.
Molt en avon veü; ençois
175   [ ] eüst nos robes chier vendues
que il les nos eüst rendues:
il en eüst assés deniers;
& sachiés que li chevaliers
a vers nos fet grant cortoisie,
180   & nos avon fet vilenie,
que riens ne li avon doné
dont il nos doie savoir gré.
Rapelon *le*, sel paion bien;
il est si povre qu'il n'a rien.
185   Nule ne soit envers li chiche,
mes feson le povre home riche. »
        Les autres li acreanterent,
le chevalier dont rapelerent
& il retorna meintenant.
190   La plus mestresse parle avant,
car des autres en ot l'otroi:
« Sire chevalier, par ma foi,

which you have stolen, come what may.
I don't care to get rich that way.
It would discredit my good name."
160 "If you're poor, you've yourself to blame,"
Huet replies, ready to quarrel.
         The knight took from him their apparel
and turned and hurried back to where
the ladies were who were so fair.
165 No sooner were they repossessed
of their clothes than the maidens dressed.
Already it had been too long.
The knight must now be moving on;
he takes his leave and rides away.
170   One of the maids has this to say
and was the first to tell the rest:
"God grant me place among the blessed,
this knight is noble and polite.
We all know that many a knight
175 would not have returned them, but sold
our clothes for silver and for gold,
and would have made a tidy sum;
and know that when this knight has come
and shown us such great courtesy,
180 we're acting most ungratefully
not to repay him in full measure
in some way that will give him pleasure.
Let's call him back for his reward.
The man's so poor his life is hard.
185 Let no one be ungenerous;
let's make the poor man prosperous."
The others said that she was right,
and so they summoned back the knight.
         He came back when he heard them call;
190 the chief of them spoke first of all.
(The others felt it was her place.)
"Sir knight," she said to him, "in faith,

ne volon pas, que il n'est droiz,
que vos einsi vos en aloiz.

195 Rendues nos avez les vies,
richement nos avez servies,
si avez fet molt que preudon,
& je vos donrai riche don,
& sachiés que ja n'i faudrés.

200 Jamés en cel leu ne vendrés
que tot le mont ne vos conjoie,
& chascuns fera de vos joie,
& si vos abandoneront
la gent tot ce que il aront;

205 ne pöez mes avoir poverte.
— Dame, ci a riche deserte,
fet li chevalier, grant merciz!
— Li mien don ne rest pas petiz,
fet l'autre pucele en aprés.

210 Ja n'irés mes ne loinz ne pres
por que truissiez fame ne beste,
mes qu'el ait .ii. euz en la teste,
se daigniez son con apeler,
qu'il nel convieigne a vos parler:

215 itel sera mes vos eürs.
De ce soiez molt bien seürs
que tel ne l'ot ne roi ne conte. »
Adont ot le chevalier honte,
si tint la pucele por fole;

220 & la tierce aprés [re]parrole,
& dit au chevalier: « Beau sire,
savez ore que vos viel dire?—
car bien est reson & droiture
que, se le con par aventure

225 avoit aucun enconbrement
qu'il ne respondist enroment,
le cul si respondroit por li,
qui qu'en eüst duel ne anui,

we think it would be wrong of us
to let you simply leave us thus.
195 You've acted like a worthy man
and gave us our lives back again,
generously came to our aid,
and I'll make sure you're well repaid.
Be sure my gift will never cease.
200 Whenever you go anyplace,
everyone will seek to please you
and be elated when they see you,
and all will give you for your own
just about everything they own.
205 Never again will you know need."
"This is a noble gift indeed,
my lady, thank you," says the knight.
"Nor is the gift I'll make you slight,"
the second lady says in turn.
210 "Whatever way your path may turn,
every woman and female beast
who've in their heads two eyes apiece
whom you meet, if you call, their cunts
will have to answer you at once.
215 Forever this will be your lot,
and you may be sure there is not
a king or count can do the same."
The knight was overcome with shame
and was convinced the girl was mad.
220 The third one next hastened to add
and asked him, "Can you guess, sir, pray,
the thing I have in mind to say?
Since it were right by reason's laws
that if the cunt for any cause
225 should happen to be too obstructed
to answer promptly as instructed,
the asshole should speak in its place,
no matter what shame or disgrace

si l'apelisiez, sanz aloigne. »

230   Dont ot li chevalier vergoigne,
& bien quide que gabé l'aient
& que por noient le deloient.
Meintenant au chemin se met;
quant a aconseü Hüet

235 trestot meintenant li aconte
si con avez oï le conte:
« Gabé m'ont celes du prael! »
& dit Hüet: « Ce m'est molt bel,
que cil est fous, par seint Germein,

240 que ce que il tient en sa mein
giete a ses piez en nonchaloir.
— Par mon chief, Hüet, tu dis voir,
fet le chevalier, ce me semble. »
  Atant es vos, si con moi semble,

245 .i. proverre tot seul de gent,
qui chevauchoit une jument.
Li prestres ert poissant & riche,
mes molt estoit aver & chiche;
le chemin voleit trespasser

250 & a une autre vile aler
qui assez pres d'iluec estoit.
Le prestre le chevalier voit,
vers li trestorne sa jument,
si descendi inellement

255 & li dist: « Sire, bien veigniez!
Je vos pri que vos remaigniez
huimés o moi por osteler.
De vos servir & honorer
ai grant envie & grant talent,

260 tot en vostre commandement
est quant que j'ai, n'en doutez ja. »
Le chevalier se merveilla
du prestre qu'il ne connoist mie,
qui de remanoir si le prie.

may come of it, once you have called."
230 When the knight hears this, he's appalled
and thinks they mock him and mislead him
and to no purpose would impede him.

Again he set out on his way,
and when he caught up with Huet,
235 he straightaway gave an account
of what you've heard this tale recount:
"By those three damsels I've been tricked!"
Huet said, "What did you expect?
That man's a fool, I'll have you know,
240 who has something and lets it go
without thought for its worth or price."
"By God, Huet, that's sound advice,
it would seem" was the knight's reply.

Just then who happens to come by?
245 A priest, and no one else was near,
and he was riding on a mare.
This priest had lots of wealth and riches,
but he was mean and avaricious.
He crossed their path while riding down
250 on his way to another town
that was located right nearby.
Now, when the knight catches his eye,
the cleric turns his mare around
and quickly gets down on the ground
255 and says, "I'm glad you've come my way!
I beg of you that you will stay
with me from now on as my guest,
for it would be much to my taste
to serve you and to do you honor.
260 All my possessions, on my honor,
I now place at your beck and call."

The knight can't understand at all
why some strange priest he doesn't know
should welcome him and fête him so.

265 Huez le sache, si li dist:
     « Biaus sires chiers, se Deus m'aïst,
     les pucelles vous ont dit voir,
     bien le pöez aparcevoir.
     Or apelez delivremant
270 le con de celle grant jumant:
     vous l'orrez ja parler, ce croi. »
     Dist li chevaliers: « Je l'otroi. »
     Tout meintenant li prist a dire:
     « Sire cons, ou va vostre sire?
275 *Dites le moi, nel celez mie.*
     —— Par foi, il va veoir s'amie,
     fait li cons, sire chevaliers.
     Si li porte de bons deniers,
     .x. livres de bone monnoie
280 qu'il a ceinz en une courroie
     pour acheter robe mardi. »
     & quant li prestres entendi
     le con qui parole si bien,
     esbaïz fu seur toute rien,
285 enchantez cuide estre & traïz,
     de la paor s'en est foïz,
     & por mielx courre inellemant
     desfuble sa chape erranmant
     & les deniers & la courroie
290 tout a getié enmi la voie,
     la jument lait, si torne en fuie.
     Quant Hüez le voit, si le huie,
     & cil s'en fuit grant aleüre
     qui de retorner n'avoit cure,
295 ainz s'en fuit par une charriere;
     por .c. mars ne tornast arriere!
     Li chevaliers les deniers prant,
     & Hüez saisi la jument
     qui molt estoit bien afautree,

265   Huet took him aside and said,
        "See here, dear master, by my head,
        all that the damsels said was true,
        as I can see and so can you.
        Now if you'll only speak, I swear,
270   to the cunt of his sturdy mare,
        you're bound to hear the thing reply."
        The knight agrees, "It's worth a try,"
        and asks it without hesitation,
        "What is your master's destination?
275   Hide nothing, Mr. Cunt; tell all."
        "Sir knight, he's off to pay a call,"
        the cunt says, "on his concubine.
        He's bringing her a gift of fine
        new-minted money worth ten pounds
280   tied in a belt he's girded 'round
        to buy a dress at Tuesday's fair."
        It gave the priest an awful scare
        to hear the verbal evidence
        that his mare's cunt could talk good sense.
285   He was sure this was sorcery,
        and out of fear he turned to flee,
        and, to ensure his quick escape,
        he hurriedly took off his cape
        and his purse with its ten-pound load,
290   and flung it all down on the road
        and left the mare and ran away.
        Deaf to the catcalls of Huet,
        he ran as with his pants on fire
        (to turn back he has no desire)
295   and headed off down a side track.
        A hundred marks won't bring him back!
            The knight picked up the purse, of course,
        and Huet took the cleric's horse,
        which was equipped with the best gear,

300 si trousse la chape feurree
& les deniers bien estoia
que li chevaliers li bailla.
Adont s'en tournerent parlant
& d'eures en autres riant
305 dou provoire qui s'en foï
pour le con que parler oï
Li chevaliers a Hüet dist:
« Hüet, fait il, se Deus m'aïst,
se je t'eüsse orainz creü!
310 Mon los eüsse descreü
se nous eüssiens retenues
les robes & lessees nues
les franches pucelles senees.
Je sai de voir, ce furent fees
315 quant tel guerredon m'ont rendu.
Ainz que nos aions despendu
cest avoir & dou tout gasté,
ravrons nous de l'autre a planté,
car teus paiera nostre escot
320 qui de tout ce ne set or mot." »
        Atant vindrent en un chastel
molt bien seant & fort & bel.
Que vous feroie je lonc conte?
En ce chastel avoit .i. conte
325 & la contesse i ert, sa fame,
qui molt estoit courtoise dame,
& clers & chevaliers assez
qui la estoient assemblez
en mi la vile senz tencier
330 pour jöer & pour solacier.
Quequ'il se vont esbanoiant,
ez vous le chevalier venant
celui qui fet les cons parler.
Tuit cil le queurent salüer

300 and packed away the cape to wear
and also pocketed the stash
of coins. (The knight gave him the cash.)
Then they continued on their path.
Time and again they had to laugh
305 to think of how the priest had fled
on hearing what the cunt had said.
The knight turned to Huet and spoke:
"So help me God, it were no joke
if, when you counseled me, I'd listened,
310 for my good name would have been lessened,
having their clothing, just to take it
and leave the ladies there stark naked,
who were so wise, well-bred, and pure.
Why, they were fairies, to be sure,
315 to make me such a princely gift.
Before we will have made short shrift
of all the wealth we got today,
plenty more's bound to come our way,
for someone's sure to foot the bill,
320 who of all this knows nothing still."
　　　Then they came to a citadel,
handsomely built and strong as well.
Why should I lengthen my account?
There in the castle dwelt a count;
325 the countess, too, was there, his wife—
courtly refinement ruled her life—
and clerics and a slew of vassals
who'd come together at the castle
in friendship and cooperation
330 for company and recreation.
While they were occupied at play,
the knight came riding by their way,
who could make cunts burst into speech.
All wanted to be first to reach

335 qui le virent & conjoïr
dont il se pot molt esjoïr;
touz li pueples court celle part,
au conte meïsmes fu tart
qu'acolé l'ait et embracié,
340 & enz en la bouche baisié;
tout autretel fet la contesse—
.xx. foiz le baisast senz permesse
se ses sires n'eust esté la,
mais pour lui atant le laissa.
345 Quant baisié l'ont & acolé
si l'en ont a joie mené
tout droit en la sale le conte.
     Que vous feroie je lonc conte?
Tantost sont assis au mengier
350 li baron & li chevalier.
Quant mengié orent a loisir
si parlerent d'aler gesir.
La contesse, qui fu courtoise,
de son oste pas ne li poise,
355 ainz li fist feire a grant delit
en une chanbre i. riche lit.
La se dort a aise & repose,
& la contesse a chief de pose
apele une soue pucelle,
360 la plus courtoise & la plus belle.
A consoil li dist: « Belle amie,
alez tost, ne vous ennuit mie,
avec ce chevalier gesir
tout bellement & a loisir,
365 dont nous amons tant la venue.
Lez lui vous couchiez toute nue,
si le servez s'il est mestiers.
Je i alasse volentiers,
que ja nou laissasse por honte

335 and greet him warmly when they saw him,
which must have been a pleasure for him.
Every last one rushed up to meet him.
The count, too, couldn't wait to greet him
and gave the knight a warm embrace,
340 kissing him squarely on the face,
nor did his wife her kisses spare.
(Were not the count, her husband, there,
she would have given him a score.
Because of him she won't give more.)
345 When all had hugged him with a will,
they gave him joyful escort till
they came into the count's great hall.
       I won't prolong my tale or stall.
They all sat down to have a bite,
350 every last nobleman and knight,
and when at length they'd been well fed,
they spoke about going to bed.
The gracious countess did her best,
nowise put out to have a guest,
355 and to a chamber richly wrought
she had the finest bedding brought.
There all alone he takes his rest,
but before long she thought it best
to call one of her maids-in-waiting
360 with charms beyond enumerating.
She told her secretly, "My friend,
if you are willing, go and spend,
for company and for delight,
this night in bed with that same knight
365 whose coming made us all so glad.
Go lie beside him all unclad
and serve him if he feels the need.
I would have gone myself, indeed,
nor would shame make me stay away,

370 ne fust pour mon seigneur le conte
    qui n'est pas encor endormi. »
    & celle i vet molt [a] enviz,
    mais escondire ne l'osa.
    Au lit ou cil se reposa
375 i va tramblant comme une fueille,
    plus tost qu'elle post se despoille,
    puis si se couche & s'estent,
    & quant li chevaliers la sent
    tantost erranment se tourna
380 & de celle se merveilla:
    « Qui est ce, fet il, delez moy?
    — Sire, nou tenez a desroi,
    fait celle qui fu simple & coie,
    que la contesse m'i envoie.
385 Une de ses pucelles sui,
    ne vous ferai mal ne ennui,
    ainz vous tastonerai le chief.
    — Par foi, ce ne m'iert mie grief, »
    dit li chevaliers, qui l'embrace,
390 la bouche li baise & la face,
    puis li pourtaste les memelles,
    qui estoient plaisanz & belles,
    & seur le con sa mein li mist.
    En aprés li chevaliers dist:
395 « Sire cons, or parlez a moi!
    Je vous veil demander pour quoi
    vostre dame est venue ci.
    — Sire, ce dist li cons, merci,
    que la contesse l'i envoie
400 pour vous faire solaz & joie.
    Je ne vous quier ja a celer. »
    Quant celle oï son con parler,
    estrangemant fu esperdue,
    dou lit sailli trestoute nue,
405 arrier a la voie s'est mise,

370 but with my husband there's no way,
because the count is still awake."

The maiden went; she dared not make
objection, though it gave her grief,
and she went trembling like a leaf
375 up to the bed where the knight slept,
took off her clothes and quickly crept
in right beside him and stretched out.
When the knight feels someone's about,
he quickly turns and wakes from slumber.
380 To find her there fills him with wonder.
"Who can this be I feel beside me?"
"My lord," she says, "please do not chide me"
(for she was simple and naïve);
"I'm sent here by my lady's leave.
385 One of her handmaidens am I;
I'll do no harm, but satisfy
you. Come, and I'll massage your head."
"In faith, I'm not displeased," he said.
He held her close in his embrace
390 and kissed her on the mouth and face,
then put his hands on and caressed
her most delicious, lovely breast,
and, moving down, began to stroke
her cunt, and, as he did, he spoke.
395 "Now speak up, Mr. Cunt, because
I'm curious to know the cause
that brought your lady here to me."
"My lord," her cunt said, "certainly.
Know that the countess sent her here
400 to pleasure you and give you cheer.
From you there's nothing I would hide."
When she heard how her cunt replied,
the maid was filled with untold dread
and jumped up naked out of bed
405 and, clutching only her chemise,

onc n'en porta que sa chemise.
Dedanz la chanbre sa dame entre,
molt li trambloit li cuers ou ventre
& la contesse si l'apelle,
410 si li demande la nouvelle:
« Pour qu'as laissié le chevalier
que ceanz herberjames ier
a cui je t'avoie envoïe? »,
mais celle fu si esbaïe
415 qu'a poines pot parler .i. mot.
Puis respondi mielx qu'elle pot
& dist: « Dame, vous ne savez!
Je cuit que cist hons est faez!
Decoste lui couchier m'alai,
420 toute nue me despoillai,
il prist mon con a apeler,
assez l'a fet a lui parler:
trestout quanqu'il li demanda
oiant moi mes cons li conta! »
425 Quant la contesse ce entant
si s'en merveille duremant,
& dist qu'elle nou crerroit mie,
& celle li jure & afie
que c'est tout voir qu'elle li conte.
430 Atant en laisserent leur conte
de ci qu'a main qu'il ajourna,
que li chevaliers s'esveilla.
Hüez se lieve, met sa selle.
La contesse sot la novelle
435 dou chevalier, qu'aler s'en viaut,
plus main se lieve qu'el ne siaut,
au chevalier vint, si li prie
qu'il ne s'en voist encore mie:
devant sempres aprés digner
440 ne s'en pourroit il pas aler.

takes to her heels, and off she flees
to where her mistress takes her rest.
Her heart was trembling in her breast.
     The countess gives the girl a call
410 and demands that she tell her all.
"Tell me why you have left the knight
whom we gave lodgings to tonight,
to whom you were expressly sent?"
But, overcome by the event,
415 she scarcely could do more than babble.
She managed as best she was able:
"You can't think what I have to tell!
This man must be under some spell!
I went to where he took his rest
420 and lay beside him all undressed,
when he turned to my cunt and spoke.
At his word into speech it broke,
and all the facts that he required
I heard my cunt state as desired."
425 Now when the countess heard this wonder
beyond all precedent, it stunned her;
she could not believe what she'd heard.
The other swore and gave her word
that what she'd told her was no lie.
430 And so they let the matter lie
till it was morning and day broke,
whereon the knight in question woke,
and Huet got the horses ready.
     The countess heard as the news spread he
435 was intending soon to go.
She rises very early so
as to go to the knight and say
he should not leave just yet, but stay.
Until they'd had their midday meal
440 he should not go was her appeal.

« Dame, fait il, se Deus me voie,
pour riens le digner n'atendroie
mais qu'il ne vous doie desplaire,
car j'ai molt grant journee a faire.

445 — Tout ce, fait elle, ne vaut rien.
Vostre journee ferez bien. »
Il voit qu'autrë estre ne puet,
si remaint, que faire l'estuet.
& quant ce vint aprés digner

450 si commancierent a parler
li chevalier de maint afaire,
mais celle qui ne se pot taire
a dit: « Seigneur, or m'entendez!
Contesse sui, si m'escoutez:

455 je vous dirai une merveille
vers qui nulle n'est sa paroille. »
La contesse parole en haut
& dist: « Seigneur, se Deus me saut,
j'ai oï parler chevaliers,

460 clers & bourgois & escuiers,
& aventures raconter,
mais nus ne s'en pourroit venter
d'une aventure qu'oï ier:
qu'il a ceans .i. chevalier

465 qui tout le monde a seurmonté,
quar il a si grant pöesté
qu'il fet les cons a lui parler.
Molt fet or teus hons a löer,
& saichiez bien, par saint Richer,

470 ce est nostre oste qui vint yer! »
Quant li chevalier ce oïrent,
molt duremant s'en esbaïrent;
au chevalier ont demandé
se la dame dit verité.

475 « Oïl, fait il, senz nule doute. »
Li cuenz s'en rit & sa gent toute,

"Lady," he says, "as God is great,
even for lunch I cannot wait,
if you will not take it too ill,
for I've a long way to go still."
445 She says, "All that is trivial.
Your journey can wait just as well."
He sees that there's no other way,
and stays because he has to stay.
Now when at last the meal was through,
450 they started speaking, as knights do,
about their many occupations.
The countess, at the end of patience,
burst out, "My lords, now lend an ear!
I am the countess, listen here!
455 The prodigy I would relate
were difficult to overstate."
The countess said, loud as she could,
"My lords, as God may bring me good,
of many knights have I heard tell,
460 and clerics, townsmen, squires as well,
and the adventures they have known,
but none could boast of as his own
the wondrous deed I heard last night.
There sits among us here a knight
465 who has exceeded everyone
by the great exploits he has done:
He makes cunts talk at his command,
which must earn praise on every hand!
Let it be known, by Saint Riquier,
470 it's our guest who came yesterday!"
When this great marvel reached their ear,
all felt astonishment and fear
and asked the knight he please reveal
if what the lady said was real.
475 "Why yes," he says, "most certainly."
The count and knights laugh heartily.

& la contesse reparole,
qui n'estoit musarde ne fole:
« Danz chevaliers, commant qu'il aille,
480   a vous veil feire une fremaille,
& si metrai .xl. livres,
que mes cons n'iert si fos ne yvres
que pour vous *parolt* .i. seul mot. »
& quant li chevaliers ce ot,
485   si dist: « Dame, se Deus me voie,
se .xl. livres avoie
jes i meïsse demanois,
mais mon cheval & mon hernois
i gagerai tout meintenant.
490   Metez encontre le vaillant.
— Je ne demanz, fait elle, plus.
Ja des deniers ne cherra nus
que .xl. livres n'aiez
se la fermaille gueeigniez,
495   & se perdez, vous en iroiz
tout a pié senz vostre hernois. »
Li chevaliers ne fu pas soz:
« Dame, dist il, jusqu'a .iii. moz
parlera il tout entreset.
500   — Ainçois, fet elle, en i ait sept
des moz, ou plus, se vous volez,
mais ençois que vous l'apelez,
irai en ma chambre .i. petit. »
A ce n'ot il nul contredit.
505   La parole fu devisee,
& la contesse s'est levee,
dedanz sa chambre s'en entra.
Oëz de quoi se pourpensa!
Plein .i. penier prist de coton,
510   si en empli trestout son con,
bien en estoupa le pertuis,
& dou poing destre feri sus;

The countess, sober and well-bred,
has this to add to what she's said:
"Sir knight, however this thing goes,
480   I have a wager to propose,
and forty pounds I'll gladly bet
my cunt would never so forget
itself to speak to you one word."
The knight responds to what he's heard,
485   "Lady, may God lead me aright,
if I had forty pounds, all right,
I'd bet them. Make my horse the stake,
and if I lose, you're free to take
my harness, too. That's all I've got.
490   Assess the value of the lot."
She answers, "That's more than sufficient.
The forty pounds won't be deficient
by so much as a single penny.
Now win the bet and get the money,
495   and if you lose, you leave on foot
and I get horse and gear to boot."
The knight's not one to hedge his bet.
"With just three words, lady, I'll get
it to speak up; I'll need no more."
500   "Why, make it seven or a score,"
she said. "I leave that up to you.
First, though, before the interview,
I'll go to my room for a while."
That much he grants without denial.

505   Thus was the wager fixed and closed,
and then the countess quickly rose
and straight up to her room she went.
Listen! I'll tell you her intent.
A basket full of cotton wad
510   she took, and plugged her cunt up hard
till the hole was completely choked;
with her right fist she pushed and poked

plus en i entra d'une livre.
Or ne fu pas li cons delivre,
515   dou parler n'i avra mais rien:
molt ira au chevalier bien
s'il ne pert armes & destrier.
La contesse retourne arrier
& en son siege se rassist;
520   en aprés au chevalier dist
qu'or face dou pis qu'il pourra,
que ja ses cons ne parlera
ne ne li contera nouvelle.
Li chevaliers le con apelle:
525   « Sire cons, fet il, or me menbre,
que quist vostre dame en sa chanbre
qu'elle s'ala si tost repondre? »
Mais li cons ne pooit respondre
car il estoit touz enossez
530   & dou coton fu enconbrez
si qu'il ne pot trot ne galot;
& quant li chevaliers ce ot
qu'au premerain mot n'a parlé,
autre foiz le ra apelé,
535   mais li cons ne li pot mot dire,
don ot li chevaliers grant ire.
Quant ne parle [ ] grant ne petit,
a Hüet conseilla & dist
que or a il trestout perdu,
540   & Hüet li a respondu:
« Sire, dit il, n'aiez paor!
Ne savez vous que la menor
des .iii. pucelles vous premist?
Elle vous enseigna & dist,
545   se li cons parler ne pooit,
que li cus pour lui respondroit.
Ne vous vost mie decevoir.
— Par mon chief, Hüet, tu diz voir! »

and stuffed inside at least a pound.
There's no way Cunt can make a sound;
515   it's all clogged up. Unless it's freed,
the knight will lose both arms and steed;
he's doing well if he can win.
That done, the countess comes back in,
sits down among the company,
520   turns to the knight, and tells him he
may do his worst, for, though he try,
he'll never make her cunt comply
or tell him anything at all.
He spoke to it and gave a call.
525   "My lady's cunt, now tell me true,
just now what did your mistress do
when she went to her room alone?"
The cunt kept silent as a stone.
Completely muzzled by the gag
530   and packed inside with cotton rag,
it's hopelessly immobilized.
When he'd asked once and realized
it wouldn't speak when first addressed,
he tried repeating his request,
535   but the cunt could not say a word,
which made him angry and disturbed.
      When it won't whisper, much less yell,
he turns to squire Huet to tell
him all is lost and seek advice.
540   Huet responded in a trice
and said, "My lord, don't be afraid.
Don't you remember what she said,
the last of the three fairies, who
both promised and instructed you?
545   If Cunt can't speak, then in that case
the butt will answer in its place.
She'd not abandon you in need."
"Huet, you've spoken true indeed!"

fait li chevaliers en riant.
550 Le cul apele meintenant,
si le conjure & si li prie
que tost la verité li die
dou con, qui parole ne muet.
Li cus respont: « Sire, il ne puet,
555 qu'il a toute la gueule plaine
ne sai de coton ou de laine
que ma dame orainz i bouta
quant en sa chambre s'enferma,
mais, se li cotons estoit hors,
560 bien sachiez qu'il parleroit lors. »
Quant li chevaliers ot cest conte,
tout meintenant a dit au conte:
« Sire, fet il, foi que vous doi,
la contesse mesprant vers moy
565 quant elle a son con estoupé.
Or saichiez qu'il eüst parlé
se ne fust ce qu'ellë i mist. »
Li cuenz a la contesse dist:
« Dont le vous covient delivrer! »
570 Celle ne l'osa refuser,
ainz s'en ala widier son con,
s'en a trait hors tout le coton
qu'il avoit englouti & mors;
a .i. crochet l'en a trait hors,
575 puis s'en vint arriere senz faille.
Bien set qu'or perdra la fermaille
qu'elle gaja, si fist que fole.
Li chevaliers au con parole,
si li demande que devoit
580 que respondu ne li avoit.
« Sire, fet il, je ne pooie
pour ce que encombrez estoie
dou coton que ma dame i mist. »
Li quens l'oï, assez s'en rist,

the knight responds with merry laughter
550 and calls upon her asshole after,
and, phrasing his request politely,
he urges it to tell him rightly
just why the cunt won't give an answer.
The asshole answers, "But it can't, sir,
555 because it has its muzzle full
either of cotton or of wool
the lady stuffed into her crack
locked in her room a while back.
Had not that wadding been inside,
560 it certainly would have replied."
The knight, hearing this explanation,
tells the count without hesitation,
"My lord, I've kept my word as promised.
With me the lady's been dishonest
565 to stuff her cunt till it was choking.
You can be sure it would have spoken
except for what she put into it."
The count said to his spouse, "Undo it!
You'd better go remove the cloth."
570 She must obey, however loth,
and rid her cunt of what she'd stowed
inside. She emptied out the load
of force-fed cotton, which she took
out of her cunt using a hook,
575 and then returned to the great hall.
As for her bet, she's lost it all,
she knows; it was a foolish stunt.
        The knight again spoke to her cunt
and asked it if it would not say
580 why it did not speak right away.
"I couldn't," Cunt said; "I was jammed
with cotton, which my lady crammed
inside me, and that's why, my lord."
When the count heard this, he guffawed,

585 & tuit li chevalier s'en ristrent;
riant a la contesse distrent
qu'elle a perdu, n'en parolt mais,
mais or face au chevalier pais.
Elle si fist, plus ne tarja,
590 .xl. livres li bailla
qu'elle avoit longuemant gardez
& par son grant senz amassez;
& cil les reçut a grant joie
qui mestier avoit de monoie
595 & qui si bon eür avoit
que touz li mondes l'enoroit
& fist puis tant comme il vesqui.
    De bone eure teus hons nasqui
cui si bons eürs fu donnez!
600 Atant est mes contes finez.
Ci faut li contes dou chevalier
qui faisoit cons & cus parler.

15. LE VILAIN ASNIER

Il avint ja a Monpellier
c'un vilein estoit costumier
de fiens chargier & amasser
a .ii. asnes terre fumer.
5   Un jor ot ses asnes chargiez;
maintenant ne s'est atargiez,
el borc entra, ses asnes maine,
devant lui chaçoit a grant paine:
sovent li estuet dire « Hez! »
10 Tant a fait que il est entrez
dedenz la rue as espiciers.
Li vallet batent les mortiers,
& quant il les espices sent,

585 and all the knights were laughing, too.
They told the countess it was true
she'd lost her bet, to make an end,
and treat the knight like a good friend.
She did so and no more delayed,
590 and thus the forty pounds were paid
which over some years gradually
she'd saved through wise economy,
and he received his winnings gladly
because he needed money badly.
595 Henceforth his fortune was assured
because so long as he endured
he had prestige throughout the earth.
    The heavens smile upon the birth
of those whom Fortune has befriended;
600 and, on that word, my tale is ended.
Now you've heard how the story runs,
how he could chat with cunts and buns.

15. THE MULETEER

This happened once in Montpellier:
    A peasant owned two asses; they
earned him his living hauling mulch or
manure for use in agriculture.
5 One day he loaded up the back
of his asses, and didn't slack,
but drove his asses to the city.
He had to call out to them pretty
often—"Geeyup!"—to keep them trotting,
10 and so he did, until he got in-
to where the spice dealers are found.
The shop boys are at work and pound
their mortars. As soon as the scent

qui li donast .c. mars d'argent
15   ne marchast il avant un pas,
ains chiet pasmez isnelepas
autresi com se il fust morz.
Iluec fu granz li desconforz
des genz qui dïent: « Dieus merci!
20   Vez de cest home qu'est morz ci! »
& ne sevent dire por quoi;
& li asne esturent tuit quoi
enmi la rue volentiers,
quar l'asne n'est pas costumiers
25   d'aler se l'en nel semonoit.
Un preudome qu'iluec estoit,
qui en la rue avoit esté,
cele part vient, s'a demandé
as genz que entor lui veoit:
30   « Seignor, fait il, se nul voloit
a faire garir cest preudom,
gel gariroie por du son. »
Maintenant li dit uns borgois:
« Garissez le tot demenois!
35   Vint solz avrez de mes deniers. »
& cil respont: « Molt volantiers. »
Donc prent la forche qu'il portoit,
a quoi il ses asnes chaçoit,
du fien a pris une palee,
40   si li [a] au nes aportee.
Quant cil sent du fiens la flairor
& perdi des herbes l'odor,
les elz oevre, s'est sus sailliz
& dist que il est toz gariz,
45   molt en est liez & joie en a;
& dit par iluec ne vendra
ja mais, se aillors puet passer.
&   por ce vos vueil ge monstrer
que cil fait & sens & mesure

hits him . . . well, there's no way he went,
15   not if you paid him, one more step,
but then and there fell in a heap
and lay there like a corpse, unconscious.
The people standing by were anxious
on his account. "Dear God," they said,
20   "see here—this poor man just dropped dead!"
Not one of them could tell you why.
(Meanwhile, the man's asses stood by
there, not unsettled in the least.
A jackass is a lazy beast
25   and only moves under duress.)
          A worthy man, who sees them press
around him, having chanced that way,
approaches them with this to say:
"Hear me, good gentlemen! If you're
30   concerned and wish for this man's cure,
I'll cure him. Now, who will agree
himself to guarantee the fee?"
A townsman cries out straightaway,
"Then heal him quickly, and I'll pay
35   for it. You'll get a twenty-shilling
fee." And he replies, "I'm willing."
          The pitchfork used to drive the asses
he takes, and he digs in and passes
beneath the peasant's nose some pure,
40   unadulterated manure.
Now that the smell of dung disguises
the odor of the herbs and spices,
his eyes open, he stands, and he
announces his recovery:
45   he's glad for it, and life is sweet.
He'll never more come down that street
if he can find a way around it.
          The moral that's herein expounded
says he who's sensible and wise

50   qui d'orgueil se desennature
   Ne se doit nus desnaturer.
   Explicit du vilein asnier.

16. LA CROTE

   A cui que il soit lait ne bel,
   commencier vos voil .i. fablel,
   por ce qu'il m'est conté et dit
   que li fablel cort et petit
5   anuient mains que li trop lonc.
        Or escoutez ci aprés donc
   que il avint a un vilain:
   sor .i. coissin tot plain d'estrain
   se degratoit delez son feu,
10   et sa fame fu en son leu
   de l'autre part seur une nate,
   et li vilains qui se degrate
   empoingne sa coille & son vit;
   sa fame apele, que il vit:
15   « Dame, foi que vos me devez,
   or devinez, se vos savez,
   qu'est ce que je tieng en mon poing. »
   & cele qui ne fu pas loing
   li respont, qui n'est pas coarde:
20   « Li maleoiz feus le vos arde!
   Je cuit que ce soit vostre andoille.
   — Par mon chief, ainçois est ma coille,
   fet li vilains, qui gist sovine.
   Vos n'iestes pas bone devine. »
25   & la dame tout coiement
   taste a son cul isnelement
   (semblant fet qu'ele se desfrote),
   s'a trové une masserote

50 will not seek pridefully to rise.
    One's rightful place no one surpasses.
    So much for the man and his asses.

16. THE PIECE OF SHIT

   Though some may like it and some no,
   I mean to tell a fabliau,
   for I've heard many folks repeat
   when fabliaux are short and sweet,
5 compared with long ones they're less dreary,
   and so here goes now. Hear ye! Hear ye!
        A peasant sat some time before
   now on a cushion filled with straw,
   scratching himself by the fireplace,
10 with his wife sitting in her place
   across from him upon some thatch.
   Right in the middle of a scratch
   the peasant grabs his cock and balls
   and, looking at his wife, he calls,
15 "Hey, woman! By your marriage vow,
   if you can tell, try guessing now
   just what I'm holding in my hand."
   She wasn't too far from him, and
   she's pretty uppity as well.
20 "May it roast in the fires of Hell!
   You've grabbed your wiener, I surmise."
   "Not so. I've got the sack that lies
   beneath it," says the peasant, "yes sir.
   You see you're not that good a guesser."
25   The woman unobtrusively
   reaches beneath her rapidly
   as if she has to scratch her ass,
   and hanging there she finds a mass

qui ert plus grosse que .i. pois;
30 a soi la sache demanois,
a tout le poil a li la tire,
a son seignor commence a dire:
« Sire, fet ele, or gaigeroie,
a vos se gagier m'i osoie,
35 qu'a .iii. moz ne devineroiz
que je tien ci entre mes dois.
— & g'i met denree de vin,
fet li vilains, par saint Martin! »
        Einsi fu faite la fermaille,
40 & cele la crote li baille.
Li vilains la prent et si taste:
« Par foi, fet il, je cuit c'est paste
por ce qu'ele est .i. petit mole.
— Par mon chief, c'est fausse parole,
45 fet la dame molt hautement;
vos mentez au commencement.
Or n'avez que .ii. moz a dire.
— Par le cuer Dé, je cuit c'est cire,
que ou que soit avez trovee.
50 — Par foi, c'est mençonge provee,
fet cele, qui le tient por sot.
Or n'avez a dire q'un mot. »
& cil en sa gole dedenz
la masche et *mere* entre ses denz,
55 que paor a que il ne perde.
« Par le sanc Dé, fet il, c'est merde!
Or m'en puis bien apercevoir.
— Par mon chief, vos avez dit voir:
c'est merde de tot a estrous!
60 Ja mes ne gaigerai a vos;
deable vos ont fait devin.
Or vos doi denree de vin. »

about the size of a small bean,
30 and quickly, without being seen,
she pulls it all out by the hair
and tells her husband, "If I'd dare
to make a bet against you, sir,
I'd wager what I'm holding here
35 between my fingers, though you try
three times, you can't identify."
"Saint Martin help me, that's just fine!
I'll bet a pennyworth of wine."
        The bet thus closed, they gave their word,
40 and his wife handed him the turd.
He takes and rubs it to and fro
between his fingers. "Is it dough?
To me it feels a little soft."
"Now by my head, you have got off
45 to a bad start," the woman calls
out loud to him, "for that is false.
Two guesses left!" The peasant racks
his brains: "By God, I bet it's wax!
I can't imagine where you found it."
50 "What you suppose is quite unfounded,"
(she takes him for a fool) she says.
"That only leaves you one last guess."
The peasant's so afraid he'll lose,
he puts it in his mouth and chews
55 and rolls it on his tongue a bit.
"God's holy blood! Why, this is shit!
Now I can tell!" the peasant said.
"You got it this time, by my head,
for shit it is, and that's for sure.
60 You get the wine; I'll bet no more
with you. Satan's made you a sage, or
else I'd have never lost our wager."

17. LA COILLE NOIRE

D'un vilain cont & de sa fame,
une molt orguilleuse dame
& felonesse & despisant;
mes ne sot pas du païsant
5   qu'il eüst la coille si noire—
se le seüst, ce est la voire,
ja ne geüst delez sa hanche,
mes el cuidoit qu'ele fust blanche
tant que par aventure avint
10   que li vilains de labor vint
& se fu a son feu assis,
mes en ses braies jusqu'a .vi.
avoit pertuis, si furent routes
tant que fors issirent trestoutes
15   ses coilles, & cele les vit.
« Lasse! dist ele, come noir vit
& com fetes coilles je voi!
Ja ne girra mes avoec moi
cist vilains qui tels coilles porte.
20   Certes, bien sui honie & morte
quant onques a moi adesa.
En maleür qu'il m'espousa
ne que a lui sui mariee;
molt en sui dolente & iree!
25   Certes, si doi je molt bien estre,
mes, par celui qui me fist nestre,
je m'en clamerai orendroit:
a l'evesque en irai tout droit
& li conterai cest afere. »
30   Li vilains fu molt debonere,
se li dist debonerement:
« Suer, alez! A Dieu vous commant;

17. BLACK BALLS

This is the story of a peasant
and of his wife, a most unpleasant
woman and a disdainful shrew.
She didn't have the faintest clue
5   that her husband had such black nuts.
Had she known, no *ifs*, *ands*, or *buts*,
she'd never have lain at his side,
but she assumed that they were white
until the following event.
10   Back from his work, the peasant went
and took a seat beside the coals,
but he'd as many as six holes
in his britches, for they were ripped.
She saw his testicles had slipped
15   through and hung down in full array.
"Alas!" she cried out in dismay,
"how black these cock and balls I see!
This peasant will not lie with me
again, since he is so endowed.
20   Indeed, I'm put to shame and cowed
to have been touched by such a one.
It was on a black day he won
my hand and he and I were wedded.
How mad I am! How I regret it!
25   Small wonder that I'm aggravated!
I swear by the God who created
me, I'll at once appeal this mishap
and lay my case before the bishop
and tell him of the whole affair."
30   The peasant, who was debonair,
said to her calmly as he could,
"Go, sister, do, and go with God,

mes se de moi fetes clamor,
ja n'aie je la Dieu amor
35   se de vous ne redi tel chose;
ja n'i avra parlé de rose.
     — Qoi, dant vilain? que dites vous?
Certes, or departirons nous!
Or ne leroie je por rien
40   que ne m'en clamaisse au dïen
ou a l'evesque ou au clergié.
.i. petit pet ne vous dout gié—
fetes du mieus que vous porrez;
par tens tels noveles orrez
45   dont vous serez molt corouciez.
Or est vostre plet empiriez
de ce que m'avez menacie! »
       Lors s'en va toute coroucie
& vint a l'evesque a Paris,
50   qui molt s'est de la clamor ris.
« Sire, devant vostre presence
vueil je bien dire en audïence
por qoi je sui a cort venue.
Bien a .vii. ans que m'a tenue
55   .i. vilain c'onques ne connui,
fors qu'ersoir primes aperçui
l'achoison que plus n'i remaingne
que je demeure en sa conpaigne.
Tesmoingnié me sera por voir,
60   mes vilains a le vit plus noir
que fers & la coille plus noire
que chape a moine n'a provoire,
s'est velue comme pel d'orse:
onques encore vielle borse
65   d'userier ne fu si enflee.
La verité vous ai contee
au mieus que dire le vous sai;
le voir reconeü vous ai. »

but accuse me or even try,
then may I lose God's love if I
35 don't point the finger. Don't suppose
you'll come out smelling like a rose."
"How so, you peasant? What's to say?
We two must separate today,
for I'll not let it drop, I reckon,
40 but lay my case before the deacon,
or else the bishop or a priest.
I do not fear you in the least
or give a fart. Do what you can!
In time you'll learn the outcome, then
45 you'll be sorry you did, because,
for sure, you've not advanced your cause
by making all those empty threats."
      Seething with anger, up she gets
and goes to the bishop in Paris,
50 who finds her plaint simply hilarious.
"My lord, I seek an audience
to let you know on what pretense
I've come to court. I have been wed
to a peasant and shared his bed
55 for seven years, unconsummated.
Last night I found corroborated
the cause, so there's clear validation
to justify our separation.
I'll testify that it's the whole
60 truth that his cock is black as coal;
as for the color of his sack,
a friar's habit's not so black,
and, like a bear, with hair it's coated,
and it's more swollen up and bloated
65 than the purse of a moneylender.
The truth, as best as I can render
it, I have laid out for you here,
the whole God's honest truth, I swear."

Lors s'en gabent trestuit & rïent
70 & en riant l'evesque dïent
qu'il face le vilain semondre
por savoir qu'il voudra respondre
& dira sor ceste besoingne.
« Je lo bien que l'en le semoingne,
75 dist li evesques, par ma foi.
Fetes li savoir de par moi
a Dant Popin le chapelain
qu'il face venir le vilain. »
L'en le fet maintenant savoir
80 a Dant Popin qu'il face avoir
celui a cort, & il si fet.
        L'en l'acuse de mauvés plet.
Il vint avant & si s'escuse.
Maintenant sa fame l'acuse
85 & dist oiant toute la cort
a qoi que la chose ne atort.
« Biaus sire, je me sui clamee—
moi ne chaut se j'en sui blasmee—
de cel vilain, qui m'a honie
90 de sa grant coille de Hongrie
qui sanble sac a charbonier.
Trop furent cil mauvés ouvrier
qui le me firent espouser!
Mes s'il se voloit escuser
95 ou respondre, je l'opposaisse,
la verité li demandaisse
por qu'il l'a plus noire que blanche. »
& cil la parole li tranche
& dist: « Biaus sire, a vous me claim
100 de ma fame, qui tout mon fain
m'a gasté a fere torchons!
—Vous mentez aval les grenons,
dist cele, dant vilain despers!
Bien a .vii. ans que ne fu ters

The court reacts with jibes and glee
70　and tells the bishop merrily
to have the peasant brought to court
in order to find out what sort
of answer he'll make in this case.
"I mean to have him summoned," says
75　the bishop, "as I love the Lord.
Therefore, on my behalf, send word
to our chaplain, Father Popina,
to issue the man a subpoena."
Popina is informed of it:
80　He is to issue him a writ
to come to court; and he obeys.

　　　The charges facing him are grave.
He comes to give justification.
His wife soon makes her accusation
85　and states before the court the basis
of her action and what her case is.
"My lord, though all the world may blame
me, I have come to make my claim
against this peasant, who appalls
90　me with his large Hungarian balls
just like a charcoal burner's sack.
Oh, what an ill-intentioned pack
has given me to him in marriage!
Whatever he says to disparage
95　my deposition, I'll oppose it.
I want the truth told, if he knows it:
Why are they black instead of white?"

　　　He cut her short. "I, too, indict
this woman, Father," he protested,
100　"for all the fodder she has wasted
on wipes and swabs for her behind."
"What lies! Are you out of your mind?
I've not used in our seven-year
marriage your hay to wipe my rear,

105   mon cul de fain ne d'autre rien.
       — Non? dist il. Je savoie bien:
       por c'est ma coille si noircie! »
       Lors n'i a nul qui ne s'en rie
       quant il oïrent la parole,
110   & la dame se tint por fole
       de la clamor que ele a fete.
       L'evesque la pais en a fete;
       racordé furent, ce me sanble,
       puis s'en retornerent ensanble.
115   Par cest fablel pöez savoir
       que fame ne fet pas savoir
       qui son seignor tient en despit
       por noire coille, por noir vit,
       qu'autant de force a il ou noir
120   comme ou blanc, ce pöez savoir.

𝟏𝟖. LE VILAIN MIRE

       Jadis avint d'un vilein riche
       qui trop avoit (mes trop ert chiche):
       trois charues ot de [.viii.] bués
       qui totes erent a son oés,
5   & .ii. jumenz & .ii. roncins,
       asez ot blé & char & vins
       & quant que mestier li estoit,
       mes por fame que il n'avoit
       le blamoient touz ses amis
10   & tote la gent du païs,
       tant qu'il leur dist qu'il en prendroit
       une bone s'il l'a trovoit,
       & cil dïent qu'il li querront
       la meillor que il troveront.
15   El païs ot .i. chevalier

105 nor any other thing you own!"
      "You've not?" he said. "I might have known.
      No wonder that my balls turned black!"
      There's no one in court can hold back
      his laughter, hearing this defense.
110 The lady saw she had no sense
      to have brought such a suit to trial.
      The bishop made them reconcile,
      and they, I think, ended their strife
      and went back home as man and wife.
115   In this fabliau you are taught
      a wife does not do as she ought
      to hate her husband or to mock
      him for black balls or a black cock,
      for whether they are black or white,
120 they're not one bit less potent, right?

18. THE PEASANT DOCTOR

      A peasant once in days long past,
      who was tightfisted, had amassed
      a fortune: For the plow three team
      of eight oxen belonged to him,
5   and two mares, two workhorses, wheat
      in plenty, also wine and meat,
      and everything a man might need,
      but he was criticized that he'd
      never been married. His friends and
10   the other people in the land
      kept at him till at length he said
      if he found a good wife, he'd wed,
      and they say that they'll look around
      and get the best that can be found.
15   A knight lived in the area,

qui estoit vieus & sanz moillier
qui une fille avoit, molt bele
& molt courtoise damoisele.
Les amis au vilein parlerent
20 & au chevalier demanderent
sa fille a oés le païsant
qui molt estoit riche & menant
(asez avoit joiaus & dras).
Que vos diroie? Enelepas
25 fu otroié le mariage.
La pucele, qui molt fu sage,
ne vot escondire son pere
car orfeline estoit de mere,
einz otria quant qu'il li plot,
30 & li vileins a l'eins qu'il pot
fist ses noces & espousa
cele qui forment en pesa
(se autre chose en osast fere).
        Quant trespassé fu son afere
35 & des noces & autre chose,
ne demora mie grant pose
que le vilein se porpensa
& dist que mal esploitié a:
n'aferist pas a son mestier
40 avoir fille de chevalier.
« Quant je serai a ma charue,
le chapelein iert en la rue,
a qui toz les jours sunt feriez,
& quant me serai esloigniez
45 de ma meson, li sougrestein
ira tant & hui & demein
que ma fame me fortrera
si que jamés ne m'amera
ne ne me prisera .i. pein.
50 Hé! las, cheitif! dist li vilein,
or ne me sai ge conseillier,

an old man and a widower,
who had a daughter, both well favored
in looks and gracious in behavior.
The friends of the peasant approached
20 the knight on his behalf and broached
the idea that his daughter marry
this wealthy peasant, who owned very
many jewels and lots of clothes.
What can I tell you? The knight chose
25 upon the spot to give consent.
The young girl was obedient,
and meekly, raising no objection,
not having a mother's protection,
did as her father said she should.
30   The peasant, then, soon as he could,
with much rejoicing went and wedded
the wellborn girl, who frankly dreaded
this marriage but dared not oppose it.
The peasant bridegroom himself knows it
35 was not a wise move on his part
and has a total change of heart.
Not long after the ceremony
he comes to question what he's done; he
now understands it wasn't right
40 to wed the daughter of a knight.
"When I'm at work behind the plow,
the village priest is bound to show
up—he's always on holiday—
and hang around while I'm away.
45 What with that clergyman about
my house both day in and day out,
he'll steal my wife from me. Before
long she won't love me anymore,
and all she'll feel for me is scorn.
50 I've no idea which way to turn.
I'm sorry now and woebegone

que repentir n'i a mestier. »
Forment se prist a porpenser
com la porra de ce garder:

55 « Dieus, fet il, se je la batoie
chascun matin quant leveroie
por aler fere mon labour,
ele ploroit au lonc du jour.
Bien sai, tant com ele plorroit,

60 que nul ne la dornoieroit,
& au soir quant je revendré,
por Dieu merci! li crierai.
Je la ferai au soir haitie
& au matin iert corocie. »

65 Quant le vilein ot ce pensé
si a a mengier demandé.
N'orent pas poison ne perdriz,
mes bons frommages & oés friz
& pein & vin a grant plenté

70 que le vilein ot amassé,
& quant la nape fu ostee,
de sa paume qu'ot grant & lee
fiert si sa fame les la face
que de ses doiz i pert la trace;

75 puis la prise par les cheveus
le vilein, tant par fu il feus,
si la batue tot ausi
com s'el l'eüst bien deservi.
Puis s'en revet as chans arer,

80 & cele commence a plorer:
« Lasse! fet ele, que ferai?
& comment me conseillerai?
. . . . .

Dieus! com sui ore mal baillie!
Dieus! com m'a mes perres traïe,

85 qui m'a donee a cest vilein!
Cuidoie ge morir de fein?

because what's done can't be undone."
All his reflections now were centered
on how that best might be prevented.
He thought, If I gave her a tanning
on waking first thing in the morning
before I had to go away
to work, she'd sit and cry all day.
I know as long as she keeps bawling
no ladies' man will come a-calling,
and when I get back in the evening,
I'll beg of her to be forgiving,
God help me! Thus, I'll treat her well
at night and by day give her hell.

When he'd decided how to deal
with her, he asked to have his meal.
They didn't dine on fish and pheasant,
but cheese and fried eggs that the peasant
had stocked up on, and plenty of
good wine to drink and a fresh loaf.
Then, when she'd tidied up the place,
he struck his wife across the face
with open palm, so that the fingers
left there the kind of mark that lingers,
then grabbed her hair as though gone mad.
A broad and heavy hand he had,
his fists upon her body drumming
as if she really had it coming.
He goes off to his fields while she
sits at home weeping bitterly.
"Alas!" she cried, "what shall I do?
Where can I turn? I wish I knew!
. . . . .

God! what wretched adversity!
My father was my enemy
to marry me to such a bully!
Was I about to starve, then? Surely

Certes, j'oi bien el cuer la rage
quant j'ostriai le mariage!
[Dieus! por quoi fu ma mere morte? »
90   Einsi cele se desconforte],
si a ploré au lonc du jour
que le vilein vint de labour;
au pié sa fame se chaoeit,
por Deus merci si li crioit:
95   « Dame, fet il, por Deu, merci!
Tot ce m'a fet fere anemi!
De ce que batue vos ai
& de quant que mesfet vos ai
j'en sui dolenz & repentans. »
100   Tant li dist le vilein puans
que cele li a pardonné;
puis a a mengier demandé,
cele l'en done a plenté
de quant qu'el a apareillié,
105   couchier alerent tot en pes.
        Au matin le vilein purnés
ra si sa fame apareillie
par poi qu'il ne l'a mehaignie,
puis s'en ala as chans arer,
110   & cele commence a plorer:
« Lasse! fet el, mal eüree!
Lasse! por quoi fui onques nee?
Bien sai que mau m'est avenu!
Dieus! fu onc mon mari batu?
115   Certes, *il ne set* que cous sunt:
[s'il le seüst, por tout le mont]
il ne m'en donast mie tant! »
& quant el s'aloit dementant,
estes vos .ii. serjanz le roi
120   chascun sor .i. grant palefroi,
qui dedenz la meson entrerent
& a disner li demanderent.

I must have been blind and demented
to marry him, yet I consented!
Why did my mother have to die?"

90   She continues to weep and cry
all day long, until from the fields
the peasant comes back home and kneels
at his wife's feet repentantly
and stammers an apology.

95   "Forgive me, lady, in God's name!"
he cries. "The Devil was to blame!
That I should have so dared to beat you
and do what I did to mistreat you
distresses me, and I repent."

100   So on and on the peasant went
till she forgave the loathsome sinner,
and then he asked her for his dinner.
She served him plenty of the fare
that she had managed to prepare,

105   and they retired and spent a pleasant
night, but the pernicious peasant
next morning again beat his wife
up within an inch of her life
and went off to his farming jobs

110   while she remains at home and sobs.
"Alas!" she cries, "I am forlorn!
Alas! Why ever was I born?
I see I've met an evil fate.
Did anybody ever beat

115   my husband? No, he couldn't know
how beatings hurt, or he'd not go
on beating me for any reason."

       While she's bewailing the state she's in,
two of the monarch's deputies

120   come riding by on large palfreys,
come into the house, and entreat
her to give them something to eat.

Cele lor dona volentiers,
puis leur a dit: « Beaus amis chiers,

125   dont estes vos ne que querez?
Ce me dites, se vos voulés. »
Li .i. respont: « Dame, par foi,
nos sommes mesagier le roi,
qui nos envoie mire querre.

130   Passer devon en Engleterre,
par foi; ma damoisele sade,
la fille au roi, est si malade,
il a passé .viii. jor entier
que ne pot boivre ne mengier,

135   que une areste de poison
li aresta eul gavion.
Li rois en iert forment iré;
se il la pert, jamés n'iert lié.
— Seignors, fet el, or m'entendez:

140   plus pres irez que ne quidez.
Je vos di bien que mon mari
est bon mire, jel vos afi;
certes, il set plus *de mecine*
ne de fisique ne d'orine

145   que ne sot onques Ipocras.
— Dame, le dites vos a gas?
— De vos gaber, fet el, n'ai cure;
mes il est de tele nature
qu'il ne veut fere nule rien

150   s'il n'est enceis batu molt bien. »
Cil responnent: « Or i parra:
ja pour batre ne demorra,
dame! Ou le troveron nos?
— Vos le troverez a estrous

155   quant vos istrez de ceste court
a .i. rivail qui la jus court
de jouste ceste vieille rue;
tote la premiere charue

She readily sees to their needs,
and then she asks, "Gentlemen, please,
125 I'd like to know where you are from
and on what errand you have come."
One answers, "Good woman, in truth,
the king himself has sent us forth.
We're off to England on a mission
130 to bring back an expert physician,
because that lovely demoiselle,
our monarch's child, is gravely ill.
It's been more than a week, I think,
since she could either eat or drink
135 because of a fish bone that's stuck
inside her throat and makes her choke.
The king her father's well-nigh wild
with fear that he may lose his child."
"My lords," she tells them, "listen here:
140 You never will believe how near
is what you seek, for, cross my heart,
my husband knows the healer's art.
He knows more about medicines
and therapies and specimens
145 than ever did Hippocrates."
"Woman, what kind of jokes are these?"
"It's not my nature to make jokes.
Still, he's one of those stubborn folks
and only acts as a physician
150 if beaten first into submission."
The officers say, "Heaven knows
he won't refuse for lack of blows!
Where will we find him? Where is he?"
"You'll come upon him readily.
155 Beyond the yard around this house
you'll see a little stream that flows
downhill along a well-worn street,
and the first acreage to meet

que vos troverez est la nostre.
160 Alez a seint Pere l'apostre,
fet elë, ou je vos commant. »
& cil s'en vont esperronnant
tant que le vilein ont trové;
de par le roi l'ont salué,
165 puis li dïent sanz demorer
qu'il vieigne au roi sans atarger.
« A que fere? dist le vileins.
— Por le sens dont vos estes pleins.
N'a si bon mire en nule terre;
170 de loing vos sommes venu qerre. »
Quant le vilein s'ot clamer mire,
si enbroncha .i. poi la chire
& dit n'en set ne tant ne quant.
« & qu'alon donques atendant?
175 dist l'un a l'autre. Bien ses tu
qu'il veust avant estre batu
que il avant nul bien nos die. »
Li .i. le fiert delés l'oïe
& li autre parmi le dos
180 d'un baston qu'il ot grant & gros;
tant l'ont entr'eus .ii. debatu
qu'a la terre l'ont abatu.
Quant le vilein senti les cous
& es espaulles & eul dos,
185 bien voit le mieusdre n'est pas son,
ençois a dit: « Mire sui bon!
Por Deu merci, lessiez m'ester!
— Or n'i a donc fors du monter,
font il, si en venez au roi. »
190   Ne quitrent autre palefroi,
einz monterent tuit enroment
le vilein sor une jument,
& quant furent venu a court,
li rois encontre li acourt;

your eye will be my husband's claim.
160 In the apostle Peter's name,"
she says, "go by the way I've shown."

    The officers go spurring on
and find the peasant laboring,
greet him in the name of the king,
165 and tell him without further fuss,
"The king commands you come with us."
"Who me? What for?" the man inquired.
"For your skill, which will be required.
The best doctor on earth you are.
170 We've come here for you from afar."
The peasant, when he heard it said
he was a doctor, bowed his head
and protested his ignorance.
One tells the other, "What he wants—
175 you know it—is a thorough beating,
so what's the use of us two waiting?
Till then he won't offer his aid."
One punched him in the ear; one laid
into his back using a stick
180 he carried with him, stout and thick.
He got a buffeting so sound,
it flattened him out on the ground.
The peasant, feeling all those blows
on back and shoulders, clearly knows
185 the hopelessness of his position
and cries out, "I'm a fine physician!
For God's sake, please leave me alone!"
They say, "There's no more needs be done
but mount and ride to the king's court."
190 No palfrey needed to be sought;
they all three mounted then and there,
the peasant seated on a mare.

    When they at last arrived at court,
the king rushed to them, for his thought

com cil qui estoit desirant
de la santé a son enfant,
demanda lor qu'il ont trové.
L'un des serjanz li a conté:
« Nos vos amenon .i. bon mire,
mes il est molt de pute orine. »
Lors li ont conté du vilein,
de queus teiches il estoit plein,
que il riens fere ne voleit
se il enceis batu n'estoit.
Li rois respont: « Mau mire a ci!
Onc mes de tel parler n'oï.
Bien, soit batu quant issi est. »
Cil responnent: « Vez nos tot prest.
Ja si tost ne commanderez
que li paieron bien ses droiz. »
Li rois le vilein apela:
« Mestre, dist il, seez vos cha;
si ferai ma fille venir,
que grant mestier a de garir.
— Certes, sire, je vos di bien,
de fisique ne sai ge rien,
ne en ma vie rien n'en soi. »
& dist li rois: « Merveilles oi!
Batez le moi! » & cil saillirent
qui asez volentiers le firent.
Quant le vilein senti les cous
sus les espaulles & el dos,
au roi a dit: « Sire, merci!
Je la guerrai, jel vos afi! »
Li rois respont: « Or le lessiez.
Mar i sera imés touchiez. »
        La pucele fu en la *sale*,
qui molt estoit & teinte & pale
que por l'areste d'un poisson
avoit enflé le gavion.

195 concerned itself with nothing else
but his beloved daughter's health,
and asked what help they had obtained.
One of the officers explained,
"We bring an excellent physician,
200 though uncouth and of low condition."
They told him all about the lout
and laid all of his failings out,
how he would not agree to treating
patients until he'd had a beating.
205 "That's one bad doctor, on my word!
The likes of this I've never heard!"
the king says. "Beat him, if you must."
They answer, "Sire, we're ready. Just
as soon as you command us, we
210 will pay in full the fellow's fee."
        The king then turned to face the peasant; he
spoke and told him, "Good doctor, presently
I'll have my child brought in. Be seated.
It's urgent that the girl be treated."
215 "I swear to you, Your Majesty,
that medicine's unknown to me,
nor have I ever known about it."
"I've heard it all now!" the king shouted.
"I want him beaten!" They hopped to it
220 ungrudgingly and glad to do it.
No sooner did he feel the blows
on back and shoulders than he chose
to cry for the king's mercy. "Sire,
I'll heal her, if you so desire!"
225 The king ordered his men, "Leave off:
I will not have him harmed henceforth."
        The king's daughter was in the hall,
and looked so weak and pale and all
from the bone sticking in her throat; it
230 made it tender, painful, and bloated.

Lors le vilein se pourpensa
comment garir il la porra,
car or set il bien que garir
li convendra ou a mourir:
235 « Je sai de voir, s'ele rioit
a tot l'esforz qu'el i metroit,
l'areste s'en voleroit fors,
car el n'est pas dedenz le cors.
Tel chose m'estuet fere & dire
240 dont je la puise fere rire. »
Au roi a dit: « Sire, merci!
Or escoutez que *je vos di*:
que vos me faciez .i. grant fu
alumer en .i. privé leu,
245 si n'i covendra nule gent
que moi & lié tot soulement,
puis si verrez que je ferai,
car, se Deus plest, je la guerrai. »
Li rois respont: « Molt volentiers. »
250 [Vallet saillent & escuiers,]
errant ont le feu alumé
la ou li rois a commandé.
En la sale *sont*, com moi semble,
le mire & la pucele ensemble.
255 La damoisele au feu s'asist
sor .i. siege que l'en li mist,
& li vilein se despoilla,
onques ses braies n'i lessa,
si s'est delés le feu assis
260 & s'est gratez & bien rostiz
(ongles ot lons & le cuir dur—
il n'a home jusqu'a Saumur,
s'il fust gratez en itel point,
qu'il ne fust molt bien mis a point),
265 & quant la pucele le voit,
a tot le grant mal qu'el avoit,

The peasant's mind raced and explored
the ways whereby she could be cured,
for she must be restored to health,
that much was clear to him, or else . . .
235   "If she'd just laugh—I know I'm right—
with all her force and all her might,
it would be coughed up and discharged,
because the bone's not deeply lodged.
I need something to do or say
240   to make her laugh in such a way."
He said to the king, "Thank you, sire.
Now listen. Here's what I require:
a roaring fire stoked up for me
in some secluded place where we
245   can be alone, just she and I,
for no one else must be nearby,
and then, please God, you will discover
what I can do, for she'll recover."
"Glad to oblige," the king replies.
250   The squires and servants quickly rise
and kindle him a blazing fire
in the hall at the king's desire,
where all alone, it seems to me,
doctor and girl keep company.
255   The lady went and took a seat
readied for her close to the heat.
The peasant takes off all his clothes—
even his britches—then he goes
and sits beside the fire and scratches
260   and roasts himself while the girl watches.
He'd long nails and thick hide; I'm sure
any man twixt here and Saumur
who scratching of that sort received
would find his itching well relieved.
265   In spite of all the pain that she's
suffering, when the maiden sees

volt rire, si s'en esforça
que de la bouche li vola
l'areste delés le foier,
270 & le vilein sans detrïer
se vesti, puis a pris l'areste,
de la sale ist fesant grant feste;
ou voit le roi, si li escrie:
« Sire, vostre fille est garie!
275 Vez ci l'areste, Deus merci. »
Le roi forment s'en esjoï:
« Certes, *maistres*, je vos di bien
que je vos aim sor tote rien;
vos m'avez ma fille rendue.
280 Benoeste soit vostre venue!
Asez arez joiaus & dras.
— Merci, sire, je n'en veil pas.
Je ne puis o vos demorer;
en mon païs m'estuet aler.
285 — Par Dieus, dist li rois, non ferois;
mon mestre & ove[c] moi serés.
— Merci, sire, dist le vilein,
en ma meson n'a point de pein.
Quant je m'en parti ier matin
290 l'en devoit aler au molin. »
Li rois respont: « Or i parra!
Batez le moi; si demorra. »
Cil saillirent tot enroment,
si le batirent vistement,
295 & le vilein prist a crïer:
« Je remeindré! Lessiez m'ester! »
      Le vilein est a court remés,
si l'a l'on bien roognié & rés,
& si ot robe d'escarlate.
300 Fors cuidoit estre de barate,
quant li malade du païs
dont il i ot, ce m'est avis,

him, she must laugh. The laughter wells
up in her mouth and thus expels
the bone, which lands beside the grate.
270 The peasant doctor didn't wait.
He got dressed and retrieved the bone
and ran rejoicing from the room,
and when he sees the king, he yells,
"Your daughter's been restored to health!
275 Here is the fish bone, praise the Lord!"
The king rejoices that she's cured
and says, "Doctor, I tell you true,
I love no man better than you.
Blessed be your coming! You've restored
280 my daughter to me, praise the Lord!
I'll give you jewels and clothes in plenty."
"Your Majesty, I don't want any.
I'm sorry, but I can't remain;
it's time I went back home again."
285 The king refused to give permission.
"You'll stay on here as my physician."
"I thank you, sire," the peasant said,
"but back at home we're out of bread.
When I left I was on my way
290 to the mill early yesterday."
The king's response was, "We shall see.
He'll stay with us. Beat him for me!"
The officers hopped to it quickly
and laid it on the peasant thickly,
295 who started crying out in pain,
"Leave off, I beg you! I'll remain!"
     The peasant has stayed on at court.
They've shaved him, they've cut his hair short,
and he has costly robes to wear.
300 He thought he'd nothing left to fear,
then sick people from all around
the country (thirty, I'll be bound,

.xxx.—ou .xl., ce *me sanble*—
vindrent au roi trestuit ensemble.
305　Chascun li a conté son estre;
li rois a dit au vilein mestre:
« De ceste gent prenez conroi.
Fetes tost, garisiez les moi. »
Dist le vilein: « Por Dieus merci,
310　trop en i a, jel vos afi! »
Li rois ses serjans en apele;
chascun a sesi une astele,
car chascun d'eus molt bien savoit
por quoi li rois les apeloit.
315　Quant le vilein venir les *vit*,
grant paour ot, au roi *a dit*:
« Sire, merci! Je les garré! »
& dist li rois: « Ja le verré! »
Le vilein fist demander laigne
320　(asez en ot, comment qu'il praigne),
en la sale alume .i. grant feu.
Il meïsmes fu mestre queu;
les malades fist arengier,
au roi dist: « Je vos voil proier
325　que vos descendez la aval,
vos & tuit cil qui n'aront mal. »
Li rois l'otroie bonement;
aval s'en vet, il & sa gent.
Le vilein as malades dist:
330　« Seignors, por le Deu qui me fist,
molt a grant peine en vos garir.
Je n'en porroie a chief venir
fors issi com je vos dirai:
tot le plus malade eslirai
335　& l'ardré tot dedenz cel feu.
Vos autres i arez grant preu,
car tuit de la poudre bevrez
& enroment gari serez. »

or even forty, I would guess)
showed up before the king en masse,
305　each one bewailing his condition.
He told his peasant court physician,
"Under your care I'm placing these
good people. Cure their maladies."
The peasant said, "God help me, there
310　are too many of them, I swear!"
The king summons his officers.
Each of them grabbed a stick because
every last one of the men knew
what the king summoned them to do.
315　The peasant saw them drawing nearer
and called out to the king in terror,
"Mercy! I'll cure them, sire! So be it!"
The king replied, "Now let me see it."
　　　　The peasant called for firewood (and
320　there was more than enough on hand)
and lit a great fire in the hall,
then, like a master chef, made all
the invalids stand in a row.
He told the king, "I bid you go
325　and stand down there to one side, please,
with all those who're free from disease."
The king follows the doctor's orders
and goes to stand down with his courtiers.
The peasant doctor told his patients,
330　"In God's name and all His creations,
good sirs, your cure's no easy thing,
nor do I think that I could bring
it off except this way: I'll choose
the one among all of you who's
335　most sick and throw him in the fire.
The rest will have your heart's desire.
His ashes I'll give you to drink,
and you'll be cured quick as a wink."

Lors a l'un l'autre regardé;
340 n'i ot si contret ni enflé
qui ostriast por Normendie
qu'il eüst greignor maladie.
Le vilein a dit au premier:
« Je te voi molt afeblïer;
345 de trestouz es tu le plus vein.
— Mestre, fet il, einz sui tot sein.
— Va donc aval! Qu'as tu ça quis? »
& celui saut, si a l'uis pris.
Li rois demande: « Es tu gari?
350 — Oïl, sire, la Deu merci,
je sui plus sein que nule pome.
Molt est li mestre gentil home! »
Que vos iroie plus contant?
Onques n'i ot petit ne grant
355 qui por nule rien otriast
que le mestre el feu le jetast,
einz s'en alerent autresi
com s'il fusent trestuit gari,
& quant li rois a ce veü,
360 de joie fu tot esperdu;
en la sale entre & dit: « Beau mestre,
je me merveil que ce puet estre
que si tost gari les avez!
— Sire, dist il, les ai charnez.
365 Je sai .i. charne qui mieus vaut
que gengibre ne citouaut.
— Mestre, dist il, or en irez
a vostre ostel quant vos vodrez.
Asez arez dras & deniers
370 & palefroiz & bon destriers,
& ne vos ferez plus ferir,
car grant honte ai de vos laidir.
— Merci, sire, dist li vileins;
je sui vostre lige de meins,

They stared at one another. No one,
340 no matter how palsied or swollen,
would own, not for all Normandy,
his was the gravest malady.
          The peasant doctor turned to speak
to the first. "I can see you're weak.
345 You are the sickest. I can tell."
He says, "No, Doctor. I am well."
"Get out! What did you come here for?"
The man turns and makes for the door,
and the king asks him, "Are you cured?"
350 "That I am, sire, praised be the Lord!
You see that I'm fit as a fiddle.
That doctor's talents are not little!"
What more is there to tell? Of all
the invalids, both great and small,
355 no way would any give permission
that he be burnt by the physician.
Instead one and all quit the field
and swore they were completely healed.
          The king was witness to this sight
360 and, overcome with pure delight,
came back and said, "Most noble doctor,
how can this be? So soon? I'm shocked! Are
you sure that all of them are cured?"
"I used a charm on them, my Lord,
365 a more potent electuary
than gingerroot or zedoary."
"Doctor," he said, "I give you leave
to return home if you so please.
I'll pay you well in cash and both
370 palfreys and steeds, and also cloth,
nor will I ever have you beaten.
I'm shamed that I gave you such treatment."
"Thank you, Your Highness," said the peasant.
"I am your vassal and your servant,

375   tot a vostre commandement. »
         De la sale ist inelement,
      puis est a son ostel venu
      & richement el païs fu,
      n'onques puis ne fu a charue,
380   ne puis ne fu par lui batue
      sa fame, ainz l'ama & chieri.
      Einsi ala com je vos di;
      par sa fame & par sa boidie
      fu puis bon mire sanz clergie.

19. BERANGIER AU LONC CUL

      Tant ai dit contes & flabiaus
      que je ai fait viez & noviaus
      ne finé passé a un an,
      foi que doi Deu & saint Johan,
5   ne cuit que j'an sache mais nul
      fors de Berangier au lonc cul
      n'avez vos mie *oï* encore,
      mais par mon chief g'en dirai ore
      si tost que ne tarderai gaire.
10   Or öez que je voil retraire
      que il avint en Lonbardie
      o la gent n'est gaires hardie,
      d'un chevalier qui ot pris fame,
      ce m'est vis une gentis *dame*,
15   fille d'un riche chastelain,
      & cil estoit fiz d'un vilain,
      d'un usurier riche & comblé
      qui molt avoit & vin & blé,
      brebiz & vaches & deniers
20   ot a monciaus & a setiers,

375 in all things at your beck and call."
He turned and quickly left the hall
and then went back to his own house
and lived in ease there with his spouse.
He never more needed to farm
380 nor ever again did her harm,
but loved and cherished her instead.
It all took place just as I said.
Thanks to his wife and his wit, he
needed no medical degree.

19. LONG BUTTHOLE BERENGIER
by Guérin

So many fabliaux I've told,
and other tales, both new and old,
I've put together this past year,
as I hold God and Saint John dear,
5 of those I know I think there's none
you've not heard yet, except for one
that's called "Long Butthole Berengier,"
and, by my head, without delay
I'll quickly lay the whole thing out.
10 Now listen while I tell about
what happened once in Lombardy,
a land not known for bravery,
about a knight who took in marriage
a well-born lady of the peerage
15 and heiress to a fief, I own,
though he was just a peasant's son.
His father lent money for gain,
was rich in wine and rich in grain,
cattle and sheep, and had a stash
20 of heaps and bushels full of cash.

& li chastelains li devoit
tant que paier ne lo pooit,
ainz dona a son fil sa fille.
Ensi lo bon lignage aville
25   & dechiet tot & va a honte,
que li chastelain & li conte
se marïent bas por avoir,
si [en] doivent grant honte avoir;
& grant domage si ont il:
30   li chevalier mauvais & vil
& coart issent de tel gent
qui miauz aiment or & argent
que il ne font chevalerie.
Ensi est largesce perie,
35   ensi dechiet enor & pris . . .
mais a ce que je ai empris
repaireré por traire a chief.
          Li chevaliers a grant meschief
maria sa fille au vilain,
40   sel fist chevalier de sa main.
Cil l'amena; si sont ensanble
plus de .x. anz, si con moi sanble.
Li chevaliers amoit repos,
il ne prisoit ne pris ne los
45   ne chevalerie .ii. auz:
tartres amoit & flaons chauz
& molt despisoit gent menue.
La dame s'est aperceüe
que ses sires est si mauvais
50   que pires de lui ne fu mais
por armes prendre ne baillier
(*mielz amast* estrain & paillier
a menoier qu'escu ne lance),
donc set ele bien sanz dotance
55   a ce que il ert molt parliers
qu'il n'est pas nez de chevaliers

So in debt to him was her father
that he could not repay him; rather,
he wed his daughter to the lad.
Thus many noble lines go bad
25 and are undone and end in shame,
and all those barons are to blame
who wed for wealth below their station.
Great harm comes from this situation,
so shame on them! The knights who're born
30 of such a union, base, forsworn,
craven, live for gold, silver, greed,
and never do a knightly deed.
When noble blood is bastardized
free, honest living is despised
35 and worth and honor soon die out.
But what I have to tell about,
it's time I told it and had done.

     Perversely, to the peasant's son
the baron had his daughter plighted
40 and by his own hand had him knighted.
He led her home, and there they stayed
together some ten years, it's said.

     He loved his comforts best on earth;
of knightly deeds, honor, and worth
45 he didn't even think to dream;
pastries he loved, and hot egg cream,
and scorned all those of lesser means.
The lady very quickly gleans
her husband's merit is so slim
50 there's never been one worse than him
when it comes to the use of arms.
He'd much sooner sleep in the barn
than ever wield a lance or sword,
and thus the lady is assured,
55 since all he does is boast, that he
is not of knightly pedigree

ne estraiz de gentil lignaje.
Don li remantoit son paraje
o tant a vaillanz chevaliers
60   & as armes & as destriers:
« A sejorner ne pris je rien! »
Donc entandi li vilains bien
q'ele nel dist se por lui non:
« Dame, dist il, j'é tel renon
65   n'avez nul si hardi parant
que je n'aie plus hardement
& plus valor & plus pröece.
Je sui chevaliers sanz perece,
lo meillor de toz par ma main,
70   seviaus tu lo verras demain.
Se mes enemis puis trover,
demain me voldrai esprover
qui m'ont desfié par envie.
Ja nus n'an portera la vie,
75   que ges metrai a tel meschief
que chascuns i perdra lo chief;
tuit seront mort, cui qu'il enuit. »
       Ensi trespasserent la nuit,
& l'andemain a l'ajornant
80   li chevaliers leva avant,
si fist ses armes aporter
& son cors richement armer,
que armes avoit il molt beles,
trestotes fresches & noveles.
85   Qant li chevaliers fu armez
& desus son cheval montez,
si se porpanse qu'il fera,
comment sa fame decevra
q'el le tingne a bon chevalier.
90   .I. bois molt grant & molt plenier
avoit molt pres de sa maison.
Li chevaliers a esperon

and all his forebears must be base,
and she reminds him of her race,
so very rich in worthy knights
60   and weapons, steeds, and valiant fights:
"How I despise an idle life!"
The scoundrel understood his wife
and knew at whom her words were aimed.
"Lady," says he, "I am so famed
65   that no one in your family
can equal me in bravery,
in valor or in knightly worth.
No slouch am I! No man on earth
can stand against me and prevail,
70   you'll see tomorrow without fail,
because it's my intent to show
my worth. Should I meet any foe
who out of envy dares defy me,
with life intact none will get by me,
75   for I'll cause such blood to be shed
that each will surely lose his head.
Like it or not, they all must die."

       And so another night went by,
and the next day at break of dawn
80   the peasant knight rose with the sun.
He had his armor taken down
and armed himself from toe to crown,
for he had weapons of the best
(and quite unused, you may have guessed).
85   Then, when his arming was completed
and on his charger he was seated,
he gave thought to a stratagem
to make his wife think well of him,
and to deceive her by some trick.

90   There was a forest, vast and thick,
not far from where their dwelling was.
The knight straightaway dug his spurs

s'an vet tot droit en la forest;
jusqu'el mileu ne fist arest.

95 Quant a mi lo bois fu venuz,
desoz un chasne est descenduz;
son cheval as resnes estache,
son escu pant a une estache
d'une branche seche *fechiee*;

100 aprés a s'espee sachiee,
si fiert en l'escu comme fos,
mien esciant, plus de .c. cous,
tot l'a tranchié & tot malmis,
puis avoit son fort espié pris,

105 sel brisa en .iiii. tro[n]çons.
Aprés est montez es arçons
de la sele de son cheval,
puis s'an vait poignant tot .i. val
tot droitement a sa maison;

110 de sa lance tint .i. tro[n]çon,
& de l'escu n'ot c'un cartier
qu'il avoit porté tot entier.
Lo cheval par la resne tint
sa fame, a l'ancontre li vint,

115 au descendre li tint l'estrié.
Li chevaliers la fiert del pié,
qui molt iert fiers de grant meniere:
« Traiez vos tost, fait il, arriere!
Que sachiez bien n'est mie droiz

120 qu'a si bon chevalier tochoiz
con je sui, ne si alosé.
Il n'a si preu ne si ossé
en tot vostre lignage au mains.
Ne sui mie truanz vilains,

125 ainz ai lous de chevalerie. »
La dame fu tote esbaïe
qant el vit son escu percié
& frait lo fust de son espié:

in and rode as fast as he could
right to the middle of the wood.
95 When he was far inside enough,
he stopped his charger and got off
beneath an oak, and there he tied him,
and on a dry branch propped beside him
he hung his shield, and stood beneath
100 and drew his sword out from its sheath,
slashed at the shield as though insane
some hundred times with might and main
till none of it was left intact,
then took his mighty lance and hacked
105 it in four pieces. When he's done,
he grasps the pommel, swings back on
up in the saddle of his horse,
goes spurring by the straightest course
till he comes back into his yard.
110 Of his lance he had just a shard
and just a quarter of his shield,
which he'd borne whole into the field.

His wife comes to help him dismount;
she grasps the halter of his mount
115 and holds the stirrup for her lord.
The peasant knight then kicked her hard,
for he was proud and arrogant.
"Step back from me!" he said. "Avaunt!
You ought to know you have no right
120 to touch so fine and praised a knight
as I am for courage and bearing.
There's none so hardy nor so daring
in all your lineage, for sure.
I am no loutish, peasant boor,
125 but am esteemed for knightliness."

The lady was in great distress
to see his shield thus slashed and battered
and his wooden lance likewise shattered,

selonc ce qu'il li fait acroire
130 ne set que dire ne que croire,
ne set el mont que ele face,
que li chevaliers la menace
que ver lui n'aut ne qu'el n'i toche.
La dame tint close la boche,
135 onques un mot ne respondi.
Que vos diroie? Ensin servi
li chevaliers de ceste guille
& tenoit la dame molt vile
& despisoit tot son lignage,
140 don *ele* nel tenoit a sage.
　　　.I. jor *refu* do bois venuz
li chevaliers, & ses escuz
fu estroiez & depeciez,
mais il n'ert cassez ne bleciez,
145 ne ses hauberz n'a point de mal,
& vit tot haitié son cheval,
qui n'est lassez ne recreüz.
N'est pas de la dame creüz
a cele foiz li chevaliers.
150 Or dit qu'il a mort ses gerriers
& ses enemis confonduz
& a force pris & panduz.
Bien set la dame & aperçoit
que par sa borde la deçoit,
155 & panse s'il i va ja mais
el bois, que ele ira aprés
& si verra qanqu'il fera
& commant il se contandra.
Ensin s'est cele porpansee;
160 & qant vint a la matinee
li chevaliers se fist armer
& dit que il ira tüer
.III. chevaliers co menaçoient
& qui son mal li porchaçoient:

for, if she would believe his tale,
130 what can she say that will avail
her, and what on earth can she do
faced with the threats of this knight who
so rudely chases her away?
She can't think of a word to say,
135 and so she keeps her mouth shut tight.
What can I tell you? Thus, the knight
makes good use of this clever ruse
to heap the lady with abuse
and scorn her family, which shows
140 his wife just how little he knows.
        Now one day, be it understood,
the knight came back home from the wood,
his shield all full of holes and pounded,
but he himself not at all wounded
145 and on his hauberk not a scratch,
a happy, healthy horse to match
without a trace of weariness,
and so this time his wife could guess
her husband's not to be believed.
150 He said his enemies received
death at his hands and were all routed,
captured, and hanged, let her not doubt it.
The lady clearly sees her lord
's boasting to her is simply fraud,
155 and thinks that if he ever goes
back to the wood she'll follow close,
see what he does with her own eyes,
how well he fights, with whom he vies.
        She settled thus on her intent,
160 and when another night was spent,
the knight armed himself for the fray
and said that he would go and slay
three knights who threatened to undo him
and to the death sought to pursue him

165   gaitant lo vont, dont molt se plaint.
La dame li dit que il maint
de sergenz armez .iii. o .iiii.,
si porra plus seür combatre.
« Dame, je n'i manrai nelui.
170   Par moi lor movré tel enui
que ja nus n'en estordra vis. »
       A tant s'est a la voie mis,
par grant aïr el bois se fiert;
& la dame unes armes quiert,
175   comme chevaliers s'est armee
& puis sor un cheval montee.
Cele qui n'a soing de sejor
s'an vait tost aprés son seignor,
qui ja s'est ou bois embatuz,
180   & ses escuz estoit panduz
a une chasne, & il i feroit,
a l'espee lo depeçoit,
si fait tel noise & tel martire
qui l'oïst il poïst bien dire
185   ce sont .c. & *mile* deiable.
Ne lo tenez vos mie a fable:
grant noise fait & grant tampeste,
& la dame .i. petit s'areste
qant ele a la chose veüe,
190   esbaïe est & esperdue;
& qant assez ot escouté
avant a lo cheval hurté
ver son mari, si li escrie:
« Vasaus, vasaus! c'est grant folie
195   que vos mon bois si decopez!
Mauvais sui se vos m'eschapez
que ne soiez mis en *uns giez*!
Vostre escu por qoi peçoiez
qui ne vos avoit rien mesfait?
200   Molt avez or meü fol plait

165   and set traps for him, he objected.
      "That you may be better protected,
      take three or four men," said his wife,
      "to help you succeed in this strife."
      "Lady, I'll take no company.
170   Since they have to contend with me,
      none will survive, they'll all be dead,"
      and off into the woods he sped
      along the road he always took.
      His wife, meanwhile, went to look
175   for arms, dressed as a knight for battle,
      called for a horse, got in the saddle.
      She set out quickly, never tarried,
      in the steps of the man she married,
      who'd gone deep in the wood by now
180   and hung his shield from an oak bough
      and with his trusty sword delivers
      such blows to break it into slivers,
      and he makes such a racket there,
      the noise you're hearing was, you'd swear,
185   a hundred thousand devils screaming.
      Don't let yourselves think that I'm dreaming.
      Such is the fracas and the storm,
      it gives the lady great alarm
      when she sees how he flails and hacks,
190   and she stops quite dead in her tracks.
              When she's sized up just what the case is,
      she rides on forward a few paces
      toward her husband and calls out,
      "What madness is this here, you lout?
195   What right have you to fell my trees?
      If I can't bring you to your knees,
      I'm worthless! They should shackle you!
      Why beat your shield? What did it do?
      Don't pick on it—it's innocent!
200   I can't think what deranged intent

que a lui avez gerre prise!
Mal dahaz ait qui or vos prise,
que vos estes coarz provez! »
Li chevaliers s'est regardez
205 qant il a les moz entanduz;
esboïz est & esperduz:
la dame n'a pas coneüe.
Do poin li chiet l'espee nue
& trestoz li sans li foï:
210 « Sire, fait il, por Deu merci,
se je vos ai de rien mesfait,
jo vos amanderai sanz plait
a vostre gré molt volantiers.
Vos donrai avoir & deniers. »
215 La dame dit: « Se Deus me gart,
vos parleroiz d'autre Renart,
car je vos partirai un jeu
ainz que vos movoiz de cest leu.
Comment que vos jostoiz a moi,
220 & je vos creant & otroi,
se vos cheez, ja n'i faudroiz—
maintenant la teste perdroiz,
que ja n'avrai de vos pitié;
ou je descendrai jus a pié,
225 devant vos m'iré abaissier,
vos me vandroiz o cul baissier
tres o mileu o par delez.
Prenez loquel que vos volez
de cez jeus; ice vos covient. »
230 Li chevaliers, qui dote & crient
& qui plains est de *coardie*,
[ ] dit *que il* n'i jostera mie:
« Sire, dist il, je ai vöé
ne josterai a home né,
235 mais descendez, si ne vos griet,
& je ferai qanque vos siet. »

leads you to wage such senseless war.
A curse on him who thinks you are
a knight, for you're a proven coward!"
The knight stops swinging and turns toward
205 her when he's heard the words she's spoken.
His courage is completely broken,
he can't see through her masquerade,
his hand lets fall his naked blade,
and all the blood drains from his face.
210 "For love of God, my lord," he says,
if I have done you injury,
I'll make amends most willingly.
I'll pay in full. Say what your wish is.
I'll give you coin and other riches."
215 The lady says, "No, by my head,
you'll sing another tune instead!
You'll not move from here or go free
until you choose. Which will it be?
Either you fight with lance and sword
220 against me—you've my solemn word
that if you fall, I'll give no quarter,
your head will come off in the slaughter,
it can't be helped—or I'll dismount,
stand in front of you, turn around,
225 bend over, and you, on your knees,
will kiss my ass, if you so please,
right on the hole or close beside it.
Now let me know what you've decided;
those are your choices. Come on, choose!"
230   The knight is shaking in his shoes.
He's filled with cowardice and fright;
he says he certainly won't fight.
"My lord," says he, "know that I've sworn
to fight no man of woman born,
235 and so dismount. Don't take offense;
I'll carry out all your intents."

La dame n'i volt respit querre;
tot maintenant descent a terre,
la robe prant a solever,
240 devant lui prant a estuper,
& dit: « Tornez ça vostre face. »
& cil esgarde la crevace
do cul & del con: ce li sanble
que trestot se tienent ensanble.
245 A lui meïsmes panse & dit
onques mais si grant cul ne vit,
don l'a baisé de l'orde pais
a guise de coart mauvais
molt pres del tro iloc endroit.
250 Bien l'a or mené a destroit!
        A tant la dame rest montee.
Li chevaliers l'a apelee:
« Biaus sire, vostre non me dites,
puis si vos en alez toz quites.
255 — Vasaus, mes nons n'ert ja celez.
Onques mais teus ne fu nomez,
de mes parans n'i a il nul:
j'é non Berangiers au lonc cul
qui a toz les coarz fait honte. »
260 A ce mot a finé son conte,
si s'an est en maison alee.
Au miauz que pot s'est desarmee,
puis a mandé .i. chevalier
que ele amoit & tenoit chier;
265 dedanz sa chanbre tot a aise
l'anmoine, si l'acole & baise.
        Estes vos li sires revient
del bois. Cele qui po lo crient
ne se daigna por li movoir;
270 son ami fait lez li seoir.
Li chevaliers toz abosmez
s'an est dedanz la chanbre entrez.

He doesn't need to tell her twice;
she has dismounted in a trice,
her tunic she begins to lift,
240   and she bends over in short shrift
and says, "I'm ready. Turn your face."
He looks over her nether place.
Asshole and cunt so close do lie,
they seem like one hole to his eye.
245   He thinks and mutters in between
his teeth, "The biggest hole I've seen!"
The filthy kiss of peace he gives
just like the lowest cur that lives
right by the hole there straightaway.
250   She's shown him up and had her way.
       His wife remounted thereupon.
The knight called out before she'd gone,
"Good my lord, let me know your name
before you go. You've won the game."
255   "Vassal, I'll not hide it from you.
The name I bear's unique and new;
my line consists of me alone:
Long Butthole Berengier, who's known
for putting cowards all to rout."
260   When she'd said this, she turned about
and rode home straight out of the wood,
disarmed herself as best she could,
then sent for a knight to come over
whom she held dear, to be her lover,
265   and to her room, where they'll be snug,
she takes him, and they kiss and hug.
       Returning from the forest, here
her husband comes. She has no fear,
nor, just because her man is present,
270   will she leave off doing what's pleasant.
She sits by him. The knight, dismayed,
came in the room and found displayed

Qant vit la dame & son ami,
sachiez point ne li abeli:
275 « Dame, fait il isnelement,
vos me servez vilainement
qui home amenez ceianz.
Vos lo comparoiz, par mes danz!
— Taisiez vos an! No dites mais!
280 Taisiez vos an, coarz malvais!
Tantost de vos me clameroie
por lo despit que j'en avroie,
si seroiez cous & jalous!
A cui vos clameroiez vos
285 de moi, par l'ame vostre pere?
A cui? A nostre chier compere
qui vos tint ja en son dongier?—
ce est mes sires Berangier
al lonc cul qui vos feroit honte. »
290 Qant cil ot que cele li conte,
molt en ot grant duel & grant ire,
onques *plus* ne li osa dire,
desconfit se sant & maté;
& cele fait sa volanté,
295 qui ne fu sote ne vilaine.
A mol pastor chie los laine.

20. LE POVRE MERCIER

Uns joliz clers qui s'estudie
a faire chose de c'on rie,
vos vueil dire chose novelle.
Se il dit chose qui soit belle,
5 elle doit bien estre escoutee,
car par biaus diz est oblïee
maintes foiz ire & cussançons

lover and wife embracing tightly;
he didn't take the matter lightly.
275 "Now, woman," he spoke up and quick,
"you're playing me a dirty trick
to bring a man inside. You'll pay
most dearly for this, let me say!"
"Shut up, you have no right to speak!
280 Shut up! You're cowardly and weak.
It's I who have cause to complain!
For all I hold you in disdain,
you've fully earned your cuckoldry.
To whom would you complain of me?
285 To whom, on your father's salvation,
would you turn in this situation?
To him who bested you today,
my lord Long Butthole Berengier?
He'd once again put you to shame."
290 When he hears her mention that name,
he has great anger and dismay
and can't think of a thing to say.
He knows he's lost; he's ill at ease.
Henceforth she'll do as she may please;
295 she's not base-born, and she's no fool.
The shepherd's weak; the wolf shits wool.

20. THE POOR PEDDLER

A merry cleric who's intent
on giving people merriment
has something new he'd like to share.
If in the telling he speaks fair,
5 then it is worthy of attention,
for often anger and contention,
when men speak fair, are set aside,

& abasies granz tançons,
car quant aucuns dit les risees,
10 les fors tançons sont oblïees.

  Uns sires, qui tenoit grant terre
[&] qui tant haoit mortel guerre
totes genz de malveisse vie
que il lour fesoit vilenie,
15 que tot maintenant les pandoit
(nunle raenson n'an prandoit),
fist crïer .i. merchié novel.
.I. povres merciers sanz revel
i vint atot son chevallet;
20 n'avoit beasse ne vallet;
petite estoit sa mercerie.
« Que ferai je, sainte Marie?
dist li merciers de son cheval.
Il ai molt grant herbe en ce val.
25 Volumtiers pestre le manroe
se perdre je ne le cuidoe,
car trop me coste ses ostages
[&] s'avoinne & ses forrages. »
.I. merchant qui l'ot escouté
30 li dit: « Ja mar sera douté
que vos perdroiz la vostre chose
en ceste pree qui est close.
Seur totes les terres dou monde,
tant com il dure a la rehonde,
35 ne trueve l'on si fort justisse,
si vos dira par quel devisse
vos lerroiz aler vostre beste:
commandez les piez & la teste
au bon seignour de ceste ville,
40 ou il n'ai ne barat ne guille.
S'il est perduz sour sa fiance,
je vos di, sanz nunle creance
vostre chevaus vos iert randuz

and mighty quarrels, too, subside,
because when someone's telling jokes,
10   resentment has no hold on folks.
        A lord who ruled a vast domain
and suffered such unheard-of pain
at the mere thought of wickedness
that criminals felt his duress—
15   he'd hang them by the neck till dead
and not accept a fine instead . . .
this lord proclaimed a market day.
        A sorry peddler, poor as they
come, came to trade there on his pony;
20   he'd little wares and still less money
and not a servant in his hire.
"If only I could find a byre,"
the peddler said, "to leave my mount!
I see lots of green grass around,
25   and I'd be glad to leave him here
to graze, were it not for my fear
that he'll get stolen. I'm not able
to pay for fodder or a stable."
A passing merchant overhears
30   and tells him, "Brother, calm your fears
of losing any property
that you leave in this fenced-off lea.
Throughout the whole wide world around
there's not a country to be found
35   where justice runs a smoother course,
so you may safely leave your horse
if you'll commend, at my direction,
it head and foot to the protection
of the good lord who rules this town.
40   There isn't a dishonest bone
in the man. If, despite his word,
you lose it, it will be restored,
your oath will have his full belief,

       & li lerres sera panduz

45   s'il est trovez en sa contree.

       Faites an ce que vos agree;

       li miens i est dois ier a nonne.

       — Par foi, dit il, a l'eure bone!

       dit li merciers. Je l'amanrei

50   & puis ou val le lesserei.

       A Deu, au seignour le comant . . . »

       & en latin & en romant

       commance prïeres a feire

       que nuns ne *puist* son cheval traire

55   du vaul ne de la praerie.

       Li fiz Deu ne l'an faillit mie,

       c'onques n'issit de la valee:

       une louve tote effamee

       vint celle part, les danz li ruhe,

60   si l'estrangle, puis le mainjue.

           L'andemain va son cheval querre

       li merciers, si le trueve a terre

       gissant, en pieces estandu.

       « Dieus! car m'eüst on or pandu!

65   dist li merciers. Je le vorroe

       de tote ma plus fort corroe!

       Ne porrai merchiez poursuïr!

       Hé las! il m'an covient foïr

       de mon païs en autre terre,

70   si me covient mon pain a querre,

       & nonporquant je m'an irei

       au seignour & se li dirai

       qu'avenuz m'est tel mescheance

       de mon cheval sor sa fiance

75   veoir se il le me randroit

       ne se il pitié l'an panroit. »

           Plorant s'an vai juqu'au seignour:

       « Sire, dit il, joe greignor

and, I declare, he'll hang the thief
45   if he's caught inside his frontiers.
Leave your horse here if that appears
best. Mine's been here since yesterday.
Good luck to you! I'm on my way."
The peddler says, "I may as well
50   leave my horse down there in the dell
in God's safekeeping and this lord's."
And using French and Latin words
the peddler lifts his voice to make
a prayer that nobody will take
55   his pony from the pasture where
he's left it.

             Jesus heard his prayer,
because it never left the dell:
A hungry she-wolf came and fell
upon his horse, which, overpowered
60   by tooth and claw, was soon devoured.
The next day, when he goes to get
his horse, he finds it lying dead,
scattered about and ripped to pieces.
"I'd sooner have been hanged, sweet Jesus!
65   I wish my stoutest belt were tied
around my neck!" the peddler cried.
"I'll go no more buying and selling,
but, forced to leave my humble dwelling,
in foreign parts I'll wend my way
70   begging my bread from day to day!
Nevertheless, I mean to try
to tell the suzerain here I
entrusted him with my poor horse
and see if he'll make good my loss
75   in light of my calamity,
or if he'll take pity on me."

        In tears, he goes to see the lord
and says, "I pray that your reward

vos doint il qu'il ne m'a donee! »
80   & li sires sanz demoree
respondit molt cortoissemant:
« Biaus amis, bon amandemant
vos doint Deus. Por quoi plorez vos?
— Biaus [douz] sires, le volez vos
85   savoir, & je le vos dirai,
que ja ne vos an mentirai.
Mon cheval mis en vo pesture,
si fis ma grant mesaventure,
car li lou l'ont trestot maingié,
90   sire, s'an ai le san changié.
On m'avoit dit, su comandoie
a vos & aprés le perdoie
en pesture ne en maison,
que vos m'an randrïez raison.
95   Sire, par sainte patenostre,
en la Deu guarde & en la vostre
le commandoi entieremant,
si vos pri pour Deu doucemant,
se la raison i entandez,
100   qu'aucunne chose m'an randez. »
Li sires respont en riant:
« N'alez mie por ce plorant,
dit li sires. Confortez vos!
Seur vostre foi me direz vos
105   de vostre cheval verité?
— Oïl, par Sainte Trinité
ne se ja Deus me gart d'essoigne.
— Se tu eüsses grant besoigne
d'ergent, por *combien* le donesses
110   & de coi denier ne lessases?
— Sire, par le peril de m'ame
ne par la foi qu'i doi Ma Dame
ne se *ja* mes cors soit essos,
il valoit bien .lx. sous.

is fairer than what God gave me!"
80 The suzerain immediately
answered him graciously: "My friend,
God bring you to a happy end!
Do tell me why you're weeping so."
"My liege lord, if you want to know,
85 I'll tell you everything because
I wouldn't dream to speak you false.
I left my pony in your lea,
and that was a catastrophe,
because the wolves entered the fold
90 and ate him up. My blood runs cold!
I'd been informed if I entrusted
him to you and then, as I just did,
indoors or out, I lost him, you'd
see to it my loss was made good.
95 My lord, by the Lord's Prayer I swear
into Your Grace's and God's care
I entrusted my mount completely,
so in God's name, I beg you sweetly,
if in your eyes this all makes sense,
100 that you grant me some recompense."
The lord says, laughing in reply,
"There is no need for you to cry
about this; take some consolation!
Swear you'll provide me information
105 about your horse that's true and honest."
"By Holy Trinity," he promised,
"and God keep me from perfidy."
"Were you in dire necessity,
what is the smallest sum of money
110 for which you'd have sold off your pony?"
"My lord, I swear upon my soul
and as I hope to be made whole
and by Our Lady, I'd be willing
to let him go for sixty shillings."

— Amis, la moitié de .lx.
vos randrai je—ce sont bien .xxx.—
car la moitié me comandestes
& l'autre moitié Deu donestes.
— Sire, je ne li doné mie,
120 ainz le mis en sa commandie!
— Amis, or prenez a li guerre,
si l'alez guagier en sa terre,
que je plus ne vos an randroe.
Se me doint Deus de mon cors joie,
125 se tout commandé le m'eussiez,
toz les .lx. sous reussiez. »
      Li merciers dou seignor se part
& s'an vai tot droit cele part
ou il avoit sa mercerie.
130 Sa delour li fu alegie
por l'ergent que randuz li ere.
« Par la foi que je doi saint Pere,
dist il, se je vos [or] tenoie
ne se seur vos povoir avoe,
135 de vostre cors l'acheteriez
que .xxx. sous me randrïez! »
Li merciers ist hors de la ville
& jure foi qu'il doit saint Gille
que molt volentiers [les] prandroit
140 sor Deu & si le vangeroit;
s'il an povoit le lué trover,
que bien s'an porroit esprover.
      Quant il ot sa raison finee,
si voit venir par mi la pree
145 un moinne que du bois se part.
Li merciers s'an va celle part,
se li dit: « A cui estes vos?
— Biaus douz sires, que volez vos?
Je suis a Deu, le Nostre Pere.

115   "My friend, settle for half of that.
   I'll pay you thirty shillings flat,
   for you commended half to me
   and gave half to the Deity."
   "My lord, I just made a request
120   He keep him safe, not a bequest!"
   "Then sue Him, friend, and make a claim
   of equal worth on His domain,
   for I'll not pay you more myself.
   As God may give me joy and health,
125   had the whole horse been in my care,
   you'd get all sixty fair and square."
    The peddler takes leave of the lord
   and turns his steps directly toward
   where he had left his goods for trade.
130   The sum he'd got had much allayed
   his sorrow and his worries, too.
   "If I could get my hands on You,"
   he called to God, "and had the muscle,
   I swear by Peter the apostle
135   that I'd compel you to redeem
   the thirty shillings of my claim!"
    The peddler now has left the town
   and in Saint Giles's name he has sworn
   that surely he'd collect the debt
140   from God and get his own back yet
   if he could just find an occasion
   to make Him give in to persuasion.
   When he has got that off his chest,
   he sees a monk who has just left
145   the forest come across the mead.
   He heads toward him, and when they meet,
   the peddler asks, "Whose man are you?"
   "Good gentleman, how do you do.
   I serve our Father, God on high."

150	— Hai! hai! dit li merciers, biaus frere[ ],
	que vos soiez li bien venuz!
	Je soie plus honiz que nuns
	se m'achapez en nule guisse,
	s'an daviez aler en chemisse,
155	tant que je serai bien paiez
	de .xxx. sous. Or tost! Traiez
	sanz contredit vostre grant chape!
	Guardez que la main ne m'eschape
	sur vostre cors par felonie,
160	car, foi qu'i doi sainte Marie,
	je vos donrai jai tel coulee
	que tele ne vos fu donee,
	que ne vos donesse greignour!
	Je vos gage por vo Seignour:
165	.xxx. sous m'a fait de domage.
	— Frere, vos faites grant domage,
	dit li moinnes, que me tenez,
	mes devant le seignor venez
	qui est justise de la terre.
170	Nuns moinnes ne doit avoir guerre.
	Se savez moi que demander,
	li sires set bien commander
	c'on doint a chescon sa droiture.
	— Si me doint Deus bone aventure,
175	dit li *merciers*, je vueil aler,
	meis s'il me davoit avaler
	en sa chartre la plus parfonde,
	s'averai je vostre reonde.
	Bailliez la moi apertemant,
180	ou, foi qu'i doi mon sauvemant,
	vous tanroiz jai malveis sentier!
	— Sirë, envis ou voleintiers,
	dit li moinnes, la vos donrai je
	[que] vos me faites grant outrage. »

150　The peddler cries out loud, "Aye! Aye!
　　　Brother, how glad I am you came!
　　　I never could live down the shame
　　　if you escape from me unhurt!
　　　You'll go about in just your shirt
155　until such time as they repay me
　　　my thirty shillings. Quick, obey me!
　　　Hand over the cloak you have on
　　　before my hand slips and I've done
　　　you injury, beaten you bloody,
160　for by the faith I owe Our Lady,
　　　the drubbing you're going to get
　　　is worse than any you've had yet.
　　　You've never felt blows half so hard!
　　　I take you hostage until God
165　has paid me back my thirty shillings."
　　　"My brother, these are evil dealings,"
　　　the monk says. "How dare you detain
　　　me? Let's go see the suzerain
　　　in charge of justice and the right.
170　A monk is not allowed to fight.
　　　If you are able to make clear
　　　your case against me, he will hear
　　　you out and give us each his due."
　　　The peddler says, "I'll go with you,
175　so may God further my just cause,
　　　but though I be taken by force
　　　and locked up in his darkest cell,
　　　I'll have your cloak. You may as well
　　　give it here without more ado
180　or, upon my salvation, you
　　　will hobble all the way to court!"
　　　"Brother, whether or not I ought,
　　　I'll give it up," the monk assents,
　　　"or else you'll do me violence."

185   Cil a la chape desvetue
        & li merciers l'ai recoillue;
        entre le moingne & le mercier
        veignent au seignour encerchier
        liquieus ai droit en la querelle.
190   « Sire, ce n'est pes chose belle,
        dist li moinnes, c'on me desrobe
        en vostre terre de ma robe,
        [ne] n'est il bien hors de memoire
        qui met sa main sus .i. provoire?
195   Sire, ma chape m'*a* tolue!
        Faites qu'ele me soit randue.
        —— Si me doint Dieux amendemant,
        dit li merciers apertemant,
        vos mentez, mes je vos an gage,
200   je ne vos demant autre outrage,
        s'an vueil le jugemant oïr.
        —— Ce me fait le cuer resjoïr,
        dit li moinnes, que vos me dites.
        Par jugemant serai toz quites.
205   Je n'ai seignor fors que lo Roi
        de Paradis. —— Par son desroi,
        dit li merciers, vos ai gagié
        & de vostre gage ostagié.
        Mon cheval li mis en sa guarde;
210   morz est; se li maus fués ne m'arde,
        vos an paieroiz la moitié.
        —— Merciers, tu es molt to[s]t coitié,
        dit li sires, de gages prandre. »
        Dit li sires: « Sans plus estandre,
215   tot maintenant je jugeroie
        du tres plus bel que je savroe.
        —— Por ce suemes nos ci venuz,
        dit li moinnes. —— Sera tenuz,
        fait li sires, ce qu'i dirai.
220   —— Sire, jai ne vos desdirai,

185   Under duress he took it off
       and gave it to the peddler. Both
       the peddler and the monk petition
       the suzerain for a decision
       on who's right in their disagreement.
190   "Sire, can you countenance such treatment,
       that in your lands I am divested
       of what I wear?" the monk protested.
       "Since when have those in holy orders
       suffered attack within your borders?
195   He took my cloak right off my back,
       my lord! Now make him give it back."
       Without reserve, the peddler says,
       "May I live to see better days,
       you lie! It's my security.
200   I'll do you no more injury,
       nor have I. I want only justice."
       The monk replies, "If it is just as
       you say it is, my heart feels light.
       It will be found I'm in the right.
205   I'm subject to the King of Heaven
       and no one else." "It was to even
       up my score with Him that I saw fit,"
       he says, "to take your cloak as forfeit.
       I put my pony in His care,
210   and now it's dead. You'll pay His share,
       may I not be burnt by Hell's fire!"
       "You're overeager to require
       these pledges, peddler," says the lord.
       "No need to say another word.
215   I will deliver judgment now
       as rightfully as I know how."
       "It was for that we came to you,"
       the monk says. "And you both must do,"
       the lord insists, "as I decide."
220   "Your judgment will not be denied

dit li moinnes. — Ne je, biaus sire, »
dit li merciers. Qui veïst rire

le seignor & sa conpaignie
de rire ne se teignest mie.
225   « Or antandez le jugemant,
dit li sires, communalmant,
car tout en haut le vos dirai.
Dan moinnes, *je* vos partirai
.ii. geus: le malveis lesserez
230   & au moillour vos an tanrés.
Se volez lessier le servisse
de Deu & de saintë Yglise
& autre seignour faire homage,
vos ravez quite tot vo gage,
235   & se vos Deu servir volez
ausi comme vos solïez,
le mercier vos covient paier
.xxx. sous por lui rapaier.
Or an faites a vostre guisse. »
240   Com li moinnes ot la devisse,
il *vosist* estre en s'abaïe;
bien voit qu'il n'achapera mie.
« Sire, avant que Deu renoiesse,
j'avroe plus chier que paiesse,
245   dit li moinnes, .xl. livres.
— De .xxx. sous serés delivres,
dit li sires, seüremant,
& porrez plus hardiemant
prandre des biens Deu sanz outrage,
250   car por lui avez cest domage. »
Li moinnes plus parler n'an osse,
meis je vos di a la parclosse
paia li moinnes dan Deniers
por Deu, .xxx. sous de deniers—
255   por Deu les paia sanz aumosne.

by me," the monk says. "Nor will I,"
the peddler says.
                        All those nearby
were laughing, and the lord was, too,
and, were you there, so would have you.
225 "I will make known how I decide
to one and all both far and wide,"
the lord declares. "Now hear my voice.
Let the monk know he has a choice
between two courses, and he should
230 reject the bad and take the good.
Brother, if you will quit the Church
and leave God's service in the lurch
to take another lord as liege,
the peddler must restore your pledge,
235 but if it's your wish to stay in
God's service as you've always been,
then you must pay the peddler money
in compensation for his pony.
Now do whatever you think best."
240 The monk knows he cannot contest
the sentence that's been handed down
and wishes he were safely home
and cloistered. "Sooner than deny
God," he replies, "more dearly I
245 would have to pay; say forty pounds."
"No, surely, thirty shillings sounds
a fair price, and from now on to
a share of God's belongings you
with a clear conscience may lay claim
250 now that you've suffered in His name."
        The monk had nothing more to say,
and so it all turned out this way:
It cost the monk a pretty penny
(some thirty shillings, that's how many)
255 paid out for God, but not as alms.

& li Sires qui toz biens done
gart cels de male destinee
qui ceste rimme ont escoutee
& celui qui l'a devisee!
260   Done moi boire, si t'agree!

21. LES .II. CHANGEORS

Qui que face rime ne fable,
je vous dirai en lieu de fable
une aventure qui avint;
de qui fu fete & a qoi vint
5   vous en dirai bien verité.
       Il avint en une cité
que .ii.. changeors i avoit
jones & biaus, & molt savoit
chascuns du change maintenir.
10   Entr'aus .ii. orent a tenir
longuement conpaignie ensanble,
mes chascuns avoit, ce me sanble,
par soi le sien herbergement.
Ainsi furent molt longuement
15   entr'aus .ii. sanz aconpaignier,
fust a perdre ou a gaaignier,
tant que l'uns d'aus se maria,
& li autres tant taria
cele que ses conpains ot prise
20   qu'ele fu de s'amor esprise,
& firent quanques bon lor fu
li uns a l'autre sanz refu.
Ainsi maintindrent lor amors
longuement qu'ainz n'en fu clamors
25   ne par privé ne par estrange.

May they all be kept out of harm's
way by God, whence all blessings flow,
who've heard this tale, and he also
who set it down with quill and ink!
260   Now, if you please, buy me a drink!

21. THE TWO MONEY CHANGERS

Whatever man may be a rhymer
or raconteur, the story I'm a-
bout to tell really did take place,
no fable. The truth of the case
5   and who's concerned will now be heard.
        In a walled town, it so occurred,
two exchangers of currency
there were, of great ability
in their profession, handsome, young,
10   and of necessity both hung
around together hours on end,
but each of them had, as I tend
to think, his own separate abode.
For a long time they kept this mode
15   of living as two bachelors, both
in times of profit and in loss,
until one of the two got married.
The other fellow so long harried
the woman his companion wed,
20   she fell in love with him, which led
to an affair, and what seemed good
to one, the other never would
refuse. Thus they indulged their love
for long, and no one gossiped of
25   it privately or publicly.

.ɪ. matin se seoit au change
li bachelers qui la fame ot,
& li autres, qui molt amot
la borgoise, jut en son lit;
30   por son bon & por son delit
l'envoia querre, & cele vient.
« Dame, fet il, il vous covient
toute nue lez moi couchier
se de rien nule m'avez chier.
35   Couchiez i vous sanz contredit!
— Amis, vous n'avez pas bien dit,
fet la dame, se Dieus me gart.
Il covient mener par esgart
amors, qui les veut maintenir,
40   que l'en nes puist por sos tenir.
Denn'est pas mes sires jalous?
Ainz avons entre moi & vous
jusques ci nostre amor eüe
c'onques par nul ne fu seüe—
45   la volez vous fere savoir?
Cil n'est mie plains de savoir
qui tout a escient s'aville.
Bien savez vous qu'en ceste vile
est mes sires sanz nule faille,
50   & s'il avient que il s'en aille
ainz que je reviegne en meson,
mestrie avra & achoison
de jalousie a toz jors mes.
— Dame, fet il, tenez nous pes;
55   je n'ai cure de preeschier.
Mes venez vous lez moi couchier
maintenant, que fere l'estuet. »
& cele voit que mieus ne puet;
despoille soi, quel que l'en chiee.
60   Si tost comme ele fu couchiee
cil fet prendre toute sa robe

The married man, one morning he
was at the exchange at his seat,
whereas the other, who was sweet
on that man's wife, lay in his bed.
30 His wish for fun and pleasure led
him to call her; she acquiesced.
"Lady," he says, "now get undressed
and lie beside me naked here,
if in the least you hold me dear.
35 Don't disobey; come lie with me."
"Dear, you're not talking suitably,"
the woman says, "so help me God.
In love one must be on one's guard
if one expects love to endure
40 or be thought careless fools. For sure
my husband's jealous, isn't he?
I have loved you and you've loved me
up until now, neither suspected
by anybody nor detected.
45 Would you, then, make this known to all?
It's not intelligent at all
intentionally to debase
yourself. You know that it's the case
that beyond any doubt my man's
50 in town, and if by any chance
he should return before I do,
he'll have both cause and the right to
be jealous of me all my days."
"Lady, no arguments," he says.
55 "No care for homilies have I.
Just get in bed with me and lie
down now. You must." The woman sees
that there's no other way to please
him and undresses, come what may.
60 Once she's in bed, without delay
he takes her clothes and has them stashed

& metre en une garde robe,
puis a son conpaignon mandé.
Cil vient la, si a demandé:
65 « Ou est li sires de ceenz?
D'autrui aises est il noienz
fors que des siens, ce m'est avis.
— Conpains, fet il, je vous plevis,
se vous saviiez orendroit
70 qui ci gist, vous avriiez droit.
De ce dirai, venez avant!
D'une haute chose me vant
dont je ne vous mentirai mie,
que j'ai la plus tres bele amie
75 qui onques fust, qui lez moi gist. »
Quant cele l'entent, si fremist.
N'est merveille se s'esbahi
quant son seignor parler oï.
Lors est cil en la chanbre entrez
80 & li dist: « Biaus conpains, moustrez
vostre amie, se Dieus vous saut. »
& cele fremist, si tressaut,
mes bien a point son vis li cuevre,
& cil les treces li descuevre,
85 qui furent de trop grant beauté:
« Conpains, par vostre lëauté,
veez! A il ci biau tesmoing.
— Je meïsmes le vous tesmoing,
fet li autres, se Dieus me gart.
90 Je cuit bien qu'ele a douz regart
quant ele est si bele deça. »
& ele adés se remuça
souz son ami, & boute & tire,
mes cil remoustre tout a tire
95 piez & jambes, cuisses & flans,
les hanches & les costez blans,
les mains, les bras & les mameles,

in a wardrobe, and then he asked
that his friend should be sent for. So
his friend arrives and wants to know:
65 "The master here, is he at home?
To no one's interests but his own
does he give thought, it seems to me."
"My friend, I promise you," says he,
"if you but knew who's lying right
70 here next to me, you would be right.
I'll tell about it; come close by.
In no way will I tell a lie.
Of my great fortune I would boast:
the woman I love is the most
75 beautiful ever. Here she lies."
When she hears this, it's no surprise
she trembles, overcome with fear,
hearing her husband's voice so near.
　　　Her husband then came in the room
80 and said to him, "Show me her, boon
companion, God grant you His grace."
The woman trembles and she shakes,
but in the nick of time she covers
her face. However, he uncovers
85 her beautiful, unequaled hair:
"Upon your honor, friend, see there
a comely piece of evidence!"
"I'll swear to that myself," assents
the other, "may God further me!
90 She must be beautiful to see
when that one feature is so fair."
　　　While he shows off her everywhere,
trying to hide herself, she snuggles
beneath her beau, and squirms and struggles:
95 feet and legs and flanks and thighs
and haunches and snowy-white sides
and hands and arms and bosoms, which

qu'ele avoit serrees & beles,
le blanc col & la blanche gorge.

100 « Conpains, foi que je doi saint Jorge,
fet cil, qui n'en connissoit mie,
n'avez pas failli a amie!
Bien devez gesir matinee
lez la plus bele qui soit nee.

105 Au tesmoing que j'en ai veü,
aucun pechié m'avoit neü
que j'ai si tost fame espousé;
mainte foiz m'en a puis pesé
& poise, ce sachiez de voir.

110 Molt par devez grant joie avoir
& de bone eure fustes nez
quant si bien estes assenez,
mes, foi que je doi saint Martin,
tart m'est que je lieve au matin! »

115 Lors a cil couverte s'amie

& dist: « Conpains, ne vous poist mie
se je ne vous moustre sa chiere.
Je la dout tant & tant l'ai chiere
que ne vueil que plus en voiez.

120 — Je m'en tieng molt bien a paiez,
fet cil, se Dieus me beneïe!
Vous avez bele conpaignie;
si la servez a sa devise
qu'el praingne en gré vostre servise. »

125 A tant li bachelers s'en torne,
& cele se vest & atorne;
de soi chaucier ne fu pas lente;
molt fu coroucie & dolente;
vers sont ostel issi s'en vint.

130 .iii. semaines aprés avint
que la dame fist .i. baing fere
& li sires en son afere

are firm, well-rounded, ripe and rich,
and her white neck and her white throat.
He sees his wife, but doesn't know't
and says, "Now, by Saint George, good pal,
in girlfriends you've not failed at all.
How right you are to lie all morn-
ing by the fairest ever born!
The testimony I have seen
shows that for some sin I have been
punished, in that too soon I wed.
Since then I've often felt regret
and I still do, it's all too true,
but what great joy must come to you,
born under such a lucky star,
for how very well-off you are!
I, by Saint Martin, though, can't wait
to get up mornings—it seems late
to me!"
        His friend replaced the cover
on her and said, "Friend, don't be over-
distressed if I don't show you more.
I love her and hold her in awe
and don't want you to see her face."
"You have rewarded me," he says,
"more than enough, God bless my soul!
Your lady's lovely. I hope you'll
serve her in her every desire
and that she likes your service, sire."
That said, the young fellow returns,
and she, who's grief-stricken and burns
with wrath, gets dressed and isn't slow
to put her shoes on and to go
back on her way home at long last.
        Then, three weeks later, here's what passed.
The woman asked to have a bath
drawn, while her husband took the path

fu alez *au change* ou aillors,
& la borgoise mande lors
135   son ami que por rien qu'aviegne
ne lest pas que a li ne viegne.
Cil vient la, si a demandé
por qoi ele l'avoit mandé.
« Amis, fet ele, tant vous aim
140   que por vous fis fere cest baing,
si nous baingnerommes ensanble.
Tout autre solaz, ce me sanble,
ai je de vostre cors eü;
nous avons ensamble geü
145   maintes foiz par nuit & par jor.
Sachiez que j'aim molt le sejor
quant je vous ai a conpaignon.
Or me plest que nous nous baignon,
lors si avrai quanques je vueil.
150   — Dame, dist il, trop grant orgueil
avez dit; ainz n'oï greignor!
Je vi ore vostre seignor,
qui revendra je ne gart l'eure.
— Par toz les sains que l'en aeure,
155   fet la dame, sachiez de fi
se nel fetes, je vous desfi
de m'amor & la vous desfent.
A pou que li cuers ne me fent
quant je onques jor de ma vie
160   oi de cest homme amer envie
qui se plaint ainz que li cops chiee!
— Dame, ainz que nostre amor dechiee,
fet li vallés, je sui tout prest
de fere quanques bon vous est,
165   puis qu'il vous plest & bon vous sanble. »

Lors sont entré el baing ensanble,
& por ce c'on nes puist sousprendre,

to the exchange or to some other
workplace, and she sends for her lover,
135 that she'll take it ill if for some
reason he should neglect to come.
He comes there and he asks her why
she had sent for him by and by.
"Dearest," she says, "I love you true,
140 and so I've drawn this bath for you
so you can bathe in it with me.
All other pleasures, certainly,
your body offers I have taken.
We've often lain together making
145 love with each other night and day.
Be sure I dearly love to stay
with you and have your company.
To bathe with you now pleases me,
and what I want, I mean to get."
150 "It's far too daring, what you've said,
lady. I've not heard worse," said he.
"I saw your husband recently.
He may come home at any moment."
"By all the saints for our atonement,"
155 the woman says, "unless you do,
I will hold back my love from you,
forbid you it, make no mistake.
My heart is just about to break
to think that I should live to see
160 me love a man who, before he
gets hurt, would whine of it already!"
"Sooner than see our love end, lady,
I'm more than willing, and will do,"
he says, "whatever pleases you,
165 if that's what you think best."
                                He got
in the bath with her. So as not
to be caught unawares, she goes

la robe au vallet a fet prendre
la dame & metre en une huche.
170   Estes vous le seignor qui huche,
que la dame ot envoié querre.
Lors vousist estre en Engleterre
cil qui se baingne, quant il ot
son conpaignon qui apelot;
175   durement en fu esbahiz:
« Dame, dist il, je sui trahiz
quant j'empris onques cest afere;
or ne sai que je puisse fere!
Metez i conseil, par vostre ame.
180   — Comment, vassaus? ce dist la dame.
Estes vous de si biau confort?
Je vous voi bel & grant & fort,
si vous desfendez comme preus.
Je cuit bien que c'est vostre preus
185   s'a desfendre vous afichiez,
ou derriere moi vous fichiez
se vous cuidiez estre sorpris. »
& cil s'est au plus legier pris;
derrier la dame s'est tapis,
190   qui d'un blanc drap & d'un tapis
ot bien fete couvrir la cuve.
Li vallés derrier li se muce
que ainsi fere li covient.
Estes vous le seignor qui vient,
195   & la dame li a dit: « Sire,
ça venez. .i. poi vous vueil dire
de chose dedenz vostre oreille. »
Cil se besse; ele li conseille:
« Sire, fet ele, ci se baingne
200   o moi une moie conpaingne,
riche borgoise & riche fame,
mes par la foi que je doi m'ame,
ele est plus noire c'une choe

and has them take the young man's clothes
and put them somewhere in a box.

170   See here—her husband calls and knocks,
for he'd been summoned by his wife.
The one who's bathing for dear life
wished that he was in England when
he heard his buddy calling them,

175   and he was terribly afraid.
"Lady," he said, "I've been betrayed
by getting in the bath with you,
and now I don't know what to do.
On your soul, show me where to hide!"

180   "What's this, my hero?" she replied.
"Do you have that much confidence?
You have the looks and size and strength.
Defend yourself, then, like a man!
I think that, if you try, you can

185   put up a good defense, all right!
Get down behind me out of sight
if you believe that you'd be bested."

        The easier plan she suggested,
to hide himself, is what he did.

190   With a sheet and rug as a lid
she covered up the tub. The youth
takes refuge behind her. In truth,
that's what he is compelled to do.

        There's her husband in front of you.

195   The woman said to him, "Come closer.
There's something I want you to know, sir,
something to whisper in your ear."
He leans down. So just he can hear,
"I have a friend of mine," says she,

200   "taking a bath in here with me,
a rich lady, a burgher's wife,
but, on my soul and on my life,
she's fatter than a wicker crate

& plus grosse c'une baschoe
205 Ainz ne vi fame si mal fete!
Ele se plaint & se deshete
de ce que vous estes ici,
si vous en vueil crier merci,
foi que devez au Sauveor,
210 c'un petit li faciez paor
seulement de sanblant moustrer
que vous volez el baing entrer.
Ele ne sera mes hui aise! »
Molt fu li vallés a mesaise,
215 qui ne sot de qoi el parloit,
& cele en haut dist si qu'il l'oit:
« Biaus sire, venez vous baignier,
& demain vous ferez sainier
que la sainie vous demeure. »
220 La chanberiere sanz demeure
vient au seignor, si le deschauce,
& li vallés forment enchauce
& pince & boute la borgoise,
qui molt se jue & molt s'envoise
225 de la paor que cil avoit:
n'est pas aaise quant il voit
son conpaignon qui se despoille;
lors joinst les mains, si s'agenoille
& dist: « Dame, por Dieu merci,
230 ne honissiez moi & vous ci,
que se vostre sires me trueve,
ja n'i avra mestier contrueve
ne parole ne serement! »
Molt losenge cil durement
235 cele qu'il tenoit a amie,
mes la dame n'i entent mie,
ainz l'a derrier son cul torné;
le musart a si atorné
qu'il ne la puet veoir el vis.

and blacker than a crow. I'd hate
205   to see a woman more misshapen!
Right now she's all upset and weeping
because you're here, so as a favor
I ask you, by Our Lord and Savior,
whom we believe in and hold dear,
210   to give her just a little scare
by putting up the pretense you
intend to get in the bath too.
Never again will she rest easy."
        The young man felt, at best, uneasy
215   because he couldn't hear a word.
Then, speaking loudly so he heard,
"Good husband, come and bathe," she said.
"Tomorrow we will have you bled.
It's been a while now you've been needing
220   one." So their servant, quickly heeding
her mistress, bends down and removes
her master's stockings and his shoes.
The young man nudges, pinches, presses
her hard, whose playful happiness is
225   all due to the fear she inspires.
He's not at ease now that her sire's
getting undressed, as he now sees,
and, hands clasped, gets down on his knees
and says, "For God's sweet mercy, dear,
230   if your husband should find me here,
no word nor oath nor fabrication
will rectify the situation.
Don't bring shame on yourself and me."
Despite all his cajolery,
235   the woman he thought was his friend
will neither listen nor attend
to what he says: She's turned her rear
and where the fool's placed he can't see 'er
(at least not look her in the face).

240 Onques nus hom, a mon avis,
     ne fu mes ausi desjouglez.
     Or n'est il pas si enjenglez
     comme il fu l'autrier en sa chanbre,
     ainz li fremissent tuit li menbre;
245 du conforter est ce neenz,
     qu'il voit le seignor de leenz
     qui toute a jus sa robe mise
     fors ses braies & sa chemise . . .
     mes ses braies maintenant oste . . .
250 si pres de la cuve s'acoste
     c'un de ses piez a el baing mis . . .
     & la dame li dist: « Amis,
     or vous chauciez, se vous volez.
     Cist bains n'est pas assez coulez;
255 ne vueil pas que vous i baingniez—
     mes molt me ples quant vous daingniez
     baingnier o moi, mieus vous en pris,—
     si ai .i. autre conseil pris.
     Demain ferai .i. baing tout froiz
260 qui sera coulez .iiii. foiz,
     si vous baingnerez, s'il vous plest. »
     A cest mot li sires se vest
     & s'atorne, puis vait au change.
     « Vassal, fet ele, tel eschange
265 doit l'en fere au musart prové!
     Or vous ai je bien esprové
     a coart & a recreant,
     mes au jor d'ui, ce vous creant,
     ert de nous .ii. la departie. »
270 Maintenant s'est du baing partie,
     si s'est en sa chanbre enfermee,
     & cil qui molt l'avoit amee
     fu de mauvés contenement
     La chanberiere isnelement

240 No man's been put back in his place
with so much contempt, as I live!
Now he is not so talkative
as in his room the other week;
his limbs are all trembling and weak
245 because how can he feel at ease
when the man of the house, he sees,
has taken off his clothes and stands
there only in his shirt and pants? . . .
And now his breeches are off, too. . . .
250 And now he's coming closer to
the tub. . . . One foot's already in. . . .
        "My friend," the woman said to him,
"get dressed again, please, for the water
is not as limpid as it ought to
255 be. I don't think it's a good time
to bathe. When you bathe with me, I'm
so happy and hold you more dear,
so I've had another idea
instead. Tomorrow I'll prepare
260 one fresh, filtered four times and clear,
and you'll bathe then, if you agree."
When she has told him all this, he
gets dressed and leaves for the exchange.
        "Brave heart," she says, "here is the change
265 a nitwit gets back for his own.
Now that I've proven and have shown
that you're a poltroon and a coward,
I promise you from this day forward
we go our own way separately."
270 She left the tub immediately,
went in her room, and locked the door,
and the man, who had loved her more
than words can tell, was feeling sorry
for himself. The maid in a hurry

275 li rent sa robe, & il s'atorne,
maintenant de l'ostel s'en torne,
mes il se tint a mal bailli
de ce que il a si failli
du tout en tout a la borgoise,
280 qui de ce fist molt que cortoise
qui s'en parti & atarja.
Ainsi la dame s'en venja.
  Par cest fablel prover vous vueil
que cil fet folie & orgueil
285 qui fame engingnier s'entremet,
quar qui fet a fame .i. mal tret,
ele en fet .x. ou .xv. ou .xx.
Ainsi ceste aventure avint.

22. LE CHEVALIER QUI FIST SA FAME CONFESSE

En Beesin molt pres de Vire
une merveille j'oï dire
d'un chevalier & de sa fame,
qui molt estoit cortoise *dame*
5 & molt proisie en sa contree,
a la meillor estoit contee,
& li sires tant se fioit
en sa moillier & tant l'amoit
que de rien cure ne prenoit.
10 Tout li ert bon quanques fesoit,
que ja nule rien ne feïst
que il seüst qu'il ne vousist.
  Ainsi vesquirent longuement
qu'entr'eus n'ot point de mautalent
15 fors tant, ne sai par quel maniere,
que la dame, qui molt fu chiere,

275 returns his clothes; he puts them on
and within moments he has gone
back home, distressed and pained to see
that he has failed so utterly
in everything and every way
280 with her, who was right to repay
him and break up and turn her back
on him. That's how she paid him back.
    I told you this fabliau meaning
to prove that mad and overweening
285 is he who tries to trick a woman.
The wrong he does she'll return to him
ten- or fifteen- or twentyfold,
as happened in the tale I've told.

22. THE KNIGHT WHO HEARD HIS WIFE'S CONFESSION

In the Bessin, not far from Vire,
a wondrous story reached my ear
that tells of a knight and his wife,
a woman of such courtly life
5 that all the region was impressed
with her and counted her the best,
and such was her lord's confidence,
his love for her was so intense,
he had no worries. As things stood,
10 to him all that she did seemed good;
as far as he knew, she would never
do aught that might cause him displeasure.
    For many years thus he and she
lived on in perfect harmony,
15 except that once—how, I don't know—
the lady whom he cherished so

devint malade & acoucha;
de .iii. semaines ne leva,
grant paor ot qu'el ne morust.
20   Tant que son terme venu fust,
de son provoire fu confesse,
du sien dona & fist grant lesse.
Ne se vout pas a tant tenir:
Son seignor fist a li venir
25   & si li dist: « Biaus sire chiers,
du conseil de moi fust mestiers.
Uns moines maint molt pres de ci;
sainz hom est molt, c'avons oï.
A m'ame fust grant preu, ce cuit,
30   se je fusse confesse a lui.
Sire, por Dieu, sanz nule aloingne
quar me fetes venir le moine.
Grant mestier ai d'a lui parler.
— Dame, dist il, vez m'i aler.
35   Nul meillor mes de moi n'i a!
Je cuit jel vous amenrai ja. »

A ces paroles s'en torna,
sor .i. cheval qu'il ot monta,
a la voie se mist anblant
40   & de sa fame molt penssant:
« Dieus, penssa s'il, tant a esté
ceste fame de grant bonté!
Ce savrai je, se Dieus m'aït,
s'ele est tant bone com l'en dit:
45   ja n'i avra confessïon,
par le cuer Dieu, se de moi non.
En leu de moine a li vendrai
& sa confessïon orrai. »
      En ce qu'en cest penssé estoit
50   & devise qu'estre en porroit,
chiés le prïor en vint manois,

fell sick and couldn't leave her bed
for three whole weeks. They were afraid
she'd die, nor would recover from
20 her illness. Since her time had come,
the lady made a full confession
and gave the Church a large donation,
but still she was not satisfied.
She called her husband to her side
25 and told him, "I cannot afford
to disregard my soul, dear lord.
A monk lives not too far away,
a very saintly man, they say.
If I confessed to him, my soul,
30 I do believe, would be made whole.
For God's sake, sire, with all due speed
go bring the monk to me. I need
to see him. It's imperative."
"I'm off," he answered. "I believe
35 that I'll return here with him very
soon. There's no better emissary
than I am."
            Having told her this,
he went out and got up on his
horse, and he set off at a trot.
40 The lady occupied his thought:
Dear God! what a devoted woman!
Her goodness goes beyond what's human.
I mean to find out, with God's aid,
if she's as good as it is said.
45 When she confesses, by God's heart,
I, too, will get to play a part:
I'll come wearing a friar's dress
and hear what she has to confess.
            Involved in thinking up this plan,
50 how he'll confess her if he can,
before you knew it, he'd arrived

qui fu preudom & molt cortois,
& quant le prïeor vit li,
en contre lui molt biau sailli,
55   bel l'apela, sel fist descendre,
puis si a fet son cheval prendre,
puis li a dit: « Par l'ordre Dé,
or m'avez vous servi a gré
quant vous m'estes venuz veoir
60   com vostre ami & remanoir!
De herbregier grant joie en ai—
por vous la cort amenderai. »
Li chevaliers li dist: « Biaus sire,
grant gré vous sai certes du dire,
65   mes ne puis mie herbregier.
Venez o moi ça conseillier. »
Quant il l'ot tret a une part,
« Sire, fet il, se Dieus me gart,
grant mestier ai de vostre aïe—
70   gardez que ne me failliez mie.
Se voz dras noirs me presterez,
ainz mienuit toz les ravrez—
& voz granz botes chaucerai
& je ma robe vous lerai;
75   ceenz avez mon palefroi
& le vostre menrai o moi. »
Li moine tout li otria
quanquë il quist & demanda,
& quant fu nuis, les dras vestit,
80   il chanja trestout son abit,
desus le palefroi monta
au moine, qui souëf ambla,
lors s'en parti demaintenant.
En sa meson en vint anblant,
85   dedenz entra; bien fu enbronc,
bien s'enbroncha ou chaperon,

where the good, gracious prior lived,
and, as soon as the monk caught sight
of him, he rose to greet the knight,
called out to him, had him dismount,
and had someone see to his mount.
He said then, "By the Eucharist,
I'm honored to have such a guest!
How pleased I am that you have come
here as a friend to share my home!
By way of hospitality
I'll decorate the priory."
"Father," replied the chevalier,
"thank you for everything you say,
but I'm afraid I can't remain.
Come here in private. I'll explain."
When he had taken him aside,
"Father," he said, "as God's my guide,
I have a favor I need done.
I hope that you won't let me down.
If you can lend me your black habit—
well before midnight you will have it
back—also your big boots to wear,
I'll leave you my own clothing here,
and, while my horse stays in your barn,
I'll borrow yours, please, and ride on."
The cleric generously granted
everything that he asked and wanted,
and when night came he donned his robes,
completely changed all of his clothes,
and mounted on the prelate's horse,
whose gait was smooth, and set his course
for home and left immediately.

   He came to his house presently
and went inside. Stooping, he stood
with his face hidden in the hood,

quar ne voloit, ce cuit je bien,
que l'en le conneüst de rien.

      La meson ert auques obscure.
90   Uns gars sailli grant aleüre
en contre lui por lui descendre;
a une fame se fist prendre
par la gonne, sel mena droit
la ou la dame se gisoit.
95   « Dame, dist el, le moine est ci
que vous mandastes des ier ci. »
& la dame si l'apela:
« Sire, dist el, seez vous ça
delez cest lit, quar molt m'enpire
100   mon mal, si crieng que je me muire,
que nuit ne jor point ne me cesse.
Si vueil de vous estre confesse.
    — Dame, dist il, ce sera sens
tant comme avez & leu & tens,
105   quar nus ne nule ne set mie
esmer de soi ne de sa vie.
Por ce vous di, ma douce dame,
qu'aiez merci de vostre ame:
pechié celé, ce truis escrit,
110   l'ame & le cors ensanble ocist.
Por ce vous di & vous chasti
que vous aiez de vous merci. »
& la dame qui ou lit fu
trestout en autre siecle fu;
115   de son seignor ne connut mie
por le grant mal qui l'ot saisie,
quar sa parole *entrechanjot*,
en la chanbre lumiere n'ot
fors d'un mortier qu'iluec ardoit—
120   point de clarté ne lor rendoit,
ne gent n'avoit en cel ostal
qui seüssent gueres de mal.

intending to remain disguised
and in no way be recognized.
The household lay in total darkness.
90   A servant came to hold his harness
and help him to dismount and greet him,
and then a woman came to lead him;
holding his robe, she showed the way
to the room where the lady lay.
95   "Lady," she said, "here's the monk from
the abbey whom you asked to come."
        The lady called him to her side:
"Come, Father," she said, "sit beside
my bed. I fear that I shall die.
100   My sufferings intensify
both night and day without remission.
I want you to hear my confession."
"Lady," he said, "that makes good sense
while you've still time. What Providence
105   wills for us all cannot be known,
and who can judge what he has done?
It's for this reason we are taught
by Scripture that we must give thought
to our soul's health, for, dearest lady,
110   the hidden sin kills soul and body.
It's for this reason that I press
you. Give thought to your soul's distress!"
Because the lady who was lying
in bed was then so close to dying
115   and so far from reality,
she didn't know her husband; he
altered his voice, and it was dark—
nothing more than a feeble spark
of one night candle lit the room
120   and threw its faint light in the gloom,
nor had the servants cause to foster
suspicion he was an impostor.

« Sire, molt ai esté proisie,
mes je sui fausse & renoïe.
125 Sachiez de voir, tele est blasmee
qui vaut molt mieus que la löee:
c'estoie je, qui los avoie
mes molt mavese fame estoie,
quar a mes garçons me livroie
130 & avoeques moi les couchoie
& d'aus fesoie mon talent.
Moie coupe! je m'en repent. »
& quant li chevaliers l'oï,
de mautalent le nez fronci;
135 molt par vousist & desirrast
que mort soubite l'acorast.
« Dame, dist il, pechié avez.
Dites avant, se vous savez,
mes bien vous deüssiez tenir,
140 dame, s'il vous fust a plesir,
a vostre espous, qui molt vaut mieus,
ce m'est avis par mes .ii. ieus,
que li garçons. Molt me merveil!
— Sire, se Dieus m'envoit conseil
145 a ceste ame, je vous dirai
la verité si com je sai.
A paine porroit l'en choisir
fame qui se puisse tenir
a son seignor tant seulement,
150 ja tant ne l'avra bel & gent,
quar la nature tele en ont
qu'eles requierent [& sel font],
& li mari si sont vilain
& de grant felonie plain,
155 si ne nous oson descouvrir
vers aus ne noz besoins gehir,
quar por putains il nous tendroient
se noz besoins par nous savoient;

"Father, men think I have no faults,
but I have been perverse and false.
125   Too often she who seems adorned
with virtue's worse than she who's scorned.
So have I been, despite men's praise.
I've always followed wicked ways
in that I surrendered myself
130   and bedded with the household help,
indulging my concupiscence.
Ah, mea culpa! Penitence!"
    When the knight heard his wife's confession,
his anger showed in his expression,
135   and he'd have found it to his taste
if Death had come and laid her waste.
He told her, "You have sinned, my lady.
If there is more, go on already,
but if you were spurred on by lust,
140   you should have been content with just
your husband, lady, who is worth
more than your lackeys. Why on earth?
That much is clear to my two eyes."
"Father, so may the Lord advise
145   my soul, I shall explain to you
as best I can a fact or two.
It would be difficult to find
even one woman who's inclined
or even capable to husband
150   her lust, however fine her husband.
Because our nature drives us to it,
we can't resist it, and we do it,
and those we marry are too dense,
too harsh, and too vindictive, hence
155   we daren't disclose ourselves to them
or speak our needs regarding men,
for they would think that we were tarts
if we admitted that our hearts

si ne puet estre en nule guise
160 que n'aions d'autrui le servise.
— Dame, dist il, bien vous en croi.
Dites avant, se savez qoi.
— Sire, dist ele, oïl, assez
dont li miens cors est molt grevez
165 & la moie ame en grant freor,
que le neveu de mon seignor—
tant l'amoie en mon corage,
ce m'estoit vis que c'estoit rage
&, sachiez bien, que je morusse
170 se mon plesir de lui n'eüsse!
Tant fis que je o lui pechai
& que .v. anz, je cuit, l'amai.
Or m'en repent vers Dieu. Aïe!
— Dame, dist il, c'estoit folie
175 que le neveu vostre seignor
amiiez de si fole amor!
Li pechiez doubles en estoit.
— Sire, se Dieus conseil m'envoit,
c'est la coustume de nous fames
180 & de nous aaisies dames,
quar cels dont l'en mains garde avra,
entor cels plus se tornera.
Por le blasme que je cremoie
le neveu mon seignor amoie,
185 quar a mes chanbres bien sovent
pooit venir veant la gent,
ja n'en fust blasme ne parole.
Ainsi j'ai fet, si fis que fole,
quar mon seignor ai grevé si
190 qu'a poi que ne l'ai tout honi,
que du tortiau puant Ligart
li ai bien fet mengier sa part.
Tant li ai fet, tant l'ai mené,
que il croit plus en moi qu'en Dé!

had such needs, so we have no choice
160 but to rely on serving boys."
"Lady," he said, "you're right, I'm sure.
Go on confessing, if there's more."
"Yes, Father. There's a grievous error
that fills my soul with mortal terror
165 and stains my body with its refuse,
because one of my husband's nephews . . .
passion for him so filled my brain,
I thought that I would go insane,
and I was ready to expire
170 if I could not have my desire.
At last I gave in to my lust
and sinned with him five years, I trust.
Now I repent before my Savior."
"Lady," he said, "what mad behavior!
175 To love with an illicit passion
your husband's nephew! In that fashion
committing one sin, you sinned twice."
"As I hope for the Lord's advice,
Father, that's what we women do,
180 and wealthy, noble ladies, too,
because those whom one least suspects
are most attractive to our sex.
Because of the blame which I feared,
my husband's nephew was endeared
185 to me, for he could often come
to my rooms seen by everyone
and no one would think to accuse us.
For my mad acts I've no excuses,
for I have wronged my lawful spouse
190 and brought dishonor on his house
and served him up a stinking slice
of Empress Messalina's pies
and led him on so shamelessly,
he trusts God less than he does me.

195 Quant ceenz vienent chevalier,
si com droit est, por herbregier,
lors demandent il a noz genz:
'Ou est la dame? — Ele est leenz.
Ja le seignor n'ert demandé
200 quar je l'ai tout aneanté,
ne ja ostel n'ert a honor
dont la dame se fet seignor,
& fames ceste coustume ont
& volentiers toz jors le font
205 qu'eles aient la seignorie
sor lor seignors. Por c'est honie
mainte meson qu'est sanz mesure,
& fame avoire par nature.
— Dame, dist il, ce puet bien estre. »
210 Del vrai Dieu, le souverain prestre,
onques riens plus ne li enquist,
mes sa coupe batre li fist
& li enjoinst sa penitance,
& ele mist en couvenance
215 que ja mes jor amor n'avroit
a autre hom s'ele vivoit.
        Lors s'en parti, molt fu iriez;
a son cheval est reperiez,
desus monta, tost s'en issi.
220 D'ire & de mautalent fremi
por sa fame qu'il seut löer
& tant prisier & tant amer,
mes en ice se confortoit
qu'encore bien s'en vengeroit
225 a l'endemain quant il li plout
a son ostel & quant il vout.
En sa meson s'en repera,
& la dame si respassa.
Grant merveille ot de son seignor,
230 qui li soloit moustrer amor

195   When, as is custom, knights now come
       and ask for shelter in our home,
       they ask our folk who see them in,
       'Where is your lady?' 'She's within.'
       The master isn't ever sought,
200   for I've reduced the man to naught.
       A household knows shame and disaster
       whose mistress makes herself the master,
       but women like to play the man
       and jump at every chance they can
205   to see to it that they hold sway
       over their husbands. In this way
       the honor of the household lessens
       and woman manifests her essence."
       "Lady," he said, "that well may be."
210   In God's true priestly sovereignty
       he asked no further of her. She
       beat her breast in humility,
       and he imposed a penance on her,
       and she gave him her word of honor
215   that never would her love be given
       to other men while she was living.
          Infuriated, he went out,
       got on his horse and turned about
       and soon rode off into the night,
220   trembling with bitterness and spite
       for the wife who for all his days
       had had his love, esteem, and praise,
       but, at the thought he could arrange
       some means by which to take revenge
225   next day at home or when he please,
       his mind was somewhat set at ease.
          He came back home intent to get her,
       and in the end his wife got better.
       Her husband's ways surprised her much,
230   who once had manifested such

& li besier & a[co]ler:
or ne daingnoit a li parler!
     Un jor par sa meson aloit
trestout ainsi com el soloit
235 & commandoit molt fierement
de ses aferes a sa gent,
& li sires sel regarda,
ireement le chief crolla,
se li a dit: « Par l'ordre Dé,
240 dame, quele est vostre fierté
& vostre orgueil! Je l'abatrai,
quar a mes poins vous ocirrai!
S'il vous menbrast de vostre vie,
honte eüssiez d'avoir baillie,
245 quar nule fame bordeliere
ne fu de si male maniere
com vous estes, orde mauvaise! »
Lors ne fu pas la dame a aise;
de son seignor se merveilla.
250 Avis li fu, de voir cuida
que il l'eüst fete confesse;
molt se doute que mal n'en nesse.
Puis li a dit demaintenant:
« Ha! mauvés homme souduiant!
255 Molt me poise que je ne dis
que tuit li chien de cest païs
le me fesoient nuit & jor,
mes plus m'estoit de ma dolor!
Ha! mauvés homme trahitier,
260 tu preïs abit d'ermitier
por me prover a desloial,
mes, merci Dieu, je sui loial!
Je n'ai voisine ne voisin
por qui je port le chief enlin,
265 je ne te criem, la merci Dé!
Tu seüsses la verité,

affection and kissed and embraced her—
he never spoke to her or faced her!

    She went around the house one day
exactly in her usual way.
235 Her husband looked at her in wrath
while she gave orders to her staff
about their work. He shook his head
to see her prideful ways and said,
"Lady, by God's own holy Mass,
240 how dare you show such haughtiness?
I'll take it down a notch or two!
Just let me get my hands on you!
I'll kill you! Your iniquity
lays forfeit your authority,
245 for not even a prostitute
has fallen in such disrepute
as you have, slut, or been so sleazy!"
Surprised, the woman felt uneasy
to hear the knight attack her so.
250 She figured he could only know
this had it been he who confessed her,
and dreaded what ill will might fester.
She quickly turned and told her sire,
"You wicked man! You knight for hire!
255 I wish I'd made you understand
that all the stray dogs in the land
had done it with me day and night,
but my pain gave me no respite!
You wicked man! Your faithlessness
260 led you to put on monkish dress
to prove that *I* had been unfaithful,
but, God be praised, I have been faithful!
Before all of our neighbors I
can, thank God, hold my head up high,
265 and with you, too, I'll hold my own.
You would have known what I had done,

quar ma honte tost fust seüe,
mes m'en estoie aperceüe
quant je vous en enquis sordois
270   en ce que dis par mon gabois.
Molt me poise, par saint Symon,
que ne vous pris au chaperon
& que ne vous deschirai tout!
Sachiez de voir, pas ne vous dout
275   de rien que j'onques vous deïsse;
se Dame Dieus mon cors garisse,
bien vous reconui au parler.
Je ne vous doi ja mes amer,
non ferai je, se Dieus me gart,
280   mauvés trahitre de male art!
Ja ne vous ert mes pardoné! »
        Tant li a dit & tant conté
que li osta tout son espoir
& bien cuida que deïst voir.
285   Granz risees & granz gabois
en firent en Beseïnois.

23. AUBEREE

Qui pres de moi se vodra trere
i. beau conte m'orra retrere
dont je me sui molt entremis.
Por ce l'ai ge en rime mis
5   tot einsi com avint a ligne.
Or öez qu'avint a Conpigne!
        En la vile avoit .i. borjois
qui molt fu sages & cortois
& riche de molt grant afere;
10   ententieus est a honor fere

for my shame would be talked about,
but I had figured your game out
when I confessed in great abandon
270 to sins I just thought up at random.
Saint Simon, how I wish I would
have grabbed you firmly by the hood
and torn you in a thousand pieces!
You've no cause to believe, by Jesus,
275 a single sin that I confessed.
May God grant me eternal rest,
your voice revealed your trickery.
Why should I love you? Certainly,
by God, I never will again,
280 most vile and treacherous of men!
Don't think you'll ever be forgiven!"
       She dunned him so, he had to give in
and lay all of his doubts to rest.
Thus in the end she got the best
285 of him. Now he's a standing joke
among all of the local folk.

23. AUBERÉE, THE GO-BETWEEN
by Jehan

Come, gather 'round me, if you're willing!
I'll entertain you all by telling
a pleasing tale: I've spent much time
to put it into verse and rhyme
5   just as it happened, nothing missing.
It happened in Compiègne. Listen!
       There lived a tradesman there in town
who'd a rich business of his own
and was both clever and polite,
10   intent on doing what is right

ausi au povre com au riche,
com cil qui n'iert aver ne chiche.
Le borgeis ot .i. molt bel fil,
qui meint denier mist a essil
15 tant com il fu en sa janesce;
de sa valour, de sa proeice,
parloit l'en par tot Beauvoisin.
Il avoit .i. povre voisin
qui une fille avoit molt cointe,
20 & li vallez de li s'acointe
& la pria molt durement.
Cele li dist apertement
que mieus le vendroit reposer
s'il ne la voleit espouser,
25 mes si li plesoit qu'il l'eüst
a moillier si come il deüst . . .
« de ce avroie je grant joie.
— M'amie, ausi aie ge joie,
fet le vallet, car molt me plest. »
30 A tant plus pres de lié se trest,
si ont d'amours asés parlé.
Quant une piece i ont esté,
si s'en revint en sa meson,
son pere en a mis a reson,
35 si li a son afere dit,
& le pere li contredit
& molt l'en blasme & molt l'en chose.
« Biau fiuz, fet il, de ceste chose
te devroies tu molt bien tere.
40 Ele n'est pas de ton afere
ne digne de toi deschaucier.
Je te vodrai plus souhaucier,
que que il me doie couster,
que je te vodré ajouster
45 au meillors gens de cest païs.
De ta folie m'esbahis

both by the well-to-do and needy,
like one who's neither cheap nor greedy.
The man had a good-looking son
who squandered quite a hefty sum
15 when he was still an adolescent,
and folk spoke of him as a decent,
hardy lad throughout Beauvaisis.
A poor man lived nearby them; he
had a most charming, clever daughter.
20 The rich man's son desired to court her
and begged her most insistently,
but the girl told him openly
he'd better put such thoughts aside
unless he first made her his bride,
25 but if it pleased him to agree
to make her his wife honestly,
their union would give her great joy.
"My darling, I, too, would enjoy
to marry you, so I concur,"
30 he says, and draws closer to her.
The two then spoke of love somewhat,
and when they'd done, the young man got
up and went back to where he lives
to speak to his father and gives
35 him an account of where things stand.
The father's quick to countermand
his wishes and chastise his son.
"I don't approve of what you've done,
young man," he says, "nor wish to hear your
40 protests, for she is our inferior,
unworthy to take off your shoes.
For you, dear boy, I mean to choose
a nobler match, whatever I
may have to spend, and thus ally
45 you with the land's best families.
It doesn't put my heart at ease

qui tel garce veus espouser.
Par foi, l'en te devroit tüer
se jamés nul jor en parolles! »
50 Le vallet voit que ses parolles
a mis ses peres a noient,
son dire ne li vaut nïent.
Le vallet esprent & atise,
que Amours le veint & justise
55 qu'il n'espousast ja la pucele;
el cors li met une estencele
qui les autres esprent & art.
Amours l'a feru de son dart.
        Trois jors aprés ice avint
60 qu'en la vile morir covint
la fame a .i. autre borgeis,
mes enceis que passast le meis
puis que la dame ot esté morte,
le borgeis, qui bel se deporte,
65 par le conseil de ses amis
a a reson le pere mis
a la pucele bele & gente
ou cil avoit mise s'entente
que j'ai amenteü en conte,
70 & le borgeis dont je vos conte
a tant sa besoigne esploitiee
que la pucele a fianciee,
& a l'eins qu'il pot, l'espousa—
mes au vallet molt en pesa,
75 qui i pensoit & jor & nuit.
Ne voit riens qui ne li anuit,
einz het [le solaz de la gent,
& het] son or & son argent
& le grant avoir que il a,
80 & jure que molt s'avila
de ce qu'a tant creü son pere:
sa grant richesce trop conpere!

when you want some tramp for your wife.
I'd rather someone took your life
than hear you speak of it again."
50　To the young man it's all too plain:
Talking won't help; his dad won't care
for his words more than empty air.
Love's conquered the young man, who burns
and suffers torments, for he yearns
55　for her who'll never be his bride.
Love's kindled a spark deep inside
his heart, and shot him with the same
arrow that's set others aflame.
　　　Just three days later to the day
60　a married woman passed away
whose husband lived in that same town.
Before another month had gone
by following his wife's demise,
the husband's closest friends advise
65　him, since he's healthy, to remarry.
He makes an offer to the very
man whose child I told you of,
whose charms had won the young man's love,
as I've explained in some detail.
70　The man's request was of avail.
He pressed his suit in such a way
that she became his fiancée,
and shortly after they were wed.
What anguish for the lad whose head
75　was filled with her both day and night!
Nothing finds favor in his sight;
he hates all human company,
hates his wealth and his property,
and hates his silver and his gold,
80　swears he's done himself harm untold
through filial obedience—
just see what his inheritance

Longuement li convint penser,
que il ne se set apensser
85   par quoi eüst nul recomfort.
       Il ot robe d'un Estanfort
teint en greine & de vert partie,
si ot fet chascune partie
a longue qeues cöer cil;
90   le sercoz fu touz a pourfil
forré de menuz escurel.
       Molt seult cil estre gent & bel
qui or a le vis teint & pale.
       .i. jour de son ostel avale,
95   son chief afublé d'un mantel;
deduiant vet par le chastel
tant que vint devant la meson
s'amie. S'iert en la seson
que il fet chaut com en aoust.
100 Que que li griet ne que li coust,
enging li estuet a trover
qu'a s'amie puisse parler;
molt l'en tint & molt s'en prist garde.
       A tant une meson esgarde
105 a une vieille costuriere;
meintenant passe la chariere,
si s'est asis sor la fenestre.
       Cele li enquiert de son estre,
qui de meint barat molt savoit,
110 si li demande qu'il avoit
qui si soloit estre envoisié
& des autres le plus proisié.
       La vieille avoit non Auberee—
ja si ne fust fame enserree
115 qu'a sa corde ne la treïst!—
& le vallet les li s'asist,
si li conte tot mot a mot
comment cele bourjoise amot

has cost him! So he turned his mind
to see if he at length could find
85   some consolation for his woes.
           He owned an outfit of fine clothes
of Stamford wool dyed red and green,
and on each article he'd seen
to it to have long tails attached;
90   the surcoat of the suit was edged
and lined with dainty squirrel fur.
Once smart and bright, his features were
now ashen and had lost their bloom.
           One day he set out from his home,
95   a short cloak tossed over his head.
Strolling for pleasure, his path led
through town until he came before
at last his stolen sweetheart's door.
Just like in August, it was hot
100 that day. He feels no matter what
the cost to him he must think of
some trick to meet up with his love.
This occupies his every thought.
An aged woman's house then caught
105 his eye, who plied a trade (she sewed),
and he was quick to cross the road
and sit down in her windowsill.
This woman had a lot of skill
in subterfuge. She asks of him
110 what's wrong that he should look so grim,
once known for gaiety and wit
as everybody's favorite.
           The woman's name was Auberée.
She could lead any wife astray
115 however strictly she was guarded.
The young man sat by her and started
in full detail to tell her of
how he was overcome with love

qui si estoit pres sa voisine:
120   s'ele li puet metre en sesine,
.xl. livres li donroit.
Ele respont, ne la savroit
le vilein si tres bien garder
que il ne la puist esgarder
125   par tens entre li & la terre.
« Alez me tost les deniers qerre,
& je penseré de ceste oevre! »
Cil s'en va, une huche oevre
ou il avoit deniers asez
130   que ses peres ot amassez.
Les deniers prent, puis si s'en torne
& ches dame Auberee tourne,
si li baille .xl. livres;
mes encore n'est pas delivres,
135   encor i metra son escot.
« Or me bailliez vostre sercot, »
fet la vieille delivrement,
& cil, qui son commandement
vout fere sanz nul contredit,
140   fet ce que la vieille li dit—
bien l'a Amours en son destroit,—
& cele plie molt estroit
le sercot & met sous s'eisele,
puis est levee de sa sele,
145   si afubla .i. mantel court;
einsi vers cel ostel s'en court.
      Ce fu a .i. jor de marchié.
La vieille ot molt bien espié
que li sire n'iert pas laiens.
150   « & Dieus, dist ele, soit ceans!
Dieus soit o vos, ma douce dame,
& il eit hui merci de l'ame
de l'autre dame qui est morte,
dont mes cuers molt se desconforte.

for the woman who was her neighbor.
120   If she could further his love's labor,
she'd earn a forty-pound reward.
"Although that fool may closely guard
his wife," she answers, "thanks to me,
before much time has passed you'll see
125   her sandwiched twixt you and the ground!
Quick, get the cash, every last pound,
while I weigh what our options are."
He goes and opens an armoire,
which held a tidy sum his father
130   had over time managed to gather.
He takes the coins and doesn't stay,
but heads straight back to Auberée
with forty pounds, paid in advance.
Will that be all, then? Not a chance—
135   there's more he has to put in hock.
"Give me that surcoat off your back,"
says the old woman speedily,
and he does as he's told, for he
intends to follow her advice
140   without having to be told twice—
Love has him in a stranglehold—
and she proceeds to neatly fold
the surcoat, gets up from her chair,
and takes out a short cloak to wear.
145   Surcoat under her arm, she's ready
to go next door to see the lady.
          This all took place on market day.
She'd checked first that it was okay
and that the husband wasn't in.
150   "God bless this house and all within,
mistress!" she said. "God be with you
and may He grant forgiveness to
the soul of the first wife, who's dead
and I remember with regret.

155 Meint jor m'a ceanz honoree.
       — Bien veigniez vos, dame Auberee,
     la dame dist. Venez seoir.
       — Ma dame, je vos vieig veoir
     car de vos acointer me voil.
160 Je ne passé puis vostre sueil
     que l'autre dame morte fu,
     qui onques ne me fist refu
     de riens que je li demandasse.
     Certes, se je li *commandasse*
165 a fere une chose molt grief,
     sel feïste ele, par mon chief.
     Dieus la soille, el me fist meint bien!
       — Dame Auberee, faut [ ] vos rien?
     Se riens vos faut, dites le nos.
170   — Oïl, dame, je vieig a vos.
     Une goute a ma fille eu flanc,
     si voil avoir de vos vin blanc
     & .i. soul de vos peins fetiz,
     mes que ce soit le plus petiz.
175 Dieus merci, com j'en sui honteuse,
     mes si m'en angoise la teuse
     qu'il le me convient demander!
     Je ne soi onques truander,
     einc ne m'en soi aidier, par m'ame.
180   — & vos en arés, » dist la dame,
     qui iert a privee mesnie.
     Cele qui bien est enresnie
     delés la bourjoise s'asiet.
     « Certes, dist ele, molt me siet,
185 que j'oi de toi si grant bien dire.
     Comment se contient or ton sire?
     Te fet il point de bele chiere?
     Ha! com il avoit l'autre chiere!
     El avoit molt de son delit.
190 Bien vodroie vöer ton lit;

155 She always showed me courtesy."
    She answered, "I'm so glad to see
    you, neighbor. Make yourself at home."
    "Lady, it's for your sake I've come,
    because I want to know you more.
160 I haven't entered through this door
    since his last wife's untimely end.
    I'd but to ask, and like a friend
    she gave to me ungrudgingly.
    I'd but to speak, and certainly,
165 however onerous the task,
    she'd do it—I had but to ask.
    Oh, she was good to me indeed,
    God comfort her!" "Are you in need,
    Auberée? If so, let us know."
170 "Of course I turn to you. Just so.
    My daughter's lower back is sore,
    so I would borrow some of your
    white wine and just one dainty roll,
    but, please, the smallest of them all.
175 God help me, I am so embarrassed
    to ask, but the poor girl has harassed
    me so, I've no alternative.
    Panhandling's not the way I live,
    nor am I one to ask for aid."
180 "They're yours to take," the lady said.
    Home all alone, she'd not a soul
    with her. Auberée, in control
    now, takes a seat beside the wife.
    "How glad I am, upon my life,"
185 she says, "for all speak in your praise.
    Tell me about your husband's ways
    and how he treats you. Is he kindly?
    I swear he loved the other blindly,
    and what a pleasant life she led!
190 I'm curious to see your bed.

lors savroie certainement
se tu gis ausi richement
com fesoit la premiere fame. »
Meintenant se lieve la dame
195 & puis dame Auberee aprés.
En une chanbre iluecques pres
andeus ensenble s'en alerent.
De plusors choses i parlerent,
mes la vieille la sert de lobes.
200 La dame li moutre ses robes,
aprés li moutre une grant couche,
puis dit la dame: « Ci se couche
misire & je les son flanc. »
Li liz fu de haut fuerre blanc
205 ou il ot grant coute de plume,
& por ce que il ne s'enplume,
a deseure une coute pointe.
La vieille ot une aguille pointe
& .i. deel en cel sercot
210 que desouz s'eissele portot.
Molt le tint pres de son costel.
Que que la dame de l'ostel
li moutre sa besoigne tote,
& la vieille meintenant boute
215 le sercot par desouz la coute,
& lors dist: « Puis la Pentecouste
ne vi ge mes si riche lit!
Plus as asez de ton delit
c'onques n'ot l'autre, ce me senble. »
220 A tant s'en issent de la chanbre,
& la vieille tor jors sermonne.
La dame meintenant li done
plein pot de vin & une miche
& une piece de sa fliche
225 & de pois une grant potee.
Bien a la bourjoise abertee

I'd know then for a certainty
if you have all the luxury
his first wife was accustomed to."
        The second wife gets up on cue
195 and Auberée follows her lead,
and so the two of them proceed
together to a room next door.
They touch on several subjects more,
but Auberée tricks and finesses
200 her always, while she shows her dresses
and next a bed of ample size,
and she explains, "In this bed lies
my husband with me by his side."
The bedding straw was thick and white
205 and covered with a feather bed,
and to make sure it wouldn't shed
a quilt was spread across on top.
The old woman had stuck a sharp
needle and thimble in the garment
210 (the one she held beneath her arm and
clutched to her body very close).
Now, while the mistress of the house
was showing off all her possessions,
beneath the quilt among the cushions
215 Mistress Auberée quickly thrust
the surcoat. "Not since Pentecost,"
she said, "have I seen such a bed!
In comforts you come out ahead
of the first wife by far, I vow!"
220 They step out of the bedroom now.
Auberée talks without a break
while the wife presses her to take
a jug of wine, a wheaten loaf,
a slab of bacon, and enough
225 peas to fill up a fair-sized pot.
The old woman has really got

la vieille, qu'ele ne set pas
qu'el a bouté desous ses dras.
Plus ne s'est la vieille arestee;
230   en sa meson est retornee.
       Du borgeis dire me convient
qui a son ostel s'en revient.
Toz seus de la vile repere,
& ot esté en son afere,
235   & dist que dormir se voleit
por ce que le chief li doleit
En sa chanbre entre, si se couche.
Tantost com il fu sus la couche
si sent le sorcot bochoier,
240   lors le commence a enpoignier
qu'il ne set que c'est qui le grieve.
Meintenant la *coute* souzlieve,
si en a tret le sercot fors,
& qui or li boutast el cors
245   .i. coutel par desouz le flanc
n'en tresist il goute de sanc,
tant est durement esbaïz.
    « Ha! las! dist il, tant sui traïz!
Onc ceste fame ne m'ama! »
250   Lors vint a l'uis, si le ferma,
meintenant a le sercot pris,
car jalosie l'a soupris,
qui est pire que mal de dens.
De fors le remire & dedens
255   qu'il senble c'achater le veille;
n'il n'a membre qui ne se dueille,
tant est pleins de corouz & d'ire.
    « Hé Dieus! dist il, que porrai dire
de cest sercot? Bien sai, par m'ame,
260   qu'il est au lecheor ma fame,
qui soulaz ele consenti
[ains qu'ele m'eüst a mari]! »

the best of her: She doesn't know
what's hidden underneath the throw.
Her business done, Auberée loiters
230 no more, and goes back to her quarters.
        I now tell of the lady's spouse
and how he came back to their house
from the town unaccompanied
(he'd been at work) and said that he'd
235 like to lie down a bit and take
a nap, for his head had an ache.
He went to his room, got in bed,
and felt the lump the surcoat made
as soon as he was lying down,
240 so he begins to feel around.
He doesn't know, but he'll discover
what's hurting him. He lifts the cover
and finds the surcoat underneath.
If you had stabbed the man beneath
245 the ribs then with a knife, you would
not have drawn the least drop of blood,
he is so very much dismayed.
"Alas," he said, "I am betrayed!
This woman has no love for me."
250 He went to the door, turned the key,
and, seized by jealousy, he's taken
hold of the surcoat. No mistaking
it—toothache doesn't hurt as much!
He continues to turn and touch
255 and look it over like a buyer,
so full of bitterness and ire
that every inch of him's in pain.
"Dear God, what does this surcoat mean?"
he asked himself. "It's all too clear
260 that my wife's lover left it here,
whose lust and passion she assuaged
before we even were engaged!"

Lors le prist & si l'estoia,
aprés sor son lit s'apoia
265 & penssa que il porra fere,
& com plus pense a son afere,
plus s'est deables en lui mis.
        Issi fu tant que il fu nuis
que les huis vit clos par la rue,
270 lors prent sa fame, si la rue
par mi l'us fors de la meson.
Cele, qui ne set l'acheson,
a poi de duel n'est acoree.
A tant es vos dame Auberee,
275 qui de lui se prenoit regart.
« Ma belle fille, Dieus vos gart,
fet la vieille, que fetes ci?
— Ha, dame Auberee, merci!
Mon sire est corocié a moi,
280 mes ne sai a dire por quoi.
Ne sai que l'en li a conté!
Car me fetes tant de bonté
qu'avec moi veigniez ches mon pere.
— Avoi! fet ele, par seint Pere,
285 je ne vodroie por grant chose!
Veus tu que tes peres te chose?
Il cuideroit que entreset
eüses a ton seignor fet
[grant vilonnie de ton cors
290 & qu'il t'eüst boutee hors],
ou qu'il t'eüst prise provee
& o ton lecheor trovee!
Or est espoir le vilein ivres
& demein en sera delivres,
295 mes je te lo en bone foi
que tu t'en vieignes avec moi,
que desor sont li rues vides.
Mieus enploias que tu ne cuides

He took it and put it away
and got back on the bed and lay
265   there thinking about what to do.
The more he thinks the matter through,
the more the Devil's overcome
him. Thus he lay till night had come
and up and down the avenue
270   the doors closed. Then he took and threw
his wife out the door in the street,
who'd no idea why he should treat
her so. She's stricken with dismay.
       Now see before you Auberée,
275   who'd been on lookout all along.
"God keep you, pretty child, what's wrong?
What are you doing in this place?"
"Please, Auberée," the woman says,
"my lord is furious with me!
280   I can't think what the cause might be
or if he's been told something hateful,
but I would be forever grateful
if you'd come with me home to father."
"Saint Peter save me, but I'd rather
285   not, whatever the price," she said.
"You want your father to upbraid
you, dear? Why, surely he'd conclude
that you must have done something lewd,
deceived your husband, been unchaste,
290   and that is why he went and chased
you from his house, a proven whore
discovered with your paramour!
Let's hope the ruffian's not sober
and that tomorrow it's all over,
295   but I'd advise you in good faith
for now to come back to my place
because the streets are all deserted.
What foresight you showed," she asserted,

le pein, la char, le vin, les pois—
300 jel te rendré a double pois
le guerredon & le servise,
& s'iert tot fet a ta devise
quant que tu savras demander.
Il ne te faut fors commander,
305 car tu seras molt bien celee
en une chanbre a recelee,
que ja ame ne t'i savra
jusqu'a tant que tes *sire* avra
trespassee tote s'ivresce. »
310 Meintenant la vieille s'adrece
vers son ostel, la dame en meine.
« Dame, dist ele, une semeine
porrïez vos molt bien ci estre,
que nus ne savra ja vostre estre. »
315 Lors la proie molt de mengier,
mes la borjoise en fist dangier
& dist que ja Deu ne pleüst
qu'ele menjast jusqu'el seüst
por quoi ele a tel honte eüe.
320 Dame Auberee s'est teüe
a cest mot de lié plus proier,
lors l'a menee por couchier
en une chanbre iluec de jouste
sor bons dras & sor bone coute,
325 [molt l'a la vieille bien coverte;
ne laissa pas la chanbre overte,
ainz] frema bien l'us a la clef,
de son ostel s'en ist söef,
lors si s'en va plus que le pas
330 pour le vallet qui ne dort pas
Torne & retorne en son lit,
molt crient la vieille ne l'oublit
de ce que li a en covent,
du cuer en soupire forment,

"in giving me the wine and peas
300 and bread and meat! How it will please
me to repay the favor double!
My dear, I'll gladly—it's no trouble—
bring you whatever you demand,
because your wish is my command.
305 I've a back room where you may stay
for now, safely hidden away,
for not a soul will know you're here,
while we wait for his mind to clear
and him to come back to his senses."

310   Thereupon Auberée advances
toward her abode, the wife in tow.
"Lady," she says, "a week or so,
you could stay here, I have no doubts,
and none would know your whereabouts."
315 She brings some dinner for her guest,
but all the wife does is protest
and say that she'll not eat a bite,
God help her, till she learns the right
cause of her dishonor and pain.
320 The old woman knows to refrain
from urging, given what she's said,
and leads the lady off to bed
in the next room, where she has laid
out her best linens and bedspread,
325 has her lie down, and covers her.
The door is not left open there;
instead she locks it with her key.

        She leaves the household furtively
and hurries quickly as she can
330 to look for the sleepless young man,
who, greatly fearful, turns and tosses
lest the old woman double-crosses
him or forgets to keep her word.
Heaving sighs from his heart and scared,

335	lors saut de son lit trestouz nuz,
	puis se vest, si en est venuz
	a une fenestre apoier;
	& la vieille, qui son loier
	veut de chief en chief deservir
340	& le vallet en gré servir,
	ne guenchist destre ne senestre.
	Le vallet trueve a la fenestre,
	qui li demande: « Quieus noveles?
	— Jes te dirai, dist ele. Beles,
345	car je tieng t'amie en mes laz.
	Avoir en puez touz tes soulaz
	jusqu'a demein aprés ceste eure. »
	Le vallet l'ot, plus ne demeure,
	que la vieille a servi a gré.
350	Söef avale le degré,
	a l'ostel s'en vienent ensemble.
	N'avoit gueres, si com moi semble,
	que la bourjoise iert endormie,
	& cil qui desiroit s'amie
355	se deschauce & si se despoille.
	« Dame, fet il, s'ele s'orgeille
	& el crie, que ferai gié?
	Ovrer veil par vostre congié,
	car bien m'avez rendu mon droit.
360	— Je te conseilleré a droit,
	fet la vieille. Va, si te couche,
	& se point vers toi se corouche
	& ele crie, & tu .ii. tans,
	lieve la robe, si entre ens.
365	Si tost com el te sentira,
	autrement la besoigne ira.
	Meintenant la verras tesir,
	s'en porras fere ton plesir. »
	Le vallet est au lit alez;
370	les la bourjoise s'est couchez

335 he leaves his bed in his bare skin,
puts on his clothes, and sits down in
the window, propped against the sill,
and the old woman, who'd fulfill
her promise and thus earn her fee
340 serving the young man honestly,
without a detour left or right,
there at the window catches sight
of the young man, who asks, "What's new?"
"Good news! I've done my best for you
345 and hold your mistress in my snare.
Take all the pleasure that you care
to till tomorrow at this time."
He hears her and hastens to climb
down the stairs quietly, for she
350 has met his wishes perfectly.
        Now back to Auberée's they go.
It seems to me, not long ago
the woman had at last dozed off.
In his desire, he's quick to doff
355 his clothing and take off his shoes.
"What tactics, lady, should I use
if she turns proud and starts in screeching?
I will be guided by your teaching
in everything, my benefactress."
360 "What I preach, you'd do well to practice,"
says the old woman. "Get in bed.
If she resists and screams in dread,
yell twice as loudly to outdo her,
lift up the bedclothes, stick it to her.
365 As soon as she feels you inside,
objections will be set aside
and she won't make another sound.
Then you'll be free to fool around."
        The young man went to bed and lay
370 beside her. Softly as he may,

& molt söef a lui adoise.
A tant s'esveilla la borjoise,
qui de paour est tressaillie
quant celi sent, si est saillie
375 hors du lit, mes cil l'embracha
& dist: « Bele, treez vos cha,
que je sui vostre chier amis
que vos avez a dolour mis,
mes tant ai fet, la Dieu merci,
380 que tote sole vos tieng ci
dedenz ceste chanbre enserree
par le conseil dame Auberee.
   — Certes, dist ele, riens ne vaut,
que je crïerai ja si haut
385 que ci verrez molt tost venue
tote la gent de ceste rue.
   — Par foi, dist il, riens ne vos monte.
Ci ne voi ge fors que vos honte
quant la grant gent & la menue
390 vos verront les moi tote nue.
Il est ja pres de mie nuit;
n'i avra .i. seul qui ne cuit
que j'aie fet a grant plenté
de vostre cors ma volenté.
395 Mieus vient asez que soit emblee
a ceus defors nostre asemblee,
que nus fors que nos trois le sache. »
A tant söef vers soi la sache,
si l'enbrace parmi les flans
400 qu'el ot molt tendres & molt blans,
la bouche li bese & la face.
La borgeise ne set que face:
mieus li vendroit estre a repos,
qu'el porroit acuillir tel los
405 par ses voisins & tel renon,

he drew his body close to hers
and, doing so, woke the bourgeoise,
who, feeling him there, shook with dread
and quickly jumped up out of bed,
375 but he embraced her earnestly
and said, "My beauty, come to me,
because I am your loving swain,
who, losing you, suffered much pain,
but I have managed by God's grace
380 to get you alone in this place,
the two of us here locked away,
by listening to Auberée."
"Be sure your efforts were in vain,"
she said. "I'll scream with might and main.
385 Before your eyes to me will flock
every last person on the block."
He said, "And what good would that do?
It will bring only shame to you
should all, both great and lowly, see
390 you lying naked next to me
here in the middle of the night.
Who wouldn't conclude at the sight
of us together I'd already
enjoyed you thoroughly, dear lady?
395 Our business were much better hidden
from prying eyes, so people didn't
know of our tryst, except we three."
He draws her to him tenderly,
embraces her and holds her tight
400 around the waist, so soft and white,
kissing her on the mouth and face.
What can she do but acquiesce?
She has to quietly submit,
for, if the town got word of it,
405 her reputation and good name

jamés n'avroit se honte non.
La bourgeise let son orgeil,
or est tornee en autre fueil,
molt l'asouage & molt l'apese,
410   & le vallet l'acole & bese,
& cele si fet bel atret,
li .i. pres de l'autre se tret,
si se jöent ensenble & font
le gieu por quoi asenblé sont.
415   Au matinet, quant l'aube crieve,
dame Auberee *si se* lieve,
si lour atorne au mieus qu'el pot
char de porc & poucins en rost,
a tant sont asis au mengier.
420   N'i a nul qu'en face dangier,
einz mengerent assez & burent,
& andui en bon gré rechurent
le servise dame Auberee,
& quant ce vint a la vespree
425   que le soleil a son droit torne,
dame Auberee lour atourne
ce qu'ele set que lor fu boen,
mes ele n'i met rien du soen.
Cele nuit ont asés soulas;
430   anbedui jurent bras a bras,
c'onques de veillier ne finerent
tant que les matines sonerent
de Seint Cornille a l'abeïe.
Tantost que la cloche a oïe,
435   dame Auberee si s'esveille,
si se vest & si s'apareille
& vient au lit ou cil se gisent
qui lor amors s'entredevisent
« Or sus, fet ele, bele fille!
440   Si [en] irons a Seint[ ] Cornille
entre moi & toi au moustier.

would be destroyed and turn to shame.
She will no longer give him grief,
but turns over another leaf.
She seeks to calm him with caresses;
410 the young man gives her hugs and kisses,
and she accepts him as a lover.
The two draw close to one another
and toy together, and the two
do what they had come there to do.
415   Early next morning, when dawn breaks
and Mistress Auberée awakes,
she readies for them in the kitchen
a roast of pork and also chicken,
and then all sit down to a feast.
420 No one is timid in the least;
instead they eat and drink their fill,
and both make use of with goodwill
the services of Auberée.
At long last comes the end of day;
425 it's evening and the sun is setting,
and Auberée goes about getting
the things she knows will please them most.
(At no expense, though, to their host.)
The two of them all through the night
430 remained awake, taking delight
in close embrace and in unbounded
pleasure until matins had sounded
in the Abbey of Saint Cornille.
When Auberée's heard the bell peal,
435 she quickly gets up in the dead
of night, gets dressed, and to the bed
she comes, where the two lie awake,
engaged in loving give-and-take.
"Time to get up," she says, "and we'll
440 be on our way to Saint Cornille,
for it's high time, my pretty child,

Des or aroies tu mestier
que tes sire a toi s'acordast. »
Le vallet molt se descordast,
445   mes il ne l'ose contredire,
& la vieille li prist a dire:
« Lai moi a mon talent ouvrer.
Encor porras bien recovrer
a t'amie & a ton delit. »
450   La vieille prist chandeles .viii.
dont chascune a plus d'une toise;
entre la vieille & la bourjoise
s'en sont issues de l'ostel,
au moustier vont devant l'autel
455   Nostre Dame, devant l'image,
& la vieille, qui molt fu sage,
la fet couchier jus a la terre
& li dist bien que de sa guerre
ne li soit pas vaillant .iii. noiz.
460   La vieille a fetes .iiii. croiz
des chandeles que ele avoit;
en une lampe ou feu ardoit
les aluma de chief en chief
l'une des croiz li mist ou chief
465   & l'autre as piez & l'autre a destre
& la quarte mist a senestre,
lors vint a lui, si l'aseüre
[& dist: « Soiez tote seüre]
& gardez, comment qu'il avieigne,
470   ne vos movez. Tant que je vieigne,
tenez vos ci endementiers.
— Dame, dist ele, volentiers. »
Einsi la dame se contient,
& la vieille sa voie tient
475   vers l'ostel au borjois tot droit,
qui por sa fame iriez estoit
si qu'il ne se set conseillier,

you and your lord were reconciled.
We two will go to church together."
The young man's grieving; he would rather
445   she stayed, but doesn't dare complain,
and Auberée tries to explain.
"Just let me carry out my plan.
Later, you and your lady can
indulge in other lovers' capers."
450   Then the old woman took eight tapers,
each of them taller than a human,
and the younger and older woman
stepped out, and not long after were
at the abbey basilica
455   before the shrine of Holy Mary,
and the old woman, who was very
clever, made her lie on the floor.
"You fret about that fight no more—
three nuts will cover all your losses!"
460   Auberée arranged in four crosses
the long tapers with which she came
and kindled them using the flame
of a lamp burning there, and put
one of the crosses at her foot,
465   one at her head, one to her right,
one to her left, all four alight,
then went to her to reassure
her, saying, "Just lie still now. You're
safe here, but make sure, come what may,
470   that you don't move. I'm on my way.
Till I get back, just lie here still."
She answered, "Auberée, I will."
    The woman did as she was told,
and the old woman briskly strolled
475   toward the husband's domicile.
He had been angry all the while
and didn't know what steps to take,

       & cele por li esveillier
       court cele part & hurte & boute.
480   Li borgeis oreille & escoute,
       qui bien vosist tel chose oïr
       dont il se poïst resjoïr.
       A tant son huis ovrir commande,
       & dame Auberee demande
485   tantost com el entra dedans:
       « Ou est, dist ele, li noiens,
       le failliz, le mal enseigniez?
       — Dame Auberee, bien veigniez,
       fet il. Qui vos meine a tele eure? »
490   Cele a respondre ne demeure:
       « Je te vieig dire sans essoigne,
       ennuit sonjai .i. molt mal songe,
       que de paor m'en esveillai,
       vesti moi & apareillai
495   que du songe fui esbahie.
       Au mostier ving a l'abeïe
       tres devant l'autel Nostre Dame.
       Iluecques vi gesir ta fame
       devant l'autel tote estendue.
500   Tote m'en sui, voir, esperdue,
       que je ne sai que ce puet estre:
       au piez, au chief, destre & senestre,
       vi chandeles iluec ardans,
       iluec se gist ta fame adans
505   devant l'autel a oreison.
       Molt par as fet grant mesprison—
       si en batras encor ta geule!—
       d'envoier a tele eure seule
       fame qui si bele fourme a!
510   De Damle Dieu qui nos forma
       soie ge, dist ele, saignie!
       Tote m'en sui espoorie,
       & si le tieng a grant merveille

while Auberée, who means to wake
him up, goes banging at his door.
480 He strains to listen. To be sure,
he'd like to receive information
that gave him cause for jubilation,
and orders his door opened for her.
No sooner was she in the foyer,
485 Auberée asked, "Say, where is he,
that monster of iniquity,
that selfish cad, that no-good bum?"
"Auberée, I am glad you've come.
What brings you here so late at night?"
490 She answered quickly as she might,
"I rushed here half-dressed and unkempt
to tell you that tonight I dreamt
a dream so evil, scared and startled,
I woke up, got dressed, then I started
495 for the church at the monastery.
There in the chapel of Saint Mary,
when I arrived, I looked and saw
your wife stretched out across the floor
before the altar. On my word,
500 I don't know when I've been so scared!
What can it mean? There at her feet
and head and right and left were lit
tapers, which had been placed around
your lady, who lay there facedown
505 before the altar, lost in prayer.
You've done her a great wrong, I swear,
and you need badly to atone
for having sent there all alone
at such an hour your lovely wife.
510 May the Lord God, who gave us life,"
she said, "bestow on me His blessing!
I find it terribly distressing
and marvel greatly at the sight

de cel enfant qui einsi veille,
515 de cel tendron qui ier fu nee,
qui deüst la grant matinee
dormir ceanz souz les cortines . . .
& vos l'envoiez a matines!
A matines! Lasse, coupable!
520 De damle Deu l'esperitable
soie je, dist ele, saignie
& ennoree & beneïe!
Veus en tu fere papelarde?
Mau feu & male flambe l'arde,
525 qui jane fame issi envoie! »
Issi la vieille le desvoie
du mal pensé qu'en son cuer ot,
& se ne fust por le seur[c]ot,
ja n'i pensast mes se bien non.
530 « Dame, por Deu & por son non,
dist le borgeis, dites vos voir?
— Lieve toi, si porras savoir,
fet la vieille, se je te ment! »
Cil se lieve delivrement,
535 n'il ot talent que plus i gise;
errant s'en vienent a l'iglise,
que du demorer n'i ot point.
Cil trueve sa fame en tel point
com la vieille li ot retret.
540 Meintenant pres de li se tret,
par la mein contremont la dresce,
en bas li dist que par ivresce
li avoit fet tel mesprison;
lors s'en revien[en]t en [ ] meson,
545 si se recouche[nt] derechief.
La bourjoise cuevre son chief,
que de dormir a grant talent.
Molt li est poi du mautalent
que ses sire a vers li eü,

of a mere child awake all night,
515 this tender babe born yesterday,
who should sleep late into the day
in a bed made with silk and satins . . .
and you dare send her off to matins!
To matins yet! Ah, woe is me!
520 May the Lord God in charity
bless me and keep me safe," she said,
"and grant me honor and His aid!
What priggish pious ostentation
would you impose? Hell and damnation
525 on all who'd treat a young wife thus!"
Auberée's fabrication does
much to allay the man's distrust.
Except for the surcoat, he must
admit, he'd no reason to blame
530 his wife. "I ask you in God's name,"
the husband said, "do you speak true?"
"Get up and find out if I do
yourself," she said. "You'll see what's what."
        The husband got up on the spot,
535 for he'd no taste to stay in bed,
and off to church with her he sped,
having no reason to delay.
He finds his wife at prayer the way
the old woman had said she was.
540 Now quickly up to her he goes,
gives her his hand to help her stand,
and gently makes her understand
he must have been drunk to mistreat her
so harshly; now it's time to lead her
545 home. When they're there, they get in bed.
She pulls the quilt over her head
because she really needs her rest.
She is not in the least distressed
because of his ill will, and soon

550 einz dort & en pes a geü,
& le borgeis tot por veir quide
que sa fame eit la teste wide
de geüner & de plorer,
& que puis ne finast d'orer
555 devant l'autel por son seignor,
& que plorast & nuit & jor.
   Einsi les sa fame se jut
le borgeis tant que jor parut
& li soleil amont se hauce.
560 Le borgeis se vest & se chauce
& let sa fame qui se gist;
de son ostel meintenant ist,
si seigne son vis & son cors,
& dame Auberee [ ] saut fors,
565 si s'escria a haute vois:
« .xxx. sous, seinte voire crois!
.xxx. sous! Dolente! cheitive!
Or ne me chaut se muire ou vive!
.xxx. sous! Lasse, doulereuse!
570 Com je sui or meseüreuse,
.xxx. sous! Lasse! .xxx. sous!
Or vendra ceanz li prevoz
por prenre cel petit que j'ai!
C'est le songe que je sonjai! »
. . . . .
575 —Dites moi, se Dieus vos aït,
[fet li borgois qui s'esbahist,]
por quoi vos fetes si grant duel.
Par mon chief, jel savrai, mon vuel!
— Sire, fet ele, jel dirai,
580 que ja ne vos en mentirai.
.i. vassal vint ci des l'autrier.
Por recoutre & pour afetier
m'ot aporté .i. sien sercot
d'escarlate & d'Estanfort,

550   the lady's sleeping like a stone.
    His wife, he thinks, must be light-headed
    because she's fasted so and fretted,
    nor would he hesitate to swear
    that she'd spent night and day in prayer
555   before the altar for his sake,
    weeping as though her heart would break.
        Beside his wife the tradesman lay
    just so until the break of day
    and in the sky the sun arose.
560   The man puts on his shoes and clothes
    and, leaving there his sleeping spouse,
    he shortly steps out of the house,
    signs the cross on his chest and forehead. . . .
    Lo! Auberée comes running toward
565   him, screaming so she must go hoarse,
    "Thirty whole sous, true Holy Cross!
    Thirty whole sous! Wretched am I!
    I don't care if I live or die!
    Thirty whole sous! Ah, woe is me!
570   Malevolent fatality!
    Thirty whole sous! Woe! Thirty! Yes!
    The provost will come repossess
    what little I have set aside,
    just as I dreamed they would!" she cried.
    · · · · ·
575   "Tell me, may God come to your aid,"
    the man asked, mightily afraid,
    "the cause of all this grief and woe.
    Yes, by my head, I'd like to know!"
    "Neighbor," she says, "I'll tell you why,
580   and, take my word, I never lie.
    A young man stopped by recently
    and left his surcoat here with me
    for alterations and resewing.
    It had three or four tails (no knowing

585   ne sai ou .iii. queues ou .iiii.
      Je le pris, si m'alai esbatre
      a tot le sorcot recousant,
      car .i. poi me senti pesant.
      Einsi o tote ma costure
590   m'en issi par mesaventure
      icel jor hors de mon ostel.
      Mescheü m'est de mon chatel,
      car j'ai icel sercot perdu
      dont j'ai mon cuer si esperdu,
595   & si ne sai, lasse, ou je fui.
      Que ferai ge se ne m'enfui
      ne je ne truis qui le m'enseigne?
      Se je ne truis qui le me raigne,
      jel ferai le matin noncier
600   & dïemenche escommenier,
      certes, par trestouz les moutiers,
      qu'il ne m'en fust ore mestiers
      de recevoir si lede perte!
      Biau sire, or oiez chose aperte:
605   si pusse je vöer Nöel,
      g'i lessé pendant mon deel
      avec m'esguille en cel seurcot,
      dont je sui, *lasse, a tel escot*
      s'einsi rendre le me convient
610   & li vallez a moi si vient
      ceanz, sire, & me demande
      .xxx. sous *ou* le sercot *rende*!
      Or sui de tel chose enconbree!
      — [Or me dites, dame Auberee,]
615   fustes vos piecha en meson?
      — Oïl, sire, por l'acheson
      d'avoir .i. petit de relief,
      que ma fille avoit mal el chief.
      Ce fu avant ier. Or m'amenbre—

585 which) and was of the finest wool
from Stamford. I went for a stroll
with both surcoat and sewing kit
because indoors I felt a bit
under the weather, but my going
590 out of the house with all my sewing
brought nothing but ill luck to me
and will cost me my property,
because the surcoat has been lost!
I'm ready to give up the ghost!
595 Whatever will become of me?
What will I do? Where will I flee?
Can't someone set me on the track
to find the thief? He'll give it back,
or else tomorrow I'll give warning
600 that in all churches Sunday morning
I'll have him excommunicated!
What a great loss! I'm devastated!
Why must these things happen to me?
But, sir, know for a certainty
605 that, as I hope to live until
next Christmas, sticking in there still
must be my thimble and my needle.
No wonder I'm more than a little
distressed, for I must give it back,
610 and the young man is on my back
dunning me for his surcoat, whose
worth is, he claims, thirty whole sous!
What a misfortune's come my way!"
"Do tell me whether, Auberée,
615 you visited my house of late."
"Why, yes, sir, when I went to get
something to ease my daughter's pain—
you know she suffers from migraine—
two days ago. Now I remember

620   la dame trovai en sa chanbre,
       car iluecques pignoit son chief,
       & iluec vi de chief en chief
       estendue une coute pointe,
       einz de mes ieus ne vi si cointe.
625   Tant i musai qu'iluec dejouste
       m'en dormi, mon chief sor la coute,
       tant que la dame m'esveilla,
       qui molt volentiers m'aporta
       ce que demandé li avoie,
630   mes je me mis lors a la voie.
       Einsi celi jor m'en avint,
       mes ne soi, lasse, que devint
       le sorcot, fors tant que je souque
       que je le lessai sous la coute. »
635   Quant li sires ot ces noveles,
       molt li furent gentes & beles;
       mes s'il i trueve le deel,
       einz n'ot tel joie en son ael
       com il avra se il l'i trueve;
640   tart li est qu'il voie la prueve.
       A tant vers son ostel se tret,
       une huche euvre, si en tret
       le seurcot [qu'il i ot mucié,
       & quant il i trueve atachié
645   le deel] a tote l'aguille,
       qui li donast demie Puille
       n'eüst il pas joie greignor.
       « Par Dieu, dist il, li mien seignor,
       or sai ge bien certainement
650   que la vieille pas ne me ment,
       car j'ai trovee la costure! »
       Einsi fu liez de s'aventure
       le borgeis, & bel se deporte,
       [& dame Auberee raporte]
655   le sercot [ ] & si li livra.

620 how I found your wife in her chamber,
where she had gone to comb her hair,
and how I saw a quilt in there,
which had been laid across the bed.
I've never seen a finer spread!
625 I gazed at it so long, I felt
tired, and with my head on the quilt
I dozed until the lady brought
to me the remedy I sought
and woke me; then I went away.
630 That's how I spent that fateful day,
but I, poor wretch, can't even guess
what's become of the coat, unless . . .
but no . . . still, I have my suspicions
I left it there among the cushions."

635   The husband hears her narrative
with pleasure. What he wouldn't give
to find her thimble in the garment!
If it *is* there, instead of torment
he'd feel his greatest joy in life.
640 He cannot wait to clear his wife,
and turns and hurries straight back home,
opens a cupboard and takes from
a shelf the surcoat he hid in
there and finds both thimble and pin
645 still stuck in it. His jubilation
exceeds what an outright donation
of half Apulia would bring.
"By God, all of creation's king,"
he says, "I now know certainly
650 the woman didn't lie to me,
for I have found the old girl's sewing!"
Thus, all the happier for knowing,
the tradesman, lighthearted and gay,
brings back to Madam Auberée
655 the surcoat. So it's been restored,

Einsi la vieille delivra
le borgeis de son mal penser,
que puis ne li lut apenser
que il fu du seurcot delivres,
660 & la vieille ot .xl. livres.
Bien a son loier deservi
quant touz .iii. sont a gré servi!

24. LA DAMME QUI FIST .III. TORS ENTOR LE MOUSTIER

Qui fame voudroit decevoir,
je li faz bien apercevoir
qu'avant decevroit l'anemi.
Au deable a champ arami
5   cil qui fame veut justicier:
chascun jor la puet conbrisier,
& l'endemain rest toute saine
por resoufrir autretel paine,
mes quant fame a fol debonere
10   & ele a riens de lui afere,
ele li dist tant de bellues,
de truffes & de fanfelues
qu'ele li fet a force entendre
que le ciel sera demain cendre;
15   issi gaaingne la querele.
Jel di por une damoisele
qui ert fame a .i. escuier,
ne sai chartrain ou berruier.
La damoisele, c'est la voire,
20   estoit amie a .i. provoire;
molt l'amoit cil & cele lui
& si ne lessast por nului

and likewise the old woman's cured
the notions the man entertained.
Now that the surcoat's been explained,
his old suspicions have no grounds.
660   The woman gets her forty pounds,
and she more than deserves her fee
because she's satisfied all three.

24. THRICE AROUND
THE CHURCH
by Rutebeuf

If any man should try to con
a woman, let me pass this on:
The Fiend's more easy to outwit.
The man who'd make his wife submit
5   faces the Devil in the lists:
For all he beats her, she resists,
and the next day she's right as rain
and ready for as much again.
When it's an easygoing dunce
10   a woman's dealing with, at once
she'll rattle off such mysteries,
absurdities and trickeries,
that he'll believe, wonder of wonders,
tomorrow's sky will burn to cinders.
15   In this way she wins the debate.
        The one for whose sake I relate
this was the wife of an equerry
from around Chartres or from Berry.
Now this young lady, let me tell it
20   straight out, was sleeping with a prelate
whom she adored, as he did her.
For no one's sake would she defer

qu'ele ne feïst son voloir,
cui qu'en deüst le cuer doloir.

25   .i. jor au partir de l'eglise
ot li prestres fet son servise,
ses vestemenz lest a ploier,
& si vint la dame proier
que le soir en .i. boschet viengne:
30 parler li veut d'une besoingne
ou je cuit que pou conquerroie
se la besoingne vous nommoie.
La dame respondi au prestre:
« Sire, vez me ci toute preste,
35 c'or est il & poins & seson.
Ausi n'est pas cil en meson. »
Or avoit en cele aventure
sanz plus itant de mespresure,
que les mesons n'estoient pas
40 l'une lez l'autre a .iiii. pas,
ainz i avoit, dont molt lor poise,
le tiers d'une liue franchoise:
chascune ert en .i. espinois
com ces mesons de Gastinois,
45 mes li boschés que je vous nomme
estoit a cel vaillant preudomme
qu'a saint Ernoul doit la chandoile.

  Le soir qu'il ot ja mainte estoile
parant el ciel, si com moi samble,
50 li prestres de sa meson s'anble
& s'en vint el boschet seoir
por ce c'on nel puisse veoir,
mes a la dame mesavint
que sire Ernous ses mariz vint
55 toz moilliez & toz engelez
ne sai dont ou il ert alez;
por ce remanoir li covint.
De son provoire li sovint,

doing with him as she saw fit,
whoever was the worse for it.

25   Once after church, it came to pass
that when he'd finished saying Mass,
his vestments laid aside, the preacher
approached the lady to beseech her
to meet him that night in the bushes;
30   he's something to tell her that touches
on some matter, but if I named
it, I don't think much would be gained.
In answer to the priest, the lady
said, "Sir, I'm waiting and I'm ready.
35   My husband's gone, and for this reason
the time is ripe and so's the season."

        Now it so happened that their guilty
plans are not without difficulty
because the homes where they reside
40   are not exactly side by side,
but were (which pains them to the heart)
a third of a French league apart,
and both houses lay in a brake,
as those in Gâtinois are placed.
45   Those bushes, though, lay in a wood
belonging to that worthy who'd
Saint Arnolphe watching over him.

        That evening, when throughout the dim
sky stars were twinkling, I believe,
50   the prelate set about to leave
his house and went straight to the wood,
sat in the bushes so none could
see him there; but a mishap scuttled
the lady's plans, because her cuckold
55   returned, soaked and chilled to the bone,
from wherever it was he'd gone,
so she could not leave for their tryst.
Still, she did not forget her priest;

si se haste d'appareillier,
60   ne le vout pas fere veillier
(por ce n'i ot .v. mes ne .iiii.).
Aprés mengier petit esbatre
le lessa, bien le vous puis dire!
Sovent li a dit: « Biaus douz sire,
65   alez gesir, si ferez bien.
Veillier grieve sor toute rien
a homme quant il est lassez.
Vous avez chevauchié assez. »
L'aler gesir tant li reprouche,
70   par pou le morsel en la bouche
ne fet celui aler gesir,
tant a d'eschaper grant desir.
Li bons escuiers i ala,
qui sa damoisele apela,
75   por ce que molt la prise & aime.

« Sire, fet ele, il me faut traime
a une toile que je fais,
& si me faut encor grant fais
dont je ne me soi garde prendre,
80   & je n'en truis nes point a vendre.
Par Dieu, si ne sai que j'en face!
— Au deable soit tel filace,
fet li vallés, comme la vostre!
Foi que je doi saint Pol l'apostre,
85   je voudroie qu'el fust en Saine! »
A tant se couche, si se saine,
& cele se part de la chanbre.
Petit sejornerent si menbre
tant qu'el vint la ou cil l'atent.
90   Li uns les braz a l'autre tent;
iluec furent a grant deduit
tant qu'il fu pres de mienuit.

instead, she hastened through her chores
60 lest he have long to wait outdoors.
    There weren't four courses, much less five,
    nor after dinner did she give
    him time, believe me, to unwind,
    but kept on saying, "Dearest, kind
65 husband, you ought to go to bed.
    Staying up's the worst thing, it's said,
    when a man suffers from fatigue,
    and you've ridden many a league."
    Her "go to bed" she keeps repeating,
70 so that he's barely finished eating
    before she's packed him off to bed,
    she longs so to go out instead.
    So the good equerry, inspired
    by his wife's urgency, retired,
75 he loved her so.

                    "Husband," she said,
    "it happens that I'm out of thread
    for the weft of some cloth I'm weaving.
    It wasn't long before this evening
    that I first had a look and saw't.
80 I can't find any to be bought.
    I don't know what to do at all."
    "As I trust the apostle Paul,
    the devil's welcome to your thread
    for all your trouble," the man said.
85 "Into the Seine I'll see it tossed!"
    He went to bed then, and he crossed
    himself. As for his wife, she left
    the room and gave her feet no rest
    till she came to her waiting lover.
90 They threw their arms around each other,
    and there they lay in great delight
    until the middle of the night.

Du premier somme cil s'esveille,
mes molt li vient a grant merveille
95 quant il ne sent lez lui sa fame.
« Chanberiere, ou est vostre dame?
— Ele est la fors en cele vile,
chiés sa commere ou ele file. »
Quant cil oï que lafors iere,
100 voirs est qu'il fist molt laide chiere;
son sorcot vest, si se leva,
sa damoisele querre va;
chiés sa commere la demande,
ne trueve qui reson l'en rande,
105 qu'ele n'i avoit esté mie.
Ez vous celui en frenesie!
Par delez cels qu'el boschet furent
ala & vint; cil ne se murent,
& quant il fu outre passez,
110 « Sire, fet ele, or est assez.
Or covient il que je m'en aille.
— Vous orrez ja noise & bataille,
fet li prestres. Ice me tue
que vous serez ja trop batue.
115 — Onques de moi ne vous soviengne,
dant prestres; de vous vous coviengne, »
dist la damoisele en riant.
Que vous iroie controuvant?—
chascuns s'en vint a son repere.
120 Cil qui se jut ne se pot tere:
« Dame orde, vieus pute provee,
vous soiez or la mal trovee!
dist li escuiers. Dont venez?
Bien pert que por fol me tenez! »
125 Cele se tut, & cil s'esfroie:
« Voiz! Por le sanc & por le foie,
por la froissure & por la teste,
ele vient d'avoec nostre prestre! »

From first sleep chancing to awaken,
the lady's husband was much shaken
95 to find himself sleeping alone.
He asked, "Where has your mistress gone?"
"She's off in town," their servant said,
"gone to the neighbors' to spin thread."
When the man heard that she'd gone out,
100 his face took on an ugly pout,
he put his surcoat on, he rose,
and off in search of her he goes.
He asks for news of her next door,
but they can tell him nothing, for
105 she hadn't stopped by there of late.
By now the man is desperate.
He twice passed by the bushes where
they were. They didn't move a hair,
but after he had gone on by,
110 the lady said, "It's high time I
went home again. We've had enough."
The priest replied, "You'll have it rough.
He'll yell a lot, and I fear you
will get a dreadful beating, too."
115 "Don't worry for me in the least;
take care of *your*self, mister priest,"
said the young woman with a smile.
Both went back to their domicile.

What more need I tell you about it?
120 Her husband, back in bed now, shouted,
"Vile, filthy woman! Proven whore!
How do you dare darken my door?
You take me for some simpleton,
that's clear enough. Where have you been?"
125 She kept mum. He cried in a fever,
"Damn! By God's blood and by God's liver
and by God's guts and by God's head,
she's been with our priest!" (What he said,

(Issi dit voir, & si nel sot).

130 Cele se tut, si ne dist mot;
quant cil ot qu'el ne se desfent,
par .i. petit d'iror ne fent
qu'il cuide bien en aventure
avoir dit la verité pure,

135 mautalenz l'arguë & atise,
sa fame a par les treces prise
por le trenchier, son coutel tret . . .
« Sire, fet el, por Dieu, a tret!
Or covient il que je vous die.

140 Or orrez ja trop grant voisdie,
j'amaisse mieus estre en la fosse.
Voirs est que je sui de vous grosse,
si m'enseigna l'en a aler
entor le moustier sanz parler

145 .iii. tors dire .iii. patre nostres
en l'onor Dieu & ses apostres,
une fosse au talon feïsse
& par .iii. jors i revenisse:
s'au tiers jor ouvert le trovoie

150 c'estoit .i. filz qu'avoir devoie,
& s'il estoit clos, c'estoit fille.
Or ne revaut tout une bille,
dist la dame, quanques j'ai fet,
mes par saint Jaque, il ert refet,

155 se vos tuër m'en deviiez! »
A tant s'est cil desavoiez
de la voie ou avoiez iere,
si parla en autre maniere:
« Dame, dist il, je que savoie

160 du voiage ne de la voie?
Se je seüsse ceste chose
dont je a tort vous blasme & chose,
je sui cil qui mot n'en deïsse,
se je anuit de cest soir isse. »

though just a guess, was true enough,
130 but she kept calm and shut her mouth.)
When she won't give an explanation
he nearly bursts from aggravation,
for he imagines that he's struck
upon the truth by purest luck.
135 Spurred on by wrath that burns and presses,
he seizes his wife by her tresses
to cut them off, he draws his knife. . . .
"Dear God, have patience!" says his wife.
"It can't be helped now, I must tell
140 you of a most uncanny spell.
I'd sooner have been dead and buried.
The truth is that I learned I carried
your child, and I was told to go
around the church (though none must know)
145 three times and thrice say the Lord's Prayer
for God and his apostles, there
scrape out a hole using the back
of my foot, for three days go back,
and if the hole remained unfilled,
150 I'd bring a son into the world,
or a girl if I found it gone.
Now everything that I have done,"
the lady said, "was all for naught,
but even though you kill me for't,
155 by Saint James, I'll do it again!"
The equerry abandoned then
the course of action he'd begun
and spoke in quite another tone.
"Lady," he told her, "what could I
160 have known of where you'd gone and why?
Why, if this thing were known to me
for which I blamed you wrongfully,
I'd not have had a word to say,
so may I live to see the day."

165   A tant se turent, si font pes
        que cil n'en doit parler ja mes:
        de chose que sa fame face
        n'en orra noise ne manace.
                Rustebeuf dist en cest fablel:
170   quant fame a fol, s'a son avel.

25. LA DOLENTE QUI FU FOTUE
SUR LA TONBE

        Entrués que volentez me vient
        de fables dire & il me tient,
        dirai, en lieu de fable, voir.
                Uns hom, qui de petit d'avoir
5   ert en grant richece embatuz,
        si com ses termes ert venuz
        li prist mort en Flandres jadis.
        Molt fu & par fais & par dis
        sa fame de sa mort irie,
10   quar fame s'est tost atirie
        a plorer & a grant duel fere
        quant ele a .i. poi de contrere
        & tost ra grant duel oublïé.
        Quant la dame vit devïé
15   son seignor qui tant l'ot amee,
        sovent s'est chetive clamee,
        de grant dolor mener se paine,
        molt i emploie bien sa paine
        qu'ele en a le molle trové,
20   si a molt bien son cuer prové,
        ce samble a toz, vers son seignor.
        Ainz fame ne fist tel dolor,
        & quant ce vint a l'enterrer,
        dont oïssiez fame crïer

165　　　　　They said no more, and no more he'd
　　　　mention the subject, they agreed;
　　　　no matter what his wife may do,
　　　　he won't raise a hullabaloo.
　　　　A woman married to a dunce,
170　　so says Rutebeuf, gets what she wants.

25. THE MOURNER WHO GOT
FUCKED AT THE GRAVE SITE

　　　　Since I'm in the mood to narrate
　　　　fables, while it lasts I'll relate,
　　　　instead of fables, something true.
　　　　　　Long past, in Flanders, a man who,
5　　　　once poor, had gained prosperity
　　　　reached that time in his life when he
　　　　must meet his end. Death laid him low.
　　　　In word and deed his wife made show
　　　　of her great grief now he was dead,
10　　　for woman easily is led
　　　　to mourning and much lamentation
　　　　upon the slightest provocation
　　　　and quickly puts sorrow behind her.
　　　　When the man's widow called to mind her
15　　　adoring husband who'd passed on,
　　　　she cried that she is woebegone;
　　　　she strives to vent her great vexation
　　　　exemplifying desperation
　　　　and put her strength in the commotion,
20　　　such that she's proven her devotion
　　　　to the departed, all agree.
　　　　No wife could show more misery
　　　　and, when time came to bury him,
　　　　you could have heard the woman scream

25 & veïssiez molt grant duel fere
    & poins detordre & cheveus trere,
    & si s'escrie deseur tous:
    « Preudom, bons hom, ou irez vous?
    Or vous met l'en en cele fosse.
30 Sire, je remaing de vous grosse—
    qui garira l'enfant & moi?
    Mien vuel, morissiens nous andoi! »
    Quant li cors fu en terre mis,
    dont s'escria a molt hauz cris,
35 si se deschire & pleure & brait,
    a la terre cheoir se lait.
    Si parent la reconfortoient;
    a l'ostel mener le voloient,
    mes ele dist qu'ele n'iroit
40 ne jamés ne s'en partiroit
    de la fosse morte ne vive.
    Tant s'en escombat & estrive
    qu'il l'ont lessie par anui.
    Avoec li ne remaint nului,
45 seule remaint sanz compaingne.
            Ez vous .i. chevalier estraingne:
    lui & son escuier venoit,
    son chemin a l'atre tenoit,
    la dame voit iluec seoir,
50 qui a trestout le sien pooir
    destruit & escillie son cors
    por son seignor qui estoit mors.
    « Voiz tu, dist il a l'escuier,
    cele dame la escillier
55 son cors? N'a mie son cuer lié.
    Certes molt en ai grant pitié.
    — Pitié? Du deable vous tient
    quant il de li pitié vous vient!
    Je gagerai, se vous volez,
60 par si que de ci vous tornez,

25 and seen her display her despair
and wring her hands and tear her hair.
She cries out as loud as she can,
"Where are you going, good, kind man?
They've laid you in this hole and piled
30 earth on your body. I'm with child.
How shall we live, your babe and I?
I wish that both of us might die!"
        When the earth hid him from her eyes,
she uttered shrill and piercing cries
35 and tore her clothes, nor ceased to weep,
but let herself fall in a heap.
Her relatives made shift to calm
the widow and to lead her home,
but she replied that she would stay,
40 nor would she ever go away
or quit his grave, dead or alive.
They reason with her and they strive
until they leave her there, tired out,
and no one else remains about.

45   She stays alone by the grave site.
A stranger comes, an errant knight;
he and his squire together come
along the path toward the tomb.
He sees the lady sitting there,
50 who in the strength of her despair
batters her face and body hard
for him who's gone to his reward.
He says to his squire, "Do you see
that lady? How sad she must be
55 to beat her body in that fashion!
Indeed, she moves me to compassion."
"Compassion? Are you so naïve
that you're convinced to see her grieve?
If you are willing, I will wager
60 that while you hide I will engage her

que je ja a molt petit plet,
si dolente comme el se fet,
la foutrai, mes que vous traiez
en tel lieu que *vous* nous voiez.

65 — Qu'as tu dit, escommenïez?
Je cuit que pas crestïens n'iez,
ainz as el cors le vif deable
quant contrové as or tel fable!
— Est ce fable? G'i gageroie

70 vers vous, se gagier m'i osoie.
— Or i parra que tu feras;
ja par moi veüs n'i seras.
Repondre m'irai souz cel pin. »
Lors descent cil de son roncin

75 a terre & fet chiere morne,
vers la dame sa voie torne,
si dist en bas, non pas en haut:
« Chiere suer, dist il, Dieus vous saut!
— Saut? fet ele, mes doinst la mort,

80 quar je sui vive a molt grant tort
quant me sire est mors, mes maris,
par qui mes cuers est si maris,
qui me geta de povreté
& me tenoit en grant chierté,

85 qui m'amoit mieus que lui meïsme!
— Suer, je sui plus dolenz la disme!
— Comment, plus? — Jel te dirai, suer:
je avoie mis tout mon cuer
a une fame que j'avoie,

90 & assez plus de moi l'amoie,
qui ert bele & cortoise & sage.
Ocise l'ai par mon outrage.
— Ocise l'as? comment, pechiere?
— En foutant, voir, ma dame chiere,

95 ne je ne voudroie plus vivre.
— Gentiz hom, vien ça, si delivre

and have no trouble, I believe,
for all that she pretends to grieve,
in getting her to fuck with me,
but you must hide where you can see."
65 "What have you said, you unbeliever?
No Christian, you—the Arch Deceiver
lives in your body, I maintain,
that you'd think up so wild a claim!"
"Some wild claim? Who am I to bet
70 against you? But I'll show you yet!"
"Well, we shall see how you make out.
I won't see much, I have no doubt.
Beneath that pine I'll go and hide."
        The squire dismounts then from astride
75 his horse, assumes a sad expression
and heads in the lady's direction,
and, speaking softly, he addressed her
thus: "May God preserve you, dear sister."
"Preserve me?" she says. "May He give
80 me death! I've no desire to live.
My husband's dead, my noble sire,
and my heart's ready to expire!
He raised me out of poverty
and treated me so tenderly
85 and loved me like himself. No . . . better!"
"Lady, my pain is ten times greater!"
"Greater? How so?" "I'll tell you all.
This heart of mine was held in thrall
by a most fair and noble woman
90 of gentle breeding and acumen,
whom more than my own self I cherished.
By my unthinking act, she perished."
"Unlucky man! You killed her? How?"
"By fucking, dear, sweet lady. Now
95 life has become hateful to me."
"You noble man, come here and free

cest siecle de moi, si me tue!
Or t'en esforce & esvertue,
& si me fai, se tu pués, pis
100 que tu ta fame ne feïs!
Tu dis qu'ele fu morte au foutre. »
Lors s'est lessie cheoir outre
ausi com s'ele fust pasmee.
Cil a la robe sus levee,
105 se li embat el con le vit
si que ses sires bien le vit,
qui se pasmoit de ris en aise.
« Me cuides tu donc tüer d'aise,
fet la dame, qui si me fous?
110 Ainz t'i deromperoies tous
que tu m'eüsses ainsi morte! »
        Ainsi la dame se conforte
qui ore demenoit tel dol.
Por ce je tieng celui a fol
115 qui trop met en fame sa cure.
Fame est de trop foible nature:
de noient rit, de noient pleure,
fame aime & het en trop poi d'eure,
tost est ses talenz remüez.
120 Qui fame croit, si est dervez.

26. LES .III. MESCHINES

Or escoutez une aventure
& puis si en dites droiture!
        A Brilli ot ja .iii. meschines.
Ne sai comme eles erent fines,
5 ne sai s'erent sages ou foles,
mes molt hantoient ces caroles
& volentiers se cointissoient

the world of me! Kill me, release
me too, I beg, if you can! Please,
with all your strength and all your force
100   do me as you did her, or worse!
You say that fucking did her in?"
          Then she fell backward under him
as if she had lost consciousness,
and the squire hoisted up her dress
105   and shoved his prick into her slit
so his liege could see all of it,
who nearly swooned away from giggling.
"You think you can kill me by tickling?"
the lady asked. "You call this fucking?
110   You'll sooner wear yourself out bucking
than finish me off at this rate!"
          Thus she, who was disconsolate,
found consolation in the end.
That man's a moron, I contend,
115   who puts much faith in woman's nature,
for woman is a weak-willed creature:
She laughs or weeps for no good reason,
her moods change quicker than the season,
she loves, she hates, she's glad, she's sad . . .
120   Who trusts in woman must be mad!

26. THE THREE GIRLS

Now here's a tale to listen to
and then give us your point of view.
          There were three girls who dwelt in Brilly.
I couldn't say if they were silly
5   or wise, nor vouch that they behaved
themselves, but most of all they craved
to go dancing, and they applied

a lor pooir & s'acesmoient.
L'une ert Brunatin apelee,
10   l'autre Agace, l'autre Sueree.
.I. jor tindrent lor parlement
d'atruper lor acesmement
por une grant place aramie
qui fu criee & aatie
15   de Boudet & de Jovincel
en ces chans vers Buesemoncel.
« Certes, dist Sueree a Agace,
tel poudre sai, qui en sa face
l'auroit mise .i. poi destenpree
20   que tantost seroit coloree.
Si lo que nous querre l'alon,
quar se le sanc ert el talon,
sel feroit ele amont venir
& le vis vermeil devenir,
25   si l'a a Roëm .i. mercier,
mes a tant poons bien marchier,
qu'il n'a el monde si tres fine. »
Dist Brunatin, l'autre meschine:
« & j'ai .iii. sous a vous prester.
30   Si vous alez tost aprester
& metez erant a la voie. »
Suerete a prise la monoie,
si s'est vers Roëm esmeüe;
a tout la poudre est revenue
35   a ses .ii. conpaingnes qu'el trueve.
         Si commencierent la bone oevre
le jor que la place dut estre
a la luor de la fenestre
d'une chanbrete ou els s'assistrent;
40   dedenz .i. test la poudre mistrent.
Dist Sueree: « Dieus nous i vaille,
mes sachiez il covient sanz faille
que o pissat soit destempree.

much effort getting prettified.
The name that each was known by was
10   Brunatin, Suerée, and Agace.
         One day they were talking about
how they would get themselves decked out
for a great tournament at arms
set to take place among the farms
15   in the region of Buesemoncel
between Boudet and Jovincel.
"Indeed, I know a powder," said
Suerée to Agace, "which, if wet
a bit and you applied a touch
20   on your face, gives a lovely blush.
Let's go and get some, I entreat,
for, though your blood were in your feet,
it would soon draw it to your head
and make your cheeks a rosy red.
25   A dealer has some in Rouen,
but we can walk that far. There's none
that's better in the whole world wide."
The third girl, Brunatin, replied,
"I've three shillings to lend to you.
30   Go and get yourself ready, do,
and quickly set off on your way."
Taking the coins with her, Suerée
left down the road to Rouen and
came back again, powder in hand,
35   to her friends, after her long journey.
         Early on the day of the tourney,
near a window for light, they set
about preparing their toilette
in a small room. I need to state
40   they put the powder in a plate.
Suerée said, "God aid us in this,
but be aware we'll need some piss
to mix it with; that's how you wet it.

Je ne sui mie reposee,
45   si me dueil del errer encore,
si me covient reposer ore,
mes fetes & j'esgarderai. »
Dist Agace: « & je pisserai
ou test & ferai mon orine. »
50   Dist Brunatin: « Bele cousine,
& je tendrai bien atiriez
le test que que vous pisserez. »
Lors li tint desouz & i garde
& i prist au plus que pot garde:
55   por mieus esgarder el se plie,
mes Agace ne pissa mie.
Se l'en la deüst escorcier,
n'i pissast el sanz esforcier,
mes ele i a mise sa force.
60   En ce que Agace s'esforce
& .i. tres grant pet li eschape;
por neent deüst taillier chape:
pet fist du cul, & poudre vole
« Qu'est ce deable, pute fole?
65   dist Brunatin. Que as tu fet?
Certes vez ci vilain mesfet!
Toute as nostre poudre souflee.
Ele m'est dusqu'es ieus volee,
si m'a enfumee trestoute.
70   Que passïon & male goute
te puisse ore en tes ieus descendre!
Ça mes .iii. sous! Tu les dois rendre;
jes aurai, par sainte Marie! »
Dist Agace: « Je nel di mie
75   que je les vous rende par droit,
que ne tenistes pas a droit
le test que tenir deviiez
endroit le con, & l'aviiez
endroit le cul, si mesfeïstes

As for me, I still haven't rested
45   and all that walking's left me sore.
I'll need to rest a bit while you're
getting it ready. I'll look on."
Agace said, "I will be the one
to piss in the plate and make water."
50   Brunatin said, "Well, then I ought to
steadily hold and aim the plate,
dear cousin, while you urinate."
Then she held it beneath her there
and took every possible care
55   and squatted down so she could see,
but Agace didn't take a pee,
though you might torture her or press her.
To pee she had to apply pressure.
She went at it with might and main,
60   forcing herself, till from the strain
she let out an enormous fart;
for all her care and skill and art,
her ass broke wind, the powder scattered.
        "The devil! What have you done, drat it,
65   you slut?" said Brunatin. "Why this is
without a doubt a filthy business!
You've blown our powder clean away.
My eyes are blinded by the spray,
I'm coated with it and smoked out.
70   May seizures, pestilence, and gout
inflame your eyes, and may you rack!
I spent three shillings. Give them back.
By Saint Marie, I'll be repaid!"
"In my opinion," Agace said,
75   "you've no right to ask them of me.
You didn't hold it properly.
You should have held the plate in front,
not of my ass, but of my cunt,
so clearly it was you who sinned

80 que la poudre nous en tolistes,
& quant ele est par vous cheüe
je di qu'ele est vostre perdue,
si covient que vous la rendez. »
Dist Brunatin: « Or entendez!
85 Vostre cul est si pres du con
que il n'est sages ne bricon
qui i veïst a paine marche—
ce sanble le cop d'une hache
qui a .i. roont trou s'aboute!—
90 & vez ci ma reson trestoute:
comment que je le test tenisse,
jamés la poudre ne perdisse
se ne fust vostre souflerie,
& quant vous l'avez hors jalie,
95 je di que vous la devez rendre.
       — S'en oserai bien droit atendre
& en romanz & en latin.
       — Bien puet estre, dist Brunatin,
mes quant vous ice saviiez
100 que vous au pissier poirriiez,
que doit que vous ne le deïstes?
Si fussiez du domage quites
s'eüssiez dit vostre maniere.
J'eüsse tret le test arriere,
105 mes vous nous avez deceües
& toutes nos colors perdues
& vilainement hors souflees,
s'en devez rendre les denrees.
       — Cest contens n'est ne bon ne gent.
110 Metons nous en sus bone gent. »
Dist Brunatin: « Jel lo bien, certes,
& qui devra *rendra* les pertes. »
Ainsi ont la chose atiree.
       « Damoiseles, ce dist Sueree,
115 que Dieus vous doint male semaine!

80　　and blew our powder to the wind,
　　　and since it's your fault it was lost,
　　　I say you ought to bear the cost.
　　　It's rightfully yours to replace."
　　　Said Brunatin, "Hear what she says?
85　　Considering your asshole lies
　　　right by your cunt, there's no one, wise
　　　or dumb, who can see a division.
　　　An ax must have made the incision
　　　to open up so round a hole,
90　　I do declare!, and that's my whole
　　　defense in this. No matter how the
　　　plate was held, never would the powder
　　　have been lost if you hadn't farted.
　　　Since by your doing it departed,
95　　I say that it's yours to replace."
　　　"I'll go to court and make my case
　　　and have judgment in French and Latin!"
　　　"Perhaps, but still the fact is that in
　　　full knowledge that it comes to pass
100　 that when you piss you may pass gas,
　　　you volunteered. You should have let
　　　us know. You'd be free of the debt
　　　if you had said you pissed that way,
　　　for I'd have pulled the plate away,
105　 but since you didn't tell us first,
　　　now our cosmetics are dispersed
　　　disgustingly, so pay the price
　　　of replacing the merchandise."
　　　"This bickering is a disgrace.
110　 Let worthy people try our case."
　　　Said Brunatin, "That's what I say,
　　　and after, she who must will pay."
　　　　　So thereupon the matter rested,
　　　but Suerée in her turn protested:
115　 "Girls, God give you an evil week!

La quele me rendra ma paine
des colors que j'ai aportees
que vous avez au cul souflees?
    — Qui perdra rende les domages,
120 font eles, & prenez bons gages
de chascune, c'est bien reson,
tant que cest afere apelon. »
Si firent comme oï avez.

        Seignors & dames, qui savez
125 de droit, jugiez sanz delaier:
qui doit ceste poudre paier,
cele qui tint le test en l'uevre
ou cele qui soufla deseure?
Molt est de gent, qoi que nus die,
130 qui bien ne pisseroient mie
en nul leu que il ne peïssent
& puis aprés ice si pissent,
si ra grant force en test tenir
endroit le con sanz avenir
135 endroit le cul, se n'est pas fable.
Or en dites droit couvenable.

27. LA DAMOISELE QUI
VOST VOLER

D'une damoisele vos voil
conter c'onques ne virent oil
si bele com elë estoit
& de biauté grant los avoit.
5   De riches clers, de chevaliers
& de borjois & d'escuiers
estoit totes eures requise,
mes ne voloit en nule guise
la prïere a nul escouter.

Who'll pay me back, who went to seek
the powder, for the work I've gone
through and which now your ass has blown?"
"For that you'll be indemnified
120 by her who loses. Till it's tried
we each will give you surety,"
they say. "That's fair, and we agree."
          They did as I've explained to you.
You noble lords and ladies, who
125 are versed in justice, speak your mind
and quickly say for whom you find:
the one who held the plate? the one
who blew it all to Kingdom Come?
Many folk, you cannot deny,
130 can't piss, however hard they try,
wherever they may be, but break
wind first and after take a leak,
nor is it easy to hold near
a cunt whatever and keep clear
135 of the behind, and that's no lie.
I bid you well and truly try.

21. THE GIRL WHO WANTED TO FLY

I'll tell you by way of example
about the most beautiful damsel
ever beheld by human eyes.
Her beauty was praised to the skies,
5 and wealthy clerics, townsmen, and
knights and their squires sued for her hand
day in, day out, insistently,
but to none of their prayers would she
give any heed in any way.

.I. jor dit qu'el voudroit voler.
Sachiez que plusors genz l'oïrent;
a mervelles s'en esbaïrent.
Eles li firent damoisel
de cire & de pennes d'oisel,

as braz & as costez li mistrent
&, ce sachiez, molt s'entremistrent
de li cointement acesmer,
mes ainz por ce ne pot voler.
.I. clers li dist: « Ce ne valt rien,

damoisele, ce sachiez bien.
Il vos convendra atorner
autrement se volez voler,
que bec vos convendra avoir
& queue, ce sachiez de voir,

que nus oisaus sanz ce ne vole.
— Je gree bien ceste parole,
fait la pucele, & je l'otroi.
Qui *fera* ce, dites lou moi?
— Damoisele, fait il, je sui.

Se vos commandez, encor hui
vos cuit je fere plus bel bec
& miaus fait *que* n'a nul *espec*;
plus bele qeue vos ferai
que poons, que ja n'i faudrai. »

A tant en une chanbre entrerent
& l'uis sor aus molt bien fermerent.
Li clers en .i. lit la cocha,
plus de .xxx. fois la besa;
ele demande que c'estoit.

Il dit que lou bec li faisoit.
« Fet lo l'en donc en tel maniere?
— Oïl. Tornez vos par derriere
que la coë i enterai.
— Danz clers, fet ele, je ferai

tot ce que vos m'ensaigneroiz,

10   She'd like to fly, she says one day.
Word of her wish soon spread around; it
left those who heard of it astounded.
For her sake young men put together
bird wings made out of wax and feathers,
15 attached them to her arms and tied
them to her ribs; yet though they tried
to deck her out as best they knew,
in spite of this, she never flew.
One student told her, "Truth to tell,
20 all this is useless, mademoiselle.
You'll need a very different getup
to put on if you mean to get up
off of the ground: a beak and tail.
Nothing else, truly, will avail,
25 for without these not any bird
can fly." "I'll take you at your word,"
the damsel said, "and I agree,
but who will make these things for me?"
"Mademoiselle, I am the one.
30 If you so wish, it will be done.
I mean today to make a better
beak for you than any woodpecker
and I'll make you a finer tail
than any peacock, without fail."
35   At that they went off to a room
and shut the door tight as a tomb.
Upon a bed the student placed her
and more than thirty times embraced her.
He said, when she asked what this was
40 for, he's making that beak of hers.
"So that's how beaks are made, you say?"
"Yeah. Turn around the other way
and I will graft the tail on you."
"Student," she says, "I'll gladly do
45 whatever you tell me I need

mes gardez que vos n'i failloiz. »
Cele se torne a estupons;
il li enbat jusqu'as coillons
lo vit el con sanz contredit,
50 & la damoisele li dit
& demande comment ce vet.
Il dit que sa cöe li fet.
« Danz clers, fet el, or esploitiez!
Botez parfont, si l'atachiez
55 si fermement qu'ele ne chiee!
Je seré si aparrelliee
quant je de vos departirai,
bien cuit que je voler porrai. »
& li clers bote adés en l'angle,
60 cui il n'est gaires de sa jangle.
Quant ot de li fet son talant,
el lit s'asist demaintenant
& la damoisele lez lui:
« Danz clers, fet ele, don n'iert hui
65 ceste qeue tote parfete?
Fetes la tost, que molt me hete. »
La boche li bese & la face,
& si li prie que il face
la qeue tost, se Dieus l'i salt:
70 « Do bec, fet ele, ne me chalt.
Ce puet assez metre en respit. »
De la queue li prie & dit
que il la face sanz demore.
Li clers dist: « Se Dieus me secore,
75 el n'iert fete devant .i. an.
— Dan clers, fet el, par saint Jehan,
ja de moi ne departiroiz
devant que vos fete l'avroiz! »
Il remest o la damoisele
80 car la parole li fu bele,
& de la queue s'entremist,

to do, but make sure you succeed."
The damsel turns around and crawls
on all fours. Right up to the balls
he rams his peter in her cunt,
50   while she wants to be told up front
exactly how his work advances.
"I'm making you a tail," he answers.
"Student," she says, "give it your all!
Stick it in deep, so it won't fall
55   off but hold firmly. I believe
that when it's time for you to leave,
I'll be so well outfitted I
will surely be able to fly."
       The student never ceased to poke,
60   indifferent to what she spoke,
and when he'd finished what he wanted
to do with her and had dismounted,
he sat beside her on the bed.
"Then it won't be today," she said,
65   "that that tail of mine is completed?
Get back to work—I really need it!"
She kisses his mouth and his face,
begs and entreats him to make haste
and finish her tail, in God's name.
70   "As for the beak, it's all the same
with me. We can leave that for later."
Still, she beseeches he not wait; her
tail must, she says, be done right now.
The student says, "By God, I vow
75   it takes a year to graft one on."
"Student, I promise, by Saint John,
I won't let you out of my sight
until that tail is put on right!"
       Since what she told him gave him joy,
80   he stayed on in the girl's employ
and diligently worked her tail,

chascun jor .i. petit en fist;
tant l'enpaint & tant i hurta
que la damoisele engroissa,

85 & dit: « Clers, vos m'avez gabee!
La queue m'est el cors germee;
je quit que je soie engroissiee.
Malement m'avez engigniee!
Je ne puis seulement aler—

90 comment porroie je voler?
Empiriee sui durement.
Bien savez engignier la gent! »
Li clers li dist: « Par saint Amant,
vos m'alez a grant tort blasmant,

95 que, par la foi que je vos doi,
n'iestes pas descreüe en moi
se grosse iestes—ce est nature,
mes ce estoit grant desmesure
que par l'air volïez voler;

100 par trop en faites a blasmer.
De poi estes apesantie. »
        En tel maniere l'a servie
com vos pöez ici oïr,
& ce l'en doit bien avenir—

105 qui otrage quiert, il li vient
Por ce de ceste me sovient
qui trop estoit desmesuree.
Issi li fu la qeue entee.

28. LA VIELLE TRUANDE

Des fables fait on les fabliaus,
et des notes les sons noviaus,
et des materes les canchons,
et des dras cauces & cauchons.

continuing to bang and flail
away a little bit each day
till she was in a family way.

85 "Student," she says, "I've been deceived!
Thanks to you, I think I've conceived:
That tail of yours has germinated!
I've been cruelly manipulated!
When I can scarcely walk upright,

90 what chance have I of taking flight?
I've seen my lot steadily worsen.
You certainly can fool a person!"
The student said, "By Saint Amant,
why turn on me? What do you want?

95 You're not diminished in your stature
when big with child—that's only nature.
You take my word for this, however,
that it was prideful beyond measure
to think you could fly through the air,

100 more shame to you! How did you dare?
Now you will be a bit less flighty."

As you can hear, it served her right. He
gave her a lesson for her cheek,
which she deserved. The more you seek

105 to rise, the harder you will fall,
and so I think of her whose gall
and hubris were on such a scale
she ended up stuck with a tail.

28. THE OLD BEGGAR WOMAN

Fabliaux are made of idle chatter,
and epic poems of weighty matter,
the latest songs of notes and pitches,
and out of cloth slippers and britches.

Pour çou vos voel dire & conter
       [ ] un fabelet *pour deliter*
       d'une fable que jou oï
       dont au dire molt m'esjoï.
       Or le vos ai torné en rime
10   tout sans batel & tot sans lime,
       si ne le vos voel plus celer.
              Dire vos voel d'un baceler
       qui cevauchoit parmi .i. bois;
       la on cuelloit sovent du bois.
15   Li bacelers dont je vos conte,
       s'il fust fius de roi u de conte,
       s'estoit il biaus a desmesure;
       çou n'estoit ne rois ne mesure
       car trop ert biaus outreement,
20   se li fabliaus ne vos en ment—
       biaus estoit & cortois & sages.
       A .i. chevalier ert messages
       qui bien estoit du païs nes,
       & cius fu si endoctrinés
25   & si cortois & si sachans
       & de paroles si trenchans
       que nus n'i peüst entremaure;
       proec qu'il vausist sa lange esmaure,
       il ne doutast .ii. avocas,
30   mais par tans ert & mus & quas
       & si mas & si abaubis
       qu'il ne sara ne blanc ne bis.
       Il cevauchoit tout une lande
       et troeve une vielle truande
35   que s'asorelle a un buisson.
       Ce fu un peu devant *meison.*
       Iloeques recousoit ses piaus,
       son mantelet & ses drapiaus,
       qui n'estoient mie tot noef,
40   ains ont veü maint an renoef:

5   That's why I now wish to recite
    a fabliau for pure delight
    based on a fable I heard tell
    which, I assure you, pleased me well.
    Shaped for you with my rhymester's palette,
10   not with a chisel or a mallet,
    I'll no longer keep it from you.
          It tells about a young man who
    rode through a forest where folk would
    often go to collect firewood.
15   The young hero of my account,
    were he son to a king or count,
    would have been reckoned very handsome
    beyond his noble rank and then some,
    for his good looks exceeded those
20   of men (if you trust fabliaux),
    he was so fair, well-bred, and bright.
    Messenger for a wellborn knight
    from those parts was his situation,
    and, thanks to his fine education,
25   the youth was so courtly and smart
    and skilled in rhetorical art
    that nobody could match his wit.
    His tongue, when he would sharpen it,
    could turn two lawyers to his side! . . .
30   But soon his glib tongue will be tied
    and he, flustered, taken aback,
    and stymied, won't know white from black.
          Across a clearing he rode on
    until he came on an old crone
35   sunning herself beside a thicket.
    The grain was ripening; they'd pick it
    shortly. The old woman was bending
    over her clothes, for she was mending
    what she wore, they the worse for wear,
40   for they'd seen many a New Year.

du premier drap i ot le mains,
ele ne pot tenir as mains
escröele ne drap ne piece
que tot n'i akeuse & assiece—
45 en .vc. des n'ot tant de poins
com ele i a de dras porpoins!
La s'asorelle & esgohele;
son pochon ot & s'escüele,
son sakelet & ses mindokes,
50 .i. ongement ot fait de dokes,
de *vif* argent & de viés oint
dont son visage & ses mains oint
pour le solel qu'il ne l'escaude,
mais ce n'estoit mie bele Aude,
55 ains estoit laide & contrefaite,
mais encor s'adoube & afaite
por çou k'encore veut siecler.
　　　Quant ele vit le baceler
venir, si tres bel a devise,
60 si fu de lui si tost esprise
k'ainc Blancheflor n'Iseus la blonde
ne nule feme de cest monde
n'ama onques si tost nului
com ele fist tantost celui.
65 « Dieus vos saut, dist il, boine fame!
Veïstes vos [ ] ci passer ame?
— Naie, certes, mes enfes dous.
Que pleüst Diu k'entre nos dous
jeüssons ore bras a bras—
70 si fesissiemes nos soulas!
— Soulas! fait il. Por les sains Diu,
porriés vos donc soffrir men giu?
— Certes, fait ele, jou ne sai,
mais or en soions a l'assai.
75 Se jou *nel* puis soffrir, si perge!
— Li maufés, fait il, vos aerge

Of the cloth of which they'd been made
little was left, it was so frayed,
and all she could hold in her hands
was resewn patches, shreds, and bands.
45   Five hundred thimbles have seen less
needlework than was in her dress!
Enjoying the sun with her riches
near her—a cup and plate (her dishes),
her little satchel, and some notions—
50   she sat and smeared herself with lotions
of old lard, quicksilver, and plants
over her face and on her hands
because the sun shone bright and hot,
but lovely Alda she was not,
55   and though repulsive and ill-favored,
attached to worldly things, she labored
and fretted over her toilette.
          The youth approached, and when they met,
his beauty set her heart on fire
60   and she was seized with a desire
far greater than the blond Yseult
or Blancheflor had ever felt,
nor has woman so suddenly
felt passion for a man as she.
65   "God keep you, good woman," he asked,
"have you seen anyone ride past?"
"No, pretty child," in reply
she said. "Please God that you and I
were lying in each other's arms
70   and had our pleasure of your charms!"
"My charms! By all God's saints above,
have you the strength for making love
with me?" "I don't know," she replies,
"but we can give it a few tries,
75   and mine be the loss if I can't, sir."
"The devil take you," is his answer,

ancois que jou por tel ju faire!
De vos soulas n'ai jou que faire!
— Non, fait ele, me douce vite,
80 je sui plus *sade* & plus *eslite*
que jou ne perce par dehors!
Si ai bien savereus le cors
et deduisant ma douce geule,
et je sui ci trestoute seule,
85 si avomes ci molt biau liu.
Descendés, dous amis, por Diu,
si me baisiés & acolés
& faites plus, se vous volés!
— Baisier, fait il, vielle pusnaise!
90 Volés vos donc que jou vos baise?
Li diable i soient tout! »
Quant cele le voit si estout
k'ele n'i puet merci trover
por prometre ne por doner,
95 lors dist c'aprés lui s'en ira,
ja cele part ne tournera.
     Prist s'escüele & sen pochon,
sen sakelet & son baston,
son drapel prent & si s'en torne;
100 de courre aprés celui s'atorne.
Tant le porsiut & tant le cache,
tant a porsivie sa trace,
k'ele le consiut & ataint
la u cius son ceval restraint
105 qui passer devoit .i. courant,
et la vielle vient acourant
qui d'amors estoit marvoïe.
« Tot si, fait ele, n'irés mie,
par le mort Diu! N'i passerés
110 s'outre l'iaue ne me portés.
— Li maufés, fait il, vos i port,
vielle pusnaise, & vos raport,

"before I ever have a share
in your delights, so much I care!"
"Not so," she says, "sweet, well-hung stud.
80   I have more charms and hotter blood
and allurements than meet the eye!
My body's made for pleasure, I
have full lips, sweet and savory,
and what better place could there be
85   than here, since I am all alone?
For God's sake, lover boy, get down
and cover me with hugs and kisses
and do whatever your heart wishes!"
"Kiss you," he says, "you aged roach?
90   You really want us two to smooch?
I wish your kisses all to hell!"
        He won't relent, and she can tell
she's no way to make him give in
to her desires, and says to him
95   that she will follow where he goes
and never leave him in repose.
She grabs her plate and drinking cup,
her stick, her satchel, and gets up,
gathers her cloak, and sets her course,
100   scampering on behind his horse.
She's so persistent in the chase,
she overtakes him at a place,
by closely following his track,
where he is holding his horse back
105   beside a river they must ford.
The old woman comes running toward
the youth, out of her mind with love.
"Wait up! What are you thinking of?"
she cries. "God's death! You will not cross
110   unless you carry me across!"
"The devil," he says, "carry you
across, old roach, and back here, too!

que ja ne vous i porterai!
— Fius, fait ele, jou te portai
115 ens en mes flans .ix. mois entiers,
si te nouri molt volentiers.
Tu es mes fius! Por Diu merci,
ne me lai[sse] pas seule ichi!
— Vos fius! fait il. Vielle brehaigne,
120 li passïons ançois vos pregne!
Que ja me mere soit si faite,
si clope ne si contrefaite,
car me mere est haute borgoise!
— Fius, fait ele, com il me poise
125 que jou vos voi si desvoié*s*!
Vo mere sui, bien le saciés;
mes fius estes tot entresait,
maugrés que tos li mons en ait!
— Vois, fait il, por le geule Diu,
130 sui bien honis! A ci boin giu
quant ceste laide vielle *torche*
se fait me mere tot a force!
Pres va que jou ne l'escervele! »
Dont se raert cius a sa sele,
135 a çou qu'il cuida monter sus;
et la vielle le rabat jus,
et si l'emporte & sace & tire.
       A çou qu'il sont en tel martire
et qu'ele le tenoit si court,
140 .i. haus hom repairoit de court
a grant conpaignie de gent,
si vint par la isnelement,
si s'enbati sor la mellee:
« A il maaille bestornee,
145 biaus amis? fait li castelains.
Ne soiés pas faus ne vilains—
paiiés la feme son argent
por k'ele a fait vostre talent.

I won't give you a ride, for one!"
"I bore you in my womb, my son,
115 for nine whole months, and let you rest
your head and suckle on my breast.
You're my own son! For God, I pray
do not abandon me this way!"
"Your son!" he cries. "Sterile old maid,
120 God's torments rain down on your head!
How could my mother be like this,
so misshapen and hideous?
My mother's a fine city lady."
"My son," she says, "your mind's unsteady.
125 What suffering must I endure!
I am your mother, that's for sure.
I say you're my son, and stand by it
though everyone on earth deny it!"
"Ugh!" he exclaims. "By the Lord's face,
130 the joke's on me! What a disgrace
when this old, ugly, ragged slut
claims I'm her son and God knows what!
I'd beat her brains in with brute force!"
He goes to get back on his horse,
135 but he's not finished mounting when
the old crone pulls him down again,
and drags and yanks and won't give way.
While they were locked in their mêlée
and she hung on as leeches do,
140 a noble and his retinue
rode by, returning from the court.
On seeing them, he pulled up short
and hurried to break up the fight.
"What is it, friend?" inquired the knight.
145 "Is there some small pittance you'd keep
back from the woman? Don't be cheap,
but pay her her fee in full measure
since she's seen fit to do your pleasure."

— Or resui, fait il, bien venus!
150 Mius ameroie estre pendus
k'eüsse fait tel vilonie! »
Et li truande haut s'escrie:
« Sire, por Diu, faites me droit
de mon enfant, qui ci endroit
155 me veut laissier ci a cest port!
Dites li, sire, qu'il m'en port
par mi cele eve outre cel tai.
C'est mes enfes! Jou le portai!
— Ha! fait li sires, dous amis,
160 qui vos a en si fait sens mis
que vos laissiés ci vostre mere?
Car l'en portés outre, biau frere! »
— Sire, fait il, vos avés tort,
qui me metés seure la mort,
165 que si me laist Dius repairier
a mon ostel sans encombrier
que jou ne soie desmembrés,
ars u pendus u traïnés,
que jou onques mais ne le vi
170 ne ne parlai encore a li,
ne ne sai qu'ele me demande!
Çou est une vielle truande,
ne jou ne le vi onques mais.
Sire, por Diu, *laissiés m'en* pais. »
175 Fait li sires: « Par saint Vincent,
[se] savoie *or* certainement
que la truande me mentist
& que ne vos apartenist,
il le vos convenroit ja foutre.
180 Jou duc ore avoir dit tot outre. »
Quant la truande ot le haut home:
« Sire, par saint Piere de Rome,
il ne m'apartient ne jou lui,
n'onques mais jor ne le connui

He says, "I see she's cooked my goose!
150 I'd sooner meet the hangman's noose
than ever to have stooped so low!"
And the old tramp begins to crow,
"I cry you justice, noble lord,
against my child, who at this ford,
155 by God, seeks to abandon me!
Sire, pray you tell him speedily
to bear me now across the water.
I bore him in my womb. He ought to!"
"Ha!" says the nobleman. "Dear friend,
160 what's in your head that you intend
to abandon your aged mother?
I bid you give her passage, brother."
"You wrong me, sire, by what you've said
and make me wish that I were dead.
165 By God, as I hope to arrive
back home in safety and alive,
may I be torn apart or slaughtered
or burnt or hanged or drawn and quartered
if ever I've laid eyes on her
170 till now or spoken to her, sir,
or know just what she wants of me!
A raggedy old tramp is she,
and I've never seen her before.
My lord, leave me be, I implore!"
175 "By Saint Vincent, I swear," says he,
"if I knew for a certainty
the beggar's statement was untrue
and that she's no mother to you . . .
You'd better fuck her. That would prove
180 it. In a word, I now so move."
     The tramp cries as soon as she's heard,
"By Saint Peter of Rome, my lord,
we are related in no way!
I only met the man today,

185   fors hui cest jor, qu'il me jura
       sor sains que il m'espousera!
       — Ahi! fait il, vielle sorciere!
       Li passïons ainçois vos fiere! »
       Fait li sires: « Or n'i a tour.
190   Foi que jou doi saint Sauveour,
       puis qu'ele ne vos apartient,
       tantost foutre le vos convient. »
       Adonc ot li vallés grant ire,
       ne sot que faire ne que dire.
195   « Sire, fait il, por Diu merci,
       vos m'averiés en fin honi,
       & grant desloiauté feroie,
       sire, se ma mere foutoie. »
       Li sires l'ot, si s'en a ris;
200   fait il: « Foi que doi saint Denis,
       ainc mais ne vi si faites gens!
       Vallés, dis tu voir u tu mens?
       — Sire, fait il, çou est ma mere.
       — Or n'i a tour c'un seul, biau frere.
205   Outre l'iaue le porterés
       u voiant tous le fouterés.
       — Sire, voir se l'i porterai,
       quar ja, voir, ne le fouterai. »
            Dont prist le vielle entre ses bras,
210   si l'en porta en es le pas
       desor son archon par devant,
       l'emporta outre le courant,
       et en la fin tant le mena
       li vielle, si c'on me conta,
215   c'ançois que il de li escape
       covint qu'il li donast se cape,
       si le baisa tot maugré suen.
       Quant de tant en ot fait son buen,
       si fu des gens grans la risee.
220   « Or l'as baisie & acolee,

185   when he gave me his guarantee
and swore the saints he'd marry me."
"You hag from hell! You unbeliever!
May you be struck dead with a fever!"
The lord says, "It's a fair solution,
190   as I hope for God's absolution.
Since you maintain you're not related,
then fuck her as I've indicated."
The young man is dismayed and vexed,
unsure what to say or do next.
195   He says, "By God's mercy, your grace,
you're forcing me into disgrace,
for it would be a felony
to know my mother carnally."
The nobleman heard this and laughed.
200   "Young man, by Saint Dennis," he asked,
is this true or duplicitous?
I've never seen people like this!"
"My lord, she truly is my mother."
"Then you've no other option, brother.
205   Either bear her across or you
will have to fuck her in plain view."
"Then must I offer passage to her,
for never ever will I screw her."
      No longer did the young man dawdle,
210   but lifted her up in the saddle
and, with the hag seated before
him, bore her to the farther shore.
What's more, as it turned out, the old,
raggedy tramp, so I was told,
215   before he made good his escape,
obliged him to give her his cape
and in spite of him got a kiss,
and so she had her way in this,
to the amusement of the crowd.
220   "These hugs and kisses are allowed,

fait li castelains, biaus amis! »
& cius s'en va tous desconfis,
cui li vielle a tant pormené
k'ele l'envoia deffublé.
225 Por çou vos di en la parfin,
teus cuide avoir le cuer molt fin
et molt repoint, n'est pas mençoigne,
qui set molt peu a le besoigne.

29. GAUTHERON ET MARION

Quant Gauteron se maria,
Marion prist, qui dit li a
que l'aime molt & est pucele.
La nuit jurent & cil & cele
5 en .i. lit souz une cortine.
Gauteron prent Marion sovine:
son vit au con li ap[r]oucha,
& Marion .i. poi guicha,
& Gauteron s'afiche, si boute,
10 par pou n'i met la coille toute,
& si roidement l'asailli
c'un grant pet du cul li sailli.
Quant il oï le pet qui saut,
« Dame, dist il, se Deus me saut,
15 je sai bien & si ai senti
que de covent m'avez menti,
car pucele n'estiez pas. »
El li respont enelepas:
« Jel fui, mes je nel sui or mie,
20 & vos fetes grant vilenie
& si me dites grant outrage.
N'ostiés vos le pucelage
qui s'en fuï quant vos boutastes?

my dear young friend," the noble said,
and the youth rode away dismayed,
so bested by the old hag's joke
that she left him without his cloak.

225   I tell you, therefore, in conclusion,
he's often reduced to confusion
in a pinch, who believes his heart
is worldly-wise and shrewd and smart.

29. WALTER AND MARION

When Walter went a-marryin',
the girl he wedded, Marion,
was still a virgin, so she said,
and loved him, too. That night in bed
5   they lay behind the draperies.
Walter on top and she beneath,
dick pressed to cunt, the couple joins,
and Marion wobbles her loins.
Walter steadies himself and butts
10   in almost burying his nuts,
and with such vigor plays his part
that from her ass comes a large fart.
When Walter heard her fart resound,
"God save me, woman, I have found
15   out certainly," he said, "and I
can tell what you swore was a lie,
because a virgin you were not."
She answers him upon the spot:
"I was one until recently,
20   and you're treating me nastily,
and it's outrageous, what you said.
Did you not take my maidenhead?
It ran out when you shoved that way,

Molt vileinement l'en chaçastes!
25 —Par le cuer Dieu, fet il, il put!
Ce poise moi que il se mut:
bien fust eul con a une part,
car g'en eüsse asez du cart;
bien i peüst estre en son lieu.
30 Por ce maudi ge que de Dieu
soit la pucele confondue
qui tant le garde que il pue. »

30. PORCELET

Or oiez un fablel cortois
d'un vallet, fil a un borjois,
qui prist fame cortoise & sage
par lo consoil de son lignage.
5 Si l'ama engoiseussement;
n'ot pas o li esté grantmant
qu'i l'ama tant que lo feïst
tunber se talant l'an preïst.
De li fist s'amie & sa dame;
10 sovant li recordoit sa grame.
      .I. jor estoient en lor lit
o il faisoient lor delit.
La dame, a cui li jeus fu buens,
dist au vallet que tot est suens:
15 « Biaz amis, car metomes non
a vostre rien & a mon con.
      — Dame, fait il, ice est droiz
que les nons amedous metoiz
teus con vostre plaisir sera.
20   — Sire, fait el, si me plaira
que mes cons ait non Porcelez
porce qu'il ne puet estre nez,

and you basely drove it away."
25 "By the Lord's heart," he says, "it smelled!
I'm sorry that it was expelled.
It's fine in cunts somewhere or other,
but one-fourth of it would quite smother
me. Where it lodged, it should have stayed.
30 So I pray God to damn the maid
who won't surrender what she's got
for so long that it starts to rot."

50. PIGGIE

This fabliau's a courtly one
about a youth, a burgher's son,
who married a proper and nice
girl on his family's advice.
5 He loved her well and tirelessly.
They'd but been married recently,
and he so loved her that she could
have made him keel over if she would.
He made her his queen and he spoke
10 often about what pains he took.
        They were lying in bed one day,
cavorting lustily at play.
She, pleased with the festivities,
said to the doting fellow, "Please,
15 let's think up names to give, my dear,
to your thing there and my cunt here."
"It's only right that you," says he,
"decide what both their names shall be.
Call them whatever pleases you."
20 "Sir," she says, "it would please me to
give the name Piggie to my cunt,
because I'm never clean in front.

& vostre rien, ne sai conmant . . .
je cuit qu'il avra non Fromant
25 car c'est biaus nons. — Et j'otroi bien,
fait li vallez, ce non au mien
des qu'il vos plaist & il vos siet.
— Sire, fait ele, or ne vos griet
que Porcelez voldra mangier.
30 Ne li faites mie dongier
de vostre Fromant, qui est boens.
— Dame, fait il, il est tot suens. »
        Ensi furent molt longuemant
tant qu'il avint (ne sai conmant)
35 que trestoz li Fromanz failli,
& la dame l'a asailli
por viande a son Porcelet.
Li vallez lait aler .i. pet
el giron de la damoisele.
40 « Que est ce or, sire? fait ele.
Q'avez vos fait en mon devant?
— Dame, ce est brans qui espant
por doner a vostre Porcel,
que, foi que je doi saint Marcel,
45 do Fromant qui est en despans
n'i est remés fors que li brans.
— Conmant, sire, est donques failliz
li Fromanz? Donc est mal bailliz
Porcelez, se Deus me doint sen,
50 qu'il n'a cure de vostre bran!
— Dame, fait li vallez, par m'ame,
fous est qui por les bons sa fame
se grieve tant con je sui faiz!
Vostre merci, laissiez m'an paiz,
55 que tant ai fait voz volantez
que toz me sui desfromantez.
Trop est vostre pors engoisseus.
Car recovrez vostre perteus

I don't know what to call your thing. . . .
It shall be christened Wheat, I think,
for it's a pretty name." "That's fine
by me," he says, "that name for mine.
If that's your pleasure, I concur."
"Now, if you've no objection, sir,
my Piggie here would like to eat.
Do not be stingy with your Wheat,
which is so good, with Piggie, please."
"Lady," he says, "what's mine is his."

They kept at it so long, at length
(I can't think why) Wheat lost his strength,
felt whacked-out, had no more to give her,
and she nagged at him to deliver
rations to satisfy her Piggie.
The young man blows a fart, a biggie,
right in the lap of the young woman.
"Now what's with this, sir?" she says to him.
"What have you left at my front door?"
"Some husks and waste I've scattered for
your Piggie's sustenance, dear lady,
for I'm at my Wheat's end already
and nothing's left, in Saint Marcel's
name, just the chaff and empty shells."
"How now, sir? Can it be that Wheat
has run dry? That's bad news indeed
for Piggie here, who has no taste,
so help me God, to eat your waste."
The young man says, "Upon my soul,
who works as hard as I's a fool—
and all to satisfy a lady!
So please, leave me alone already,
for I've so catered to your need
I've drained my granary of seed.
Your hog is a voracious glutton.
You can go cover up your butt and

& vostre con, qui est punais.

60 Ja par moi ne manjera mais.
Qant plus manjue, plus fain a.
Fous fu qui primes l'estrova! »

31. LE VALLET AUS
.XII. FAMES

Il avint ja, que que nus die,
en la terre de Lombardie—
ce dist cil a qui je l'apris—
que .i. vallet de molt haut pris
5 se volt eul païs marïer,
mes il prist forment a jurer
ja une fame ne prendroit
se .x. ou .xii. n'en avoit.
« Fiuz, dist son pere, que dis tu?
10 Une m'a en si court tenu
que je ne puis ne ho ne jo.
Je deïse volentiers ho
s'a tant m'en peüse passer,
mes ele m'a si fet lasser
15 que je ne me puis mes aider.
Fiuz, or prenez une moillier,
si essaiez que ce sera
tant que cist ans passé sera,
& s'une ne vos puet durer
20 je vos en feré .ii. doner
ou .iii. ou .iiii. ou .v. ou .vi.
ou .vii. ou .viii. ou .ix. ou .x.
ou tant com vos onques vodrez,
ja mar de ce en douterez.
25 — Pere, fet il, je le veil bien,
mes une ne m'en feroit rien. »

your cunt as well; it's slovenly
60 and won't be fed again by me.
The more it gets, the more it wants.
What idiot invented cunts?"

31. THE FELLOW WITH
A DOZEN WIVES

Though there are some who'll disagree,
this happened once in Lombardy
(so he who told me it avers).
    A popular young man there was
5 who wished to marry locally,
but swore it was a certainty
that not just one wife would he wed—
he must have ten or twelve instead.
His father said, "What's this you wish?
10 *One's* kept me on so short a leash
that I'm not free to stop or go.
I'd more than happily cry 'Whoa!'
if words were all that were required,
but she has left me so damn tired,
15 when it comes to my interests I'm
unfit to act. Son, this first time
try it out marrying just one
wife until the first year is done,
and if one's not enough for you,
20 I'll see to it that you get two
or three or four, five, six, or seven,
or eight or nine, ten or eleven,
however many you may wish;
don't ever doubt my word on this."
25 "Father," he answers, "I am willing,
but I won't find just one fulfilling."

Que volez? Tant en a parlé
a ses amis & devisé
qu'il li donent une pucele
30 auques courtoise & asés bele,
& cele ot oï bien sovent
du bacheler le serement
que fame nule ne prendroit
se .x. ou .xii. n'en avoit,
35 mes ele dit tot en requoi
qu'einz .i. an le fera si quoi
s'ele le tient entre ses bras
que d'une en sera il tot las.
      Il la prist, espousee l'eut,
40 & sa fame le vos aqueult
aussi com ore ja parra,
& cil qui veintre la quida
la raqueult aussi vistement
& nuit & jor asaut li rent.
45 *Ains que passast le* demi ans
fu il si las, si recreans,
si ot si megres li *meiseles*
que ce semble .ii. viez asteles,
s'est plus jaune que pié d'escoufle
50 son cors, ne vaut une viez moufle,
si a les euz si enfossez
& si parfont el chief plantez
que ce samble qu'il eit langui.
Sa fame le vos aqueult si
55 & nuit & jor a dornoier,
a acoler & a besier.
      « Sire, fet ele, c'avez vos?
Si soulïez estre jalos,
si viguereus, si remuant
60 & si aigres & si ardant
que ne me lessïez dormir,
& or vos voi si quoi tenir

What do you want?—he asked around
and let his friends know till they found
a young girl for his son to wed,
30 both very lovely and well-bred,
who had herself quite often heard
how the lad had given his word
that he would never marry any
wife if he couldn't have as many
35 as twelve, but to herself she swore,
once she laid hands on him, before
a year'd gone by she'd stop his boasting,
and he'd find one more than exhausting.

He took her for his wife and wedded
40 her, and she made sure he was bedded
in the way you'll hear shortly after,
while he, who thought he'd be the master,
gave her as vigorously back
around-the-clock counterattack.

45 Even before a half a year he
appears so tuckered out and weary,
so wan and haggard are his cheeks
they look like two old dried up sticks,
he's yellower than a hawk's feet 'n'
50 as worthless as a worn-out mitten,
and his eyes are so deeply sunk in
their sockets and hopelessly shrunken,
that clearly the poor boy is wasting
away. His wife goes on insisting
55 by night and day he give her kisses
and hugs and intimate caresses.
"Husband, what is it?" she inquires.
"You used to have such hot desires
and were so vigorous of late,
60 eager, lusty, and passionate,
you wouldn't ever let me sleep,
and now instead I see you keep

qu'il me semble en bone foi
que vos amez autre de moi.
65   — Amer? fet il. Deus n'i soit mie
a foi en ceste jalousie!
D'amer ai ore grant besoing,
molt en avez ore grant soing.
— Si ai, sire, se Deus m'aït,
70   car vos me tenez en despit.
Por quoi ne fetes vos deduiz?
— Par Deu, dame, que je ne puis!
Qui tant a fet qu'il n'en puet mes,
hon le doit bien lesser en pes. »
75   Einsi furent une seson.
Le pere au vallet fu preudon;
il a mis son fiz a reson
quant il en vint a sa meson:
« Fiuz, i vos covient encore hui
80   prendre fame. Querez .i. lui
o vos puisiez vos noces fere,
que j'ai bien enquis vostre afere:
une en avez, j'en ai quis .xi.
Or vos en recovient il .xii.
85   — .xii.? fet il, Deable i soient!
.C. *homes ne* les meintendroient!
Une m'a fet si recreant
que je n'ai mes ne char ne sanc.
Lessez m'ester, por Deu merci. »
90   Einsi le lesserent andui
tant qu'il avint par aventure
c'on prist .i. leu en la pasture
droit en la vile ou cil manoit,
qui grant domage leur fesoit:
95   ne remanoit vache el païs,
oue ne pourcel ne berbis
ne jument nule qu'il n'ocie.
Molt fu la vile espoorie;

so to yourself, I think, in faith,
you love another in my place."
65 "What? I in love?" he tells her. "Hardly!
I find your jealousy ungodly.
I'm nearly dead from making love,
and this is all you're thinking of!"
"Most surely, husband, God protect
70 me, for you treat me with neglect.
Why won't you have your way with me?"
"I haven't the capacity,
by God! Who's given all that he's
able to should be left in peace."
75   For the time being, so things stood.
His father, a worthy and good
man, broached the subject with his son
one day when he'd stopped by his home:
"My boy, the time has come around
80 for you to wed. It's time you found
somewhere to hold the celebration.
I've looked into your situation.
You've one wife now; I've found eleven
to bring it to an even dozen."
85 "To Satan let the twelve be given!
What hundred men could keep up with 'em?
Just one's unmanned me so that I
have no flesh left, have been bled dry.
For God's sake, just lay off of me!"
90   So the two let the matter be,
until by chance, in that same village
he lived in, they caught near the tillage
a wolf who over time had done
great injury to everyone.
95 For miles there wasn't a cow whose
life he'd not taken, nor a goose
nor piglet, ewe or even mare,
so all the village lived in fear

molt furent lié quant l'orent pris,
si l'amenerent, ce m'est vis,
au plus qu'il porent onques tost
as esquevins & au prevost.
Li .i. le juge a mehaignier,
l'autre le juge a escorchier,
le tiers le juge a lïer
a une atache pour berser,
& li quars l'a jugié a pendre,
& li quinz a ardoir en cendre.
Quant orent tot dit lor voleir,
de l'escorchier ou de l'ardoir
ou de fere languir de fein,
si vint le vallet daarrain,
li marïez dont dit vos ai
qui seut avoir le cuer si gai,
el monde n'ot si merveilleus.
Or est son cors devenu tieus
qu'a peine se puet il rescorre
des mouches qui li corent sore.
Cil parla quant tuit orent dit:
« Or oiez, seignor, .i. petit
& volentiers le vos dirai
& molt bien le vos aprendrai
comment cest leu porrez honir
tout sanz lui batre ne ferir.
Se vos l'escorchez ou tuëz,
cil martires iert tost passez;
fetes le a tel dolor vivre
qu'il ne s'en voie ja delivre. »
& il dïent: « & vos comment?
— Jel vos dirai, fet il, briément,
se Deus me doint joie de m'ame:
fetes li tost espouser fame,
si l'avrez dont si bien honi
c'onques ne fu si mau bailli! »

and was delighted he'd been caught,
100 I rather think, and had him brought,
dragging him quickly as they can,
before the sheriff and his men.
"Torture and maim him!" the first said;
the second thought he should be flayed;
105 the third said, "Tie him up to act as
a bull's-eye for our target practice!";
the fourth would hang him by the neck;
the fifth cried, "Burn him at the stake!"
When everyone had had his say
110 whether to starve to death or to flay
or set the wolf on fire and burn
him up, it was the young man's turn,
that bridegroom I've been telling of
who'd once been lighthearted above
115 all men on earth, but who of late
has been in such a sorry state
he's barely fit to lift his hand
to brush the flies off when they land
on him. When all had spoken, he
120 said, "Listen, gentlemen, to me
a bit and I'll be glad to spell
it out for you, for I can tell
you how best to lay this wolf low
without striking a single blow.
125 Were you to have him flayed or killed,
his sufferings would soon be stilled.
Make him live on in agony
beyond all hope of getting free."
And they reply, "How can we do it?"
130 "Let me explain. There's nothing to it,"
he says, "God grant me joy in life.
Give him a woman for a wife,
and he'll know the worst martyrdom
on earth from now till Kingdom Come!"

135   & trestouz commencent a rire,
      & sa fame li prent a dire:
      « Alon nos en, beaus douz amis;
      bon conseil lor avez apris! »
      Cele qui fu & sage & cointe,
140   bien enluminee & bien jointe,
      son baron prist, si l'en mena
      & molt soavet le baigna,
      assés le fist boivre & mengier
      & sovent rere & roongnier,
145   & par li seul le fist gesir,
      reposer le fist & dormir
      & avoir trestouz ses degras
      & tant qu'il fu devenu gras
      & *avoit* tute sa vertu.
150   Or a son paiement eü
      de l'outrage qu'il demandoit
      de .xii. fames qu'il voloit,
      mes sa fame li volt oster.
          Cist fableaus dit au definer:
155   qui croit sa fame plus que lui
      sovent avra duel & anui,
      por ce ne doit nul aastir
      de chose qu'il ne puet fornir,
      por ce est droiz qui mal porchace
160   qu'a la fiee mau li face.

32. LE CLERC QUI FU REPUS DERIERE L'ESCRIN

Unes gens sont qui anchois oient
une truffe & plus le conjoient
k'une bien grande auctorité;

135 All present laughed uproariously.
His wife turned to the lad and she
said, "Come, my friend, it's time we went
back home. Your counsel's excellent."
     The lady was clever and smart
140 and levelheaded and well taught.
She took her husband by the hand
and led him home and bathed him and
had him shaven and cut his hair,
and saw he drank and had three square
145 meals every day and had a place
where he could sleep alone in peace,
and made sure all his needs were met
till he'd filled out and put on weight
and regained his vitality.
150 He paid a heavy penalty
for rashly asking they join him in
the bonds of marriage with twelve women.
His wife taught him a lesson, though.
     The last word of this fabliau:
155 Who more than himself trusts his wife
will have his share of woe and strife,
that none should boast of things that he
has not in his capacity,
that who pursues an evil end
160 will suffer evil in the end.

52. THE CLERIC BEHIND
THE CHEST

by Jean de Condé

There are some folks who'd sooner hear
(they find it gives them much more cheer)
some trifle than a thing of weight,

pour ce, truffe de verité
5   vous vorrai ci ramentevoir
si c'om le me conta de voir.

     En Haynau ot une bourgoise
en une ville, assez courtoise,
plaine de jeu et de soulas
10 k'Amours le tenoit en ses las.
Dont ele fu & de son non
ne vous veul faire nul renon,
c'on le porroit teil part retraire
u il tourneroit a contraire
15 et en seroit plus grans *criee.*
La bourgoise estoit mariee,
si estoit bele & saverouse,
gaie, envoisie & amourouse.
Un jour en sa chambre aveuc li
20 avoit .i. clerc cointe & joli;
si mangoient & si buvoient,
car viande & vin tant avoient
com il lor vint a volenté;
maint mot ot dit d'amours enté
25 et bien se porent aaisier
et d'acoler & de baisier.
(Ne sai s'autre jeu y ot point.)
Sicom il ierent en teil point,
en la maison s'en vint atant
30 uns biaus vallés, & vint hurtant
a la chambre. Li clers l'oÿ.
Sachiés point ne s'en esjoï:
« Dame, dist il, ke devenrai?
En queil guise me maintenrai?
35 — Amis, dist elle, vous ireis
deriere l'escrin, si gireis
tous cois tant que raleis s'en iert.
Je ne sai qu'il veut ne k'il quiert. »
Deriere l'escrin chieus mucha,

and that is why I will relate
5   here, just as someone told it to
me once, a trifle that is true.
         There lived in Hainaut, in a city,
a burgher woman, charming, pretty,
who loved her pleasures and was gay
10   because Love held her in his sway.
I don't want to reveal her name
or tell you from what town she came
because it just might be repeated
somewhere where the news would be greeted
15   with scandal and ruin her life,
the woman being someone's wife.
She was attractive, glamorous,
merry, playful, and amorous.
         She had a cleric with her one
20   day in her room, handsome and fun-
loving. They were drinking and eating
as much as they wanted, not needing
more wine and food than was prepared.
They spoke many a loving word
25   and, making good use of their tryst,
in privacy they hugged and kissed.
(I don't know whether they did more.)
Then there came knocking at the door
of the room a handsome young man
30   and cut short what the two of them
were doing. When the cleric heard this,
he wasn't happy; he was nervous.
"Lady," he said, "I can't think how
I should behave. What happens now?"
35   "My dear," she said, "here's what to do:
Go hide behind the chest, where you
'll keep quiet till he's gone away.
Just what he's come for, I can't say."
He went behind the chest to hide

40 et li vallés molt fort hucha;
la dame ens le laist a ce mot.
Li vallés aveuc la dame ot
souvent priveement esté.
Quant il a veü apresté
45 ensi a boivre & a mengier,
il s'est assis sans nul dangier.
La dame povre chiere fist
car li jeus pas ne li souffist
car compaignon laiens avoit,
50 que li vallés pas ne savoit.
« Dame, dist li vallés adonques,
de vous teil chiere ne vi onques.
Vous saveis tant de nostre affaire
que bone chiere devez faire. »
55 La dame atant se rapaisa;
chieus l'acola & le baisa
c'onques cele n'i mist defois—
teil vie ot mené autre fois
et plus avant un point loiié;—
60 assés ont but & dosnoiié
tant qu'il lor agrea & plot,
mais au clerc durement desplot
ki repus s'estoit & tapis,
et la chose qui li fait pis,
65 ce est que le vallet veoit
qui deleis la dame seoit
et y menoit si grant dosnoi;
au cuer en avoit grant anoi.
          Tant ala que li viespres vint.
70 Li maris la dame revint
en sa maison, car il ert nuis.
Ce fu au vallet grant anuis
ki l'oÿ; molt s'en effrea;
a la dame point n'agrea.

40 while the handsome young fellow cried
out loudly, and she let him in.
        This young fellow had often been
alone in secret with the lady.
When he saw everything there ready
45 and waiting for eating and drinking,
he sat down to it, never thinking
about it twice, but she received
him coldly, because she was grieved
since she was with another beau,
50 which the young fellow didn't know.
The youth then said, "I've never seen
your face, lady, look quite so mean.
You know how intimately we
two are involved, so smile at me."
55 The woman put aside what bugged her,
and the young fellow kissed and hugged her,
and she did not stand in his way.
He'd done as much before that day
and done a whole lot more that bound
60 them together. They fooled around
and drank a lot, just as they pleased.
The cleric, though, was much displeased,
hidden away behind the chest,
and what hurt him more than the rest
65 of it was having in plain sight
the young fellow sitting there right
beside her, flirting all the while.
It filled his heart with bitter bile.
        So it went on until the evening.
70 The husband whom she was deceiving
then came back home, for it was night.
It gave the youth an awful fright;
he heard him and was in distress.
The lady liked it even less.

75 « Dame, dist chieus, queil part irai? »
Dist la dame: « Jel vous dirai;
n'i sai chose plus profitable:
il a la drecie une table.
Teneis vous y celeement.

80 Je menrai grant effreement
et vorrai mon mari tenchier
tant que je le ferai couchier,
et quant point & heure en veés,
d'en voie aler vous pourveés. »

85 Chieus se repust au mieus qu'il sot.
Li maris a guise de sot
hurta a l'huis hasteement.
La dame ouvri ireement
et laidement le recueilli

90 et par paroles l'acueilli:
« Dont veneis, chaitis dolereus,
mesceans & mal eüreus?
Vous n'iestes onques en maison!
Vous iestes uns hons sans raison,

95 un ort usage mainteneis
car de la taverne veneis,
si me laissiés toute jour seule,
honnie soit vo gloute geule!
Alons dormir; il en est tans.

100 — Bele suer, ne soiiés hastans.
Il me couvient ançois mengier. »
Cele le prent a laidengier,
et chieus s'assist, si demanda
a mengier & du vin manda,

105 dont la bourgoise se courouche
et s'amere, forment en grouche.
« Suer, dist il, pour Dieu vous taisiés
et par amours vous apaisiez.
Honnis soit qui s'esmaiera,

75   "Lady," he asked, "where shall I go?"
She said, "I'll tell you. I don't know
what else to do. The table's set
up over there. Why don't you get
down next to it out of his sight?
80   I'll put on a big show of fright
and argue with him and act fed
up till I get him into bed,
then when you see the coast is clear,
see to it you get out of here."
85   He hid himself as best he could.
      As stupid as a block of wood,
her husband knocked with undue haste
on the door, and she with distaste
opened for him uncivilly
90   and launched into him evilly.
"You sorry wretch! You useless, mean
piece of bad luck! Where have you been?
You're never at home nowadays,
but keep on with your filthy ways,
95   a dissolute man who can't govern
himself! Why, you've been in the tavern!
You leave me all alone and guzzle
all day, God damn your greedy muzzle!
Let's go to sleep. It's getting late."
100   "Why hurry, dear? The bed can wait.
I have to eat my supper first."
While she insulted him and cursed
with vehemence, he took a seat
and asked for wine and food to eat,
105   which made her angry, and she grumbled
loudly, resentful and disgruntled.
"For God's sake, calm yourself, my pet.
We can afford it; don't you fret.
That's where the money's coming from,

110 car chieus la trestout paiera. »
De nul hoste ne se gardoit;
son escrin enseignoit au doit,
qui adont estoit bien garnis.
Li clers cuida estre escharnis;
115 bien cuida que la le seüst
et qu'au venir veü l'eüst,
si douta vers li ne venist.
Pour ce, ains que baston tenist,
issi hors & si s'en ala
120 vers le bourgois & si parla:
« Sire, fait il, par le mort Beu,
mal a point partiriés le jeu
se chieus n'en paioit autretant
qui la derriere est en estant
125 deleis cele table apoiiés. »
Or fu li bourgois avoiiés,
qui en son osteil ot teis hostes—
bien pooient reire ses costes
qui ensi du sien s'aaisoient!
130 (Mais son ouvrage li faisoient.)
Il fu deboinaires & frans;
car il estoit wihos soffrans,
tous cois fu, n'ot soing de meslee,
si a la besoigne celee,
135 n'a a iaus mot dit ne parlé,
& il s'en sont em pais alé.
          Ne di plus qu'entre iaus lor avint
ne coument la dame en couvint;
ne fu mie trop entreprise
140 car du mestier estoit aprise.
Vrais wihos estoit ses maris!—
se ses cuers fu un pou maris,
bien le sot tout a point remetre.
Point ne m'en couvient entremettre

110   so quit your griping and keep mum."
       He, ignorant of any guest,
       pointed his finger at the chest,
       which at the moment was well stocked.
       The cleric thought he's being mocked
115   and that his presence there was known,
       that he'd seen him when he got home.
       He feared he'd come at him, so quick,
       before he'd time to grab a stick,
       he came out from his hiding place,
120   approached him, and said to his face,
       "See here, sir, by God's death and passion,
       the cost's not split in a fair fashion
       if that man doesn't pay his share—
       the fellow by that table there,
125   leaning against it where it's standing.
       The husband had an understanding
       at last of what guests had dropped by.
       They'd easily have bled him dry,
       his larder empty when they're through.
130   (But they were doing for him, too.)
       With largesse and politeness, he
       calmly accepted cuckoldry,
       made no fuss, for he didn't care
       for fights, and hushed up the affair.
135   He hadn't anything to say
       to them. In peace they went away.
              I will not say what next took place
       or what the woman had to face,
       not that she much lost countenance:
140   She'd had too much experience.
       (Her man's a cuckold to the hilt.)
       His little heartache was soon stilled
       because he knew how to control
       (himself, at least). It's not my role

de dire qu'ele respondi
ne comment ele s'escondi:
ele en sot si bien a chief traire
ke je atant m'en vorrai taire.

33. SIRE HAIN ET DAME ANIEUSE

Hues Piaucele, qui trova
cest fablel, par reson prova
que cil qui a fame rubeste
est garnis de mauvese beste,
5 si le prueve par cest reclaim
d'Anieuse & de sire Hain.
Sire Hains savoit bon mestier,
quar il savoit bien rafetier
les coteles & les mantiaus.
10 Toz jors erent a chavestriaus
entre lui & dame Anieuse,
qui n'estoit pas trop volenteuse
de lui servir a son voloir,
quar quant li preudom veut avoir
15 poree, se li fesoit pois
& si estoit tout seur son pois,
& quant il voloit pois mengier,
se li fesoit por engaignier
.i. poi de poree mal cuite.
20 Anieuse ert de mal porcuite
vers son seignor quanqu'ele pot,
quar quant il voloit char en pot,
dont li fesoit ele rostir
& toute en la cendre honir
25 por ce qu'il n'en peüst gouster.

145   to tell you just what explanation
      she offered in this situation.
      She knew exactly what to do
      to end it. I'll be silent too.

55. MASTER HAM AND NAGGIE, HIS WIFE

by Hues Piaucele

Hugh Paucel, who made and narrated
this fable, clearly demonstrated
that a man married to a shrew
has problems. Here is proof for you,
5   a tale about marital strife:
      "Master Ham and Naggie, His Wife."
            Master Ham worked a useful trade,
      for he was a tailor who made
      alterations on people's coats,
10   but ever at each other's throats
      were Mistress Naggie and poor Ham,
      because she didn't give a damn
      for making an attempt to please
      her husband. She would give him peas
15   and act up as if in a snit
      when he had asked for greens to eat,
      and when he asked his wife for beans,
      she'd serve him up some sorry greens
      she'd ruined just to make him mad.
20   A special talent Naggie had
      for giving her poor husband grief:
      When he desired to have boiled beef,
      she'd fix it for him as a roast,
      dropped in the ashes like burnt toast
25   to take his appetite away.

Se vous me volez escouter,
je vous dirai bon helemot.
Rien ne vaut se chascuns ne m'ot,
quar cil pert molt bien l'auleluye
30 qui par .i. noiseus le desluie,
[& si en faut bien a son conte
quant .i. poi de noise sormonte]—
c'est por noient, n'i faudrai mie.
        Sire Hains a dit: « Douce amie,
35 alez me achater du poisson.
        —Vous en avrez a grant foison,
dist Anieuse, par saint Cire,
mes or me dites, biaus douz sire,
se vous le volez d'eve douce. »
40 & cil qui volentiers l'adouce
li a dit: « Mes de mer, amie. »
Anieuse ne tarda mie,
qui molt fu plaine de mal art;
au pont vient, si trueve Guillart,
45 qui estoit ses cousins germains.
« Guillart, dist ele, c'est du mains,
je vueil avoir des espinoches.
Mon mari, qui de males broches
ait crevez les ieus de la teste,
50 demande poisson a areste. »
& cil, qui fu de male part,
li a tornees d'une part,
se li a mis en son platel;
puis les cuevre de son mantel,
55 en sa meson en vint tout droit.
Sire Hains, quant venir la voit,
li a dit: « Bien veigniez vous, dame!
Foi que vous devez Nostre Dame,
est ce raïë ou chien de mer?
60 — L'en faut molt bien a son esmer,

Now listen well to what I say
and learn a legal precedent.
(Unless you all do, I'll have spent
my breath for naught. You lose your count
30   with just a little noise around
to act as a distraction to you,
which messes up the *Alleluia*.
Don't worry; I won't lose the thread.)
      "My dearest wife," Master Ham said,
35   "I bid you go and buy me fish."
"I'll get you as much as you wish,"
said Mistress Naggie, "by Saint Cyr,
but you must tell me, husband dear,
is it freshwater fish you want?"
40   And he, whose chief goal is détente,
said, "Dearest, I'd prefer saltwater."
Then Mistress Naggie didn't loiter
(the woman's quarrelsome and hard);
close by the bridge she finds Guillard,
45   who was her not-too-distant cousin.
"What I require is next to nothing,"
she said; "I'd like some stickleback,
because my husband—may a black
day blind him!—wants fish that are bony."
50   Cousin Guillard, who's just as stony
hearted, was able to discover
a batch he'd stowed somewhere or other
and placed them for her in her bucket.
Hidden beneath her cloak, she took it
55   and went directly home again.
Master Ham called out to her when
he saw her coming, "Welcome, dearie.
Say, by the blessed Virgin Mary,
did you buy dogfish? Is it skate?"
60   "It's a bit soon to celebrate,

fait Anieuse, sire Hain!
Volez vous lïer vostre estrain,
qui me demandez tel viande?
Molt est ore fols qui demande
65   chose que l'en ne puet avoir!
Vous savez bien trestout de voir
qu'il a anuit toute nuit plut.
Toz li poissons de la hors put.
— Put? fet sire Hains, Dieu merci,
70   j'en vi ore porter par ci
de si bons dedenz .i. panier!
— Vous en porrez ja tant pledier,
fet cele qui le het de cuer,
que je geterai ja tout puer! »
75   Dehait qui le dit s'il nel fet:
les espinoches tout a fet
a semees aval la cort.
« Dieus! fet Hains, com tu me tiens cort!
A paines os je dire mot!
80   Grant honte ai quant mon voisin m'ot
que tu me maines si viument.
— Ba! si en prenez vengement,
fet ele, se vous l'osez fere!
— Tais toi, fame de pute afere!
85   fet sire Hains. Lai moi ester!
Ne fust por ma chose haster
por aler au marchié demain,
tu le conpraisses aparmain!
— Comperaisse? fet Anieuse,
90   par mon chief, je vous en di beuse!
Quant vous volez, si commenciez! »
       Sire Hains fu molt corouciez;
.i. petitelet se porpensse,
a pres a dit ce que il pensse
95   quant fu apoiez sor son coute:

Ham," she replies. "It would avail
you just about as much to bale
loose straw as ask for such a dish!
Only an idiot would wish
65 for things that cannot be obtained.
You know damn well, last night it rained,
so local fish are to be had,
but the rest stink; they've all gone bad."
"They stink?" says Master Ham. "I saw
70 pass by here not too long before
a basketful of first-rate fish."
"Make something of it, if you wish,"
his wife (who hates him) starts to shout.
"I'll just go dump the whole lot out!"
75   It's wrong to utter empty threats.
She dumps all of it out and lets
the stickleback spill on the floor.
Says Master Ham, "God help me, you're
so touchy, I can't say a word!
80 I'd hate to think our neighbor heard
you treat me so contemptibly!"
"Bah! Just you dare get back at me!"
she says. "I'd like to see you try it!"
"You rotten-tempered woman! Quiet!"
85 says Master Ham. "Will you leave off?
Except for all the market stuff
for the next day that must be done,
you'd pay for all of this and soon!"
Naggie defies him: "*I* would pay?
90 Bullshit I would, that's what I say!
If that's what you want, come and get it!"
    Master Ham was most irritated.
He mulled things over for a while,
almost expressing his thoughts while
95 leaning his elbows on his knees.

« Anieuse, fet il, ç'acoute.
Il m'est avis & si me sanble
que ja ne serons bien ensanble
se nous ne tornons a .i. chief.
100 — Or dites donques derechief,
fet ele, se vous l'osez fere,
a quel chief vous en volez trere.
— Oïl, fet il, bien l'ose dire:
le matinet, sanz contredire,
105 voudrai mes braies deschaucier
& en mi nostre cort couchier,
& qui conquerre les porra
par bone reson mousterra
qu'il ert sire & dame du nostre.
110 — Je l'otroi bien, par saint apostre,
fet Anieuse, de bon cuer;
& se je les braies conquer,
cui en trerai a tesmoingnage?
— Nous prendrons en nostre visnage
115 .i. homme que nous mieus amon.
— Je l'otroi bien. Prenons Symon
& ma commere dame Aupais—
que qu'il aviegne de la pais,
cil dui garderont bien au droit.
120 Hucherai les je orendroit?
— Dieus! fet Hains, com tu es hastiue!
Or cuides bien que ja soit tiue
la baillie de no meson?—
ainz avras de molt fort poison
125 beü. Foi que doi saint Climent,
molt va pres que je ne comment!
— Commencier? fet dame Anieuse;
je sui assez plus covoiteuse
que vous n'estes del commencier!
130 — Or n'i a fors que del huchier

"Naggie," he tells her, "come here, please.
As I see it, apparently
there'll be no peace twixt you and me
if we can't reach a compromise."
100 "Well, out with it," Naggie replies,
"and quickly, if you have the pluck!
What kind of bargain might be struck?"
"Indeed," he says, "I have the guts.
Tomorrow, no *ifs*, *ands*, or *buts*,
105 I'll slip out of the pants I wear
and lay them in our yard right there.
Who wins them fairly in a fight
will prove that he or she by right
is lord and master and should rule."
110 "Agreed, by the apostle Paul,
so be it!" Mistress Naggie grants.
"If I prevail and seize the pants,
who will attest my victory?"
"Some man in the vicinity
115 whose judgment both of us respect."
"Agreed. It's Simon I suggest,
and Mistress Opie, my dear friend.
Whatever way the match may end,
those two will see justice is done.
120 I'll go and get them on the run."
"Good God!" says Ham. "What hastiness!
Do you imagine you possess
the sovereignty here already?
Not so fast! Over my dead body!
125 Why, in Saint Clement's name, I vow
I'm almost ready to start now!"
"*You're* ready?" is Naggie's reply;
"there's no one readier than I
am to start in—you, least of all!"
130 "There's nothing left to do but call

noz voisins. — Certes, ce n'a mon.
Sire Symon! Sire Symon!
quar venez avant, biaus conpere,
& si amenez ma commere!
135 S'orrez ce que nous volons dire.
— Je l'otroi bien sanz contredire, »
fet Symons debonerement.
Adonc s'en vindrent esraument,
si s'assieent l'un delez l'autre.
140 Sire Hains l'un mot aprés l'autre
lor a contee la reson
& descouverte l'achoison
por qoi la bataille doit estre.
« Ha! fet Symons, ce ne puet estre
145 que vous ainsi vous combatez! »
Anieuse dist: « Escoutez:
li plais est pris en tel maniere
que nus n'en puet aler arriere.
Foi que doi au baron saint Leu,
150 je vueil que soiez en no leu,
si ferons que fere devons. »
Dont primes a parlé Symons:
« Je ne vous porroie achoisier
ne acorder ne apesier,
155 ainz avrez esprové voz forces.
Or garde bien que tu ne porces,
Anieuse, se ton poing non;
sire Hain, je vous di par non,
gardez bien que vous ne porciez
160 nule chose dont vous faciez
vo fame mal fors de voz mains.
— Sire, si m'aït saint Germains,
fet sir Hains, non ferai gié,
mes or nous donez le congié
165 de no meslee commencier. »

the neighbors, then." "No, surely not.
Hey, Master Simon! Come on out,
good friend and neighbor, Master Simon,
and bring along the little woman
135   to hear what we two have to say."
"We're coming over right away,"
says Simon, nicely as he can,
and both he and his missus ran
over and sat down side by side.
140   In full detail Ham specified
the nature of the situation
and what had caused their altercation
and why a battle must take place.
Says Simon, "Can it be the case
145   that you've no choice except to fight?"
Says Naggie in reply, "That's right.
The situation's so far gone
that neither of us can back down.
As I have trust in Saint Loup, I'll
150   thank you to referee our trial,
and we'll play our part as we ought to."
Then Simon called them all to order:
"Since you will not be mollified
nor reconciled nor pacified,
155   but will decide by trial by combat,
I stipulate you only come at
him, Mistress Naggie, with your fist,
and I explicitly insist
that Master Ham carry no arm
160   with which to do his consort harm
and only use his hands to fight with."
"By Saint Germain, that's quite all right with
me, sir. Now give the signal, please,
to open the hostilities
165   so we can start," Master Ham said.

Il n'i a fors del deschaucier
les braies dont la noise monte.
Que vous feroie plus lonc conte?
Les braies furent deschaucies
170 & enz en mi la cort lancies,
chascuns s'apresta de conbatre;
ja lor verra lor os debatre
sire Symons, qui le parc garde.
Ainz que Hains s'en fust donez garde,
175 le fiert Anieuse a plains braz:
« Vilains, dist ele, je te haz!
Or me garde ceste alemite!
— Ha! dist Hains, tres orde traïtre,
m'es tu ja venue ferir?
180 Je ne porroie plus souffrir
puis que tu m'as avant requis;
mes, si m'aït sainz Esperis,
je te ferai male nuit trere!
— Par Dieu, je ne vous doute guere,
185 fet cele, por vostre manace!
Puis que nous sommes en la place,
face chascuns du pis qu'il puet! »
A cest mot sire Hains s'esmuet,
d'ire & de mautalent espris.
190 La cors fu granz & li porpris,
bien s'i pooit l'en retorner,
& quant cele vit atorner
son baron por li domagier,
onques ne se vout esmaier,
195 ainz li cort sus a plain eslais.
Huimés devendra li jeux lais,
quar sire Hains sa fame ataint
si grant cop que trestout li taint
le cuir sor le sorcil en pers.
200 « Anieuse, dist il, tu pers!
Or t'ai ta colee rendue! »

There's nothing left to do but shed
Ham's pants, which are the *casus belli*.
Why draw out what I have to tell? He
takes his pants off, which they fling
170 into the middle of the ring,
and both get ready to do battle.
Soon Simon will see their bones rattle;
it's he who's umpiring the bout.
    Before her husband can watch out,
175 Naggie swings at him, hitting hard.
"I hate you," she cries out, "you clod!
Here's something to settle our score!"
Ham says, "You underhanded whore,
have you gone and begun the round
180 already? I won't sit around
since you went and attacked me first.
I'll see to it this night's the worst
you've ever spent, you have my word!"
"Pooh!" she replies. "I am not scared,
185 not of your threats and not of you.
Now that it's come to this, we two
will go at it with might and main."
    Then Master Ham did not restrain
himself, fuming with wrath and spite.
190 The courtyard was both large and wide,
so both of them had lots of space,
and when she saw her husband brace
himself to go on the offensive,
she wasn't at all apprehensive,
195 but flew at him with breakneck speed.
Now things will turn ugly indeed,
for Master Ham at once lets fly
and punches his wife in the eye
and leaves her with an ugly bruise.
200 "Naggie," he calls to her, "you lose!
That punch you gave me is repaid."

Cele ne fu mie esperdue,
ainz li cort sus isnelement,
se li done hastivement
205 .i. cop par deseur le sorcil
qu'a poi que delez .i. bercil
ne l'abati trestout envers.
« Trop vous estiiez descouvers,
fet Anieuse, ceste part! »
210 Puis a esgardé d'autre part,
s'a veü les braies gesir,
hastivement les cort sesir,
si les lieve par le braioel,
& li vilains par le tijuel
215 les enpoingne par molt grant ire.
Li uns sache, li autres tire,
la toile desront & despiece,
par la cort en gist mainte piece.
Par vive force jus les metent;
220 a la meslee se remetent.
Hains fiert sa fame en mi les denz
tel cop que la bouche dedenz
li a toute emplie de sanc.
« Tien ore! dist sire Hain. Anc!
225 je cuit que je t'ai bien atainte:
or t'ai je de .ii. colors tainte!
— J'avrai les braies toutes voies,
dist Anieuse, ainz que tu voies
le jor de demain au matin!
230 Chanteras tu d'autre Martin,
que je ne te pris .ii. mellenz,
filz a putain! Vilains pullenz,
me cuides tu avoir sorprise? »
A cest mot, de grant ire esprise
235 le fiert Anieuse esraument.
Li cops vint par grant mautalent

She was not in the least afraid,
but ran at him immediately
and landed on him rapidly
205   another punch right in the eye
that nearly knocked him over by
the sheepfold, stretched out in the yard.
"You shouldn't have let down your guard,"
taunts Mistress Naggie, "on that side!"
210   Then, looking off a bit, she spied
the trousers lying on the ground
and ran to seize them at a bound
and lifted them up by the waist,
while Ham, consumed with anger, raced
215   and grabbed hold of them by the cuffs.
The first one pulls, the second tugs,
the fabric rips, and torn and tattered
pieces lie in the courtyard, scattered.
      Letting go of the trousers, they
220   return undaunted to the fray.
Ham landed one right on her chin
that packed such power that within
her mouth it flooded up with blood.
Master Ham said, "You hear that thud?
225   I think my fist made a connection
and gave you a two-tone complexion!"
"But all the same, I'll have those pants,"
said Naggie, "before you've a chance
to see another morning dawn!
230   You'll learn to sing another song,
'cause I don't care for you a fig,
son of a bitch! You stinking pig,
you won't get the better of me!"
Then, filled with animosity,
235   she struck again without a pause.
A mighty blow it was, because

que dame Anieuse geta:
delez l'oreille l'acosta;
que toute sa force i emploie,
240 a sire Hain l'eschine ploie,
quar del grant cop molt se detort.
« Vilains, dist ele, tu as tort,
qui ne me lais les braies prendre! »
Fet sire Hains: « Or puis aprendre
245 que tu ne m'espargnes noient,
mes se par tens ne le te rent
sire Hains, dont li faille Dieus!
Or croist a double tes granz dieus,
quar je te tuerai ancui! »
250 Anieuse respondi: « Qui
tuerez vous, sire vilains?
Se je vous puis tenir aus mains
je te ferai en mon Dieu croire!
 — Vous ne me verrez ja recroire!
255 — Ainz morras ainçois que m'eschapes!
 — Tien ore ainçois ces .ii. soupapes,
fet sire Hains, ainz que je muire!
 — Je te le metrai molt bien cuire
se j'en puis venir en desus! »
260 A cest mot se recorent sus,
si s'entredonent molt granz caus.
Sire Hains fu hastis & chaus,
qui del ferir molt se coitoit;
n'en pot mes, quar molt le hastoit
265 Anieuse, qui pas nel doute;
del .ii. poins si forment le boute
que sire Hains va chancelant.
   Que vous iroie je contant?
Tout furent sanglent lor drapel,
270 quar maint cop & maint hatipel
se sont doné par grant aïr.
Anieuse le cort sesir,

Naggie was moved by bitter spite
and had swung out with all her might
and caught him right beside the ear
so heavily that from the sheer
pain of it Ham bent over double.
"Lowlife," she said, "you're in big trouble
for not letting me take those breeches!"
Master Ham answers, "Well, that teaches
me you intend to show no mercy.
Now Master Ham deserves God's curse, he
swears, if he can't pay you back
soon! You're going to writhe and rack,
because I'll do you in for sure!"
Naggie retorted, "And just who're
you going to do it to, you dunce?
If I get hold of you, for once
I'll make you follow my religion!"
"You'll never see me budge a smidgen!"
"Before you break free, you'll be dead!"
"Here, take the old one-two instead!
I'm far from giving up the ghost."
"You'll get a basting; you will roast
if ever I come out on top!"
They go back to it then nonstop,
both giving as good as they got.
        Master Ham is hard-pressed and hot
and hankering to land some punches,
but he can't, because Naggie lunges
at him; she's not at all afraid.
Flailing with both her fists, she laid
it on him thick; Ham reeled and staggered.
What else is there? Their clothes were ragged
and bloodied; what with all the drubbing,
the punching, swinging, hitting, slugging,
they'd both given and got the same.
Naggie, who's neither slight nor lame,

qui n'ert pas petite ne manche;
sire Hains au tor de la hanche
275 l'abat si durement sus coste
qu'a poi ne li brise une coste;
cele chose forment li grieve,
mes Anieuse se relieve,
.i. petit s'est arriere traite.
280 Aupais le voit, si se deshaite,
qui le parc garde o son baron:
« Ha! por Dieu, fet ele, Symon,
[qu]ar parlons ore de la pes!
— [Hé]! dist Symons, lai moi en pes!
285 [Si] t'aït or saint Bertremieus,
[que] s'Anieuse en fust au mieus
que tu m'en priaisses aussi!
Non feïsses, par saint Forsi,
tu ne m'en priaisses a piece!
290 Or atent encore une piece
tant que li uns le pis en ait,
autrement n'avront il ja fait
Souffrir te covient, se tu veus. »
Cil refurent ja par cheveux,
295 qui erent en molt grant destrece:
Hains tient sa fame par la trece,
& cele, qui de duel esprent,
son baron par les cheveus prent,
si le sache que tout l'enbronche.
300 Aupais le voit, en haut s'esfronche
por enhardir dame Anieuse.
Quant Symons a choisi s'espeuse
& l'esme qu'ele li a fete,
« Aupais, dist il, tu es mesfete;
305 a poi que ferir ne te vois!
Se tu fez plus oïr ta vois
des que li uns en soit au mieus,

grabs hold of Master Ham, who punches
her with such strength square in the haunches,
275   it knocks her down. The jab he gives
is quite enough to break her ribs,
but, in spite of her grievous hurt,
Naggie gets back up from the dirt
and draws back somewhat in retreat.
280   Opie's more than upset to see't,
who, with her husband, referees,
and says, "For God's sake, Simon, please,
we must call for an armistice!"
"Ha!" Simon says. "Now what is this?
285   So help you Saint Bartholomew,
were Mistress Naggie winning, you
would not ask me to intercede!
No, by Saint Fursey, no indeed,
you wouldn't be so quick to end it!
290   Just wait a bit until it's ended
and one of them has clearly won,
or else they'll just go on and on.
It's something you'll just have to bear."
       The two have grabbed each other's hair
295   meanwhile, and how great their distress is!
Ham tugs away at his wife's tresses
while Naggie, overcome with pain,
has dug into her husband's mane
and yanks until his head is bowed.
300   Opie looks on and cheers aloud
to give Naggie encouragement,
but Simon knew what his wife meant
to do and saw the sign she gave.
"Opie," he said, "don't misbehave,
305   or else I'll take a stick to you!
Say nothing more, for if you do,
once their fight has come to a stop

tu le conperras, par mes ieus! »
Cele se tut, qui le cremi.

310   Tant ont feru & escremi
cil qui se conbatent ensanble
que li contes dit, ce me sanble,
qu'Anieuse le pis en ot,
quar sire Hains a force l'ot
315   reculee encontre une treille;
encoste avoit une corbeille,
Anieuse i cheï arriere
quar a ses talons par derriere
estoit, si ne s'en donoit garde,
320   & quant sire Hains la regarde,
s'en a .i. poi ris de mal cuer:
« Anieuse, fet il, ma suer,
tu es el paradis Bertran!
Or pués tu chanter de Tristran
325   ou de plus longue, se tu sez!
Se je fusse autressi versez,
tu me tenisses ja molt cort! »
A tant vers les braies s'en cort,
si les prist & si les chauça;
330   vers sa fame se radreça,
qui en la corbeille ert versee;
malement l'eüst confessee,
ne fust Symons, qui li escrie:
« Fui toi, musart, n'en tue mie!
335   Bien voi que tu es au desus.
Anieuse, veus en tu plus?
fet Symons qui la va gabant.
Bien a abatu ton beubant
sire Hains par ceste meslee.
340   Seras tu mes si emparlee
com tu as esté jusqu'a ore?
— Sire, foi que doi saint Grigoire,

you'll pay, I promise." She shut up
out of fear of the man she'd married.
310   The two combatants punched and parried
until at long last, I suppose,
it happened, so the story goes,
that Mistress Naggie got the worst
of it, because Master Ham forced
315 her to back up against a trellis.
A basket lay nearby, they tell us,
and since it was behind her heels,
Naggie trips over it and reels
and tumbles in, caught off her guard.
320 When Master Ham saw her ensnared,
he gloated over her disaster
and said, "Now Naggie, dear soul sister,
you're stuck in the mud like Bertrand!
Now sing the lament of Tristan
325 or something longer, if it's known
to you! Were I thus overthrown,
would you let me go free, perchance?"
      He runs to grab hold of the pants
and picks up and puts on his trousers.
330 Then he turns back to where his spouse is
wedged in and stuck. In penitence
she'd have faced dreadful punishments
if Master Simon hadn't shouted,
"Hold off! Don't do her in, you hothead!
335 I can see you've settled her score.
Naggie, do you want any more?"
says Simon to her in derision.
"Ham's conquered in this competition
and deflated your vanity.
340 Will you still be as uppity
as you have acted up till now?"
"Sir, by Saint Gregory, I vow,"

fet cele, ne fusse hui lassee
se je ne fusse ci versee,
345   mes or vous proi par amistez,
biaus sire, que vous m'en getez. »
Fet Symons: « Ainz qu'isses issi,
fianceras orendroit ci
que tu jamés ne mesferas
350   & que en la merci seras
sire Hain a toz les jors mes
& que tu ne feras jamés
chose nule qu'il te desfenge.
— Ba! deable! & s'il me ledenge,
355   fet Anieuse, ne cort seure
& j'en puis venir a deseure,
ne me desfenderai je mie?
— Escoute de ceste anemie,
fet Symons, qu'ele a respondu!
360   Aupais, en as tu entendu?
— Oïl voir, sire, bien l'entent.
Anieuse je te blastent
que tu respons si fetement,
quar tu vois bien apertement
365   que tu ne pués plus maintenant,
si te covient d'ore en avant
fere del tout a son plesir,
quar de ci ne pués tu issir
se par son commandement non. »
370   Anieuse respondi: « Non!
Conseilliez moi que je ferai.
— Par foi, dist Aupais, non ferai,
que tu ne m'en croiroies mie.
— Si ferai, bele douce amie;
375   je m'en tendrai a vostre esgart.
— Or t'estuet il, se Dieus me gart,
orendroit fiancier ta foi
(je ne sai se ce ert en foi,

she says, "that I'd have not been humbled
today, were it not that I stumbled.
345 In friendship's name, I beg you, dear
neighbor, help me get out of here."
Says Simon, "Before you're set free
you must promise us solemnly
that henceforth you will mend your ways
350 and until the end of your days
always submit to Master Ham
and that you'll never do again
anything to oppose his will."
"The devil! If he treats me ill
355 or raises his hand to me, and
I'm like to gain the upper hand,
am I to hold back and be meek?"
"Just listen to that hellcat speak
and what response the woman made!
360 Did you hear, Opie?" Simon said.
"I well and truly did, sir. Look you,
Naggie, I fault you and rebuke you
for answering in such a way
when you can see as plain as day
365 there's nothing more that you can do,
so from now on it's your place to
obey him utterly whatever
he says, for only at his pleasure
can you escape your present fix."
370 Mistress Naggie responded, "Nix!
Advise me what I should do now."
"I won't," said Opie, "for, I vow,
you'll not listen to me at all."
"Not so, dearest of friends! I shall
375 be guided by your point of view."
"God keep me, then it falls to you
here and now to swear under oath
(I don't know if you'll tell the truth,

403 ❧ THE FABLIAUX

mes toutes voies le feras)
380 que tu ton baron serviras
si com preude fame doit fere,
ne [j]amés por nul mal afere
ne te dreceras contre lui. »
Anieuse dist sans delui:
385 « Par foi, bien le vueil creanter
por que je m'en puisse garder;
ainsi en vueil fere l'otroi. »
A cest mot en risent tuit troi,
sire Hains, Symons & Aupais,
390 toutes voies firent la pais,
de la corbeille la geterent
& en meson la ramenerent.
Molt sovent s'est clamee lasse,
mes Dieus i mist tant de sa grace
395 que puis cele nuit en avant
onques ne s'ala percevant
sire Hains qu'el ne li feïst
trestout ce qu'il li requeïst,
de lui servir s'avolentoit
400 & por ce que les cops doutoit
nel desdisoit de nule chose.
Si vous di bien, a la parclose
en fu a sire Hain molt bel.

Ainz que je aie cest fablel
405 finé, vous di je bien en foi,
se voz fames mainent bufoi
deseur vous nul jor par male art,
que ne soiez pas si musart
que vous le souffrez longuement,
410 mes fetes ausi fetement
comme Hains fist de sa moillier,
qui ainc ne le vout adaingnier
fors tout le mains que ele pot

but all the same, it must be promised)
380 that you will do as every honest
woman must do, obey and serve
your man and never have the nerve
to cross his will in any way."
Naggie replied without delay,
385 "I'd gladly give my word, except
by such as me, can it be kept?
That's all that I can guarantee."
Then they laughed heartily, all three,
Simon, Opie, and Master Ham,
390 reinstituting peace and calm.
Out of the basket she was pried
loose, and they led her back inside.
She frequently bemoaned her case,
but God conferred on her His grace,
395 so that never after that night
did Master Ham ever catch sight
or find she wouldn't carry through
whatever he asked her to do.
She did her utmost to obey
400 and would on no account gainsay
her man for fear of being struck.
As it turned out, Ham had good luck
and a good life, I tell you so.
Before I end this fabliau,
405 I say in all sincerity
that if your wives through perfidy
oppose you and will not be led,
don't be the kind of knucklehead
who puts up with their insolence.
410 Make use of the expedients
by which Ham brought his wife in tow,
who wouldn't deign to stoop so low
as do more than the least she could

dusques atant que il li ot
415   batu & les os & l'eschine.
Tout issi cis fabliaus define.

𝟑𝟒.   LA DAME ESCOILLIEE

Seignor, qui les femes avez
& qui sor vos trop les levez
ques faites sor vos seignorir,
vos ne faites que vos honir.
5   Öez une essanple petite
qui por vos est issi escrite;
bien i pöez pranre essanplaire
que vos ne devez mie faire
du tot le bon a voz molliers
10   que mains ne vos en tignent chiers.
Les foles devez chastoier,
& si les faites ensaignier
que n'en doivent enorguillir
vers lor seignor ne seignorir,
15   mais chier tenir & bien amer
& obeïr & onorer;
s'eles ne font, ce est lor honte.
Huimais descendrai en mon conte
de l'essanple que doi conter
20   que cil doivent bien escouter
qui de lor femes font seignor,
dont il lor avient deshenor,
qu'an dirai, ce pöez savoir,
n'est si mal gas comme le voir.
25   Un riches hom jadis estoit
a qui grant richece apendoit;
chevaliers ert, tint grant hennor,

for him until he beat her good
415 so every bone was black-and-blue.
So there! This fabliau is through.

54. THE GELDED LADY

You, noble lords, who have a spouse
whom you've made master of your house,
above your very selves exalted,
with your own shame are to be faulted.
5   To this exemplum lend an ear,
which for your sake is written here,
by which you'll learn beyond a doubt
that you ought not to carry out
whatever your wives bid you do;
10   they'll only think the less of you.
If they're wrongheaded, then chastise
your wives and open up their eyes
that they must never be so forward
as dare lord it over their lord,
15   but love and cherish, as is fit,
and do him honor, and submit.
If they do not, theirs is the shame.
But now it were high time I came
to telling what I have to tell,
20   to which those men should listen well
who act as vassals to their wives
and bring dishonor on their lives.
This much I'll say: You can be sure,
compared with truth, no joke hurts more.
25   A noble man lived in times past
whose riches and estates were vast,
a knight who led a noble life,

mais tant avoit amé s'ossor
que desor lui l'avoit levee
30 & seignorie abandonee
de sa terre, de sa maison,
& de tot otroié le don,
dont la dame le tint si vill
& tint si bas, que quanque cil
35 disoit, & ele desdisoit
& desfaisoit quanqu'il faisoit.
Une fille avoient molt bele.
Tant en ala loing la novele
de sa beauté & ça & la,
40 renomee tant en palla,
que .i. quens en oï parler;
sempres la prist molt a amer.
Ainz ne la vit, & nequedent
si l'amoit il; ç'avient sovent,
45 & por löer bien aimë on
tot sanz veoir, ce sanble bon.
N'avoit point de feme li quens,
joenes estoit & de grant sens,
& si ert plains de grant savoir,
50 qui mielz li valt que nul avoir.
La pucele dont l'en li dist,
molt volentiers il la veïst
se l'en dit voir ou se l'en ment.
Puis la vit il: öez coment.
55 Li quens ala .i. jor chacier,
avesques lui .iii. chevalier;
les chiens mainent li veneor.
En la forest ont tote jor
chacié de si que aprés none,
60 que aive monte, forment tone,
esclairë & molt a pleü.
Dessevrez sont & deperdu

but because he so loved his wife,
he raised her even over him
30   and let her govern at her whim
all that he had. Household and lands,
he put it all into her hands,
which so debased him in her sight
and cheapened him that if the knight
35   said yes, she would say no instead
and undid everything he did.
        They had a daughter. She was fair,
and word of her spread everywhere,
her beauty praised hither and yon
40   till news of her so far had gone
that a count heard her spoken of
and he began to fall in love.
He'd never seen her, yet for all
that he loved her. Such things befall:
45   Inspired by praise, any man could
love someone sight unseen; it's good.
The count was not in wedlock bound,
but young in years, in judgment sound,
and full of good sense beyond measure,
50   worth more to him than any treasure.
The girl of whom he had been told
he very gladly would behold
to see if it were truth or lie.
Hear how he saw her by and by.
55   The count went out to hunt one day,
along with him three chevaliers
and hunters with the dogs on leash.
All day within the forest each
pursued the game till after noon,
60   when came a storm, a true monsoon
with thunder, lightning, pelting rain.
The greater part of the count's men

la gent le conte, fors li quart,
qui se traient a une part.
65 A escons tornoit li solaus;
dit li quens: « Quels ert li consaus?
Ge ne sai que nos puission faire.
Nos ne poons en huimais traire
a nesune de *nos* maisons.
70 Li solaus s'en vait a escons,
ne ge ne sai ou noz genz sont,
fors tant que ge cuit qu'il s'en vont.
Nos estuet traire a .i. ostel,
mais ge ne sai mie a quel. »
75 Que que li quens si se demente,
avalez sont par une sente
en .i. jardin lez .i. vivier
a la maison au chevalier,
celui qui la bele fille a.
80 Estes les vos chevalchant la:
cel jor plut & ne fist pas bel;
la descendent soz .i. ormel.
Sor .i. perron siet li frans hom
cui devoit estre la maison.
85 Ez vos le conte: gentement
le salue, & cil bel li rent
son salu & puis se leva;
li quens son ostel li rouva.
« Sire, ce dit li chevaliers,
90 herbergasse vos volentiers,
que mestier avez de repos,
mais herbegier pas ne vos os.
— N'osez? Por quoi? — Por ma moillier,
qu'a nul fuer ne velt otroier
95 chose que face ne que die.
Desor moi a la seignorie,
de ma maison a la justice,

lost their way, scattered by the weather,
except those four, who stuck together.
65 The night approached, soon set the sun.
The count spoke up: "What's to be done?
I do not know what we can do.
By now there's no way for us to
return to any of our homes—
70 the sun is sinking, nightfall comes—
nor do I know where we can find
our men. I guess we're left behind.
To lodgings we must now repair,
though I know not to which or where."
75   Thus while the count is fretting still,
they go along a path downhill
beside a pond of flowing water
where the knight with the lovely daughter
has his residence in a park.
80 It's raining hard; the sky is dark.
In ride the three men and the count;
beneath an elm they all dismount
and, seated on the doorstep, see
the man whose house this ought to be.
85 See how the count politely gives
him greeting, how courteous his
answer. Then he gets to his feet.
For lodgings the count would entreat
him. "Noble lord," so says the knight,
90 "I'd gladly put you up tonight,
for you are weary and in need,
but I do not dare do this deed."
"Not dare? And why?" "Because I can't.
I know my wife will never grant
95 whatever thing I do or say,
for she's the one here who holds sway,
decides for me and for my folk.

de trestot a la commandise,
si ne li chalt s'en ai enuie:
100   ge ne li sui fors chape a pluie,
a son bon fait, noient au mien;
de mon commant ne feroit rien. »
Li quens s'en rist & si li dist:
« Se fussiez preuz, pas nel feïst.
105   — Sire, dit il, si l'a apris,
sel vorra maintenir toz dis
se Dieus de moi n'en a merci.
Mais or soffrez .i. pou ici;
g'irai lassus, venez aprés,
110   l'ostel me querrez a engrés
& ge vos en escondirai,
& s'ele l'ot, tres bien le sai
que vos seroiz bien ostelez
por ce que vos avrai veez. »
115   Il remainent, il va amont;
quant il fu enz, aprés lui vont,
dit li quens: « Dieus salt le seignor!
A vos & a nos doint henor!
— Sire quens, Dieus vos beneïe,
120   & vos & vostre conpaignie.
— Herbergiez nos. — Ge non ferai.
— Por quoi, sire? — Ge ne voldrai.
— Si feroiz par vostre franchise.
— Non ferai, voir, en nule guise.
125   — Par gerredon & par amor,
herbergiez nos de si *au jor.*
— Non ferai en nule maniere,
ne par amor ne par proiere. »
La dame l'ot, si salt avent,
130   qui fera ja le sien comant:
« Sire quens, bien soiez venuz!
Lieement seroiz receüz!
Descendez tost. » Il descendirent,

Here everything's under her yoke.
She doesn't care if I complain.
100 I'm just a coat she wears for rain;
she does her will, but never mine.
If it's my will, she will decline."
The count laughs and replies, "You're wrong.
She wouldn't dare if you were strong."
105 "My lord," he says, "she's set the law
and means to go on as before,
unless the Lord pity my fate.
If you'll permit, I bid you wait
while I go up; then presently
110 come ask my hospitality
and I'll refuse you, for I know
when she hears this how things will go.
You'll be housed well, as you require,
because it counters my desire."
115   They stay outside, and he goes in.
Once he's inside, they follow him.
"God protect the lord of the manor,"
the count says, "and give us all honor."
"Count, may the Lord His blessings bring
120 to you and all your following."
"Do put us up." "That I refuse."
"Why not, sir, pray?" "For so I choose."
"Do, out of generosity."
"Indeed, I won't; it shall not be."
125 "For payment and from kindliness,
from now till day here let us rest."
"That I will not in any way,
from kindness nor for what you say."
Hearing these words, up jumps the lady;
130 to have her way she's always ready.
"My lord count, you're most welcome here.
We give you lodgings with good cheer.
Come in." So they entered the hall,

& li sergant bien les servirent,
135 que la dame l'ot commandé.
[Ce] dit li sires: « [ ] Par mon gré,
ne mengeront de mes poissons,
ne de mes bones venoisons,
de mes viez vins, de mes ferrez
140 ne mes oiseaus ne mes pastez. »
Dit la dame: « Or vos aesiez;
de ses diz ne vos esmaiez,
que por ses diz, ne plus ne mains,
par senblant est li sires grains.
145 Molt beau li est de tel servise. »
          Molt s'en est la dame entremise,
de servir les forment se paine,
li cheval ont assez aveine
a plenté, por ce que li sire
150 l'avoit osé nes contredire.
La dame haste le mengier;
molt en a fait apareillier
de venoison, de voleïlle.
En la chanbre cela sa fille;
155 ne volt que li quens la veïst,
mais li sires bien le vosist:
« Dame, dit il, laissez laiens
mangier ma fille avuec noz genz
en la chambre, non ça defors.
160 Tant a beauté, tant a gent cors,
li quens est joenes, s'il la voit
tel flor, molt tost la *covoitroit*. »
Ce dit la dame: « Or i venra
mengier o nos; si la verra. »
165 La dame molt bien l'aparelle;
lors fu gente, clere, vermeille
El la maine; li quens l'a prise
par la mein, l'a lez lui assise.
Molt li fu sa beautez löee,

and servants at their beck and call
135   offered their help at her command.
"No venison found on my land,"
the host insists, "nor any fish
shall these men taste, for so I wish,
nor of my wines, meat from my grill,
140   my birds and pasties eat their fill."
The lady says, "Come take your ease,
and let him say as he may please.
The man's all bark, no more, no less,
and just wants to look gruff, I guess.
145   To serve you gives him satisfaction."
        The lady has sprung into action,
to serve them well takes every pain;
their horses get their fill of grain,
and all because her rightful lord
150   with their request had not concurred.
She bids her household to make haste
and put together quite a feast
and serve much game and poultry to 'em.
Her daughter she hid in her room;
155   she doesn't want the count to see her.
        Her husband has his own idea:
"Lady, my daughter should be told
to stay inside with your household
and have her meal, not in this place.
160   She has such beauty and such grace,
if this young count caught a glimpse of
this flower, he'd soon fall in love."
The lady says, "Let her appear
and eat with us so he can see 'er."
165   The lady dresses her with care
and made her rosy, bright, and fair.
She leads her in. The count, to guide
her, took her hand and by his side
he sat her. Seeing her, he thought

170   mais il li a graignor trovee,
        ce li ert vis, que molt est bele:
        Amor le fiert soz la memele,
        qui tant la li fist a amer
        qu'il la vorra avoir a per.
175   Or ont lavé & sont assis;

        li quens, qui est d'Amors espris,
        mengue o la bele meschine.
        Molt par fu riche la quisine,
        molt ot beüz vins & morez,
180   & molt fu li quens honorez.
        Aprés mengier si ont deduit
        de paroles, puis si ont fruit.
        Dit li quens: « Sire, ge vos quier
        vostre bele fille a moillier.
185   Plus bele ne virent mi hueil.
        Donez la moi, quar ge la vuell. »
        Dist li peres: « Nel ferai pas,
        quar ge la vueil doner plus bas.
        Ge la donrai bien endroit *li.* »
190   La dame l'ot, en piez sailli.
        « Sire, dit ele, vos l'aroiz,
        ne ja *nul* gré ne *l'en* savroiz,
        que li donners n'est pas a lui.
        Ge la vos doins, *& avuec* lui
195   ai assez, & or & argent,
        si ai maint riche garnement.
        Donrai la vos; si la prenez! »
        Li quens respont: « Merciz & grez.
        Ge l'aim tant que la vueil avoir
200   por sa beauté, non por avoir.
        Qui l'avra, n'avra pas petit. »
        Adonc si furent fait li lit,
        couchier se vont. Dorment li troi;
        Amors met le conte en effroi;

170   the praises he'd heard fell far short,
    she seemed so fair. He was impressed;
    Love struck him deep inside his breast
    and made him love her so, he planned
    right then that he'd ask for her hand.

175   They've washed their hands; now they
                            are sitting.
    The count, whom Love's completely smitten,
    eats alongside the lovely maiden.
    The table with rich food was laden,
    wines and liqueurs in vast amount,

180   and all honor was paid the count.
    Then they conversed some to divert
    themselves, and had fruit for dessert.

          The count says, "Sire, I would demand
    you grant me your fair daughter's hand.

185   I've never seen beauty so rich.
    Give her to me, for so I wish."
    Her father said, "That I will not.
    A lower match will be her lot;
    I'll find her such a one instead."

190   His wife heard him, jumped up, and said,
    "My lord, you and she shall be wedded,
    no thanks to him! Let it be said, it
    is not his business to decide.
    I give her up, and with your bride

195   I've gold and silver, too, to offer,
    and of rich clothing a full coffer.
    I give her to you. Take your prize."
    "I thank you, but," the count replies,
    "I love her so, I seek no wealth

200   besides her beauty, just herself.
    He has a lot, who has this lady."
    That settled, their beds were made ready,
    and all retired. Though three find rest,
    Love has the count so much distressed

205 auques dormi, & *plus* veilla,
Amors son bon li conseilla.

  Au matin, quant levé se sont,
maintenant au mostier en vont,
la pucele ont o aus menee.
210 Li quens l'a d'argent honoree;
la dame grant avoir li offre,
dras & deniers, vaisseaus en coffre;
li quens dit qu'a assez avoir—
le lor aient, si dist por voir:
215 « Molt a qui bone feme prant;
qui male prant, ne prant nïent. »
Dist li peres: « Fille, entendez!
Se vos honeur avoir volez,
cremez vostre seignor le conte;
220 se nel faites, c'ert vostre honte. »
Dist la *mere*: « Parlez a moi,
bele fille, ça en requoi.
  —Volentiers, mere, » dit la fille.
Ele li comende en l'orille:
225 « Bele fille, levez la chiere!
Vers vostre seignor soiez fiere.
Pranez essample a vostre mere,
qui toz jors desdit vostre pere:
ainz ne dist riens ne desdeïst
230 ne ne commenda c'on feïst.
Se vos volez avoir henor,
si desdites vostre seignor,
metez l'arriere & vos avant,
petit faites de son coumant.
235 S'ainsi faites, ma fille estrés;
se nel faites, vos conparrez.
  — Gel ferai, fait ele, se puis,
se ge vers mon seignor le truis. »
« Sire quens, dist li riches hom,
240 de ma fille vos ai fet don.

205 that sleep mostly eluded him,
for Love harangued the man at whim.
     Come morning, and with all due speed
they get up and to church proceed,
the maid with them. To do her honor,
210 the count showers silver upon her.
By way of wealth her mother offers
cloth, coins, and vessels from her coffers.
"No, keep what's yours. I have no use
for more," the count says, "for in truth,
215 who finds a good wife needs no more,
while he whose wife is bad is poor."
Her father says, "Child, listen here.
If you wish to have honor, fear
the count your husband, keep your place;
220 if not, we'll only have disgrace."
Her mother says, "A word with you,
my daughter, just between us two."
"Gladly," she answers, "mother dear."
She whispers in her daughter's ear
225 and says, "Hold your head high, my child,
nor with your husband be too mild,
but adopt as your model rather
the way I override your father.
For all he's ordered, vetoed, said,
230 he never once has been obeyed.
If you wish to have honor, speak
up to your husband, don't be meek,
put yourself first and put him last,
do little of what you are asked.
235 Prove you're my daughter in this way.
If you do not, you'll surely pay."
"I'll try to do as you advise
if the occasion should arise."
     "Lord Count," the man says, "by your leave,
240 along with this girl whom I give,

Pranez par amors, sire quens,
cest palefroi qui molt est boens,
& cez .ii. levriers qui sont bel
& preuz & hardi & *isnel.* »
245 Li quens les prant, si l'en mercie,
le congié prant, sa fame enguie.
  Molt se vait li quens porpenssant
par quel art & par quel senblant
face sa fame vers lui vraie,
250 que a sa mere ne retraie,
qui si estoit fiere & grifaigne.
Lors entrent en une chanpaigne.
.i. *lievres* saut devant aus pres;
dit li quens: « Or levrier, aprés!
255 Quant vos si preu & isnel estes,
ge vos commant desur les testes
[ençois le tiers champ l'aiez pris! »
La dame l'ot, si en a ris.
Le lievre fuit, qui crient la mort;
260 molt fuit, mes pas ne lor estort:
el quint champ l'ont pris & tenu.
Es vos la le conte venu;
il descent, si a tret l'espee,
la teste andeus lor a coupee.
265 Des .ii. levriers molt s'esmerveille
la dame, ot la face vermeille,
porpense soi: « Cist quens est fiers,
qu'ensi a ocis ces levriers! »
Le lievre pranent, si s'en vont,
270 a lor chemin revenu sont;
li palefrois au conte ceste.
« Je te commant desour la teste,]
dit li quens, ne *ceste* autre foiz! »
Ne l'entendi li palefroiz;
275 a chief de pose *recesta.*

in proof of my affection, Count,
also accept this goodly mount
and these two greyhounds as a gift.
They're handsome, fine, courageous, swift."
245 Taking leave, he with thanks accepts them
and sets off with his new wife next him.
　　　　The count rides on engrossed in thought.
What conduct and what bearing ought
he to take to make his wife true
250 to him, unlike her mother, who
's puffed up with shrewishness and pride?
They come into a countryside,
when close in front a rabbit bounds.
The count cries out, "Go get 'im, hounds!
255 Since you're so swift and hardy, too,
now, by your heads, I order you
to catch that hare before it clears
the second field!" The lady hears
and laughs. Feared for its life, it bounds
260 and leaps, but can't escape the hounds;
they catch it when they've crossed four fields.
See, now the count arrives, who wields
his sword, and then and there dismounts
and strikes the heads off both his hounds.
265 The lady's face has turned bright red,
surprised to see them stricken dead,
and thinks, How fierce this count must be
to kill those dogs so recklessly!
Taking the hare, directly they
270 returned to where their road home lay,
when something startled their lord's mount.
"Don't stumble again," says the count,
"by your head! That is my command."
The palfrey didn't understand
275 and before long once more it tripped.

Li quens descent, si li coupa
la teste, sor .i. autre monte.
« Sire, ce dit la dame au conte,
cel palefroi & cez levriers
280   deüssiez vos avoir molt chiers
por mon pere, non pas por moi.
Morz les avez; non *sai* por quoi. »
Ce dit li quens: « Por seul itant
que trespasserent mon commant. »
285   Va s'en li quens, sa feme emmaine,
de losangier forment se paine,
& vient a sa maistre cité.
Iluec estoient assanblé
li baron & li vavassor,
290   que molt pesoit de lor seignor
qu'il cuidoient avoir perdu.
Ez les vos au pont descendu,
encontre vont, joie li font,
li auquant demandé li ont
295   qui cele bele dame estoit.
« Seignor, c'est vostre dame a droit.
— Nostre dame? — Voire, par foi,
que mis li a[i] l'enel el doi.
— Dame, bien soit ele venue! »
300   A grant joie l'ont receüe.
         Li quens ses noces apareille,
le queu apele & li consaille
& li conmende qu'il li face
savors teles dont gré li sache
305   & sauxes molt assavorees:
« Que nos genz soient honorees
por l'onor la novele dame,
[que de li portent bonne fame]! »
Dit li queus: « Ge m'en apareil. »
310   La dame li dit a conseil:
« Que t'a dit li quens? — Que savors

The count changed horses and was swift
to strike off the offender's head.
"Indeed, my lord," the lady said,
"that palfrey and those greyhounds, too,
280 ought to have been most dear to you
for my father's sake, not for mine.
You've killed them. Why, I can't divine."
The count replied, "The only cause
was that they disobeyed my laws."
285   He rides on in her company,
takes care to speak with courtesy,
till he comes to his capital,
and there he finds assembled all
his knights with the rest of his court,
290 who thought his life had been cut short
and were in mourning for his loss.
At the bridge everybody draws
close, and all greet him joyfully,
and some inquired who she might be,
295 that lovely lady at his side.
"Lords, she's your mistress," he replied.
"Our mistress, sire?" "Yes, by my life.
With that ring I made her my wife."
"By God, she is most welcome here!"
300 and they received her with good cheer.
     A wedding feast the count prepares.
He summons his cook and confers
with him and lets him know what flavors
on this occasion he most favors
305 and with what highly seasoned sauces
to fête his people, which, of course, is
to do all honor to his bride,
that she be welcomed nationwide.
Says cook, "I'll do it in a trice."
310 The lady offers this advice:
"What did the count say?" "That he wishes

li face bones & plusors.
— Vielz avoir mon gré? — Dame, aol.
— Garde que il n'i ait .i. sol
315 ou il ait savors fors ailliee,
mais que bien soit apareilliee.
— Ge n'oseroie. — Si feras.
Ja de lui mal gré n'en avras
s'il set que l'aie commandé,
320 & tu doiz bien faire mon gré:
ge te puis aidier & nuisir.
— Dame, dit il, vostre plaisir
ferai, mais que honte n'en aie!
Du tot sui en vostre menaie. »
325 Li queus s'en va en la quisine,
de ses mes atorner ne fine;
s'aillie a li queus atornee.
Atant a l'on l'eve cornee;
levent, si s'assieent as dois.
330 Li mes vienent molt a esplois
as barons & a la mesniee;
a chascun mes si a ailliee,
mais de bon vin i ot assez.
Toz en fu li quens trespenssez;
335 ne sot que faire, tant soffri
que les genz furent departi.
En la chanbre mande son queu;
il i vint, non mie a son preu;
il ot poor, si vint tranblant.
340 « Vassal, fist il, par quel conment
avés vos fait tantes ailliees
& les savors avez laissiees
que ge vos commendai a faire? »
Li queux l'entent, ne sait que faire:
345 « Sire, fait il, gel vos dirai.
Par ma dame, *sire, fet l'ai*,
por vostre dame, voire, sire,

a meal both varied and delicious."
"May I advise you?" "Yes, of course."
"See to it that there's not one course
315 where garlic doesn't dominate,
but lavish care on every plate."
"I wouldn't dare." "You'll do just this.
Be sure he won't take it amiss
if he knows it was my desire;
320 and you must do as I require.
I can advance you or undo you."
"Lady," he says, "I'll listen to you,
pray God I do not suffer for't!
I put my trust in your support."
325 Then to the kitchen he withdraws,
works on the dishes without pause
in which strong garlic sauce abounds.

  The horn announcing dinner sounds;
they wash their hands and take their place;
330 the wedding meats arrive apace
to feed the barons and the guests,
but everything of garlic tastes,
although enough good wine is served.
The count, however much disturbed,
335 bore with it—what else could be done?—
and waited till his guests were gone.
He summoned his cook to appear.
The man arrived, trembling in fear,
nor was he pleasantly rewarded.
340 "Now, vassal," said the count, "who ordered
garlic be put in every dish
and, in defiance of my wish,
no other seasonings be used?"
When the cook hears this, he's confused
345 and answers, "Sire, I must admit it.
On your wife's orders, sire, I did it,
believe me, on account of her

que ge ne l'osai contredire.
  — Par les sainz que on por Dieu quiert,
350 que ja garant ne vos en ert
de trespasser ma commendise! »
Du queu fist li *quens* la justise:
l'ueil li crieve & tolt li l'orille
& une main & puis l'essille
355 de sa terre que n'i remaigne,
puis a parlé a sa conpaigne:
« Dame, dit il, par quel conseil
nos avez fait cest apareil?
  — Par le mien, sire, si mespris.
360 — Non feïstes, par seint Denis,
par le vostre ne fu ce mie.
Mais or me dites, douce amie,
itel conseil qui vous dona.
  — Sire, ma mere le loa
365 que ge [de] li ne forlignasse
ne voz commanz pas n'ostroiasse,
mais avant alassent li mien,
si m'en venroit honeur & bien.
A ceste foiz l'ai fait ainsi,
370 or m'en repent, por Dieu merci.
  — Bele, ce dit li quens, par Dé,
ja ne vos sera pardoné
sans le vostre chastiement! »
Il saut, par les cheveus la prant,
375 a la terre la met encline,
tant la bat d'un baston d'espine
qu'il l'a laissiee presque morte;
tote pasmee el lit la porte.
Iluec jut ele bien .iii. mois
380 qu'ele ne pot seoir as dois;
iluec la fist li quens garir,
tant li a faite bien servir.

to whom I'm bound, sire, to defer."
"By all the saints who intercede
350 on our behalf, you did not heed
my orders, and no one can shield
you from my justice!" His fate's sealed:
One eye is plucked out and a hand
and ear cut off; then from the land
355 he's exiled, never to return.
      The count spoke to his wife in turn.
"Lady," he said, "now whose idea
was it to have you interfere?"
"I am at fault, sire. Mine alone."
360 "You weren't acting on your own,
by Saint Dennis, it wasn't you.
Now tell me freely, darling, who
advised and prompted you to do it."
"My mother, sire, put me up to it
365 and told me that I must not stray
from her path, but should disobey
and give the orders. By this scheme
would I have honor and esteem.
I did as she advised this time.
370 God help me, I repent my crime."
"My beauty, as God is my witness,"
the count says, "don't expect forgiveness
till you've been punished." Then and there
he jumps up, grabs her by the hair,
375 and hurls her down before his feet
and with a thorn branch starts to beat
her till she's lying nearly dead.
Unconscious, she is put to bed.
Three months had passed till she was able
380 to come and take her place at table.
Meanwhile, the count saw to her cure
and that she got just what was due 'er.

D'un autre essanple öez la somme:
a la fiere feme au preudome
385   est prist volentez de veoir
sa fille; el demain velt movoir.
.vi. chevaliers apareilla
molt noblement, a cort ala;
son seignor dit, com ele sielt,
390   qu'aprés *li* viegne se il velt.
Au conte mande qu'ele vient;
li quens a grant orgueil le tient
quant ele mande & non li sire,
qui vient lui autre, ce ot dire;
395   nequedent bel ator fait faire
de mengier & de luminaire.
Ez vos la dame receüe:
ne fu [pas] trop bel recuillue,
li quens li fist baseste chere.
400   Atant ez vos venu le pere:
a l'encontre li quens li saut,
« Bien viegnoiz! » dit il tot en halt,
qeurt a l'estrier, & cil s'en ire,
& dit li quens: « Or soffrez, sire,
405   que l'en vos serve en vo meson
volentiers, quant il vos est bon, »
prist par la mein, lez lui l'assist,
deshueser & servir le fist.
La contesse issi de la chanbre,
410   qui vers sa mere ot le cuer tendre,
& nequedent le conte crient
por le baston dont li *sovient.*
Primes son pere salua,
& il li rent, puis la baisa,
415   puis a sa mere salüee.
(Molt volentiers i fust alee,
mais li quens l'assist lez son pere—
la mere en fist pesante chere.)

I've one more lesson left to write.
The proud wife of the worthy knight
385 thought she would leave for a short stay
with her daughter on the next day.
Six richly fitted knights she brought
to swell her train, and left for court.
She told her husband that he may
390 follow behind; such was her way.
She sent on word of her arrival.
The count takes it as prideful drivel
that she, and not her lord, sends word,
who's also coming, he has heard,
395 but all the same makes preparations
for feasting and illuminations.

    See how they welcomed her at court
less royally than she had thought.
The count showed her a sullen face,
400 but when her husband reached the place,
how he sprang up and ran to meet him!
"Welcome!" he calls out loud to greet him
and holds his stirrup. He protests;
"Allow me, lord," the count insists,
405 "to see we gladly meet your needs
here in your house, if you so please,"
leads him beside him to a seat,
has his boots taken off his feet.
The countess comes down to them. She
410 yearns for her mother tenderly,
but still she holds the count in awe,
knowing he's thrashed her once before.
She welcomes first her father, who
gives greeting and kisses her, too,
415 and she welcomes her mother second.
(She'd go with her, but the count's beckoned
her to sit by her father's place.)
Her mother takes it in bad grace.

Le mengier hasterent li queu;
420   devant les dois ont fait bon feu;
laivent, s'assieent au mengier.
Li quens tint son seignor molt chier,
de lez lui l'assist hautement;
molt furent servi richement,
425   molt ont bons mes & bons viez vins
& bons morez & clarez fins.
La fiere dame & li sien .vi.
sont en .i. banc en loig assis,
ne furent pas si bien servi;
430   ce fist li quens tot por *celi*
qui a son seignor ert contraire.
Mengié ont, les napes font traire,
deduit se sont & envoisié,
le fruit ont, puis se sont coschié.
435   La nuit s'en va, li jors apert,
li quens lieve, qui dolenz ert
de son seignor, qui feme a male.
Il l'en apele en mi la sale:
« Sire, alez chacier en mon parc
440   o chiens, o reseus & o arc;
alez chacier a venoison
que a grant plenté en aion.
N'i ait serjant ne chevalier
ovuec *vos* ne voisent chacier,
445   avuec cez dames demorrai.
Li chiés me dielt, grant mal i ai. »
Or sont montez, n'atendent plus,
tuit vont chacier, n'i remaint nus
fors le conte & .iiii. serjant
450   fort & menbruz & fier & grant.
Il le conseille a .i. sien mor:
« Va querre les coilles d'un tor,
les coillons a tot le *focel*,
si les m'aporte, & .i. *tonel*

Comes time to eat, the cooks don't wait,
420 a roaring fire burns in the grate;
all wash and take their place at table.
The count did all that he was able
and placed his guest in the high seat,
where they were served the finest meat
425 in great abundance, wines of price,
liqueurs and drinks with fragrant spice.
The haughty lady and her train
on a far bench had to remain,
where they were served less handsomely.
430 The count treated them thus for she
thwarted the man she should have feared.
They ate and, when the boards were cleared,
amused themselves as they liked best,
had fruit, and then retired to rest.
435 Night passed, and a new day began.
The count wakes, troubled for the man
whose wife's so brazen she would steer him.
Called to the hall, the man comes near him.
The count says, "Sire, I pray you, go
440 and hunt with dogs and net and bow
on my estates. Big game abounds
most plentifully on these grounds.
Let all my household take their place
as your companions in the chase;
445 here with the ladies I'll remain.
I have a headache; I'm in pain."
All took to horse without delay
and went to hunt, leaving to stay
the count with four of his attendants,
450 large, fierce, and rugged, in attendance.
"Go find a bull, cut off its nuts,
and bring them to me with the guts
that cling to them," he tells his Moor,
"a basin, too, and one thing more:

455   & .i. rasoir bien afilé.
Si le m'aporte en recelé, »
& il si fist sanz demorance.
Il prist *la* dame par la manche,
lez lui l'assist, si li a dit:
460   « Dites moi, se Dieus vos aïst,
dites moi ce que vos querrai.
— Volentiers, sire, se gel sai.
— Dont avez vous icest orgueil?
Molt volentiers savoir le vuel,
465   que vos avez en tel despit
vostre seignor &, quanque dit,
vos dites ce que li desplait
& commandez si sera fait.
Feme ne fait vilté graignor
470   que de vill tenir son seignor.
— Sire, plus sai que il ne set,
& si ne fait riens qui m'agret.
— Dame, bien sai dont ce vos vient:
ceste fiertez es rains vos tient.
475   Ge l'ai bien veü a vostre hueil
que vos avez de *nostre* orgueil;
vos avez coilles comme nos,
s'en est vostre cuers orgueillous.
Ge vos i vueil faire taster;
480   s'il i sont, ses ferai oster. »
Dit la dame: « Taisiez, beau sire!
Gas ne me devrïez vos dire. »
Li quens ne volt plus atargier,
ses serjanz commence a huschier:
485   « Estendez la bien tost a terre
as *denz*! *Es rains* li ferai querre. »
Cil estendent la dame encline.
Lors s'escrie: « Lasse! *frarine*! »
.i. des serjanz le rasoir prant,
490   demi pié la nache li fent,

455   a razor, newly sharpened, keen.
      Go do it without being seen."
      The Moor immediately obeyed.
      The count approached the wife and said
      (he sat her by him, held her sleeve):
460   "Now tell me, lady, by your leave,
      something that I should like to know."
      "If I can, sir, I'll tell you so."
      "Where is it that you get your pride,
      I wonder, where does it reside?—
465   for you so scorn your sovereign lord
      that he can scarcely say a word,
      but you will contradict and fight him
      and hand down orders just to spite him.
      A wife can do nothing more base
470   than scorn her husband to his face."
      "My lord, I know much more than he,
      and nothing he does pleases me."
      "I know the cause," the count rejoins.
      "Your pride's engendered in your loins.
475   I have observed it in your glance:
      your self-assurance is a man's,
      and, like us men, you are endowed
      with testicles, so your heart's proud.
      You'll undergo examination
480   and, if they're there, emasculation."
      "Be quiet, sir! What have you spoken?
      Such matters are unfit for joking."
      He means to set to work right then
      and, with a call, summons his men.
485   "Quick, stretch her out there on the ground
      facedown, so we can feel around."
      They hold her down, expose her ass;
      the lady cries out, "Woe! Alas!"
      A servant took the razor blade
490   and with it in her buttock made

son poig i met enz & tot clos
.i. des coillons au tor molt gros,
ça & la tire, & ele brait.
Senblant fet que du cors li trait
495 [tout sanglent, le giete el bacin.
La dame cuide bien enfin
que ce soit voir, & cil revint
qui en sa mein le rasoir tint,
demi pié li fent l'autre nache,
500 semblant fet cil que fors l'esrache,]
tot sanglent el bacin le rue;
cele se pasme qui fu mue.
   Quant ele vint de pasmoison,
« Dame, dit li quens, or avon
505 l'orgueil dom estïez si ose:
or seroiz mais molt simple chose!
Mais ge dout qu'aucune racine
n'i remaigne se nel quisinne . . .
Or tost! .i. costre m'eschaufez
510 *dont* les racines *arderez!* »
Dit la dame: « Sire, merci,
certes lealment vos affi
& sor sainz le vos jurerai
que mon seignor ne desdirai;
515 servirai le si com ge doi.
Tenez, gel vos affi par foi.
 — Or atendez donc sa venue,
jurrez li, s'en seroiz creüe. »
La contesse a forment ploré:
520 « Ça, dit li quens, savez m'en gré
de ce que vostre mere ai fait,
que son orgueill fors li ai trait.
Ge crieng que a lui ne traiez
& cest orgueil es rains n'aiez;
525 mais or soffrez—ge tasterai
& se ges truis, ges osterai.

a six-inch gash, stuck in his fist
with one of the balls, gave a twist
or two, or more, as though to drag
it out. She bellowed like a stag.
495   He tossed the organ in a pail,
all bloody, and she thought it real.
Holding the razor in his hands,
the servant comes back and pretends
to rip the other from her butt,
500   and makes another six-inch cut
and throws it, bloody, in the pail.
She faints, giving a final wail.
  When she's recovered consciousness,
the count says, "Lady, now I guess
505   we've found the pride that made you bold;
from now on you'll do as you're told.
Still, if the roots remain, no doubt
they'll grow unless I burn them out.
Go quickly, heat an iron coulter
510   to cauterize them till they smolder."
The lady says, "Have mercy, lord!
In loyalty I give my word,
on relics I will gladly swear
against my lord never to dare
515   speak out, but serve him as is fit.
Yes, on my oath I promise it."
"Wait till the man's come back here, lady.
Swear it to him, and you'll persuade me."
  The countess wept and sobbed and cried.
520   "Come," says the count, "her willful pride
I've cut out of your mother's flanks,
for which, I think, you owe me thanks.
Since you're her daughter, I am worried
that in your loins this pride lies buried,
525   so come to me and let me feel you.
If I find testicles, I'll heal you."

— Merci, sire, por Dieu le voir!
Sire, bien le devez savoir,
tant i avez sovent tasté,
530   se il i sont—nenil, par Dé!
Ge ne sui pas de la nature
ma mere, qui est fiere & dure;
ge retrai plus, sire, a mon pere
que ge ne faz voir a ma mere.
535   Ainc vostre comment ne desdis
que une foiz, si m'en fu pis,
si en preïstes la venjance.
Ge vos en fais asseürance
que ge ferai quanque volrez
540   & amerai quanqu'amerez.
Se nel faz, le chief me tranchiez. »
Ce dist li quens: « Bele, or sachiez
q'or soffrerai, mais se ge voi
que voilliez reveler vers moi,
545   ostez vos seront li coillon
si com a vostre mere avon,
que ce sachiez, par cez grenotes
sont les femes fieres & sotes. »
          De chacier vint li riches hom;
550   assez a prise venoison.
La dame l'a oï, si pleure,
& il i ala en es l'eure,
si li demande qu'elë a.
Li quens l'encontre, si parla:
555   « Sire, que ge li ai ostez
ce dont el menoit tel fiertez,
cez .ii. coillons qu'es rains avoit
dont ainsi orgueillouse estoit.
Vez les coillons en cel bacin!—
560   n'i meïssiez autrement fin.
Les racines vueil quisiner,
mais ele velt sor sainz jurer

"I thank you, sire. As God is true,
how I am fixed is known to you.
You've often felt around down there.
530 How could I have? No way, I swear!
My mother's nature differs greatly
from mine. She's proud and hard innately;
I'm more my father's child instead
of like the woman whom he wed.
535 When have I ever disobeyed
except for once? And then I paid.
Your retribution was most just.
I give my word, take it on trust,
to do only as you approve
540 and love whatever you may love.
Cut off my head if I rebel."
The count says, "Fair one, listen well.
I'll let it pass, but if I see
you trying to stand up to me,
545 I'll cut your balls out on the spot.
You'll get just what your mother got.
Such kernels have no place in wenches;
they make them prideful and pretentious."
    The rich man came back from the hunt;
550 he'd caught a generous amount
of game. His wife heard through her tears,
and he immediately appears
and asks her what the matter is.
The count comes up and tells him this:
555 "My lord, she weeps because I've cut
the testicles out of her butt,
which caused her to be arrogant
and willful to such an extent.
See her balls lying in that pail!
560 No other treatment would avail.
The roots I ought to cauterize,
but she's said she'll swear to the skies

que jamais ne vos desdira
& volentiers vos servira. »
565 Cil quide que trestot voir soit
por les coillons que iluec voit;
por la dame qu'il voit navree,
cuide qu'ele soit amendee.
Le soirement & la fiance
570 fist la dame sanz demorance;
ses plaies li font reloier
& la letiere apareillier,
si l'enportent sor .ii. chevaus.
Ses plaies ne sont pas mortaus;
575 bon mire ot qui bien la gari:
son seignor ama & servi,
onques puis nel desdist de rien.
       Molt par esploita li quens bien,
benoit soit il!, & cil si soient
580 qui lor males femes chastoient!
[Honi soient, & il si ierent,
cil qui lour fames trop dangierent!]
Les bones devez molt amer
& chier tenir & hennorer,
585 & il otroit mal & contraire
a ramposneuse de put aire:
teus est de cest flabel la some.
Dahet feme qui despit home!

35. LE PESCHEOR DE PONT-SUR-SEINE

J'oï conter l'autre semaine
c'uns peschieres de Pont seur Saine
espousa fame baudement;
assez i prist vin & forment

never to gainsay your command
and wait upon you foot and hand."
565 Her husband credits the count's tale,
seeing the testes in the pail
and likewise fresh wounds on his wife,
so he's convinced she'll change her life.
Scarcely a moment passed before
570 the lady made her pledge and swore.
They bind her wounds and rig a gurney
to bear her on her homeward journey,
tied to two horses and suspended.
Don't think from these wounds her life ended.
575 She had an excellent physician.
She loved her lord with due submission:
When he said something, she agreed.
    The count performed a noble deed,
God bless him! And on all a blessing
580 who teach a wicked wife a lesson!
And shame on all those men who've come
to live under a woman's thumb!
Good women deserve our affection
and high esteem and close protection,
585 while ruthless treatment and abuse
we save for heinous, stinking shrews;
such is the moral of our text.
God curse the wife who disrespects!

35. THE FISHERMAN OF PONT-SUR-SEINE

Last week I heard a fisherman
who plied his trade at Pont-sur-Seine
married a woman lustily
with wine and wheat as dowry,

& .v. vaches & .x. brebis.
La meschinete & ses maris
s'entramoient de bone amor.
Li vallés aloit chascun jor
peschier en Saine en son batel,
& si fesoit argent novel
toutes les foiz que il peschoit;
assez en vendoit & menjoit
& s'en pessoit molt bien sa fame.
Il estoit sire & ele dame
de lui & de quanqu'il avoit;
comme preudom se maintenoit
& la fottoit au mieus qu'il pot.
Qui ce ne fet, l'amor se tolt
de jone fame quant il l'a,
ja bone joie n'en avra,
quar jone fame bien peüe
sovent voudroit estre fotue.

     Un jor gisoient en lor lit,
au bacheler tendi le vit
que il avoit & lon*c* & *gros*;
ou poing sa fame l'ot enclos,
si nel senti ne mol ne vain.
« Sire, dist ele, plus vous aim
que je ne faz Perrot mon frere,
voire, par Dieu, plus que ma mere
ne que mon pere ne ma suer.
   — Je ne t'en croiroie a nul fuer,
fet cil, que tu m'amaisses tant
comme tu me fez entendant,
ainz cuit que tu le dis par guile.
   — Non faz, dist ele, par saint Gile!
Je vous aim por ce que m'amez;
vous me chauciez bien & vestez
& donez assez a mengier,

Nathaniel E. Dubin ❧ 440

5 and five milch cows, also ten ewes.
Each of the married couple views
the other with a tender heart.
Each day the young man would depart
to fish in his boat on the Seine,
10 and he made profitable gain
whenever he went out to fish;
they ate some, sold some to get rich,
and he supported her this way.
He was her lord, and she held sway
15 over him and all he possessed.
This upstanding man did his best
and fucked his wife diligently.
Unless a husband does so, he
loses the love of a young wife
20 and will have no joy in his life,
for a young wife who gets her food
will frequently want to be screwed.

One day when they lay in their bed
the young man's cock reared up its head—
25 he had one long and thick and grand.
The woman held it in her hand
and didn't feel it limp or drained.
"I love you more," his wife maintained,
"more than I love Pierrot, my brother,
30 even, by God, more than my mother,
more than my sister or my father."
"There's no way I'd believe your blather,"
he said. "You don't have so much love
for me as what you're talking of.
35 All that you say is woman's wiles."
"It's not," she said, "no, by Saint Giles!
I love you for the love you show me,
because you buy me shoes and clothe me,
and see to it I always have

40   & si m'achetastes l'autrier
      bone cote & bon sorcot bleu.
      —Tu m'ameroies, fet il, peu
      se plus ne te savoie fere.
      D'aillors covient amor atrere!
45   Se je ne te fotoye bien
      tu me harroies plus c'un chien.
      Je m'en esfors por toi sovent.
      Ja fame por nul garniment
      n'amera si bien son mari
50   com por fere ce que je di. »
      Cele fist molt le grimouart:
      « Fi!, fet ele, que Dieus m'en gart
      que je vous aime por ce fere!
      Molt m'anuieroit vostre afere
55   se le vous osoie veer,
      ja ne vous leroie bouter
      vostre longaigne de boiel.
      Cuidiez vous or qu'il m'en soit bel?—
      ce est la riens qui plus m'anuie.
60   Mengié l'eüst ore une truie,
      mes que vous n'en eüssiez mort.
      — Suer, dist il, tu avroies tort.
      Se j'avoie le vit perdu,
      il me seroit trop mescheü;
65   tu ne m'ameroies ja mes.
      — Si feroie plus c'onques mes,
      fet cele qui volentiers ment.
      Molt me poise quant je le sent,
      tel deable de pendeloche
70   qui entre les jambes vous loche.
      Quar pleüst ore au vrai cors Dé
      que .i. chien en fust enossé! »
            Or ne set son mari de voir
      s'ele ment ou ele dist voir

40   enough to eat, and just now gave
        me a fine new blue coat and jacket."
        He said, "All that still wouldn't hack it
        if I could not do something more.
        More's needed to make love secure!
45   If I did not do you know what,
        you'd hate me like a mangy mutt.
        I push myself to do my stuff
        for your sake. Clothes are not enough
        to keep a wife's love; satisfaction
50   depends much more on fucking action."
        She answered him, making a face,
        "For shame! By God, it's not the case
        that I love you for such a thing!
        You never would quit pestering
55   me if I ever dared refuse,
        or else I'd never let you use
        your little hanging bit of bowel.
        There's nothing else I find more foul.
        Do you think it gives me a thrill?
60   I wish a sow'd eaten her fill
        of it, but you might lose your life."
        "You would be wrong," he told his wife.
        "To lose my cock would be for me
        a terrible calamity.
65   You wouldn't love me any more."
        "I'd love you better than before,"
        she answered, glibly fabricating.
        "To feel it is most aggravating,
        that devilish dingle-dangle thing
70   between your legs that's free to swing.
        God grant that like a bone it were
        stuck in the throat of some stray cur!"
            The man has no way to decide
        whether she told the truth or lied,

75 tant qu'un example li moustra
 par qoi molt tres bien l'esprova.
 Il se leva .i. jor bien main,
 son aviron prist en sa main
 & prist sa roi & son trüel,
80 si s'en entra en son batel
 & s'en rala peschier en Saine
 tant qu'il vint a la mestre vaine
 de l'eve qui estoit corant.
 Lors a veü venir flotant
85 .i. provoire qui ert noié;
 si vous dirai par quel pechié.
  Uns chevaliers le mescreoit
 qui por sa fame le haoit;
 s'en fu espris de jalousie.
90 Tant le gueta & tant l'espie
 que il trova la char jumele,
 le masle deseur la femele
 trova ensanble nu a nu.
 Cil saut en piez, le vit tendu,
95 en l'eve sailli, qui ert grant;
 noier le covint maintenant,
 mes onques nul lieu n'aresta
 & li peschierres le trova.
 Ausi tost comme il a lui vint,
100 de sa fame lors li souvint
 qui dist que rien ne haoit tant
 qui fust en cest siecle vivant
 comme ele fesoit son ostil.
 Le vit rez a rez du poinil
105 li a a son coutel trenchié,
 puis l'a bien lavé & torchié,
 si l'a mis dedenz son giron.
  Atant comme il ot de poisson,
 s'en vint en sa meson arriere;

75　until an event came about
　　which allowed him to find her out.
　　One day he got up well before
　　the dawn and went and took his oar,
　　and also took his net and seine,
80　and shoved his boat out on the Seine
　　and rowed on out until he reached
　　the central stream, because he fished
　　there, where the current was most strong.
　　Then he caught sight, floating along
85　toward him, of a priest who had drowned.
　　Now I will tell you on what grounds.

　　　　A knight who had a strong suspicion
　　about his wife was his perdition,
　　because his jealousy was such
90　he spied on him and kept close watch
　　and found the two joined at the tail,
　　the female underneath the male,
　　body to naked body pressed.
　　Sporting a hard-on, up he gets,
95　leaps in the water (which was high),
　　and cannot help but drown and die.
　　He floated on without a stop
　　until the fisher picked him up,
　　who, when he floated by him dead,
100　remembered what his wife had said,
　　how no one thing made her as sick
　　in all the world as did his prick.
　　He took his knife and amputated
　　the cleric's tool, still much inflated,
105　right at the spot it joined the paunch.
　　He rinsed off all the blood and stanched
　　it and wrapped it up in his coat.

　　　　With what fish he had in his boat
　　he rowed on back to where he lived,

110   si a fet une tele chiere
       comme s'il deüst lors morrir.
       Sa fame le cort conjoïr
       & il li dist: « Suer, tré te en la!
       Jamés mon cuer joie n'avra,
115   quar je sui mors & mal bailli.
       Troi chevalier m'ont assailli
       ou ne trovai nule merite
       fors qu'il me mistrent a eslite:
       il me distrent que je perdroie
120   lequel menbre que je voudroie.
       S'il me tolissent la veüe,
       toute joie eüsse perdue;
       s'il me trenchaissent les oreilles,
       li mons en parlast a merveilles;
125   je dis c'on me copast le vit
       por ce que tu avoies dit
       que tu n'en avoies que faire. »
       Le vit a geté en mi l'aire,
       & cele l'a bien regardé,
130   si le vit gros & [rebou]lé
       & connut bien que c'estoit vit.
       « Fi! fet ele, com fet despit!
       Dieus vous envoit corte duree!
       Or n'est il riens que je tant hee
135   comme je faz le cors de vous.
       Certes or departirons nous.
       — Qoi, bele suer? Ja deïs tu,
       se j'avoie le vit perdu,
       que tu ne m'en harroies ja.
140   Je me merveil comment ce va.
       — Encor, dist ele, di je bien
       qu'il ne me chaut de vostre rien
       se de vostre mauvestié non.
       Jamés ensanble ne girron. »

110 wearing a face so very grieved,
  as if he had no hope of life.
  The happy greeting of his wife
  he answered, saying, "Don't come near me!
  Nothing again will ever cheer me;
115 I'm good as dead and badly shaken
  because by three knights I was taken,
  from whom I could get no concession
  but that I must make a decision,
  saying that I would have to lose
120 whatever body part I choose.
  Now if they took away my eyes,
  I'd lose the joy that I most prize;
  and if they sliced off both my ears,
  the world would speak of it for years.
125 I asked them to cut off my member
  because you told me once—remember?—
  you hated having it around."
    He flung the prick down on the ground.
  She turned and saw the stiffened rod,
130 she looked it over long and hard,
  and she could tell it was a prick.
  She cried, "Oh, what a dirty trick!
  I pray to God you soon will die!
  Your body is the thing that I
135 now most hold in abomination.
  It's time we got a separation."
  "What's this, dear wife? Did you not say
  that if they took my prick away,
  you wouldn't hate me just for this?
140 I wonder what the matter is."
  "Again, your thing or things do not
  matter to me an awful lot
  except this evil," she replied.
  "No more will we lie side by side."

145	Une baiasse ot amenee
	qui estoit de la vile nee,
	ne sai sa niece ou sa cousine;
	ele l'apele: « Ysabeline,
	cueil ces vaches par cel porpris;
150	maine les en par cel postis.
	Je m'en irai par l'uis derriere. »
	Il i avoit une faviere
	qui ja estoit toute cossee;
	oiez de qoi s'est porpenssee.
155	Ele en apele Ysaberon:
	« Bele niece, fai bon giron,
	eslis de ces plus beles cosses,
	& je cueillerai des plus grosses,
	si en enplirai tout mon sain.
160	Ja n'en leroie une au vilain
	se les en peüsse porter! »
	Cil *la* commence a rapeler:
	« Douce amie, quant je t'oi prise,
	je te promis en sainte yglise
165	que je te porteroie foi.
	J'ai bien .xx. & .vi. sous sor moi.
	Vien avant, pren en la moitié;
	g'i cuideroie avoir pechié
	se je t'en toloie ta part.
170	Vien avant & si les depart,
	pren la moitié, l'autre me lesse. »
	& cele contreval s'abesse,
	se li cerche entor le braier,
	si a trové .i. vit si fier
175	qui en ses braies li pantoise,
	ele le paumoie & souspoise,
	si le senti & dur & chaut,
	de joie toz li cuers li saut.
	« Qu'est ce, dist ele, que je sent?
180	— C'est mon vit, dist il, qui me tent

145   Their maid, whom she had brought to live
with her (a niece or relative
who was from the same town as they),
she calls for now: "Isabelle, hey!
Round up the cattle in the croft

150   and drive them through that gate!" she scoffed.
"I'll take the back way to go out."
Now hear what else she thought about.
He'd planted beans out in his field;
the time had come to pick their yield.

155   She gives a call to Isabelle,
"Come, niece," she tells her, "make a well
in your skirt. Fill it with the best
beans you can find. I'll pick the rest
and fill my shift by the same means,

160   for I won't leave the scoundrel beans
if I can cart them all away."
         The fisherman has this to say:
"My darling, when I married you,
I made a vow that I'd be true

165   to you, in church before the saints.
I have here on me what remains—
twenty-six shillings. Half is yours,
for I'd be breaking Heaven's laws,
I think, if I should take your share,

170   so let's divide it up. Come here
and take your half, leave me the rest."
She bends to carry out her quest
and puts her hand into his breeches
and feels around until she reaches

175   a proud prick straining at the bit;
she cups her hand and fondles it
and finds it heavy, hard, and hot.
With joy her heart leaps like a shot.
"What's this I feel?" she said. "What is it?"

180   "My prick," he said, "which has gone rigid,

itel com je soloie avoir.
— Gabez me vous? — Ainz *te* di voir.
— Comment vous est il revenu?
— Ja l'a Dieus fet par sa vertu,
185   qui ne voloit mie, ce croi,
que tu te partisses de moi. »
     Lors le commence a acoler,
a besier & a langueter,
& tint la main au vit toz dis:
190   « Ha! biaus frere, biaus douz amis,
tant m'avez hui espöentee!
Onques puis l'eure que fui nee
ne fu mon cuer plus a malaise. »
Tout maintenant l'acole & baise.
195   El rapele sa chamberiere:
« Ramaine les bestes arriere!,
ele li crie a grant alaine.
Ramaine les bestes, ramaine!
Me sire a son vit recouvré.
200   Nostre Sires i a ouvré! »
     Seignor, fols est qui fame croit
fors tant comme il l'ot & la voit.
Je di en la fin de mon conte
que s'une fame avoit .i. conte,
205   le plus bel & le plus adroit
& le plus alosé qui soit,
& fust chevaliers de sa main
meillor c'onques ne fu Gavain,
por tant que il fust escoillié,
210   tost le voudroit avoir changié
au pïor de tout son ostel
por tant qu'ele le trovast tel
qu'il la foutist tost & sovent.
Se dames dïent que je ment,
215   soufrir le vueil, atant m'en tais.
De m'aventure n'i a mais.

just like it used to do of old."
"Is this a joke?" "It's as I've told."
"But how did it return to you?"
"As the Lord wills, so He can do,
185   and it was not His will, believe me,
that my dear wife should ever leave me."
    Around his neck her arms she flung
and kissed him deeply with her tongue,
still clasping his rod in her hand.
190   "My darling husband, dearest friend,
today you gave me such a fright!
Never since I first saw the light
of day has my heart known such pain!"
She hugs and kisses him again.
195   She calls her servant straightaway:
"Bring back the animals, I say!"
She calls out loud, "Bring back the beef!
Return the stock! It's my belief
my husband's meat has been restored
200   by God, our wonder-working Lord."
    Believing women is absurd
except for what you've seen and heard.
My lords, I'll finish my account
and say, though married to a count,
205   the handsomest and the most skilled
and the most famous in the world,
a better knight by might and main
than ever was the lord Gauvain,
if by some chance he'd been castrated,
210   a wife would ask to have him traded
in for the meanest in her house
were he more ready than her spouse
to fuck her hard and frequently.
If ladies doubt my honesty,
215   I'll let them talk, and I'll be mute.
My story's done; that's all there's to't.

Qui wet au siecle a honeur vivre
& la vie de ceux ensuyvre
qui beent a avoir chevance
molt trueve au siecle de nuisance,
5   qu'il at mesdizans d'avantage
qui de ligier li font damage
& si est touz plains d'envïeux.
Ja n'iert tant biaux ne gracïeux,
se .x. en sunt chiez lui assis,
10   des mesdizans i avra .vi.
& d'envïeux i avra nuef;
par derrier nel prient un oef
& par devant li font teil feste,
chacuns l'encline de la teste.
15   Coument n'avront de lui envie
cil qui n'amendent de sa vie
quant cil l'ont qui sont de sa table,
qui ne li sont ferm ne metable?
Ce ne puet estre, c'est la voire.
20   Je le vos di por un prouvoire
qui avoit une bone esglise,
si ot toute s'entente mise
a lui chevir & faire avoir;
a ce ot tornei son savoir.
25   Asseiz ot robes & deniers
& de bleif toz plains ses greniers,
que li prestres savoit bien vendre
& pour la vendue atendre
de Paques a la saint Remi,
30   & si n'eüst si boen ami

36. THE DONKEY'S LEGACY

by Rutebeuf

Who'd live in honor and pursue
the way of life of all those who
hanker after prosperity
will know the world's severity,
5   for it's our lot to live among
envious folk of evil tongue
who're quick to do harm out of spite.
Though he be gracious and upright,
out of ten of his guests, six persons
10   will slander him and cast aspersions,
and envy's sure to gnaw at nine.
Behind his back they call him swine,
and to his face they make a show
of praising him and bowing low.
15   What else but envy can he get
from those who are not in his debt
when the disloyal men who feed
at his own board are filled with greed?
Impossible. Can't be. No way.
20   I mention this for a curé
who had a gainful benefice
and whose purpose in life was this:
acquiring more riches and wealth;
in fact, he thought of little else.
25   He'd chests of clothes, a treasury
of coins, wheat in his granary,
his skills at salesmanship were great,
and before selling he could wait
twixt Easter and September's end,
30   and no one, even a close friend,

qui en peüst riens nee traire
s'om ne li fait a force faire.
Une asne avoit en sa maison,
mais teil asne ne vit mais hom,
35   qui vint ans entiers le servi;
mais ne sai s'onques teil serf vi.
Li asnes morut de viellesce
qui molt aida a la richesce.
Tant tint li prestres son cors chier
40   c'onques nou laissat acorchier
& l'enfoÿ ou semetiere.
Ici lairai ceste matiere.

      L'esvesques ert d'autre maniere,
que covoiteux ne eschars n'iere,
45   mais cortois & bien afaitiez,
que s'il fust jai bien deshaitiez
& veïst preudome venir,
nuns nel peüst el list tenir.
Compeigne de boens crestïens
50   estoit ces droiz fisicïens:
touzjors estoit plaine sa sale,
sa maignie n'estoit pas male.
Mais quanque li sires voloit
nuns de ses sers ne s'en doloit;
55   s'il ot mueble, ce fut de dete,
car qui trop despent, il s'endete.

      Un jour grant compaignie avoit
li preudons, qui toz biens savoit,
si parla l'en de ces clers riches
60   & des prestres avers & chiches
qui ne font bontei ne honour
a evesque ne a seignour.
Cil prestres i fut emputeiz
qui tant fu riches & monteiz.
65   Ausi bien fut sa vie dite

could get him to sell at a loss
the smallest item, save by force.
He kept a donkey in his stable—
none ever saw a beast so able—
35 who, in his twenty years of service,
gave new meaning to what a serf is.
This donkey, having multiplied
his master's riches, at length died.
The priest held him so dear, he made
40 provision that he not be flayed,
but in the churchyard laid to rest.
        So much for him. What happened next
concerns his bishop, who's the kind
of man toward envy uninclined,
45 who's generous and well-disposed,
who, although he were indisposed,
if any good man came around,
you couldn't keep him lying down.
To all good Christians this good doctor
50 was both a friend and benefactor;
his dining hall was always thronged,
and only honest folk belonged
to his household; if he was moved
to do something, his staff approved.
55 All that he owned he'd bought on credit.
(Who spends too much ends up indebted.)
        One day this man, who made so free
with all he had, had company.
Their talk turned to the wealthy clergy
60 and to those priests, grasping and stingy,
who no honor nor good accord
to bishop or to overlord.
That cleric soon was implicated
who was so rich and self-inflated,
65 the details of his life laid out

con s'il la veïssent escrite,
& li dona l'en plus d'avoir
que troi n'em peüssent avoir,
car hom dit trop plus de la choze
70 que hom n'i trueve a la parcloze.
« Ancor at il teil choze faite
dont granz monoie seroit traite
s'estoit qui la meïst avant,
fait cil qui wet servir devant,
75 & s'en devroit grant guerredon.
    — & qu'a il fait? dit li preudom.
    — Il at pis fait c'un Beduÿn,
qu'il at son asne Bauduÿn
mis en la terre beneoite.
80   — Sa vie soit la maleoite,
fait l'esvesques, se ce est voirs!
Honiz soit il & ses avoirs!
Gautier, faites le nos semondre,
si orrons le prestre respondre
85 a ce que Robers li mest seure;
& je di, se Deus me secoure,
se c'est voirs, j'en avrai l'amende.
    — Je vos otroi que l'an me pande
se ce n'est voirs que j'ai contei.
90 Si ne vos fist onques bontei. »
        Il fut semons. Li prestres vient:
venuz est, respondre couvient
a son evesque de cest quas,
dont li prestres doit estre quas.
95 « Faus deslëaux, Deu anemis,
ou aveiz vos vostre asne mis?
dist l'esvesques. Mout aveiz fait
a sainte esglise grant meffait—
onques mais nuns si grant n'oÿ!—
100 qui aveiz votre asne enfoÿ

like something they had read about,
and all the riches rumor gave
to him were more than three could have,
for people will exaggerate
70 beyond what they can demonstrate.
"Moreover, he has done a thing
which, were it known, would surely bring
in a stiff fine or something graver,"
somebody said to curry favor.
75 "His informer should be rewarded."
The bishop said, "Say what the boor did."
"Why, much worse than a Bedouin!
He had his donkey, Baudouin,
interred in consecrated earth!"
80 "His wretched life will not be worth
much," said the bishop, "if it's true!
Disgraced be he and his wealth, too!
Go summon the priest to appear
before us, Gautier, and we'll hear
85 him answer Robert's accusation.
I swear, as God is my salvation,
that if it's true, I'll make him pay."
"If not, I promise you, you may
have me turned over to the gallows.
90 His attitude toward you is callous."
        The priest was sent for. He presents
himself at court, where some defense
before his bishop must be made.
He's every cause to be afraid.
95 "False traitor! Enemy of God!
Where did you have your ass interred?"
the bishop asks. "You dare besmirch
and defile Holy Mother Church—
I never heard the like!—and bury
100 your donkey in the cemetery

la ou on met gent crestïenne.
Par Marie l'Egyptïenne,
s'il puet estre choze provee
ne par la bone gent trovee,
105 je vos ferai metre en prison,
c'onques n'oÿ teil mesprison! »
Dist li prestres: « Biaus tres dolz sire,
toute parole se lait dire,
mais je demant jor de conseil,
110 qu'il est droiz que je me conseil
de ceste choze, s'il vos plait,
non pas que jë i bee en plait.
      — Je wel bien, le conseil aiez,
mais ne me tieng paz a paiez
115 de ceste choze, s'ele est voire.
      — Sire, ce ne fait pas a croire. »
Lors se part li vesques dou prestre,
qui ne tient pas le fait a feste.
Li prestres ne s'esmaie mie,
120 qu'il seit bien qu'il at bone amie:
c'est sa borce, qui ne li faut
por amende ne por defaut.
            Que que foz dort & termes vient.
Li termes vint & cil revient.
125 .XX. livres en une corroie,
touz ses & de bone monoie,
aporta li prestres o soi;
n'a garde qu'il ait fain ne soi.
Quant l'esvesques le voit venir,
130 de parleir ne se pot tenir:
« Prestres, consoil aveiz eü,
qui aveiz votre senz beü?
      — Sire, consoil oi ge sens faille,
mais a consoil n'afiert bataille,
135 ne vos en deveiz mervillier
qu'a consoil doit on concillier.

as if it were a baptized Christian!
By saintly Mary the Egyptian,
if this thing can be demonstrated
and witnesses substantiate it,
105 I'll have you locked up in a cell!
A graver crime I've not heard tell."
"Reverend Bishop," says the priest,
"people will always talk. At least
grant me one day to give it thought
110 before I have my day in court,
if you'll allow, as is my right . . .
not that I hanker for a fight."
"Though I grant a delay in action,
don't think I'll forgo satisfaction
115 if this be true and we so find."
"Father, it never crossed my mind."
       The bishop left after he spoke
and didn't think the case a joke.
The priest was not upset; he reckoned
120 he could count on his faithful second.
(I mean his wallet, in which he'd
enough to buy off his misdeed.)
       Time passes while the heedless sleep.
The day arrives when he must keep
125 his word. The priest ties round his loins
a purse with twenty pounds in coins
of his own money. (He'd dispense
far more and not know indigence!)
The bishop, seeing him approach,
130 cannot resist one more reproach
and says, "Well, priest, have you had time
to grasp the folly of your crime?"
"It's had my full consideration
and without lengthy litigation
135 may be resolved. Don't be astounded
if we can talk our way around it.

Dire vos weul ma conscïence,
& s'il i afiert penitance,
ou soit d'avoir ou soit de cors,
140 adons si me corrigiez lors. »
Li evesques de li s'aprouche
que parleir i pout bouche a bouche,
& li prestres lieve la chiere,
qui lors n'out pas monoie chiere.
145 Desoz sa chape tint l'argent
(ne l'ozat montreir por la gent),
en concillant conta son conte:
« Sire, ci n'afiert plus lonc conte.
Mes asnes at lonc tans vescu,
150 mout avoie en li boen escu:
il m'at servi & volentiers
molt loiaument .xx. ans entiers.
Se je soie de Dieu assoux,
chacun an gaaingnoit .xx. soux,
155 tant qu'il at espairgnié .xx. livres.
Pour ce qu'il soit d'enfer delivres,
les vos laisse en son testament. »
& dist l'esvesques: « Dieus l'ament
& si li pardoint ses meffais
160 & toz les pechiez qu'il at fais. »
Ensi com vos aveiz oÿ,
dou riche prestre s'esjoÿ
l'evesques por ce qu'il mesprit;
a bontei faire li aprist.
165   Rutebués nos dist & enseigne:
qui deniers porte a sa besoingne
ne doit douteir mauvais lÿens.
Li asnes remest crestïens—
atant la rime vos en lais—
170 qu'il paiat bien & bel son lais.

I'll tell you what I have in mind,
and if you rule I should be fined
or beaten as my penalty,
140   so be it, Father; sentence me."
          The bishop rises and comes close
so they can confer nose to nose,
and the priest looks him in the face.
Money's no issue in this case:
145   He'd twenty pounds beneath his cloak,
well hidden from the gathered folk.
"Father, there's nothing to be gained
by lengthy speeches," he explained
hush-hush. "While my ass lived, all told
150   his help was worth his weight in gold.
He served me well and willingly
for twenty years in loyalty.
As I hold my salvation dear,
he earned twenty shillings a year
155   and had put twenty pounds aside.
He willed them to you when he died
so he'd be rescued from damnation."
The bishop said, "God grant salvation
to him and pardon him his faults,
160   his misdeeds and whatever else!"
          As you have heard, it turned out well
for the bishop that his priest fell
into sin; he was glad that he
'd learned from it holy charity.
165   Here's the opinion of Rutebeuf:
Whoever has money enough
need not fear life's impediments,
and that is how my fable ends.
The donkey's legacy paid well
170   and earned him Christian burial.

57. LE PET AU VILAIN

En paradis l'esperitable
ont grant part la gent charitable,
mes cil qu'en aus n'ont charité
ne sens ne bien ne verité
5 si ont failli a cele joie,
ne ne cuit que ja nus en joie
s'il n'a en lui pitié humaine.
Ce di je por la gent vilaine
c'onques n'amerent clerc ne prestre,
10 si ne cuit pas que Dieus lor preste
en paradis ne leu ne place.
Onques a Jhesucrist ne place
que vilains ait herbregerie
avoec le filz sainte Marie,
15 quar il n'est reson ne droiture.
Ce trovons nous en escripture,
paradis ne pueent avoir
por deniers ne por autre avoir,
& a enfer ront il failli
20 dont li maufé sont mal bailli.
Si orrez par quel mesprison
il perdirent cele prison.
         Jadis fu uns vilains enfers.
Appareilliez estoit enfers
25 por l'ame au vilain recevoir.
Ice vous di je bien de voir,
uns deables i ert venuz
par qui li droiz ert maintenuz.
Maintenant que leenz descent
30 .i. sac de cuir au cul li pent,
quar li maufez cuide sans faille

37. THE PEASANT'S FART

by Rutebeuf

The Heavenly Realm of Our Lord
is where the just reap their reward,
but those who know not charity,
wisdom, good deeds, nor honesty
5   have cut themselves off from this joy,
nor do I think one may enjoy
Heaven who lacks humanity.
I say this for the peasantry,
who have no love for clergymen,
10   so I don't think God holds for them
a place or seat in Paradise.
Heaven forfend that Jesus Christ
countenance that a peasant lodge
alongside Mary's son and God's!
15   It's injudicious and unfit.
We find laid down in Holy Writ
that Paradise they cannot gain
through wealth nor goods nor other gain;
and they are shut off from Hell, too.
20   (The devils, then, can't have their due.)
You'll hear now by what accident
they lost eternal punishment.

     A peasant was feeling unwell
once long ago, and all of Hell
25   made preparations to receive
the peasant's soul, you may believe
my words. A devil was sent forth
to see that justice take its course.
This devil held, when he came near,
30   a leather bag up to his rear,
convinced the peasant's soul would pass

que l'ame par le cul s'en aille,
mes li vilains por garison
avoit ce soir prise poison:

35 tant ot mengié bon buef as aus
& du cras humé qui fu chaus
que la pance n'estoit pas mole,
ainz li tent com corde a citole;
n'a mes doute qu'il soit periz:

40 s'or puet poirre, si est gariz.
A cest enfort forment s'esforce,
a cest esfort met il sa force,
tant s'esforce, tant s'esvertue,
tant se torne, tant se remue,

45 c'uns pes en saut qui se desroie.
Li sas enplist, & cil le loie,
quar li maufez por penitance
li ot aus piez foulé la pance,
& l'en dit bien en reprovier

50 que trop estraindre fet chiier.
Tant ala cil qu'il vint a porte
a tout le pet qu'el sac en porte,
en enfer gete sac & tout,
& li pes en sailli a bout.

55 Estes vous chascun des maufez
mautalentiz & eschaufez,
& maudïent ame a vilain.
Chapitre tindrent l'endemain
& s'acordent a cel acort

60 que ja mes nus ame n'aport
qui de vilain sera issue:
ne puet estre qu'ele ne pue!
A ce s'acorderent jadis,
qu'en enfer ne en paradis

65 ne puet vilains entrer sanz doute.
      Oï avez la reson toute.
Rustebués ne set entremetre

assuredly out through his ass,
but in hope of recovery
he's just downed as a remedy
35 so much beef cooked with garlic cloves
and rendered fat hot from the stove
that both his guts and belly are
taut as a string on a guitar
and he no longer fears his end.
40 If he can only fart, he'll mend.
     Toward this end he strains and forces,
and all his effort and his force is
put to it; he so tries and strives
and rolls around and twists and writhes
45 until at last a fart explodes.
The bag filled up, and the imp closed
it. (For the fellow's sins he'd been
stomping on the man's abdomen.
Indeed, the proverb states, and rightly:
50 "One lets loose when one grips too tightly.")
     The imp came to the gates of Hell
toting both bag and fart as well,
and tossed the bag down when he entered,
and thereupon the fart was vented.
55 Then you could hear the devils holler,
nettled and hot under the collar,
and lay a curse on peasants' souls.
On the next day the chapter holds
a meeting and agrees to make
60 it law that henceforth no one take
any soul a peasant expels.
There's no avoiding it—it smells!
     They agreed on this long ago.
Beyond a doubt, peasants can't go
65 either to Heaven or to Hell,
and for the reason you've heard tell.
Rutebeuf isn't one to know

ou l'en puisse ame a vilain metre
qu'ele a failli a ces .ii. raignes.
70   Or voist chanter avoec les raines,
que c'est li mieudres qu'il i voie,
ou el tiegne droite la voie
por sa penitance alegier
en la terre au pere Audegier.
75   (C'est en la terre de Coccuce
ou Audegiers chie en s'aumuce.)

𝟑𝟖. L'ARME QUI GUANGNA
   PARADIS PAR PLAIT

Nos trovomes en escriture
une mervellose aventure
qui jadis avint d'un vilain.
Mors fu par un venresdi main;
5   tels aventure li avint
q'angles ne deables ne vint
a cele eure que il fu mors;
qant l'ame s'en isci del cors
ne trueve qui rien li demant
10   ne nule cosse li commant;
saciés que molt fu eürouse.
L'ame, qui molt fu paorose,
garda sor destre vers le ciel
& vit l'arcangle saint Miciel
15   qui portoit une ame a grant joie;
aprés li a tenu sa voie.
Tant suï l'angle, ce m'est vis,
que il entra em paradis;
aprés lui est laiens entree.
20   Sains Pieres, qui gardoit l'entree,
reçut l'ame que l'angles porte

just where those peasants' souls can go,
banished from Satan's realm and God's.
70   Let them go sing among the frogs!
That seems to him the best solution . . .
or, to lighten their absolution,
let them go straight off and remain
in Audigier's father's domain.
75   (It's called Cuckoldia, and that
's where Audigier shits in his hat.)

𝟛𝟠. THE SOUL THAT ARGUED
ITS WAY INTO HEAVEN

We can find manuscripts which tell
a wondrous thing that once befell
a peasant in the distant past.
Early one Friday the man passed
5   away. By chance, at his demise
no angel came from Paradise
nor did a demon come from Hell;
when his soul quit its mortal shell,
it found no one to ask it questions
10   or give it orders or directions.
(In this it was most fortunate.)
The soul, still very scared as yet,
looked up toward Heaven on its right.
Archangel Michael in plain sight
15   was bearing a soul, jubilant,
and, following, the peasant went
behind the angel, till he spies
them enter into Paradise
and enters Heaven, as had they.
20   Saint Peter watched the entranceway.
He took the soul the angel bore,

& puis retorna vers la porte,
l'ame encontra qui seule estoit,
demanda li quil conduissoit:
25 « Çaiens n'a nus herbergement
se n'est par mon commandement.
Ensorquetot, par saint Germain,
nos n'avons cure de vilain
& vilains n'a rien en cest estre.
30 Plus vilains de vos n'i puet estre! »
Fait li ame: « Beaus sire Piere,
tostans fustes plus durs que piere!
Fols fu, par *sainte patenostre*,
cil qui fist de vos son apostre.
35 Petit i conquestas d'onor
quant renoias Nostre Segnor;
molt fu petite vostre fois,
quel renoiastes par trois fois
que n'estiiés de sa conpagne.
40 Ceste maisons ne vos adagne,
ains het vos & vostre manoir;
ne devés pas les cles avoir—
alés fors o les desloiaus!—
mais je sui prodom & loiaus,
45 s'i doi bien estre par droit conte. »
        Sains Pieres ot estrange honte;
tornés s'en est, taisans & mas.
Il a encontré Saint Tumas,
se li a conté a droiture
50 trestote sa mesaventure
& son contraire & son anui.
Fait Sains Tumas: « G'irai a lui.
N'i remanra, ja Deu ne place! »
A l'ame s'en vient en la place:
55 « Vilain, ce li dist li apostres,
icil manoirs est cuites nostres
& as martirs & as confés.

and then he turned back to the door
and faced the soul who stood alone
and asked it with whom it had come.
25 "Within these halls none come to live
who do not do so by my leave.
Foremost and first, by Saint Germain,
we've no desire to entertain
a peasant. They've nothing to do
30 here. That goes for the likes of you!"
"Peter, my dear sir," the soul spoke,
"you always were harder than rock.
I swear that he was crazy who
made an apostle out of you!
35 It redounds little to your pride
that by you Our Lord was denied.
Your faith must have been very small,
for you denied three times in all
that you were of His retinue.
40 This dwelling wasn't made for you;
it hates you and your living here.
You shouldn't have the keys you wear—
go join the traitors and disloyal!
By every right, I, as a loyal
45 and good man, may stay in this place."
        Saint Peter felt untold disgrace
and turned aside, dumbstruck and flummoxed,
and then he met up with Saint Thomas,
to whom he made a full narration,
50 detailing his humiliation,
misfortune, and discomfiture.
"Please God, he won't stay, to be sure.
I'll go to him," Saint Thomas added,
and straight off to the soul he headed.
55 "Peasant, the Lord God made this place
for us apostles," Thomas says,
"and His confessors and His martyrs.

En quel liu as tu les biens fes
par qoi tu dois çaiens manoir?
60   Il n'i doit vilains remanoir:
ço est la maizons as cortois.
    — Tumas, Tumas, plus estes cois
des responsaus que nus legistes!
En estes vos ce qui desistes
65   as apostres, dont ert seü
que il avoient Deu veü
emprés le resusitement?
Vos fesistes vo sairement
que vos ja ne le kerriiés
70   se vos les plaies ne veiés
qu'en crois avoit reçut vos Mestre.
Çaiens ne devés vos pas estre,
car faus fustes & mescreans! »
Sains Tumas fu lués recreans
75   de tenchier & basce le col;
venus en est droit a Saint Pol,
se li conte de cief en cief.
Fait Sains Pols: « G'irai, par mon cief,
s'orai qu'il me volra respondre. »
80   L'ame n'ot cure de repondre;
aval paradis se deduist.
« Vilain, fait il, qui vos conduist?
Çaiens ne doit vilains entrer
ne herbergier ne habiter.
85   Ou fesistes vos la deserte
que la porte vos fu overte?
Wide paradis, vilains faus!
    — Cui, fait l'ame, dans Pols li caus,
estes vos? As sains? As tirans?
90   Tant fustes oribles tirans,
jamais si crueus ne sera;
Sains Estevenes le conpara,
cui vos fesistes lapider.

Where did you do good works, and what is
it that says that you may reside
60   in a place peasants are denied?
For genteel souls this place was meant."
"Thomas, Thomas, more reticent
than lawyers are to testify!
Could the apostles certify,
65   you yourself asked them, the man who
they'd seen was God and how they knew,
after He'd risen from the dead?
You swore you doubted this and said
that this could never be believed
70   until you saw the wounds received
on the cross where the Master died.
You are not worthy to abide
here, disbelieving and dishonest."
Afraid to argue more, Saint Thomas
75   thereupon bowed his head in shame;
directly to Saint Paul he came
and to him he disclosed it all.
"By my head, I'll go," says Saint Paul.
"Let's hear what it would say to me."
80   Undaunted, the soul openly
was finding Paradise most pleasant.
He asks it, "Who brought you here, peasant?
No peasant is allowed to come
here to shelter or make his home.
85   What worthy actions did you do
that Heaven's gates opened for you?
Get out of Heaven, base-born soul!"
"Whose man are *you*, bald-headed Paul?"
it asks. "The saints'? The torturers'?
90   A crueler tyrant never was,
nor will there ever be a harder.
You made blessed Stephen a martyr
and had him stoned. Let me retell

Bien sai vo vie recorder:
95   les commans a Deu desdegniés,
en quel liu que vos veniés
tot estoient mort li saint ome,
Deus vos dona sor cele some
une bufë a main enflee—
100 del marcié & de le paumee
devés vos enqore le vin.
Ha, Deus! quel saint & quel devin!
Qant çaiens ont li buen confort,
par foit, vos i estes a tort!
105 [Cu]idiés que bien ne vos conoisce? »
[Sains] Pols en ot honte & angoisce,
[tor]nés s'en est mornes & mas;
[reve]nus est a Saint Tumas,
qui a Saint Piere estroit conselle.
110 Il li raconte la mervelle,
si com li vilains l'ot maté:
« Endroit moi a il conquesté.
Paradis quite li otroi. »
        A Deu s'en vont clamer tot troi.
115 Sains Pieres bonement li conte
del vilain qui lor a dit honte:
« Par parole nos a vaincus.
Je meïsmes sui si conclus
que ja mais, voir, n'en parlerai. »
120 Fait Nostre Sire: « Jo irai
por solement ceste novele. »
Il vient a l'ame, si l'apele,
demande li comment avint
que sans conduit la dedens vint:
125 « Çaiens n'entra onques mais ame
sans conduit, o d'ome o de fame.
Mes apostles as blastengiés
& avilliés & laidengiés.
Comment cuidiés ci remanoir?

your sinful life. I know it well!
95 You scorned the laws God instituted,
and saintly men were executed
wherever you were to be found.
God struck you down on that account;
with His own mighty hand He laid
100 you out, and for the deal you made
you've yet to pay the round of wine.
God! What a saint! What a divine!
When this is where the just belong,
to find you here is clearly wrong.
105 You think you are unknown to me?"
    Anguished at this indignity,
crestfallen, bested, Saint Paul went
back to Saint Thomas, who with Saint
Peter was speaking privately.
110 He told them of the prodigy
and how the peasant won the day.
"For all I care, he's free to stay
up here. He's won a victory."
    They go appeal to God, all three.
115 Saint Peter clearly states their case,
of what was said to their disgrace.
"By argument the peasant vanquished
us all. I am myself so anguished,
I never wish to say a word
120 about it." "*I'll* go," says Our Lord,
"just on account of what you've told
Me." He went to the soul and called
it, asking how it came about
that it had entered there without
125 an escort. "Here no soul may enter,
woman's or man's, that's not been sent for.
When My apostles you've defamed
and vilified and roundly blamed,
by what right do you think to stay?"

130 — Sire, ausi bien i doi manoir
 com il font, se jugement ai,
 car onques ne vos renoiai,
 n'onques ne mescreï vo cors,
 ne par moi ne fu sains om mors,
135 mais tot ce firent il jadis
 & si sont ore em paradis.
 Tant que mes cors vesqui al monde
 nete vie mena & monde:
 as povres dona de son pain,
140 ausmosniers ert & soir & main,
 onques n'ama tençon ne lime,
 volentiers dona droite dime,
 les povres o lui osteloit
 & volentiers les herbergoit,
145 si les escaufoit a son fu,
 maint en garda tant que mors fu
 & puis les portoit a l'eglise,
 mainte braie, mainte cemisse
 mis sor cels qui erent despris.
150 Qant la mors ot mon cors sopris,
 si fu confés veraiement
 & reçut vo cors netement;
 qui ensi muert, on nos sermone
 que Deus ses pecciés li pardone.
155 Vos savés bien se j'ai voir dit.
 Çaiens entrai sans contredit.
 Quant çaiens sui, por que en iroie?—
 vostre parole desdiroie,
 car otroié avés sans falle
160 qui çaiens est, puis ne s'en alle.
 Vos ne mentirés ja por moi!
 — Amis, fait Deus, & je t'otroi
 paradis. Si m'as araisnié
 que par plaidier l'as desraisnié.

130   "Lord, I have as much right as they
       to be here. Right is on my side.
       By me You never were denied,
       nor did I waver in my trust
       nor raise my hand against the just.
135   Transgressions they all have behind them,
       yet here in Paradise we find them.
       When my body lived in the world,
       it led a life pure and unsoiled:
       It shared its bread among the poor,
140   it had no love for strife or war,
       at all times gave to charity
       and paid the tithe unstintingly,
       and always kept an open door
       and offered shelter to the poor,
145   who warmed themselves beside its hearth;
       it cared for many till their death
       and carried them to church; whose back
       was bare of clothing did not lack
       for shirt and trousers—it provided;
150   and when it breathed its last and died, it
       in full contrition was confessed
       and received Holy Eucharist,
       and we are told God will erase
       the sins of those who die in grace.
155   You know the truth of what I've said.
       That I am here can't be gainsaid.
       When I'm here, should I be evicted?
       Your own word would be contradicted,
       for by Your promise You made clear
160   none shall be seized who shelter here.
       For my sake would You be belied?"
       "Friend," says the Lord, "you may abide
       with us. I have heard you bear witness
       and clearly demonstrate your fitness

165 Bien ses avant metre ta verbe! »
　　　　Li vilains dist en son proverbe
que mains om a a tort *requis*
ce qu'en plaidier a puis conquis:
noreture vaint mais nature,
170 fausetés amorce droiture,
tors va avant & drois a orce,
mels valt engiens que ne fait force.

165   By eloquent and skillful speech."
        Here's what the peasant's proverbs teach:
    By argument are vindicated
    many claims falsely arrogated;
    nature is overcome by nurture;
170   the truth falls prey to those who perjure;
    wrong flourishes and cripples right;
    cleverness is worth more than might.

II.

The COMEDY of ERRORS

*N*EARLY ALL FABLIAUX involve some kind of trickery. Again and again, we find people preying on the vanity and gullibility of others. The preceding section has provided numerous examples. It may suffice just to lie (#24, "Thrice Around the Church"), or one may enlist the help of others (#6, "The Priest and Alison") or concoct elaborate schemes (#23, "Auberée, the Go-Between"). They very often rely on twisting language to mislead their victim, or a victim may use the ambiguities of language to circumvent an oppressor (#9, "The Cunt Blessed by a Bishop"). A ruse may also backfire, and some would-be tricksters, like the countess in "The Knight Who Made Cunts Talk" (#14), end up caught in their own trap and have "to drink what they've brewed," as a favorite fabliau proverb puts it.

People resort to tricks for personal gain, to enjoy illicit sex, to cover up their misdeeds, to get even, or for the sheer pleasure of making a fool of someone else. It sometimes happens that one person deceives another unintentionally, or a person may pretend to be deceived and play along with the ruse. Such tales straddle the boundary between "trickster" and "trickster tricked." We also find stories where language and appearances may take over the trickster's role. When communication breaks down because of someone's ignorance or a chance statement ambiguously phrased, what results may not much differ from an intentional trick. Finally, a deception gets out of hand and chaos ensues, sometimes with unwanted results. Fabliau authors enjoyed narrating a good free-for-all.

Often enough, the author tacked on a moral condemning the deception and warning against cheats, but that does not fool the reader. In this genre, cleverness vindicates dishonesty, and while an author may have shown sympathy for the underdog, very few sided with a fool or the loser. In this way, the fabliaux most resemble fables that teach savvy rather than virtuous behavior, and the people in them are more exemplary than individualized. ◆◆◆

Des or, que que j'aie targié
puis qu'il m'a esté enchargié,
voudré [je] .i. fabliau ja fere
dom la matiere oï retrere
5   a Vercelai devant les changes.
Cil ne sert mie de losenges
qui la m'a racontee & dite—
ele est & brieve & petite,
mais or oie qui oïr vialt.
10   Ce dit Garins, qui dire sialt,
que jadis fu .i. chastelains
qui ne fu ne fous ne vilains,
ainz ert cortois & bien apris.
Une fille avoit de haut pris
15   qui estoit bele a desmesure,
mes li chastelains n'avoit cure
qu'en la veïst se petit non
ne que a li parlast nul hom.
Tant l'avoit chiere & tant l'amoit
20   que en une tor l'enfermoit;
n'avoit o li que sa norice,
qui n'estoit ne fole ne nice,
ainz ert molt sage & molt savoit;
la pucele gardee avoit,
25   molt l'avoit bien endotrinee.
           .i. jor par une matinee
vost la norice aparellier
a la damoisele a mengier,
si li failli une escüelle.
30   Tot maintenant s'en corut cele
a lor ostel qui n'est pas loing

39. THE CRANE
by Garin

However much I have been lax
since first I was set to this task,
I'll now compose a fabliau
about something I came to know
5   in Vézelay by the exchange.
It's not at all within the range
of my purpose to say who told it;
it's short enough and soon unfolded,
but listen, if you're curious.
10   Garin the storyteller says
that once there lived a castellan,
neither a fool nor uncouth man,
but courtly, and well-cultured, too.
He had a worthy daughter, who
15   was beautiful beyond compare,
but the castellan didn't care
that any man have conversations
or see her, save on rare occasions.
He kept her shut up in a tower,
20   he loved her so, and would allow her
only her nurse for company.
No silly, foolish woman, she,
but worldly-wise and disciplined,
who saw to it her charge was penned
25   and oversaw her education.
            While engaged in the preparation
of the girl's breakfast, it occurs
on one fine morning to the nurse
that they could use another plate,
30   and off she hurries, doesn't wait,
back to their home, which was quite near,

querre ce dont avoit besoing
L'uis de la tor overt laissa.
Atant .i. vaslet trespassa
35 par devant la tor, qui portoit
une grue que prise avoit;
si la tenoit en sa main destre.

La pucele ert a la fenestre,
a l'esgarder hors se deporte,
40 le vaslet qui la grue porte
apela, si li dist: « Biaus frere,
or me di, par l'arme ton pere,
quel oisel est ce que tu tiens?
— Dame, par toz les sains d'Orliens,
45 c'est une grue grant & bele.
— En non Dieu, fet la damoisele,
ele est molt granz & parcreüe!
Ainz tele mes ne fu veüe.
Je l'achetasse ja de toi.
50 — Dame, fet li vaslez, par foi,
s'il vos plest, je la vos vendré.
— Or di donc que je t'en donré.
— Dame, por .i. foutre soit vostre.
— Foi que doi saint Pere l'apostre,
55 je n'ai nul foutre por changier!
Ja ne t'en feïsse dangier
se l'eüsse, se Dieus me voie,
tantost fust ja la grue moie.
— Dame, fait il, ice est gas:
60 ice ne querroie je pas
que de foutre a plenté n'aiez!—
mes fetes tost, si me paiez. »
El jure, se Dieus li aït,
c'onques encor foutre ne vit:
65 « Vaslez, fet ele, vien amont,
si quier & aval & amont,

to fetch the needed kitchen gear.
She didn't think to lock the tower.
A young man at that very hour
35 came walking by there, and he had
a crane he recently had bagged
clutched in his right hand.

                              Now, the girl,
who liked to look out at the world,
was sitting by the windowpane
40 and saw him pass by with the crane.
She called to him and said, "My friend,
what bird have you there in your hand,
on your father's soul?" He explains,
"By Orléans and all her saints,
45 my lady, it's a large, fine crane."
The girl replies, "In God's own name,
it's fat and fair and just mature;
I've never seen its like, I'm sure.
I'd buy it from you, if I could."
50 "My lady," he says, "well and good.
If that would please you, I will sell."
"What are you asking for it, tell?"
"My lady, for a fuck it's yours."
"Saint Peter help me now, because
55 I haven't any fuck to trade!
God knows, if I had, we'd have made
a bargain quickly—I'm not cheap—
and the crane would be mine to keep."
"Lady," he says, "surely you jest.
60 I certainly would not suggest
a fuck unless you had a lot.
Be quick and pay me what you've got."
She swears to God that, just her luck,
she's never laid eyes on a fuck.
65 "Young man," she says, "come on up now
and look for yourself high and low,

soz bans, soz lit, partot querras,
savoir se foutre i troveras.
Li vaslez fu assez cortois;
70   en la tor entra demenois,
sanblant fet de querre partot.
« Dame, fet il, je me redot
qu'il ne soit soz vostre pelice. »
Cele qui fu & sote & nice
75   li dist: « Vaslez, vien, si i garde! »
& li vaslez plus ne s'i tarde:
la damoisele a enbraciee
qui de la grue estoit molt liee,
sor lou lit l'a cochiee & mise,
80   puis li solieve la chemise,
les james li leva en haut,
au con trover mie ne faut;
lo vit i bote roidement.
« Vaslez, tu quiers trop durement! »
85   fet la pucele, qui sospire.
Li vaslez commença a rire,
qui est espris de la besoingne:
« Drois est, fet il, que je vos doingne
ma grue; *est* vostre tot[e] quite.
90   — Tu as bone parrole dite,
fet la meschine; or t'en torne. »
      Cil la lessa pensive & morne,
si s'en issi de la tor fors,
& la norice i entra lors,
95   si a aparceü la grue.
Toz li sans li fremist & mue;
lors a parlé tost & isnel:
« Qui aporta ci cest oisel,
damoisele? Dites lou moi!
100   — Je l'achetai or, par ma foi;
je l'ai d'un vaslet achetee
qui çaienz la m'a aportee.

'neath bed and benches, all around,
to see if a fuck can't be found."

      The youth, who was well-bred and courtly,
70   came to her in the tower shortly,
pretending to search thoroughly.
"Lady," he said, "it seems to me
there may be one under your dress."
She'd not much sense and knew still less.
75   She told him, "Come, fellow, and look."
Without delay the young man took
her in his arms with might and main
who was enamored of his crane,
placed her in bed and grabbed her shift
80   and hiked it up, went on to lift
her legs way up and held them high,
and her cunt quickly caught his eye,
and roughly he thrust in his rod.
"Young man, you're searching much too hard!"
85   the maiden says, sighing and gasping.
The young man couldn't keep from laughing,
involved to the hilt in his game.
"It's just I'm giving you my crane.
Take full possession of the bird."
90   "You never spoke a truer word,"
the girl says. "Now be off with you!"

      He left her sad and thoughtful, too,
went from the tower and traveled on,
and her nurse came back thereupon
95   and saw the damsel with the crane.
She trembled, and the blood did drain
out of her face, and she was short:
"Young lady, what's this bird? Who brought
it here? Now tell the truth to me!"
100   "I bought it just now, honestly,
from a young man, who sold the bird
and brought it in here, you've my word."

— Qu'i donastes? — .i. foutre, dame.
Il n'en ot plus de moi, par m'ame.
105 — .i. foutre? Lasse! dolerouse!
Or sui je trop maleürouse
quant je vos ai leissiee sole!
.c. dahaiz ait mauvese gole
quant onques menjé en ma vie!
110 Or ai ge bien mort deservie,
& je l'avré, ge cuit, par tens! »
Par pou n'est issue do sens
la norrice & chiet jus pasmee,
& *neporquant si* a plumee
115 la grue, & bien aparrelliee:
ja n'i avra, ce dit, ailliee,
ainz en voudra mengier au poivre.
(Sovent ai oï amentoivre
& dire & conter en main[t] leu:
120 « Li domages qui bout au feu
vaut miaus que cil qui ne fet aise. »)
Qui que soit bel ne qui desplaise,
la grue atorne bien & bel,
puis si reva querre .i. cotel
125 dom ele vialt ovrir la grue,
& la meschine est revenue
a la fenestre regarder.
Si vit lou vaslet trespasser,
qui molt est liez de s'aventure,
130 & la damoisele a droiture
li dist: « Vaslez, venez tost ça!
Ma norrice se correça
de ce que mon foutre enportastes
& vostre grue me laissastes.
135 Por amor, venez lou moi rendre!
Ne devez pas vers moi mesprendre;
venez, si fetes pes a moi.
— Ma damoisele, je l'otroi, »

"What did you pay?" "One fuck, no more;
I gave him nothing else, be sure."
105 "Wretch that I am! Woe's me! A fuck?
How could I have such awful luck
as to have left you here alone?
I curse my mouth for what I've done
that ever it ate or drew breath!
110 I deserve to be put to death
and will be, too, I think, quite soon!"
You'd think the nurse about to swoon
and fall to the floor altogether,
but still she sets out to defeather
115 the crane and dress it for the pot.
A garlic sauce, she says, is not
what's called for; pepper's her intention.
(I often have heard people mention
in many places that I've been:
120 "Adversity that ends up in
the pot at least gives some small comfort.")
Some it may please and some discomfit,
so what?—the nurse seasons the crane
and then has to go out again
125 to get a knife to open it,
and the young girl returns to sit
down by the window and look out.
       She saw the young man, still about
and glad of what had taken place.
130 The maiden called him straightaways
and said, "Come back here, sir, and quick!
My nurse was angered to the quick
because you took my fuck away
when you sold me your crane today.
135 Do give it back, and be so kind
not to begrudge it me or mind.
Come here, and let us two make peace."
"Missy, I'll do just as you please,"

fet li vaslés; lors monte sus,
140 la damoisele giete jus
& entre les janbes li entre,
si li enbat lou foutre el ventre.
    Quant ot fet, tantost s'en ala,
mes la grue pas n'i lessa,
145 ainz l'en a avec soi portee,
& la norice est retornee,
qui la grue vialt enhaster.
« Dame, ne vos estuet haster,
fet la meschine, qu'i[l] l'enporte
150 qui s'en est issuz par la porte.
Desfoutue m'a, jel vos di. »
Quant la norice l'entendi,
lors se debat, lors se devore,
& dit que maudite soit l'ore
155 [qu'ele est hui de la tor issue
quant sa fille li est foutue:]
    « Que je onques de vos fui garde?
Trop en ai fet mauvese garde
quant si avez esté foutue
160 & si n'ai mie de la grue!
Je meïsmes li ai fet leu:
la male garde pest lo leu. »

40. LE PRESTRE QUI ABEVETE

Ichi aprés vous voel conter,
se vous me volés escouter,
.i. flablel courtois & petit,
si com Garis le conte & dit,
5 d'un vilain qui ot femme prise
sage, courtoise & bien aprise.

the young man said; then up he came
140　and stretched her out and did the same.
He went between her legs and pounded
the fuck right back where he had found it.
　　　When he had done, he didn't stay,
but took his crane and went away
145　instead of leaving it behind.
The nurse returned, thinking she'd find
the crane and put it up to roast.
"Don't hurry; it's all labor lost,"
the maiden told the woman, "for
150　the man who just went out that door
unfucked me and took back his bird."
The nurse, no sooner had she heard,
made of her grief such a display
and called down curses on the day
155　she'd left the maiden in the tower
that day for some man to deflower.
"Why was I given you to watch?
So heedlessly have I kept watch
that here you have been fucked again
160　and I don't get a bit of crane!
I gave the man his chance myself:
The careless shepherd feeds the wolf!"

40. THE PEEKABOO PRIEST
by Garin

Next, if you will just hear me out,
here's something you should know about
and which I, Garin, like to tell
that's charming and quite short as well.
5　　　My fabliau concerns a peasant
whose wife was courtly, lovely, pleasant,

Biele ert & de grant parenté;
Molt le tenoit en grant certé
li vilains & bien le servoit,
10 & cele le prestre amoit;
vers lui avoit tout son cuer mis.
Li prestres ert de li souspris,
tant que .i. jour se pourpensa
que a li parler en ira.
15   Vers le maison s'est esmeüs,
mais ains qu'il i fust parvenus
fu li vilains, ce m'est avis,
au digner o sa femme asis.
Andoi furent tant seulement,
20 & li prestres plus n'i atent,
ains vint a l'uis tous abrievés,
mais il estoit clos & fremés.
Quant il i vint, si s'aresta
pres de l'uis & si esgarda
25 par .i. pertuis, garde & si voit
que li vilains mengue & boit
& sa femme delés lui sist
(au prestre volentiers desist
quel vie ses maris li mainne,
30 que nul deduit de femme n'aimme),
&, quant il ot tout esgardé,
esraument .i. mot a sonné:
« Que faites vous la, boine gent? »
Li vilains respondi briefment:
35 « Par ma foi, sire, nous mengons.
Venés ens, si vous en dourons.
— Mengiés, faites? vous i mentés!
Il m'est avis que vous foutés!
—Taisiés, sire, non faisons voir!
40 Nous mengons, ce pöés veoir. »
Dist li prestres: « Je n'en dout rien.
Vous foutés, car je le voi bien!

and smart, nor could you fault her birth.
He, beyond any man on earth,
kept his vow to honor and cherish
10   her, who loved the priest of their parish,
to whom she had given her heart.
The priest, who likewise felt Love's smart
for her, one day decided to
go see her on a rendezvous.
15   He beats a path to where she lives,
but some time before he arrives
her peasant husband with his missus
sits down to eat, or so my guess is—
yes, just the two of them together.
20   The priest didn't just loiter; rather,
he went straight to the doorway, but
he found the entrance barred and shut.
He came to a stop as he neared
the door. Gluing his eye, he peered
25   inside and observed the two people
eating and drinking through a peephole,
the man with his wife by his side.
          The priest (to whom she would confide
the peasant's lack of inclination
30   to meet a husband's obligation),
having seen what there was to see,
called out to them deliberately,
"What's this you're up to, honest folk?"
Answering him, the peasant spoke
35   concisely: "Father, eating dinner.
We'll share it with you. Come on in here."
"Eating, you call it? Nothing doing!
To me it looks more like you're screwing!"
"How can you say that, Father? We
40   are eating dinner, as you see."
The priest replied, "Beyond a doubt,
you're fucking, and I've found you out!

Bien me volés ore avuler!
O moi venés cha fors ester
45 & je m'en irai la seoir,
lors porrés [bien] appercevoir
se j'ai voir dit u j'ai menti. »
Li vilains tantost sus sali,
a l'uis vint, si le desfrema,
50 & li prestres dedens entra,
si frema l'uis a le keville.
Adont ne le prise une bille:
jusqu'a la dame ne s'areste,
maintenant le prent par le teste,
55 si l'a desous lui enversee,
la roube li a souslevee,
si li a fait icele cose
que femme aimme sor toute cose.
[Le vit li a ou con bouté],
60 puis a tant feru & hurté
que il fist che que il queroit,
& li vilains abeuwetoit
a l'huis & vit tout en apert
le cul sa femme descouvert
65 & le prestre [si] par desseure:
« & qu'est chou, se Dius vous sequeure?
fait li vilains. Est che a gas? »
& li prestres eneslepas
respont: « Que vous en est avis?
70 Ne veés vous?—je sui assis
pour mengier chi a ceste table.
— Par le cuer Dieu, ce samble fable,
dist li vilains. Ja nel creïse,
s'anchois dire nel vous oïsce,
75 que vous ne foutissiés ma femme.
— Non fach, sire, taisiés! Par m'ame,
autrestel sambloit ore a moi. »
Dist li vilains: « Bien vous en croi. »

What do you think I am, then? Blind?
Come on out here, if you don't mind,
45 while I go take a seat inside
and leave it to you to decide
if what I've said is false or true."
        The peasant quickly rose and drew
the bolt back and opened the door;
50 the priest strode in and with no more
ado shut it and turned the key.
Without a thought for the man, he
rushed to his wife and went ahead
and grabbed her tightly by the head
55 to hold her under him inert,
reached down and lifted up her skirt
and did to her the very thing
women love more than everything.
He finds her cunt, and then he puts
60 his prick in, and he thrusts and butts
and gets from her what he's been seeking,
and, while he does, the peasant peeking
sees through the door how his wife shows her
fair derrière in full exposure
65 while over her the priest lies spread.
"What's this, the Lord preserve you?" said
the peasant. "Can this be for real?"
The priest goes right on with his meal
and says, "So, how does it appear?
70 Don't you see I'm just sitting here
eating my dinner at this table?"
"By God, I'd swear that was a fable,"
the peasant says. "To trust my eyes,
had you not told me otherwise,
75 I'd say you're humping on my wife."
"Not I, sir! Hush! Upon my life,
that's just what it looked like to me."
"You must be right, then. Well, I'll be!"

Ensi fu li vilains gabés
80 & decheüs & encantés
& par le prestre & par son sans
qu'il n'i ot paine ne ahans,
& pour ce que li vis fu tius.
Dist on encor: Maint fol paist Dius.

41. LE VILAIN DE BAILLEUL

Se fabliaus puet veritez estre,
dont avint il, ce dist mon mestre,
c'uns vilains a Bailluel manoit;
formenz & terres ahanoit,
5 n'estoit useriers ne changiere.
.I. jor a eure de prangiere
vint en meson molt fameilleus.
Il estoit granz & merveilleus
& maufez & de laide hure;
10 sa fame n'avoit de lui cure
quar fols ert & de lait pelain,
& cele amoit le chapelain,
s'avoit mis jor d'ensanble a estre
le jor entre li & le prestre.
15 Bien avoit fet son appareil,
ja ert li vins enz ou bareil,
& si avoit le chapon cuit,
& li gastiaus, si com je cuit,
estoit couvers d'une touaille.
20 Ez vous le vilain qui baaille
& de famine & de mesaise:
cele li cort ouvrir la haise,
contre lui est corant venue,
mes n'eüst soing de sa venue—

That's how the peasant was deceived,
80 duped, and bewitched, so he believed
he hadn't suffered in the least,
tricked by his senses and the priest,
and how he saw things helped besides.
What fools men are! But God provides.

41. THE PEASANT OF BAILLEUL

by Jean Bodel

If fabliaux can have an ounce
of truth in them, by all accounts,
my master says, in Bailleul village
a peasant dwelt and had his tillage.
5   He didn't practice usury.
      At noon one day, at mealtime he
returned home hungry as a bear.
The man was hideous, I swear,
ugly as sin, loathsome, and burly.
10 His wife, since he was dense and surly,
had no love for him in the least;
instead, she loved the local priest
and had invited him to come
and spend the day with her alone.
15 She had made lavish preparation:
The wine was tapped for their collation,
the capon roasted, by the hearth
a fresh cake covered with a cloth,
I do believe, to keep it warm.
20   Here comes the peasant. See him yawn
from hunger—it's high time he ate.
She hurries to unlock the gate
and goes to meet him at a run,
but isn't glad that he has come.

mieus amast autrui recevoir. 25
Puis li dist por lui decevoir
si com cele qui sanz ressort
l'amast mieus enfouï que mort:
« Sire, fet ele, Dieus me saint,
com vous voi or desfet & taint! 30
N'avez que les os & le cuir!
— Erme, j'ai tel fain que je muir,
fet il. Sont boilli li maton?
— Morez, certes, ce fetes mon!—
jamés plus voir dire n'orrez! 35
Couchiez vous tost, quar vous morez!
Or m'est il mal, lasse! chetive!
Aprés vous n'ai soing que je vive
puis que de moi vous dessanblez,
sire, com vous [m'est]es anblez. 40
Vous devïerez a cort terme.
— Gabez me vous, fet il, dame Erme?
Je oi si bien no vache muire,
je ne cuit mie que je muire,
ainz porroie encore bien vivre. 45
— Sire, la mort qui vous enyvre
vous taint si le cuer & enconbre
qu'il n'a mes en vous fors que l'ombre.
Par tens vous tornera au cuer.
— Couchiez me donques, bele suer, 50
fet il, quant je sui si atains! »
Cele se haste ne puet ains
de lui deçoivre par sa jangle;
d'une part li fist en .i. angle
.i. lit de fuerre & de pesas 55
& de linceus de chanevas,
puis le despoille, si le couche,
les ieus li a clos & la bouche,
puis se lest cheoir sor le cors.
« Frere, dist ele, tu es mors, 60

25   She'd sooner have a different guest!
      Then, to deceive him, she addressed
      him in this manner (and no wonder—
      she wished that he were six feet under!).
      "Husband, the Lord bless me," she stated,
30   "you look flushed and emaciated!
      Why, you're reduced to bones and skin!"
      "My hunger's like to do me in,
      Erma. Say, are the curds aboil?"
      "Surely you're dying, on my soul!
35   A truer word was never said.
      You're dying! Quickly go to bed!
      What a mischance for me, your wife,
      alas! I have no taste for life
      after you, husband dear, have gone
40   out of my life and have passed on.
      Before long you'll be laid to rest."
      "Erma," he says, "is this some jest?
      I hear so clearly our cows lowing
      that I cannot believe I'm going
45   to die. No, I'll live on a bit!"
      "Approaching death, which clouds your wit,
      darkens your heart and ruins your health.
      You're just a shadow of yourself.
      Your heart will stop, and you'll be dead."
50   "Beloved wife, get me to bed,"
      he says, "since I am so far gone."
            Racing to carry out the con
      she has cooked up, the bogus mourner
      fixes up for him in a corner
55   a bed of dry pea stalks and straw
      and hempen linen on the floor,
      undresses him and lays him out
      and sees his eyes and mouth are shut,
      then faints across his last remains.
60   "Husband, you're dead now," she complains;

499   ❧   THE FABLIAUX

Dieus ait merci de la teue ame!
Que fera ta lasse de fame
qui por toi s'ocirra de duel? »
    Li vilains gist souz le linçuel,
65 qui entresait cuide mors estre,
& cele s'en va por le prestre,
qui molt fu viseuse & repointe;
de son vilain tout li acointe
& entendre fet la folie.
70 Cil en fu liez & cele lie
de ce qu'ainsi est avenu.
Ensanble s'en sont revenu
tout conseillant de lor deduis.
Lués que li prestres entre en l'uis
75 commença a lire ses saumes
& la dame a batre ses paumes,
mes si se set faindre dame Erme
qu'ainz de ses ieus ne cheï lerme;
envis le fet & tost le lesse,
80 & li prestres fist corte lesse—
n'avoit soing de commander l'ame.
Par le poing a prise la dame,
d'une part vont en une açainte,
desloïe l'a & desçainte;
85 sor le fuerre noviau batu
se sont andui entrabatu,
cil a denz & cele souvine.
Li vilains vit tout le couvine,
qui du linçuel ert acouvers,
90 quar il tenoit ses ieus ouvers,
si veoit bien l'estrain hocier
& vit le *chaperon* locier;
bien sot ce fu li chapelains.
« Ahi! ahi! dist li vilains
95 au prestre, filz a putain ors,
certes, se je ne fusse mors,

"may God be merciful to you!
What can your grieving widow do
but kill herself?" she cries aloud.
The peasant underneath his shroud
65 really believes that he's deceased,
and she goes running for the priest.

She, who was full of tricks and wily,
explained how she had acted slyly
and told him of the peasant's folly.
70 Both he and she were very jolly
that things had worked out as she'd planned.
They walked to her house hand in hand
while they laid plans for their amour.
The priest was scarcely in the door
75 when he began singing his psalms,
and she beat her breast with her palms,
but in spite of her knack for drama,
no tear was shed by Mistress Erma;
her heart's not in it. She soon lay
80 off, and the priest cut short his say
and left the man's soul uncommended.
He took her wrist, and the two wended
their way to an adjacent loft,
where he took all her clothing off,
85 and on the newly beaten hay
the couple tumbled down and lay,
with him facedown and her stretched flat.

The peasant saw what they were at.
Beneath the sheet where he reposed,
90 because his eyelids were not closed,
he watched the hay tossing about
and the cowl bounce. He had no doubt
where the priest had gone and what for.
"You stinker! You son of a whore!
95 I wager you," the peasant said,
"that surely, if I were not dead,

mar vous i fussiez enbatuz!
Ainz hom ne fu si bien batuz
com vous seriez ja, sire prestre!
100 — Amis, fet il, ce puet bien estre,
& sachiez, se vous fussiez vis,
g'i venisse molt a envis
tant que l'ame vous fust ou cors,
mes de ce que vous estes mors
105 me doit il bien estre de mieus.
Gisiez vous cois! clöez voz ieus!
Nes devez mes tenir ouvers. »
Dont a cil ses ieus recouvers,
si se recommence a tesir,
110 & li prestres fist son plesir
sanz paor & sanz resoingnier.
        Ce ne vous sai je tesmoingnier
s'il l'enfouïrent au matin,
mes li fabliaus dist en la fin
115 c'on doit por fol tenir celui
qui mieus croit sa fame que lui.

42. LE PRESTRE ET LA DAME

Icil qui les mençonges trueve
a fait ceste trestote nueve.
        Quar il avint a un mardi
que uns prestres devers Lardi
5 s'aloit a Estanpes deduire,
mais ses deduiz li dut bien nuire,
ainsi com vos m'orroiz ja dire,
mais conter vos vueil tot a tire
comment une cointe borgoise,
10 qui estoit mignote & cortoise,

you'd soon come to regret your humping!
No man ever had such a thumping
as you, sir priest, would get today!"
100 "Friend, it may well be as you say,
and be assured, were you still living,
I'd not have come without misgiving
as long as your body had breath
in it, but since you've met your death,
105 why shouldn't I have fun?" replies
the priest. "Lie still and close your eyes.
They have no business being open."
He shut them once the priest had spoken
and never said another word.
110 Nothing to fear and undisturbed,
the prelate went about his business.
        Though there's no way that I can witness
if he was buried in the morning,
the fabliau ends with this warning:
115 There's nobody on earth as dense as
who trusts his wife more than his senses.

42. THE PRIEST AND
THE WOMAN

Here is another, wholly new,
from him who tells things that aren't true.
        On a Tuesday it came to be
that a priest from around Lardy
5 went to Étampes, where he chased skirt,
but his pleasure was like to hurt
him, as you'll hear me soon explain,
but first I need to make it plain
how a chic woman in that city,
10 who was well-mannered and quite pretty,

li ot mandé, n'est mie guile,
que ses sires a une vile
devoit cel jor au marchié estre;
bien li ot tot conté son estre.

15　Que vos iroie plus contant?
Li prestres s'i esploita tant
& tant de la dame s'aprime
qu'il fu a l'ostel devant prime
ou fu receü sanz dangier.

20　La baiesse atorne a mangier
char cuite en pot, pastez au poivre
& bon vin cler & sain a boivre,
& li bains estoit ja chauffez
quant .i. deables, .i. mauffez,

25　le seignor la dame amena
quant au marchié ot esté ja,
le cheval qui soëf le porte.
Il s'en vint droit devant la porte,
si la trouva molt bien fermee,

30　que la barre ert tote coulee.
Quant il parla, si dit: « Ovrez
errant & point n'i demorez!
Por quoi m'avez la porte close? »
& la borgoise molt en poise

35　cui li covient la porte ovrir,
mais cele fist avant covrir
les pastez soz une touaille,
& puis aprés se retravaille
de repondre le chanteor,

40　qui de soi avoit grant paor.
Au provoire loe & conseille
qu'il entrast en une corbeille
qui ert mise dedenz la porte,
& cil qui ne se desconforte

45　cel conseil ne refusa mie,
ainz entra sanz nule aïe

had summoned him and made it known
her husband would be out of town
that day at market, honestly,
and told him just when she'd be free,
15   et cetera. Need I say more?
           The priest was at the woman's door
well before prime, such was his zeal
and haste to see the woman. She'll
give him a very friendly greeting!
20   The serving girl prepares for eating
peppered pasties, meat in a pot,
and good, clear, wholesome wine. A hot
bath was set out, ready and steaming,
but just then some devil, some demon,
25   brought the woman's husband back home.
To market he had gone and come
back again. (He has a good horse.)
He went to go in, but the door's
shut fast, as he found out, and closed
30   because somebody's drawn the bolts.
When he spoke—"Open up," he says,
"and quickly! I'll brook no delays.
Why have you locked the gate on me?"—
his wife must of necessity
35   open for him. She's more than bothered,
but first she had the pasties covered
beneath a towel, and then she tried
to come up with a place to hide
the man who sings the Mass and psalms,
40   whom this sudden return alarms.
She admonishes him to get
in a large basket by the gate,
which someone had put there. The priest
felt no compunction in the least
45   in following what she suggested
and climbed inside it unassisted,

que geter se velt de la frape,
mais il laissa aval sa chape;
plus ne repostrent ne ne firent,
50 tot maintenant la porte ovrirent
au borgois qui tendoit la muse.
Cil entra enz & partot muse
tant qu'il a la cuve veüe
ou la dame estoit tote nue;
55 ainz nul barat n'i entendi.
Tantost du cheval descendi,
si l'a fait molt tost establer,
& cil qui n'a soig de fabler,
qui repoz ert en la corbeille,
60 icil ne dort ne ne someille,
mais si fort de poor trestranble
que la corbeille & lui ensanble
encontre terre aval chaïrent.
Cil de l'ostel pas ne le virent.
65 Quant il vit qu'il estoit cheüz
& qu'il n'estoit mie veüz,
si s'en vient enmi la meson,
hardiement dist sa reson;
ne parla pas comme noienz.
70 « Dieus, fait li prestres, soit ceanz!
Ge vos raport vostre corbeille. »
Au borgois vint a grant merveille
quant il vit ainsi le provoire,
& la dame li fait acroire
75 que ele li avoit prestee.
Bien est la dame asseüree:
« Certes que ge en ai bon gaige.
—Dame, vos feïstes outraige,
fait li borgois, quant en preïstes
80 son gaige ne *le* retenistes. »
Or est li prestres fors de foire:
« Dame, fait il, ma chape noire,

not wanting to get knocked around.
His cape, though, he left on the ground.
They hid nor did not one thing more
50   and quickly opened up the door
for him who stood cooling his heels.
          Coming directly in, he steals
a glance around and in a minute
saw the tub and his wife, nude, in it,
55   so, not suspecting any trick,
he then dismounted and was quick
to have his horse put in the barn.
The priest's no mind to prattle on
inside the basket that they chose
60   to hide him in, nor does he doze,
but shakes with fear so forcefully
the large wicker basket and he
together tumble to the ground.
The others didn't turn around
65   to look, and when he saw his fall
was unperceived by one and all,
he walked right in and, unafraid,
said whatever came in his head,
but not like some nonentity.
70   "May God dwell in this house!" says he.
"Your basket, I've come to return it."
          Her husband was surprised to learn it
and see the priest out of the blue,
and his wife makes him think it's true
75   that he had borrowed it from her
and tells her husband, to make sure,
"He gave something in surety."
"Woman, you acted shamefully.
To think you'd want," her husband says,
80   "and take and hang on to his pledge!"
          So now the priest is in the clear.
"Lady," he says, "my black cape here,

se vos plaist, quar me faites rendre.
Ge n'ai mestier de plus atendre—
85 & ma toaille & mes pastez.
　　　—Sire prestres, trop vos hastez.
Mais viengiez avuec mon siegnor,
si l'i faites itant d'ennor. »
& li prestres dit, « Ge l'otroie »
90 qui du remanoir ot grant joie.
Il est remés sanz grant dangier;
lors vont laver & puis mengier.
La table sist sor .ii. coissins;
desor la nape ot .ii. broissins
95 ou il avoit cierges d'argent,
molt [par] estoient bel & gent;
lors despiecent pastez & froissent.
La dame & li prestres s'angoissent
de verser vin a grant foison
100 tant qu'au seignor de la maison
ont tant doné de vin a boivre
& mengier des pastez au poivre
que il fu maintenant toz yvres:
si ot vaillant plus de .m. livres
105 en son chatel que au matin,
lors commence a paller latin
& postroillaz & alemant
& puis tyois & puis flenmanc,
& se ventoit de *sa largesce*
110 & d'une trop fiere proësce
que il soloit faire en s'anfance—
li vins l'avoit fet roi de France!
Lors dist li prestres, ce me sanble,
que .iii. genz leveroit ensanble,
115 mais li borgois li contredist
& dit, « Merveilles avez dit.
Ice ne porroit pas voir estre.
Merveille avez dit, sire prestre. »

please give it back, as I require.
To linger I have no desire. . . .
85 Oh, yes—my towel, too, and pasties."
"I can't think, Father, what your haste is.
Do visit with my husband, Father.
He would be honored. It's no bother."
The priest, who was most glad to stay,
90 says to them, "I will, if I may."
So he stayed on with right goodwill.
        They washed and went to eat their fill.
The table was placed on two props;
a pair of wood candlesticks tops
95 the cloth, with silver candles, which
were lovely, elegant, and rich.
They cut the pasties up and break
them, and the priest and woman make
an effort to pour lots of wine
100 until they've given, by design,
him so much alcohol to drink
and peppered pies, beyond the brink
of total drunkenness has passed
the master of the house. Just last
105 morning he had a thousand pounds
stashed somewhere on the castle grounds!
He eloquently undertook
to speak Latin, gobbledygook,
German and two Dutch dialects,
110 boasted of his largesse, and next
told one of his wild, youthful stunts.
The wine had made him *roi de France!*
The priest, I do believe, then vaunts
he'll lift three people all at once,
115 but the good citizen protested.
"You're talking marvels," he insisted.
"It can't be true, Father; no way.
You're talking miracles, I'd say."

Fait li prestres, « & g'i metroie.

120 —& qu'i metroiz? fait il. —Une oie,
fait li prestres. —Se vos volez,

. . . . .

fait li borgois, qui le devee;
la parole au provoir agree,

125 & molt li plaist & atalente.
Lors vient au borgois, si l'adente
tot estendu encontre terre,
& puis va la baiasse querre,
si l'a mise sor son seignor;

130 a la dame fist tant d'onor
que sor li lieve la chemise,
aprés si l'a enverse mise,
entre les cuisses si li entre
par le pertuis li entre el ventre;

135 la a mis son fuiron privé.
(Molt seroit malvais au civé
li connins que li fuirons chace;
molt est fous qui tel connin trace.
mielz li venroit trover .ii. lievres,

140 quar cil connins est si enrievres
qu'il ne puet faire bele chiere
s'il n'a fuiron en sa tesniere.)
Deci au borjois vos rameine:
de lui relever molt se paine

145 que quant li prestres boute & saiche
li borgois dit qu'il les esquasche
& que desor lui a .ii. rosches,
& li prestres sone .ii. closches,
qui avoit faite sa besoigne;

150 au borgois a dit sanz aloigne,
« Levez sus, que ge ne porroie
ces .iii. lever por riens que j'oie,
porquant s'en ai tel paine eüe
que tote la coille m'en sue

"I'll bet," the priest says, "and won't lose."
120 "What will you bet?" he asks. "A goose,"
the priest says. "I leave it to you,"
. . . . .

the husband answers, unconvinced.
He's on; the bargain has been clinched,
125 which makes the priest feel very glad.
       He went to the husband and had
him stretch out facedown on the floor,
and then he went out to look for
the maid; on top of him he gave her
130 orders to lie, then, as a favor
to the woman, lifts her skirts
and over those two he inverts
her, and between her thighs goes in
the hole below her abdomen.
135 He put his own pet ferret there.
(I personally wouldn't care
to partake of a coney stew
from one that ferret would pursue!
To hunt coneys like this is mad—
140 better two hares! Their mood is bad,
because these coneys feel depressed
when there's no ferret in their nest.)
       Let's turn to the husband again.
He tries hard to get up, for when
145 the priest humps up and down and pushes,
the man complains because it squooshes
them and it feels as if he's weighted
down by two stones. Once the priest's sated
and he has rung out both his bells,
150 with no further delay he tells
the husband, "Get up. I could not
lift you three whatever I got.
My efforts and determination
have drenched my balls with perspiration.

155 de l'angoisse & de l'efforz. »
Dist la dame: « N'estes si forz
que ausi forz ou plus ne soit.
Or paiez l'oie, car c'est droit.
—Dame, fait il, par bone estraine!
160 Soffrez vos jusqu'a diemeine.
Vos l'avrez grasse, par ma foi. »
Dit le borgois, « & ge l'otroi.
Si l'acheterez au marchié.
Bien ai eü le col charchié.
165 Alez a Dieu beneïçon. »
A tant s'en vait en sa maison,
que saigement a esploitié.
C'est de tel vente, tel marchié.
        Par cest flabel poez savoir
170 molt sont femes de grant savoir,
teus i a, & de grant voisdie.
Molt set feme de renardie,
quant en tel maniere servi
son bon seignor por son ami.

43. GOMBERT

En iceste fable parolle
de .ii. clers qui vindrent d'escole,
s'orent despendu lor avoir
& en folie & en savoir.
5 Ostel pristrent ches .i. vilein.
De sa fame, dame Gillein,
fu l'un des clers des qu'il la vint
si fous qüe amer li covint,
mes ne set comment s'en acointe.
10 La dame estoit mignote & cointe,

What pain and suffering I had!"
"You're not so strong," the woman said,
"that there's none stronger or as good.
Pay us the goose now, as you should."
"Lady, a lucky turn of Fate.
Be patient till tomorrow; wait.
You'll have a fat one, I dare say!"
Her husband answers, "That's okay.
You'll buy one in the marketplace.
Good-bye for now. Go with God's grace.
That's one load taken off my back!"
　　　　So thereupon the priest goes back
to his house. He's done very well.
As goes the market, buy or sell.
　　　　By this fabliau we may know
women are really in the know,
at least some are, and very clever.
A woman is a skilled deceiver,
since this one made a cuckold of a
kind, loving husband for her lover.

43. GOMBERT

by Jean Bodel

Now here in this next fable you'll
hear of two students, fresh from school,
who'd spent whatever wealth they had
in sensible ways and in bad.
　　　　Once they lodged at a peasant's house.
One of the two fell for his spouse,
named Jill, as soon as he had come,
so madly he must make love some-
how with her, but where should he start?
The woman was comely and smart

s'ot clers les euz comme cristal;
tote jor l'esgarde a estal
li clers, si c'autre part ne cille.
Li autres aama sa fille
15 si qu'adés i metoit ses euz.
Cil mist encore s'entente mieus,
car sa fille ert & jane & bele,
& je di c'amor de pucele
quant faus cuer n'i est ententis
20 est sor totes amors gentis
com est li ostour au terçueil.
.i. petit enfant el berçueil
pessoit la prodefame en l'estre.
Que qu'ele l'entendoit a pestre
25 l'un des clers les li s'acosta,
fors de la paalete osta
l'anelet ou ele pendoit,
si le bouta *enson* son doit
si cointement que nus nel sot.
30   Tieus biens com frere Gonbers ot
orent la nuit asez si oste—
let bouli, frommage & conposte—
ce fu asez commë a vile.
Molt fu tote nuit dame Gille
35 regardee de l'un des clers;
les ieus i avoit si aers
que il nes en poeit retrere.
Li vileins, qui bien cuidoit fere
& n'i entendoit el que bien,
40 fist leur lit fere les le sien,
ses a couchiez & bien covers,
dont s'est couchié sire Gonbers
quant fu chaufé au feu d'estouble,
& sa fille jut tote sole.
45   Des que li gent fu endormie
li clers ne s'entroublia mie:

and she had eyes so crystal clear
that all day long he stares at her
fixedly, without even blinking.
The other student had been thinking
15 of her daughter since he first saw
her, so his heart aimed higher, for
the girl was beautiful and young,
and I say such love is among
the best, surpassing every other,
20 just as a goshawk ranks above a
tercel, if one's heart means no ill.

     A baby, in the cradle still,
the good woman was nursing by
the hearth. One of the two came nigh
25 while she was nursing him and took
the ring from a pot, used to hook
it up over the fire; then he
on his fingertip stealthily
slipped it so that nobody knew.

30   All the good things Gombert had to
give them, his guests enjoyed that night:
boiled milk and cheese and stewed fruit, quite
the ordinary country fare.
One of the students fixed his stare
35 on Jill all evening long, so eager
he couldn't get his glance to leave her
or turn aside. The peasant, who
was only thinking how to do
right by them, as he thought was best,
40 alongside his had their bed placed,
covered them well, and had them turn
in, and then it was Gombert's turn,
warmed by the straw fire he had made.
His daughter slept alone in bed.

45   When he saw everyone was sleeping,
the first student, who had been keeping

molt li bat le cuer & flaelle;
o tot l'anel de la paelle
au lit la pucele s'en vint.
50 Or oiez com il li avint!
Les li se couche & les dras euvre.
« Qui est ce or qui me descuevre?
fet ele quant ele le sent.
Sire, por Deu omnipotent,
55 qu'avez vos quis ci a tele eure?
— Bele, se Jhesu me sequeure,
n'aiez paour que sus vos voise,
mes tesiez vos, ne fetes noise
que vostre perre ne s'esveille,
60 car il cuideroit ja merveille
s'il savoit qu'avec vos geüse:
il quideroit que jë eüse
de vos fetes mes volentez.
Mes se mon bon me consentez,
65 grant bien vos en vendra encor
& s'avrés ja mon anel d'or,
qui plus vaut de .iiii. besanz.
Sentez mon com il est pesanz:
il m'est trop grant au doi manel! »
70 A tant li a bouté l'anel
el doi, si li passe la jointe,
& cele s'est envers li jointe
& jure *que ja nel* prendroit.
Toute voies, qu'a tort qu'a droit,
75 l'uns vers l'autre tant s'umelie
que li clers li fist la folie;
mes com il plus acole & bese
plus est ses conpains en malese
c'a la dame ne puet venir,
80 car cil le fet resovenir
que il ot fere ses deliz.

watch with a palpitating heart,
with the ring he took from the pot
approached the bed where the girl lay.
50 Listen! It happened in this way:
He lies down and takes off the covers.
"What person is this who uncovers
me?" she says, feeling him by her.
"By God all-powerful, kind sir,
55 what do you want here at this hour?"
"Fair one, fear not if I come now or—
God forbid!—that I'll do you harm.
Hush up and don't raise an alarm,
for if your father should awaken,
60 he would believe that I had taken
advantage of you. If he knew
that I was lying here with you,
great would be his astonishment.
If you will give me your consent
65 to do my pleasure, it will bring
you great wealth. You shall have my ring
of gold, worth over four besants.
Feel how it's heavy in my hands:
My finger isn't large enough!"
70 With that he proceeded to stuff
it on her finger past the joint,
and she turned to him and enjoined
him, no! and swore she can't accept
it, come what may, and so they kept
75 on exchanging these courtesies
till the student did what he pleased.

      The more he kisses and embraces,
the greater his companion's stress is
that he cannot get at the woman,
80 for the other brings it home to him
when he listens to his delights.

Ce qu'a l'un estoit paradis
estoit a l'autre droit enfers.
    Dont s'est drecié sire Gonbers,
85 si se leva pissier touz nuz,
& li clers est au lit venuz
a l'esponde par dedevant,
si prent le bers atot l'enfant,
au lit lo met ou ot geü.
90 *Ez* vos dant Gonbert deceü,
car tot a costume tenoit
la nuit quant de pisier venoit
qu'il gardoit au berçueil premier.
Si comme il estoit coustumier,
95 vint atastant sire Gombers
au lit, mes n'i fu pas li bers.
Quant il n'a le berçuel trové,
lors se tint por musart prové;
il cuide avoir voie changie:
100 « Deable, fet il, me charie,
car en cest lit gisent mi oste. »
Lors vint a l'autre lit encoste,
si sent le berz o le mailluel,
& le clerc jouste le paluel
105 se tret que *li vilains nel* sente.
Lors fist Gonbert chiere dolente
quant il n'a sa fame trovee;
cuide qu'ele soit relevee
pissier & fere ses degras.
110 Li vilein senti chaus les dras,
si se muce entre les linceus;
le someil li fu pres des eus,
si s'en dormi enelepas;
& li clers ne s'oublia pas:
115 avec la dame ala couchier;
einz ne li lut son nes mouchier
s'ot esté .iii. fois a s'amie.

One of them was in Paradise;
Hell held the other in its throes.

    It was then that Gombert arose
85 and went out to piss in the raw.
The student went and stood before
the foot of the bed, where the lady
was left alone, and moved the baby
and cradle next to his own bed.
90 You see how Gombert was misled,
because he was habituated
at night after he'd urinated
to have the cradle orient
him on his way. So Gombert went
95 as always, and he felt around
the bed. No cradle's to be found.
When it turned out he couldn't spot it,
he had to be, he thought, besotted
and had managed to lose his way.
100 "The Devil's leading me astray,"
he says. "In this bed are my guests!"
He went on and felt by the next
the cradle and the swaddling clothes.
Close to the wall the student goes
105 so he will not be recognized.
Gombert was saddened and surprised
when he found his wife wasn't there,
and thinks she must have gone somewhere
at Nature's call to take a whiz.
110   How warm the peasant's bedding is!
Nestled between the sheets he lies,
sleep closes in over his eyes,
and off to slumberland he speeds.
The student won't neglect his needs.
115 Into the woman's bed he goes;
before she could have wiped her nose
he's been with her three times around.

Or a Gombert bone mesnie—
molt *le mainent* de male pile!

120 « Sire Gonbert, fet dame Gille,
si vieus com estes & usez,
trop estes anuit eschaufez,
ne sai de quoi il vos *sovint*;
grant piece a mes ne vos avint—

125 cuidiez vos qu'il ne m'en anuit?
Vos avez fet ausi anuit
com s'il n'en fust nul recovriers.
Trop estes anuit bons ovriers;
n'avez gueres esté oiseus! »

130 Cil ne fu mie trop noiseus,
einz fist totes voies son bon
& *li laissa* fere le son;
ne l'en est pas a une bille.

Li clers qui jut avec sa fille,
135 quant assez ot fet son delit,
penssa qu'il iroit a son lit
ainz que li jours fust esclairiez.
A son lit s'en est reperiez
ou Gonbert se gisoit, ses ostes,

140 & cil le fiert delés les costes
grant coup du poing a tot le coute.
« Cheitis, bien as gardé la coute!
fet cil. Tu ne vauz une tarte,
mes ençois que de ci me parte,

145 te dirai bien fete merveille! »
A tant sire Gonbert s'esveille,
si s'est tantost aperceüz
qu'il est gabez & deceüz
par les clers & par lor engiens:

150 « Di moi dont, fet il, dont tu viens.
— Dont? fet cil, si nomma tot outre:
Par le cuer Dieu, je vien de foutre,
mes que ce fu la fille a l'oste!

Now how those baleful pestles pound
Gombert's big, happy family!
120 "Gombert," says his wife, Jill, "I see
that, old as you are and depleted,
tonight you're awfully overheated.
I don't know what's come over you,
and it's been such a long time, too—
125 you think I liked going without it?—
and now tonight you've gone about it
like it was going out of style.
For sure, tonight you've not been idle,
and made good work of it, at that!"
130 The student, in no mood to chat,
went right back to having his fun,
allowing her to have her own,
no matter if he's out of order.
The student who lay with the daughter,
135 when he had had enough delight,
thought that before the sky grew light
it would be time for him to head
back where he slept. Back to his bed
he went, where his host lay, Gombert,
140 and in the ribs gave him a smart
jab with his forearm, and he said,
"You sorry, timid slugabed,
your exploits are not worth a pie!
Before I get up from here I
145 will tell you wonders." When he spoke
to him, Mr. Gombert awoke
and in no time flat he's perceived
he's been deluded and deceived
both by the students and their game.
150 "Tell me," he says, "where you just came
from." "Where?" he says, and spits it out:
"By God's heart, from a fucking bout,
and with the daughter of our host!

Sin ai pris deriere & encoste,
155   afeuré li ai son tonnel,
      & si li ai donné l'anel
      de la paalete de fer.
         — Ce soit par trestouz ceus d'enfer,
      fet cil, les cens & les milliers! »
160   A tant l'aert par les iliers,
      sel fiert du poing delés l'oïe,
      & cil li rent tele joïe
      que tuit li oeil li estencelent,
      & par les cheveus *s'entre aficelent*
165   si fort—qu'en diroie je el?—
      c'on les poïst sor .i. tinel
      porter de chief en chief la vile.

      « Sire Gonbert, fet dame Gille,
      levez tost sus, car il me senble
170   que li clerc conbatent ensenble!
      Je ne sai qu'il ont a partir.
         — Dame, jes irai departir »,
      fet cil; lors s'en vet cele part.
      Venuz i dut estre trop tart,
175   que ses conpainz ert abatuz.
      Quant cil s'est sor eus enbatuz,
      dont en ot le peour Gombers,
      car cil l'ont ambedui aers:
      li .i. le bat, l'autre le fautre,
180   tant le boute li .i. sor l'autre
      qu'il ot, par le mien encïentre,
      si mol le dos comme le ventre.
      Quant ainsi l'orent atorné,
      andui sont en fuie torné
185   par l'uis, si le lessent tot ample.
              Ceste fable dist por essample
      que nus hons qui bele fame ait
      por nule *proiere* ne lait

I took her backward, sideways, thrust
155 into her vat like anything,
and also let her have the ring
I took off of the iron pot."
"By all the devils Hell has got,
hundreds and thousands of them!" cries
160 Gombert, and grabs him by the sides
and punches him beside the ear,
and in return, so stars appear
to his eyes, he's punched in the jaw.
They grip each other's hair—what more
165 can I say?—so strongly and yank,
you could have borne them on a plank
from end to end right through the vill-
age.
        "Hey, Gombert!" says his wife, Jill,
"get up quick, for I have no doubt
170 those students are slugging it out.
I don't know what's got them so heated."
"Lady, I'll get them separated,"
her student says, and heads their way.
Almost too late he joined the fray,
175 for his friend was already down,
but when the second trounced upon
them, Gombert had the worst of it,
for both go at him. One man hit
him while the other man lambasted
180 him; one after the other wasted
him so bad that, as I heard tell, he
felt his back was soft as his belly.
The two, after they'd thus ill-treated
him, fled through the door and retreated,
185 leaving it wide open behind.
        This little fable calls to mind
that no man with a pretty wife
should ever permit, on his life,

jesir clerc dedenz son ostel
190   qu'il ne li face autretel.
Qui bien lor fet sovent le pert,
ce dit le fablel de Gombert.

44. LA SAINERESSE

D'un borgois vous acont la vie
qui se vanta de grant folie
que fame nel porroit bouler.
Sa fame en a oï parler,
5   si en parla priveement
& en jura .i. serement
qu'ele le fera mençongier,
ja tant ne s'i savra guetier.
.i. jor erent en lor meson;
10   la gentil dame & le preudon
en .i. banc sistrent lez a lez.
N'i furent gueres demorez,
ez vous .i. pautonier a l'uis
molt cointe & noble, & sanbloit plus
15   fame que homme la moitié,
vestu d'un chainsse deliié,
d'une guinple bien safrenee,
& vint menant molt grant posnee.
Ventouses porte a ventouser,
20   & vait le borgois salüer
en mi l'aire de sa meson:
« Dieus soit o vous, sire preudon,
& vous & vostre conpaignie!
— Dieus vous gart, dist cil, bele amie!
25   Venez seoir lez moi ici.
— Sire, dist il, vostre merci,
je ne sui mie trop lassee.

a student to lodge with him lest
190 he do the same. Give them your best
and it's all to your loss. I show
that here in Gombert's fabliau.

𝟦𝟦. THE HEALER

I'll tell you the biography
of a burgher, who foolishly
boasted no woman could outsmart him.
His wife, it happened, overheard him
5   and spoke about it on the sly,
swearing an oath that she would try
to make him out to be a liar
however closely he might eye her.
            One day these two were in their house,
10   the good man and his well-bred spouse
on a bench, sitting side by side.
Before long—behold!—who should stride
up to their door? Some low riffraff
so all dolled up, he seemed by half
15   more like a woman than a male
in the loose-fitting gown and pale
wimple he wore of saffron yellow.
He has with him, the cheeky fellow,
a set of cups for bleeding patients,
20   and goes and offers salutations
to the burgher who's sitting there.
"God be with you, most worthy sir,
and with all those who live with you!"
"You lovely lass, God keep you, too,"
25   he said. "Come sit beside me here."
"I thank you, sir," he said. "I swear
that I am not the least bit tired.

Dame, vous m'avez ci mandee
& m'avez ci fete venir;
30 or me dites vostre plesir. »
Cele ne fu pas esbahie:
« Vous dites voir, ma douce amie.
Montez lasus en cel solier;
il m'estuet de vostre mestier.
35 Ne vous poist, dist ele au borgois,
quar nous revendrons demanois.
J'ai goute es rains molt merveillouse,
& por ce que sui si goutouse,
m'estuet il fere .i. poi sainier. »
40 Lors monte aprés le pautonier.
Les huis clostrent demaintenant.
Le pautonier le prent esrant;
en .i. lit l'avoit estendue
tant que il l'a .iii. foiz foutue.
45 Quant il orent assez joué,
foutu, besié & acolé,
si se descendent de perrin
contre val les degrez; en fin
vindrent esrant en la meson.
50 Cil ne fu pas fol ne bricon,
ainz le salua demanois:
« Sire, a Dieu, dist il au borgois.
— Dieus vous saut, dist il, bele amie.
Dame, se dieus vous beneïe,
55 paiez cele fame molt bien.
Ne retenez de son droit rien
de ce que vous sert en manaie.
— Sire, que vous chaut de ma paie?
dist la borgoise a son seignor.
60 Je vous oi parler de folor,
quar nous .ii. bien en convendra! »
    Cil s'en va, plus ne demora;
la poche aus ventouses a prise.

Madam, I believe you desired
me to come here. You sent for me.
30   Tell me, what may your pleasure be?"
His wife was not the least bit shaken.
"Dear woman, you are not mistaken.
Go on upstairs; wait for me there,
because I need a surgeon's care."
35   She told her husband, "Do not worry,
for we'll be back down in a hurry.
My loins are swollen up with gout,
and I've been feeling down-and-out
and in need of a bleeder's skill."
40   She goes to join the ne'er-do-well.
They quickly close the chamber door;
the rogue grabs hold of her before
you know it, lays her in bed, climbs
on top, and fucks her hard three times.
45   When they had had their share of pleasure,
and fucked and kissed and hugged at leisure,
they came out of the room and went
quickly downstairs, so in the end
they wound up back on the main floor.
50   Neither a numbskull nor a boor,
he gave her husband a fair greeting
and said, "Good-bye till our next meeting."
"May God keep you, bewitching creature."
He turned to his wife to beseech her
55   to pay the girl generously.
"Don't stint in giving her her fee
for her attentive services."
"What the price of the service is
does not concern you," his wife said.
60   "Don't talk off the top of your head.
We two can settle our accounts."
            The fellow goes away at once
with his equipment for bloodletting.

La borgoise se rest assise
65   lez son seignor bien aboufee.
« Dame, molt estes afouee,
& si avez trop demoré.
— Sire, merci, por amor Dé!
Ja ai je esté trop traveillie:
70   si ne pooie estre sainie,
& m'a plus de .c. cops ferue
tant que je sui toute molue.
N'onques tant cop n'i sot ferir
c'onques sans en peüst issir.
75   Par .iii. rebinees me prist,
& a chascune foiz m'assist
sor mes rains .ii. de ses peçons
& me feroit uns cops si lons,
toute me sui fet martirier,
80   & si ne poi onques sainier.
Granz cops me feroit & sovent!
Morte fusse, mon escïent,
s'un trop bon oingnement ne fust—
qui de tel oingnement eüst
85   ja ne fust mes de mal grevee—
& quant m'ot tant demartelee,
si m'a aprés ointes mes plaies,
qui molt par erent granz & laies,
tant que je fui toute guerie.
90   Tel oingnement ne haz je mie
& il ne fet pas a haïr,
& si ne vous en quier mentir:
l'oingnement issoit d'un tuiel
& si descendoit d'un forel
95   d'une pel molt noire & hideuse,
mes molt par estoit savoreuse. »
Dist li borgois: « Ma bele amie,
a poi ne fustes mal baillie!

The burgher's wife, breathless and sweating,
65 sits back down where her husband's seated.
"Lady, you're very overheated,
and both of you sure took your time!"
"In God's name, sir, pardon me, I'm
worn out after all the exertion!
70 I just could not be bled. My person
more than a hundred times was battered,
and now I feel completely shattered.
No matter how forceful the blow,
we couldn't get the blood to flow.
75 Three times I needed to be tapped,
and each time the bloodletter slapped
two instruments against my haunches
and struck at me with such deep punches
that it was like a martyrdom,
80 and even then no blood would come.
How often those mighty blows fell!
I should have died, I know it well,
were it not for a potent salve.
Whoever has the luck to have
85 a salve like that will soon recover!
At last, after that working-over,
the healer took the salve and wiped
the lesions, which were deep and wide,
until I was made whole again.
90 I don't scorn such a medicine,
nor ought one to find fault with it,
nor would I lie to you one bit
about the ointment. It came out
of a tube fashioned with a spout,
95 squeezed from a black and ugly pelt,
but oh, how wonderful it felt!"
The burgher said, "My lovely wife,
you've had the drubbing of your life.

Bon oingnement avez eü! »
100 Cil ne s'est pas aperceü
de la borde qu'ele conta,
& cele nule honte n'a
de la lecherie essaucier.
Por tant le veut bien essaier:
105 ja n'en fust paié a garant
se ne li contast maintenant.

Por ce tieng je celui a fol
qui jure son chief & son col
que fame nel porroit bouler
110 & que bien s'en savroit garder,
mais il n'est pas en cest païs
cil qui tant soit de sens espris
qui mie se peüst guetier
que fame nel puist engingnier,
115 quant cele qui ot mal es rains
boula son seignor premerains!

45. LE BOUCHIER D'ABEVILE

Segnour, oiés une merveille—
c'onques n'oïstes sa pareille—
que je vous voel dire & conter.
Or metés cuer a l'escouter:
5 parole qui n'est entendue,
sachiés qu'ele est en fin perdue.

A Abevile eut .i. bouchier
que si voisin eurent molt chier;
n'estoit pas fel ne mesdisans,
10 mais cortois, sages & vaillans
& loiaus hom de son mestier,
& s'avoit souvent grant mestier

How fortunate you had that cream!"
100   The cuckolded man didn't dream
what kind of yarn his wife was spinning,
who gave an account of her sinning
quite brazenly, but free from blame.
To prove him wrong had been her aim,
105   and she thought her revenge would fall
short if she didn't tell him all.
      Therefore I think a man's a ninny
to swear on his head that not any
woman can fool him for he knows
110   well enough to keep on his toes.
In all the land you'll never find
a man, however sharp his mind,
whose watchful wariness protects
him from the tricks of the fair sex.
115   Just see how this one, racked with gout
in her loins, paid her husband out!

45. THE BUTCHER OF ABBEVILLE

by Eustache d'Amiens

My lords, here's something marvelous!
You've never heard the like of this
which I am now about to tell,
so set your minds to listen well,
5   for words, when no one lends an ear,
in the end simply disappear.
      In Abbeville a butcher dwelt.
In high esteem the man was held:
He wasn't base or slanderous,
10   but wise, well-bred, and virtuous;
he plied his trade with honesty
and often in adversity

ses povres voisins soufraiteus;
n'estoit avers ne covoiteus.

15   Entor feste Toussains avint
c'a Oisemont au markiet vint
li bouchiers bestes acater,
mais n'i fist fors voie gaster:
trop i trova kieres les bestes,
20 les cochons felons & rubestes,
felons & de mauvais afaire—
ne puet a iaus nul markiet faire;
povrement sa voie emploia,
c'onques derniers n'i emploia.

25 Aprés espars markié s'en torne,
de torst errer molt bien s'atorne,
se cape porte sur s'espee,
& pres estoit de la vespree.
Oiiés comment il esploita:
30 droit a Bailluel li anuita,
en mi voie de son manoir
avespré fu, si fist molt noir;
pense c'uimais avant n'ira,
mais en la vile remanra.

35 Molt redoute la male gente,
c'on ne li toille son argent
dont il avoit a grant fuison.
En l'entree d'une maison
vit une povre fame estant,
40 si li demanda & dist: « Tant
a il en ceste vile a vendre
nule riens ou on puist despendre
le sien por son cors aaisier,
c'onques n'amai autrui dangier? »
45 Li bone fame li respont:
« Sire, par tous les sains du mont,
ce dist mes barons, sire Mile,
de vin n'a point en ceste vile

helped out his neighbors who were needy,
nor was he covetous or greedy.

15   One All Saints' Day, as was his wont,
the butcher went to Oisemont
to purchase livestock at the fair,
but all his time was wasted there.
He found the animals too pricey,
20 the pigs looked dangerous and feisty,
a wretched and degraded breed;
nothing was there that met his need.
His whole trip was to no avail;
he'd keep his cash, forget the sale!
25 His meager marketing now done,
he quickly turned his steps toward home
with cape and sword, since day was ending
and twilight soon would be descending.
Listen, and you'll hear how he fared.
30   Night overtook him unprepared
when halfway home, there in Bailleul.
The day was gone, the night was full;
it was so dark, he thought he'd stay
and go no farther on his way,
35 because he feared the many robbers
the countryside around there harbors
might steal the money he had brought.
Before the entrance to a court-
yard he caught sight of a poor woman.
40 He asked of her, calling her to him,
"Say, do you know some place nearby
where for a price a man can buy
the basic comforts for his body?
I'd not intrude on anybody."
45 The worthy woman in reply
said, "Sir, by all the world's saints, my
employer here, good Master Miles,
says there's no wine around for miles,

fors nos prestres, sire Gautiers.
50 .ii. touniaus en a tous entiers
qu'il amena de Nojentel;
tous jors a il vin en tounel.
Alés avec lui ostel prendre.
— Dame, g'irai sans plus atendre,
55 fait li bouchiers, & Dius vous saut!
— A foi, sire, & Il vous consaut. »
        Li dïens seoit sor son suel,
qui molt avoit en li d'orguel.
Chieus le salue & se li dist:
60 « Biaus sire, se Dieus vous aït,
herbegiés moi par carité;
si ferés honor & bonté.
— Prodom, fait il, Dieus vous herbert!
Foi que jou doi a saint Hubert,
65 lais hons chaiens nuit ne gerra;
bien iert qui vos herbergera
en cele vile la aval.
Querés tant amont & aval
que vous puissiés ostel avoir,
70 & sachiés vraiement por voir
ja ne gerrés en mon porpris.
Autre gent ont cest ostel pris,
ne ce n'est droiturë a prestre
que vilains hom gise en son estre.
75 — Vilains, sire? c'avés vos dit?
Tenés vos lai home en despit?
— Oie [ ], voir, & si ai raison.
Alés ensus de ma maison!
Ce m'est avis ce soit ramprosne.
80 — Non est, sire, ains seroit aumosne
se huimais me prestiés l'ostel,
car je n'en puis trover nul tel,
que je sai bien le mien despendre.
Se *rien nule* me volés vendre,

except Father Gautier, our priest,
50 has two casks at the very least,
brought all the way from Nogentel.
There's always wine there, I hear tell.
See if he'll put you up tonight."
The butcher said, "I'll go there right
55 away, good woman, God defend you."
"Sir, to His keeping I commend you."
         Before his doorstep he found seated
the deacon, who was most conceited.
The butcher greeted him and said,
60 "Father, as God may send you aid,
I ask your hospitality
in honor and in charity."
"Go seek your shelter with the Lord!
By Saint Hubert, I'll not accord
65 a layman lodgings for the night!
You'll find some other place, all right,
where you can stay somewhere in town.
Just go on searching up and down
till someone offers you a bed.
70 I promise you, I'll not be led
to let you spend the night inside
this house of mine—it's occupied;
nor should a priest in any case
open his home to someone base."
75 "Base, Father? Are you telling me
that you despise the laity?"
"Indeed I do, and I am right.
You've shown me disrespect and spite.
Now get off of my property!"
80 "What spite? It would be charity
for you to let me stay here, Father,
for I'm not like to find another.
I spend my money willingly.
If you've something to sell to me,

85   grasses & gres vos en saroie
    & volentiers l'acateroie;
    [riens nule ne vos vueil couster.
    — Ausi bien vos venroit hurter]
    vo teste a cele bise pierre,
90   ce dist li dïens. Par saint Pierre,
    ja ne gerrés en mon manoir!
    — Diable i puissent remanoir,
    fait li bouchiers, faus capelains!
    Pautoniers estes & vilains! »
95   A tant s'em part, n'i vaut plus dire;
    plains fu de grans courous & d'ire.
         Or oiés comment li avint:
    sicom hors de la vile vint,
    devant une gaste maison
100   dont furent keü li chievron
    encontre .i. grant tropé d'oëlles.
    Par Dieu, or escoutés mervelles!
    Il salue le pastourel,
    qui mainte vache & maint torel
105   avoit gardé en se joneche:
    « Paistres, se Dius te doinst leeche,
    cui cis avoirs? — Sire, no prestre,
    a foi. — De par Dieu, puist çou estre? »
    Or orrés que li bouchiers fist:
110   si coiement .i. mouton prist
    k'ains li paistres ne s'en perchut;
    bien l'a engingnié & dechut
    qu'il ne le vit ne mot n'en seut.
    Li bouchiers au plus tost qu'il peut
115   maintenant a son col le rue,
    par mi une foraine rue
    au mes le prestre en vient ariere,
    qui molt ert fiers de grant maniere,
    sicom il dut clorre la porte,
120   & chieus ki le mouton aporte

85   I'll buy it of you, never fret,
and be in your eternal debt.
I'd never dream, sir, to impose."
"You'd do as well to knock, Lord knows,
against a stone wall with your head,
90   by Saint Peter!" the deacon said.
"I won't give you a place to rest."
"The Devil come and be your guest,"
the butcher said, "dishonest priest!
You are a scoundrel and a beast!"
95   He went away—why waste his breath?—
but he was smoldering with wrath.
      What happened to him? Be it known
that just as he was leaving town,
before an old abandoned shelter
100   with rafters fallen helter-skelter
he met up with a flock of ewes.
Now you will hear a piece of news!
He gave the herding man a call,
who'd had many a cow and bull
105   under his care back in his youth.
"God give you joy, shepherd. In truth,
whose beasts are these?" "Our priest's, in faith."
"God! can this really be the case?"
Hear what the butcher did next! He
110   purloined a sheep so cleverly,
the shepherd didn't see the theft;
he was so tricky and so deft,
it all escaped the shepherd's eyes.
      The butcher quickly takes his prize
115   and hoists it up onto his back
and takes a detour to go back,
arriving at the deacon's manse,
who's so puffed up with arrogance
as he's about to close the door,
120   and, saddled with a sheep, once more

li dist: « Sire, chieus Dius vos saut
qui seur tous homes puet & vaut! »
Li dïens son salut li rent,
puis li demanda erranment:
125 « Dont es tu? — D'Abevile sui.
D'Oisemont vieng; au markié fui.
N'i acatai c'un seul mouton,
mais chieus a molt cras le crepon.
Sire, anuit mais me herbergiés,
130 car bien voel estrë aaisiés.
Je ne sui avers ne escars:
anuit iert mengïe la chars
de cest mouton, mais q'il vos plaise,
c'aporté l'ai a grant malaise.
135 Il est grans, si a char assés;
cascuns en avra bien son ses. »
Li dïens pense qu'il dist voir,
qui molt goulouse autrui avoir—
mius aime .i. mort que .iiii. vis,
140 ensi com moi en est avis.
« Oie, certes! Molt volentiers!
Se vos estiés ore vos tiers,
si ariés ostel a talent,
c'ains nus hom ne me trova lent
145 de courtoisie & d'onor faire.
Vos me sanlés de bon afaire;
dites moi comment avés non.
— Sire, par Dieu & par son non,
j'ai non Davis en droit baptesme
150 quant je rechuc & oile & cresme.
Traveilliés fui en ceste voie—
ja Dieus de ses sains ieus ne voie
celui cui ceste beste fu!—
huimais seroie pres du fu. »
155 A tant entrent en le maison,
[ ] u li fus estoit de saison;

he said, "May God, who rules mankind,
be good to you, Father, and kind."
The deacon bid the man the same
and promptly asked from whence he came.
125 "From Abbeville. Today I went
to market down in Oisemont.
This sheep is all I found to buy,
but it looks meaty in the thigh.
Will you not let me be your guest
130 tonight, for I'm in need of rest?
I'm not a stingy man, nor cheap.
Tonight we'll cook and eat the sheep
if you would like to, 'cause I've found
it quite a load to tote around.
135 It's big, and it has so much meat,
we all will have enough to eat."
The priest approves. He has intense
desire to dine at his expense.
(He loves a funeral, which brings
140 him in more than four christenings.)
"Why certainly, sir, with a will!
If there were three of you here, still
I'd house you all and you would lack
for nothing. I'm not one to slack
145 on honor and consideration!
You seem to be a man of station,
and I would like to know your name."
"Father, by God, know that I came
to be called David by baptism
150 when I received the oil and chrism.
May God not smile on in the least
the man who raised so large a beast!
I'm tired from bearing such a load.
Your hearth means rest after the road."
155   They went inside then. At that late
hour a fire sparkled in the grate.

lors a sa beste mise jus,
puis a regardé sus & jus,
une cuingnie a demandee,
160   on l'i a tantost aportee,
se beste asome & puis l'escorce,
a .i. bauch ki fu la d'encoste
pendi le pel lor ieus voian*t*.
« Sire, dist il, venés avant,
165   por amor Dieu! Or esgardés
com cis moutons est amendés!
Veés com est cras & refais!—
mais molt m'en a pesés li fais
que de si loins l'ai aporté.
170   Or en faites vo volenté!
Cuisiés les espaules en rost,
s'en faites metre plain .i. pot
en essiau avec le maisnie.
Je ne di mie vilenie
175   c'onques plus bele chars ne fu.
Metés le rostir sor le fu!
Veés com est tenre & refaite—
enchois que li saveurs soit faite
ert ele cuite vraiement!
180   Biaus ostes, faites vo talent—
sor vos ne m'en sai entremetre.
Dont faites tost la table metre,
c'est prest! N'i a fors du laver
& des candeilles alumer. »
185   Segnour, ne vos mentirai mie:
li dïens avoit une amie
dont il si fins jalous estoit
toutes les fois c'ostes avoit
le faisoit en sa cambre entrer,
190   mais cele nuit le fist souper
a la table avoec le bouchier;
[sanblant li fait qu'il l'ait molt chier].

He put the sheep down on the ground
and turned his head and looked around,
requesting someone bring an ax,
160   which came as soon as he had asked.
He killed the beast and skinned it. After,
he hung the skin up from a rafter
nearby for all of them to see.
"Father," he said, "what quality!
165   See for yourself, for love of God,
what first-class meat marbled with lard—
it's even better than I thought!
I must admit that having brought
it so far hurt my neck a bit.
170   Now do with it as you see fit.
Make a roast of the shoulder quarter
and a pot full of boiling water
for stock for all the house to share
around. I think that it is fair
175   to say that this meat is the most
fine I've seen. Put it up to roast.
How tender and juicy it looks!
It will be done before the cooks
have even finished with the sauce!
180   I won't give orders; you're the boss,
good host. You've but to say the word,
so have them quickly lay the board:
It's ready! Let's wash up a bit
and have some candles brought and lit."

185   Here's something now that's just for your
ears. The priest had a paramour
for whom he felt such jealousy
whenever he had company,
he sent her to stay in her room,
190   but on this night he called her to 'im
to table to join their repast
with him he called his special guest.

Quant il eut mengié a delit,
la dame fist parer .i. lit
195 a ués son oste bon & bel,
de blans dras büé de novel.
Li dïens se meschine apele:
« Je te commant, fait il, suer bele,
que nos ostes sire Davis
200 soit aaisiés a son devis
si qu'il n'ait riens qui li desplaise.
Par lui avons esté bien aaise. »
A tant s'en vont couchier ensamble
il & la dame, ce me samble,
205 & li bouchiers remest au fu;
ains mais plus a aise ne fu:
bon ostel ot, & biau samblant.
« Baissele, dist il, vien avant,
trai toi en cha, parle a mi,
210 & si fai de moi ton ami.
Tu i porras avoir grant preu.
— Taisiés! Queles ne dites preu?
Dieus! com cist home sont vilain!
Laissié me em pais! Ostés vo main!
215 Je n'apris onques tel afaire!
— Par foi, il le te convient faire
par covent ke je te dirai.
— Dites donques, & je l'orrai.
— Se tu vieus avec moi gesir,
220 faire mon bon & mon desir,
par Dieu, que de vrai cuer apel,
de men mouton aras le pel.
— Taisiés! onques mais ce ne dites!
Par Dieu, vos n'estes mie erites
225 qui tel cose me requerés—
molt estes de mal apensés!
Dieu merchi, com vos sanlés sos!
Vo bon fesise, mais je n'os:

When they had eaten royally,
the lady made especially
195   for their guest's comfort a fine bed
with white fresh-laundered sheets and spread.
The deacon called his serving maid.
"I order you, sister," he said,
"that Master David here, our guest,
200   be waited on as he likes best.
Let nothing at all disagree
with him. He's been good company."
The deacon went off to his room.
(His lady friend, too, I assume.)
205   The butcher remained by the fire.
He'd everything to his desire:
good lodgings, also bonhomie.
He called the maid. "Come here to me.
A word with you, wench, come on over.
210   Grant me your favors, be my lover,
and you will get a princely gift."
"How dare you? Hush!" she answered, miffed.
"Lord! Men are such ill-mannered beasts!
Hands off, you! Let me be in peace!
215   What do I know of such a sin?"
"In faith, I'm sure that you'll give in
when you have heard my proposition."
"Come, out with it, and I will listen."
"If you will sleep with me tonight
220   and give me pleasure and delight,
I swear to God, I'll let you keep
in payment the skin of my sheep."
"Don't even think it! Stop your noise!
I see you don't go in for boys,
225   by God, to ask that thing of me!
Your mind is full of lechery;
you're such a crazy fool, I swear!
I'd do it, but I just don't dare.

vous le diriés demain madame.
230 — Suer, se Dius ait pitié de m'ame,
en ma vie ne li dirai
ne ja ne vous encuserai. »
Dont li a cele creanté
qu'ele fera sa volenté.

235 *Avec li jut* tant ke jours fu,
puis se leva, si fist le fu,
son harnas fait & trait ses bestes;
dont primes s'est levés li prestres.
Il & ses clers vont au mostier
240 canter & dire leur sautier,
& li dame remest dormant;
& li bouchiers demaintenant
se vest & cauche sans demeure,
que bien en fu saisons & eure.

245 En le cambre sans plus atendre
vint a s'ostesse congié prendre,
le clenke sache, l'uis ouvri.
Le bele dame s'esperi,
ses ieus ovri, son oste voit
250 (devant s'esponde *estait* tout droit);
lors s'esmerveille dont il vient
& de quel cose il li souvient.
« Dame, fait il, grasse vos rent;
herbegié m'avés a talent
255 & molt m'avés biau sanlant fait. »
A tant vers le cavech se trait,
son chief mist seur le cavechuel,
puis traist ariere le linchuel,
si vit le gorge blanke & bele
260 & se poitrine & se mamele:
« É Dieus! fait il, je voi miracles!
Sainte Marie! Sains Roumacles!
com est li dïens bien venus
qui o tel dame gist tous nus!

Tomorrow you would tell Madame."
230 "I'll keep it secret like a clam,
God bless my soul! I'd never use you,
then turn around, dear, and accuse you."
So she agreed to do his whim
and promptly gave herself to him.
235   She lay with him until day broke.
She lit the fire when she awoke,
then did her chores and milked the cow.
The deacon, too, has woken now.
He leaves for church, where at the altar
240 he and his cleric sing the Psalter,
and lets his concubine sleep late.
        David the butcher doesn't wait
now that it's morning and time presses,
but quickly grabs his shoes and dresses.
245 To the room where his hostess lies
he now goes to say his good-byes,
draws back the latch, opens the door.
To see her guest standing before
her bed when she opens her eyes,
250 the lovely lady shows surprise
and can't imagine to what ends
he's come there and what he intends.
"Let me express my gratitude,
lady," he says. "Nobody could
255 have shown more hospitality
and gracious generosity."
Having said this, he draws up closer
and lays his head down on the bolster,
pulls back the sheet, and catches sight
260 of her breasts, beautiful and white.
"My God," he says, "now here's a wonder!
Sweet blessed Virgin! Yes, by thunder,
this deacon really has it good
to lie with such a lady nude.

265 Ausi m'aït sains Honourés,
    un rois en fust tous honorés!
    Se j'avoie tant de loisir
    que peüsse une nuit gesir,
    refais seroie & respassés!
270 — Biaus ostes, ce n'est mie assés
    que vous dites, par saint Germain!
    Alés lahors! Ostés vo main!
    Mesires ara ja canté;
    molt se tenroit a engané
275 se en se cambre vos trovoit!
    Ja mais nul jour ne m'ameroit,
    si m'ariés maubaillie & morte! »
    & chieus molt biau le reconforte:
    « Dame, fait il, por Dieu merchi,
280 ja mais ne mouverai de chi
    pour nul home vivant qui soit
    ne, se li dïens i venoit,
    pour qu'il desist une parole
    qui fust orguellouse ne fole.
285 Je l'ochirroie maintenant
    se de riens nule aloit grouchant!
    Mais faites çou ke je vaurai:
    me pel, amie, vous donrai.
    Ele vaut molt de bon argent.
290 — Je n'oseroie pour la gent,
    car je vous sench a si estout
    que demain le diriés partout!
    — Dame, fait il, ma foi tenés,
    tant com je soie vis ne nes
295 ne le dirai fame ne home,
    par tous les sains qui sont en Rome. »
    Tant li dist & tant li pormet
    li dame en se merchi se met,
    & li bouchiers bien s'en refait
300 tant qu'il en eut tout son bon fait.

265 So help me Saint Honorius,
a king would be content with less!
If it were given to me to
lie here at night in bed with you,
I'd be contented and made whole!"

270 "By Saint Germain, it's not your role,
David, to say the things you say!
Now leave me! Get your hands away!
My man won't be in church that long.
He'd think we've done him grievous wrong

275 if he came in the room and saw;
he wouldn't love me anymore,
thanks to you. It would cost me dear."
He does his best to calm her fear.
"Lady," he tells her, "I will not,

280 for love of God, move from this spot
for any man alive. The same
holds for the deacon. If he came
and uttered so much as a word,
however prideful and absurd,

285 in protest like some uncouth villain,
I wouldn't hesitate to kill him.
But if you'll satisfy my wish,
sweet lady, I will make you rich.
That first-rate sheepskin will be yours."

290 "But what will people say?—because
I think that you're so indiscreet,
you'll blab it all over the street."
"Will you not trust me when I've promised
that while I live I will be honest?

295 No one will know, woman or man,
by the saints in the Vatican."
He goes on urging and insists
until no longer she resists
and lets the butcher at his pleasure

300 enjoy her favors in full measure.

A tant s'em part; n'i vaut plus estre,
ains vint au mostier ou li prestre
ot commenchie sa lechon;
ainques n'i fist arestison.

305 Sicom dist *Jube domine*,
é le vous ou mostier entré:
« Sire, fait il, gres vos en rent.
Herbergiet m'avés a talent
& molt m'avés fait bel samblant,

310 mais une cose vos demant
& proi que vos me fesissiés:
sire, me pel acatissiés,
si m'ariés delivré de paine.
Bien i a .iii. livres de laine;

315 ele est bone. Si m'aït Deus,
.iii. sous vaut—vos l'arés por deus,
& molt bon gré vos en sarai.
— Biaus ostes, & je le ferai
pour l'amor de vos volentiers!

320 Bons compains estes & entiers;
revenés me veoir souvent. »
Se pel meïsme chius li vent,
puis prist congié & s'en ala.

Li fame au prestre se leva,
325 qui molt fu jolie & mignote,
si se vesti d'une vert cote
molt bien faudee a plois rampans,
& si eut escorchiés ses pans
a se chainture par orguel;

330 vair & riant furent si ouel,
bele, plaisans ert a devise;
en le caiere s'est asise.
Li baissele sans plus atendre
vint a le pel, si le vaut prendre,

335 quant li dame li desfendi:
« Diva, baissele! Car me di

After, he left—why hang around?—
went to the church, and there he found
the priest, who had begun the readings
and never halted the proceedings.
305 Right at the *Jube domine*
the butcher came to him to say,
"Let me express my gratitude
for housing me. Nobody could
have done so more hospitably.
310 But I would ask you to agree
to do something for me and buy
the skin of that fine sheep that I
brought you, for it would ease my road.
The wool must be a three-pound load
315 and first-rate. I'll sell it to you,
though it's worth three, for only two
shillings, and be grateful to boot."
"Most welcome guest, for you I'll do 't
gladly, if it's expedient.
320 Your company is excellent.
Come back and visit frequently."
He sells him his own skin; then he
bids him farewell, and off he goes.
       The deacon's lady friend arose,
325 who was so lovely and flirtatious
(her bluish gray eyes were vivacious),
and chose to wear a bright green gown
with deep and large pleats hanging down
and tucked in tightly at the waist.
330 Such vanity suited her taste;
she was, in short, coquette and fair.
She went and sat down in a chair,
whereon without delay the maid
approached the skin and would have laid
335 her hands on it, had not her mistress
forbid her, saying, "Now what business

c'as tu de cele pel a faire?
— Dame, j'en feirai mon afaire.
Je le voel au soleil porter
340 por le cuirien a escaufer.
— Non feras. Lai le toute coie
qu'ele pent chi hors de le voie,
si fai çou ke tu as a faire.
— Dame, j'ai fait; je n'ai ke faire.
345 Je levai plus matin de vous.
— A foi? — Mau gres en aiés vous!
Vous en deüssiés bien parler!
— Trai te ensus! Lai le pel ester.
Warde que te main plus n'i mete
350 ne que plus ne t'en entremete.
— En non Dieu, dame, si ferai;
toute m'en entremeterai!
J'en ferai comme de la moie.
— As tu dit que le pel est toie?
355 — Oie, je l'ai dit. — Voirement?
Met jus le pel! Va, si te pent
ou te noie en une longaingne!
Molt me torne ore a grant engaingne
quant tu deviens si orguelleuse!
360 Pute! ribaude! poueilleuse!
Va! si aroie te maison!
— Dame, vos dites desraison
quant pour le mien me lesdengiés.
Se vos sor sains juré l'aviés,
365 s'est ele mieue toute voie.
— Wide mon ostel! Va te voie!
Je n'ai cure de ton serviche,
car trop iés pautoniere & nice!
Se me sires juré l'avoit,
370 chaiens ne te warandiroit,
tant t'ai forment cueilli en hé!
— Parmi le col ait mal dehé

do you have with that sheepskin there?"
"Lady, I think that's my affair.
I mean to hang it up outside
340   in the bright sunshine till it's dried."
"Oh no you won't! You do your chores
and leave it hanging here indoors.
It's not disturbing anyone."
"But mistress, all my chores are done.
345   I got up earlier than you."
"I bet!" "Well, anyway, it's true,
while you slept late, so hold your peace."
"Be off! And don't dare touch that fleece!
Don't you so much as lay a hand
350   or fiddle with it, understand?"
"In God's name, lady, and why not?
I'll fiddle with it a whole lot.
I may, since it belongs to me."
"You say the skin's your property?"
355   "Indeed I do." "Oh, is that so?
You put that sheepskin down and go
hang yourself! Drown in a latrine!
I'm livid! Who has ever seen
a servant try to be so bossy?
360   You two-faced, stinking, brazen hussy!
Go take care of some other chore."
"What do you carry on so for,
and why insult me for what's mine?
So what if you'd swear on divine
365   relics? It's mine beyond a doubt."
"Get out before I throw you out!
Your service here is terminated!
You're shameless and you're self-inflated!
The priest himself might contradict it,
370   but all the same you'd be evicted,
you fill me with such strong dislike!"
"I'm going—may the black plague strike

qui ja mais jour vos servira!
J'atendrai tant que il venra,
375   me sire, & puis si m'en irai.
De vos a lui me clamerai!
— Vos clamerés? Pute boufarde!
Puslente ribaude! Bastarde!
— Bastarde, dame? Vous dites mal!
380   Li vostre enfant sont molt loial
que vos du prestre avés eüs!
— Par le passïon, met le jus,
me pel, ou tu le comperras!
Mieus vos venroit estre a Arras,
385   par les nons Dieu, voire a Coloingne!
& la dame prent sa *queloingne*,
un coup l'en fiert, & cele crie:
« Par le vertu Sainte Marie,
mar m'avés ore a tort batue!
390   Li piaus vos iert molt bien vendue
anchois que je muire de mort! »
Lors pleure & fait .i. duel molt fort.
     A le noise & a le tenchon
entra li prestres en maison.
395   « Qu'esce? dist il, qui *t'a* çou fait?
— Sire, madame, sans mesfait!
— Por Dieu, por noient ne fu mie!
Di me voir, si ne me ment mie!
— Certes, sire, por le pel fu
400   qui la pent encoste le fu.
Biaus sire, vos me commandastes
ersoir quant vos couchier alastes
que nos ostes, sire Davis,
fust aaisiés a son devis,
405   & je fis vo commandement,
& il me douna voirement
le pel. Sor sains *le jurerai*
que molt bien deservie l'ai! »

who works for you a single day!—
but till the master comes I'll stay.
375   I mean to let him know completely,
in every detail, how you treat me."
"How *I* treat *you*? What cheek! You blasted
immoral bitch! You trull! You bastard!"
"Me? Bastard? If you say so, that's
380   because the deacon sired your brats,
no doubt, in a more legal fashion!"
"Put down my sheepskin, by God's Passion,
or you'll come to a sorry pass!
You'll wish that you were in Arras,
385   or even in Cologne, by God!"
And then the woman struck her hard
using her distaff. The maid shouted,
"That skin will cost you, never doubt it!
By Saint Marie's pure reputation,
390   you hit me without provocation!
Though it may kill me, you shall pay!"
She burst in tears and wailed away.
        Amid the ruckus and the fight
the priest returned and said, "All right,
395   who struck you? What's this argument?"
"My mistress, but I'm innocent!"
"She had some cause, and you know why,
so let me hear it, and don't lie."
"Indeed, sir, it was for the hide
400   that's hanging there by the fireside.
Remember, master, how you said
last evening when you went to bed
that I should do my level best
to entertain David, our guest?
405   I did as you commanded. He
in gratitude presented me
the sheepskin, and, by all that's holy,
I swear to you I earned it fully."

Li dïens l'ot & aperchoit
410 as paroles qu'ele disoit
que ses ostes l'ot enganee:
pour ce li ot sa pel dounee.
S'en fu courechiés & plains d'ire,
mais son penser n'en ose dire:
415 « Dame, fait il, se Dius me saut,
vos avés fait trop vilain saut!
Petit me prisiés & doutés
qui me maisnie me batés!
— Ba! qu'ele viout no pel avoir!
420 Certes, se vous saviés le voir
ne le honte k'ele m'a dite,
vous l'en renderiés le merite,
que vos enfans m'a reprouvés!
Mauvaisement, voir, vos provés
425 quant souffrés qu'ele me lesdenge
& hounist, li orde puslente!
Je ne sai qu'il en avenra,
mais me piaus ne li remanra—
je di qu'ele n'est mie soie!
430 — Qui esce donques? — Par foi, moie.
— Vostre? — Voire. — Par quel raison?
— Nos ostes jut en no maison,
sor no kuite & sor nos lincheus,
&, maugrés en ait Sains Acheus,
435 si volés ore tout savoir!
— Bele suer, or me dites voir
par cele foi que me pluevistes
quant vos premiers chaiens venistes,
cele piaus doit ele estre vostre?
440 — Oïl, par Saint Pierre l'apostre! »
& li baissele dist adonques:
« Ha, sire! ne le creés onkes!
Ele me fu anchois dounee!
— Ha, pute! mal feussiés vos nee!

The deacon heard her and deduced

410 from what she said, she'd been seduced
and their guest had given his word
to make the sheepskin her reward.
It raised the hackles on his back,
but still he kept his true thoughts back

415 and said, "Now, lady, by our Savior,
I don't approve of your behavior.
You flaunt me and make a disturbance
and beat up on my household servants."
"What? Just because she wants our fleece?

420 I'm sure if you knew but a piece
of the shame she heaped on my head,
you'd pay her back for what she said.
The things she said about your children!
What kind of man are you, who're willing

425 to permit me to be the butt
of insults for this foulmouthed slut?
Whatever else you may decide,
I will not let her have my hide.
I say the sheepskin isn't hers."

430 "Whose is it, then?" "Why, mine, of course."
"It's yours?" "Why, yes." "Why should that be?"
"We showed him hospitality;
we gave him covers, sheets, a roof.
I'd think that was sufficient proof,

435 yet here I stand interrogated!"
"Dear lady, say, is what you've stated
true, by your promised honesty
when you first came to live with me?
Are you the owner of the pelt?"

440 "Saint Peter, yes! You heard me tell't!"
Just then the serving maid broke in,
"It was to me he gave the skin!
She's handing you a pack of lies!"
"Whore! What foul stars were in the skies

445   On vous douna le passïon!
        Alés ent hors de ma maison!
        Que male honte vos aviegne!
        — Par le saint singne de Compiegne,
        dist li prestres, vos avés tort.
450   — Non ai, car je le hac de mort
        por çou qu'ele est si menteresse,
        cele ribaude larrenesse!
        — Dame, ke vous ai jou emblé?
        — M'avainne & mon orge & mon blé,
455   mes pois, mon lart, men pain faitich!
        Sire, com vous estes caitis
        qui tant l'avés chaiens soufferte!
        Sire, paiés li se deserte!
        Pour Dieu, si vos en delivrés!
460   — Dame, fait il, or m'entendés:
        par saint Denis, je voel savoir
        liquele doit le pel avoir.
        Dites moi ki le vous dona.
        — Nos ostes, quant il s'en ala.
465   — & pour les boiaus saint Martin,
        il se leva jehui matin
        ains que levés fust li solaus!
        — Dieus! com vos estes desloiaus
        qui si jurés escortement!
470   Il prist congié molt belement
        a moi quant il s'en dut aler.
        — Fu il donques a vo lever?
        — Nenil. — Quant dont? — Je me gisoie;
        de lui garde ne me dounoie
475   quant je le vi devant m'esponde.
        Or convient que je vos desponde?
        — & que dist il au congié prendre?
        — Sire, trop me volés sousprendre!
        Il dist: 'Dame, a Dieu vos commant,'
480   adonc s'em parti a itant,

445 when you were born? He had his way
with you! Clear out of here today!
For shame! to boast of it aloud!"
The priest said, "By the sacred shroud
of Compiègne, control yourself!"
450 "I hate her more than death itself!
When she speaks, there is no believing
her, and I've caught the baggage thieving!"
"What did I ever take from you?"
"My oats, my wheat, my barley, too,
455 my peas, my lard, my fresh-baked loaves!
How can you treat her with kid gloves
and let her so get on our nerves,
sir? Let her have what she deserves!
For God's sake, get rid of this menace!"
460 "Lady," he answered, "by Saint Dennis,
listen to me. I want to know
to which of you the skin should go.
Now tell me who made you this gift."
"Our guest did, right before he left."
465 "How so? For, by Saint Martin's maw,
this morning he got up before
the sun had risen in the sky!"
"How blasphemous! I can't think why
you need to swear with such élan.
470 When it was time to go, the man
took fitting leave and was well-bred."
"He saw you getting out of bed?"
"No way!" "Then when?" "I was reposing
and scarcely noticed in my dozing
475 when he came up to me. I fail
to see the need for such detail."
"With what words did he bid farewell?"
"You're out to trap me, I can tell!
He said, 'Lady, farewell. God bless!'
480 That's all he did or said—no less,

c'ainc plus n'i fist ne plus n'i dist
ne riens autre ne m'i requist
qui vos tornast a vilonie,
mes vos i entechiés folie!
485   [Onques ne fui de vos creüe,
& si n'avez en moi veüe,
grasce Deu, se molt grant bien non,
mes vos me fetes desreson,
qui m'avez en tel ire mise
490   dont ma char est teinte & remise!]
— Ahi, fait il, fole mauvaise!
je t'ai norrie trop a aise!
A peu ke ne te fier ou tue!
Vraiement sai qu'il t'a foutue!
495   Di me pour coi ne crias tu?—
il t'estuet rompre le festu!
Va t'ent! si wide mon ostel!
Je jüerrai sur mon autel
ja mais en ton lit ne gerrai!
500   Orendroit te fourjüerai! »
        Par ire s'est li prestre assis,
dolans & tristres & pensis.
Quant la dame aïré le voit,
se li poise que ele avoit
505   tenchiet ni estrivé a lui,
si crient que ne li fache anui;
en le cambre entre maintenant,
& li paistres entre acourant,
qui ses moutons avoit contés.
510   Ersoir l'en fu li uns emblés,
si ne set qu'il est devenus;
grant aleüre en est venus,
gratant ses hines, en maison.
Li dïens siet seur sen leson,
515   tous courechiés & escaufés:
« K'es çou el non de vis maufés,

no more—and so he took his leave.
He asked for nothing, I believe,
to cause you any harm or shame,
and now you're seeking to place blame!
485   You never did believe in me,
and yet there's nothing there to see
except great virtue, God be praised!
Still, you accuse me as if crazed
and anger me in such a fashion,
490   my flesh turns colors out of passion."
"Aha!" he cries. "Deceitful shrew!
I went too far in coddling you!
I'll have you thrashed! I'll see you dead!
I know he fucked you in that bed!
495   You could have cried out. Tell me why
you had to break our sacred tie?
I cast you out! Get out of here!
On the church altar I will swear
no more to lie beside you naked
500   in bed. You are repudiated!"
      The priest sat, overcome with choler,
sorrow, despondency, and dolor.
On seeing him so irritated,
the lady heartily regretted
505   she'd been so headstrong and perverse
and, fearing he might yet do worse,
went to her room. Right then in sallied
the shepherd, who, it seems, had tallied
all of his sheep, and the count proved
510   that one of them had been removed.
He's no idea what has become
of his sheep, and came at a run
to the priest's house, scratching his crotch.
The priest sat, taken down a notch,
515   on a bench, hot and angry, too.
"The devil take you! What's with you,

ribaus mauvais? Dont reviens tu?
Qu'es çou? Comfait samblant fais tu,
fius a putain? Vilains rubestes,
520 tu deüsses garder tes bestes!
A peu ne te fier d'un baston!
— Sire, n'ai mie d'un mouton,
tout le plus bel de vo tropé!
Je ne sai qui l'a atrapé.
525 — As tu donques mouton perdu?
On te deüst avoir pendu!
Mauvaisement les as gardés!
— Sire, fait il, or m'entendés!
Ersoir quant *en la vile* entrai,
530 un estrange home i encontrai
que onkes mais veü n'avoie
en camp ni en chemin n'en voie,
qui molt mes bestes esgarda
& molt m'enquist & demanda
535 cui cis biaus avoirs pooit estre,
& je li dis: 'Sire, no prestre.'
Cil le m'embla, ce m'est avis.
— Par le cuer bieu, ce fu Davis
nos ostes, qui chaiens a giut!
540 Bien m'a enginiet & dechut
[ ] qui ma m[esn]ie m'a foutue:
me pel meïsme m'a vendue!
De ma mance m'a ters mon nes!
En mal eure fuisse jou nes
545 quant je ne m'en seuch garde prendre—
on puet cascun jor molt aprendre!
De me paste me fait tortel.
Counisteroie tu le pel?
— Que dites vos, biau sire? Avoi!
550 oie, si bien, se je le voi.
Je l'ai eü .vii. ans en garde. »
Cius prent le pel, si le regarde;

you no-good bum? What brings you here?
What's with this frown from ear to ear,
son of a bitch? You hick! You creep!
520   You should be out watching your sheep!
I ought to give you a good shaking."
"But one of your sheep has been taken,
master, the best of all the herd!
I can't think how or what occurred."
525   "So, now you've gone and lost a sheep!
That shows what kind of watch you keep!
You should be hanged or thrown in prison!"
The shepherd answered, "Master, listen.
Late in the evening yesterday
530   I met a stranger on the way
back into town, whom I had never
seen in the fields or road, wherever,
who eyed my flock most carefully
and made a point of asking me
535   who owned such admirable beasts,
and I said, 'Sir, they are our priest's.'
He, I imagine, was the thief."
"David, by my Christian belief!
Our guest last night!" exclaimed the priest.
540   "I've been outsmarted! I've been fleeced!
He's fucked all of the women in
my house and sold me my own skin!
He's wiped my nose on my own sleeve!
I must be a born fool to live
545   so long and still be caught off guard!
You're always learning, if you're smart.
With my own crust he bakes me pies!
The sheepskin, would you recognize
it?" "Master, what? If I've a chance
550   to look, I'll know it at a glance.
For seven years I've had that flock."
He takes the hide and has a look.

as oreilles & a la teste
connut bien le pel de se beste.
555 « Ha la! ce dist li pastouriaus,
par Dieu, sire, c'est Cornuiaus,
le beste ou mont que plus amoie!
En no tropel n'avoit si coie,
foi que je doi a saint Vincent,
560 n'avoit si cras mouton en cent.
Mieudres de lui ne pooit estre. »
« Cha venés, dame, dist li prestre,
parlés a moi, je vous commant.
& tu, baissele, vien avant;
565 parole a moi quant je t'apel:
que claimes tu sour cele pel?
— Foi que doi vos, que je molt aim,
sire, trestoute le piau claim.
— & vos que dites, bele dame?
570 — Sire, se Dieus ait part de m'ame,
ele doit par droit estre moie.
— Ele n'iert ne vostre ne soie:
je l'acatai de mon avoir,
ele me doit bien remanoir.
575 Il m'en vint priier au moustier,
lau ge lisoie men sautier.
Par Saint Pierre le vrai apostre,
ele n'iert ne soie ne vostre
se par jugement ne l'avés! »
580   Segnor, vos qui les bien savés,
Wistasses d'Amiens vos demande
par amors & prie & commande
que vous fachiés ce jucement
bien & a droit & loiaument,
585 s'en die cascuns son savoir:
liqueus doit mieus le pel avoir—
ou li prestres ou li prestresse
ou li meschine piprenesse?

The ears and head identified
the sheep that had supplied the hide.
"Aha! By God," the shepherd shouted,
"sir, that's Cornello, don't you doubt it,
my most favorite animal
and much the gentlest of them all!
By Saint Vincent, whose faith I keep,
I'd say out of a hundred sheep
there's no fatter or finer beast."
"You come here, lady," said the priest,
"and state your case, I order you;
and you, our servant, come here, too,
and speak, for I'll not be denied.
What claim do you have on the hide?"
"I swear that as I love you, sire,
it's mine alone, whole and entire."
"And you, fair lady, what's your claim?"
"Sir, God forgive me, all the same,
it should be mine, and for good cause."
"It will be neither hers nor yours.
I paid good money for the fleece
and mean to keep the entire piece.
He asked I buy it at the altar
when I was reading from my Psalter,
so, by God's true apostle Peter,
it won't be yours, no, nor hers either
unless a magistrate decides!"
    To you, my lords, who all are wise,
I, Eustace d'Amiens, submit
their case that you may settle it,
and ask you with due courtesy
to render judgment loyally.
Each one of you will speak his piece
and say who most deserves the fleece:
His deacon host? The deaconess?
Their maid, who showed such sauciness?

46. LES .III. AVUGLES
DE COMPIGNE

Une matere ci dirai
d'un fablel que vous conterai.
On tient le menestrel a sage
qui met en trover son usage
5   de fere biaus dis & biaus contes
c'on dit devant dus, devant contes.
Fablel sont bon a escouter;
maint duel, maint mal font mesconter
& maint anui & maint mesfet.
10   Corte Barbe a cest fablel fet,
si croi bien qu'encor l'en soviegne.
      Il avint ja defors Conpiegne
troi avugle .i. chemin aloient;
entr'eus nis .i. garçon n'avoient
15   qui les menast ne conduisist
ne le chemin lor apresist;
chascuns avoit son hanepel;
molt povre estoient lor drapel
quar vestu furent povrement;
20   tout le chemin si fetement
s'en aloient devers Senlis.
Uns clers qui venoit de Paris,
qui bien & mal assez savoit,
escuier & sommier avoit
25   & bel palefroi chevauchant,
les avugles vint aprochant
quar grant ambleüre venoit,
si vit que nus ne les menoit,
*lors se pensa qu'*aucuns [ ] en voie,
30   comment alaissent il la voie?

46. THE THREE BLIND MEN
OF COMPIÈGNE

by Cortebarbe

First I will say something about
the fabliau I'm laying out.
That minstrel shows his erudition
who turns his hand to composition
5   and writes fine poems and fair accounts
to be performed for dukes and counts.
It's good to hear a fabliau:
They dispel evil, also woe
and many griefs, life's stings and barbs.
10 This fabliau is Cortebarbe's.
I think his memory won't fail.
        Outside Compiègne, says our tale,
three blind men were making their way.
Not so much as a boy had they
15 to guide them so that they could learn
what path to take, which way to turn.
Each had that cup with which one begs,
their meager clothing was in rags,
and they were very meanly dressed.
20 Thus down the road the three progressed
toward Senlis, where they were going.
Coming from Paris, a most knowing
scholar, schooled in both good and bad,
with a pack horse and servant lad
25 and riding on a sprightly mount,
drew near the blind men on account
of the speed at which he was riding
and noticed that no one was guiding
their steps. He wonders how the three
30 could find their way, so one must see,

puis dist: El cors me fiere goute
se je ne sai s'il voient goute! »
Li avugle venir l'oïrent;
erraument d'une part se *tirent*,
35   si s'escrïent: « Fetes nous bien!
Povres sommes sor toute rien;
cil est molt povre qui ne voit. »
Li clers esraument se porvoit,
qui les veut aler falordant:
40   « Vez ici, fet il, .i. besant
que je vous done entre vous .iii.
— Dieus le vous mire & sainte croiz,
fet chascuns; ci n'a pas don lait! »
(Chascuns cuide ses conpains l'ait).
45   Li clers maintenant s'en depart,
puis dist qu'il veut vir lor depart:
esraument a pié descendi,
si escouta & entendi
quanque li avugle disoient
50   & comment entr'eus devisoient.
Li plus mestres des .iii. a dit:
« Ne nous a or mie escondit
qui a nous cest besant dona—
en .i. besant molt bon don a!
55   Savez, fet il, que nous ferons?
Vers Conpiegne retornerons:
grant tens a ne fumes a aise,
or est bien droiz que chascuns s'aise!
Conpiegne est de toz biens plentive.
60   — Com ci a parole soutive!
chascuns des autres li respont.
C'or eüssons passé le pont
& fuissimes entaverné! »
Vers Conpiegne sont retorné.
65   Molt furent lié, baut & joiant;
li clers les va adés sivant

and he thinks, If I can't find out,
let my body be racked with gout!
　　　　The blind men, hearing someone ride
their way, hurriedly step aside
35　and call out, "Give us charity!
We are reduced to poverty.
His need is great who's lost his sight."
The student soon sees how he might
play them a trick—that's what he wants.
40　"Here, have one of my gold besants,"
he tells them, "for all three to spend."
"May God and the Holy Cross send
you blessings! What a fine gift, brother!"
(Each thinks he gave it to the other.)
45　　　　The student turned his horse about;
he wished to see them share it out,
and so dismounted then and there
and listened close so he could hear
every word of the blind men's speech
50　and what decision they would reach.
The leader of the three then stated,
"We weren't abused, chased, and upbraided—
instead, he gave us a besant!
What finer gift could a man want?
55　Know what I think we should do next?
To Compiègne we'll retrace our steps.
It's been so long since we've had pleasure,
let's take advantage of our treasure.
Compiègne's stocked with luxuries!"
60　Each of the other two agrees
that his idea is really great:
"I can't wait till we're through the gate
and set ourselves up at an inn!"
They head back to Compiègne again,
65　whooping it up with rowdy laughter.
The scholar follows shortly after

& dist que adés les sivrra
desi adont que il savra
lor fin. Dedenz la vile entrerent,

70 si oïrent & escouterent
c'on crioit par mi le chastel:
« Ci a bon vin fres & novel,
ça d'Auçoirre, ça de Soissons,
pain & char, *pastez* & poissons!
75 Ceenz fet bon despendre argent!
Ostel i a a toute gent—
ceenz fet molt bon herbregier! »
Cele part vont tout sanz dangier,
si s'en entrent en la meson,
80 le borgois ont mis a reson:
« Entendez ça a nous, font il,
ne nous tenez mie por vil
se nous sommes si povrement.
Estre volons priveement.
85 Mieus vous paierons que plus cointe,
ce li ont dit & li acointe,
quar nous volons assez avoir. »
L'ostes pensse qu'il dïent voir
(si fete gent ont deniers granz).
90 D'aus aaisier fu molt engranz;
en la haute loge les maine.
« Seignor, fet il, une semaine
porriez ci estre bien & bel.
En la vile n'a bon morsel
95 que vous n'aiez se vous volez.
— Sire, font il, or tost alez,
si nous fetes assez venir!
— Or m'en lessiez dont couvenir, »
fet li borgois, puis si s'en torne,
100 de .v. mes pleniers lor atorne
pain & char, pastez & chapons

and says that he will follow close
behind the three until he knows
how they'll make out.
                              They reached the town
70 and heard a man go up and down
proclaiming loudly through the square:
"We've wines from Soissons and Auxerre!
The latest vintage! And to eat
we've bread and pasties, fish and meat!
75 If you have cash, here's where to spend it!
Whoever comes will be befriended!
There is no better place to stay!"
They don't think twice, but go that way
and enter the establishment
80 and tell the owner their intent.
"Listen to us and be forewarned
lest you assume we should be scorned
because we're dressed so shabbily.
We want a room for just us three.
85 We'll spend more recklessly, by gosh,
than someone who looks chic and posh,"
they say. "We mean to celebrate."
A beggar's earnings can be great,
and so the innkeeper believes them
90 and very readily receives them.
"Come on upstairs. Here's what you're seeking,
my lords. You'll spend a pleasant week in
accommodations such as these.
All of the town's delicacies
95 are yours. You only have to ask."
"Good sir," they say, "hop to it fast,
and make sure we're served copiously."
The host replies, "Leave that to me,"
and goes to order them a feast.
100 Five heaping courses at the least—
pâtés, roast capons, meat and bread,

& vins—mes que ce fu des bons!—
puis si lor fist lasus trametre
& fist du charbon el feu metre.

105 Assis se sont a haute table.
Li vallés au clerc en l'estable
tret ses chevaus, l'ostel a pris.
Li clers, qui molt ert bien apris
& bien vestuz & cointement,

110 avoec l'oste molt hautement
sist au mengier la matinee
& puis au souper la vespree,
& li avugle du solier
furent servi com chevalier.

115 Chascuns grant paticle menoit;
l'uns a l'autre le vin donoit:
« Tien, je t'en doing; aprés m'en done!
Cis crut sor une vingne bone! »
Ne cuidiez pas qu'il lor anuit!

120 Ainsi jusqu'a la mienuit
furent en solaz sanz dangier.
Li lit sont fet; si vont couchier
jusqu'au matin qu'il fu bele eure,

& li clers tout adés demeure
125 por ce qu'il veut savoir lor fin.
        L[i] ostes *ert* levez matin
& son vallet, puis si conterent
conbien char & poisson cousterent.
Dist li vallés: « En verité,

130 li pains, li vins & li pasté
ont bien cousté plus de .x. saus,
tant ont il bien eü entre aus!
Li clers en a .v. sous par lui.
— De lui ne puis avoir anui.

135 Va lasus, si me fai paier. »
& li vallés sanz delaier

expensive wines, a noble spread—
are sent upstairs as they desire,
and extra charcoal for the fire.
105 They sat down to a lavish table.
        The student's servant went to stable
their mounts and took rooms at the inn.
The well-heeled scholar soon fell in
with his host, whom he had impressed
110 by how he acted and was dressed.
The two of them together ate
the morning meal, also the late,
while the blind men lodging upstairs
were served like noble cavaliers.
115 The rafters rang, they lived it up,
in turn each filled the other's cup:
"You pour for me, I'll pour for you!
Let's toast the vintner and his *cru!*"
Without a care, to their delight
120 they reveled on till late at night.
I'd scarcely think they'd cause to weep!
Their beds are made; they go to sleep
till morning because it was high
time.
        The scholar remains close by
125 to see the ending of his joke.
The owner and his servant woke
early and figured out a statement
of what was owed to them in payment.
"Quite honestly," the servant says,
130 "the bread, the wine, and the pâtés
come to ten shillings at the least,
because they certainly did feast.
Count five more for the scholar's bill."
"I'm not concerned for him. He will
135 pay up. Go collect from the three."
The servant went up speedily

vint aus avugles, si lor dist
que chascuns errant se vestist,
ses sires veut estre paiez.

140   Font il: « Or ne vous esmaiez,
quar molt tres bien li paierons!
Savez, font il, que nous devons?
— Oïl, dist il, .x. sous devez.
Bien le vaut. » Chascuns s'est levez,

145   tuit troi sont aval descendu.
(Li clers a tout ce entendu,
qui se chauçoit devant son lit.)
Li troi avugle a l'oste ont dit:
« Sire, nous avons .i. besant.

150   Je croi qu'i est molt bien pesant.
Quar nous en rendez le sorplus
ainçois que du vostre aions plus.
— Volentiers, li ostes respont.
Fet li uns: Quar li baille dont

155   li quels l'a. — Bé, je n'en ai mie.
— Dont l'a Robers barbe florie.
— Non ai, mes vous l'avez, bien sai!
— Par le cuer bieu, mie n'en ai!
— Li quels l'a dont? — Tu l'as! — Mes tu!

160   — Fetes, ou vous serez batu,
dist li ostes, seignor truant,
& mis en longaingne puant
ançois que vous partez de ci! »
Il li crïent: « Por Dieu, merci,

165   sire! Molt bien vous paierons! »
Dont recommence lor tençons:
« Robert, fet l'uns, quar li donez
le besant. Devant nous menez.
Vous le reçustes premerains.

170   — Mes vous qui venez daarrains
li bailliez, quar je n'en ai point!
— Or sui je bien venuz a point,

to the room where the blind men stayed
and said their host wished to be paid
and they should get dressed in a hurry.
140 They answer, "There's no need to worry,
for we'll pay everything we owe.
Just how much is it? Do you know?"
"Why yes, ten shillings," he replies,
"worth every penny." Then they rise
145 and all three find their way downstairs.
Beside his bed, the student hears
what's said while putting on his shoes.
The blind men don't suspect his ruse
and tell their host, "We've a besant.
150 I don't believe its weight is scant.
We'll pay and get the change before
we spend a single penny more."
The host responds, "That's fine with me."
"Whoever has it, pay the fee,"
155 the first one says. "Well, I don't have it."
"To white-beard Bob, then, the man gave it."
"Not I! You have the coin, I know."
"I swear to God I haven't, though."
"Then who?" "Why, you!" "I don't!" "Do too!"
160 "Pay, or I'll thrash all three of you,
you thieving lordlings," says the host,
"and in the cesspool you'll be tossed
before I let you get away!"
"Good sir, be merciful," they say,
165 "for God's sake, for we'll pay you well."
Then each begins to scream and yell.
"Bob, give him the besant I say,
It's always you who leads the way,
and you got it first when he passed."
170 "And you're the one he was with last,
so you pay, for I haven't got it!"
The host cries, "What's this scam you've plotted

fet li ostes, quant on me truffe! »
L'un va doner une grant buffe,
175   puis fet aporter .ii. lingnas.
Li clers qui fu a biau harnas,
qui le conte forment amoit,
de ris en aise se pasmoit
quant il vit le ledengement.
180   A l'oste vint isnelement,
se li demande qu'il avoit,
quel chose ces genz demandoit.
Fet l'ostes: « Du mien ont eü
.x. sous c'ont mengié & beü,
185   si ne m'en font fors escharnir,
mes de ce les vueil bien garnir!
Chascun avra de son cors honte!
— Ainçois le metez sor mon conte,
fet li clers; .xv. sous vous doi.
190   Mal fet povre gent fere anoi. »
L'ostes respont: « Molt volentiers!
Vaillanz clers estes & entiers. »
Li avugle s'en vont tout cuite.
       Or oiez com fete refuite
195   li clers porpenssa maintenant!
On aloit la messe sonant;
a l'oste vint, si l'aresone:
« Ostes, fet il, vostre persone
du moustier dont ne connissiez?
200   Ces .xv. sous bien li croiriez
se por moi les vous voloit rendre?
— De ce ne sui mie a aprendre,
fet li borgois, par saint Silvestre,
que je croiroie nostre prestre
205   s'il voloit plus de .xxx. livres!
— Dont dites j'en soie delivres
a l'ostel quant je revendrai.
Au moustier paier vous ferai. »

to cheat me? I can take no more!"
and lets one have it on the jaw
175 and called for two stout sticks to wield.
       Amused, the scholar, who's well-heeled,
watched the course the events were taking
and laughed so hard that he was shaking,
enjoying their predicament.
180 Then straight up to the host he went
and asked him why he was distressed
and what he wanted of these guests.
"They owe ten shillings," the host said,
"for food and drink and for their bed,
185 and now they think that they can stiff me!
They'll rue the day they grappled with me!
A beating will settle their score!"
"It is a sin to harm the poor,"
the scholar says. "Add that amount
190 to my bill—fifteen on account."
The host replies, "So let it be.
You're a man of integrity."
       Thus were the three blind men redeemed.
Here's how the clever scholar schemed
195 to clear the debt from his accounts.
He hears the bells ring to announce
Mass and turns to his host to say,
"Of course, you must know the curé
of your church. Say, can he be trusted
200 for fifteen shillings, if entrusted
to discharge the debt I've incurred?"
"I've no doubt there—he'll keep his word,"
he answers him, "by Saint Sylvester!
I'd trust him, if he acquiesced or
205 promised me, for thirty-some pounds."
"Then say I've settled all accounts,
once I return, for board and bed.
Let's go to church, where you'll be paid."

L'ostes le commande esraument,
210 & li clers ainsi fetement
dist son garçon qu'il atornast
son palefroi & qu'il troussast
que tout soit prest quant il reviegne;
a l'oste a dit que il s'en viegne.
215   Anbedui el moustier en vont,
dedenz le chancel entré sont.
Li clers qui les .xv. sous doit
a pris son oste par le doit,
si l'a fet delez lui assir,
220 puis dist: « Je n'ai mie loisir
de demorer dusqu'aprés messe.
Avoir vous ferai vo promesse.
Je l'irai dire qu'il vous pait
.xv. sous trestout entresait
225 tantost que il avra chanté.
      — Fetes en vostre volenté,
fet li borgois, qui bien le croit.
Li prestres revestuz estoit
qui maintenant devoit chanter;
230 li clers vint devant lui ester,
qui bien sot dire sa reson.
(Bien sanbloit estre gentiz hon,
n'avoit pas la chiere reborse.)
.xii. deniers tret de sa borse,
235 le prestre les met en la main:
« Sire, fet il, por saint Germain,
entendez ça .i. poi a mi.
Tuit li clerc doivent estre ami,
por ce vieng je pres de l'autel.
240 Je giuc anuit a .i. ostel
chiés a .i. borgois qui molt vaut.
Li douz Jhesu Criz le consaut,
quar preudon est & sanz boisdie!—
mes une cruël maladie

The innkeeper has no objections.
210 The student gives his boy directions
to go and get the horses harnessed
and pack their bags and do his darnedest
so they can set out no time lost.
"Now come with me," he tells his host.

215 　　The two together went to church
and entered the chancel in search
of the curé. The man in debt
took his host by the hand and led
him to a bench, where both sat down,
220 and told him, "I can't hang around
till Mass is over, I'm afraid,
but I'll see that your bill is paid.
I'll tell him that, soon as he's through
with Mass, he is to pay to you
225 the fifteen shillings for my bill."
"Arrange it any way you will,"
the host replied in perfect trust.

　　The priest came, wearing what he must
for Mass, to start the Kyrie.
230 The scholar went up straightaway
(he was most skillful at misleading
people—he seemed a man of breeding
and his face bespoke innocence)
and, handing to the priest twelve pence
235 from his purse, started to explain.
"Father," he said, "by Saint Germain,
men of the cloth should all be friends.
If my coming up here offends
you, please forgive. I'll keep it short.
240 It happened that last night I sought
my lodgings at an inn. The host—
sweet Jesus Christ protect this most
worthy man for his honesty!—
was stricken with a malady,

245 li prist ersoir dedenz sa teste
     entrués que nous demeniens feste
     si qu'il fu trestoz marvoiez.
     Dieu merci! or est ravoiez,
     mes encore li deut li chiez,
250 si vous pri que vous li lisiez,
     aprés chanter, une evangile
     desus son chief. — & par saint Gille,
     fet li prestres, je li lirai. »
     Au borgois dist: « Je le ferai
255 tantost com j'avrai messe dite.
     — Dont en claime je le clerc cuite,
     fet li borgois, mieus ne demant,
     sire prestre. — A Dieu vous commant,
     fet li clers. — A Dieu, biaus [douz] mestre. »
260   Li prestres a l'autel va estre,
     hautement grant messe commence;
     par .i. jor fu de diemenche,
     au moustier vindrent molt de genz.
     Li clers, qui fu & biaus & genz,
265 vint a son oste congié prendre,
     & li borgois sanz plus atendre
     dusqu'a son ostel le convoie.
     Li clers monte, si va sa voie,
     & li borgois tantost aprés
270 vint au moustier. Molt fu engrés
     de ses .xv. sous recevoir—
     avoir les cuide tout por voir!
     Enz el chancel tant atendi
     que li prestres se desvesti
275 & que la messe fu chantee,
     & li prestres sanz demoree
     a pris le livre & puis l'estole,
     si a huchié: « Sire Nichole,
     venez avant. Agenoilliez. »
280 De ces paroles n'est pas liez

245 a cruel affliction of the brain,
which made him act as if insane
while we were partying last night.
Thank God, for now he seems all right,
although his head is aching still.
250 Pray read a chapter, if you will,
of Gospel over the man's head."
"Yes, by Saint Giles, it shall be read,"
he says; then to the host: "Wait till
the Mass is over. Then I will."
255 "The student has settled his score
then," says the host. "I ask no more."
"Father, farewell, God's will be done,"
the scholar says. "God's peace, my son,
be with you. Go now with my blessing."
260   The priest steps forth to read the lesson
at the altar and say High Mass.
The people all arrived en masse
because it was a Sunday morning.
The gracious scholar, on returning
265 to his host, said it's getting late,
he must be off. So they don't wait;
back to the inn without delay
they go; the student rides away.
The host, then, without hesitation
270 set off for church in great elation,
expecting fifteen shillings now.
He thought he'd get them, too, I vow!
Inside the chancel there, he waited
until Mass had been celebrated
275 and the priest had removed his surplice.
Immediately after the service,
the priest went to retrieve his holy
book and he also took his stole.
"Come, Nicholas, down on your knees!"
280 he called, but his words didn't please

li borgois, ainz li respondi:
« Je ne ving mie por ce ci;
mais mes .xv. sous me paiez!
— Voirement est il marvoiez,
285   dist li prestres, nomini Dame!
Aidiez a cest preudomme a l'ame!
Je sai de voir qu'il est dervez.
— Öez, dist li borgois, öez
com cis prestres or m'escharnist!
290   Por poi que mes cuers du sens n'ist
quant son livre m'a ci tramis!
— Je vous dirai, biaus douz amis,
fet li prestres. Comment qu'il praingne,
tout adés de Dieu vous souviegne,
295   si ne pöez avoir meschief. »
Le livre li mist sor le chief,
l'evangille li voloit lire,
& li borgois commence a dire:
« J'ai en meson besoingne a fere.
300   Je n'ai cure de tel afere,
mes paiez moi tost ma monnoie! »
Au prestre durement anoie;
toz ses parroschïens apele—
chascuns entor lui s'atropele—
305   puis dist: « Cest homme me tenez!
Bien sai de voir qu'il est dervez!
— Non sui, fet il, par saint Cornille
ne par la foi que doi ma fille,
mais .xv. sous me paierez!
310   Ja ainsi ne me gaberez!
— Prenez le tost! » le prestre a dit.
Li parroschien sanz contredit
le vont tantost molt fort prenant,
les mains li vont trestuit tenant,
315   chascuns molt bel le reconforte,
& li prestres le livre aporte,

the innkeeper, who made reply,
"If I've come here, that isn't why!
Now pay me fifteen shillings, Father."
"The fever's struck again, I gather,"
285 the priest cried out. "Father in Heaven,
let this poor sinner be forgiven!
Now I can tell he's lost his senses!"
"Just listen to this priest's pretenses!"
the host exclaimed. "He'd rob me blind!
290 I think I'll go out of my mind!
Just why has he brought that book here?"
"I'll tell you," the priest says, "my dear,
sweet friend. Come what may, take my word,
and if you have faith in the Lord,
295 you surely will be cured in full."
He placed the Gospel on his skull
and tried to read from Holy Writ,
but the host would have none of it:
"I've business to see to at home.
300 Stop playing games! Leave me alone!
I want you to give me my money!"
The curé didn't find it funny,
summoned his parish, who obeyed
and faithfully flocked to his aid.
305 He told them, "Hold him on the ground,
for I am sure his mind's unsound."
"By the faith owed my child and Saint
Cornelius," he says, "I ain't!
Now pay me every single shilling!
310 I'll not be cheated thus, God willing!"
The priest cried out, "Don't let him go!"
and his parishioners all do
their best to keep the man immobile,
try to allay his fears with noble
315 sentiments, hold his arms in place.
The curé brought the book apace

se[l] li a mis deseur son chief,
l'evangille de chief en chief
li lut, l'estole entor le col
320 (mes a tort le tenoit por fol),
puis l'esproha d'eve benoite,
& li borgois forment covoite
qu'a son ostel fust revenuz.
Lessiez fu, ne fu plus tenuz;
325 li prestres de sa main le saine,
puis dist: « Esté avez en paine. »
& li borgois s'est toz cois teus,
corouciez est & molt honteus
de ce qu'il fu si atrapez.
330 Liez fu quant il fu eschapez;
a son ostel en vint tout droit.
  Corte Barbe dist orendroit
c'on fet a tort maint homme honte.
A tant definerai mon conte.

47. LES .III. DAMES QUI
TROVERENT L'ANEL

Oiez, seignor, .i. bon fablel!
Uns clers le fist por .i. anel
que .iii. dames .i. main troverent.
Entre eles .iii. Jhesu jurerent
5 que icele l'anel avroit
qui son mari mieus guileroit
por fere a son ami son buen:
l'anel avroit & seroit suen.
  La premiere se porpenssa
10 en quel guise l'anel avra.
Son ami a tantost mandé;
quant il sot qu'el l'ot commandé

and held it over the man's skull
and read out the Gospel in full
from end to end, wearing his stole,
320 convinced (though wrong) of the man's folly,
and sprinkled him with holy water.
As for the innkeeper, he thought a
quick escape would please him the most.
They loosed their grip and freed the host.
325 Signing the cross in benediction,
the priest said, "God cure your affliction."
Despite his anger and his shame,
the host kept quiet all the same,
perceiving that he had been taken.
330 Happy to get away, but shaken,
he returned to his hostelry.

       Cortebarbe thinks that you'll agree
that guiltless men often get punished.
So ends my tale. Now it is finished.

47. THE THREE WOMEN
WHO FOUND A RING

Hear this good fabliau, good sirs!
A cleric made it up because
of a ring that three ladies found.
They've sworn by Jesus and are bound
5 that she will win the bauble who'll
best play her husband for a fool
to please and satisfy her lover.
She'll get the ring, and no one other.

       The first gave thought how to secure
10 the ring and make it hers for sure.
She bid her lover come to her.
When he knew what her wishes were,

si vint a li delivrement,
quar il l'amoit molt durement
15 & ele lui, si n'ot pas tort.
Del meillor vin & del plus fort
c'on pot trover en cele terre
fist la dame maintenant querre,
& si ot quis dras moniaus
20 qui assez furent bons & biaus.
Del vin dona a son mari;
il en but tant, je le vous di,
qu'il ne savoit ou il estoit
(a coustume pas ne l'avoit).
25 Quant li preudom fu endormi,
entre la dame & son ami
l'ont pris & rez & l'ont tondu
& coroné: tant ot beü
que l'en le peüst escorchier!
30 La dame & son douz ami chier
le prenent & si l'ont porté
droit devant la porte a l'abé
dont il erent assez prochain.
Iluec jut jusqu'a l'endemain
35 que Dame Dieus dona le jor.
Il s'esveilla, si ot paor
quant il se vit si atorné.
« Dieus, dist il, qui m'a coroné?
Est ce donc par vostre voloir?
40 Oïl, ce puet on bien savoir
que nus fors vous ne le m'a fait!
Or n'i a point donc de deshait:
vous volez que je soie moine,
& jel serai sanz nul essoine. »
45 Maintenant sor ses piez se drece
grant oirre, que ne s'aperece,
vient a la porte, si apele.
Li abés ert a la chapele,

he went to her immediately
because he loved her tenderly
15 as she did him, so was he wrong?
The very finest and most strong
wine that in those parts could be bought
the woman sent for, and she sought
to lay hold of a good and fair
20 habit, the kind monastics wear.
She gave the vintage to her mate,
who drank himself into the state
you don't know where you are at all,
being unused to alcohol.
25 Then, while the worthy slept it off,
the lady and her lover both
took him and shaved him like a monk
and tonsured him. He was so drunk
they could as easily have flayed him!
30 The lady and her lover laid him
by the door of a monastery
whither they carried him, not very
distant from where their home was found.
There he lay stretched out on the ground
35 till God made the sun rise next day.
          He woke. Imagine his dismay
when he saw himself thus attired!
"God!" he exclaimed. "Who has conspired
to tonsure me? Thy will be done!
40 Amen. It's all too clear no one
but You has done this thing to me,
so who am I to disagree?
To holy orders You have called me;
I'll gladly become what You've told me."
45 The man now gets up on his feet,
does not delay, but with due speed
comes to the door and calls. Just then
the abbot was in chapel. When

qui maintenant l'a entendu,
50 la porte ouvri. Quant l'a veü
a pié & sanz ame, toz sous,
« Frere, fet il, qui estes vous?
— Sire, dist il, je sui uns hom.
Estre vueil de relegion.
55 De ci pres sui vostre voisin;
sachiez que encore ier matin
ne savoie cest aventure,
mes Dame Dieus, qui tout figure,
m'en a doné si bon talent
60 & moustré si cortoisement,
sire, com vous m'oëz conter,
quar il m'a fet ci aporter
tout coroné & tout tondu
comme autre moine revestu.
65 Fetes moi mander ma moillier,
& se li ferai otroier
de ma terre & de mon avoir.
Vous ferai tant ceenz avoir
que toute en avrez ma partie
70 por estre de vostre abeïe. »
Li abés covoita la terre,
si envoia la dame querre,
& ele i vint delivrement,
quar bien savoit a escïent
75 por qoi li abés l'ot mandee;
& quant el fu leenz entree
& ele a veü son seignor:
« Sire, por Dieu le creator,
volez vous moines devenir?
80 Je nel porroie pas soufrir! »
A la terre cheï pasmee
par faint sanblant: s'est demoree
une grande piece a la terre,
sanblant fet que le cuer li serre.

he heard him, he opened the door
50 and said to the man when he saw
him standing there alone, no other,
just him alone, "Who are you, brother?"
"Father, I'm a man from this region
who would lead his life in religion,"
55 he said. "I live very close by.
Truly, yesterday morning I
was ignorant of my vocation,
but God, the Lord of all creation,
has filled my heart with such desire
60 and nobly shown me the way, sire,
as you are now about to hear,
because He had me carried here,
my head having received the tonsure
and myself dressed just as your monks are.
65 If you'll have my wife sent to me,
I'll assign her some property,
land and belongings, and will cede
to you and to your house by deed,
holding back nothing, all my share
70 so that I may be your confrere."
      The abbot coveted the land.
He had the lady sent for, and
without delay she hurried there,
since she was very well aware
75 what cause the abbot had to summon
her there. No sooner did she come in
and see him than she gave a cry
and said, "Husband, by God on high,
are you becoming a monastic?
80 How can I bear something so drastic?"
She fell to the ground in a faint
(it's all an act), and she remained
there on the ground a long time, making
it look as if her heart was breaking.

85   Li abés li dist franchement:
      « Dame, cest duel est por neent.
      Vous deüssiez mener grant joie!
      Vostre sire est en bone voie:
      Dieus l'aime, ce poëz savoir,
90   qui a son oés le veut avoir. »
      El l'otria a quelque paine.
      Uns gars a son ostel l'en maine
      ou ele trova son ami.

      Maint preudomme a esté trahi
95   par fame & par sa puterie!
      Cil fu moines en l'abeïe,
      ou *il vesqui* molt longuement.
      Por ce chasti je toute gent
      qui cest fablel oient conter
100   qu'il ne se doivent pas fier
      en lor fames n'en lor mesnies
      se il nes ont ainz essaïes
      que plaines soient de vertuz.
      Mains hom a esté deceüz
105   par fame & par lor trahison:
      cil fu moines contre reson,
      qui ja en sa vie nel fust
      se sa fame nel deceüst.
        La seconde a molt grant envie
110   de l'anel: ne s'oublia mie,
      ainz se porpensse comment l'ait;
      molt fu plaine de grant agait.
      Il avint a .i. vendredi
      tout ainsi com vous orrez ci.
115   Ses sire ert au mengier assis;
      anguilles avoit jusqu'a .vi.
      Les anguilles erent salees
      & sechies & enfumees.
      « Dame, dist il, quar prenez tost

85   The abbot told her openly,
    "Lady, you're grieving needlessly;
    be happy for him, as you should.
    The path your husband's on is good,
    as you can see. He has God's favor
90   who has been chosen for His labor."
    Though she gave in, she still did grouse.
    A lad led her back to her house,
    where she met up with her adoring
    lover.
          A woman and her whoring
95   have betrayed many! Her disorders
    landed this man in holy orders,
    and there he stayed. . . . Who knows till when?
    That's why I caution all you men
    who hear this story and advise
100   you not to place trust in your wives
    or those who live under your roof
    unless you've tried them and have proof
    they're honest and can be believed.
    Many a man has been deceived
105   by his wife and her wicked treason,
    like this one, cloistered without reason,
    who'd never have become a monk
    had he not fallen for her bunk.
          The second, whose desire is great
110   for the ring, won't procrastinate,
    but thinks how she can lay her hands
    on it. She's lots of clever plans.
    Toward noon one Friday it befell
    exactly as you'll hear me tell.
115   Her husband sat down for his meal
    at table; they were having eel,
    some six of them, salted and smoke-
    preserved and dried. The husband spoke.
    "Take these eels, woman. It's my will

120 ces anguilles, cuisiez en rost!
   — Sire, ceenz n'a point de feu.
   — & ja en a il en maint leu
   ci pres! Alez i vistement! »
   La dame les anguilles prent
125 & trespassa outre la rue;
   chiés son ami en est venue.
   Quant il la vit, molt ot grant joie
   com se il fust sire de Troie,
   & la dame grant joie maine.
130 Iluec fu toute la semaine
   & l'autre jusqu'au vendredi.
   Quant vint a eure de midi
   la dame apela .i. garçon:
   « Gars, dist ele, va en meson
135 & saches que mon seignor fait. »
   Li gars molt tost a l'ostel vait:
   la table ert mise & sus .ii. pains,
   & li preudom lavoit les mains;
   asseïr devoit maintenant.
140 Li gars vint arriere corant
   & dist: « Vostre mari menjue. »
   Cele ne fu mie esperdue:
   chiés son voisin en est entree,
   & le preudom l'a saluee
145 & la dame le resalue.
   « Sire, dist el, je sui venue
   anguilles cuire a mon seignor.
   Nous avons juné toute jor.
   Jel lessai or molt deshaitié
150 qu'il n'avoit encore hui mengié. »
   Les anguilles rosti molt tost;
   quant il fu droiz que on les ost,
   si les a prises en son poing.
   Son ostel n'estoit gueres loing,
155 & ele i fu molt tost venue.

120 to have them roasted on the grill."
"Husband, I can't. Our fire is out."
"We're not the only hearth about
the neighborhood. Now get to work!"
The woman picked them up and took
125 them out the door and down the road
and stopped at her lover's abode.
Seeing her there, he felt more joy
than if he had been king of Troy,
and the lady was joyful, too.
130 She stayed with him the whole week through,
till it was Friday once again.
She waited till the noon hour came,
called for a servant, told him, "Go
back to my house, boy. Let me know
135 what my husband is up to, please."
The lad hurries on back and sees
two loaves with just one table setting,
the husband washing his hands, getting
ready to take his place at table,
140 then ran back fast as he was able.
"Your husband's having lunch," he said
to her. The lady kept her head.
Straight to her neighbor's she proceeded
and went into his house and greeted
145 him in turn when he welcomed her.
"My husband sent me here, good sir,
to grill him up a plate of eel.
We've not yet had our midday meal.
I left him in a surly mood
150 caused by a total lack of food."
         It wasn't long before the grilled
eels were back in the plate she held;
before you knew it, they were ready,
and, since she lived nearby, the lady
155 was shortly back in her own house.

Tres devant son mari les rue:
« Huis! dist el, je sui eschaudee! »
& li preudom l'a regardee,
sur ses piez saut comme dervé:
160 « Pute, ou avez vous tant esté?
Vous venez de vo puterie! »
& la dame a haute voiz crie:
« Harou! aïde, bone gent! »
& il i vindrent esraument,
165 & li preudom i fu venu
chiés qui la pautoniere fu
por les .vi. aguilles rostir.
« Sire, dist el, venez veïr!
Mes sire est de son sens issu!
170 Ne sai quel mal il a eü:
je me parti ore de ci . . .
—Voire, pute, des vendredi! »
Cil entendirent qu'il a dit
qu'ele au vendredi s'en partit;
175 cil de toutes pars l'ont saisi.
Li preudom si fu esbahi
que il ne sot qu'il peüst dire:
chascuns le desache & detire,
les mains li lïent & les piez—
180 bien est matez & cunchïez!—
puis s'en issirent de l'ostel,
quar la pute ne queroit el.
L'en lor demande ou ont esté:
« Chiés Dant Jehan, qui est dervé.
185 Si est grant duel & grant domage,
quar orendroit li prist la rage
qu'il voloit sa fame tüer! »
Cele ne se volt oblïer,
ainçois a mandé son ami,
190 & il vint maintenant a li;
en sa chanbre l'en a mené,

She put them down before her spouse
and said, "Whew! I'm perspired and hot!"
The good man stared; quick as a shot
he jumped up like a maniac.
160 "Where were you, bitch? Already back
from your filthy debauchery?"
The woman called full-throatedly,
"Good people, help! Haroo! Haroo!"
and to her aid the neighbors flew,
165 that good man also in the throng
to whom the debauchee had gone
to bring her six smoked eels for grilling.
"See here, sir," she said, "there's no telling
just what it was that brought it on,
170 but my poor husband's mind is gone.
I left the house shortly before . . ."
"Why, you've been gone since Friday, whore!"
When the neighbors heard him attest
that it was Friday when she left,
175 they rushed to grab him from all sides.
The worthy man was so surprised
that he could not utter a sound.
They pushed and pulled at him and bound
him firmly by the hands and feet
180 in ignominious defeat
and then went home and left him, for
the floozy hadn't asked for more
of them. When asked where they had gone,
they said, "He's lost his mind, has John!
185 What a misfortune and how sad!
Just now he went stark raving mad
and tried to do his missus in."
     She wasn't idle. To begin
with, straightaway she called her lover
190 and then and there he hurried over.
She led him off into her room

par .i. pertuis li a moustré
com li vilains estoit liié.
Bien l'a maté & cunchiié
195   & bien vaincu par son barat!
Li vilains reproche du chat
qu'il set bien qui barbes il leche:
cestui a servi de la meche,
mes s'il eüst cuer de preudomme,
200   il s'en venjast a la parsomme.
      Or oiez de la daerraine,
qui nuit & jor fu en grant paine
en quel guise l'anel avra.
Son ami ot que molt ama:
205   sachiez, point n'en remest sor lui;
molt s'entramerent anbedui.
.i. jor l'ot la dame mandé;
quant il sot qu'el l'ot commandé
si vint a li tout sanz demeure,
210   & la dame en meïsmes l'eure
li dist: « Biaus amis, longuement
vous ai amé molt folement.
Toz jors porroie ainsi muser,
bien porroie mon tens user
215   en fole vie & en mauvaise!
Se vous de moi avez mesaise,
molt seroie fole & musarde!
Maus feus & male flambe m'arde
se vous ja mes o moi gisez
220   se vous demain ne m'espousez!
    — Dame, dist il, por Dieu merci,
ja avez vous vostre mari!
Comment porroit ce avenir?
De grant folie oi plet tenir! »
225   Dist ele: « J'en pensserai bien:
ja mar en douterez de rien,
mes vous ferez a mon talent.

and through a peephole she showed to 'im
how the clodhopper lay hog-tied,
whom she'd managed to override,
195   vanquish, and humble by her tricks.
        The cat knows whose whiskers it licks,
or so the peasant's proverb goes.
She's tweaked her husband on the nose,
but if the fellow's heart is strong,
200   this won't go unavenged for long.
        You'll hear about the last one now,
who day and night racked her brains how
to make sure the ring would be hers.
She had a lover, and he was
205   much loved—know that he had it all—
and their great love was mutual.
One day she bid him come to her;
when he knew what her wishes were,
he went to her immediately,
210   and as soon as he got there she
told him, "Sweet love, a long time now
I've loved you. God only knows how
much! I could easily forever
go on living like this and savor
215   this culpable insanity!
If you should ever tire of me,
I'd see how foolish I have been.
May Heaven damn me for my sin
if ever you come in my bed
220   unless tomorrow we are wed."
"Merciful God!" her lover parried,
"but, lady, you're already married!
How could this ever be arranged?
What you propose is quite deranged."
225   The lady said, "I'll think it out.
There's nothing you need fret about,
but make sure you do as I say."

— Dame, a vostre commandement
ferai, ja n'en ert desdaingnié. »
230 Lors li a la dame enseignié
qu'au soir viegne por son mari
& si le maint avoeques li
chiés Dant Huistasse, le fil Tiesse . . .
« ou il a une bele niece
235 que volez prendre & espouser
se il la vous voloit doner;
& g'irai la sanz demorer—
ja tant ne vous savrez haster
que je n'i soie avant de vous.
240 Iluec nous troverez andous
ou j'avrai mon afere fait
a Huistasse tout entresait
en tel guise que vous m'avrez,
se Dieu plest, & me recevrez
245 tres par devant nostre provoire.
Mon seignor ne savra que croire,
qu'il m'avra aprés lui lessie.
Je serai si appareillie
que je avrai chancgiez mes dras
250 que il ne me connoistra pas,
& me fiancerez demain
tres par devant no chapelain.
A mon mari direz: 'Biaus sire,
el non Dieu & el non saint Sire,
255 ceste fame me saisissiez.'
Il en sera joianz & liez,
& bien sai que il me donra
a vous & grant joie en avra,
& s'il ainsi me veut doner,
260 je di que ce n'est pas prester! »
Issi fu fet, issi avint:
toute sa vie cil la tint
a cui son mari la dona;

"I shall. Never in any way
will what you tell me be neglected."

230   Now here's what the lady instructed
he do: that he come for her spouse
that night and bring him to the house
of Eustace, Tess's son, "for he's
the guardian of his lovely niece.

235 Say that if her uncle will grant
it, you intend to seek her hand.
I'll go there, too, no time to waste.
It doesn't matter how much haste
you make; I'll be first to arrive.

240 By the time you're there you'll find I've
let Eustace know what I have planned
and have the business well in hand
in such a way that I'll be yours,
please God, and you'll have me because

245 it will be done before the priest.
My husband won't know in the least
because he'll think he left me here.
I'll change my clothes and so appear
before him in such a disguise

250 that he will never realize
who I am. You'll plight me your troth
before our priest and take an oath.
Say to my husband: 'By Saint Cyr
and in God's name, this woman here

255 give me as mine from this day forth.'
He, with a light heart and unforced,
I know it, will give me to you
and be more than delighted to.
If he freely makes me your own,

260 I say, a gift is not a loan."
      So it was, and what's done is done:
Her husband gave her, so the one
he gave her to kept her for life.

por ce que il ne la presta,
265   ne la pot onques puis ravoir.
           Mes or vueil je par vous savoir
      la quele doit avoir l'anel:
      je di que cele ouvra molt bel
      qui moine fist de son seignor;
270   & cele rot el grant honor
      qui le suen fist prendre & loier
      & par estavoir otroier
      & toz les .viii. jors mesconter;
      ceste se refist espouser
275   en tel maniere a son ami.
      Or dites voir, n'i ait menti,
      & si jugiez reson & voir
      la quele doit l'anel avoir.

ᚠ𝑆. BOIVIN DE PROVINS

      Molt bons lechierres fu Boivins;
      porpenssa soi que a Provins
      a la foire voudra aler
      & s'i fera de lui parler.
5   Ainsi le fet com l'a empris:
      vestuz se fu d'un burel gris,
      cote & sorcot & chape ensanble,
      qui fu tout d'un, si com moi sanble,
      & si ot coiffe de borras,
10   ses sollers ne sont mie a las,
      ainz sont de vache dur & fort,
      & cil qui molt de barat sot
      .i. mois & plus estoit remese
      sa barbe, qu'ele ne fu rese.
15   .i. aguillon prist en sa main

Because he didn't *lend* his wife,
265   he couldn't get her back again.
          But now I want you to explain
      which one you think should have the ring.
      I say she did a lovely thing
      who made her husband a monastic;
270   but she was equally fantastic
      who had her husband tied and bound
      till he was forced to come around
      and admit he had lost eight days;
      and that one, too, we have to praise
275   who made herself her lover's bride.
      Let's have no lies, now; *you* decide,
      and honestly and wisely choose.
      The ring in question should be whose?

48. BOIVIN DE PROVINS

   by Boivin (?)

      Boivin was quite the entertainer:
      He turned his thought to how to gain a
      name for himself at Provins fair
      and make folk talk about him there,
5   which he succeeded in in full.
      He put on clothes of coarse gray wool—
      his blouse, his jacket, and his cloak
      were all of the cloth that I spoke
      of, likewise the cap on his head—
10   no laces on his shoes, instead
      they were of cowhide, hard and sturdy,
      and for a month or more his beard he
      allowed to grow and didn't shave,
      and then the slick and cunning knave
15   procured himself a rough-hewn crook

por ce que mieus sanblast vilain;
une borse grant acheta,
.xii. deniers dedenz mis a
(que il n'avoit ne plus ne mains),
20 & vint en la rue aus putains
tout droit devant l'ostel Mabile,
qui plus savoit barat & guile
que fame nule qui i fust;
iluec s'assist desus .i. fust
25 qui estoit delez sa meson,
delez lui mist son aguillon,
.i. poi torna son dos vers l'uis.
      Huimés orrez que il fist puis:
« Par foi, fet il, ce est la voire,
30 puis que je sui hors de la foire
& en bon lieu & loing de gent,
deüsse bien de mon argent
tout seul par moi savoir la somme;
ainsi le font tuit li sage homme.
35 J'oi de Rouget .xxxix. saus—
.xii. deniers en ot Giraus,
qui mes .ii. bués m'aida a vendre . . .
A males forches puist li pendre
por ce qu'il retint mes deniers!—
40 .xii. en retint li pautoniers,
& se li ai je fet maint bien!
Or est ainsi, ce ne vaut rien.
Il me vendra mes bués requerre
quant il voudra arer sa terre
45 & il devra semer son orge . . .
mal dehez ait toute ma gorge
s'il a ja mes de moi nul preu!—
je li molt cuit bien metre en leu,
honiz soit il & toute s'aire!
50 Or parlerai de mon afaire:
j'oi de Sorin .xix. saus;

to give himself a peasant look.
He bought himself an ample purse
and put in all he had, a scarce
twelve pennies' worth, and then the fellow
20 headed straight for Mabile's bordello
in the street where the whores resided—
for scheming and deceit she prided
herself the best woman in town—
and there Boivin sat himself down
25 on an overturned log before
her house, his back turned to the door,
and set his staff down in the street.
      Hear how he managed his deceit!
He mutters loudly, "Well, I swear,
30 now that I've gone and left the fair,
in this safe place with none around,
I really ought to make a count
and see how much money I've earned.
That's what smart people do, I've learned.
35 Thirty-nine shillings Roger paid,
and twelve pence went for Gerald's aid
in selling off my pair of oxen,
may he go hang! An evil pox on
him, making me pay for his labor!
40 I've helped the scoundrel like a neighbor,
and he keeps twelve pence of my money!
But what's the use? What's done is done. He
is sure to ask me anyhow
for oxen when it's time to plow
45 his field for barley. Let him stow't!
May I be stricken in the throat
if he gets anything from me!
I'll give him what for, certainly!
A curse on him and all his kind!
50 But I've my own affairs to mind. . . .
I got for the ox Sorin bought

de ceus ne fui je mie faus,
quar mon conpere, dans Gautiers,
ne m'en donast pas tant deniers
55 com j'ai eü, de tout le mendre—
por ce fet bon au marchié vendre.
Il vousist ja creance avoir,
& j'ai assanblé mon avoir,
.xix. saus & .xxxix.—
60 itant furent vendu mi buef.
Dieus! c'or ne sai que tout ce monte—
s'i meïsse tout en .i. conte,
je ne le savroie sommer,
qui me devroit tout assommer.
65 Ne le savroie je des mois
se n'avoie feves ou pois . . .
que chascuns pois feïst .i. sout,
ainsi le savroie je tout,
& neporquant me dist *Girous*
70 que j'oi des bués .l. sous,
qui les conta, si les reçut . . .
mes je ne sai s'il m'en deçut
ne s'il m'en a neant emblé,
qu'entre .ii. sestiere de blé
75 & ma jument & mes porciaus
& la laine de mes aigniaus
me rendirent tout autrestant.
.ii. foiz .l. ce sont .c.,
ce dist uns gars qui fist mon conte;
80 .v. livres, dist, que tout ce monte.
Or ne lerai por nule paine
que ma borse, qu'est toute plaine,
ne soit vuidie en mon giron. »
& li houlier de la meson
85 dïent: « Ça vien, Mabile, escoute!
Cil denier sont nostre, sanz doute,
se tu mes ceenz ce vilain.

nineteen shillings, nor was I short-
changed in this, for Walter, my pal,
would never have paid me as well
55 for my worst ox. For merchandise
the market brings in the best price,
and Walter would have bought on credit,
and now I've all this cash instead! It
must total . . . nineteen . . . thirty-nine . . .
60 in all for those oxen of mine. . . .
God! To how much does that all come?
I couldn't figure out the sum,
not even if I made a list!
Though someone beat me with his fist,
65 it would take months. If I had peas
or beans, then it would be a breeze:
I'd make each pea count for a shilling
and so figure it out, God willing. . . .
But didn't Gerald say to me,
70 who counted when he took his fee,
that my two oxen brought in fifty
shillings? . . . But maybe he was shifty
and ripped me off by some deceit,
because for two bushels of wheat,
75 my piglets also, and my mare
and the wool I sold at the fair
I got exactly the same price.
One hundred, now that's fifty twice.
A chap who added my accounts
80 said so—in all, he said, five pounds.
Well, come what may, I'll have to pull
my money bag out—it's chock full—
and empty it out in my lap!"
         The brothel's pimps, eyeing the chap,
85 say, "Come and listen here, Mabile!
This guy's cash will be ours for real
if you can lure the peasant in.

Il ne sont mie a son oés sain. »
Dist Mabile: « Lessiez le en pes,
90   lessiez le conter tout adés,
lessiez le conter tout en pes,
qu'il ne me puet eschaper mes!
Toz les deniers, je les vos doi,
les ieus me crevez, je l'otroi,
95   se il en est a dire uns seus! »
Mes autrement ira li geus
qu'ele ne cuide, ce me sanble,
quar li vilains conte & assanble
.xii. deniers sanz plus qu'il a.
100   Tant va contant & ça & la
qu'il dist: « Or est .xx. sous .v. foiz.
Des ore mes est il bien droiz
que je les gart—ce sera sens,
mes d'une chose me porpens:
105   s'or eüsse ma douce niece
qui fu fille de ma suer Tiece,
dame fust or de mon avoir.
El s'en ala por fol savoir
hors du païs en autre terre,
110   & je l'ai fete maint jor querre
en maint païs, en mainte vile.
Ahi! douce niece Mabile,
tant estiiez de bon lingnage!
Dont vous vint ore cel corage?
115   Or sont tuit troi mort mi enfant
& ma fame, dame Siersant.
Jamés en mon cuer n'avrai joie
devant cele eure que je voie
ma douce niece en aucun tans,
120   lors me rendisse moines blans,
dame fust or de mon avoir,
riche mari peüst avoir. »

It ain't fit for the likes of him!"
Mabile said, "Leave the man alone
90   and let him count up what's his own!
I tell you, let the fellow be;
he's no match for the likes of me!
I'll stand you everything he's got.
Poke out my eyes if I do not
95   bilk him of every single penny!"
(But I doubt it will turn out any-
thing at all like what she has planned,
for Boivin counts his money and
those twelve pence are all that he's worth.)
100   He goes on counting back and forth
till he says, "That's twenty times five.
Now I'd better put back what I've
just tallied; that's the wisest course.
Now I'm reminded of my loss!
105   If only my sweet niece were here,
the daughter of my sister, dear
Tess, I would give her all I own.
Some wild fancy made her leave home
and run away and go abroad.
110   How many lands and towns I've sought
her in and for how long, but she's
not anywhere! Mabile, sweet niece,
descended from such genteel stock,
what made you give us such a shock?
115   Now my two children and my wife,
Siersant, have passed on from this life,
and my heart never will find peace
till I find my beloved niece.
I'd put an end to my exertions
120   and go to live with the Cistercians,
and she, as mistress of my fortune,
would land a wealthy marriage portion."

Ainsi la plaint, ainsi la pleure,
& Mabile saut en cele eure,
125 lez lui s'assist & dist: « Preudom,
dont estes vous, & vostre non?
— Je ai non Fouchier de la Brouce . . .
Mes vous sanblez ma niece douce
plus que nule fame qui fust. »
130 Cele se pasme sor le fust;
quant se redrece, si dist tant:
« Or ai je ce que je demant! »
puis si l'acole & si l'embrace,
& puis li baise bouche & face
135 que ja n'en sanble estre saoule,
& celui qui molt sot de boule
estraint les denz & puis souspire:
« Bele niece, ne vous puis dire
la grant joie que j'ai au cuer!
140 Estes vous fille de ma suer?
— Oïl, sire, de dame Tiece.
— Molt ai esté por vous grant piece,
fet li vilains, sanz avoir aise! »
Estroitement l'acole & baise.
145 Ainsi aus .ii. mainent grant joie,
& .ii. houliers en mi la voie
issirent fors de la meson.
Font li houlier: « Icist preudom,
est il or nez de vostre vile?
150 — Voir, c'est mon oncle, dist Mabile,
dont vous avoie tant bien dit. »
Vers aus se retorne .i. petit
& tret la langue & tuert la joe,
& li houlier refont la moe:
155 « Est il donc vostre oncle? — Oïl, voir.
— Grant honor i pöez avoir,
& il en vous, sanz nul redout;
& vous, preudom, du tout en tout,

While he thus mourns and carries on,
Mabile comes out and thereupon
125 sits next to him and says, "I came
to ask where you're from and your name."
"My name is Fouchier de la Brouce.
You seem to bear a far more close
resemblance to my niece than any."
130 Mabile pretends to pass out when he
says so, and says when she comes to,
"Now all my wishes have come true!"
gives him a hug and an embrace
and showers kisses on his face,
135 nor can she get enough, it seems,
while he, whose expertise is schemes,
clenches his teeth and heaves a sigh.
"Niece, I can't speak the great joy I
feel in my heart—it's running wild!
140 Say, can you be my sister's child?"
"Yes, sir, my mother's name was Tess."
"I cannot tell you what distress
I've long felt on account of you."
He gives her hugs and kisses, too,
145 and, now that their joy is complete,
two pimps come out into the street,
who have been watching from within,
and say, "Was this good man born in
the city from which you, too, come?"
150 "Indeed, this man's my uncle, whom
you know from all the good I've said!"
Mabile then slightly turns her head,
sticks out her tongue, and twists her cheek.
The pimps make the same face and speak.
155 "Is he your uncle?" "Yes, it's true."
"He can be very proud of you,
and you of him, of that be sure,
and we're in every way at your

font li houlier, sommes tuit vostre.
160 Par saint Piere le bon apostre,
l'ostel avrez saint Julïen—
il n'a homme jusqu'a Gïen
que plus de vous eüssons chier! »
        Par les braz prenent dant Fouchier,
165 si l'ont dedenz lor ostel mis.
« Or tost, ce dist Mabile, amis,
achatez oes & chapons!
— Dame, font il, venez ça dons.
Ja n'avons nous goute d'argent.
170 —Tesiez, fet el, mauvese gent!
Metez houces! metez sorcos!—
sor le vilain ert li escos.
Cis escos vous sera bien saus;
sempres avrez plus de .c. saus. »
175 Que vous iroie je contant?
Li dui houlier demaintenant,
comment qu'il aient fet chevance,
.ii. cras chapons sanz demorance
ont aporté avoec .ii. oes,
180 & Boivin lor a fet les moes.
En tant comme il se sont tornez
Mabile lor dist: « Or soiez
preu & vistes d'appareillier! »
Qui donc veïst com li houlier
185 plument chapons & plument oies,
& Ysane fist toutes voies
le feu & ce qu'ele ot a fere,
& Mabile ne se pot tere
qu'el ne parlast a son vilain:
190 « Biaus oncles, sont ore tuit sain
vostre fame & mi dui neveu?
Je cuit qu'il sont ore molt preu. »
& li vilains se li respont:
« Bele niece, tuit troi mort sont.

service, good sir," the pimps aver.
160 "Saint Julian the hosteler
himself will house you, by Saint Peter.
From here to Gien you will not meet a
man we so cherish and applaud."
      They take Fouchier's arms and escort
165 him in the house. Mabile says, "Please,
friends, go and buy capons and geese."
"Come here, lady," they say. "With what
are we supposed to pay? We've got
no money at all here between us."
170 "Hush up," Mabile replies, "you heinous
men! Just pawn your cloak or your jacket.
This peasant will pick up the packet.
You won't be risking what you stake—
you'll have some hundred shillings' take!"
175   Why prolong what I have to say?
The two procurers right away
somehow or other found the sums
they needed and brought back at once
both geese and capons, four fat fowl,
180 oblivious to Boivin's scowl.
No sooner were they back, Mabile
said, "Get to work; prepare the meal
quickly now; make yourselves of use."
They went and plucked capon and goose—
185 who ever saw such industry!
Ysane got busy, too, and she
kindled the fire and did her chores,
while Mabile prattled without pause
on with her peasant, fit to bust.
190 "Are all in health, uncle? I trust
your wife and my two cousins both
are doing well, upon my oath."
To this last question he replied,
"My dearest niece, all three have died!

195 Par pou de duel n'ai esté mors;
or serez vous toz mes confors
en mon païs, en nostre vile.
— Ahi! lasse! ce dist Mabile,
bien deüsse or vive enragier!
200 Lasse! s'il fust aprés mengier
il n'alast pas si malement!
Lasse! je vi en mon dormant
ceste aventure en ceste nuit!
— Dame, li chapon sont tout cuit
205 & les .ii. oies en .i. haste,
ce dist Ysane, qui les haste.
Ma douce dame, alez laver
& si lessiez vostre plorer! »
Adonc font au vilain le lorgne,
210 & li vilains, qui n'ert pas borgne
qu'il le moquent en la meson.
Font li houlier: « Sire, preudom,
n'estes pas sages, ce m'est vis.
Lessons les mors, prenons les vis! »
215 Adonc sont assis a la table,
mes du mengier ne fu pas fable:
assez en orent a plenté,
de bons vins n'orent pas chierté.
Assez en font au vilain boivre
220 por enyvrer & por deçoivre,
mes il ne les crient ne ne doute;
desouz sa chape sa main boute
& fet sanblant de trere argent.
Dist Mabile: « Qu'alez querant,
225 biaus douz oncles? Dites le moi.
— Bele niece, bien sai & voi
que molt vous couste cis mengiers.
Je metrai ci .xii. deniers. »
Mabile jure & li houlier
230 que il ja n'i metra denier.

195 I nearly passed away from grief.
Now you will be my sole relief
back in my country, in our city."
"Alas," Mabile cries, "what a pity!
I'm like to lose my mind, poor sinner!
200 If you had told me after dinner,
alas, perhaps the news would seem
less cruel! Last night in my dream
I saw that they were dead and gone!"
"Madam, the capons are both done
205 and likewise the geese on the spit,"
Ysane interrupts. "Step on it
and wash for dinner, dearest lady.
You've wept more than enough already."
Then they all made a face behind
210 the peasant's back, who wasn't blind
to how they laughed at his expense.
"Good sir, you're not making much sense,
I think," the two procurers said.
"Treasure the living, leave the dead."
215   They sat down. On the boards was such an
array, there wasn't much discussion
of all the morsels they were packing
away, nor were the fine wines lacking.
They gave the peasant lots of liquor
220 to make him drunk and dupe him quicker,
but he was not at all afraid.
He reached beneath his cape and made
as if to take some money out.
Mabile said, "What are you about,
225 beloved uncle? Answer me."
"My lovely niece, I plainly see
this dinner is a great expense
for you. Let me put in twelve pence."
Mabile and the procurers swear
230 that they won't let him pay his share.

La table ostent quant ont mengié,
& Mabile a doné congié
aus .ii. houlier d'aler la hors:
« Si vous sera bons li essors
235   que bien avez eü disner.
Or prenez garde du souper. »
Li dui houlier s'en sont torné;
aprés aus sont li huis fermé.
Mabile prist a demander:
240   « Biaus douz oncles, ne me celer
s'eüstes pieça conpaignie
a fame, nel me celez mie,
puis que vostre fame fu morte.
Il est molt fols qui trop sorporte
245   talent de fame; c'est folie
autressi comme defamie.
    — Niece, il a bien .vii. anz toz plains,
tant a il bien a tout le mains,
ne de ce n'ai je nul talant.
250   — Tesiez, oncles! Dieus vous avant!
Mes regardez ceste meschine . . . »
Adonc bat .iii. foiz sa poitrine:
« Oncles, je ai molt fort pechié,
qu'a ses parenz *la fortrechié*.
255   Por seul son pucelage avoir
eüsse je molt grant avoir,
mes vous l'avrez, que je le vueil. »
A Ysane cluingne de l'ueil
que la borse li soit copee.
260   Li vilains ot bien en penssee
de coper la avant qu'Isane;
la borse prent & si la trenche
dans Fouchier, & puis si l'estuie;
en son sain pres de sa char nue
265   la mist, & puis si s'en retorne,
vers Ysane sa chiere torne,

They cleared the boards after the meal,
and as for the two pimps, Mabile
sent them outside to take the air:
"You ate a lot of hearty fare
235 and need to build your appetite
before we have supper tonight."
The two procurers up and left;
the doors were closed behind them. Next
Mabile proceeded to inquire,
240 "Beloved uncle, don't be shy or
try to keep it secret from me
whether you've known the company
of women since your wife's demise.
Such self-denial's most unwise.
245 To hold in check one's manly craving
is a depraved way of behaving."
"Full seven years have now gone by
or more, niece, since the last time I . . .
but, really, I've no inclination."
250 "Hush, uncle, upon your salvation!
Do take a good look at my maid. . . ."
She beat her breast three times and said,
"Uncle, I've sinned, for I beguiled
her parents to get at this child.
255 The sale of her virginity
would make a rich woman of me,
but you shall have her, I insist."
She gives Ysane a wink to lift
the peasant's purse and cut the strings,
260 but he is onto her and thinks
to do so before she's a chance.
Thus Fouchier cuts them in advance
and tucks it safely in his breast
under his shirt against the flesh,
265 and then, proceeding with his con,
he turns around to face Ysane.

& s'en vindrent li uns vers l'autre.
Andui se vont couchier el piautre.
  Ysane va avant couchier
270 & molt pria a dant Fouchier
por Dieu que il ne la bleçast.
Adonc covint que il ostast
la coiffe au cul por fere l'uevre,
de sa chemise la descuevre,
275 puis si commence a arecier
& cele la borse a cerchier.
Que qu'ele cerche, & cil l'estraint,
de la pointe du vit la point,
el con li met jusqu'a la coille,
280 dont li bat le cul & rooille
tant, ce m'est vis, qu'il ot foutu.
Ses braies monte, s'a veü
de sa borse les .ii. pendanz:
« Ha! las! fet il, chetiz dolans!
285 tant ai hui fet male jornee!
Niece, ma borse m'est copee!
Ceste fame le m'a trenchie! »
Mabile l'ot, s'en fu molt lie,
qui bien cuide que ce soit voir,
290 qu'ele covoitoit molt l'avoir.
Maintenant a son huis desclos;
« Dant vilain, fet ele, alez hors!
— Dont me fetes ma borse rendre!
— Je vous baudrai la hart a pendre!
295 Alez tost hors de ma meson
ainçois que je praingne .i. baston! »
Cele .i. tison prent a .ii. mains;
adonc s'en va hors li vilains,
qui n'ot cure d'avoir des cops.
300 Aprés lui fu tost li huis clos.
  Tout entor lui chascuns assanble,

The two of them approach each other
and go off to lie down together.
    Ysane was first to get in bed,
270   and, calling on God's name, she pled
insistently Fouchier not hurt
her, so he had to lift her skirt
to do his business, and pulled off,
to bare her rump, her nether coif,
275   and while his member grew more solid,
she groped around to find his wallet.
She feels around, and he embraces
her tightly, and his prick he places
in her cunt, shoves it to the nuts,
280   beats them against her ass and ruts,
which means he's fucked her, I suppose.
He sees, while hiking up his hose,
his two cut purse straps hanging free.
"Alas!" he cries. "Oh, woe is me!
285   This day for me has been a curse!
Mabile! Niece! Someone's cut my purse!
I'm sure this woman did it, too!"
Mabile hears him. Thinking it's true
(which makes her most extremely glad
290   because she coveted the wad),
she flings the door wide, starts to shout
at him, "You peasant! Quick, get out!"
"First make her give my wallet back!"
"I'll give you a rope for your neck!
295   Just get out of my house and quick,
before I go and get a stick!"
In both her hands she grabbed some wood,
and he left quickly as he could,
not being in the mood for blows.
300   The door behind him was shut close.
The people gather and surround him,

& il lor moustre a toz ensanble
que sa borse li ont copee;
& Mabile l'a demandee
305   a Ysane: « Baille ça tost,
que li vilains va au provost!
    — Foi que je doi saint Nicholas,
dist Ysane, je ne l'ai pas,
si l'ai je molt cerchie & quise.
310   — Par .i. poi que je ne te brise,
pute orde vieus, toutes les danz!
Enne vi je les .ii. pendanz
que tu copas? Jel sai de voir.
Cuides les tu par toi avoir?
315   Se tu m'en fez plus dire mot . . .
Pute vielle, baille ça tost!
    — Dame, comment vous baillerai,
dist Ysane, ce que je n'ai? »
& Mabile aus cheveus li cort,
320   qui n'estoient mie trop cort,
que jusqu'a la terre l'abat,
aus piez & aus poins la debat
qu'ele le fet poirre et chïer:
« Par Dieu, pute, ce n'a mestier!
325   — Dame, or lessiez! Je les querrai
tant se puis que les troverai,
se de ci me lessiez torner.
    — Va, fet ele, sanz demorer! »
Mes Mabile l'estrain reborse,
330   qu'ele cuide trover la borse.
« Dame, or entent, ce dist Ysane,
perdre puisse je cors & ame
s'onques la borse soi ne vi!
Or me pöez tuer ici.
335   —Par Dieu, pute, tu i morras! »
Par les cheveus & par les dras

and he shows everyone around him
how his purse strings have been cut through,
while, in the house, Mabile calls to
305 Ysane, "Give it here quickly. He's
gone to get the authorities."
"But, by Saint Nicholas, I swear,"
Ysane replies, "it wasn't there,
however much I searched and sought."
310 "I wouldn't give a second thought
to break your teeth, you shit-faced whore!
And what about the strings I saw?
I know you cut them, on my soul!
Do you think you'll keep what you stole?
315 Why, if I have to say another
word . . . Stinking hag! Quick, hand it over!"
"How, madam, can I give you what,"
Ysane protests, "I haven't got?"
Mabile runs up and takes a strong
320 grip on her hair, which was quite long,
and, throwing her down to the ground,
with feet and fists begins to pound
so hard, she makes her fart and shit.
"Whore! You won't get away with it!"
325 "Let me go, mistress, and I'll look
in every cranny, every nook
and find it, if you let me go."
She says, "Then do it; don't be slow!"
Mabile looks under the reverse
330 side of the mattress for the purse.
"Listen here, mistress, it's no use,"
Ysane asserts, "and may I lose
body and soul both if I saw it,
even though you may kill me for it!"
335 "Get ready, whore, to meet your Maker!"
She grabs her hair and clothes to shake her

l'a tiree jusqu'a ses piez,
& ele crie: « Aidiez! aidiez! »

Quant son houlier dehors l'entent,
340 cele part cort isnelement,
l'uis fiert du pié sanz demorer
si qu'il le fet des gons voler;
Mabile prist par la chevece
si qu'il la deront par destrece—
345 tant est la robe deronpue
que dusqu'au cul en remest nue—
puis l'a prise par les chevols,
du poing li done de granz cops
parmi le vis en mi les joes
350 si qu'eles sont perses & bloes.
Mes ele avra par tens secors,
que son ami i vient le cors,
qui au crïer l'a entendue;
tout maintenant sanz atendue
355 s'entreprenent li dui glouton.
Lors veïssiez enplir meson
& de houliers & de putains;
chascuns i mist adonc les mains.
Lors veïssiez cheveus tirer,
360 tisons voler, dras deschirer,
& l'un desouz l'autre cheïr.
Li marcheant corent veïr
ceus qui orent rouge testee,
que molt i ot dure meslee,
365 & se s'i mistrent de tel gent
qui ne s'en partirent pas gent:
teus i entra a robe vaire
qui la trest rouge & a refere.
Boivin s'en vint droit au provost,
370 se li a conté mot a mot
de chief en chief la verité,

and throws her down upon the floor.
"Help! Help!" she calls.
                              Outside the door
her pimp hears her cry out in need
340 and comes a-running at top speed,
kicks the door open with a vengeance
to send it flying from its hinges,
and seizes Mabile by the collar,
so yanking at it in his choler
345 that her whole dress behind her rips,
exposing her below the hips,
and then he holds her by the hair
and lands some heavy punches square
upon her face across her two
350 cheeks such that they turn black-and-blue.
But she will have help presently:
Her fancy man has heard, and he
comes running to his wench's aid.
Without so much as one word said
355 the two toughs lay into each other.
Then in that house you'd have seen gather
a crowd of pimps and also trollops
who set about exchanging wallops;
there you would have seen hair pulled out,
360 clothes ripped and torn, sticks flung about,
bodies above, bodies below.
Storekeepers flocked to see the row
and the heads bloodied in the brawl,
which had become a free-for-all,
365 and many joined the fighting there,
only to leave the worse for wear.
Whatever clothes they wore were showing
red stains and cried out for resewing.
           Boivin went to the magistrate
370 and told him the whole story straight
from end to end and word for word,

& li provos l'a escouté,
qui molt ama la lecherie;
sovent li fist conter sa vie
375   a ses parens, a ses amis,
qui molt s'en sont joué & ris.
Boivin remest .iii. jors entiers,
se li dona de ses deniers
li provos .x. sous a Boivins,
380   qui cest fablel fist a Provins.

49. LA BORGOISE D'ORLIANS

Plest vos oïr d'une bourjoise
une aventure asés courtoise?
Nee & norrie estoit d'Orliens,
& ses sires estoit d'Amiens,
5   riche & menant a desmesure;
de marchaandise & d'usure
savoit touz les tours & les poins,
& quant que il tenoit as poins
estoit molt richement tenu.
10   De Normendie estoit venu
.iiii. clers normant, escolier,
portant lour sas comme colier
ou lor livres sunt & lor dras.
Li clerc furent & gros & gras
15   & bien chantant & envoisié
& en la rue bien proisié
ou il avoient ostel pris.
.i. en i ot de molt grant pris
qui chantoit par ches ces borjois;
20   s'estoit tenuz por trop courtois
a la bourjoise voirement:

and when the dignitary heard,
who had a taste for ribaldry,
he had him tell his family
375 and friends the many things he'd done,
a source of merriment and fun.
Boivin stayed three days as his guest,
and the provost made a bequest
to him of half a pound. Boivin
380 made this fabliau in Provins.

49. THE GOOD WOMAN
OF ORLÉANS

Say, how would you all like to hear
a townswoman's courtly affair?
She born and bred in Orléans,
while her husband hailed from Amiens,
5 a wealthy merchant of high standing.
About retail and moneylending
the man knew all the turns and twists;
whatever he held in his fists
he hung on to tenaciously.
10   Four lay brothers from Normandy,
all students, had arrived in town,
wearing their duffels slung around
their necks, with all their books and clothes.
Large and well fed from head to toes,
15 they sang and partied throughout town,
esteemed by all and widely known
in the street where their lodgings were.
One of them in particular,
who for the townsfolk used to sing,
20 seemed courtlier than anything
in the eyes of the merchant's wife,

plesoit molt son acointement
dont je vos ai avant conté,
quant que cil dist li vint a gré.
25   Tant vint li clerc & tant ala
que li bourjois s'en apenssa
& par semblant & par parole
que cil la trera a s'escole
s'il a tant en poeit venir
30   qu'il la peüst seule tenir.
Laienz ot une *seue* niece
qu'il avoit norrie grant piece;
priveement a soi l'apele,
si li promist une cotele
35   mes que au clerc li soit espie
& que la verité li die.
Cele li a tot otroié,
& l'escolier a tant proié
que la bourjoise a mise en voie,
40   & la meschine tote voie
a tant escouté & oï
comment il ont lor plet basti.
Au borjois vint demeintenant,
si li conte le convenant,
45   que li parlemenz tel estoit
que la dame au cler manderoit
quant li bourjois n'i seroit mie,
qu'il seroit en *marchaandie*
fors de la vile conquester;
50   a tant vendroit sanz demorer
le clerc droit a .i. huis ferré
qu'ele li avoit devisé
qui estoit devers le cortil,
ou il fesoit bel & gentil.
55   La bourjoise li afia
qu'ele seroit contre li la.

who loved the way he led his life
(and how he lived you've just now heard).
She hung upon his every word.
25 So often did he come to see 'er,
it gave the merchant the idea
his body language and his speech
would get her to learn what he'd teach
her if only he could arrive at
30 some way to be with her in private.
        A niece was living in his home
whom he had brought up as his own.
He called her confidentially,
and promised her some cutlery
35 if she would spy upon the youth
for him and tell him all the truth.
With this she readily complied,
and the youth diligently tried
till he broke down the wife's resistance.
40 Meanwhile the girl spied with insistence
for her uncle, heard what was said,
and knew the plan that they had laid.
She went to him with all due speed
and told him what had been agreed,
45 how they'd decided it was prudent
to have her send word to the student
when the merchant would not be there,
when he'd have gone to sell his ware
and make a profit out of town.
50 The student then would hurry down
straight to an iron-studded door
she had described to him before
that led into their garden plot,
a very fair and charming spot.
55 The woman promised she would wait
and meet him there inside the gate.

Li bourjois entent la parrolle,
entrez est en male rïolle
quant il entent qu'a l'anuitier
60 vendroit li clerc. Sanz atargier,
com ainz puet a la dame vient:
« Dame, fet il, il me convient
aler en ma marchaandie.
Gardez l'ostel, ma douce amie,
65 comme preudefame doit fere,
car rien ne sai de mon repaire.
— Sire, fet ele, volentiers. »
Cil atorne ses charetiers
& dit qu'il s'ira herbergier
70 pour ses jornees avancier
dusqu'a trois lieues de la vile.
La dame ne sot pas la guile;
tost fist au clerc l'euvre savoir.
Cil qui la cuida decevoir
75 s'en est tornez sanz atargier,
ses charetiers fist herbergier
molt pres d'iluec a .i. recet,
si lour a dit tot *soavet*
qu'il le convient avant aler,
80 a .i. riche home veut parler.
Cil otrïent sa volenté,
qui ne se sunt garde doné
du retour que il devoit fere,
& cil s'en vint vers son repere,
85 tant qu'il fu vespre s'atarja,
& quant il vit qu'il anuit*a*,
que la nuit fu au jor merllee,
au vergier vint a recelee.
A l'uis ferré qu'il bien savoit
90 s'en est venuz li borjois droit;
a l'uis hurta .i. petitet.
Cele qui ne sot pas l'abet

The merchant, when he understood,
was taken by an ugly mood
to hear as soon as day was gone
60   the student would come. Thereupon,
soon as he can he goes to see 'er
and says, "The time has come, my dear,
for me to go away on business.
See to the house like a good mistress,
65   my darling wife, while I'm away.
When I'll be back, I cannot say."
"Husband, I will," replies the lady.
        He has his cartage men get ready
and says he'll find a place to sleep
70   to get a head start on his trip
some three leagues off from where they lived.
        His wife knew none of this. Deceived,
she let the student know and quick.
The man who thought that he would trick
75   his wife set out without delay,
found for his men a place to stay
quite nearby at a hostelry
and explained to them patiently
he'd go on ahead by himself
80   to consult with a man of wealth.
They fell in with what he proposed—
not one of them ever supposed
that he'd go back where they'd come from—
and he retraced his steps toward home.
85   Till evening came he just sat tight,
and when he saw that it was night,
in the half-light of fading day
up to their yard he made his way
in stealth. The iron-studded gate
90   the merchant knew, and he went straight
on up to it and gave a rap.
She, unaware it was a trap,

s'en vint a l'uis & si l'ovri,
entre ses braz le recoilli,
95   qu'el cuida que ses amis soit—
mes esperrance la deçoit.
Son mari salue enroment
& li a dit molt doucement:
« Amis, bien soiez vos venus! »
100   Cil s'est de haut parler tenuz,
si li rent son salu en bas.
Tout meintenant, enelepas,
par .i. destroit de la meson
menoit la dame son baron
105   & vers sa chanbre trestout droit.
Quant de celui reson ne voit
que cil ne sonne .i. tot soul mot
qui tel senblant d'amour fet ot,
celi tient sa chiere encline,
110   .i. petitet vers li s'acline,
par desouz le chaperon garde;
de traïson se done garde
& voit tres bien & aperçoit
c'est ses maris qui la deçoit.
115   Quant el [le] prist a aperchoivre,
si s'apense de li dechoivre—
fames ont molt le sens agu,
eles ont meint homes dechut,
si fera ceste son vilein:
120   metre le fera en pelein
& li fera .i. mal jöel!
« Amis, fet ele, molt m'est bel
que tenir vos puis & avoir!
Je vos donré de mon avoir
125   dont vos porrez vos gages trere
se vos celez bien cest afere.
O moi vendrez celeement;
je vos metrai priveement

came to the door, opened it wide,
and, hugging him, drew him inside
95 because she thought he was her lover.
(That hope deceives her, she'll discover.)
She hastens to welcome her lord
and greets him with a tender word.
"Your coming, love, makes me rejoice."
100 He kept from speaking in full voice
and, when he answered, murmured low.
Immediately they quickly go
through a small hallway in the house;
straight on the lady leads her spouse
105 toward her chamber on the sly.
When she can see no reason why
he should keep quiet in this fashion
who had made such a show of passion,
the woman keeps her head bent forward
110 and turns it just so slightly toward
him to see underneath his hood.
His treachery she understood,
she recognized him and perceived
that by her husband she's deceived.
115 Enlightened now by this perception,
she thinks to repay his deception.
A woman's mind is very quick,
they've played many a man a trick,
and so will she on him she married,
120 she'll see to it that he is harried—
a painful keepsake will be his!
"My love," she says, "how sweet it is
to hold you and to know you're mine!
From what I own I'll give you fine
125 gifts for you to keep for your own
if you'll tell no one what we've done.
Now come with me in secrecy.
I'll put you under lock and key

en .i. perrin dont j'ai la clef,
130 la si m'atendrez tot söef
tant que nos gens aront mengié,
& quant il seront tuit couchié,
lors vos metrai souz la cortine.
Ja nus ne sara la covine.
135 — Dame, dist il, bien avez dit. »
Dieus! com cil savoit or petit
ce que sa fame li porpose,
que li uns pensoit une chose
& li autres penssoit tot el!
140 Encui avra mavés ostel,
car, quant la dame enfermé l'ot
el perrin dont issir ne pot;
a l'uis du vergier retorna,
son ami prist qu'el i trova,
145 si l'enbrace & acole & bese.
Or est, ce quit, asés plus *ese*
li segont douz que le premier!

Quant passé fu tot li vergier,
droit en la chanbre sunt venu
150 ou li drap furent portendu.
La dame son ami i meine
desi en sa chanbre le meine,
si l'a souz la cortine mis,
& il s'est tantost entremis
155 du gieu que Amours li commande,
car ne prisast mie une amande
tout l'autre gieu se cil ne fust,
ne cele gré ne l'en seüst.
          Quant asez se sunt envoisié
160 & ont acolé & besié,
« Amis, fet ele, or m'entendez:
.i. petit ici m'atendez,
& je m'en irai la dedenz

in a safe room built all of stone,
130 where you'll wait calmly while I'm gone
until our people have been fed,
and, when they all have gone to bed,
I'll bed you down beneath the covers.
No one will ever know we're lovers."
135 "Lady, what you have said is good."
(Lord! how little he understood
the scheme his better half has laid,
for he had one thing in his head
and she harbored another thought!)
140 In a sad scrape will he be caught
today, for once she shut him in,
no way could he get out again,
and to the garden she returned
and found the man for whom she yearned,
145 gave him a kiss, a hug, a squeeze.
(The second suitor's more at ease,
I rather think, than the first to
arrive there!)
When they had gone through
the garden, they proceeded right
150 to her room, readied for their night
together. She, acting as guide,
ushered her paramour inside
and got him underneath the quilt,
and right away he went to tilt
155 in the tourney prescribed by Love.
Less than a nut's all he thought of
playing at any other game,
and, as for her, she felt the same.
When their delight is satiated
160 and hugs and kisses have abated,
she says, "Now listen to me, dear.
A little while wait for me here,"
and she explains to him that she'll

& si ferai souper nos genz.
165 — Dame, a vostre commandement. »
Cele s'en vet molt lieement,
en la sale entre ou sa mesnie,
a son poeir l'a enhaitie.
Quant li mengiers fu aprestez,
170 mengerent & burent assez,
& quant il orent tuit mengié,
ençois que fusent desrengié,
la dame apele sa mesnie,
si parrolle comme afetie
175 as .ii. neveuz que li sire ot.
(Autre mesnee assez i ot—
il i avoit .i. grant Breton
qu'eve portoit en la meson,
& chanberieres dusqu'a .iii.,
180 si i fu la niece au bourjois,
& .ii. garchons & .i. ribaut.)
« Seignor, fet el, se Dieus me saut,
or entendez a ma reson.
Vos avez en ceste meson
185 veü sovent .i. clerc venir
qui ne me let en pes tenir.
D'amour m'a requise lonc tens,
je l'en ai fet torjors desfens;
quant vi que je n'i gariroie,
190 je li otriai tote voie
que je feroie tot son gré
quant mon seignor seroit alé
quere loinz sa marcheandie.
Or est alé, Dieus le conduie!
195 Li faus clerc qui tant m'a proïe,
de folie fere ennoïe,
a bien de mon seignor seü
que fors de la vile est issu.
Enbatuz s'est anuit ceanz;

go let the servants have their meal.
165 "Lady, let it be as you say."
          The lady goes her merry way
and joins her household in the hall;
to make them glad she gives her all.
When the food was set on the table,
170 they ate and drank all they were able,
and when they'd all eaten their fill
and all were at the table still,
the lady called a household session,
addressing with taste and discretion
175 two nephews whom her husband hired.
With them, she'd what help she required:
a Breton man, sound as a bell,
who carried water from the well,
three chambermaids to clean the house,
180 the niece who had spied for her spouse,
two hired hands, and a renegade.
"God save me, good people," she said,
"now listen well and hear me out.
You've seen around the house, no doubt,
185 a student who comes frequently
and simply will not let me be.
He pesters me to sleep with him,
and I have never given in,
but, when I saw he'd not relent,
190 I went along with his intent
and said that he could have his way
when my husband had gone away
on business to barter and sell.
Now he has gone, may he fare well!
195 That low-life student who'd harass
me into doing something crass
has somehow learned my husband's gone
and is no longer around town.
He forced his way in here tonight,

je l'ai enfermé la dedanz,
        lasus amont en cel perrin.
        Je vos donré du meillor vin
        qui ceanz soit une corgie,
        mes que je soie bien vengie!
205   Sus el perrin amont alez,
        o bons batons le me batez
        encontre terre & en estant,
        & d'orbes cous li donez tant
        que jamés jor ne li en chaille
210   de preudefame qui riens vaille! »
                Quant la mesnee l'uevre entent,
        il saillent sus molt vistement.
        L'un prent baston, l'autre tinel,
        l'autre pesteil qu'il n'i ot el,
215   & la dame la clef lor baille.
        Qui tous les cous meïst en taille,
        a bon conteor le tenisse!
        Ne suefre[nt] pas que il s'en isse;
        einz l'acueillent el perrin haut:
220   « Par Deu, clerjastre, ne vos vaut!
        Ja vos avron decepliné! »
        Li .i. l'a a l'autre geté
        & par le chaperon saisi,
        parmi la gorge l'estreint si
225   que il ne puet .i. mot sonner.
        Cil l'en acoillent a doner;
        du batre ne sunt mie escha[r]s
        se il eüst doné .c. mars.
        Par meintes foiz l'ont tooillié:
230   bien li ont son hauberc roullé,
        li dui neveu molt fierement
        sor lor oncle fierent sovent,
        primes desus & puis en haut,
        & la dame s'escrie en haut:
235   « Or du ferir, bone mesnie!

200 and now I have him locked up tight
upstairs there in the stone-walled room.
Avenge me! Let him meet his doom,
and I'll let you drink several kegs
of our best wine down to the dregs!

205 Go on upstairs to where I've locked
him up. Bring sticks—I want him knocked
about, flattened or on his feet.
Don't stop the blows or cease to beat,
so that while he yet lives on earth

210 he'll not pursue women of worth!"
        When the household hears what's expected
of them, they jump up as directed.
One grabs a stick, one takes a cudgel,
this one a pestle, that a shovel;

215 the key she gives them; off they sally.
I'd say the man who'd keep a tally
of every blow 's some raconteur!
They won't let him get through the door,
but corner him inside the room.

220 "You corrupt cleric, meet your doom!
We'll cane you like a lazy scholar!"
One grabs his throat around the collar
so tightly he can't make a sound;
they shove and push the man around,

225 hiding his face beneath his hood.
They really give it to him good:
They wouldn't miss a chance to thrash
him for a hundred marks in cash.
They didn't cease to dun and dog him;

230 they rained down blows upon his noggin;
the nephews with ferocity
displayed their animosity
and beat their uncle high and low;
and all the while she yelled, "Now go!

235 Pummel him soundly! Lay him flat!

Fetes tant a ceste foïe
le [cle]rjastre, le renoié
qui de folie m'a proié,
que jamés jor ne soit tant os
240   de tolir dame son bon los,
mes gardez bien ne le tüez!
Quant vos en avrés fet assez,
si le lanciez lafors au vent,
qu'autre foiz n'i vieigne noient! »
245   Le bourjois voit bien c'on l'afole
& de sa fame ot la parrolle,
qui si se fet du clerc vengier.
Ce le refet asouagier;
n'ose sonner .i. tot sol mot,
250   einz suefre tot quant que lor plot,
& cil firent lor volenté.

      Quant du batre se sunt lassé,
la bourjoise haut lour escrie:
« Or est assez, franche mesnie!
255   Je ne vueil mie qu'il i muire;
bien nos porroit a trestouz nuire. »
Quant il ont lor dame entendue,
si le pranent sanz atendue,
chascun de ceus le saisi bien,
260   hors le traïnent comme .i. chien,
si l'ont en .i. fumier flati;
puis sunt ariere resorti
& si ont bien les huis serrez,
& puis burent a grant plentez
265   & des blans & des Auchorrois
autant com se chascun fust rois,
& la dame ot pastez & vin
& blanche toaille de lin
& grosse chandele de cire:
270   a son ami tint son concire

This time, good people, make sure that
this lay brother, this uncouth student
who pleaded that I be imprudent,
will never dare give provocation
240 or ruin a woman's reputation,
but don't make him give up the ghost.
Then, when you're done, let him be tossed
into the street, so he will learn
we mean him never to return!"
245 The merchant suffers the attack,
hears his wife say she's getting back
at him for his unasked flirtation,
and feels some little consolation.
He doesn't dare raise an objection
250 and just submits to their correction,
which they went about with a will.
When all the household had their fill
of beating him, the lady spoke
and cried out, "That's enough, good folk!
255 I don't want you to kill the duffer,
for, if he dies, we all may suffer."
When they have grasped their lady's whim,
they quickly grab ahold of him
and drag him like a dog. They flung
260 him out onto a pile of dung.
All had performed well, as required;
back to the homestead they retired
and tightly bolted up the doors;
then they drank deeply from their stores
265 of white wines and wines from Auxerre
just like a king, a royal share.
The lady got pasties and wine,
and a white napkin made of fine
linen, and a tall beeswax taper,
270 and went to cut another caper

quant sa mesnee fu couchie,
qui de boivre fu aesie.

     & cil qui el femier jesoit,
qu'il ont tenu a grant destroit,
275   se traïna au mieus qu'il pot
la ou son hernois lessié ot.
Quant sa gent si batu le virent,
molt durement s'en esbahirent,
demandent li comment li va.
280   « Mauvesement, fet il, m'esta.
En grant peril ai esté puis,
mes plus dire ne vos en puis.
En ma chareste me metez,
a mon ostel me remenez
285   tantost com jor iert aparus,
& si ne me demandez plus. »
La nuit sejornent duc'au jour,
si apareillent lor atour,
sus la chareste l'ont chargié,
290   vers lor ostel sunt avoié;
& la bourjoise d'autre part
de son ami enviz se part,
mes quant le jor vit esclairier
si le met hors par le vergier
295   & de revenir le proia
quant la dame le mandera,
& cil li dist: « Molt volentiers! »
   · · · · ·

A tant li clerc se departi,
300   & la bourjoise reverti
droit en sa chanbre, si se couche.
     Ez vos le bourjois en la couche
qui molt a son cuer adoulé,
mes ce l'a molt reconforté
305   qu'il sent sa fame si loial
qu'il n'i set .i. seul point de mal

with her swain while the household lay
asleep in drunken disarray.
      The merchant lying in the midden,
the one they very nearly did in,

275   dragged himself on by might and main
and so rejoined his baggage train.
When his men saw him bruised and frayed,
they were enormously afraid
and asked him about his condition.

280   "I narrowly escaped perdition,"
he answered, "and I feel half dead,
but that is all that can be said.
There in my wagon lay me up
and carry me back home nonstop

285   just as soon as dawn has appeared,
and don't ask me another word."
They stay the night and, when the day
breaks, pack their gear and head away;
the merchant added to their load,

290   they trudge along their homeward road.
The merchant's wife, though, for her part
is loath to see her swain depart,
but, once she's seen day light the sky,
she sees him out and says good-bye,

295   requesting that he come again
whenever she may send for him,
and he replies, "With greatest pleasure!"
· · · · ·

The student then bade her adieu,
300   and she went back directly to
her room and got in bed, you betcha!
      Here comes her husband on a stretcher.
For all his heart is sorely grieved,
on this one point he's been relieved

305   to feel his wife is so devoted
to him that she cannot be doubted,

& pense, se il puet garir,
molt la voudra torjors chierir.
A son ostel s'en va tot droit,
310 &sa fame bel le rechoit,
o bone erbes li fist [ ] baing,
tost le garist de cel mehaig.
Demanda li com il avint:
« Dame, dist il, il me covint
315 par .i. peril destroit passer
ou l'en me fist les os casser. »
Cil de la meson li conterent
du clerc, comment il l'atraperent,
comment la dame l'ot bailli:
320 « Par mon chief, el se desfendi
comme dame cortoise & sage! »
Onques puis en tot son aage
de nule rien ne la mescrut.
Einsi la bourjoise deçut
325 son mari qui la vot deçoivre:
il meïsmes brasça son boivre!

𝟓𝟎. LE MAUNIER D'ALEUS

Qui se melle de biaus dis dire
ne doit commenchier a mesdire,
mais de biaus dis dire & conter.
Des or vos vaurai raconter
5 une aventure ke je sai,
car plus celer ne le vaurai.
      A Palluiel, le bon trespas,
.i. maunier i ot, Jakemars;
cointes estoit & envoisiés.
10 A Aleus estoit il mauniers;

and he thinks if he can recover,
he'll always cherish her and love her.
He comes straight to his dwelling, where
310 his wife greets him with loving care.
She bathed his wounds with healing plants
and cured the fruits of his mischance.
"What happened," she asked, "for God's sake?"
He told her, "When I had to take
315 a narrow passage full of danger,
my bones were broken by a stranger."
The servants in the house related
how they had caught and castigated
a student, whom their mistress punished.
320 "For sure, her honor's as untarnished
as noblewomen of the court!"
Never did a suspicious thought
cross his mind so long as he lived.
　　　That's how the good woman deceived
325 the husband who thought he could trick her.
He, in the end, brewed his own liquor!

𝟓𝟎. THE MILLER OF ARLEUX

by Enguerrant d'Oisy

He must refrain from speaking ill
whose job is telling stories; he'll
tell only those that are first-rate.
At this time I mean to relate
5 something that came to my attention.
Concealing it's not my intention.
　　　At Palluel, where the crossings are,
a miller lived, one Jackemar,
a jolly man and clever, too.
10 The mill he owned was in Arleux;

le blé moloit il & Mousés,
qui *desoz* lui estoit varlés.
.I. jour estoient au molin
en un demierkes au matin.

15 De maintes viles i ot gent
qui au molin *moloit* sovent;
il i ot molt blé & asnees.
Maroie, fille Gerart d'Estrees,
vint au molin a tout son blé;
20 le maunier en a apielé.
Ele l'apiele par son non:
« Hé! Jaques, fait el, de Sanson!
par cele foi ke me devés,
molés mon blé, si me hastés
25 que je m'en puisse repairier.
Atorner m'estuet a mangier
por mon pere, ki est a chans. »
Jakes li a dit maintenans:
« Ma douce amie, or vous seés
30 .I. petit, si vous reposés.
Il a molt blé chi devant nous
que doivent maure devent vous,
mais vous morrés qant jou porrai,
& si n'en soiés en esmai,
35 car se il puet & vespres vient,
je vous ostelerai molt bien
a ma maison a Paluiel.
Sachiés k'a ma feme en ert biel,
car jou dirai k'estes ma nieche. »
40   Mousés ot ja moulut grant pieche;
les gens furent ja ostelé
et a leur villes retorné.
Mousés voit bien & aperçoit
tout cho ke ses maistres pensoit.
45 Andoi orent une pensee
por decevoir Marien d'Estree:

there they milled wheat for flour, he and,
beneath him, Moses, his hired hand.
There at the mill there were one day—
a Wednesday morning, by the way—
15 people from many towns who came
there frequently to mill their grain;
donkeyloads full of wheat they'd brought there.
Maray, Gerard of Estrées' daughter,
came by with her wheat to be milled,
20 and hailed the miller, whom she called
by his full name, saying, "Hola
there, Samson's Jack! You, Jackemar!
By your good faith, which is my due,
grind up my wheat, and quickly, too,
25 because I've got to get home real
soon to prepare my father's meal,
who's working in the fields today."
Jackemar said without delay
and told her, "Sister, take a seat
30 for a short while and rest your feet.
We've lots to mill for people who
must have their turn ahead of you,
but when I can, I'll get to yours.
Don't fret about it, though, because
35 if by some chance before tonight
I don't, I'll put you up all right
at my house back in Palluel.
My wife will take it very well,
for I'll say you're my cousin's child."
40 Moses had milled for a long while
and all the people had gone home
back to the towns where they'd come from.
Moses could tell (he wasn't blind)
just what's on his employer's mind.
45 Both had the same idea: how they
would seduce Maray of Estrées

jesir cuident entre ses bras,
mais il n'en aront ja solas,
ains en sera Jakes decheus,
50 tristres, dolens, *corchiés* & mus.
Mousés a son maistre apielé:
« Sire, dist il, or entendés:
il a molt poi d'iaue el vivier.
Il vous covient euvre laissier;
55 nos molins ne puet morre tor.
  — Or n'i a il nul autre tor,
fait li mauniers. Clot le molin. »

Li solaus traioit a declin.
La damoisele ert plainne d'ire;
60 pleure des ieus, de cuer soupire:
« Lasse! fait ele, que ferai?
Or voi jou bien ke g'i morrai
se je m'en vois encui par nuit.
Jou isterai dou sens, je cuit! »
65 Mousés l'a prise a conforter:
« Biele, fait il, or m'entendés:
vous [en] irés avuec mon maistre.
Il vos en pora grans biens naistre.
  — Voire, fait Jakes entressait,
70 mais meuture n'avra ui mais
el ne ses peres ne sa gent. »
Par le main maintenant le prent:
« Levés sus, biele, s'en alons
a Paluiel en mes maisons.
75 La serés vous bien ostelee.
Vous mangerés a la vespree
pain & tarte, car & poisson,
& buverés vin affuison,
mais gardés ke sace ma feme
80 que soiés el ke ma parente,
car defors ma cambre girés,

and how they would lie in her arms.
But neither will enjoy her charms;
instead it's Jack who will be had,
50 rueful, irate, stymied, and sad.

Moses called to his master. "Sir,"
he told the miller, "listen here.
There's not much water in the brook.
You'll have to leave off work now. Look,
55 the mill wheel can't turn anymore."
"If that's so, there's nothing else for
us to do here," he answered, "so
shut down the mill."

The sun was low,
and the girl was very upset,
60 and heaved a sigh; her eyes grew wet.
"Woe!" she lamented. "What can I
do now? I'm sure that I shall die
if I have to walk home at night.
I think I'll lose my mind from fright!"
65 Moses spoke up to reassure
her: "Listen here, my lovely. You're
to go home tonight with my boss,
nor will you come out at a loss."
"Indeed no," added Jack, "God willing,
70 but today there'll be no more milling
for her, her father, or her folk."
He held her by the hand and spoke:
"Get up now, child. To Palluel
we're going now. That's where I dwell;
75 I'll put you up there. You'll be fine.
This very evening you will dine
on bread and tarts and meat and fish,
and you'll drink all the wine you wish.
Be careful my wife doesn't know
80 you're not related to me, though,
for right outside my room you'll lie,

douce amie, se vous volés,
& jou girai a ma moillier.
A Aleus m'estuet repairier
85 por mon molin batre & lever;
adont me vaurai retorner
& choucerai lé vous, amie. »
Cele s'estut molt esbahie,
qui dou maunier n'avoit talent;
90 ens en son cuer bon consel prent,
dist: « Se Dieus plaist, n'avenra mie! »
      Tout .iii. en vienent a la vile
de Paluiel chiés le maunier;
or sont venu au herbegier.
95 Li mauniers apiela sa fame,
se li dist: « Dame, que vous sanble?
Que mangerons nous au souper?
— Sire, chou dist la dame, assés.
Qui est ceste meschine ichi?
100 — Ma cousine est, sachiés de fi.
Faites li feste & grant honor.
— Volentiers, la dame respont.
Bien soiés vous venue, amie!
— Dame, fait el, Dius beneïe. »
105 De mangier n'estuet tenir plait
de chou ke promesse avoit fait:
pain & vin, car, tarte & poison
orent assés a grant fuisson.
Qant orent mangié & beü,
110 li lis fu fait dalés le fu
u la meschine dut couchier:
kieute mole, lincheus molt chier
& covertoir chaut & forré.
Li mauniers en a apielé
115 sa fame k'il ot espoussee:
« Dame, fait il, s'i vous agree,

dear girl, if you desire, and I
will sleep there with my wife until
I have to head out to the mill
85   at Arleux and adjust the stone.
Then I'll come back soon as I'm done
and get in bed with you, my sweet."
Her consternation is complete;
she's no desire for Jackemar,
90   and in her heart of hearts she swore
and said, "Please God, that will not be."
        So back they went to town, all three,
to Palluel, where the miller lives,
and came to where his dwelling is.
95   The miller called out to his wife,
"Say, lady, what do things look like?
What will we have to eat tonight?"
"Oh, we've more than enough, all right,"
the woman says, "but who is *she*?"
100 "My cousin, for a certainty.
Receive her like an honored guest."
"With pleasure, sir," his wife says next.
"Sweet child, you are most welcome here."
"God bless and keep you, lady dear."
105   About the meal what needs be said,
that he had promised she would get?
Of bread and wine, meat, pies, and fish
they had as much as they could wish,
and after they all drank and ate
110 a bed was made up by the grate,
where the girl was supposed to sleep:
a feather quilt, comfy and deep,
fine sheets, and a warm, fur-lined cover.
The miller, Jackemar, called over
115 to him the wife whom he had wed.
"Lady, if it's all right," he said,

volentiers iroie au molin;
il le m'estuet batre matin.
Il i a molt blé ens es sas. »

120   La dame dist: « Se Dieus me gart,
ichou est molt tres bon a faire. »
A tant li mauniers se repaire,
mais anchois ot dit a sa feme
qu'ele pense de sa parente.

125   « Alés a Diu, chou dist la dame.
Pis n'avra com[e] se fust m'ame. »
         A tant s'en va. Cele demeure;
del cuer souspire & des ieus pleure,
& dist la dame: « K'avés vous?

130   Dites le moi, tout par amors!
Nous avons or esté si aisse,
& or nous metés en malaisse—
qui vous a riens meffait ne dit?
       — Dame, fait el, se Dieus m'aït,

135   je me loc molt de vostre ostel,
mais mes cuers est molt destorbés,
se je l'osoie descovrir . . .
j'en sui forment en grant desir.
       — []Oïl, fait la dame erramment,

140   dites le moi hardiement.
Ja ne sera si grans anuis
ne vous en oste, se je puis. »
Dist la pucele: « Grant merchi,
jel vous dirai sans contredit.

145   Hui main vinc por maure a Aleus,
& vo barons si me dist leus
que ne porroie maure a pieche.
Iluec me detria grant pieche;
l'autre gent molut erramment;

150   le molin clot delivrement
car Mousés li ot ensaigniet

"I'd like to head off to the mill.
Tomorrow come early I will
have sacks and sacks of wheat for milling."
120 The woman answered, "Yes, God willing,
that's something that is well worth doing."
It's high time the miller got going,
but first he tells his wife that she's
to be attentive to his niece.
125 "Go with the Lord," his wife replies.
"I'll treat her like my own two eyes."
         The girl stays, and the miller leaves.
Her eyes weep and a sigh she heaves,
and the wife asks her, "What's amiss?
130 As you love me, do tell me this!
Why, just now we were all so merry,
and now you're making us all worried.
What could have someone done or said?"
"As I hope, lady, for God's aid,
135 there's nothing that I can complain
of here, but my heart's in great pain.
I don't know if I dare to tell it,
but I'm most anxious to reveal it."
"Do," said the wife unflinchingly;
140 "hold nothing back, confide in me.
However difficult your plight,
if I can, I will set things right."
"A thousand thanks," replied the girl,
"I'll tell you all there is to tell.
145 When I came at an early hour
to Arleux, where we grind our flour,
your husband told me, 'Not just yet,'
and for a long time made me wait.
The others soon all got to mill;
150 then suddenly he closed the mill
because Moses had said to him

qu'il ot molt poi d'iaue el vivier.
Tant *ilueques* seoir me fissent
que nuis me prist & viespres vi[n]rent.
155   Chi m'amena por herbegier
car vaura dalés moi chouchier
se Jhesus & vous ne m'aïe.
— Or vous taisié, ma douce amie,
fait la dame, ki fu senee.
160   Vous en serés bien destornee,
car vous girés ens en mon lit
en ma cambre, tout en serit,
& jou girai chi en cestui.
Se mes maris i vient encui,
165   qu'il veulle gesir aveuc vous,
trover me pora a estrous
& soufferai chou k'i vaura. »
La damoisele s'escria:
« Dame, fait ele, grant merchi!
170   Bien avés dit, se Dieus m'aït!
— Il ert merit, se Dius plait bien,
dist la dame, chou croi jou bien!
C'est bien & autre tout ensanble. »
A tant s'en entrent dans la cambre
175   u la pucele se coucha,
& la dame se retorna,
a l'uis s'en vint, si l'entrovri,
puis est venue droit au lit
qui fais estoit les le fouier
180   u la pucele dut chouchier.
Ele s'i chouce, plus n'arieste,
Saingna son cors, saigna sa tieste,
a Diu se rent & au saint Piere
qu'il lui doinst bone nuit entiere.
185   Si fara il, mien ensïent,
se l'aventure ne nous ment,

the water was low in the stream.
They had me sit there such a long
time, it came time for evensong.
155 He's offered hospitality
because he means to sleep with me
if you and Jesus will not help."
"Dear, gentle girl, do calm yourself,"
the wife said, who'd much common sense.
160 "You shall escape what he intends,
for you'll be lying in my bed
in my room, sheltered from his threat,
and here in this one I shall lie,
so if my husband should come by
165 intending to bed down with you,
he'll find me, as he's bound to do,
and I'll take what he has to give."
The girl exclaimed, "Why, as I live,
thank you! That is well spoken, lady.
170 I'm in your debt, so may God aid me."
"Please God, what he deserves, he'll get,"
the woman says. "That's a safe bet.
It's good and, at the same time, not."
      Then to her room, where the girl got
175 into her bed, they went, and then
the woman came back out again,
went to the door, left it ajar,
then turned and went to the place where
the bed was made up by the fire,
180 where the young girl was to retire.
Without delay she gets in bed,
signs the cross on body and head,
and prays that God and that Saint Pet-
er give her a good night of it.
185 And so they shall, or so think I,
if our adventure doesn't lie,

car ses maris mauniers qui[v]ert,
il & Mousés sont repairiet;
par mi la rue vont tout droit,
190   del molin viennent ambedoit

Por jesir avuec la meschine
revint Jakes, ki le desire.
Mousés l'en a mis a raison:
« Sire, dist il, por saint Simon,
195   car faites .i. markiet a mi.
Certes, j'ai un porchiel nouri
il a passé .v. mois entiers.
Celui avrés molt volentiers,
foi ke doi Diu, sainte Marie,
200   se jesir puis o le meschine.
— Oïl, fait Jakes entresait,
se guerpir volés sans nul plait
le porcelet ke nouri as,
gesir te ferai en[] ses bras.
205   — Oïl, fait il, par tel marchiés
le vous guerpisse volentiers.
— Or m'atent dont a cest perron.
Je m'en irai a no maison,
se choucerai o la pucele
210   qui tant [par] est gentieus & biele. »
Chou dist Mousés: « A Diu alés.
Qant vous poés, si revenés. »
& Jakes li mauniers s'en torne,
dusc'a la maison ne destorne.
215   Il a trové l'uis entrovert;
tout souëf l'a ariere ouvert,
ens est entrés, puis le referme,
mais molt se doute de sa feme,
qu'il cuide k'en sa cambre gisse
220   (mais je cuic la mescine i gisse).
Au lit en vint les le fouier

for here come Moses and the miller,
her husband, the false double-dealer,
returning from the mill.

                  They both
190   come down the road, hired hand and boss.
To lie with the girl whom he's yearning
to possess, Jackemar's returning.
Moses addressed him in this way
and said, "Sir, by Saint Simon, say
195   if you will make a deal with me.
I've been raising this piglet, see,
going on almost half a year.
By God and Saint Marie, I swear
you can have my pig in return
200   if with the girl I get a turn."
On the spot Jackemar says, "Aye,
in her embrace I'll let you lie
in payment for surrendering
that piglet you've been fattening."
205   "Yes," he says, "you can have my hog on
condition that you keep your bargain."
"Wait for me by this marker stone.
First of all I will go back home
and get in bed beside Maray,
210   who's lovelier than I can say."
"Go with God," answered Moses, "then
come back and get me when you can."

      Then Jackemar the miller goes
in a straight line up to the house.
215   He found the door open a crack,
and cautiously he pulled it back
and stepped inside, then shut the door,
because of his wife none too sure.
(He thinks she's sleeping in their room,
220   but *I* think the girl's in their room.)
He went up to the bed beside

dalés sa feme tost choucier.
Il cuide qu'e[l] soit la meschine,
si l'a acolee & baisie,
225   .v. fois li fist le giu d'amors,
ains ne se mut nient plus c'uns hors.
            Il iert ja priés de mienuit.
Li mauniers crient *Mousés* n'anuit,
qui l'atent seant a la piere;
230   ses demoures forment li grieve.
A la dame a dit: « Je m'en vois,
mais ke [vous] n'en aiés irois,
car il est plus de mienuit.
Je revenrai encore anuit.
235   — Qant vous poés, si revenés,
chou dist la dame. A Diu alés. »
Jakes en est dou lit partis,
si s'est rechauciés & viestis
(gieut cuide avoir o la pucele—
240   on li a cangiet le merielle!),
a Mouset en est retornés,
qui dehors l'uis est akeutés.
« Vien cha, amis, errant jesir!
Je wel le porcel deservir.
245   .v. fois [li] a[i] fait bien hastés,
or il para quel le ferés. »
Che dist Mousés: « Que dirai jou
qant *jou venrai* en la maison? »
& cil a dit: « Au lit alés,
250   se vous chouciés dalé son les.
Ne dites mot, mais taisiés vous;
ja nel sara par nul de nous.
Faites de li vos volentés. »
A tant en est Mousés tornés
255   & vint au lit, si se despoulle,
maintenant o la dame chouce;
.v. fois li fist en molt poi d'eure.

the hearth and lay by his wife's side.
Thinking mistakenly that this is
the girl, he gives her hugs and kisses,
225 and five times he made love to her,
hanging around her like a bear.

       By now, as the midnight hour closes
in, the miller's afraid that Moses
is losing patience out there sitting
230 on that stone, that the delay's eating
at him. He tells her, "I must go.
Do not let it upset you, though.
Since it's the middle of the night,
I'll come to you again tonight."
235 "Go with God," said the woman, "then
come back here to me when you can."
Jack gets up out of bed and goes
and puts his shoes on and his clothes
(he thinks it was the girl he lay with—
240 the chips were switched he had to play with!)
and goes where Moses, left to wait,
had come to lean outside the gate.
"Come on now, pal. I want to earn
that piglet, so go take your turn.
245 I did it five times in a row.
Let's see how well you can do now."
"What shall I say when I get in
the house?" asked Moses. He told him,
"Go straightaway to the bedside
250 and lie down in it by her side.
Don't say a word, but just be quiet—
she'll never know the difference by it—
and have it your way with the lassie."
Thereupon Moses goes in as he
255 said, comes to the bed, gets undressed,
quickly climbs in and lies down next
to the wife and does her five times

A tant Moussés plus n'i demoure;
congiet a pris, si se viesti.

260 La dame croit, saciés de fi,
que ce ne soit fors ses barons,
& cil revint a Jakemon,
se li a dit: « J'ai fait .v. fois.
— Dont [en] a ele eü despois?

265 chou a dit Jakes li wihos.
Li porchiaus esciet en mon los.
— Voire, fait Mousés, en non Dé.
Or venés, prenc qant vous volés
li porcelet ki estoit mien.

270 Vous l'en menrés par le loien. »
A tant s'en sont d'iluec parti.

    Qant li jours fu bien eslarchi,
la damoisele s'est levee,
si s'est viestue & atornee,

275 [ ] la dame *a congiet* demandet
& [ ] merchie de son hostel.
Ele li dist: « Ma douce amie
perdue avés bone nuitie,
car mes maris .x. fois ennuit

280 m'en a doné par grant deduit.
Pour vous l'a fait, ne l'en sai gré—
ou lit vous *cuide* avoir trové.
— Gret m'en sachiés », fait la mescine.
A tant plus n'arieste ne fine,

285 a Hestrees tout droit s'en va,
& li mauniers tost repaira,
si amainne le porchelet.
Par dalés lui s'en vint Mousés,
qui le porciel li ot vendu;

290 bien le cuidoit avoir perdu.
Qant la dame perçut les a,
sachiés ke pas nes bienvina;
le sien marit trestout avant

in quick succession; then he climbs
out right away, gets dressed, and leaves.
260   The woman for a fact believes
that this man was her husband, Jack,
to whom, meanwhile, Moses went back
and told him, "I did it five times."
"Well, then, and did she seem to mind?"
265 so Jackemar, the cuckold, asked.
"The piglet falls to me at last."
Says Moses, "In God's name, that's true.
Now come along. Whenever you
want to take my pig, you can lead
270 it back home with you by the lead."
The two of them then went away.
        As soon as it was fully day,
the girl in the bedroom arose,
got ready and put on her clothes,
275 and, taking leave of the wife, she
thanked her for hospitality.
She answered her, "My pretty child,
I'd say you missed out on a wild
night of it, for ten times last night
280 my husband took me with delight.
To him I'm not the least indebted,
since it was you he thought he bedded."
"Thank *me* for it, then," says Maray.
Not one more minute does she stay;
285 straight back home to Estrées she goes.
        Soon after comes the miller, who's
bringing the piglet he's acquired.
Moses is walking by his side,
who sold it to him and now is
290 convinced that it's no longer his.
The miller's wife, seeing them come,
in no way bid them welcome home,
but rushed to her husband, the miller,

tost li a dit: « Ribaut puant!
.xiiii. ans ai o vous estet.
Ains ne vous poc mais tel mener
ne tant acoler ne basier,
servir a gré ne solacier
que ja i ffussë envaïe
.ii. fois en une nuit entiere.
Por la mescine euc voir ennuit
.x. fois u plus par grant deduit!
Cele m'a fait ceste bontet
cui vous cuidastes recovrer.
En mon lit [ ] *cocha*. En non Dé,
or avés vous cangié le dé! »
Qant Jakemars l'ot & entent
qu'il est wihos certainnement,
saciés que point ne l'abielist,
& Mousés tout errant li dist:
« Sire, mon porciel me rendés,
c'a tort & a pechiet l'avés!
— Qu'esse, diable? dist Jakemars.
Tu as ennuit entre les bras
[ ] ma feme jut & fait ton biel,
& tu vieus ravoir ton porchiel?
Saciés que tu n'en ravras mie!
— Si arai, fait Mousés, biaus sire,
car je duc gire o la pucele,
qui estoit grasse, tenre & biele,
ke mieus vauroit ele sentir
que de vo feme nul delit.
Saciés je m'en irai clamer;
tost a Oisi vaurai aler. »
        Mousés en va droit a Oisi,
si en est clamé au bailli,
& li baillius les ajorna;
a tant Mousés s'en retorna.

and cried, "You stinking lady-killer,
295 for fourteen years I've been with you!
No matter what I tried to do,
for all my hugs and all my kisses
and playing along with your wishes,
not any night could I entice
300 you to possess me even twice.
For that girl's sake I was possessed
ten times last night—and with what zest!
I owe this bounty to the maid,
the one whom you assume you laid.
305 She slept in my bed. In God's name,
I turned the tables on your game!"
        When Jackemar hears and finds out
he's cuckolded beyond all doubt,
it isn't something that amuses
310 him in the least, and quickly Moses
said, "Give my piglet back to me,
for you got it dishonestly!"
"What the devil?" Jackemar said.
"You spent the night in my wife's bed
315 and lay with her and had your will
and want to keep your piglet still?
No way on earth will it be yours!"
"I'll have it," Moses says, "because
it was agreed I could make love
320 with the girl, lovely, plump, and suave.
Who sleeps with her would know what bliss is
more than one who's slept with your missus.
I'll sue you! I'll go right away
to court at Oisy-le-Verger."
325   Off to Oisy Moses goes straight
and files suit with the magistrate,
who fixes a date for their trial;
then Moses goes back home awhile.

Qant li termes & li jors vint
330 que li baillius les siens plais tint,
li mauniers i vint & Mousés
por conquerre le porchelet.
Mousés a sa raison contee;
li eskievim l'ont escoutee.
335 Que vous feroie jou lonc conte?—
toute leur raison [leur] raconte,
ensi con Jakemés li cous
li ot falit de tout en tout . . .
« car o la pucele deuc *gire*
340 & o sa feme m'a fait *gire* »,
qu'il ne prent mie en paiement;
ains veut que Jakes li ament,
car deut jesir o la pucele
qui tant est avenans & biele.
345 Se li esquievin li otrïent,
communaument ensanble dïent
que il li tiegne ses markiés.
Li mauniers est levés en piés:
« Signor, fait [il], entendés nous!
350 Je sui wihos & si sui cous.
Je doi bien cuite aler par tant,
car sachiés il m'anui*t* forment
chou que il avint a ma feme.
Car ses porchiaus ne m'atalente! »
355 Li baillius a grant ris eüt,
puis si lor a ramenteüt:
« Volés de chou oïr le droit?
— Oïl, dist Mousés, par ma foit.
— & vous, mauniers? fait li baliu.
360 — Voire bien, de par Dame Diu,
que il me doinst cuites aler. »
Li baillius prist a conjurer
les eskievins pour *dire voir*;
« Si ferons nous a no pooir,

When the time and the day in question
330 came 'round for court to be in session,
Moses and Jackemar came to 't
to win the piglet in dispute.
First Moses states his case and presses
it in court before the assessors.
335 What more is there to tell about?
He lays all of the details out
of how the cuckold Jackemar
reneged on him, "for though we were
agreed that I'd lie with the maid,
340 he put me with his wife instead,
whom I'll not accept as my fee.
He'll have to make it good to me,
for on the girl we had agreed,
who is so lovely and so sweet.
345 If the assessors find this binding,
then let them all agree in finding
he keep his deal as stipulated."
The miller then stood up and stated,
"Gentlemen, hear us two both out.
350 I'm cuckolded beyond all doubt,
which really ought to be enough.
You can be sure I take it rough
that this should happen to my wife.
His piglet wasn't worth the price!"
355   The magistrate addressed them after
he'd given vent to hearty laughter.
"Would you hear how we judge this case?"
"Yes," Moses answered him, "in faith."
"Miller, you want to hear it, too?"
360 "By the Lord God, I truly do;
may He have you find in my favor."
The assessors he bade endeavor
to find what was most just and fair.
"We'll gladly do the best that we're

365 sire, font il, molt volentiers. »
A tant [ ] prende[n]t a consillier;

a ce consel en sont alé,
plus tost k'il peurent sont []torné.
« Sire, font il, entendé[s] nous.
370 Par jugement nous vous disons
ke vous Mouset *faites* ravoir
son porchelet, car chou est drois,
& commandés a Jakemon
qu'il li renge tout sans renchon
375 u la meschine li ramaint
por faire son bon & son plain. »
Li baillius li a commandé,
& Jakes li a delivré
le porchelet tout errammant,
380 & li baillius maintenant prent
par le loien le porchelet
& puis si a dit a Mouset:
« Amis, or ne vous en *courchiés*,
je vous renderai en deniers
385 .xxx. sous por le porchelet.
Mangiés sera a grant reviel
des bons conpaingnons del païs. »
          Jakes s'en part tous esbahis,
qui demeure chous & wihos.
390 Cho fu droit que le honte en ot,
car raisons ensaigne & droiture
que nus ne puet metre sa cure
en mal faire ni en [mal] dire
tous jors ne l'en soit siens li pire,
395 & ausi fist il le maunier,
qui en demoura cunquïet,
mais ne me chaut—chou fu raisons;
& li baillius a tout semons
les escuiers & les puceles,

365 capable of, my lord," they said,
     and off they went to put their heads
     together on it.
                    Now they've gone,
     and back they come soon as they're done.
     "Good sir," they tell him, "pay us heed;
370 we'll let you know what we've decreed.
     Let the pig be returned to Moses,
     whose, we've determined, the just cause is,
     and Jackemar, we've stipulated,
     must give it back uncompensated
375 or else provide the maiden, who
     must do all that he wants her to."
     That's what the magistrate commanded,
     and Jackemar with due speed handed
     the piglet to the magistrate,
380 who took the pig. He didn't wait;
     holding it tightly by the leash,
     he turned to Moses with this speech:
     "Don't take this ill, friend. If you're willing,
     I'm offering you thirty shillings
385 to buy your piglet, in hard cash.
     I'll roast it and I'll host a bash,
     and all high-livers are invited."
     Jackemar left, distraught and blighted,
     for, come what may, he'll stay a cuckold.
390 It's justice he was shamed and knuckled
     under, for right and fairness teach us
     that none should seek his fellow creatures'
     harm in the things he does or says;
     he'll get the worst of it always,
395 as did the miller of Arleux,
     who was humiliated through
     this fault. So what? It served him right.
             The judge proceeded to invite
     the squires, the knights, the damsels, and

400   les chevaliers, les dames bieles,
si a fait mangier le porciel
a grant joie & a reviel.
       Engerrans li clers, ki d'Oisi
a esté & nes & nori,
405   ne vaut ke tele aventure
fust ne perie ne perdue,
si le nous a mis en escrit
& vous anonce bien & dist
c'onques ne vous prenge talens
410   de faire honte a bone gens.
Qui s'en garde, il fait ke sages,
& Dius le nous meche en corage
a faire bien, le mal laissier.
Chi faut li ronmans del maunier.

51. JOUGLET

Jadis en coste Monferrant
out une viellete manant
en une vilete champestre.
Un fiz avoit, qui menoit pestre
5   toz les jors en champ ses brebis,
molt estoit fol e estordiz,
de fol sens e de fole chiere;
sa mere n'avoit rien tant chiere,
quer ele n'avoit plus d'esfanz.
10   Li enfez crut e devint granz;
s'il fust sagez, molt par fust genz,
mes il croissoit devant son sens,
com font oncore tez i a.
La vielle sa mere espia
15   .i. vavasor molt endeté;

400 the lovely ladies in the land,
     and saw to it the pig was eaten
     amid much revelry and feasting.
          Enguerrant, the good cleric, who
     was born in Oisy and who grew
405 up there, lest a tale like this one
     should pass into oblivion
     and so be lost, for us has written
     it down, for by it you're all bidden
     never to let it cross your mind
410 to do folks harm of any kind;
     who keeps from doing so is smart.
     So may God move every man's heart
     to do good and quit evil, too.
     So ends "The Miller of Arleux."

51. JOUGLET
by Colin Malet

     A rich old woman once resided
     in a small country town (beside it
     lay Montferrand) in bygone days.
     She had a son, who led to graze
5   her sheep flock each day in the lea.
     A simple, foolish lad was he,
     ingenuous and not too smart;
     love for him filled his mother's heart.
     (He was the only child she had.)
10   When he grew up, a finer lad,
     had he been bright, were hard to find;
     his body grew, but not his mind.
     (There're quite a few like him around.)
          The old woman, his mother, found
15   a most debt-ridden vavasor

une file out de grant biauté
qui bien e mal assez savoit,
e por ce que celui avoit
biau porpris e bel eritage,
20   espia biau le mariage
dou vaslet e de la meschine.
Un jor por voier le covigne
a pris la vielle son mantel,
de .ii. qu'ele en out le plus bel,
25   de moutons locuz & de chaz,
a l'ostel vint isnel le pas
la ou le vavasor manoit:
« Or sui venue. — Dieus i soit!
Bien viengiés vous, dame Ermenjart!
30   — Que fetes vos, sire Girart?
Coment vos barentez vos ore?
— Par foi, je doi assez oncore,
mien escïent .xl. livres.
— En vouleis vos estre delivres?
35   — Oïl, se savoie comment.
— Je vos diroi confaitement
n'en devreis vallant une bille:
que me doinsiez Mahaut vos fille
a femme mon fiz Robinet.
40   Trop bele branche de vaslet
a en lui e trop bien seant,
e si ne seit ne tant ne quant
ne de tavernes ne de jus. »
Tant parlerent e sus e jus
45   *qu'il* en ont fet le mariage;
si les doit tenir de mesnage
le vavasor .i. an entier.
       Le voir vos diroi sanz noisier,
tout apertement, sanz gloser.
50   Quant vint le jor de l'espouser,
la vielle charja Robinet

with a fair daughter, and, what's more,
she'd wit and shrewdness to her merit,
and since her son stood to inherit
a tidy sum and property,
20   the woman thought it likely he
would make a fine match for the lady.
One day when she felt good and ready
to strike a deal, she took her cape
(she'd two, but one's in better shape,
25   made of cat's fur and curly wool)
and hurried off to pay a call
on the poor vavasor, her neighbor.
"Well, here I am." "By God our Savior,
I bid you welcome, Ermengard."
30   "What are you up to, Sir Girard?
I wonder, how does business go?"
"It seems to me that I still owe
some forty pounds, sad to relate."
"Wouldn't you like to clear the slate?"
35   "Yes, but I don't know how I can."
"Listen to me. I have a plan
to pay back every cent that's owed:
that you give your daughter Mahaud
in marriage to Robin, my child.
40   The boy is well behaved and mild
mannered, nor does he even think
of partying, gambling, or drink.
I'm sure you'll never find his better."
They spoke at length about the matter
45   and closed the match right then and there.
The vavasor would house the pair
with him for their first year together.
That said, I will dispense with blather
and exegesis, and speak plain.
50   When the day of the wedding came,
Robin was placed under the wing

a un menest[e]reil, Juglet,
que il au mostier le menast
e apreïst e ensegnast.
55 Juglet molt volentiers le prist,
mes onques bien ne li aprist
ne rien qui li eüst mestier,
quer einz que fussent au mostier
le mena par .i. plesseïz
60 a .i. perier d'estrangleïz,
puis le fet haut tout sus monter,
e Robin se prist a user
de ces poires a grant esploit,
mes cil Juglet, qui le dechoit,
65 metoit les coues en .i. gant
e li proia qu'il menjast tant
de ces poires a tout le meins
que son gant fust de cöes pleinz,
e Robin dist qu'il ne porroit
70 quer ja est son ventre si roit
e si enflé e si bargié
que por tout l'avoir de Blangié
ne feroit il ce qu'il li roeve,
mes Juglet, qui la borde troeve,
75 dit que fere li covenoit
quer puis qu'ome a femme venoit
c'estoit le droit e la costume.
Robin en fait molt laide frume,
mes il ne l'ose corocier.
80 Tant l'a fet Juglet esforcier
que par .i. poi que il ne crieve,
mes oncors plus assez le grieve
ce que il nou lesse chïer;
s'il peüst son ventre vïer,
85 il ne l'eüst pas tant maumis.
« Par foi, fait Juglet, biaus amis,
sachiez que l'en ne chie mie

of a *jongleur*, Jouglet, who'd bring
him to the church, and also who
was to instruct him what to do.
55   Jouglet accepted the assignment
but didn't teach the lad refinement
or help him out in any way;
instead, while they were on their way
to church, the minstrel led him through
60   a grove where a choke pear tree grew,
in which he makes him take a seat
and tells him he should pick and eat
the choke pears quickly as he can,
while he, Jouglet, that wily man,
65   collects the stem ends in his glove,
and he should eat as many of
the pears as needed for Jouglet
to fill the glove up in this way.
Robin said that he can't, by gum,
70   his stomach's tighter than a drum
and he's so bloated and so stuffed,
all Blangy's wealth is not enough
to make him do as he has said.
Jouglet, who thought up this charade,
75   explains that he's obliged to do
as every other bridegroom who
first takes a wife; such is the custom.
Though Robin made a face and cussed him,
he didn't dare to contradict him.
80   Jouglet insists so, that his victim
eats until he's about to burst,
but in all this the very worst
is that he's not allowed to shit.
His belly, could he empty it,
85   would not torment him in this way.
"Honestly, good friend," says Jouglet,
"know that a man who moves his bowels

le jor qu'en espouse s'amie,
quer ce seroit trop grant ledure! »
90 Robin au mieus qu'il poet endure,
quer son ventre li douloit molt.
Ja estoient au mostier tout
li parent a la damoisele.
Juglet a prise sa vïele,
95 si les en meine vïelant . . .
Que vos iroie je contant?
Au mostier vindrent sanz atendre,
Robin fist on sa fame prendre,
espousa la, espousé fu,
100 a l'ostel s'en sunt revenu.
Cel jor furent bien atorné,
quer il orent a grant plenté
boens flaons e boens mortereus,
qui qu'en eüst ire ne deus,
105 en boen lait bien bolli e cuit.
Robin en menjast bien, ce cuit,
s'il n'eüst si mal en son ventre—
toz jors aloit Juglet söentre,
ou Robin tant ne sout proier
110 Juget ne tant bel esforcier
qu'il le lesast chïer .i. pou,
s'a il plus angoissous d'un clou
li ventre, si grant comme il est!
        Au vespre furent li lit prest;
115 la bru si se couche premiers.
Robin n'iert mie costumiers
de couchier au vespre si fars.
« Biau fiz doz, dist dame Ermengars,
comme or feites hui mate chiere!
120 — Par foi, fet Juglet le lechierre,
vostre fiz est .i. poi plus pris
por ce qu'il n'avoit mie apris
de fame aissi fete evre. »

when it's his wedding day befouls
the dignity of the occasion."
90 Robin, although his gut is raging,
does all he can to hold it in.
      Already all the lady's kin
were gathered for the sacrament,
and Jouglet took his instrument
95 and played a tune to lead the way.
Why prolong what I have to say?
They went to church and never tarried
till Robin and the girl were married
and he became her lawful spouse,
100 and then they went back to the house.
That day they feasted handsomely
and were served a great quantity
of fragrant flans and hearty stews
simmered in milk and fine ragouts,
105 so no one had cause to complain,
nor would have Robin, I maintain,
but for the colic that's inside him.
Throughout, Jouglet stays close beside him,
while Robin tries to beg and pray
110 and wheedle to convince Jouglet
to let him crap, to no avail.
It hurts more than an iron nail
lodged in his gut, he's so distended.
      The beds were made when the day ended,
115 the bride retired to their chamber,
and Robin? . . . He could not remember
going to bed when he's so full.
"My son," said Ermengard, "why pull
such a long face? You seem so dour!"
120 "I think," said Jouglet the *jongleur*,
"that your son feels a wee bit tense
because he lacks experience
with women. This is his first time."

Robin se couche e l'en le cuevre,
125 puis fist on la cambre voidier,
mes cele ne seit que cuidier
de ce que Robin ne l'adoise.
« Lasse! fet ele, tant me poise
de cest chetif las asoté
130 qui a femme de tel beauté
com je sui e de tel afeire,
[mes] il ne seit que l'en doit fere!
Il ne [me] traite ne manie.
Par la char Dieu, bien sui honie
135 quant cest vilain gist delez mi!
Se fusse or ovec mon ami,
il me besast e acolast
entre ses braz, & m'aaisast
e m'estreinsist molt durement.
140 Maudit soient tuit mi parent
qui m'ont donee a ceste beste! »
Mes Robin n'out cure de feste;
par le lit se vet detornant,
les linceus d'angoise mordant
145 e disant: « Las! que porrey fere? »
Celle escouta tout son afere,
qui n'out cure de somellier,
forment se prent a merveillier
quel chose Robin puet avoir,
150 mes ele le voudra savoir
par bel parler ou par bel feindre.
De poor se commence a pleindre
e dist: « Mon segnor, qu'avez vos?
N'esmes nous tout un entre nous?
155 A moi deüssiez bien parler,
ne me deüssiez pas celer
vostre afere ne vos querele.
— Par foi, fet Robin, damoisele,
je ne vos oseroie dire.

The company watch Robin climb
125　in bed, and then they leave the couple.
When Robin makes no move to couple,
the lady can't imagine why
and thinks, What a disaster I
am stuck with this poor, worthless booby
130　who marries such a peerless beauty
as I am, and has not a clue
just what a wife and husband do!
He doesn't touch me or caress me.
God's blood, how much it does distress me
135　to have this peasant alongside me!
Now if my lover lay beside me,
he'd kiss and hold me in his arms
so tight! How I'd enjoy his charms
and all the pleasure that he gives!
140　God's curse on all my relatives
for giving me to such a one!
But Robin's in no mood for fun.
Tossing in bed contortedly,
he bites the sheets in agony
145　and says, "Oh God, how can I bear it?"
The lady is surprised to hear it,
and, since she's not in the least tired,
she thinks it's time that she inquired
just what Robin's problem may be.
150　Through pretense and cajolery
she'll learn what makes him twist and turn,
and with a great show of concern
she said, "Husband, what's ailing you?
Are we not of one flesh, we two?
155　You ought to open up to me
and not keep back in secrecy
the burden that perturbs you so."
"Lady, in truth, I do not know
if I dare tell you," Robin said.

160 — Comment donc? n'estes vos mi sire?
Si ne devez estre hontous.
Vos me semblez molt angoissous;
qu'avez vos, ne quel mal vos tient?
— Rien, damoisele, je n'ai nient.
165 — Comment? Si n'en saroi le voir?
Moi le direz! — Nou feroi, voir,
por tout l'avoir de ceste vile! »
e cele qui molt sout de guile
li dist ausi comme en plorant:
170 « Biau doz freire, por seint Amant
e por Dieu e por Seint Espir,
ne vos lessiez mie morir!
S'os morez e je soie vive,
que devendra ceste chaitive
175 qui tant vos aime lëaument,
se vos morez si faitement? »
Tant le commencha a proier
qu'il li dist: « Je muir de chïer! »
e qu'eissi l'a Juglet servi.
180 « Qu'est? Por Ceste ne por Celui,
se vos a eissi atorné,
or tost, n'i ait plus demoré:
il gist coste cele paroit;
chïez a son chevez tout droit,
185 tout droit encoste cel espuer!
— Or dites vos bien, bele suer,
fait Robin, par seint Nicholay! »
Dou lit se lieve sanz delay,
au lit s'en va ou Juglet gist,
190 a son chevez tout droit s'asist,
puis a desempli sa ventree.
(*Jouglés ot beü* la vespree,
por ce ne s'esvella cil mie.)
Robin s'en revient lez s'amie,
195 si se couche entre .ii. linceus,

160   "How now? And aren't we two now wed?
      You have no cause to be defensive.
      Your anguish makes me apprehensive.
      What's wrong? What is causing your suff'ring?"
      "It's nothing, lady, really. Nothing."
165   "What? Why won't you confide in me?
      Tell me the truth!" "I'll not agree
      to tell for all the wealth in town!"
      She knew just how to get around
      a man and started to complain,
170   tears in her eyes, "Husband, explain,
      for God's sake and the Holy Ghost!
      If you should die, I would be lost!
      Alas, if you should lose your life
      and I, your loving, loyal wife,
175   were left behind to pine and grieve!
      If you should die, how could I live?"
          She begged him so, at last he said,
      "If I can't take a shit, I'm dead,"
      and told her all that Jouglet did.
180   "Is that the long and short of it?
      By God, since he played you that trick,
      don't put it off! Go to it quick:
      He's sleeping just beyond that wall.
      Rush to his bedside, shit it all
185   out on the headboard of his bed."
      "That's good advice, wife," Robin said,
      "yes, by Saint Nick!" Quick as a shot
      he went directly off to squat
      on the bed Jouglet lay at rest in
190   and emptied out his large intestine.
      (Because that evening at the party
      he had been drinking deep and hearty,
      what he did didn't wake Jouglet.)
      Robin went back to bed and lay
195   between the sheets beside the lady,

mes lors fu il plus angoisseus
que il n'avoit esté d'assez.
« Robin, estes vos respassez,
fet dame Mahaut, e gariz?
200   — Nai, dame, ains sui plus marriz
e plus corocié que devant.
          — Poi avez fet; alés avant,
fait cele, biaus amis Robert!
Poi goste d'autrui qui ne pert:
205   alez chïer joste s'esponde.
          — Avoi, dame, Deus me confonde
se bien ne voil c'on le deçoive!
Qui merde brace, merde boive,
quer ce est bien reson e droiz. »
210   E Robin, qui molt fu des[t]roiz,
tantost de son lit se leva,
au lit Juglet tantost s'en va,
si pres de l'esponde chia
qu'andeus les linceus conchia;
215   e sachiez bien qu'il ne fu pas
tout autretant, sanz mot de gaz,
comme d'aler jusqu'a l'uis hors
que son ventre le reprist lors,
quer les poires li avaloient,
220   qui de son ventre iessir voloient.
Issi soufreit *male esquitele!*
« Robin, fet dame Mahaut, quele[ ]?
Cel ventre vos deut il or mes?
          — Oïl, dame, plus que j[a]més!
225   Je n'oi imés si mal comme ore.
          — Il vos convient chïer oncore,
fait ele; n'i a autre tor.
Alez a son lit tout entor!
Alez a l'esponde de la! »
230   Robin maintenant se leva,
au lit s'en va tout a droiture.

but the pains had returned already
and worse than they had been before.
"Robin," said Mahaud, "I hope you're
now feeling well and whole again?"
200   "No, lady, I'm in greater pain
than earlier, and more distressed."
"Robin, go back and do your best,"
she says. "If one can't even see
what's given, little joy has he.
205   You must do more. Shit on the frame."
"Yes, lady, I'd deserve God's blame
not to pay back his trick, I think!
It's only right that one should drink
shit, when it's shit that one has brewed."
210   So Robin, whose insides were skewed,
got out of bed and made his way
back to the bed where Jouglet lay,
and took a shit so very near,
the sheets were covered with the smear.
215   And be assured that he had not
made it to the door from that spot—
I kid you not!—before he felt
more gurgling sounds below the belt,
because the pears he had ingested
220   were passing through him half digested.
Lord, what a case of diarrhea!
Mahaud said, "What now, Robin dear?
Say, does your tummy hurt you still?"
"Lady, I've never been this ill!
225   Till now I've never known such pain!"
"Then you'll just have to shit again,"
she says, "there's no way to avoid it.
Go back and crap until you're voided!
Surround his bed with excrement!"
230   Robin got up and quickly went
straight to the bed, where, by some chance,

Juglet par sa mesaventure
avoit la ses braies jetees,
tout coi les i out oblïees
235   a l'esponde devers le fu,
e Robin, qui angoisiez fu,
n'i atendi ne meins ne plus,
ainz a chïé ausi droit sus
comme se il s'en fust gagié.
240   Un poi a son ventre alegié,
puis se recoucha a itant,
mes or li va reborbetant
le ventre quant il fu couchié—
molt s'en estoit esmervellié
245   quant il se sent si borbellier
c'on l'oïst bien desverdellier
d'une hüee de corsin.
« Or estes vos gariz a fin,
Robin, fet ele, biau doz freire?
250   — Nenil, par l'arme de mon pere,
fait il, a prisme me muir jen!
— Faites? A mal eür soit cen!
Maudit soit hui le cors Juglet!
Tant vos avez mal gibelet
255   a afaitier ceste avespree!
Honie soit ceste ventree
que il covient esvuier tant! »
        Que vos iroie je *contant*?
Ele li fist le feu covrir,
260   chïer enz e puis recovrir
c'on n'i peüst merde cuidier,
puis li fist le seel voidier,
l'evë espandre e chïer enz,
mes oncore fu ce neenz
265   a ce que ele li fist fere,
quer la vïele li fist trere
qui iert pendue a .i. postel,

he came upon the pair of pants
Jouglet had taken off and tossed
and left to lie, much to his cost,
235   beside the bed, close by the grate.
Not one moment did Robin wait
(his gut was ready to explode),
but went again and dumped his load
as though it were a solemn duty.
240   He lay down. Having passed more fruit, he
felt a bit better, though not lots,
because his guts cramped up in knots
no sooner was he back in bed.
He thought he'd go out of his head
245   to feel his stomach churn and rumble
so loudly you'd liken its wamble
to how a horse whinnies and snorts.
"Robin, are you still out of sorts,
my friend," she asked, "or are you whole?"
250   "No way, upon my father's soul,"
he says, "I doubt that I'll pull through."
"How can that be? What devil's stew
simmers tonight inside of him?
I curse Jouglet in life and limb!
255   I curse that stomachload of shit
so full no one can empty it
and wish its contents all to hell!"
Why prolong what I have to tell?
She made him cover up the fire,
260   douse it with shit and hide the mire
beneath the ash so none would know,
and then she made her husband go
empty the water pail and shit
inside, but that's not all of it.
265   She made him take the minstrel's fiddle
from its case, which hung in the middle
of the room on a post, and crap

puis le fist chïer ou forrel
e remetre enz e refremer.
270 « Dame, par le cors seint Omer,
fet Robin, or sui je gariz
dou mal dont estoie marriz.
— Robin, fet ele, ce voil jen. »
Il l'acole. « Boi! mes qu'est cen,
275 fait ele, que vos voulez faire?
— Par ma foi, je ne soi que fere,
fet Robin, qui molt fu bisnars,
mes ma mere, dame Hermengars,
me dist que eissi vos feïsse
280 anciés qu'a feme vos preïsse,
quant je vinc de vos fiancier,
mes je ne sai ou commencier
se vos ne m'aprenez a fere. »
Cele s'en rist, ne se pout tere
285 qui li donast .xl. livres:
« Robin, fet ele, estes vos ivres?
e ne savez vos des piecha
qu'en requiert sa fame de cha
par devers l'orelle senestre?
290 — Par foi, fet il, ce puet bien estre. »
Lor afere a moi plus ne monte;
d'eus ne voil alognier le conte,
moi ne chaut comme il lor en prengne:
se il n'en seit eil, si aprengne,
295 e s'il n'en fait, s'en ait soufrete!
    A l'endemain, quant le jor jete
sa lumiere par tout li mont,
dame Maheut se lieve amont,
si s'est assise sus son lit,
300 l'us de la cambre evre .i. petit;
come cele qui molt sout d'abet:
« Ha, fet ele, Juglet! Juglet!
Comë estez ore endormi?

inside, then put it back and clap
it shut and hang it up again.
270 "By Saint Omer," said Robin then,
"lady, now I am cured at last,
and what tormented me has passed."
"Robin," she says, "that's a relief."
    He hugs her. She cries out, "Good grief!
275 And now what do you mean to do?"
"To tell the truth, I wish I knew,"
says Robin, who has not a shard
of sense. "My mother, Ermengard,
before the two of us were wed,
280 right after our engagement, said
that that's how I should play my part,
but I don't know quite where to start
unless you'll take charge of my training."
Then she cracks up; there's no restraining
285 her, not for forty pounds' reward.
"Robin, are you out of your gourd?
You must have known for all your life
that one asks such things of one's wife
by whispering in her left ear!"
290 He says, "That may well be, my dear. . . ."
But that is really their affair.
I'd not prolong my tale, nor care
much how they work the matter out.
If he knows naught, let him find out,
295 and, if he doesn't, well, too bad.
    Next morning, when the daylight had
arrived and made the whole world bright,
Mahaud arises at first light
and, sitting straight up in the sack,
300 opens the chamber door a crack.
Like one who has a trick to play,
she calls out, "Hey, Jouglet! Jouglet!
How is it you're not yet awake?

Levez tost sus, biau doz ami,
305   ne soiés parechous ne lent.
Il m'es[t] pris trop tres grant talent
d'oïr .i. petit vïeler. »
Quant Juglet s'oït apeler
le cuer de joie l'en soslieve:
310   « Ha, fet il, dame, je me lieve
se j'avoie pris ma chemise. »
Il taste a son chief, si a mise
tantost en la merde sa main:
« Vez, por les paumes seint Germain,
315   fet il, qui si m'a conchïé
qu'il a a mon cheveiz chïé?
Ja ne sui je mie ribaut!
— Biaus amis, fet dame Mahaut,
tastez a l'esponde devant. »
320   Cil a bouté sa main avant
(si n'a soing que dou soen rien perde),
sa main a bouté en la merde,
qui ne li put mie .i. pou:
« Vez, fet il, por le digne clou,
325   qui m'a ci ceste merde mise?
Puis que j'ai perdu ma chemise,
je chaucerai seveaus mes braies. »
Il salli sus jurant les plaies,
ses braies asaut por chaucier,
330   mes en lui n'ou[t] que corocier
quant il senti la merde flaire;
ses braies jeta en mi l'aire
e jure comme renoiez:
« De males eaus *soit* il noiez,
335   fait il, qui m'a fait cen!
— Juglet, fet ele, que est cen?
Qui vos a einsi eschaufé?
— Qui, dame? fet il. Li maufé
qui ont esté entor mon lit

Get up, good friend, for heaven's sake,
305 and don't be such a slugabed!
I've taken it into my head
to hear you play a little tune."
Jouglet's heart jumps for joy as soon
as he hears Lady Mahaud summon.
310 "Okay, lady," he says, "I'm coming
as soon as I put on some clothes."
He feels his head, and his hand goes
right in the shit. "By Saint Germain's
palms . . . Holy crap!" Jouglet exclaims.
315 "I'm not some tramp. Who's shitting me
so very unbefittingly
and on my bedstead left this load?"
"My friend," suggests Lady Mahaud,
"try feeling elsewhere on the frame."
320 To lose his things would be a shame.
He feels around; his hand falls slap
into another pile of crap,
which stinks more than a little bit.
"Who's covered me with all this shit,
325 by the precious nail of the Cross?
Since my shirt is a total loss,
at least I'll get into my breeches."
He hops up out of bed and reaches
for his pants, swearing like a heathen.
330 He thinks that he will lose his reason
to smell more shit rise to his nose;
back on the floor he drops his clothes
and curses like a heretic.
"Who's played me such a dirty trick?
335 May he drown in the devil's ocean!"
"What now, Jouglet? Why this commotion?
Who could have made you so upset?"
"Who, lady? Why, some devil's get
who visited my bed last night

qu'il n'i a liu grant ne petit
ou je n'aie merde trovee
e ma chemise toute ordee,
si sunt mes braies deslavees.
Ce sunt ci les bones soudees
que j'arai de vos noces fere!
— Je n'aie coupes en cest afere,
fet ele, Juglet, biaus amis.
Je ne sai qui mal i a mis
ne que ce est ne que ce fu,
mes alez alumer le fu.
Qui ne voit, il est mal balli. »
Juglet est cele part salli
comme home qui molt fu iré,
mes de ce fu mal atiré
que il n'out verge ne baston,
mes il n'[i] out feu ne ch[arbon]
fors merde qui dedens [estoit];
toute sa main e [tuit si doit]
en furent toollié tout ensemble.
Il tresue d'aïr e tremble
e maudit l'ore qu'il fu né
quant il est einsi atorné,
ne que *onques* devint juglere.
— Juglet, fet ele, bel doz freire,
qu'est ce? Est le feu desteint dont?
— Oïl, dame, il est un estront!
Il n'i a feu ne autre chose
fors merde qui i est enclose!
— Juglet, fet ele, biaus amis,
puis c'ous estes deu tout honis,
alez vos laver au seel.
Il pent en coste cel postel
tout droit a l'uis devers la cort. »
Juglet tout droit cele part cort,
qui out talent de soi mollier,

340 and covered everything in sight
with shit. There's not an inch of space
where he's not left his shitty trace.
My shirt and pants are all becrudded.
Indeed, I'm handsomely rewarded
345 for having played at your reception!"
"I had no hand in this deception,
my friend, you have my word upon it.
I can't imagine who has done it
nor how it ever came about.
350 But light the fire; it has gone out.
You're worse off when you cannot see."
  He set to work immediately
like someone in a rotten mood,
but this time he was really screwed,
355 in that he couldn't find a stick.
There's no charcoal or fire, just thick
shit everywhere; he can't avoid it.
When he reached his hand in, oh boy, did
he coat his fingers with the mess!
360 He sweats and trembles in distress,
curses the hour his mother bore him
and the sad destiny before him
and that he'd taken up the fiddle.
"Jouglet," she says, "explain this riddle.
365 Has the fire died? What has occurred?"
"No fire, my lady, just a turd!
No fire, no nothing—this recess is
filled to the brim with shitty messes!"
She says to him, "My friend Jouglet,
370 if you're as filthy as you say,
go wash your hands there in the pail.
You'll find it hanging from a nail
close to the yard door on a post."
Jouglet runs to the bucket, most
375 anxious to rinse off thoroughly,

ses mains a pris a toollier
enz ou seel e a froter;
la merde sent esclabouter
qui molt puant au nes li flaire;
380 il s'escrie, ne se puet taire:
« Li maufez soient en cest estre!
Toz deables i puissent estre,
trestoz ceus d'enfer a .i. mot!
[Quar se] j'eüsse mon sercot
385 [& ma vï]ele solement,
[je m'en] alasse vistement! »
[Cil ve]t avant, son sercot prent
[& sa vïe]le a son col pent.
[Ne flere] pas clous de girofle!
390   [Cel] jor [fu] feste seint Cristofle,
ce m'est avis, a .i. di luns,
que l'en out benee[i]t les fons
a une vile ou il passa.
Entor lui grant gent amassa
395 droit a l'entree dou mostier:
« Mestre, font il, de vos *mestier*
vos covient paier le travers! »
Il torne la teste a travers
e dit qu'il n'iert mie hetiez;
400 « Ne vos chaut, bien serez paiez,
font li vilain, qui rude sont.
— Tenez, fet il, deslïez dont
cest forrel ci li .i. de vos. »
Li .i. l'a mis sus ses genoz
405 e li autre l'a desnöé;
toute sa main a emböé
en la merde qui jus avale.
Cele jornee fu molt male
a cil Juglet, quer li vilain
410 le mistrent en molt mal pelain,
quer contre terre l'abatirent,

sticks both his hands in hurriedly,
and starts to rub them back and forth.
He's spattered with a shitty froth
that fills his nostrils with the reek.
380 He cries out loud, he has to speak,
"May all the devils that carouse
in Hell find lodgings in this house!
I'd gladly leave the place behind
me now if I could only find
385 my fiddle and my overcoat.
The devil take it by the throat!"
He shoulders his fiddle and cape
and quickly makes good his escape.
He doesn't smell like cloves or bay!
390   It was a Saint Christopher's Day,
a Monday, so it seems to me.
They'd come to bless the baptistry
in a city through which he passed.
A crowd of townspeople amassed
395 around him close by the church door.
"We won't let you pass by," they swore,
"unless you pay us with a song."
He turns his head and pulls a long,
sad face and says that he's unwell.
400 "Don't worry, we will pay you well,"
the peasants say, who seem ill-bred.
"Here, open up the case," he said,
"and take my fiddle out for me."
One of them placed it on his knee
405 and one reached for the instrument.
His hand was smeared with excrement
when all the shit came pouring down.
The peasants flung him to the ground
and beat the minstrel blue and black
410 and pounded him both front and back.
That day was a catastrophe

tant le ferirent e batirent
entor dos e entor le ventre
qu'en li peüst, mien encïentre,
415   toz les os en la pel hochier;
de cel an ne se pout aidier.
Eissi fu conchïé Juglet.
       Segnors, ce dit Colin Malet:
Tel cuide conchïer autrui
420   qui assez miez conchie lui.

𝟧2. LES .II. VILAINS

Gautiers, qui fist de Conebert
& del sot chevalier Robiert,
nos aconte d'une aventure
qu'il a fait metre en escriture,
5   qu'il avint deus vilains de Rasce
qui s'en alevent en Tierasce.
       Levé furent a l'ajornee;
molt fisent cel jor grant jornee.
Qant il furent a l'ostel trait,
10   molt furent lasset & estrait;
li ainsnés en fu si atains
qu'il en fu tos pales & tains,
q'ainc cele nuit ne peut mangier,
ainc tant ne l'en seut on blangier,
15   plus que le mole de deus tors
qu'il avoit pelés tot entors
& un navel en l'aistre cuit.
Cel manja il, si com je cuit,
& li autres manja assés,
20   qui n'estoit mie si lassés,

for poor Jouglet, it seems to me!
They very nearly did him in,
his bones were rattling in his skin,
415 and it was a full year before
he walked again, he was so sore.
That's how Jouglet got in deep shit.
　　　Colin Malet has said his bit,
my lords. They say the man who dumps
420 on others always gets his lumps.

52. THE TWO PEASANTS
by Gautier le Leu

Gautier le Loup, the author who
wrote of Conbert and Robert, too,
the one he called "The Stupid Knight,"
for our sake set himself to write
5 of two peasants who hailed from Raches
and what befell them in Thiérache.
　　　They both had risen with the sun
and traveled far ere day was done,
so, when they found a place to stay,
10 so tired and tuckered out were they,
the older of them was so bushed,
he was at once both pale and flushed
and couldn't eat at all that night,
nor could they whet his appetite
15 by any means. The tender heart
(he scraped away the outer part)
of two cabbage stems and one roast
turnip was all he ate, at most.
The other man ate his fair share—he,
20 unlike his friend, was not so weary —

puis se colcierent en .i. lit,
car lassé erent & delit.

Asés dormirent cele nuit
desci qu'aprés le mienuit,
25   que li ainsnés s'est esvelliés,
qui plus ot esté travelliés.
Son conpagnon apele & bote:
« Diva, fait il, en os te gote?
Jo ai si fain, ce m'est avis,
30   a poi que je n'enrage vis
& s[i] en cuit perdre le sens.
Savees nient en nul asens
u il ait pain n'autre despense? »
Atant li vallés se porpense;
35   « Amis, fait il, por nul avoir
ne poroie je pain avoir
se je men oste n'esvelloie
& je molt ne m'en travelloie,
& si seroit certes molt lait,
40   mais d'un grumel boli au lait
remest ersoir demis un pos.
Or soiés tos qois en repos
& si vos *saciés* deporter:
je vos en corrai aporter
45   se je puis au pot avenir.
Vos en arés au revenir. »

Lors s'est levés del lit tos nus,
desci qu'el flage en est venus,
tant quist le pot qu'il l'a trovet,
50   puis a son destre braç levet,
le loce prent par le pumel
qui estequieve ens el grumel,
fors l'en a trait tot hovee,
puis l'a encontremont levee,
55   si est ariere repairiés.
Mais il est auques desairiés

and then they lay down side by side
in bed, sleepy and satisfied,
where they slept on soundly and tight
till past the middle of the night,
25   when the older peasant awoke,
who'd felt so tired, he thought he'd croak.
     He nudged his partner there in bed.
"Psst, are you listening?" he said.
"I am so famished, I don't doubt
30   that I am ready to pass out
or maybe go stark raving mad.
Is there anything to be had
that you know of, vittles or bread?"
The younger peasant racks his head
35   and tells him, "Friend, I don't see how
at any price I'd find bread now
unless I go and wake my host
and strain myself to the utmost,
which surely wouldn't be polite,
40   but half a pot remained last night
of a thick milk and batter gruel.
Just lie here patiently. If you'll
behave yourself and keep your calm,
I'll hurry up and get you some,
45   and you can have your fill of what
's left over if I find the pot."
     Then he rose, naked as a jay-
bird, and to the stores made his way
and searched till he found the pot and
50   reached out, lifting up his right hand,
and grabbed the ladle by the stem
and picked it up, filled to the brim
(they'd left it standing in the gruel),
and, with the ladle overfull,
55   he then proceeded to return,
but doing so took a wrong turn,

car il ne set le liu ne l'estre:
tant a alet devers senestre
qu'il est venus au lit sen oste.

60   Puis dist tot coiement: « En os te?
Vois ci ce que jo t'ai promis. »
& li dame avoit sen cul mis
sor l'esponde tot descovert,
si tenoit tot le trau overt,

65   mais ele ert si fer endormie
qu'ele celui n'entendoit mie,
ains sonjoit une grant mervelle
qu'il s'en aleve a une velle,
si estoit a ore tornee.

70   Or entendés la destinee!
Li vallés qui le louce aporte
estoit fils Rogier de la Porte
& si ert cousins au preudome.
Qant il perçoit le cul le dome

75   & il le vit oscurement,
il cuida bien visablement
que ce fust cil qui l'atendoit.
Deseur le trau a mis sen doit,
si senti qu'il estoit velus,

80   & ses conpaing estoit barbus,
lors cuide estre bien asenés.
Molt pres del trau a mis sen nes.
Qant il le senti mu & qoit,
il dist qoiement en reqoit:

85   « Cis est pasmés, jel sai de fit.
Li famine l'a desconfit,
mais je l'en ferai ja mecine
tot sans erbes & sans racine. »
Puis le baissa demaintenant

90   plus de trois fois en .i. tenant.
Ce fist il por lui revenir,
car on voit sovent avenir

for unfamiliar with the lay-
out there, in the end he went way
off left and came to his host's bed.
60 "Can you hear me?" he softly said.
"See here: I've brought it as agreed."
         Off the edge of the bed, where she'd
moved it, the wife's ass hung undraped.
Between her cheeks her asshole gaped,
65 but since her sleep was so profound,
the woman didn't hear a sound
the lad made, lost in an entrancing
dream in which she had gone out dancing.
What's more, she'd turned away her face.
70   Hear what's in store now from the Fates!
The boy who for the gruel had gone
was Roger de la Porte's own son
and thus related to his host.
When he made out the woman's post-
75 erior dimly in the gloom,
he naturally did assume
that this must be his hungry friend.
He placed his hand on her rear end
and, feeling the hair there on her, he,
80 since his friend's bearded, too, and furry,
has come to the right place, he knows.
Close to her hole he moved his nose,
and softly, hearing that it uttered
not a sound, to himself he muttered,
85 "I knew it; he is in a faint.
It's clear to me his hunger's gained
the upper hand. I'll pull him through't
without recourse to herb or root."
He then proceeded to bestow
90 on it three kisses in a row.
He did this to revive the man,
as one often sees happen when

c'on baise çaus qui pasmé sont
si ami qui entor lui sont.
95   Entrués qu'il *baise le* crenel,
li saut uns vens fors de l'anel
qui rendi grant noise & grans pous.
Il cuida qu'il soflast le pous.
« Ahi! fait il, mal eüreus,
100   vos n'estes gaires famelleus
qui le soflés & s'est tos frois!
Del bu cuidiés ce soit Lanfrois?
Bien faites ço c'on doit lascier.
Je vos vi bien ersoir mascier
105   les tors pelés & les naviaus.
Vostre alainne n'est pas reviaus,
ains est plus orde & plus pusnaise
que ne soit vesse de pasnaise.
Vo feme n'en puet nient em part
110   se ele aimme Robert Lopart,
car molt i a bel baceler,
certes, je nel quier a celer.
Pusnais doit bien estre wihos. »
Atant resofle li buhos
115   ens el nes celui derecief,
& il en a croslet le cief.
« Ahi, fait il, caitis cucus,
vos pués plus que face uns cus!
Mais je sai bien, par saint Germain,
120   se vos ne lociés aparmain,
je vos ferrai ens el viaire. »
A icest mot li cus s'esclaire,
si gieta une grant gillorde.
Dist li vallés: « Cist fols m'alorde
125   qui ci me fait a lui entendre! »
Atant lait le loce destendre,
si l'en fiert si plain le havart
que Conebers en eut sa part

his or her friends standing about
will kiss a person who's passed out.
95 No sooner did he start to kiss her
than wind broke forth out of the fissure,
gusty and loud, as if to cool
(he thought) the ladleful of gruel.
"No need to blow on it, you old
100 scoundrel," he tells him, "since it's cold.
You're not so hungry, then, I see.
You think it's Mr. Lanfroy's tree?
What oughtn't to be done, you do.
Last night I clearly saw you chew
105 those turnips and the cabbage stalks.
As for your breath, it really irks
me, for it's more malodorous
and fetid than a parsnip is.
Your wife can't help but love another.
110 If Robert Lopart is her lover,
he's quite the handsome man, he is,
so why should I be secretive?
Men who stink should be cuckolded."
        Then blow again, her bowel did,
115 right in the fellow's nose, and he
wrenched his head back spasmodically.
"You lousy cuckold," says the lad,
"an asshole doesn't smell as bad
as you. By Saint Germain, I swear
120 if you don't get your ass in gear,
I'll punch you squarely in the nose."
At that instant her ass explodes
and thunders forth a hearty one.
The lad says, "He's leading me on,
125 making me listen to his bleating!"
He swings the ladle at her, beating
and striking her across her bottom,
so even her private parts got some,

& contremont desci qu'es nages
130 fu respandus li conpenages,
& li dame s'est esvellie,
qui del songier ert travellie;
son cul, qui tos estoit solliés,
tos grumeleus & tos molliés,
135 fiça en l'escorç sen marit,
qui molt en ot le sens marit
qant il s'esvelle & il le sent.
« Ahi! fait il, dame Mainsent,
honit m'avés, de fi le sai!
140 J'amasse mels estre en Ausai
u deci qu'as mons de Mongiu!
Certes ci a molt vilain giu:
s'or le savoient vo parent
& un voisin de ci par ent,
145 vos en seriés molt avillie,
& vos & tote vo lignie. »
     Qant li vallés l'a entendut,
il a son destre braç tendut;
tant s'est de totes par erciés
150 qu'il est a son lit aderciés.
Son conpagnon conta l'afaire,
& li prodom fist .i. baing faire,
si se sont bagniet & lavet,
& cil sont al matin levet,
155 s'ont a lor oste congiet pris.
Cil fu cortois & bien apris,
si les a a Deu commandés
& si lor a deus pains mandés,
qu'il lor dona de bone estrine;
160 & li dame fu molt estrine
vers son segnor & molt sogite,
car ele cuidoit estre engite
& si cuide bien avoit fait

because the gruel spreads out and leaks
130   across and down her nether cheeks.
            The woman then woke with a start
because her dreams pressed on her hard.
Her fundament, completely soiled,
dripping with porridge and befouled,
135   she shoved against her husband's lap,
who took offense at all that crap
when he awoke and felt it there.
He says, "We are disgraced, I swear!
Madam Mainsent, what's on your ass?
140   I wish I were off in Alsace
or far off in the Alps. Oh, this is
a dirty trick, a loathsome business.
If ever your relations knew
about this, and the neighbors, too,
145   you'd be degraded shamefully,
both you and all your family."
            When the young man heard what he said,
he made his way back to his bed,
feeling and groping with his right
150   arm in the darkness of the night.
He told his friend the accident.
Their worthy host meanwhile went
and drew a bath, and they scrubbed down.
The men, when morning came around,
155   got up and took leave of their host,
who, being courteous and most
well brought up, wished them both Godspeed
and handed them two loaves that he'd
for them as a gift of farewell.
160   Humbled before her man as well
as shamed, the woman's ill at ease,
for, thinking she had lain so, she's
of the opinion that she had

le vilonie & le mesfait
165 poruec qu'ele l'avoit songiet;
& cil qui eurent pris congiet
sont revenu en Ostrevant
la dont il furent mut devant.
    Saciés de fit que li Goulius
170 le raconta en tamains lius,
a Saint Amant & a Marcienes.
Uns bacelers de Valencienes
qui avoit esté ens el leu
le raconta Gautier le Leu,
175 & il mist le fablel en rime.
.x. en a fait; vesci l'onsime.
Car fuscent or si atornees
totes les dames mestornees
qui ont les maris bons & beaus,
180 ses honiscent par lor lembeaus!

𝕾𝕾. LES .III. BOÇUS

Seignor, se vous volez atendre
& .i. seul petitet entendre,
ja de mot ne vous mentirai,
mes tout en rime vous dirai
5 d'une aventure le fablel.
    Jadis avint a .i. chastel
(mes le non oblïé en ai—
or soit aussi comme a Douay)
.i. borgois i avoit manant
10 qui du sien vivoit belemant;
biaus hom ert & de bons amis,
des borgois toz li plus eslis,
mes n'avoit mie grant avoir,

really done something foul and bad,
165 since in her sleep she'd dreamt she did.
      After the two peasants had bid
their host farewell, they turned and went
back where they'd come from: Ostrevant.
      I'd have you know that Golias
170 spread it around from place to place,
in Saint-Amand and in Marchiennes.
A young man out of Valenciennes
was thereabouts. He it was who
made it known to Gautier le Loup,
175 who rhymed this fabliau. So then
here's his eleventh. (He'd done ten
already.) May all wayward women
fare as she did—they have it coming!
When they have worthy husbands, why
180 do they disgrace them on the sly?

55. THE THREE HUNCHBACKS
by Durant

My lords, if you have time to spare,
though but a moment, you may hear
a little fabliau I wrote
in rhyme, based on an anecdote,
5 and not one word of it's a lie.
      In a walled town in days gone by
(but I've forgotten the town's name—
let's say Douai; it's all the same)
there dwelt a worthy citizen
10 of decent means, the best of men,
who among his good friends could count
the foremost tradespeople around,
and, though he did not have great wealth,

si s'en savoit si bien a voir
15 que molt ert creüz par la vile.
Il avoit une bele fille,
si bele que c'ert uns delis,
&, se le voir vous en devis,
je ne cuit qu'ainz feïst Nature
20 nule plus bele creature.
De sa biauté n'ai or que fere
a raconter ne a retrere
quar, se je mesler m'en voloie,
assez tost mesprendre i porroie,
25 si m'en vient mieus tere orendroit
que dire chose qui n'i soit.
En la vile avoit .i. boçu;
onques ne vi si malostru:
de teste estoit molt bien garnis.
30 (Je cuit bien que Nature ot mis
grant entencïon a lui fere.)
A toute riens estoit contrere,
trop estoit de laide faiture:
grant teste avoit & laide hure,
35 cort col & les espaules lees,
& les avoit haut encröees . . .
de folie se peneroit
qui tout raconter vous voudroit.
Sa façon trop par estoit lais:
40 toute sa vie fu entais
a grant avoir amonceler;
por voir vous puis dire & conter
trop estoit riches durement,
se li aventure ne ment,
45 en la vile n'ot si riche homme.
Que vous diroie?—c'est la somme
du boçu, comment a ouvré.
Por l'avoir qu'il ot amassé,
li ont donee la pucele

who was respected for himself
15 and his good sense throughout the city.
He had a daughter. She was pretty;
so pretty, she was a delight.
If I were to describe her right,
I doubt that Nature ever made
20 a creature fairer than this maid,
but I do not intend to dwell
on how she looked or try to tell
her beauty, because I'm afraid
you'd just discredit what I said,
25 so better leave the matter be
than understate reality.
      In that same town, not far from them,
a hunchback lived, a ruffian,
whose head was his outstanding feature.
30 Nature, I think, who made this creature,
struggled immensely when she formed
him. Nothing else was so deformed
and hideous beyond compare:
He'd a large head and shaggy hair,
35 a short neck and, as huge as boulders,
set too high up, enormous shoulders.
The man who'd foolishly detail
his ugliness is bound to fail.
His vicious way of life accorded
40 with how he looked, because he hoarded
all of his life to pile up gain.
To tell you truly and speak plain,
this hunchback was richer than Croesus.
Unless report of him deceives us,
45 none in town had more wealth than he.
What can I say? From A to Z,
that's how the hunchback's life was led.
Because of all the wealth he had,
his friends arranged to wed the lout

si ami, qui tant estoit bele,   50
mes ainz puis qu'il l'ot espousee
ne fu il .i. jor sanz penssee
por la grant biauté qu'ele avoit;
li boçus si jalous estoit
qu'il ne pooit avoir repos.   55
Toute jor estoit ses huis clos,
ja ne vousist que nus entrast
en sa meson s'il n'aportast
ou s'il enprunter ne vousist.

    Toute jor a son sueil seïst   60
tant qu'il avint a .i. Nöel
que troi boçu menesterel
vindrent a lui ou il estoit,
se li dist chascuns qu'il voloit
fere cele feste avoec lui   65
quar en la vile n'a nului
ou le deüssent fere mieus
por ce qu'il ert de lor parieus
& boçus ausi comme il sont.
Lors les maine li sire amont,   70
quar la meson ert a degrez;
li mengiers estoit aprestez,
tuit se sont au disner assis,
&, se le voir vous en devis,
li disners ert & biaus & riches.   75
Li boçus n'ert avers ne chiches,
ainz assist bien ses conpaignons,
pois au lart orent & chapons,
& quant ce vint aprés disner
si lor fist li sires doner   80
aus .iii. boçus, ce m'est avis,
chascun .xx. sous de parisis,
& aprés lor a desfendu
qu'il ne soient jamés veü
en la meson ne el porpris   85

50 to the fair maid I told about,
but from the moment they were wed
he couldn't get out of his head
the beauty which she was endowed
with, and his jealousy allowed
55 him not a second of respite.
He always kept his doors shut tight
and let nobody in his home
who hadn't come there for a loan
or else had money to repay.

60   Thus he sat keeping watch all day,
till once on Christmas there came three
strolling players, humpbacked as he,
where he was standing by the door
and said that they'd like nothing more
65 than to observe the holiday
with him. Since he's humpbacked as they
and in the town there's no one else
as much like them as he himself,
they'd not do better anywheres.
70 He led the three of them upstairs
(for his house had a second floor),
where a repast was ready for
them all, and they sat down to dine.
Their meal was copious and fine,
75 to tell the truth, for this time he
was neither tight nor niggardly,
but offered his guests to partake in
a capon roast and peas with bacon,
and, when at length dinner was done,
80 distributed to every one
of the three hunchback minstrels plenty
of Paris pennies. (I think twenty.)
Last of all, he forbade the men
that they ever appear again
85 inside his house or in his yard.

quar, s'il i estoient repris,
il avroient .i. baing crüel
de la froide eve du chanel.
(La meson ert sor la riviere,
90 qui molt estoit granz & pleniere.)
& quant li boçu l'ont oï,
tantost sont de l'ostel parti
volentiers & a chiere lie,
quar bien avoient enploïe
95 lor jornee, ce lor fu vis,
& li sires s'en est partis,
puis est deseur le pont venuz.
          La dame, qui ot les boçus
oï chanter & solacier,
100 les fist toz .iii. mander arrier
quar oïr les voloit chanter;
si a bien fet les huis fermer.
Ainsi com li boçu chantoient
& o la dame s'envoisoient,
105 ez vous revenu le seignor,
qui n'ot pas fet trop lonc demor.
A l'uis apela fierement;
la dame son seignor entent,
a la voiz le connut molt bien,
110 ne sot en cest mont terrïen
que peüst fere des boçuz
ne comment il soient repus.
.i. chaaliz ot lez le fouier
c'on soloit fere charriier,
115 el chaaliz ot .iii. escrins.
Que vous diroie? C'est la fins:
en chascun a mis .i. boçu.
Ez vous le seignor revenu,
si s'est delez la dame assis
120 *cui* molt par seoit ses delis,
mes il n'i sist pas longuement;

If caught there, then things would go hard:
They'd have a bath to make them shiver
in the cold water of the river.
(His house was set on the canal,
90   and it was wide, and deep as well.)
The hunchbacks listened to their host
and left his house directly, most
willingly, in a festive mood,
because that day had been a good
95   one for them, of that they'd no doubt.
And then their host also went out
to the bridge and took up his station.
      His wife, who'd heard the celebration
and how the hunchbacks sang and played,
100   sent for them to come back and bade
them sing for her for her delight,
and had the household doors shut tight.
Now, while the hunchbacks sang their air
and entertained the lady there,
105   her husband, who had not been gone
too long, came back home thereupon.
He called in a commanding voice
from the door. When she heard the noise,
she recognized him in a wink.
110   For all the world she couldn't think
of anyplace where she could hide
the hunchbacks she had asked inside.
There was a bed beside the hearth
they used to carry back and forth
115   with three drawers built inside of it.
What can I say? Here's what she did:
She put one hunchback in each drawer
and let her husband in the door,
who went and sat by her, since he
120   took pleasure in her company,
but not for too long did he stay

de leenz ist & si descent
de la meson & si s'en va.
A la dame point n'anuia
125 quant son mari voit avaler;
les boçus en vout fere aler
qu'ele avoit repus es escrins,
mes toz .iii. les trova estins
quant ele les escrins ouvri.
130 De ce molt forment s'esbahi.
     Quant les .iii. boçus mors trova,
a l'uis vint corant, s'apela
.i. porteur qu'ele a avisé;
a soi l'a la dame apelé.
135 Quant li bachelers l'a oïe,
a li corut, n'atarja mie;
« Amis, dist ele, enten a moi:
se tu me veus plevir ta foi
que tu ja ne m'encuseras
140 d'une rien que dire m'orras,
molt sera riches tes loiers;
.xxx. livres de bons deniers
te donrai quant tu l'avras fet. »
Quant li porteres ot tel plet,
145 fiancié li a volentiers,
quar il covoitoit les deniers,
& s'estoit auques entestez.
Le grant cors monta les degrez,
la dame ouvri l'un des escrins:
150 « Amis, ne soiez esbahis.
Cest mort en l'eve me portez,
si m'avrez molt servi a grez. »
.i. sac li baille, & cil le prant,
le boçu bouta enz errant,
155 puis si l'a a son col levé,
si a les degrez avalé,
a la riviere vint corant

before he rose and went away,
climbed back downstairs and left the house.
It didn't incommode his spouse
125   her husband didn't hang about;
she wished to get the hunchbacks out,
the three she'd hidden in the drawers.
She had an awful shock, because,
when she had opened up the bed
130   and looked inside, she found them dead.
       When she saw all three had expired,
she ran to the door and required
a passing porter she waylaid
in God's name to come to her aid.
135   The young man, when he heard her call,
came running, didn't wait at all.
"My friend," she said, "I have a question.
Say, can I count on your discretion
and promise not to inculpate
140   me in the matter I'll relate?
I'll see to it it's worth your while,
for when you've done my errand, I'll
reward you thirty pounds in cash."
The porter heard and in a flash
145   agreed to get her business done. (He
wasn't a man to turn down money,
and so the job was to his taste.)
He followed her upstairs in haste.
She opened one drawer in the bed;
150   "No need to be afraid," she said.
"Just dump this corpse in the canal
and I will say you've served me well."
She gave him a sack; in a minute
he'd packed away the hunchback in it,
155   and then he lifted up the sack,
went downstairs with it on his back,
ran straight down to the river's edge

tout droit sor le grant pont devant,
en l'eve geta le boçu;
160   onques n'i plus atendu,
ainz retorna vers la meson.
La dame a ataint du leson
l'un des boçus a molt grant paine,
a poi ne li failli l'alaine,
165   molt fu au lever traveillie,
puis s'en est .i. pou esloingnie.
Cil revint arrier eslessiez:
« Dame, dist il, or me paiez.
Du nain vous ai bien delivree.
170   — Por qoi m'avez vous or gabee,
dist cele, sire? Fols vilains,
ja est ci revenuz li nains.
Ainz en l'eve ne le getastes;
ensanble o vous le ramenastes.
175   Vez le la, se ne m'en creez!
— Comment .c. deables maufez
est il donc revenuz ceanz?
Por lui sui forment merveillanz:
il estoit mors. Ce m'est avis,
180   c'est uns deable antecris!
Mes ne li vaut, par saint Remi! »
A tant l'autre boçu saisi,
el sac le mist, puis si le lieve
a son col si que poi li grieve,
185   de la meson ist vistement,
& la dame tout maintenant
de l'escrin tret le tiers boçu,
si l'a couchié delez le fu,
a tant s'en est vers l'uis venue.

190   Li porterres en l'eve rue
le boçu la teste desouz:
« Alez! que honis soiez vous,

and up onto the highest bridge
and tossed the hunchback in the drink.
160   He didn't take the time to blink,
but set off back home on the double.
          The lady, with no end of trouble,
had taken out one hunchback more.
Lifting him up was quite a chore,
165   and, out of breath from her endeavor,
she drew aside from the cadaver.
The porter came back much elated.
"It's time that I were compensated,
lady. I got rid of your dwarf."
170   "What kind of joke would you pull off,
mister?" she said. "You dunce! You bounder!
The dwarf's come back; he's still around here.
I don't think that you ever threw
him in. You brought him back with you.
175   If you don't trust me, look and see!"
"How in the name of Hell could he
have ever come back here, by thunder?
It baffles me. I'm filled with wonder.
Why, he was dead! I'd be surprised
180   if he were not the Antichrist!
Saint Remy, that won't help him any!"
He grabbed the second hunchback; then he
shoved him into the sack and lifted
it on his shoulders; then he shifted
185   the weight for comfort and set out,
whereon the woman turned about,
opened the third drawer and drew forth
the hunchback, laid him by the hearth,
and waited at the door.
                         The porter
190   emptied the sack into the water,
letting the hunchback fall headfirst,
and told him, "May you be accursed

dist il, se vous *me* revenez! »
puis est le grant cors retornez.
195 A la dame dist que li pait,
& cele sanz nul autre plait
li dist que bien li paiera.
A tant au fouier le mena
ausi com se rien ne seüst
200 du tiers boçu qui la se jut.
« Voiés, dist ele, grant merveille!
Qui oï ainc mes la pareille?
Revez la le boçu ou gist! »
Li bachelers pas ne s'en rist
205 quant le voit gesir lez le fu:
« Voiz! dist il, por le saint cuer bu,
qui ainc mes vit tel menestrel?
Ne ferai je dont huimés el
que porter ce vilain boçu?
210 Toz jors le truis ci revenu
quant je l'ai en l'eve rué! »
Lors a le tiers ou sac bouté,
a son col fierement le rue
d'ire & de duel, d'aïr tressue,
215 a tant s'en torne ireement,
toz les degrez aval descent.
Le tiers boçu a descarchié,
dedenz l'eve l'a balancié:
« Va t'en, dist il, au vif maufé!
220 Tant t'averai hui conporté,
se te voi meshui revenir,
tu vendras tart au repentir!
Je cuit que tu m'as enchanté,
mes, par le Dieu qui me fist né,
225 se tu viens meshui aprés moi
& je truis baston ou espoi,
tel te donrai el haterel

if you come back to me! Now go!"
and hurried back. He wasn't slow
195   to ask the lady for his fee,
which she accorded readily
and told him he would be well paid.
Then back to the fireplace she led
him, as if she were not aware
200   the third hunchback was lying there.
"What's this?" she said. "As God may strike
me dead, who's ever heard the like
of this? See where our hunchback's lying!"
The long-suffering porter, spying
205   him by the fire, was not amused
and cried, "Christ! Will my day be used
up lugging this damned dwarf around?
God's carcass! Was there ever found
a more persistent minstrel? Never!
210   I go and toss him in the river,
only to find that he's come back!"
He stuffs the third one in the sack
and heaves it up onto his shoulders.
With anger and dismay he smolders,
215   irately turns and goes to trundle
back down the stairs toting his bundle,
unloads the third and final dwarf,
and from the bridge tosses him off.
"Good riddance, and the devil take you!
220   I've lugged you all day. I can't shake you,
but if again I catch you headed
back home, I tell you, you'll regret it!
You have bewitched me, I believe,
but, by God, by Whose grace I breathe,
225   if you come following behind,
with the first sword or stick I find
I'll strike your neck in such a manner

dont tu avras rouge bendel! »
A icest mot est retornez
230 & sus en la meson montez.
      Ainz qu'eüst les degrez monté
si a derrier lui regardé
& voit le seignor qui revient.
Li bons hom pas a geu nel tient;
235 de sa main s'est .iii. foiz sainiez:
« Nomini dame! Dieus aidiez! »
Molt li anuie en son corage:
« Par foi, dist il, cis a la rage
qui si pres des talons me siut
240 que par poi qu'il ne me consiut!
Par la röele saint Morant,
il me tient bien por païsant,
que je nel puis tant conporter
que ja se vueille deporter
245 d'aprés moi adés revenir! »
Lors cort a ses .ii. poins sesir
.i. pestel qu'a l'uis voit pendant,
puis revint au degré corant;
li sires ert ja pres *montez*.
250 « Comment? Sire boçus, tornez!
Or me sanble ce enresdie,
mes par le cors sainte Marie,
mar retornastes ceste part.
Vous me tenez bien por musart! »
255 A tant a le pestel levé,
si l'en a .i. tel cop doné
sor la teste qu'il ot molt grant
que la cervele li espant;
mort l'abati sor le degré
260 & puis si l'a ou sac bouté,
d'une corde la bouche loie,
le grant cors se met a la voie,
si l'a en l'eve balancié

to leave you with a red bandanna!"
This said, he went straight back and strode
230 on up the steps of her abode.
          Now, well before he reached the top,
he glanced behind, came to a stop,
seeing her husband on his way
home again. In no mood for play,
235 he signed the cross thrice in succession
and prayed for divine intercession,
exclaiming, stricken to the quick,
"In God's name, is the creature sick
with rabies to tag after me
240 and dog me through eternity?
By the halo of Saint Mauront,
am I some peasant he can flaunt?
I just keep toting; when I'm done,
it's his idea of having fun
245 to come back for another ride!"
He grabbed a club that hung beside
the door with both fists; then he ran
back to the flight of stairs again.
The husband was close to the top.
250 "How, Mr. Hunchback? Go back! Stop!
How stubborn can a person be?
I promise you, by Saint Marie,
you'll rue having come back once more!
What kind of stooge d'you take me for?"
255 Without a pause he raised the club
and brought it down with such a thud
on the hunchback's enormous head
that on the stairs he struck him dead,
with his brains spattered left and right,
260 then bagged him, tied the sack up tight
with a cord, then went at a run
the same way he had often gone
and pitched his burden in the river,

a tout le sac qu'il ot lïé
265   quar paör avoit duremant
qu'il encor ne l'alast sivant.
« Va jus, dist il, a mal eür!
Or cuit je estre plus asseür
que tu ne doies revenir,
270   si verra l'en les bois foillir! »
        A la dame s'en vint errant,
si demande son paiement
que molt bien a son commant fet.
La dame n'ot cure de plet,
275   le bacheler paia molt bien
.xxx. livres, n'en falut rien;
trestout a son gré l'a paié
que molt fu lie du marchié;
dist que fet a bone jornee
280   despuis que il l'a delivree
de son mari qui tant ert lais:
bien cuide qu'ele n'ait jamais
anui nul jor qu'ele puist vivre
quant de son mari est delivre.
285   Durans, qui son conte define,
dist c'onques Dieus ne fist meschine
c'on ne puist por deniers avoir,
ne Dieus ne fist si chier avoir,
tant soit bons ne de grant chierté,
290   qui voudroit dire verité
que por deniers ne soit eüs:
por ses deniers ot li boçus
la dame qui tant bele estoit.
Honiz soit li hom, quels qu'il soit,
295   qui trop prise mauvés deniers,
& qui les fist fere premiers.
Amen.

hunchback and sack, the two together,
265 for he was scared that for the fourth
time he'd be followed by the dwarf.
"Bad luck to you!" he said. "Now sink!
This time I can be sure, I think,
you won't return to give me grief
270 until the forests are in leaf!"
	He went right back to see the lady
and asked her if he might be paid; he
had done her errand to perfection.
The woman offered no objection,
275 but gave the young man his reward
of thirty pounds, not one cent short,
freely and generously paid,
the best bargain she'd ever made,
she said, delighted with her day,
280 because he'd got out of the way
her husband, who was so disfigured.
For the rest of her days, she figured,
she'd never suffer pain or strife
now her spouse is out of her life.
285	Durant says, rounding off his tale,
that everything on earth's for sale—
there's not a girl that can't be bought,
nor any treasure that God wrought,
however valuable and good,
290 that, if the truth be understood,
cannot be had for the right price.
The hunchback used wealth to entice
his marriage with a lady fair.
Shame on the man whose only care
295 is massing money for his purse!
And on who coined it first, a curse!
Amen.

54. LE SEGRETAIN MOINE

D'un moigne vos dirai la vie.
Segrestein fu d'une abeïe,
si aama une bourgeise
qui molt iert vaillant & cortoise;
5   Idoine ot non, & son seignor
dant Guillaume le changeor.
Idoine fu bien enseignie,
simple, cortoise & afetie,
& Guillaumes sot bien changier;
10   molt s'entremist de gaagnier.
Il n'iert mie tavernerez,
ses ostieus estoit beaus & nez,
la huche au pein n'iert pas fermee,
a touz estoit abandonee—
15   s'un lechierres li demandast
du sien, volentiers l'en donnast.
Riche gent furent a merveille,
mes deables, qui torjorz veille,
s'entremist tant d'eus enginier
20   que il les fist apovrïer;
a Guillaume estut enprunter,
ne pot plus au change arester.
A la foire ala a Provinz
& si i porta .iiii. vinz
25   livres de bons provenoisiens;
aprés s'en revint par Amiens,
dras achetoit, si s'en venoit.
Por ce que bon marchié avoit
fesoit Guillaumes molt grant joie,
30   mes larrons guetoient la voie
& le trespas & le chemin.
Venuz s'en erent si voisin,

About a monk I'll tell the story,
sacristan of his monastery,
who loved a woman in the city
who was discreet, charming, and pretty,
5   named Idwaine, and her husband, he
was Guillaume, who changed currency.
Idwaine was wise, as I have said,
and unaffected and well-bred,
and Guillaume kept his business thriving,
10   knew his trade and made a good living.
He shunned the taverns and disorder
and always kept his house in order,
nor was he stingy: To his pantry
to all in need he granted entry,
15   and any down-and-out who asked
could count on him for a repast.

     They were exceptionally wealthy.
The Devil, envious and stealthy,
set his hand to arrange events
20   to reduce them to indigence.
He lost the place he had held once
on the exchange, and borrowed funds
with which he set out for the fair
in Provins, having in his care
25   eighty pounds minted in Provins,
and came back by way of Amiens,
where he bought cloth, then left for home.
His fruitful trading put Guillaume
in best of spirits, but a mass
30   of thieves watched the road he would pass.
His neighbors had gone on before,
while he stayed on there two days more

       & il remest .ii. jors aprés
       por ce que il menoit grant fes,
35   mes n'orent pas grantment erré
       quant en la forest sunt entré
       iluec ou li laron estoient
       qui les marchaans desroboient.
       Quant Guillaume virent venir,
40   de totes pars le vont saisir,
       jus le trebuchent du cheval;
       ne li firent point d'autre mal
       mes qu'il li tolent sa coroie.
       Puis ont veü enmi la voie
45   son serjant qui aprés venoit
       & qui le sommier amenoit:
       li mau larron seure li queurent,
       a lor couteaus tot le deveurent;
       quant Guillaumes le vit morir,
50   a pié s'en commence a fuïr;
       Guillaumes s'en fuï a pié.
       Or n'a il gueres gaagnié,
       car cil qui baillié li avoient
       lor avoir, que avoir devoient
55   quant il revendroit de la foire,
       dïent: « Ci a mavés afere!
       Qu'avez vos fet de nostre argent?
       Rendez le nos delivrement! »
       Guillaumes dit a ses voisins:
60   « Seignor, j'ai encore .ii. molins
       qui de farine muelent molt.
       Or ne soiez pas si estout:
       prenez les; en pes me lessiez
       tant que me soie porchaciez. »
65   Il lor livra, & cil s'en vont,
       car tuit a lor gré paié sunt,
       & cil remest avec sa fame,
       qui molt estoit cortoise dame.

before he set off on the road
because he had a so big a load.
35   They'd not gone far with all his goods
when they came to those very woods
where the thieves had set up to prey
on merchants who came by that way.
As soon as they saw Guillaume ride
40   by, they attacked from every side,
seized him and pulled him off his horse,
but, thank God, they did nothing worse
than take his trappings and his mount.
Then, looking down the road, they found
45   his servant following, who came
along with all the baggage train,
and, rushing down on him, the thieves
hacked him to pieces with their knives.
When Guillaume saw his servant dead,
50   on foot he quickly turned and fled,
escaped all the way home on foot.
The bandits, though, had all his loot,
and those who'd given him the loan,
who'd thought that when he came back home
55   from Provins fair they'd be repaid,
cursed their largesse to him and said,
"What have you done with what we lent?
Pay us back quickly, every cent!"
Guillaume answered his creditors,
60   "I still own two fine grain mills, sirs,
which turn out quantities of flour.
You needn't be so harsh and sour.
Until I'm back on my feet, please
take them, and let me be in peace."
65   They gladly took the mills in place
of what he owed and quit the place,
leaving him behind to remain
at home with his good wife, Idwaine.

Por ce qu'il la vit corocie,
70 « Idoine, fet il, bele amie,
se Nostre Sire a consentu
que j'aie mon avoir perdu,
encor est Il la ou Il seut—
Il nos edera bien s'Il veut. »
75 Ele respont: « Certes, beau sire.
Si m'aït Dieus, ne sai que dire.
Molt me poise de vostre perte
& molt a fet male deserte
li serjant qui en est ocis,
80 mes moi ne chaut quant estes vis,
car perte puet l'en recovrer,
mes mort ne puet nul restorer. »
      Icele nuit furent einsi.
A l'endemein devant midi
85 ala Idoine a l'abaïe
pröer le fiuz Seinte Marie,
de quoi l'iglise estoit fondee.
Une chandele out alumee.
      Que Damle Dieus la conseillast,
90 a son seignor g[a]ain donast,
desus l'autel mist la chandele;
de ses eulz qui semblent estoile
plora & de son cuer soupire,
que s'oreison ne li lut dire.
95 Li sougrestein l'a escoutee,
qui longuement l'avoit amee.
Il vint avant, si la salue:
« Dame, bien soiez vos venue,
dist li moignes, & bien trovee! »
100 Cele ne fu pas enpruntee,
einz tert ses euz, si li respont:
« Sire, dist el, Dieus bien vos dont.
— Bien, dame? dist le segresteins,
je ne demant ne plus ne meins

Because he saw she was upset,
70 he told her, "Now, Idwaine, my pet,
if it's by the Lord's will that we
are thus reduced to penury,
He still is up in Paradise to
give us His help when He decides to."
75 She answered, "Be that as it may,
so help me God, what can I say,
husband? I grieve for what you've lost,
and for the servant, whom it cost
his life unjustly, also grieve,
80 but I'm consoled since you still live,
for what's been lost you can regain,
but the dead don't come back again."
    They spent the whole night in this way,
and before noon on the next day
85 Idwaine went to the monastery
to pray to Jesus, son of Mary,
to whom their church was dedicated.
She took a candle, and she lit it
that God relieve her misery
90 and grant them both prosperity.
Tears welling in her starlike eyes
and her poor heart heaving with sighs,
so overburdened with her cares
she scarcely could recite her prayers,
95 she placed the candle on the altar.
The sacristan approached and called her,
who'd overheard and had been smitten
with love for her so long, "Thus meeting
you is a pleasure!" When she heard it,
100 she was in no way disconcerted,
but answered, lifting up her face
to him, "Father, God give you grace."
"*His* grace, dear lady?" the monk said.
"I ask no other grace instead

105 de bien avoir fors c'avec moi
vos tenissë en .i. requoi;
adont avroie achevé
ce que lonc tens ai desiré.
Je sui de ceanz tresorier,
110 si vos donnrai molt bon loier:
vos avrez .c. livres du mien
dont vos porrez vivre molt bien
& aquiter d'une partie.
J'ai bien vostre conpleinte oïe. »
115 Idoine ot .c. livres nommer,
commença soi a porpenser
savoir se les prendroit ou non
(car en .c. livres a beau don!),
mes ele amoit de grant amour
120 dant Guillaume le changeour;
puis dist a soi meïme en bas:
« Sanz congié nes prendré ge pas. »
Li moine autre foiz l'aresonne:
« [Dame, fait il, par nostre gone,]
125 bien a .iiii. anz que je vos aim;
certes ainz n'atocha ma mein
a vos, mes or i touchera! »
Lors l'acole, si la besa;
du besier li a force fete.
130 Idoine s'est ariere trete
& dist: « Beau sire, en cest moustier
ne deüsiez pas dornoier!
Je m'en irai a ma meson,
s'en parlerai a mon baron
135 & l'en demanderé conseil.
— Dame, dist il, molt me merveil
s'a li conseil en querïez! »
Dist ele: « Ne vos esmaiez—
l'en fet asez por gaagnier!
140 Mon seignor quit si losengier

105   of being able to possess
      your graceful self in secretness.
      Then would I have what I've aspired
      to for so long and so desired.
      I am entrusted with our treasure
110   here and will pay you for this pleasure:
      a hundred pounds will you receive,
      which will permit you both to live
      well and repay some of your debt.
      I overheard all that you said."
115   When Idwaine heard him say a hundred
      pounds, she quite naturally wondered
      should she accept them, no or yes?
      A hundred pounds is generous,
      but so deep her affection ran,
120   she felt such true love for her man,
      the money changer, that she thought,
      Without his leave I'll not be bought.
      Again the monk went on to court her:
      "Now, by the habit of my order,
125   for four years I've desired your charms
      and never took you in my arms,
      but this time I will not resist."
      He took her in his arms and kissed
      her by brute force passionately.
130   Idwaine managed to struggle free
      and told him, "Sir, this house of worship
      is not a fitting place for courtship!
      I'm going straight back to my house
      to consult with my lawful spouse
135   on his opinion in this matter."
      "Lady," he said, "I marvel that a
      husband be asked for such advice!"
      The lady answered, "At that price
      men have few scruples. Don't dismay!
140   I'll wheedle him in such a way,

que je feré vostre proiere. »
Dont tret le moine une aumosniere—
.x. sous i ot—& puis li tent.
Idoine volentiers les prent,
145   a Deu la commande & el lui;
einsi departirent andui.

     Idoine vint a son ostel,
ou il n'avoit ne pein ne sel,
que poverté les destreignoit
150   & la perte que fet avoit
sire Guillaumes en la forest.
Ele parla, & il se test:
« Sire, dist ele, entendez moi:
tel conseil vos dirai, ce croi,
155   que dont serez riche clamez
ja ne verrez .ii. *jours* passez.
   — Dame, dist il, en quel maniere? »
Dont tret Idoine l'aumoniere
que li moigne li ot donee,
160   hastivement l'a desfermee—
.x. sous i ot—& puis li tent
(Guillaumes volentiers les prent),
& puis [li dis]t: « Guillaume, sire,
por Deu nel tenez pas a ire
165   se je vos di ma priveté. »
De chief en chief li a conté
comment li moigne la pria
el moustier quant il la trova
& com .c. livres li promist.
170   Guillaumes l'entent, si s'en rist
& dist que por tot le tresor
Ostevïen & Nabugor
ne souferroit il c'ome nez
fust de li charnelment privez,
175   il vodroit mieus querre son pein

I think, that you'll be satisfied."
The monk reached for his purse—inside
was half a pound—and gave it to
Idwaine, who gladly took it, too!
145 He said good-bye, and so did she,
and so they parted amiably.
         She went back to her empty house.
(Their bread would not have fed a mouse,
for poverty pressed on them hard
150 after the loss Guillaume incurred
out in the woods the other day.)
He heard out what she had to say.
"Husband," she said, "listen to this.
I have a plan that cannot miss
155 and also, if I'm right, by which
within two days will make you rich."
"Lady," he said, "how can we gain
as much as that?" Right then Idwaine
took out the purse the sacristan
160 had given—half a pound was in
it—opened it and gave them to
Guillaume, who took them gladly, too!
She told him, "Husband, dear Guillaume,
when you hear what I will make known,
165 do not, for God's sake, be irate."
She then proceeded to relate
how when she'd gone to church to pray,
the monk had asked to have his way
with her, and how much it was worth.
170 Her story filled Guillaume with mirth;
he said that not for all the treasure
of Caesar and Nebuchadnezzar
was there a man whom he'd permit
to be carnally intimate
175 with her; he'd sooner beg his bread

& par terre morir de fein.
Quant Idoine l'a entendu
molt belement a respondu:
« Sire, fet ele, qui seüst
180 enging querre que l'en peüst
le sougrestein si decevoir
c'on peüst les deniers avoir,
il m'est avis ce seroit bien.
Il ne s'en clameroit por rien
185 ne a prïor ne a abé. »
Il respont: « N'avez pas gabé!
Ce vodroie je volentiers,
que nos eüson les deniers
par covent qu'il n'en eüst mie
190 a vos charnelment conpaignie.
Il s'en feroit bon entremetre
quel conseil i porrons nos metre.
— Sire, dist el, je l'i metrai.
Or escoutez que je dirai:
195 g'irai au moustier le matin;
droit a l'autel de Seint Martin
m'irai soër & arester.
Se puis au segrestein parler,
je li dirai que o moi vieigne
200 & que le convenant me tiegne
qu'il me pramist—il le tendra,
bien sai. Volentiers i vendra!—
& aport o soi la coroie
trestote pleine de monnoie.
205 — Dame, fet il, or i parra!
Malöest soit qui s'en faudra!
— Voire, fet ele, de ma part.
— Dame, dist il, il est molt tart.
Des or deüson bien penser
210 que nos mengeron a souper.

till hunger made him fall down dead.
When she had heard her husband's side,
the lady graciously replied,
"Husband, if someone could devise
180 how to pull wool over his eyes
and play the friar for a fool
and get the hundred pounds in full,
it would be in our interest,
I think. He'd never dare protest,
185 not to the abbot nor the prior."
He answered, "Well, I swear, you're slier
than I thought! It would be a pleasure
to lay our hands on all that treasure,
provided without fail that he
190 won't need to know you carnally.
To decide on what course we ought
to take, let's give the matter thought."
"Husband," she said, "I've an idea;
listen to what I tell you here.
195 I'll go to church and sit apart in
the chapel honoring Saint Martin
tomorrow early. If I can,
I will accost the sacristan
and let him know that he may come
200 provided that he bring the sum
he promised—oh, he will not fail!
I'm sure he'll come; I know him well!—
but let him have the leather purse in
which the money is on his person."
205 "Wife, we'll see how your plan will serve.
Woe to the one who loses nerve."
"Indeed, I heartily agree."
"It's getting late, Idwaine, and we
would do well now to turn our mind
210 to see what supper we can find."

— Sire, dist el, vos avez droit.
Alez acheter orendroit
tel viande com vos plera. »

Tantost les .x. sous li bailla;
215 Guillaumes est as estaus alez,
pein & char acheta assez,
puis s'en revint a sa meson.
Idoine apela .i. garçon
qu'el avoit envoié au vin
220 & au poivrë & au commin;
li meïsmes fist la savour,
& puis sunt asis; par amour
il menjuent priveement,
eus & li garchon seulement.
225 Quant orent mengié & beü,
puis se coucherent quant tens fu
& beserent & acolerent.
Onques cele nuit ne parlerent
de povreté ne de mesese,
230 qu'il sunt braz a braz molt a ese!
    Au matin, quant il ajorna,
Idoine se vest & chauça.
Quant ele fu apareilliee,
bien afulee & bien liee
235 d'une bele guimple de soie,
droit au moustier a pris sa voie,
mes ençois qu'el i fust entree,
estoit ja la messe chantee
& du moutier la gent issoient
240 qui la messe oïe avoient,
& Idoine passa avant;
droit a Seint Martin meintenant
s'est arestee pour orer.
Le moigne vint abooster
245 pour savoir quant ele vendroit—

"Husband," she said, "that's very true.
Go out right now and buy what you
like most."
                    The monk's coins in his pocket,
Guillaume set off at once for market
215 and bought a quantity of meat
and bread for both of them to eat,
then came back home. His wife, Idwaine,
had sent a boy out to get wine
and caraway and pepper, too,
220 and with those spices she made do
to make a dinner full of flavor,
and then all three sat down to savor
their meal in mutual regard
and love, wife, husband, and the lad.
225 After they drank their wine and ate,
they went to bed, for it was late,
and hugged and kissed like tender lovers,
and all that night under the covers
they didn't speak of want or harm,
230 but lay together arm in arm.
                    When morning came and the sun rose,
Idwaine put on her shoes and clothes,
and when she was completely dressed
and had tied on her very best
235 wimple of silk over her hair,
she set out for the minster, where
about the time that she arrived
they'd finished singing Mass inside
and the assembled congregation
240 was leaving after the oblation.
Idwaine continued on ahead
to Saint Martin's shrine, where she stayed
to make her solitary prayer.
The monk was watching for her there,
245 unsure if she in fact would show.

molt par fu liez quant il la voit!
Il vint avant, si li a dit:
« Molt me grieve vostre respit!
Or me dites vostre corage,
250 car por vos ai el cors la rage,
que je ne bui ne ne menjai
des ier matin qu'a vos parlai. »
El respont: « Ne vos esmaiez,
mes tot asseür en soiez,
255 car enquenuit dedenz mon lit
ferez de moi vostre delit
se vos me tenez covenant. »
Li moigne respont meintenant:
« Dame, dist il, n'en doutez plus
260 que .c. livres n'i port ou plus.
Bien est reson que ges i port,
car se de vos ai le deport,
je ne quier riens plus ne demant,
foi que doi Deu omnipotant! »
265 De ses deniers asez li baille
por acheter de la vitaille;
puis prent congié, si s'en repere,
& cil pense de son afere,
de cerchier boites & aumoires
270 & les escrins as saintuaires
ou la gent ont l'ofrende mise
qui orent oï le servise.
Une coroie en a enplie,
& de ce ne *menti* il mie
275 que bien .c. livres n'i eüst,
& se encor en il peüst,
encore en i eüst mis.
Molt a grant joie li chaitis
encontre sa male aventure!
280 Idoine plus ne s'aseüre
qu'ele n'apareut a mengier.

(He was most glad to see her, though!)
He went straight up to her to say,
"I was distressed at your delay;
let me know quickly how you feel.
250 You can't imagine my ordeal!
I've given up drinking and eating
as of yesterday morning's meeting."
She answers him, "Don't be distressed,
but be assured of all the best,
255 because in bed with me tonight
you'll have full measure of delight,
provided that you bring the cash."
The monk responded in a flash,
"Lady, don't fear on that account.
260 I'll bring at least the full amount!
I wish for nothing else in lieu
of the chance to make love to you,
and I will think the sum well spent,
I swear by God omnipotent!"
265 He gave the lady enough copper
to purchase them a special supper,
and then she said good-bye and left.
The monk now gives thought to his gift
and searches all the monastery
270 chests and even the sanctuary
till, where the faithful congregation
who have heard Mass place their donation.
He fills a belt with what he's rifled,
so you can see he hasn't trifled
275 in promising a hundred pounds,
and if he found more on the grounds
he wouldn't scruple to include it.
Thus joyfully the poor deluded
monk sets off on his peccadillo.
280 Idwaine thinks no more of the fellow
beyond getting some dinner ready.

Guillaumes menja tot premier,
qui en son lit s'ala couchier
por le moigne desbareter,
285 & porte en sa mein .i. gibet
qu'il ot enprunté .i. vallet.

   Quant li moigne de l'abeïe
orent chanté & dit conplie,
el dortor s'alerent couchier;
290 li moigne remest el moustier.
Sachiez qu'il ne se coucha mie,
einz li remenbre de s'amie,
dont s'en issi priveement
par .i. postiz tot coiement,
295 droit a l'ostel Guillaume vet,
ou il avoit basti son plet.
Il vint a l'us, si apela,
& Idoine li desferma,
puis le refeerma aprés lui.
300 Or sunt en la meson andui,
& Guillaumes el lit se jut,
& li moignes menja & but
priveement avec sa drue
qui molt li sera chier vendue.
305 Ele li dist: « Beaus douz amis,
ou est ce que m'avez pramis? »
Le moigne li respont: « Tenez
ceste coroie & la gardez:
il i a .c. livres molt bien,
310 je n'en mentiroie por rien. »
Idoine les va estuier,
puis a veü les le foier
les cles que cil i ot ruees,
desus le banc les ot getees.
315 Idoine fu & bele & gente;
sa beauté le moigne tormente.
Il se leva; croitre la vost

Guillaume ate first; then off to bed he
hurried to carry out their plan
to double-cross the sacristan,
285   in his hand holding a shillelagh
that he had borrowed from a valet.
       When the brothers had finished saying
compline and were all done with praying
and it was time that they retire,
290   the sacristan stayed in the choir.
Of course he didn't go to bed,
but thought about Idwaine instead,
and so he went out stealthily
by a back door in secrecy
295   and hurried off to Guillaume's gate,
where he'd arranged his tête-à-tête.
He reached the house and called out for
Idwaine, who unbolted the door
and closed it again after him.
300   So now the two of them were in
the house, and, off in bed, Guillaume.
The pair sat down to eat alone,
the cleric and his paramour,
whom he would pay most dearly for.
305   She said to him, "Sweetest of charmers,
where is it? Have you kept your promise?"
"Take this," the monk said, and he gave
to her the money belt to have.
"Your hundred pounds are all inside,
310   so, as you see, I haven't lied."
When Idwaine put the belt away
she noticed the monk's keys, which lay
off to the side on a bench placed
beside the hearth, tossed down in haste.
315   She was so graceful and so fair,
he rose to take her then and there;
spurred on by beauty and desire,

de jouste le foier en roust,
quant ele dit: « Por Deu merci,
320 ambedui serïon honi,
que je crien que la gent nos voie
qui trespassent parmi la voie.
En cele chanbre me merrez,
la si ferez vos volentez. »
325 Quant li moignes l'ot, si se lieve—
& sachiez bien que molt li grieve
qu'ele le va si deleant—
en la chanbre entre meintenant,
desor .i. lit la giete enverse.
330 Guillaumes saut a la traverse
& li dist: « Moigne, par Seint Pol,
sachiez que je vos tieng por fol,
qui ma fame honir volez!
Molt seroie mal eürez
335 se ainsi le vos consentoie—
ja puis Damle Deu ne le voie
qui ja le vos consentira! »
Li moigne l'ot, si se leva;
prendre le volt, mes cil li done
340 tel coup du gibet qu'il l'estone,
& quant il l'ot si estoné,
Guillaumes a son coup recovré
& le refiert el haterel
si que il li espant le cervel,
345 & li moignes chaï atant.
Isi va fol sa mort querant.
  Quant Idoine le vit morir,
du cuer a geté .i. soupir:
« Lasse! cheitive! fet Idoine,
350 car fuse je en Babiloine!
Doulereuse! mal eüree!
mar fuse je de mere nee
quant por moi est basti tel plet!

he'd spit her right before the fire.
"For God's sake," she objected, "we
320   must give some thought to modesty.
What we do here might catch the eye,
I fear, of any passersby.
Come to my room. In privacy
I'll let you have your will of me."
325   The monk hears and gets to his feet,
more than a little peeved to meet
all this resistance and delay,
and goes to the room straightaway,
where down across the bed he throws
330   her. Guillaume, quick to interpose,
jumps up and cries, "Monk, by Saint Paul,
in my opinion you're a fool
to bring dishonor on my wife!
I would regret it all my life
335   if I should let it be committed.
May God on high never permit it
and curse the man who gives consent!"
The monk gets up with the intent
of grabbing him, but he comes down
340   so hard with the club on his crown,
he leaves him stunned, and then he swings
at him a second time and brings
it down behind his neck with full
force and splits open the monk's skull,
345   and he falls dead upon the spot.
The fly drowns in the honey pot.
       When Idwaine saw the cleric die,
she gasped and heaved a heartfelt sigh.
"My God, we're lost!" she babbled on,
350   "I wish I was in Babylon!
I'm the most wretched one on earth!
Why did my mother give me birth
that by my doing this should come

Guillaumes, pour qu'as tu ce fet?
355 — Dame, dist il, je le doutoie
por ce que si grant le veoie,
que il ne me preïst as braz.
Amïez vos dont son soulaz
entre vos jambes a sentir?
360 Or n'i a mes que du fuïr
& d'aler en estrange terre,
si loinz c'on ne nos sache ou querre!
— Sire, dist el, nos ne poon,
si vos dirai par quel reson:
365 les portes du bourc sunt fermees
& les gaites en haut montees. »
Cele pleure, Guillaumes pense—
molt remeint de ce que fol pense.
Quant Guillaumes ot .i. poi pensé,
370 son chief drece, si a parlé
& dit: « Idoine, bele amie,
par ou vint il de l'abeïe?
— Sire, dist el, par le postiz
qui est devers le roilleïz.
375 Je vis or les cles sor le banc. »
Guillaumes a pris .i. drapel blanc,
s'a au moigne le chief bendé
& puis l'a a son col levé;
atot le moigne s'en torna,
380 & dame Idoine aprés ala.
Qui li deüst couper la geule,
ne remeinsist iluecques seule!—
einz s'asit sor une fenestre.
De ce fu Guillaumes bon mestre
385 qu'il est droit au postiz venuz
par ou li moignes fu venuz;
il le mist jus, puis desferma
le postiz, puis le recharja.
Guillaumes entre en .i. sentier

to pass? Guillaume, why have you done
355   this?" "Lady, from anxiety
that he would get his hands on me,
seeing how big he was. I trust
you didn't wish to feel his lust
between your legs? All we can do
360   now is run off and escape to
some foreign land so very far
that no one will know where we are."
"Husband," she said, "how can we fly
from here? You know the reason why:
365   The gates are shut; they've posted sentries
who challenge all exits and entries."
She wept and wailed while Guillaume thought.
      A foolish plan will come to naught.
After a little more reflection,
370   he looked up and made this suggestion:
"Do you know by what way he came
here from the abbey, dear Idwaine?"
"He went out by the postern door
beside the log-rail fence. I saw
375   his keys on the bench by the hearth."
Guillaume took a piece of white cloth
to bind the cleric's wounded skull
and put him on his back to haul
him off and went out, while Idwaine
380   followed close by. She'd not remain
alone inside there, where he'd smote
him dead—she'd sooner slit her throat!
She sat by the window instead,
while Guillaume kept a level head
385   and went straight to the postern gate
the way the monk had come of late,
put down the corpse, unlocked the door,
then lifted it up as before
and followed down a path that led

par ou li moigne vont pissier,   390
tout droit a la chanbre s'en entre
ou l'en garist du mal du ventre,
puis l'asist au premier pertus,
& puis a regardé vers l'us.
.i. fet de fein i vit gesir   395
de quoi li moigne au departir
de la chambre terdent lor reins;
Guillaumes ne fu pas vileins:
.i. torchon fist, si li bouta
dedenz son poing, puis s'en torna   400
parmi le funz d'une viez rue;
tel poor a que tot tressue.
Idoine, sa fame, a trovee,
qui forment est espöentee;
andui en lour ostel entrerent   405
& durement se conforterent:
bien cuident estre delivré
du moigne qu'il orent tüé.

Li moigne siet geule baee
qui ot reçut male colee,   410
& li autre sunt en dortour.
En .i. lit les le refretour
jut le priour de l'abeïe;
trop ot mengié, si ne pot mie
plus demorer que il n'alast   415
en aucun leu ou se vidast.
Atant en la chanbre entra,
au premier pertus qu'il trova
s'est aresté por lui widier,
lors se commence a escourcier;   420
son chief drece, si a veü
le sougrestein qui tüé fu,
qui ne movoit ne pié ne mein.
« Ahi! dist il, com est vilein
li sougrestein qui ci se dort!   425

390 to the communal toilet shed
where the monks went to urinate
or to relieve their tummy ache.
He seated him in the first stall;
then, looking toward the entrance wall,
395 he spied a bundle of dry grass
with which the brothers wiped their ass
after they'd obeyed Nature's call.
Guillaume was really on the ball:
He took a handful, gave a twist,
400 and stuck it in the cleric's fist;
then taking a deserted street
he hurried home, all in a sweat.
Idwaine was waiting for him there,
just about to collapse from fear.
405 They went back in their domicile
and did their best to try to smile,
believing they were now delivered
of the monk whose skull they had slivered.
    The monk who had sustained the blow
410 sat on the pot, jaw hanging low;
the other brothers lay in slumber.
Near where they ate, one of their number
had his bed. He was the abbey's prior,
who'd overeaten and had dire
415 need to go out and defecate;
in fact, he didn't dare to wait.
No sooner had he reached the privies,
he started to remove his skivvies
at the first toilet in the john,
420 sensing his movement coming on.
He looked up and found that place filled
by the sacristan who'd been killed
and sat there quite immobilized.
"Disgusting!" he exclaimed, surprised.
425 "The sacristan sleeps in the loo!

S'il le conpere n'est pas tort
demein quant seron en chapistre.
S'il eüst failli a l'ipistre
n'eüst il mie plus mesfet! »
430   Por esveillier signe li fet:
« Dant sougrestein, dist le priour,
mieus vos venist ore en dortour
dormir que en ceste longaigne!
Honie soit vostre gaaigne
435   qui si vos a grant honte fete!
Ençois me fust la cuise frete
& le cors ars en .i. chaut feu
que je dormise en si vil lieu! »
Quant il ot fet ce que il quist,
440   par le sougrestein vient, si dist:
« Dant sougrestein, esveilliez vos! »
& cil qui fu morz a estrous
si est chaü tot a travers
seur l'es de la privee envers.
445   Quant li prieur chaer le vit:
« Qu'est ce, por le Seint Esperit?
fet il. Est dont cest moigne mort?
Or avoie ge molt grant tort
quant je de lui m'entremetoie;
450   *je mar venisse* hui ceste voie!
Dieus! com me porrai conseillier?
Il tença molt a moi l'autrier
& je a lui, c'est verité.
Or dira l'en devant l'abé
455   qu'en traïson l'avrai murdri! »
Touz fu li prieur esbahi;
porpensa soi, ne set que fere
comment en porroit a chief trere;
dont dist que *il* le porteroit
460   dedenz le bourc & le leroit
a l'us a aucune bourjoise,

I'll see he's punished for it, too,
tomorrow at the chapter meeting.
Had he dozed off during the reading,
it wouldn't be a graver sin!"
430 He signaled to the sacristan
to wake him up and told him, "Father,
sleep in the dormitory rather
than make your bed in the latrine!
What kind of shameful and unclean
435 misdeeds have placed you in here? I
would sooner let them break my thigh
and roast me over burning coal
than fall asleep in such a hole!"
      When he had finished in the can,
440 he went to wake the sacristan
and said, "Get up now, sleepyhead!"
and he, who actually was dead,
fell upside down that very minute
across the plank with the hole in it,
445 and when the prior saw him totter,
he cried, "Dear Lord! What is the matter?
Can this good confrere be deceased?
If so, I acted like a beast
when I gave him a talking-to!
450 It was an evil wind that blew
me here! What can I do about
it? We two had a falling-out
the day before, and each ill used
the other. Now I'll be accused
455 of his murder before the abbot!"
The prior, frightened as a rabbit,
racked his brain to think up devices
whereby to remedy the crisis,
and hit on carrying the corpse
460 to town and then dumping it off
before some charming woman's door,

la plus bele, la plus courtoise
qui soit en tot le tenement,
si diront au matin la gent
465   qu'iluecques l'avra l'on tüé.
Dont a le moigne remüé,
a son col le lieve tot droit
& en aprés si s'en tornoit,
sel porte droit a la meson
470   ou li moigne prist la poison
dont *ja mais nul jor ne garra*;
[a l'uis Ydoine l'apoia,
puis lo gerpi, si s'an depart].
Or pri Guillaume qu' il se gart,
475   que s'en l'i trueve le matin,
je quit qu'il iert pres de sa fin!

       Guillaumes & Idoine se jurent,
qui forment espouenté furent,
& se confortent bonement,
480   quant une boufee de vent
s'est es dras le moigne ferue,
qui tot le soulieve & remue;
a la porte le fet hurter.
Dist Idoine: « Por seint Omer,
485   sire Guillaume, levez sus!
Il a ne sé qui a nostre us.
Molt nos a anuit aguetiez! »
Atant s'est Guillaumes dreciez,
son gibet prent inellement,
490   a l'us s'en vient hastivement;
molt vistement fu desfermez,
& li moignes qui fu tuez
li est cheü sus la poitrine
& Guillaumes chiet sor l'eschine.
495   Quant Guillaumes se sent cheü,
molt se merveille qui ce fu;
a haute voiz sa fame escrie:

the fairest in the district, for
the people would be bound to say
when someone found it the next day
465 that those who lived there killed the monk.
He grabbed his confrere by the trunk
and hoisted him up on his back
and turned and carried him straight back
to that same house where this Lord's vicar
470 had had a taste of that strong liquor
which he'll recover from no more,
and propped him up by Idwaine's door
and left him there and went back home.
Unless he's careful now, Guillaume
475 is like to lose his life, I gather,
should someone find the monk's cadaver.
     Guillaume and Idwaine in their bed,
gripped by an overwhelming dread,
tried to put each other at ease
480 when a strong gust of nighttime breeze
caught the monk's habit like a kite,
lifted him up, and blew him right
against their front door with a thump.
Idwaine said, "Guillaume, husband, jump
485 up quickly, by Saint Omer, for
there's someone knocking at our door.
I fear we've been spied on tonight!"
Guillaume got up and hurried right
to where the club lay, and he took
490 it and ran to the door to look
and in a flash drew back the lock,
and the dead monk, much to his shock,
fell onto his chest through the door,
knocking him backward on the floor.
495 When Guillaume senses he has fallen,
in a loud voice he begins calling,
wondering who this man could be,

« Idoine! fet il, car m'aïe!
Ne sai qui est sor moi chaest!
500   De Dieu soie ge malöest,
se ce est hons, se je nel tue! »
Idoine saut trestote nue,
au feu corut, si l'aluma;
le moigne vit & regarda:
505   « Guillaume! nos sommes traï!
[C'est li sogretains qui gist ci!]
— Dame, dist il, vos dites voir!
Malöest soit mavés savoir
& covoitise & traïson,
510   qu'il n'en puet venir se mal non!
— Dont est il mort? — Certes, oïl. »
Molt se merveille cele & cil
& dïent bien que c'est maufé
qu'iluecques le rout aporté.
515   Guillaumes le prent derechief,
& Idoine li baille .i. brief
ou li non Dieu furent escrit,
& il molt volentiers le prist,
car molt durement s'i fia;
520   atout le moigne s'en torna
tant que il vint sour le femier
sire Tibout le *moitoier*,
qui les blez as moignes gardot
& des deniers avoit plein pot
525   & d'autre richesce plenté.
.i. grant bacon avoit tüé
d'un porc qu'il ot en sa meson
encressié tote la seson,
si l'ot pendu pour essuier.
530   Emblé li ot .i. pautonnier
Le[ ] soir devant & mucié l'ot
dedenz le femier dant Tibout.
(Encore n'en savoit autre essoigne.)

"Idwaine! I need help! Come to me!
I don't know who has knocked me over,
500   but, help me God, when I recover,
if it's a man, I'll do him in."
Idwaine jumps up in just her skin,
runs to the hearth and starts to fan
the coals, and sees the sacristan.
505   "Guillaume, it's he!" he hears her shout.
"The sacristan! We've been found out!"
"You're right, lady! He's the one! Yes!
I curse our wicked cleverness,
our avarice and our sedition!
510   They'll only lead to our perdition."
"Is he still dead, then?" "Very, yes."
Nor he nor she can start to guess
how he got there; the Evil One it
must have been, they say, who's done it.

515   He seizes the corpse; thereupon
Idwaine gives him a parchment on
which God's most holy names are writ,
and Guillaume takes the amulet,
for in its strength he has great trust.
520   Setting off with the cleric trussed
up on his back, he came to stand
by Tibaut's yard, who farmed some land
the abbey owned and kept their store
of wheat, and had a chest or more
525   packed full of coins and was well-heeled.
It happened that Tibaut had killed
a pig he'd fattened in his sty
all season and had hung to dry
the side of pork up in his pantry.
530   That night a robber had gained entry,
stolen the meat, and hid it deep
in Master Tibaut's compost heap,
having no better place to stow't.

Guillaumes, qui portoit le moigne,
535 s'est *sour* le femier aresté.
     Sachoiz que molt estoit lassé
     de lui porter parmi la vile.
     Il se porpense par quel guile
     il s'en porra mieus delivrer:
540 el femier le vout enterrer
     dedenz le fiens & le lera.
     Atant le moigne mis jus a,
     .i. grant crués i fet a sa mein
     por enfoïr le sougrestein,
545 *le sac trouva ou le larron*
     avoit enfoui le bacon;
     puis le commence a deslïer;
     la couane vit [ ] nerçoier.
     Ce dit Guillaumes: « Tot por voir,
550 ci a .i. autre moigne noir,
     qui molt nercie, ce me semble!
     Or les metrai andui ensenble. »
     Fere le vot, mes il ne pot:
     « Qu'est ce, por le baron seint Lot? »
555 fet Guillaumes, si n'i porra.
     Lors se porpense qu'il verra
     quel moigne c'est qui est tüé,
     dont a le bacon remüé:
     « Dieus aïe! fet il, ce est char!
560 Or n'ai pas perdu tot mon char
     qu'en la forest me fu enblez—
     or ai char & deniers assez! »
     Le moigne dedenz le sac met
     & du courir molt s'entremet;
565 autresi com il fu devant
     o le bacon s'en va corant,
     vers son ostel est retorné.
     Quant sa fame *lo vit trossé,*
     si dist: « Rest ce le sougrestein?

Guillaume came carrying his load
535 of monk and stopped beside the pile.
He'd toted him a weary mile
across town and was now exhausted,
and gave some thought how he might foist it
off somehow and at last be rid
540 of it. It struck him, if he hid
it in the compost, he'd be free.
Unloading the cadaver, he
with his bare hands scraped out a wide,
deep hole where he proposed to hide
545 the monk, and found the sack in which
the robber had wrapped up the flitch,
and when he started to unbind
the sack, he saw the blackened rind
and said, "I do believe this sack
550 contains another Cluniac,
his skin much blackened by the weather.
I'll put the two of them together."
He tries to do so but cannot.
"What's this," he wonders, "by Saint Lot?"
555 He tries, but without much success,
and then, since he is curious,
he looks to see what monk's been killed
and finds instead the sack is filled
with cured pork. "God be praised! It's meat!
560 Now we have wealth and food to eat!
It's like I'd never lost the goods
the thieves took from me in the woods."
He stuffs his monk into the sack
and quickly turns and hurries back
565 by the same path he has just taken,
and thus Guillaume brings home the bacon.
When she saw him approach the house
still carrying a load, his spouse
cries, "Not that sacristan again!"

570   — Nenil, dame, par seint Germein,
       einz est .i. bacon gras & gros.
       Nos avon char; querez des chos! »
              Celi qui le bacon ot pris
       ches dant Tibout, si com je dis,
575   en une taverne joout;
       vin ot asez, boivre ne pout,
       puis a dit a ses conpaignons:
       « Seignors, dist il, quel la ferons?
       Je croi bien se nos eüson
580   charbonee d'un cras bacon
       que nos en beüsson molt mieus! »
       Chascun li respont: « Par mes ieus,
       beaus douz frere, vos dites voir,
       mes nos n'en paons point avoir,
585   car couchié se sunt li bouchier.
       Par foi, si n'avon nul denier!
       — Seignors, dist il, je en ai .i.
       que je vos metrai en commun;
       molt lieement le vos donrai.
590   Gras est & gros, & si l'emblai
       ches dant Tibout le *metoier*,
       mes jel muçai en .i. fumier.
       — Va le querre! font il, esploite! »
       Cil qui meinte chose ot toleite
595   s'en est droit au femier alé
       ou il ot le bacon bouté,
       a son col le moigne leva,
       en la taverne le porta.
       Chascun dit: « Vez ci chose bone! »
600   & cil a geté jus sa somme,
       puis leur a dit: « Seignors, molt poise! »
       Atant ont apelé Cortoise,
       la chanberiere de l'ostel:
       « Diva, font il, ou a nul pel?—
605   nos volon fere charbonees.

570 "No, lady, no, by Saint Germain—
a side of pork, large, fat, and sweet!
Go get the cabbage; we have meat!"
　　　　The man I told you of, who'd taken
from Tibaut's house the side of bacon,
575 was gambling at a hostelry.
Though there was wine in plenty, he
just couldn't drink, and so he shouted,
"Hey, mates, what shall we do about it?
It seems to me that if we had
580 a freshly grilled fat bacon slab,
we'd have more of a taste for drinking!"
"Yes, damn my eyes, now there's good thinking,
good buddy!" all of them agreed.
"But how can we get what we need?
585 All of the butcher shops are shut
and not a penny have we got."
"But I have got one," said the snitch,
"and I'll be glad to share my flitch.
It's big and fat, stolen, you know,
590 from the monks' sharecropper, Tibaut,
and safely stowed. If you wish, I'll
retrieve it from his compost pile."
"Well, go and get it! Quickly bring us
the meat!" The man with sticky fingers
595 went straight off to the compost heap
where he had put the pork to keep,
and, shouldering the sacristan,
he came back to the inn again.
"Good grub!" they said when he came back,
600 and he was glad to drop the sack,
remarking, "Boy, this weighs a ton!"
They called the tavern maid: "Come on,
Cortoise, and help us! Step on it!
You know where we can find a spit
605 to grill some pork? That's what we mean

Sont tes escuielles lavees?
Esploite tost, & nos iron
querre buche ci environ. »
Ele fet lour commandement,
610 & cil s'en vont inelement
tot droitement a .i. paliz
ou il avoit grant pieus fentiz.
Chascun a le sien esraché,
puis sunt ariere reperé,
615 s'ont demandé une coignie;
ele lour fu molt tost baillie.
Cele ot sa paelle lavee;
au sac estoit corant alee,
puis le deslie comme sote,
620 le moigne sesi par la bote,
trenchier en volt, mes el ne puet.
« Vez com cele garce se muet!
font li larron. El ne fet rien! »
La beasse les entent bien,
625 dont respont: « Par seint Lïenart,
cest bacon est plus dur que hart!
Si est chauciez, ce m'est avis! »
Chascun s'en est en piez saillis:
« Chaucié? funt il, & il comment? »
630 Cele lor moutre apertement
le moigne qui el sac estoit,
& cil qui aporté l'avoit
s'est ne sé quantes fois saigniés.
« Garnot, ce dit li taverniers,
635 por quoi as tu cel moigne mort?
— Sire, dist il, vos avez tort!
Onques par tous seins nel touchai,
mes c'est deable, bien le sai,
qui *a fet moine* de bacon.
640 Se Deus me doint confessïon,
ce fu .i. bacon que je pris!

to do! Say, are your dishes clean?
Be quick! And we'll find sticks of wood
lying around the neighborhood."
While Cortoise followed their commands,
610 they rushed directly to a fence
where every one of them could pick
out his personal toasting stick.
They ripped out what pickets they needed
and to the inn again proceeded,
615 where they requested they provide
an ax to split them; she complied.

When she had washed her frying pan,
straight to the sack the barmaid ran,
then, like a silly goose, untied
620 the sack, grabbed the monk's boot, and tried
to carve it, but it was too tough.
"That maid don't move half fast enough,"
the thieves say. "Nothing's getting done."
She says, hearing them harping on
625 her slowness, "By Saint Léonard,
it's like a rope, this meat's so hard!
I also think it's wearing shoes."
They jump to their feet at the news.
"Shoes?" they exclaim. "How can that be?"
630 Cortoise then shows them openly
the sacristan stuffed in the sack,
and the one who had brought him back
crossed himself countless times in dread.
"Garnot," the tavern keeper said,
635 "you've killed a monk! Now tell us why."
"No, sir," he said, "it wasn't I!
For sure it was the Devil's work
to make a monk from salted pork!
I never laid a hand on him,
640 by all the saints! Forgive my sin,
dear God, but what I took was bacon.

Or s'est deable en guise mis
du moigne por nos enconbrer,
mes bien vos en quit delivrer:
645 jel porteré ches dant Tibout.
—Va dont! funt il, esploite tost,
& si le pent droit au chevron
la ou tu ostas le bacon!
— Si ferai ge, par seint Denis! »
650 Adonques ra le moigne pris;
desor son col li ont levé.
Ez le vos el chemin entré,
puis a veü en .i. cortil
jesir .i. grant vieil charetil,
655 encontre la meson le drece,
& Garnot a monter s'adrece
droit au pertus qu'il avoit fet,
par la ou ot le bacon tret
puis l'a bien droit parmi bouté
660 & a la hart l'a bien nöé
par mi le col & fermement,
a terre s'en vient vistement;
en la taverne est retorné,
a ses conpaignons a conté
665 com il a le moigne pendu
a la hart ou le bacon fu.
        Des larrons vos lerai ester,
du *vilain vos vorrai* conter
qui gesoit avoit sa moillier;
670 ele commence a esveillier.
« Sire, dist el, ja iert matin
& bien tens d'aler au molin,
que nos n'avos mes que .ii. peins.
— Dame, ce respont li vileins,
675 je sui malade tier jor a.
Esveilliez Martin, si ira,

No doubt the Devil must have taken
the monk's shape to give us a fright,
but I think I can set things right.
645 I'll carry him back to Tibaut's."
"Then hurry! There's no time to lose.
On that same rafter hang the bacon
from which you took it at the break-in."
"Well, by Saint Dennis, here I go!"
650 Once more he took the monk in tow;
all helped lift the sack back in place.
No sooner back at Tibaut's place,
there in a pen the robber came
on an abandoned carriage frame.
655 Against the house he propped it up,
by which means Garnot climbed on top
of the roof, where he'd made a hole
the time that he broke in and stole
the pork, and when he'd pushed it through,
660 he used a rope to tie him to
the beam, knotted around his neck,
got off the roof, and ran like heck
back to the tavern, where his friends
heard how he'd tied up the loose ends
665 and left the monk a-dangling from
the beam from which the pork had come.
        I'll say no more of the thieves and
speak of the brothers' farming hand
and his wife. He lay next to her
670 in bed, and she began to stir.
"Husband," she said, "soon morning will
break and you must go to the mill.
We only have two loaves of bread."
"Wife, I shall not," the peasant said.
675 "I've been ill for three days or so.
Wake Martin up, and let him go,

[ce mercherot qui chascun mois
couche ceens .ii. fois ou .iii.],
& si li prametez tortel.
680 — Sire, dist ele, ce m'est bel.
Martinet, dist el, lieve toi.
— Dame, dist il, & je por quoi?
— Au molin te covient aler.
— Avoi, dame! or du gaber!
685 Quant tuastes vostre porcel
de fressure ne de bouel
ne m'esforchastes de mengier.
Sui ge ore en vostre dangier
por ce se gis en vostre estrain?
690 En cest païs n'a pas vilein
qui assez plus ne m'en prestast
& volentiers ne m'en donast
tot autresi c'on ceanz fet.
— Martin, fet el, or ne fei plet.
695 Se je te don de mon bacon
charbonnee sor le charbon
& du pein a desgeüner,
porroie je vers toi trover
que tu feïses ma proiere?
700 — Dame, fet il, a bele chiere
ferai lors quant que vos vodrois.
— Martin, fet ele, c'est bien drois
que *tun* aies, si aras tu. »
Du coute a son mari feru:
705 — Sire, fet ele, sus levez!
Alez au bacon, si coupez
une charbonee a Martin
& puis si ira au molin. »
Le vilein monte en son cenail:
710 « Par ou veus tu que je t'en tail?
— Sire, par ou ou bon vos iert.

that little haberdasher who
each month stays here a day or two.
Just promise him a loaf of bread."
680 "That's fine with me," the woman said.
"Little Martin, get up already!"
He answered her, "Why should I, lady?"
"I need you to go to the mill."
"You must be joking! First you kill
685 your hog and don't give me a taste
of chitterlings, then say, posthaste,
that I should go and do your chores!
Am I your servant just because
you let me lie down on your straw?
690 Why, the first peasant that I saw
around here would have willingly
given me more and treated me
at least as well as any here!"
"Martin, don't give me a full ear.
695 If I should let you grill a whole
slab of my bacon on the coal
to breakfast on, and also bread,
then do you think you could be led
to do for me as I've requested?"
700 "In that case I'd be interested,
lady, and do it with good grace."
"Martin," she told him, "in that case
you'll have some, as is only fitting."
Then she said to her husband, hitting
705 him with her elbow, "Sir, arise,
go get the bacon, cut a slice
for Martin's breakfast, and he will
go run our errand at the mill."
        The peasant goes up to his larder
710 and asks exactly from what quarter
he wants it cut. "From where you please.

Fous est qui de ce conseil quiert—
plus est il vostre qu'il n'est mien.
— Par foi, dist Tibout, tu dis bien.
715 Esclere le feu, si verré.
— Par ma foi, sire, non feré,
que vos savez bien ou il pent. »
& li vileins sa mein i tent;
qui cuida prendre son bacon
720 le moigne prent par le talon.
Prendre en volt une charbonnee
(la hart fu seiche & enfumee)
quant ele ront, si est cheü,
mes dant Tibout a si feru
725 desor le chief qu'il le trebuche
desus le fonz d'une vielz huche.
Quant dant Tibout cheü se sent,
« [Martinet! escrie forment.]
Martinet! fet il, lieve toi!
730 Le bacon est cheü sor moi. »
Atant Martinet se leva,
au feu corut, si l'aluma;
le moigne voit tot requisniez,
plus de .xxx. foiz s'est seigniez:
735 « Sire, sire, ce dist Martin,
par la foi que doi seint Martin,
n'est pas bacon, einz est maufez,
qu'il senble moigne coronnez,
si est chaucié, se Deus me saut.
740 Li bacons qui pendoit en haut
n'est mie; perdu l'avon.
Nos avon moigne por bacon!
— Las! dist Tibout, or sui ge mort!
Demain serai pendu *a tort*,
745 que tot le mont dira demein
que j'avrai mort le sougrestein!
— Sire, sire, dist Martinet,

What kind of questions, sir, are these?
It isn't my pig, as you know."
"In faith, you're right," responds Tibaut.
715   "Stir up the hearth to give me light."
"Indeed I won't, for you know right
where it's hanging." He goes to feel
around for it and grabs the heel
of the monk, which, there in the dark,
720   he takes to be the side of pork.
He means to cut a rasher, but it
(the rope, that is) is dry and rotted
from smoke, and so it breaks in two
and falls on Tibaut's noggin, who
725   gets knocked over and tumbles in-
to an old unused kneading bin.
When Tibaut senses he has fallen,
he gives a shout and starts in calling,
"Martin! Get up! Give me a hand!
730   The pork has fallen on me!" And
Martin got up and ran apace
to stoke the coals in the fireplace
and saw the monk stiff as a board,
crossed himself, and called on the Lord
735   some thirty times or more. "By Saint
Martin," he said, "why, sir, this ain't
a side of pork, but it's a devil!
May God protect me from this evil,
it looks more like a tonsured monk
740   dead with his boots on, while our hunk
of pork has disappeared, been taken,
and we have monk in place of bacon!"
"Alas," says Tibaut, "I'm undone!
They'll hang me, because everyone
745   will say tomorrow, to a man,
that I have killed the sacristan!"
"Sir," Martin tells him, "let me speak.

dementer n'i vaut .i. poret.
Porpensez vos en quel maniere
750 le moigne soit portez ariere
a l'abeïe dont il mut.
Penduz fust il or a .i. [fust]
ou la defors a .i. booull
qui nos a mis en tel triboul!
755 — Martinet, ce dit le vilein,
va, si m'ameine mon polein:
se j'ai le moigne dont lïer,
je quit, j'en ferai chevalier. »
Martinet le polein ameine;
760 de lui lïer molt bien se peine
es arçons molt estroitement.
Ce dit Martin: « Par seint Climent,
je vois une lance aporter,
& puis si ira bohorder
765 laïs aval en cele court,
& vos crïez quel part qu'il tourt:
'Harou! harou! le sougrestein
en meine a force mon polein!' »
Dont est le polein fors boutez,
770 & le vilein s'est escrïez:
« Harou! harou! » molt hautement.
Aprés le moigne en vont tieus cent
qu'il quident bien qu'il soit desvé,
& li poleins a tant alé
775 que il est entré en la porte.
Le sougrestein qui l'escu porte
a le soupriour encontré,
qui estoit trop matin levé,
puis le feri si de la lance
780 que jus du palefroi le lance,
que il s'en merveillerent tuit
& escrïent tuit a .i. bruit:

Your fretting isn't worth a leek;
instead you ought to be concerned
750 with how to get the monk returned
back to the abbey whence he came.
The person who thought up this game
deserves to be hanged from a birch
or any handy nearby perch!"
755 Tibaut replied, "Martin, my crony,
go to the barn and fetch my pony.
If there's some way he can be tied
on top, I'll send him for a ride."
      He brings the pony from the stable,
760 and Tibaut does all he is able
to strap him to the saddle bow,
and Martin tells him, "I will go
and get a lance, by Saint Clément,
to send him on a tournament
765 outside, down over in the yard,
while you pursue him, yelling hard,
'Haroo! The sacristan's got hold
of and has run off with my colt!'"
They pushed pony and monk outside;
770 Tibaut ran after them and cried
with all his might, "Haroo! Haroo!"
joined by some hundred people who
were sure the monk had gone insane.
The pony ran until it came
775 to the abbey and rode on in.
The fully armored sacristan
came charging down on the subprior.
Had he slept till the sun was higher,
he'd not have been struck with the lance
780 and thrown beneath the sacristan's
horse. Everybody was amazed
and cried, "The sacristan is crazed!

« Mal eürez, fuiez! fuiez!
Li sougrestein est forsenez!
785 Qui l'atendra ja sera mort! »
Onques n'i ot foible ne fort
qu'iluecques vosist demorer;
el moustier se vont enserrer
& li poleins saut es cuisines:
790 depeçant va ces ofecines,
ces escuielles, ces mortiers
& ces plateaus & ces doubliers;
l'escu fet hurter as paroiz
en .i. randon plus de .c. foiz
795 tant que la lance est peçoïe.
Tote la noise est abessie,
& li poleins a tant alé
qu'il est venuz a .i. fossé,
puis se force par tel aïr
800 por le grant fossé tressaillir
que totes les cengles deront.
Ambedui chieent en .i. mont
enz el fonz du fossé aval,
& li moignes & li cheval.
805 A cros de fer l'en ont fors tret.
Le moigne ne crie ne bret,
que piecha que tüez estoit.
Einsi ot Guillaumes son droit
du moigne qui par son avoir
810 cuida sa fame decevoir,
le bacon ot & les .c. livres.
Einsi fu du moigne delivres
que onques puis blasmé n'en fu,
mes dant Tibout i ot perdu
815 & son bacon & son polein.
Einsi fu mort le sougrestein.

Woe to us all! Head for the hills!
Whoever waits around, he kills!"

785   There was nobody in the throng
who dared to stay. Both weak and strong
seek shelter in the sanctuary,
while all throughout the monastery
the colt wreaks havoc: He invades
790   the kitchens, smashing all the plates,
mortars and pestles, platters, too;
the tablecloths get all ripped through;
the shield goes crash against the wall
more than a hundred times in all
795   until the lance shatters in pieces
and all the noise and chaos ceases.
The colt then breaks out, upon which
it gallops straight on toward a ditch,
and, from the effort that it makes
800   to clear it, every last strap breaks,
so when he takes a mighty leap,
the two of them in one big heap
fall straight into the ditch, kerplunk!,
both Tibaut's horse and the dead monk.
805   They use a hook to fish him out,
but the monk doesn't cry or shout,
since he was killed way in advance.

        Thus Guillaume had his recompense
from the monk who tried for a price
810   to have his wife indulge his vice:
revenge, a hundred pounds, and meat.
He dumped the monk off and was freed
from even the least hint of blame,
but in the process Tibaut came
815   to lose both pork and colt. Such, then,
was the end of the sacristan.

Ma paine vueil metre & ma cure
en raconter une aventure
de sire Constant du Hamel—
or en escoutez le fablel—
5   & de dame Ysabiau, sa fame
qui molt estoit cortoise dame
& preus & sage & avenant;
el païs n'avoit si vaillant,
tant covoitie a decevoir.

10   Li prestres i mist son pooir
a li requerre de s'amor;
ensanble o li parla maint jor,
si la requist de druerie
& dist se devenoit s'amie,
15   il li donroit assez joiaus,
fermaus, çaintures & aniaus,
& deniers assez a despendre,
mes la dame n'en vout nus prendre,
ainz dist que ja par covoitise
20   ne fera au prestre servise
por tant qu'ele en doie estre pire,
puis dist: « Sire, j'ai oï dire
que se vostre soingnant estoie,
l'amor de Dieu en perderoie.
25   Je sui cele qui vous en faut. »
Li prestres sovent la rassaut,
si la prie bel & li offre
.xx. livres qu'il a en son coffre,
mes il la trueve si repointe,
30   guetant & escoutant & cointe
& felonesse a entamer
que il n'i puet rien conquester.
Molt est dolenz quant il s'en part;

55. CONSTANT DU HAMEL

I'll put my effort and my thought
into the telling of a short
tale about Constant du Hamel—
now lend an ear and listen well!—
5   and Goody Ysabel, his wife,
who led a decent, virtuous life,
a woman fair, genteel, and gracious.
None in the shire roused such salacious
thoughts in men, who would seduce her.
10   The priest, in order to induce her
to grant her favors, did his best.
Day in, day out he would request
her love to get her into bed.
If only she'd be his, he said,
15   he'd give her many lovely things,
jewels and buckles, clasps and rings,
and all the money she could use.
The woman hastened to refuse
and said that never out of greed
20   would she service the cleric's need
no matter what mischief befell
her. She said, "Father, I've heard tell
that were I to become your bawd,
I'd lose the love of God our Lord.
25   I'm one catch that will get away."
The cleric returns to the fray
and presses her and even offers
twenty pounds sterling from his coffers,
but he finds her so very hard,
30   alert and wary and on guard,
and so averse to his request
that he's no hope of her conquest.
He goes away; great is his sorrow;

malement est blecié du dart
35 d'Amors, qui l'a ou cors navré
&l'a si durement hurté
que d'angoisse tressue & gient;
a quel que paine a l'ostel vient;
poi li a value sa guile.
40   Oiez du provost de la vile,
qui les prisons a en baillie.
Icil a la dame essaïe,
se li fet .i. cembel novel
por ce qu'ele se porte bel
45 & qu'il l'a vit bel & cortoise:
« Ha, dame, fet il, molt me poise
que cil vilains vous a en garde.
Maus feus & male flanbe m'arde
se je estoie comme vous
50 se je ne le fesoie cous,
qu'il est plus aspres c'une ronsce!
Mieus vaut de mon solaz une once
que du sien ne fet une livre,
que je sui plaisanz & delivres
55 *&* il est gros & malostrus,
il n'est sovent rez ne tondus,
ainz est & ors & deslavez;
mes se vous croire me volez,
je serai voz amis delivres,
60 si vous donrai du mien .x. livres
por consentir ma volenté. »
& la dame l'a regardé,
se li dist: « Sire, ne puet estre.
Je voudroie mieus estre a nestre
65 que je feïsse tel outrage!
Bien avez or el cors la rage
qui me volez issi honir;
certes, mieus voudroie morir
que j'eüsse fet itel saut.

he's sorely wounded by the arrow
35 of Love, deep in his body stuck,
which most distressingly has struck
him. Longing makes him sweat and moan;
in torment he drags himself home.
His trickery has let him down.
40   Hear of the magistrate in town,
who's master of the prison's vaults.
He, too, made numerous assaults
to dun the woman to submission,
seeing she was in prime condition
45 and likewise gracious and well-bred.
"It grieves me, lady," the man said,
"that you belong to such a clod!
If I tell lies, let me be charred
by Hell's own fire! If I were you
50 I'd cuckold him, that's what I'd do.
A man like him chafes and distresses;
a single ounce of my caresses
is worth a pound of that man's pawing,
for I'm refined and he's annoying,
55 I'm elegant and he is coarse,
his hair's uncut, his beard is worse,
he doesn't wash, the man's unsightly,
so, if you'll understand me rightly,
I'll be your lover with great pleasure.
60 I'll give you ten pounds from my treasure
in return for your dalliance."
The lady gave the man a glance.
"It cannot be, sir," she said to 'im.
"I'd rather still be in the womb
65 than ever commit such a sin.
What lunacy's under your skin
to urge an action that would shame me?
I'd sooner that death overcame me
than to submit to such a stain!

70   Vostre sermon poi vous i vaut
    & voz deniers—bien les gardez,
    que dans Constans m'e[n] trueve assez,
    qui molt doucement m'a norrie,
    & je feroie grant folie
75   se je por bien mal li rendoie. »
    A tant le guerpist en la voie
    & il remest toz trespenssez;
    molt fu dolenz & abosmez
    quant il ne la puet convertir.
80   Ice l'en fet resouvenir
    qu'ele a gent cors & avenant,
    le vis traitis & biau sanblant,
    les ieus vairs, la bouche petite;
    ne porroit pas estre descrite
85   par le provost sa grant biauté.
    « Je sui, fet il, musart prové!
    Amerai la je dont a force:
    quant je n'en puis percier l'escorce
    malement avroie son cuer.
90   Or me vueil je trop geter puer;
    amerai la, puis qu'el ne m'aime. »
    Ainsi a soi son cuer reclaime
    li provos quant il mieus ne puet:
    grant chose a en fere l'estuet.
95   La dame a l'ostel est venue;
    a l'endemain s'est esmeüe,
    si est alee a sainte yglise.
    Quant ele ot oï le servise,
    vers son ostel est retornee;
100   li forestiers l'a encontree,
    qui gardoit le bois au seignor;
    molt fu biaus & de bel ator
    & bien armez d'arc & d'espee.
    Il a la dame saluee.
105   Ele li rent salu molt bel.

70 Your pretty speech is all in vain,
and your coins. You can keep your stuff!
Constant provides me with enough
and looks after me tenderly.
It were the height of infamy
75 to repay kindness with deceit."
She left him standing in the street,
and he stood there greatly distressed
and disappointed and depressed
that he could not make her believe him,
80 but still her image will not leave him:
her shapely body, her sweet face,
her lovely features and her grace,
her little mouth, her gray-blue eyes.
The judge knows no word that describes
85 her inconsummate loveliness.
"That proves it," he says. "I'm an ass!
I'll use constraint to make her yield
if sweet talk won't break through her shield.
I mean to go to any length
90 and fight for her with all my strength.
Love me or not, I'll have her yet!"
Since that's the most that he can get
the judge's heart makes these demands.
He's quite a project on his hands!
95   The lady went back where she lived.
Come morning she was still so grieved,
she went to church to ease her cares,
and when she'd finished with her prayers,
she set off on her way back home.
100 The gamekeeper happened to come,
who oversaw his lordship's park,
a well-dressed man, a handsome spark,
and well armed with his bow and sword.
He addressed her a friendly word
105 and she made some polite remark.

Il trait esraument .i. anel
de son doit—bien valoit .i. marc:
« Dame, ne vous doins pas mon arc,
fet il, mes l'anel vous doins gié
110   por seulement avoir congié
de besier cele bele bouche
dont la douçor au cuer me touche. »
Ele respont comme cortoise:
« Certes, sire, pas ne me poise
115   se l'arc & l'anel vous remaint,
quar nul besoing ne me soufraint
par qoi vous m'aiez si sorprise.
Je ne vous ferai ja servise
par vilonie que je sache;
120   ja por paor de vostre hache
ne por le don de vostre anel
ne ferai rien dont vous soit bel
por tant qu'a mon seignor desplaise.
Ralez vous en tout a vostre aise
125   & je m'en irai a l'ostel.
Je ne pris pas .i. don de sel
homme qui est si garçonier.
Vostre fame se plaint l'autrier
qu'el n'avoit o vous se mal non.
130   Vous en avrez mal gerredon
quant que ce soit, ou tost ou tart. »
A cest mot de li se depart
& il remest plus chaut que brese.
Qui li eüst la teste rese
135   sanz eve a .i. coutel d'acier
ou les cheveus fet esrachier
si l'en fust il assez plus bel.
Me sire Constant du Hamel
ne savoit mot de tout cest plet.
140   Or oiez que la dame a fet:
a son ostel en vint errant,

A ring worth well over a mark
of pure gold he took from his hand.
"The bow's mine, lady, understand,"
he said, "but this ring is for you
110 if only you'll allow me to
show you how your mouth should be kissed,
so sweet, how can my heart resist?"
The lady's answer showed her virtue.
"Keep your bow, sir, nor will it hurt you
115 to keep that ring on your own finger.
I'm not so pressed by need or danger
that you should think I'm for the taking.
I'll not submit to your lovemaking,
nor will I suffer shame or harm.
120 Your ax does not cause me alarm,
nor am I tempted by your ring
to grant your wish for dallying
and give my husband cause for sorrow.
Now off with you, sir, and good morrow!
125 I wouldn't give a piece of dirt
for fellows who go chasing skirt.
I'm going back where I belong.
Your wife's told me how all along
she's had nothing from you but trouble.
130 Be sure that you'll be paid back double
sooner or later, come what may!"
She turned and went off on her way
and left him fuming then and there.
If someone had shaved off his hair
135 with a dry blade of rusty steel
or plucked his hair out, he would feel
that he'd been treated just as well.
           But back to Constant du Hamel,
who of all this was ignorant,
140 and to his wife, who simply went
back home as quickly as she could

s'a fet mengier le païsant,
puis l'envoia en son labor
ou il seut aler chascun jor.

145   Un jor avint, ce dist mon mestre,
que le forestier & le prestre
& le provost, si com moi sanble,
alerent boivre tuit ensanble.
Quant il orent beü assez

150   tant qu'il furent toz eschaufez,
« Sire, dist le provost au prestre,
dont ne feroit il or bon estre
o la fame sire Constan[z].
On en devroit juner .vii. anz

155   en pain & en eve & en sel
& en viande quaresmel
por *une nuit avoir sa* joie.
— Ci n'a que nous .iii. qui nous oie,
ce respondi le forestier.

160   Qui porroit sa bouche besier,
il en devroit souffrir la mort. »
Dist li prestres: « Vous avez tort.
Tant jeüner & mort reçoivre
por une tel fame deçoivre

165   n'est mie bone chose a fere.
Pensser covendroit d'autre afere
celui qui la voudroit amer,
quar nului ne veut escouter.
Qui de li se vueille entremetre

170   de son chatel l'estuet jus metre
tant que besoing, poverte & fain
la face venir a reclaim.
Ainsi doit on servir vilaine;
fols est qui autrement s'en paine. »

175   Or oiez du conseil au prestre:
por le vin qui le fist fol estre
a dit a ses .ii. conpaingnons:

and gave her workingman his food
and sent him to his daily toil
of planting crops and tilling soil.

145   It came to pass, my sources state,
the gamekeeper and magistrate
and parish priest, I truly think,
went out together for a drink.
When they'd been drinking for some time,
150   their temperature began to climb.
The judge said to the prelate, "Father,
do you not think it would be rather
pleasant to lie with Constant's missus?
I'd fast for seven years, my guess is,
155   with only bread and salt to eat,
and water with some Lenten meat,
for just one night with her in bed."
"There's just the three of us," then said
the gamekeeper, "who're in on this.
160   To have her lovely mouth to kiss
one would agree to meet his death!"
The priest observed, "Don't waste your breath.
Just to enjoy some woman, why
should one go hungry, much less die?
165   That attitude is lunacy.
We'll need some other strategy
if we're to have hope of succeeding,
for she'll not listen to our pleading.
The man who's going to seduce her
170   must rob her blind and thus reduce her
to poverty and near starvation;
then he'll have her cooperation.
Now that's the way to treat a peasant,
and he's a fool who says it isn't!"
175   A worthy plan, no doubt, and priestly!
The wine is making him act beastly,
and he says to the other two,

« Or escoutez que nous ferons.
Ne sommes nous assez poissant
180   por amaigroier dant Constant?
Pelez dela & je deça.
Dehez ait qui ja en faudra! »
Ce respont chascuns endroit soi:
« Or soions conpaignon tuit troi.
185   Bien poons souffrir cest marchié. »
A cest mot se sont destachié,
si departirent de l'escot.
Mes sire Constans pas ne sot
que l'en li ait tel plet basti.
190   .I. diemenche avint issi
que le provoire sermona;
aval le moustier regarda,
si vit dant Constant devant soi.
Il ne li dist pas en reqoi,
195   mes si haut que tuit l'entendirent:
« Tuit cil qui Sainte Yglise empirent
sont de dame Dieu dessevrez.
Seignors & dames, escoutez!
Vez la dant Constant du Hamel,
200   qui est maris dame Ysabel:
il a espousé sa commere,
si est bien droiz qu'il le compere,
quar cil qui les forfez encerque
si l'a conté a l'archevesque,
205   si m'a mandé que je li main
lui & sa fame hui ou demain,
si les fera l'en departir,
que la loi ne le puet souffrir.
Sire Constant, issiez vous ent
210   de cest moustier isnelement!
Je vous congié de Sainte Yglise.
Il n'i avra chanté servise
tant comme vous ceenz serez. »

"Now listen. Here is what we'll do.
Have not we three the clout and force
180 to ruin poor Constant? Of course.
You work the left, I'll work the right,
and cursed be he whose effort's slight!"
They both responded to his call:
"It's all for one and one for all!
185 We'll all work in association."
So ended their negotiation.
The three chipped in to pay the bill.
Constant du Hamel, meanwhile, still
knew nothing of this, had no warning.
190   It happened that one Sunday morning
the priest began to sermonize.
Over his flock he cast his eyes
and espied Constant in the crowd.
He didn't whisper, but spoke loud
195 to be heard by the rank and file.
"Those who God's holy Church defile,
good Christians, are proven to be
God's enemies. Listen to me,
and see there Constant du Hamel,
200 who's taken to wife Ysabel,
his godchild's godmother, so it's very
right he pay for his adultery.
The archbishop knows of the matter
through the parish investigator,
205 and he's summoned me to indict
these two before tomorrow night,
and he will have them separated
because the law won't tolerate it.
Leave us at once, Constant! I chase
210 and cast you from this holy place!
So long as you remain among
us, Holy Mass will not be sung.
From the faithful you are cut off."

Dont fu Constans forment irez
215 quant li prestres li dist tel conte,
toz fu esbahiz de la honte
si qu'il ne set qu'il doie dire;
pales, descolorez, plains d'ire
s'en est fors du moustier issuz,
220 a l'ostel le prestre est venuz;
& quant la messe fu chantee
& la gent en fu toute alee,
li prestres vint a son ostel,
& dans Constans n'atendoit el;
225 contre lui est en corant venuz.
« Fui de ci, vilains malostruz!
fet li prestres, ce ne vaut riens.
Je serai por toi toz raiens
que j'ai souffert ton avoltire.
230 — Por amor Dieu, biaus tres douz sire,
fet dans Constans, donez du mien
a l'archevesque & au doien
por moi fere cuites clamer.
— & que voudroies tu doner?
235 — Sire, .vii. livres vous otri.
— A quant paier? — A mercredi.
— Or te haste de l'aquiter.
Se tu pués por tant eschaper,
Dieus t'avra donee sa chape! »
240 A tant sire Constans eschape,
si est a son ostel venu,
& quant sa fame l'a veü,
bien voit qu'il estoit corouciez;
ses braz li a au col ploiez:
245 « & qu'avez vous, fet ele, amis?
— Dame, fet il, mal sui baillis.
A .vii. livres m'a mis le prestre
se nous volons plus ensanble estre
moi & vous, *quar* il nous envie

Poor Constant du Hamel was wroth
215 and likewise overcome with shame
to hear the preacher thus defame
him, but knows not how to reply.
He blanches, reddens, and in high
dudgeon flees from the church and leaves
220 and heads for where the preacher lives;
and when at length the Mass was done
and all the people had gone home,
the priest returned to his abode,
just as Constant was sure he would.
225 He runs to him to have it out.
"Be off," the priest says, "peasant lout!
There's not a thing that you can do.
Myself, I'm like to be fined, too,
for your incest, which I've allowed."
230 "Most kind sir, for the love of God,"
Constant says, "I'll pay off the deacon
and His Grace, too, if you'll but speak in
my behalf that I be forgiven."
"How much were you thinking of giving?"
235 "I'll give you seven pounds." "And when
will you pay up?" "On Wednesday." "Then
be quick about keeping your word.
At that price, if you can be cleared,
God's surely watching over you."
240   That settled, Constant turned and flew
back to his house, and Ysabel
took one look at him and could tell
her husband was a nervous wreck.
Winding her arms around his neck,
245 she asks, "What's wrong? What's going on?"
"Lady," he answers, "I'm undone.
There's seven pounds I have to pay
the priest if we two want to stay
together or else, as he's stated,

250 que demain ert la departie.
Quel conseil en porrons nous prendre?
Ne sai qui li a fet entendre
que vous estiiez ma commere
— Or ne vous chaut, fet ele, frere;
255 toz pres les ai, ses paierai.
Ja mar en serez en esmai
ne plus que por .i. oef de quaille:
plus avons nous deniers que paille,
s'en donrons .x. livres ou .xx.
260 Bien sai dont ceste chose vint;
ne vous en chaille a coroucier,
mes alons liement mengier. »
A tant s'assistrent esraument,
mes n'orent pas mengié graument,
265 estes vous le mes au provost:
« Levez sus, dant Constant, or tost,
fet il, si venez a la cort!
— N'avra il loisir qu'il s'atort?
dist la dame. Ce que puet estre?
270 — Par foi, dame, fet il, mon mestre
l'a molt de tost venir hasté. »
A icest mot s'en est torné,
si vint au provost, qui l'abee;
onques n'i ot reson contee
275 fors que Constans le salua,
& li provos le rooilla,
sanz plus dire el cep l'a assis:
« Dans vilains, encor avrez pis,
que vous serez mis au gibet! »
280 Puis dist a Clingnart, son vallet:
« Va tost! si di a mon seignor
que je ai pris le trahitor
qui li a son forment emblé;
& plus d'un mui en a osté
285 & par nuit sa grange brisie. »

250 tomorrow we'll be separated.
We must take steps, but I don't see a
way out. What gave him the idea
that we're related to each other?"
"Don't fret yourself," she tells him, "brother.
255 The money's on hand, and I'll pay.
You've really no cause for dismay.
A quail's egg even could do more
harm, for we have more cash than straw
to spare ten pounds or twice that sum.
260 I'm well aware how this has come
about. No need to get worked up or
keep us from sitting down to supper."
        The two of them then took a seat,
but when they'd just begun to eat,
265 the judge's messenger shows up.
"Get up, Constant," he calls, "and drop
what you're doing. Here's a subpoena."
"What is it? Can't he finish dinner,"
the lady said, "and then get ready?"
270 "To tell the truth, my master, lady,
wants him to come without delay."
So Constant set off on his way
to see the judge, who's well prepared
to deal with him, but not a word
275 did he offer. Constant came forward
to greet the magistrate, who glowered
at him and put him on the stand.
"You churl, you'll meet a sorry end,
hung by the neck until you're dead!"
280 To his servant, Clignart, he said,
"Hurry, and let his lordship know
I have the criminal in tow
who at night broke into the store
of wheat in his barn and took more
285 than a bushel of it, the thief!"

Or ot dant Constant grant haschie
quant larrecin s'ot metre seure:
« Ha, sire! Se Dieus me sequeure,
fet dans Constans, je n'i ai coupes! »
290 Dist li provos: « Ce sont estoupes
dont vous me volez estouper!
Ausi bien vous venist harper
& hurter vo chief au greïl,
que dusqu'au chief de vo cortil
295 fu du blé la trace sivie.
— Sire, fet il, c'est par envie
que l'en m'a mis seure tel oevre,
mes ainçois que plus en descuevre,
prenez du mien por pais avoir.
300 Je n'ai ou mont si chier avoir
que ne vousisse avoir doné
ainz c'on m'eüst ici trové
en cest cep a tel deshonor.
— Que donras tu a mon seignor
305 se je te faz estre delivres?
— Sire, je li donrai .xx. livres.
— Or t'en reva en ta meson.
Je serai por toi champion. »
A tant l'a hors du cep osté,
310 & dant Constans s'en est torné.
        Tres par mi l'eur d'une couture,
estes vous poingnant a droiture
contre lui son bouvier, Robet.
« Qu'as tu, fet il, qu'as tu, vallet?
315 *Qui te chace*? Comment vas tu?
— Sire, mal vous est avenu!
Li forestier voz bués enmaine.
Il dist que en l'autre semaine
li emblastes par nuit .iii. chesnes
320 qui vous cousteront .iiii. braines,
& mercredi au soir .i. hestre.

Constant was overcome with grief
to be accused of larceny.
"So help me God, my lord," says he,
"I'm innocent. It wasn't I."
290 "A pretty feeble alibi
that won't take me in!" the judge said.
"Rattle your jail bars, bash your head
against them! That won't set you free,
either! Right to your property
295 we traced the trail of wheat you left."
"Whoever's accused me of theft,"
he says, "sir, did so out of spite.
I'll lay all facts bare in plain sight,
but first, if just to clear the air,
300 what can I give? Nothing's so dear
to me I'd not give it away
sooner than be seen here today
up in the docket in dishonor."
"And how much will you pay His Honor
305 if I arrange to set you free?"
"That's twenty pounds he'll get from me."
"Now go back home. In your defense
I'll speak out for your innocence."
Freed from the docket, Constant du
310 Hamel left without more ado.
        Now see who's coming on apace
across a cultivated space
in search of him: Robbie, his cowherd.
"What gives, boy? Anything untoward?
315 How've you been doing? What's your hurry?"
"For you, boss, just hassles and worry.
The gamekeeper has confiscated
your herd, because Wednesday, he stated,
you felled and took a beech of his
320 and last week three of his oak trees,
and that will cost you four young steer."

« Dieus! dist Constans, ce que puet estre?
Tant ai hui tret male jornee! »
Lors a sa chape desfublee,
325   si cort aprés le forestier;
en haut li commence a huchier:
« Por Dieu, biaus sire, atendez moi!
— Ha! dans vilains de pute foi,
tant avez or le cul pesant!
330   Se vous venez .i. poi avant
je vous ferai du cors domage!
Se m'aportiiez .i. frommage
en vostre giron & .v. oés
bien cuideriez ravoir vos bués,
335   mes voir tout autrement ira.
Vostre pechié vous encombra
quant nostre bois nous essartastes
& a mienuit l'enportastes. »
Or fu dans Constans molt iriez,
340   molt fu dolenz & corouciez,
& dist: « Sire, vous i mentez!
Se je fusse ausi bien armez
comme vous estes parigal
sor vous en revenist le mal,
345   ou se j'eüsse mon hoël
je vous ferisse el haterel,
nel lessaisse pour vous, viellart:
vous eüssiez chauciés trop tart
voz .ii. brochetes en voz piez. »
350   Lors fu li forestiers iriez,
si le regarde fierement:
« Vilains, dont te vient hardement
que tu te veus a moi conbatre?
Por le cuer bieu, veus me tu batre?
355   Tu sanbles mieus leu qu'autre beste
de braz, de janbes & de teste.
Par les ieus bieu, mar le penssas;

"God!" said Constant. "What's this I hear?
Today I'm having such a rough
day!" Then, taking his mantle off,
325   he runs to catch up with the game-
keeper, calling to him by name.
"For God's sake, wait for me, good sir!"
"Hah! Mr. Stinking Peasant Cur
with your fat ass dragging behind!
330   Don't you come one step closer, mind,
or I will make your body hurt!
Bringing me one cheese in your shirt
and five eggs to buy back your cattle . . .
You think so? No way, mister. That'll
335   be the day! Because of your crime
you're gonna have an awful time
of it, to dare to clear our woods
at night and run off with the goods."
By now Constant was irritated,
340   disgruntled, and exasperated.
He said to him, "That's all a lie.
If, just as well as you are, I
had weapons on me and were armed,
you are the one who would be harmed.
345   If I were carrying my hoe,
your neck would quickly feel the blow,
old man. I wouldn't spare your skin,
nor would it help you to be in
that pair of spurs there on your feet."
350   The gamekeeper could feel the heat
rise to his cheeks and faced him proudly.
"How is it, cur, that you dare loudly
say you'll take me on and defeat me?
God's body, just you try to beat me!
355   You look more like a wolf instead
of a man to me, by your head,
arms, and legs. God's eyes, what a thought!

jamés franc homme n'assaudras!
Ta pance t'estuet descarchier—
360   par li vent on les pois si chier!
Ja ton hoel ne t'ert garant. »
Lors li torne le glaive avant;
dont fu Constans en grant esfroi
quant il le vit venir vers soi.
365   «Sire, dist il, por Dieu merci,
acordons nous, je vous en pri.
Ne me devez tenir si cort;
Se vous me menez a la cort
n'i avrez mie grant porfit.
370   J'ai en ma chanbre lez mon lit
.c. sous de deniers a vostre oés,
mes que je raie en pes mes bués
& racordez soie par tant. »
& cil, qui n'aloit el querant
375   mes qu'il eüst vers lui l'avoir,
li dist: « Quant les porrai avoir? »
Cil li respont: « Dedenz juesdi.
— Fai m'en seür. — Jel vous afi.
— & je la praing, comment qu'il aille.
380   Or en pués remener t'aumaille. »
      Dans Constans a l'ostel repere;
molt est dolenz, ne set que fere,
il n'a menbre qui ne li faille,
aus chans a lessie s'aumaille;
385   en meson est venuz berçant,
onques ne dist ne tant ne quant,
sor .i. lit s'est lessiez verser.
Sa fame li cort demander:
« Sire Constant, qu'avez trové?
390   — Dame, puis l'eure que fui né
n'oi autrestant mal ne dolor
com j'ai eü hui en cest jor. »
Lors li conte le destorbier

Attack a free man? Why, you ought
to see to it your belly's clear.
360   It makes the price of peas too dear!
What defense would your hoe afford?"
He draws and turns on him his sword,
which gave Constant reason to fear,
seeing an armed man coming near.
365   "For God's sake, sir, can't we agree
to settle this amicably?
What good is it to press me sore?
If you charged me in court of law,
there's not much profit to be had,
370   but in my room beside my bed
I've five pounds for you in loose change.
Give me my herd back in exchange
and let's be on good terms once more."
He, who was only looking for
375   some way to get his money, said
to him, "So when will I be paid?"
"Sometime on Thursday," says Constant.
"You promise?" "Whatever you want."
"And, come what may, I'll take your word.
380   Now you can take charge of your herd."
        Back home goes Constant du Hamel,
unsure of what to do, unwell;
his arms and legs all shake and rattle;
left behind in the fields, his cattle.
385   He's staggered back into the house
and, mute and quiet as a mouse,
he falls in a heap on his bed.
His wife ran up to him and said,
"Constant! My husband! What on earth . . ."
390   "Wife, not since the hour of my birth
have I known grief and misery
such as today have stricken me."
Then he proceeded to relate

de provost & du forestier:
395 comme il est issus de prison
por .xx. livres de raençon,
aprés li conte le meschief
du forestier de chief en chief,
a cui il doit .c. sous paier.
400 « Dame, molt me doi esmaier,
que je n'en sai denier ou prendre!
Or me covient m'avaine vendre
& le blé que devons mengier.
— Sire, ne vous chaut d'esmaier,
405 fet la dame, qui molt fu sage.
Ja n'en metrai mantel en gage
por vous oster de ceste paine,
ja n'en vendrez blé ne avaine;
bien vous metrai hors de la trape,
410 & cil remaindront en la frape,
dont vous serez autrestant lié
comme avez esté coroucié. »
Tant se pena du conforter
que il sont assis au souper.
415 Quant Constans ot assez mengié,
si l'ot dame Ysabiaus couchié;
au matin va a la charrue.
        La dame ne fu esperdue,
ainz apele sa chanberiere,
420 une gorlee pautoniere;
la garce ot a non Galestrot,
molt sot de fart & de tripot.
La dame l'apela a soi:
« Galestrot, or entent a moi.
425 Que dame Dieus nous doinst gaaing,
va moi appareillier .i. baing. »
Cele se haste ne puet plus,
ainz mist la paiele desus,
puis mist l'eve chaude en la cuve

his troubles with the magistrate,
395 who, just to keep him out of jail,
demands twenty pounds without fail;
then in detail he tells to her
his problems with the gamekeeper
and of the five pounds it will cost.
400 "Ysabel, everything is lost!
I don't know where I'll find the money.
Now you and I will both go hungry.
I'll have to sell our oats and wheat."
"Husband, don't you admit defeat,"
405 replies his wife, who's very smart.
"Without pawning the smallest part
of my wardrobe, all will be well,
and you, without having to sell
your wheat or oats, will go scot-free,
410 while they will be hard-pressed. I'll see
to it. You'll be even more glad
than you are now depressed and sad."
She took such pains to make him feel
better, soon they could have their meal.
415 After her husband had been fed,
Ysabel had him go to bed.

Next morning he goes off to plow.
The woman's not short on know-how.
She calls her chambermaid, who is
420 adept at schemes and artifice,
a cunning, moneygrubbing slut
whose given name was Galestrot.
The lady calls her to come near
and says, "Galestrot, listen here.
425 May God grant us prosperity,
go and prepare a bath for me."
Quick as she can, she put a pot
of water on to make it hot,
poured the tub full up in a stream,

430   & dras desus por fere estuve;
       a sa dame revint errant:
       « Dame, j'ai fet vostre commant.
       — Galestrot, bele douce amie,
       je te commant deseur ta vie
435   que tu soies preus & isnele
       & si saches de la favele
       tant que nostre preu en traion.
       Va; si gaaigne .i. peliçon.
       Di le prestre qui tant me prise
440   que sui preste de son servise
       se il me tient ma couvenance.
       Di qu'il m'aport sanz delaiance
       les .xx. livres & les joiaus. »
       Cele a escorcié ses trumiaus
445   qui sont gros devers les talons;
       onques vache que point tahons
       ne vi si galoper par chaut
       comme Galestrot va le saut;
       molt se paine de tost aler.
450   Le prestre ert venuz de chanter;
       tantost le tret a une part:
       « Sire, dist ele, Dieus vous gart.
       Je cuit j'ai ma paine perdue.
       Tant me sui por vous conbatue
455   que j'ai ma dame convertie;
       tant ai fait que c'est vostre amie.
       Or soiez larges & cortois:
       vous n'i avenissiez des mois
       se je ne m'en fusse entremise.
460   Ci n'afiert pas longue devise:
       aportez li tost sa promesse . . .
       & je n'ai point de guimple espesse. »
       Le prestre l'acole, si rist:
       « Galestrot, ne te soit petit:
465   tien or .xx. sous a .i. pliçon.

430   with sheets across to hold the steam,
    and then came back and told the lady,
    "Mistress, I've done. Your bath is ready."
    "Good friend and trusty Galestrot,
    upon your life, I'll tell you what
435   to do. Use ingenuity
    and turn your phrases cleverly,
    keeping our benefit in view.
    Go—there's a cloak in it for you—
    and tell that priest who's tried to win
440   my love I'm ready to give in
    if he'll keep the promise he made me.
    Tell him to bring, soon as he's ready,
    the jewels and the twenty pounds."
    The maid hitched up her skirt around
445   her calves, which grow thick toward her heels.
    No cow, not even when it feels
    a gadfly's sting, have I seen trot
    as speedily as Galestrot,
    who would not keep her mistress waiting.
450   The priest had finished celebrating
    the Mass. She draws him privately
    aside. "God keep you, sir," said she.
    "It's not in my best interest,
    but for your sake I've so hard pressed
455   my mistress that she's been won over
    by me and will become your lover.
    Be kind to me and openhanded.
    Months would have passed before you ended
    up here, had I not interceded.
460   A detailed story isn't needed;
    just quickly bring her what you said.
    I've no warm wimple for my head."
    The priest chuckles and hugs her hard.
    "Galestrot, you'll have your reward.
465   Here's twenty sous, a tidy sum

Est or li vilains en meson?
— Nenil, li las, il n'i est mie.
Sire, j'ai ma dame trahie
se vous n'estes molt debonere. »
470 Cele qui bien sot son preu fere
bouta les .xx. sous en son sain,
puis se parti du chapelain,
& il est coruz aus deniers;
tant en a pris, cens & milliers,
475 c'une grant borse en a emplie,
& les joiaus n'oublia mie,
ainz a tout mis en .i. sachel,
puis a affublé .i. mantel
vair d'escarlate taint en graine;
480 si com fortune le demaine
de son ostel s'en ist atant,
molt se vait sovent soufachant
que li sachés li poise aval.
Or oiez com li avint mal!
485 En mi sa voie a encontree
une geline piëlee
qui pasturoit en la charriere;
a poi ne s'en retorne arriere
por ce qu'il i entendoit sort;
490 a ses piez trueve .i. baston tort,
a la geline lest aler,
& ele s'en prist a voler,
en son langage le maudist:
« Honte li viegne! » et il si fist.
495 Qui donc veïst le prestre aler,
le chief bessier & esgarder
tant qu'il entra enz ou hamel.
Contre lui vient dame Ysabel,
qui molt li fet blondete chiere,
500 puis apela sa chanberiere:
« Va tost cel seignor deschaucier,

to buy a cloak. Is her man home?"
"Not he, poor fellow. No, he's not.
I've put my mistress in a spot,
Father, if you don't do right by her."
470 She knew her business—there's none slier—
tucked the twenty sous in her breast
and took leave of the parish priest,
and he ran to take from his penny
stash hundreds, thousands, very many,
475 until his largest purse was full,
nor did he leave out any jewel,
but put it all in a small sack
and tossed a coat over his back
of fine wool, mottled and dyed red.
480 He followed where his fortune led.
He passes through his courtyard gate,
bent over for the heavy weight
of the sack that he carries on him.
    Now hear what ill luck fell upon him.
485 He met halfway along the track
a pullet mottled white and black
pecking away there in the road
and almost turned back, for it showed,
he thought, misfortune lay in wait
490 for him. A stick lay at his feet.
He picks it up and goes to lay
into the hen, who flies away
and curses at him with a cluck
(and it turned out so): "Have bad luck!"
495 The priest went on, looking around
him, shoulders hunched, head to the ground,
till he arrived where he was going.
Ysabel came to meet him, showing
a welcoming and gracious air.
500 She called her chambermaid to her.
"Quickly remove the Father's shoes.

que je le vueil fere baingnier,
& je me baingnerai aprés,
si nous solacerons huimés,
505   si m'embelira plus son estre.
— Par foi, dame, ce dist le prestre,
je ne vous osai pas mentir. »
Lors li commence a descouvrir
le sachet, qui n'ert pas petit,
510   & el le gete sus son lit;
onques au conter n'i mist paine.
La dame, qui n'ert pas vilaine,
le sot tant de ses diz lober
qu'el le fist enz el baing entrer,
515   puis prist la robe & les deniers—
ainz n'i lessa nis les chauciers,
en sa chanbre a trestout geté.
Or sont cil mis a sauveté.
    A Galestrot va conseillier:
520   « Va toi bien tost apareillier,
si me fai venir le provost.
Di li que il m'aport bien tost
ce que il m'ot en couvenant. »
& cele i ala esraument
525   qu'ele en fet voler les esclas.
S'ele puet tenir en ses las
le provost, il li rendra conte!
De parler a lui n'a pas honte,
ainz le salue hautement:
530   « J'ai en vous, dist el, mal parent,
dant provost, por vostre richoise,
mais j'ai vers vous fet que cortoise
que ne me vueil desnaturer.
Qui me deüst .c. sous doner
535   ne me fusse plus entremise.
Nuit & jor de vostre servise
tant ai ma dame coru seure

He'll have a bath. That's what I choose
to do, and I'll have my bath next,
and then we'll have a little sex.
505   That way I'll be all the more pleased."
"Indeed, lady," then said the priest,
"I'd not deceive you nor go back
on my word." Then he shows the sack
of coins to her—little it wasn't.
510   She throws it on her bed but doesn't
count them; it isn't worth her while.
The woman knew how to beguile
him with the winning words she spoke,
politely coaxed him in to soak,
515   then took his money and his clothes,
not leaving so much as his hose,
and tossed them all into her room.
They're safe there now. He can't get to 'em.
        She goes and says to Galestrot,
520   "Get ready now. It's time you got
the magistrate to come to me.
Tell him to bring me presently
the things he promised I would get."
And off she goes, lickety-split,
525   making the sparks fly in her wake.
If she succeeds to snare and take
the judge in, he'll be in a bind.
She's not ashamed to speak her mind,
but gives him greetings openly.
530   "You quite neglect your family,
Sir Magistrate, despite your riches,
but seeing we're of one blood, which is
thicker than water, I've done you
a good turn. For somebody who
535   gave me five pounds I'd not do more.
Night and day on behalf of your
desires I have so dunned my lady

que ele est maintenant en l'eure
de fere tout vostre plesir,
540   mes hastez vous de tost venir
& si ne devez pas lessier
ce que vous deïstes l'autrier.
Ma dame a molt d'argent a fere;
ele est si franche & debonere
545   que molt bien le vous savra rendre,
mes ele a or mestier de prendre. »
Quant li provos ot & entent
que la chose est a son talent,
« Galestrot, dist il, douce amie,
550   je ne te doi oublier mie,
que tu m'as servi bien & bel.
Tien or .xx. sous a .i. mantel. »
Il li mist ou giron devant,
& ele s'en torna atant,
555   vers sa meson s'en va tout droit.
Li provos aprés li aloit,
a l'uis est venuz, si apele.
« Lasse! ci a male novele!
fet la dame. C'est mon seignor!
560   — Dame, por Dieu le creator,
dist le prestre, que porrai faire?
Voz maris est de si put aire
qu'il m'avra ja tout esmié.
Il est vers moi forment irié.
565   — Sire, dist el, n'aiez paor.
Je vous metrai en tel destor
ou il ne vous savroit ouän.
En cel tonnel desoz cel van
il n'i a rien que plume mole. »
570   Li prestres crut bien sa parole;
el tonnel saut de plain eslés,
si le refist couvrir aprés.

that at this moment she is ready
and willing to fulfill your wants,
540 but hurry up and go at once,
and don't forget to bring with you
what some time back you promised to.
My mistress is in need of money,
but, what with her open and sunny
545 disposition, you'll be rewarded.
She needs cash, and you can afford it."
As soon as the judge catches on
that so far everything has gone
just as he wished, he says, "My dear
550 girl, I will not forget you. Here
are twenty shillings for a coat.
You've served me well in this; I know't."
He tucked the money in her blouse,
and she set off back to her house
555 and didn't loiter on the way.
          The judge follows soon as he may,
comes to the door and gives a call.
"What a misfortune! Hang it all!"
the woman says. "My husband's here!"
560 "By God, who made the earth and air,"
the priest said, "how can I get out
of this one? Your man's such a lout,
he's like to tear me into bits.
He's mad enough at me as is!"
565 She answered, "Father, never fear.
I'll have you hide in a place where
he'll never guess that you would ever
be, in this barrel full of feathers
that's stowed beneath the winnow there."
570 The priest did not suspect her snare.
He jumped quickly inside and hid;
she used the winnow as a lid.

Estes vous le provost errant.
La dame li fist biau sanblant;
575   il la vout maintenant besier.
« Sire, dist el, ce n'a mestier;
que savez vous qui nous esgarde?
Honte m'i fet vers vous couarde,
mes Amors m'i fera hardie
580   quant je serai de vous sesie.
— Dame, fet il, c'est verité;
mes je vous ai ci aporté
ne sai quans deniers que j'avoie. »
A tant li baille la corroie,
585   qui molt estoit plaine & farsie.
La dame n'en refusa mie,
ainz l'a en sa chanbre portee.
Je ne vueil fere demoree
n'aconter chascune parole,
590   mes la dame par sa parole
li dist tant qu'il entra ou baing.
Or li est doubles son gaaing
que sa robe a en sauf portee,
puis a Galestrot apelee;
595   en bas li prist a conseillier:
« Va moi querre le forestier;
di li au mieus com tu savras.
Se nous poons metre ses dras
o les autres, ce m'ert molt bel.
600   Di li que il m'aport l'anel
qu'il me vout l'autre jor doner. »
Qui donc veïst cele troter
par mi la rue au plus que puet!
Or sachiez que venir estuet
605   au forestier s'ele l'ataint!
Quant el le vit, pas ne se faint
de bien portretier sa parole:
« Je sui, dist el, musarde fole.

Here comes the magistrate apace.
The lady showed him a fair face.
He wants to kiss her then and there,
but she says to him, "Sir, take care.
Are you so sure that no one sees me?
Modesty makes me feel uneasy
with you, but once you've taken hold
of me, love's sure to make me bold."
"Lady," says he, "that's very true.
But see here. I have brought for you"—
he holds the money belt aloft
for her to see, and it was stuffed—
"all that I have. Who knows how much!"
She didn't turn it down, I'll vouch,
but took the money to her chamber.
It's not my business to remember
their every word and drag things out,
but she, cajoling, brought about
his getting in the bath, so she
has thus doubled her salary
and locked his clothing up as well.
She then called Galestrot to tell
her secretly what she must do.
"Go bring me the gamekeeper, too.
Use words with him as you know best.
We'll put his clothes there with the rest
of them. Make sure to have him bring
what he has promised me—the ring.
Then I can have my satisfaction."

Watch Galestrot go into action
and see her hurry down the street!
You know what fate's going to meet
the gamekeeper if she can seize him.
She doesn't hold back when she sees him,
but thinks how she should turn her phrases:
I'm such a dummy! What the blazes

Qu'ai je de cest vassal afere?
610   Se il ne fust si debonere
je n'alaisse por lui plain pas! »
Puis li dist souavet en bas:
« Venez a ma dame parler.
El ne fina puis de pensser
615   qu'ele vous geta l'autrier puer,
mes je l'ai pointe jusqu'au cuer,
sovent & menu l'ai tastee
tant que por vous est eschaufee.
Vostre anel d'or li aportez;
620   el vous donra du suen assez. »
Le forestier de joie saut:
« É, Galestrot, se Dieus me saut,
bon le feïs, se je puis vivre!
Que je la tenisse a delivre,
625   ma dame, qui tant par est simple.
Tien or .x. sous a une guimple. »
Cele les a pris comme sage,
& celui i lera tel gage
qu'il ne ravra mes de semaine.
630   Tant a corut a longue alaine
qu'ele vint en meson batant;
la dame trova deschauçant
que molt le hastoit le provost.
      Ez vous le forestier tantost;
635   a la porte vient, si apele.
« Lasse, ci a froide novele!
fet la dame. Mon seignor vient. »
Li provos molt forment le crient
por ce qu'il l'avoit coroucié.
640   « Dame, vous m'avez engingnié,
fet il, s'or n'en prenez conroi.
— Sire, ne soiez en esfroi,
fet la dame. Muciez vous çà,
que mon seignor s'en ira ja. »

have I to do with this young punk?
610 Were he not a bit of a hunk,
I'd not give him the time of day!
She softly whispered to him, "Hey,
come see my mistress for a chat.
She can't get out of her mind that
615 the other day she kept her distance
from you, but thanks to my insistence
I've touched her heart in such a fashion
that now she's burning up with passion.
Just come and bring your golden ring
620 and she'll allow you everything."
For joy he jumps up like a shot.
"May God protect me, Galestrot,
upon my life, good job, I say!
I would embrace, soon as I may,
625 my lady, who's so sweet and simple.
Here, take ten shillings for a wimple."
She took his money, mild and meek,
but he will wait many a week
to recover the pledge he's leaving.
630 She ran so hard, her breast was heaving,
and by the time she reached their yard,
she found her mistress half unshod
because the judge was urging her.
    Now see—here comes the gamekeeper;
635 he's at the door; "I'm here," he cries.
"Oh dear, what a nasty surprise!"
the lady says. "My husband's here!"
The magistrate trembles with fear
because he made him hopping mad.
640 "Lady," he says, "I have been had,
unless you save me in a hurry."
"Sir," says the lady, "not to worry.
Get in that barrel there and hide
till my husband goes back outside."

645   A tant le tonnel descouvri,
       & il i est joins piez sailli.
       A poi qu'il ne creva le prestre.
       « Ha, las! dist il, ce que puet estre?
       Or sont deable descendu! »
650   Quant li provos l'a entendu
       a poi qu'il n'est du sens mariz:
       « Ha, las! dist il, com sui trahiz!
       — Trahiz, por les angoisses Dé!
       Qui es tu qui m'a afronté?
655   — Mes tu qui es? — Je sui le prestre.
       Li deable te font ci estre,
       cil d'enfer qui pas ne sommeillent,
       qui por la gent engingnier veillent.
       Hui furent il trop esveillié
660   qu'il m'ont trahi & engingnié.
       & tu qui es? Di le moi tost!
       — Ba! je sui le chetif provost.
       — Le provost? Donques n'ai je mal. »
       Ainsi s'acointent parigal
665   l'un a l'autre lor aventure.
       Le forestier ne s'asseüre,
       ainz entre en l'ostel bel & cointe.
       La dame s'est pres de lui jointe,
       tant le blandi & tant le lie
670   qu'ele fu de l'anel sesie,
       puis si le fist el baing entrer.
       Anuiz seroit a raconter
       chascun dit & chascune afere,
       mes bien en sot la dame trere
675   l'anel & ce qu'en pot avoir.
          A son seignor a fet savoir
       qu'il viegne tost qu'ele a besoing.
       La charrue n'ert gueres loing;
       ez le vous entré en la porte.
680   « Lasse! dist ele, or sui je morte!

645 Then she lifted the barrel lid,
     and he jumped in feetfirst and hid,
     crushing the parish priest, who's under-
     neath. "Ha!" he cried. "What's this? I wonder.
     The devils have come in a host!"
650 Hearing him speak, the judge almost
     lost his mind, he was so dismayed.
     "Alas," he cried, "I am betrayed!"
     "Betrayed? By all God's agonies,
     who are you who've clobbered me, please?"
655 "But who are you?" "Why, I'm the priest.
     The devils, who have never ceased
     from raising hell and everywhere
     seduce good Christians, brought you here!
     Today they're so on the alert,
660 they've tricked me and made me get hurt.
     Now tell me who you are. Don't wait."
     "I'm the unlucky magistrate."
     "The magistrate? Well then, things ain't
     so bad." They go on to acquaint
665 each other with how things have gone.
          The gamekeeper, who isn't on
     his guard, bursts noisily inside.
     The lady comes close to his side
     and wheedles him with blandishments,
670 then, once the ring is in her hands,
     shows him the tub. He got inside.
     It would be boring to describe
     everything that they said and did,
     but it was no trouble to rid
675 him of the ring and of his clothes.
     She sees to it her husband knows
     he's needed home without delay.
     The tillage wasn't far away;
     before long he is at the door.
680 "I'm done for! My husband!" she swore.

Mes sires vient; oëz le la,
mes bien sai qu'il s'en rira ja.
Il n'est pas tens de dosnoier.
— Dame, ce dist le forestier,
685   vostre sires *me* het de mort
se ne prenez de moi confort. »
Dist la dame: « Fetes isnel,
si en entrez en cel tonnel. »
Ele corut le van oster,
690   & cil saut en sanz arester;
le prestre ataint en la poitrine,
au provost fet ploier l'eschine,
mes nus d'aus n'en osa groucier.
« Ha, las! ce dist le forestier,
695   com sui folement embatuz!
— Qu'est ce? Mal soiez vous venuz,
dist le provost; traiez vous la!
Je cuit que je creverai ja
se nous sommes ci longuement.
700   — Ha, las! dist le prestre dolent,
com ci a dolente poitrine!
— Mes je ai brisie l'eschine,
dist le provost, au mien cuidier!
— Ha, las! ce dist le forestier,
705   a poi que li oeil ne me saillent!
Les vies qui tant nous travaillent
soient honies hui cest jor.
que nous vivons a grant dolor! »
      Estes vous dant Constant bruiant,
710   une grant hache paumoiant.
Dame Ysabiaus l'a acené,
tout belement li a conté
comme el les a mis el tonel:
« Por Dieu, sire, or en ouvrez bel!
715   Fetes en ce que il feïssent
se au desus de nous venissent:

"Can't you hear? He'll discover us,
and he won't find it humorous.
This is no time to bill and coo."
The gamekeeper said, "Lady, you
685 know just how much your husband hates me.
I beg of you, see to my safety."
"Then hurry up," the lady cried.
"Get in that barrel there and hide."
She took the winnow off the top,
690 and in he jumps—he doesn't stop
to wait—and lands on the priest's ribs;
the judge's backbone bends and gives,
but neither dared to vent his spleen.
"Ha!" said the gamekeeper. "I've been
695 careless and hasty, and will pay."
"Who asked you in here? Go away!"
the magistrate said. "I am sure
I'll croak if we spend any more
time cooped up in this dreadful place."
700 Said the priest, sore and in disgrace,
"Woe's me! Ow! How my chest is aching!"
"And as for me, my back is breaking,"
the magistrate says, "on my word."
"Alas," the gamekeeper concurred,
705 "my eyes will pop out of my head!
A curse upon the lives we've led
that make us suffer so today,
for it hurts more than I can say!"
Now Constant enters, making noise,
710 with a large ax held in his paws.
Ysabel beckons him come near
and whispers plainly in his ear
how she's put them all in the barrel.
"For God's sake, sir, avenge your quarrel!
715 Do unto them as they'd have done
to us if they had overcome.

il voloient a moi gesir.
Je ferai lor fames venir,
si ferez sanblant & tout outre;
720   la premiere vous covient foutre
& puis les .ii., se vous poez;
ses avrez honiz & matez.
Je vueil que ainsi le faciez,
si les avrez a droit paiez;
725   & tenez adés ceste hache,
quar ele vaut une manache:
donez lor en se nus se muet.
— Dame, dist il, fere l'estuet.
— Galestrot! vien ça, pute asnesse!
730   Va moi tost querre la prestresse;
di li qu'el viegne o moi baingnier.
& vous, alez appareillier
la dejouste cele grant mait,
si soiez toz diz en agait.
735   — Dame, vostre plesir ferai.
Galestrot s'en va par le tai;
tant a la prestresse hastee
que a l'ostel l'a amenee.
La dame la fet deschaucier
740   & de toz ses dras despoillier
fors seulement de sa chemise.
Li vilains a *la face bise*,
qui molt bien sanble espoentail,
de sa chanbre ist a tout .i. mail:
745   « Qui est ce la & qui est ceste?
Ja n'i querrai ore plus preste!
Couchiez vous tost; si vous foutray! »
Cele le vit hideus & lai,
si n'osa parler ne grondir.
750   Cil la vait aus janbes saisir,
si l'a couchie toute enverse—
ne la prist pas a la traverse,

They all wanted to lie with me;
I'll send for the wives of those three,
and nonchalantly in you'll burst.
720 I mean for you to fuck the first
and, if you can, the other two,
so you'll have shamed and licked them, too.
You do exactly as I've said
and they'll be suitably repaid.
725 Then swiftly grab hold of your ax.
It's threat enough, but give them whacks
if any of them tries to flee."
"Lady," he answered, "willingly."
        "Galestrot! Donkey! Rise and shine!
730 Go fetch the preacher's concubine
and invite her to come and take
a bath with me. You, husband, make
ready. Go stand beside that pole
and keep close watch on one and all."
735 "Lady, I'll do what you think good."
Galestrot races through the mud,
urges the priest's sweetheart to come,
and soon has brought the woman home.
Her mistress quickly has her doff
740 her shoes and take her clothing off,
until she's wearing just her shirt.
The peasant, his face dark as dirt,
much like a scarecrow, comes in quick
from his room, carrying a stick.
745 "What's going on and who is she?
She seems ready for it to me.
Now go lie down and you'll get screwed."
He looked so ugly and so crude
to her, she didn't dare talk back.
750 He turns her over on her back,
grabbing her legs so he can ride
her standing up, not on his side,

ainz l'a acueillie de bout,
& ele li livra trestout,
755 ne li vea janbe ne cuisse,
mes au prestre, que ele puisse,
ne s'en plaindra mes de semaine,
qui ou tonnel est a grant paine
qu'il en fet le vertuel voler.
760 Li provos prist a esgarder,
si vit le vilain braoillier;
au prestre moustre sa moillier:
« Qu'est ce, dist il, que je voi la?
Or esgardez ce que sera:
765 ce puet bien estre la prestresse.
La *connoistrez* vous a la fesse
& aus estres qui sont entor?
L'en la demaine a grant dolor. »
Lors n'i a nul des .ii. ne rie;
770 au prestre est l'alaine faillie
du duel qu'il a & de la honte,
mes ne vueil aloingnier mon conte.
        Quant dant Constant l'ot bien corbee,
si l'a fors de l'ostel boutee;
775 ele s'en va molt coroucie.
Galestrot ert ja envoïe
por fere venir la provoste.
Dant Constans d'une part s'acoste
tant qu'ele fust leenz venue;
780 quant ele se fu desvestue
& el cuida el baing entrer,
dant Constans li va demander:
« Que requiert ceste dame ci?
— Avoi, dant Constant, Dieu merci,
785 g'i sui venue mainte foiz.
— Par foi, dame, si est bien droiz
que vous ore i soiez foutue. »
La dame fu toute esperdue,

and in that position he plowed
her straightaways, and she allowed
755   him all her treasures, leg and thigh,
but, if she can, be sure she'll try
to keep the priest from knowing of it,
who, shut up in the barrel, suffered
so that the stopper popped right out.
760   The judge began to look about
and saw the peasant busy humping.
He shows her to the priest: "There's something
out there," he said. "What's that I see?
Now look! Tell me what it can be.
765   Why, isn't that the priestess there?
You'll know her by her derrière
and other features that surround it.
I'd say she's really getting pounded."
Then both the other two men laughed
770   at the poor priest, who, breathless, gasped
from sorrow and humiliation.
      I will not prolong my narration.
When Constant du Hamel had fucked her,
then right out of the house he chucked her,
775   and off she went, distraught and spent.
Galestrot was already sent
to bring back the magistrate's bride.
Our hero stood off to the side
until the judge's wife had come,
780   and when she'd no more clothing on
and she thought she'd get in the bath,
Constant comes up to her to ask,
"And just what does this lady want?"
"As God is my witness, Constant,
785   I've often come here for a visit."
"Right. Then it's not unfitting, is it,
that this time around you get laid."
The woman, utterly dismayed,

si se poroffri a desfendre,
790 & cil la vait aus janbes prendre,
se li a levees amont,
les genouz li hurta au front.
Por ce qu'ele se desfendoit
l'a il corbee si estroit
795 c'on i peüst jouer aus dez.
Se li prestres fu eschaufez,
li provos fu autant ou plus
quant il la vit par le pertuis
demener si vilainement.
800 Le forestier s'en rist forment
& le prestre, quant il la voit:
« Or en voi une a grant destroit!
Provost, connois tu cele la?
Je cuit qu'ele tumbera ja. »
805 Ainsi chascuns le contralie;
le provos ne set que il die
de duel qu'il ne se puet vengier;
qui li donast tout Monpellier,
n'issist il .i. mot de sa bouche.
810 Dant Constans sovent la retouche
d'un fusil qu'il avoit molt gros.
Lor cul erent plus noir que mors,
qui molt estoient pres a pres.
Cil les esgardent tout adés
815 qui ou tonnel erent mucié.
Onques cele ne prist congié;
quant sire Constans l'ot corbee,
hors de son ostel l'a boutee;
ainz n'en porta mantel ne cote.
820   Galestrot par la vile trote,
si amena la forestiere.
Cele i vint a poi de proiere;
quant a l'ostel en fu venue
& ele se fu desvestue,

with all her might tried to prevent it.
790 He grabbed her ankles and upended
her legs and raised them in the air
till each knee pressed against an ear.
Since she was putting up a fight,
he bent her backward so you might
795 have played a dice game on her bottom.
If the priest had before been hot 'n'
bothered, this time the judge was, too,
when through the hole he had a view
of her abused so shoddily.
800 The gamekeeper laughs heartily,
and the priest also, when they spot
her. "Look! Someone's in a tight spot,
judge! Do you recognize your own?
How does she keep from falling down?"
805 Thus these two needled and provoked
the judge, who, silent, nearly choked,
unable to retaliate.
Though you offered the magistrate
Montpellier, still he couldn't utter
810 a word while he watched Constant futter
her tinderbox using his very
large flint tool. Blacker than a berry,
their asses were pressed cheek to cheek
in plain sight of them, who can peek
815 out of the barrel where they lie.
The woman didn't say good-bye,
for Constant simply up and chucked her
out of his house, once he had fucked her,
without her mantle or her coat.
820 Then off through town went Galestrot
and fetched back the gamekeeper's spouse,
who willingly came to their house,
and after she was safe inside
and had put all her clothes aside,

825   se li restuet avoir sa paie.
        Dans Constans, qui pas ne s'esmaie,
        qui molt est d'anieus couvine
        & plus veluz c'une esclavine,
        por ce qu'il la vit esbahie:
830   « Ceste, dist il, sera m'amie.
        Je la fouterai jusqu'au pas.
        — Avoi, dant Constant, est ce gas?
        — Gas? Vous le verrez ja par tans! »
        A poi n'est issue du sans,
835   quar il la prist de tel ravine
        qu'il la fist cheoir sor l'eschine;
        il l'a si durement corbee
        c'on i peüst veoir l'entree
        de bien loing, qui s'en preïst garde.
840   « Esgarde, forestier, esgarde!
        dist le provost. Ce que puet estre?
        — Je le voi bien, ce dist le prestre,
        lor mireor si sont molt orbes! »
        (Lor cul erent plus noir que torbes.)
845   Le forestier est si plains d'ire
        que il ne set qu'il doie dire,
        mes ce li fet reconforter
        que l'un ne puet l'autre gaber,
        & bien voient qu'il l'a corbee
850   & rabessie & restupee,
        puis li renseigne a l'uis la voie.
        Si souëf la dame convoie
        qu'il la fet voler ou putel;
        son peliçon & son mantel
855   & sa cote remest en gage.
           Molt par fu dame Ysabiaus sage;
        toz diz tint la hache en sa main.
        Or escoutez de son vilain:
        au tonnel vint, sel descouvri:
860   « Por le cuer bieu, & qu'est ce ci?

825 it was her turn to be repaid.
Constant is not at all afraid
and just the sight of him is scary
and, like a pilgrim's shirt, he's hairy.
Because he sees she's terrified,
830 he says, "This one will be my bride.
I'll fuck her right here on the spot."
"You're joking, Constant, are you not?"
"Joking? Before too long you'll find
that out!" She nearly lost her mind,
835 because he launched such an attack
that she fell over on her back,
and then he folded her in two
and brought her chasm into view
from far off, if you only took
840 a look. "Look here, gamekeeper, look!"
chided the judge. "What can that be?"
The priest piped up, "Yes, I can see
their peep show, somewhat of a blur."
(As black as peat their asses were.)
845 The gamekeeper's so overwrought,
he can't imagine what he ought
to say, but it's some consolation
that all share the humiliation.
All three can see how he has flopped her
850 over and laid her down and topped her;
and now he's showing her the road.
With so much graciousness he showed
it to her, she fell in the mud
and left her mantle, cloak, and hood
855 in earnest (as collateral).
        A wise woman was Ysabel;
she held on to the ax throughout.
Two things you need to hear about:
Constant, the barrel. He came near,
860 lifted the lid. . . . "God! What's in here?

Qui a cest tonnel emplumé
la ou je doi metre mon blé?
Par le cuer bieu, je l'ardrai ja! »
Lors prent le feu, se l'i bouta,
865 & la plume prist a bruller,
le tonnel fist jus roeler.
Fors s'en issent, chascuns s'en fuit:
molt mainent grant noise & grant bruit,
tuit estoient de plume enclos;
870 il n'i paroit ventre ne dos,
teste ne jambe ne costé
que tuit ne fussent enplumé.
Aus chans issent par une rue,
& Constans prist une maçue,
875 si s'en vait aprés eus corant,
toz jors lor vait les chiens huant:
« Houre, Gibet! Houre, Manssel!
Par l'ame d'Anquetin *Hamel*,
mon chier pere qui me norri,
880 ainz mes puis l'eure que nasqui
n'oï mes parler de teus bestes!
Se j'en peüsse avoir les testes,
jes presentaisse mon seignor. »
Or ot chascuns d'aus grant paor,
885 si s'esploitent de tost fuir;
& chien commencent a venir.
Baloufart, le chien au provost,
le sesi aus jambes tantost,
si en porta plaine sa goule.
890 Le prestre rest en male foule,
quar Esmeraude, sa levriere,
le sesi aus naces derriere,
qui molt ert grant & merveilleuse—
por noient i meïst venteuse
895 puis qu'Esmeraude s'i est prise;
por trestout l'or qui est en Frise

Who'll tell me why this barrel's feathered?
Where will I put the wheat I gathered?
I'll burn the whole lot, in God's name!"
He took the fire, set it aflame;
865   the feathers caught on fire and burned;
the barrel fell over and turned.
The men crawl out and run away,
making a racket and a fray,
covered with feathers head to toe,
870   with every part of them on show—
head, stomach, back, sides, legs—and every
last inch of those three men is feathery.
Off toward the fields on the double
they head, and Constant grabs a cudgel
875   and takes off after the three men
and sets his pack of dogs on them.
"Sic 'em, Gibet! Sic 'em, Mansel!
On the soul of old man Hamel,
my loving dad who brought me up,
880   not ever since I was a pup
have I heard tell of beasts like these.
I'll chop their heads off. It would please
my lord to get them as a present."
Frightened by the dogs of the peasant,
885   all run like hell to get away.
The dogs see them and start to bay.
Baloufart, who pursued the judge,
pounced on his legs and took a huge
bite out of them that filled his jaws.
890   The priest's in jeopardy, because
Esmeralda, his greyhound bitch,
sank her teeth in his backside, which
she clung to. She's a big one, which is
why there's no need to apply leeches
895   when that dog latches on. You know
till she's drawn blood, she won't let go

n'en partist ele sanz du sanc.
Li prestres fu las & estanc,
si se lest cheoir a la terre.
900 Dant Constant l'est alez requerre;
a tot sa maçue gouesche
tel cop li done en la *ventreske*
que .iii. tors le fist roeler;
vueille ou non le fist jus verser.
905 Quant il li ot les chiens ostez,
aprés les .ii. en est alez.
Li provos avoit .i. levrier
qui consivi le forestier;
des cuisses li tret a braons.
910 Estes vous plus de .vii. gaingnons
qui vers le provost se hericent;
sovent le mordent & pelicent.
Constans i est venuz corant
o tout .i. grant baston pesant
915 qui pesoit plain .i. vessiau d'orge;
au provost a sauvé la gorge
que li chien orent adenté;
tantost l'eüssent estranglé,
mes il fuient por le baston;
920 ja li avoient le crepon
en plus de .xx. lieu deschiré.
Le forestier ont adenté,
& il crie: « Constant, aïe!
Por Dieu, le filz sainte Marie,
925 ne me lesse mie mengier!
Jamés ne te toudrai denier. »
& dans Constans les chiens li oste,
qui l'ont & devant & d'encoste
en plus de .xxx. lieus plaié,
930 & cil se tient a bien paié.
Quant li chien li furent osté,
forment li sainent li costé.

for all of Friesland's wealth and gold.
The priest, exhausted, cannot hold
up any longer; down he falls.
900 Constant now sets on him and hauls
off with his heavy club and puts
so great a dent inside his guts,
spinning three times around he sends him.
Like it or lump it, he upends him.
905 He called the dogs off him, and then
he went after the other men.
The judge was fleeing from a cur
that went after the gamekeeper
and shredded his thighs in his jowls.
910 With hackles raised and fearsome growls,
seven mastiffs or more close in,
chomp down on him and flay his skin
off. Constant comes a-running up
to them, swinging his mighty club
915 that weighed at least four pecks of barley,
and saves the judge's neck, who barely
could lift himself back up, and scatters
the dogs, who'd have left him in tatters,
but they're afraid of being beaten.
920 His buttocks were already bitten
and torn in more than twenty places.
As for the gamekeeper, his face is
ground in the dirt. "Constant, my brother,
for Mary's sake, God's holy mother,
925 don't let them eat me! True as true,
I'll never take a cent from you."
At that Constant calls off the pack.
In more than thirty places, back,
side, and front have been mutilated;
930 he thinks himself well compensated.
    When the mongrels had finished feeding,
their bodies were left torn and bleeding.

Ez vous la presse qui engroisse;
toute la gent de la parroisse
935   i corurent de toutes pars,
& par buissons & par essars.
Molt i ot grant noise & grant presse,
& chascuns d'aus veoir s'engresse
por ce que mal atorné erent——
940   a poi que li chien nes tuerent——
par lor pechié, par lor envie,
tant qu'il jurerent sor lor vie,
seur la croiz & seur le sautier
& seur tos les sainz du moustier
945   qu'a sire Constant du Hamel
n'a sa fame dame Ysabel
ne diront mes riens se bien non;
& la dame est en sa meson,
qui deniers a a grant plenté
950   por ce que qu'a sagement ouvré:
les deniers ot & les joiaus,
& si furent quites de ciaus
que dans Constans avoit promis.
     En cest fablel n'avra plus mis
955   quar a tant en fine le conte.
Que Dieus nous gart trestoz de honte!

See all the people who surround
them, who've arrived from miles around,
935   across the fields and through the bush,
the entire parish, making such
a throng and such a brouhaha,
eager to see them, for they are
in poor condition—in a word,
940   Constant's dogs nearly massacred
them—for their sins and lechery.
All three took an oath solemnly
on their lives, on the cross, the Psalter,
and all the saints above the altar,
945   never of Constant du Hamel
or his wife, Goody Ysabel,
to breathe a word of calumny.
The lady's safe at home, where she
has riches to her heart's content.
950   By being so intelligent,
she had both jewelry and money,
and they were henceforth free of any
promise Constant had to make good.
        The story's done, so I won't put
955   any more in this fabliau.
God save us all from shame and woe!

III.

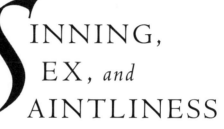

SINNING, SEX, and SAINTLINESS

THE FABLIAUX DO NOT present a flattering view of the human condition. They accept egotism and unruliness as a given, and while they pretend to deplore this situation, they obviously relish it and mine it for comedic purposes. We encounter just about every human failing, including all seven deadly sins. Examples of pride, wrath, and envy abound. Lust figures prominently in more than half the corpus, and one gets the impression that fabliau authors considered it a natural, even healthy, vice. They acknowledged its sinfulness but tended to reserve their invective for women and the clergy. On the other hand, greed, which Chaucer's Pardoner calls the root of all evil, they always found unforgivable, and approved of people indulging in every other sin in order to punish it. Not one avaricious person in the fabliaux has any admirable qualities. Even sloth makes an appearance in "Long Butthole Berengier" (#19)—a theologian might also include "The Fucker" (#59)—though lethargy generally does not offer much opportunity for humor.

The first three tales in this section focus on gluttony; then we again turn our attention to Lust with eight fabliaux in which the male and female genitals receive particular scrutiny. These stories correspond most closely to how people who have heard of the genre, but never read any, imagine the fabliaux. It might surprise them to learn that the three moral tales that close this collection belong to the same genre. In theory, any text that claims to teach a lesson—and over two-thirds of the fabliaux do so—qualify as a moral tale or exemplum. What makes these poems fabliaux is their humor, the trickery perpetrated by or on the principal character, and wordplay. Moreover, Christ's parables exemplify virtue, not vice. Therefore we cannot always credit the seriousness of the moral intent fabliau authors professed, and should regard their supposed didacticism as a burlesquing of the sermon. "Brownie, the Priest's Cow" (#68), for example, reads like an authentic disingenuous parable. Its irony, irreverence, and amorality, its warped literal interpretation of Scripture, and the way the simple but none-too-pious farmer gets the better of his exploitative priest, make it a quintessential fabliau. ◆◆◆

56. LES PERDRIS

Por ce que fabliaus dire sueil,
en lieu de fable dire vueil
une aventure qui est vraie
d'un vilain qui delez sa haie
5   prist .ii. pertris par aventure.
        En l'atorner mist molt sa cure;
sa fame les fist au feu metre.
Ele s'en sot bien entremetre:
le feu a fet, la haste atorne,
10   & li vilains tantost s'en torne,
por le prestre s'en va corant,
mes au revenir tarda tant
que cuites furent les pertris.
La dame a le haste jus mis,
15   s'en pinça une peleüre,
quar molt ama la lecheüre:
quant Dieus li dona a avoir,
ne beoit pas a grant avoir,
mes a toz ses bons aconplir.
20   L'une pertris cort envaïr,
an.ii. les eles en menjue,
puis est alee en mi la rue
savoir se ses sires venoit.
Quant ele venir ne le voit,
25   tantost arriere s'en retorne
& le remanant tel atorne,
mal du morsel qui remainsist!
Adonc s'apenssa & si dist
que l'autre encore mengera—
30   molt tres bien set qu'ele dira
s'on li demande que devindrent:
ele dira que li chat vindrent
quant ele les ot arrier tretes,

56. THE PARTRIDGES

Since I tell mostly fabliaux,
this time I want to let you know,
instead of fables, something true
about a peasant who found two
5   partridges in his shrubbery.
His heart set on roast partridge, he
had his wife put them up to roast.
She knew her business well; she trussed
them on a spit and lit the fire,
10   while he went running to inquire
if the priest would share their repast,
but he was gone so long, at last
the birds were roasted to a turn.
She takes them out so they won't burn
15   and pinches off a piece of skin,
for gluttony's her special sin.
When God is generous, she itches
not for possessions, not for riches,
but just to satisfy her craving.
20   She starts one of the birds she's saving,
and both the wings are soon devoured;
then she steps out and gazes toward
the town to see if she can spot
her husband coming, but he's not,
25   so she goes straight back in the kitchen
to the half-eaten bird to pitch in
and finish it off every bite.
Considering, she thinks she might
eat up the other one as well.
30   She knows exactly what she'll tell
anybody who asks her why
they're gone: She'll say the cats came by
when she set the birds out to stand

tost li orent des mains retretes,
35 & chascuns la seue en porta;
ainsi, ce dist, eschapera.
Puis va en mi la rue ester
por son mari abeveter,
& quant ele nel voit venir,
40 la langue li prist a fremir
sus la pertris qu'ele ot lessie—
ja ert toute vive enragie
s'encor n'en a .i. petitet.
Le col en tret tout souavet,
45 si le menja par grant douçor,
ses dois en leche tout entor:
« Lasse, fet ele, que ferai
se tout menjue? Que dirai?
& comment le porrai lessier?
50 J'en ai molt tres grant desirrier!
Or aviegne qu'avenir puet,
quar toute mengier le m'estuet! »
            Tant dura cele demoree
que la dame fu saoulee,
55 & li vilains ne tarda mie;
a l'ostel vint, en haut s'escrie:
« Diva, sont cuites les pertris?
— Sire, dist ele, ançois va pis,
quar mengies les a li chas! »
60 Li vilains saut isnel le pas,
seure li cort comme enragiez,
ja li eüst les ieus sachiez
quant el crie: « C'est gas! c'est gas!
Fuiez, fet ele, Sathanas!
65 Couvertes sont por tenir chaudes. »
« Ja vous chantaisse putes laudes,
fet il, foi que je doi saint Ladre!
Or ça mon bon hanap de madre
& ma plus bele blanche nape!

and quickly snatched them from her hand,
35   and each ran off dragging its quarry.
"That's how it goes," she'll say. "I'm sorry."
        She stands out in the road again
to look for her husband, and when
the man's not anywhere in sight,
40   partridge two whets her appetite.
She felt her mouth tingle and water;
she had to have some more; she thought her
mind might just snap if she resisted.
She gently took the neck and twisted
45   it off and ate it, licked her lips,
and sucked her greasy fingertips,
and said, "How can I get away
with eating both? What will I say?
How can I leave it on the plate
50   when the temptation is so great?
No matter what may come of it,
I'll eat it all. I just can't quit!"
        The peasant stayed away until
the woman had eaten her fill.
55   Not too long after, he came back
to where they lived and was not slack
to ask, "Well, now can we eat partridge?"
"You can't imagine what an outrage!
The cat has eaten both the birds!"
60   He jumped up quickly at her words
and rushed at her, as if demented,
to pluck her eyes out. She repented:
"I've covered them to keep them warm!
God shield me from the Devil's harm,
65   it's just a joke! I spoke in jest!"
"I almost beat you to a paste,
by my faith in Saint Lazarus!
Now fetch my wooden drinking glass
and choose a clean white cloth. I'll drape

70   Si l'estenderai sus ma chape
     souz cele treille en cel praiel
        — Mes vous prenez vostre coutel
     qui grant mestier a d'aguisier,
     si le fetes .i. pou trenchier
75   a cele pierre en cele cort. »
     Li vilains se despoille & cort,
     le coutel tout nu en sa main.
          A tant ez vous le chapelain
     qui leenz venoit por mengier.
80   A la dame vint sanz targier,
     si l'acole molt doucement,
     & cele li dist simplement:
     « Sire, dist el, fuiez! fuiez!
     Ja ne serai ou vous soiez
85   honiz ne malmis de vo cors!
     Mes sires est alez lafors
     por son grant coutel aguisier,
     & dist qu'il vous voudra trenchier
     les coilles s'il vous puet tenir!
90   — De Dieu te puist il souvenir,
     dist li prestres, qu'est que tu dis?
     Nous devons mengier .ii. pertris
     que tes sires prist hui matin. »
     Cele li dist: « Par saint Martin
95   ceenz n'a pertris ne oisel—
     de vo mengier me seroit bel
     & moi peseroit de vo mal!
     Mes ore esgardez la aval
     comme il aguise son coutel!
100   — Jel voi, dist il, par mon chapel!
     Je cuit bien que tu as voir dit! »
     Leenz demora molt petit,
     ainz s'en fuï grant aleüre,
     & cele crie: « A bone eüre
105 venez vous en, sire Gombaut!

70   it in the arbor on my cape
     in that small field," the peasant said.
     "You'd better take your carving blade—
     it's not been whetted for an age—
     and go and hone the cutting edge
75   there at the grindstone." So he ran,
     without his cape and, in his hand,
     unsheathed, one of his carving knives.
              Now finally the priest arrives
     in expectation of a feeding
80   and comes straight up to her, proceeding
     to hug her very warmly, too.
     She said without further ado,
     "Be quick about it, Father! Flee!
     I'd hate to be around to see
85   your person maimed and vilified!
     My husband just now went outside
     to sharpen an enormous blade,
     and if he catches you, he said
     he'll cut your balls off on the spot!"
90   "God help you," the priest answers, "what?
     We were supposed to eat, I thought,
     two partridges your husband caught,
     which he asked me here to take part in."
     The woman tells him, "By Saint Martin,
95   what partridges? We've no birds here.
     You won't enjoy your meal, I fear!
     If you were harmed, I'd take it hard!
     Look over there across the yard
     and see him sharpening his knife!"
100 "I see him, yes," he told the wife.
     "Upon my cowl, I think you're right!"
              The priest takes to his heels in flight;
     he doesn't stay a moment more.
     Soon as he's gone, she gives a roar:
105 "Come quickly, Gombaut! On the double!"

— Qu'as tu, dist il, se Dieus te saut?
— Que j'ai? Tout a tens le savrez,
mes se tost corre ne pöez,
perte i avrez si com je croi,
110   quar, par la foi que je vous doi,
li prestre en porte voz pertris! »
Li preudom fu toz aatis,
le coutel porte en sa main,
s'en cort aprés le chapelain.
115   Quant il le vit, se li escrie:
« Ainsi nes en porterez mie! »
Puis s'escrie a granz alenees:
« Bien les en portez eschaufees;
ça les lerez, se vous ataing!
120   Vous serïez mauvés conpaign
se vous les mengiiez sanz moi! »
Li prestre esgarde derrier soi
& voit acorre le vilain.
Quant voit le coutel en sa main
125   mors cuide estre se il l'ataint;
de tost corre pas ne se faint,
& li vilains penssoit de corre,
qui les pertris cuidoit rescorre,
mes li prestres de grant randon
130   s'est enfermez en sa meson.
A l'ostel li vilains retorne
& lors sa fame en aresone:
« Diva, fet il, & quar me dis
comment tu perdis les pertris. »
135   Cele li dist: « Se Dieus m'aït,
tantost que li prestres me vit,
si me pria se tant l'amaisse
que je les pertris li moustraisse
quar molt volentiers les verroit,
140   & je le menai la tout droit
ou je les avoie couvertes.

"God help you, what can be the trouble?"
"The trouble? You'll know soon enough!
If you don't get up off your duff,
you'll be the loser, mark my words.
110 The priest has run off with our birds.
And I mean everything I say!"
The good man is filled with dismay,
and, holding the knife in his hand,
he runs after the clergyman,
115 and, catching sight of him, he cries,
"You won't take them away nowise!"
He calls to him, panting a lot,
"You can't escape—the goods are hot!
What kind of comrade would you be
120 to go and eat them without me?
If I catch you, you'll leave them here!"
The cleric looks back to the rear
and sees the man in hot pursuit,
clutching a carving knife, to boot,
125 and thinks, if caught, that he's undone.
He doesn't just pretend to run,
and his pursuer did the same,
since he'd two partridge to reclaim.
The priest, though, much too swift to catch,
130 gets home, runs in, and bolts the latch.
        The peasant goes back to his house
then and interrogates his spouse.
"Well, tell me how," the man demands,
"our partridge fell into his hands."
135 "So help me God," his wife replies,
"as soon as the priest laid his eyes
on me, he asked if I'd agree,
in friendship's name, to let him see
the partridges; he'd like a look.
140 I didn't hesitate, but took
him where I'd set them out to stand,

Il ot tantost les mains ouvertes,
si les prist & si s'en fuï,
mes je gueres ne le sivi,
145 ainz le vous fis molt tost savoir. »
Cil respont: « Bien pués dire voir.
Or le lessons a itant estre. »
Ainsi fu engingniez le prestre
& Gombaus, qui les pertris prist.
150   Par example cis fabliaus dist
fame est fete por decevoir,
mençonge fet devenir voir
& voir fet devenir mençonge.
Cil n'i vout metre plus d'alonge
155 qui fist cest fablel & ces dis.
Ci faut li fabliaus des pertris.

57. L'OUE AU CHAPELAIN

Jadis avint d'un chapelein
qui ne fu ne fous ne vilein;
molt ot a mengier & a boivre
sus la rivïere de Suevre,
5 qui de poison est plenteïve;
le chapelein ot a non Ive.
Por ce que ja ne se remue
une crasse oue avoit en mue;
c'est .i. oisel de primevere.
10   Or orrez ja com le provoire
fu bien servi de sa crasse oie,
com [ ] en avendra contrejoie.
    Li prestres a s'oue tuee,
si a sa meschine mandee,
15 qui n'avoit pas la bouche amere
(il en ot fete sa commere

and on the spot he reached his hand
out, grabbed them, and took off apace,
but I refrained from giving chase.
145   Instead I quickly let you know."
He answers her, "That may be so.
For now we'll let the matter stand."
In that way was the cleric scammed,
and Gombaut, too, whose birds they were.
150   By this example we infer
that woman's made for trickery;
she makes a lie reality
and turns what's real into a lie.
This author will not amplify
155   on this small fable he's composed.
The partridge story now is closed.

5 7. THE CHAPLAIN'S GOOSE

This happened to a chaplain once,
a man of breeding and good sense
who dwelt nearby the river Sèvres;
of food and drink he had whatever
5   he needed (many fishes live
there), and the chaplain's name was Yves.
The chaplain owned a fine fat goose,
which he kept shut up in his mews,
hatched just that spring, a tender bird.
10   It's high time now that you all heard
just how the chaplain's goose was cooked
and he gave up the usufruct.
       The chaplain, when his goose was slaughtered,
invited his sweetheart, who sure did
15   have a sweet mouth that drove him wild
(she's godmother to his godchild,

por coverture de la gent
por ce qu'il la besoit sovent).
Quant l'oë fu molt tres bien cuite
20 a grant loisir & sanz grant luite,
li prestres a s'oë coverte
& le clerc a la sause fete
blanche & espesse & bien molue
si que tot le cors l'en tressue.
25 (Sa part en a bien deservie,
mes li prestres ne doute mie
qu'il en face ses grenons bruire,
einz s'en cuide molt bien deduire
& s'amie bien saouller . . .
30 mes en .c. muis de fol penser
nen a mie plein poing de sens,
que Salemon dist en son tens
qu'entre la bouche & la cuillier
avient sovent grant enconbrier).
35 Li prestres a sa table mise
& si a sa commere asise
sor .i. coisin & pres du feu
por ce qu'el fu el plus bel leu,
& porce qu'il veïst sa chiere
40 l'avoit trete .i. petit ariere.
      Le prestre s'asist a la table;
einz qu'il eüst fet son saignacle
.i. mesage vint a la porte
qui tieus noveles li aporte
45 dont li prestre n'ot point de joie.
Si dist au clerc: « Va, pren cele oie
& cel gastel & cel pichier
& si t'en va en cel moustier. »
Le clerc fist son commandement,
50 puis retorna inellement,
prist le henap & la toaille
& le coutel qui soëf taille,

so people will not raise a scandal
for all that they may kiss and fondle),
and when at last the roast goose was
20 done (slowly and without much fuss),
he covered up the bird because
his clerk had yet to make the sauce,
which turned out thick, smooth, creamy, rich,
which makes the clerk's whole body itch
25 to have his fully deserved share.
The priest, however, doesn't care
to let his clerk get his beard greasy,
for he intends to take it easy
and eat his fill with his beloved.
30 (A pinch of sense can't be discovered
drowned in a cistern full of twaddle,
so a wise man takes as his model
King Solomon's "Many a slip
often occurs twixt cup and lip.")
35   The table's set; the priest has called
his lady friend and has installed
her on a cushion by the grate,
where he can better contemplate
her lovely features and where she's
40 afforded the amenities.
The priest sat down and took his place.
Before he'd a chance to say grace,
a messenger came to the door
bringing him information for
45 which he'd no interest or use.
He was put out. "Quick, take the goose
and cake and pitcher to the kirk
and keep them there," he told his clerk.
The clerk did as instructed; then
50 he rushed back to the room again
and grabbed the cup and tablecloth
and the sharp knife; then he took off,

& puis referma l'us sor soi—
or puet bien boivre s'il a soi!—
55 & le prestre si est levé,
a une huche en est alé.
Li prestres a pris sa commere;
en la huche qui iluec iere
inelement enz l'enferma
60 & la clef o soi en porta,
devant la porte en vint grant erre:
« Qui est ila, dist le proverre,
qui si or hurtés durement?
— Sire, au prestre sui dant Climent,
65 qui unes lettres vos envoie.
— Sire, se Deus m'otroit grant joie,
molt m'envoie lettres sovent
desce qu'il ot .i. poi de vent
du commandement son seignor!
70 Molt m'aime ore de grant amor,
je ne li sai gré de ceste oevre. »
Le prestre le guichet li euvre,
prist la lettre veille ou ne veille,
& li clers taste a l'oueille,
75 qui molt [i] avoit a atendre.
Tot hors en a trenchié .i. menbre . . .
mes d'un trop bel barat s'amenbre
que onques nul clerc ne fist tel:
il s'en monta desus l'autel,
80 au crucefiz a oint la bouche
si que a autre chose ne touche,
la cuisse li mist el poing destre
& fera ja acroire au prestre
que le crucefiz a mengiee
85 l'oue & le gastel & l'ailliee
& le vin du pichier beü.
A tant le prestre est revenu
qui du vallet s'est delivrez,

closing the door behind him first. He
now can drink deep if he is thirsty!

55   There was a chest there in the room.
The priest told his sweetheart to come,
stood up, went up to it, and placed
her carefully inside the chest
and closed the lid and shut her in
60   and took the key away with him.
Thus having tidied up, he sped
to the door. "Who is there," he said,
"banging away like a berserk?"
"Father, it's me, Dom Clement's clerk.
65   He's sent me to you with a letter."
"As if the man had nothing better
to do, as I trust in the Lord!
At the slightest hint of a word
from our bishop, he writes to me.
70   For all his camaraderie,
I just wish he'd get off my back!"
The priest opened the door a crack
and took the letter willy-nilly.

        His clerk, meanwhile, can eat his fill; he
75   has lots of time for banqueting,
and cuts a drumstick or a wing. . . .
Before long, he's imagining
the neatest scam you ever heard.
He climbed on the altar and smeared
80   with goose fat just the mouth and lips
of the Christ on the crucifix
and stuck a drumstick in His fist.
He's sure he can convince the priest
he stood and watched the icon toss
85   down goose and cake and garlic sauce
and drink a pitcherful of wine.

        At length the priest comes back to dine.
He's sent Dom Clement's clerk away,

droit a la huche en est alez,
90   sa commere a tret de la huche.
A tant li clerc s'escrie & huche:
« Venez ça, tote bone gent! »
Li prestres va inellement
tot droit a l'uis, & cil li oevre.
95   « Or esgardez, dist il, quel oevre!
Ne sai deable ou anemis
s'est en vostre crucefiz mis,
car il a trestote mengiee
l'oue & le gastel & l'ailliee
100   & le vin beü du plomé,
mes ce ne fu pas a mon gré.
Esgardez com il s'en fet cointes—
com il en a les barbes ointes! »
        Bien a fet au prestre la moue!
105   Or puet mengier le prestre s'oue
& fere soupes d'autre pein—
si fu servi le chapelein.

58. LE PRESTRE QUI MENGA MORES

Qui qu'an ait ire ne despit,
sanz terme pranre ne respit
vos dirai d'un provoire .i. conte,
sicom Guerins le nos raconte,
5   qui au marchié voloit aler.
        Sa jument a fait ensseler,
qui granz estoit & bien peüe—
.ii. anz l'ot li prestres tenue,
n'avoit gaires ne soi ne fain,
10   assez avoit aveine & fain.

gone to the chest, and straightaway
90 has helped his lady friend climb out.
The clerk begins to yell and shout:
"Come quickly, Christian gentlefolk!"
The chaplain runs to have a look.
His clerk throws the door open wide.
95 "See what has happened here!" he cried.
  "Who knows what kind of devil's tricks
could have possessed your crucifix,
for only now I saw it make
a meal out of your goose and cake
100 and gravy, and drink all the wine!
I tried to stop it. See the fine
mess it has made, and see how smug
it looks with goose grease on its mug!"
    So now you've heard how the clerk's feast
105 was underwritten by the priest.
The chaplain's polished off his goose.
His bread will serve some other use.

𝟓𝟖. THE PRIEST WHO ATE
   BLACKBERRIES

by Guérin

Though there are some who'll take it ill,
with no further delay I will
tell you a story that Guérin
tells us about a clergyman
5 who wanted to go to the fair.
    He had his groom saddle his mare,
a sturdy and well-nourished beast,
which he'd owned for two years at least,
never thirsty for lack of water
10 or shortchanged on her oats and fodder.

Li prestre son chemin atorne,
ne fait que monter, si s'en torne
vers le marchié sor la jument.
Se l'estoire ne nos en ment,
15   por icele saison me manbre—
bien sai que ce fu en setenbre—
qu'il estoit grant plenté de meures.
Li prestre vait disant ses eures,
ses matines & ses vegiles,
20   mais a l'entree de la vile
plus loing que ne giete une fonde
avoit une rue parfonde;
en .i. buisson avoit gardé,
des meures i vit grant plenté,
25   grosses & noires & meüres,
& li prestres tot a droiture
dist que se Jhesus li aïst,
si beles meures mais ne vit.
Grant fain en ot, si ot talent;
30   la jument fait aler plus lent,
si s'arrestut tot a estal,
mais une chose li fist mal,
que les espines li nuisirent,
& les meures, qui si halt furent
35   (les plus beles el front devant)
qu'avenir n'i pot en seant.
Adonc est li prestres dreciez,
sor la sele monte a .ii. piez,
sor le buisson s'abaisse & cline,
40   puis menjue de grant ravine
des plus beles qu'il i eslut.
Ainz la jument ne se remut,
& quant il oit mengié assez
tant que il en fu toz lassez,
45   vers terre garde & ne se mut
& vit la jument qui s'estut

The priest made ready for the road,
got on his mare, and off he rode
toward the town where the market was.
Unless the story lies to us
15 about the season, I remember—
in fact, I know—it was September,
and blackberries grew everywhere.
The priest, preoccupied in prayer,
matins, and vigils, rides straight on,
20 but near the entrance to the town,
no more than a stone's throw away,
a path ran deep along the way.
He looked and saw, as he was going
by, a bush on which there were growing
25 lots of big, dark, ripe blackberries,
and the priest rightly says that he's
never seen, Jesus help him, bushes
laden with blackberries so luscious.

        They tempted him; he had to try them.
30 He slowed his mare and reined in by them
and halted there, but though he yearned
to eat some, still, he was concerned
that he'd get scratched up by the briar
patch, and the blackberries lay higher
35 above his head (where the most sweet
were) than he could reach from his seat.
Hoisting himself up, the priest stood
on the saddle as best he could.
Bending across the bushes, he
40 began to gobble avidly
the finest fruit that he could pick.
The priest's mare never moved a lick.
        He went on eating them until
he had consumed more than his fill.
45 He stood immobile and looked down,
his glance alighting on his mount

vers le *ronchoi* trestote quoie.
S'en ot li prestres molt grant joie,
qui a .ii. piez est sus montez:

50 « Dieus, fait il, qui or diroit 'Hez!' »
Il le pensa & dit ensanble,
& la jument de poor tranble,
.i. saut a fait tot a bandon,
& li prestres chiet el buisson

55 en tel maniere entre les ronces,
qui d'argent li donast .c. onces
n'alast arriere ne avant,
& la jument s'en vait fuiant.

Chiés le provoire est revenue.

60 Quant li serjant l'ont conneüe,
chascun se maudit & se blasme,
& la feme au prestre pasme
qu'ele quide que il soit morz;
ci fu molt granz li desconforz.

65 Corant s'en vont vers le marchié;
tant ont alé & tant marchié,
el buisson vienent trestot droit
ou le prestre en malaise estoit,
& quant il les ot dementer,

70 commença lor a escrïer:
« Diva! diva! ou alez vos?
Ge sui ici molt doulerous,
pensis, dolenz, molt esmaiez,
quar trop sui malmis & bleciez

75 & poinz de ronces & d'espines
don j'ai sanglentes les eschines. »
Li serjant li ont demandé:
« Sire, qui vos a la monté?
— Pechié, fait il, m'i enbati

80 hui matin quant ge vi[n]g par ci.
Que j'aloie disant mes ores,
si me prist molt grant fain de mores

waiting calmly in place beside
the bush, and his heart swelled with pride.
Standing, he thought, "What a mishap
50   if somebody said 'Giddyap!'"
He actually speaks his thoughts
and, doing so, startles his horse,
who of a sudden bolts and rushes
off, and the priest lands in the bushes,
55   caught in the thorns so hopelessly
that no way can he struggle free,
not for a hundred ounces of
silver; and his mare gallops off.
        Straight to the priest's she gallops home,
60   and when the servants see her come,
they curse themselves and rue the day,
and the priest's wife faints clean away
because she thinks that he is dead.
They nearly went out of their head.
65   Off they go running toward the fair,
not stopping until they come where
the path is with the blackberries
and the priest hanging ill at ease,
who hears them mourning his demise
70   and opens his mouth wide and cries,
"Hey there! Hey there! Where are you headed?
I'm up here in the thorns, embedded,
disconsolate, in pain, astounded,
uncomfortable and gravely wounded,
75   skewered by brambles, with my body
scratched up all over, cut, and bloody."
        His servants ask him and inquire,
"Who on earth stuck you up there, sire?"
"My sins," he tells them, "put me here.
80   This morning, riding to the fair,
I, involved in my rosary,
was so possessed by gluttony

que por rien nule avant n'alasse
devant que assez en mengasse,
85   si m'en est ainsi avenu
que li buissons m'a retenu.
Quar m'aidiez tant que fors en soie,
quar autre chose ne querroie
mais que ge fusse a garison
90   & a repos en ma maison. »
          Por cest flabel pöez savoir
que cil ne fait mie savoir
qui tot son pensé dit & conte,
quar maint domaige en vient & honte
95   a mainte gent, ce est la voire,
ainsi com il fist au provoire.

59. LE FOTEOR

Qui fabloier velt, si fabloit,
mais que son dit n'en affebloit
por dire chose desresnable.
L'en puet si bel dire une fable
5   qu'ele puet ainsi com voir plaire.
D'un vallet vos vuel conte faire
qui n'avoit mie grant avoir,
mais il n'ert mie sanz savoir,
neporquant bien vestuz estoit,
10   cote & mantel d'un drap avoit
et nueve espee & uns nués ganz.
Beaus vallez ert & avenanz,
entor .xxvi. anz avoit;
nus mestier faire ne savoit:
15   de vile en vile aloit toz jors,
par chevaliers, *par* vavassors,

for blackberries, I'd not the power
to go on, but had to devour
85   my fill of them. While picking samples,
I got entangled in the brambles.
Come help me get out of this mess.
There's nothing I want more, unless
it's to be back home once more, resting
90   in bed and safely convalescing."
        This fabliau clearly explains
that a man must be short on brains
to speak all that is on his mind,
for misfortune and shame, you'll find,
95   are the reward of those who do,
as happened to this prelate, too.

59. THE FUCKER

Let fabulists confabulate;
but tales too fabulous deflate
a fable's worth and make it feeble.
A tale well told can please the people
5   as pleasantly as gospel truth.
I want to tell you of a youth
who had no claim to affluence,
but more than his share of good sense.
Though poor, he went about well clad;
10   his coat and cape matched, and he had
new gloves and also a new sword,
and he was handsome as a lord.
His age was twenty-six or so.
He had no trade, but used to go
15   from town to town, where in the castles
of various and sundry vassals

si mengoit en autruiz osteus
quar petiz estoit ses chasteus.
.I. jor vint a une cité—
20 ge en ai le non oblïé,
or soit ainsinc com a Soissons.
Pains & vins & char & poissons
menja la nuit a grant plenté;
ses ostes a sa volenté
25 li fist venir de quanqu'il volt,
& il li dit tot a brief mot:
« Beaus dolz ostes, cestui escot
paiera teus qui n'en set mot.
Or me dites, *foi* [que] devez
30 la riens que vos plus chier amez
& que Dieus joie vos ameint,
ou la plus bele dame meint
de Soissons. — La plus bele? Voire,
par foi, si c'on nos fait acroire
35 moi & toz çaus de ceste vile,
madame Marge qui ne file,
la feme Guion de la place,
c'est la plus bele que g'i saiche.
Neïs ses mariz le tesmoigne,
40 qu'el n'aime mie une escaloigne
mains li que lui, mais plus encor.
Por quoi le demandez vos or?
— Beaus hostes, foi que me devez,
puis que conjuré m'en avez,
45 or escoutez: menestreus sui,
si sui & a li & a lui
envoiez de par .i. haut home.
Or vos en ai dite la some,
beaus ostes. — C'est .i. marcheanz
50 molt larges & molt despendanz,
& sa feme riens ne l'en doit.
Beau vos sera s'ele vos voit.

he lodged and ate at their expense,
since he himself had meager rents.

20   He arrived in a town one day;
which one it was, I couldn't say.
(I'll make it Soissons, if you wish.)
That night he dined on meat and fish
and bread and wine in quantities.
25   His host did all he could to please
him; everything he craved, he brought.
He told his host, keeping it short,
"Someone, good host, will pay my bill. . . .
Just *who* will doesn't know it still.
Now tell me, as you would be true
30   to that which is most dear to you
and as you trust God's loving care,
who's the loveliest woman here
in Soissons?" "The most lovely? Well,
in faith, to believe what they tell
35   me and my fellow citizens,
it's Marjorie, who never spins,
Guy's wife, who lives in the main square.
I know of nobody more fair,
as her own husband will confess,
40   whom she does not love any less
than her own person, if not more.
How come you're asking, and what for?"
"Innkeeper, by the faith you've shown
me, since you've asked, I'll make it known.
45   An itinerant minstrel I,
and I've been sent here to them by
a high-born man's recommendation.
So, now you know my situation."
"Her husband is a merchant. He
50   spends money openhandedly,
and his wife is of equal virtue.
Getting to know her cannot hurt you."

—Voir, oïl, voir! Molt tres matin
li dirai ge en mon latin,
55   se ge puis, mon messaige bien. »
Enprés ce ne distrent puis rien,
ainz s'en alerent lués gesir,
mais cil qui estoit en desir
de la bele dame veoir
60   ne pot onques avoir pooir
de dormir jusqu'a l'ainzjornee,
& lués que l'aube fu crevee
leva sus, si s'apareilla
& enprés son oste esveilla,
65   si li pria qu'il retenist
s'espee tresqu'il revenist
en gaiges por l'escot du soir,
& il li dist: « Volentiers, voir,
beaus ostes; alez de par Dieu.
70   Dieus vos doint venir en tel leu
ou auques puissoiz gaagnier!
Lessiez vos ençois ensaignier
l'ostel ou vos aler devez
que vos de ci mais remüez. »
75   Lors s'en va cil a molt grant joie
quant monstree li fu la voie.

      A l'ostel molt droit assena
sicom la voie le mena,
mais n'ert encore nus levez;
80   d'autre part la voie ert alez
droit endroit l'us sor .i. estal,
se sist, mais ce li fist molt mal
que si longuement vit clos l'uis,
quar il i sist grant piece puis
85   ainz que levast la chanberiere,
qui n'estoit mie costumiere
d'espïer cascun jor le jor,
mais por ce ot plus grant laisor

"Indeed, indeed! Soon as it's day
I'll go and see her, if I may,
55   and state my errand in fair speech."
       After, they said no more, and each
of them directly went to bed.
Thoughts of her beauty filled his head.
He must see her! His expectations
60   made him unable to have patience
to sleep until morning had come,
and at the same time as the sun
rose he got up. When he was dressed,
he wakened his host to request
65   he be so good as to accord,
till he returned, to keep his sword
as collateral for his bill,
and he replied, "Of course I will,
my friend! Go forth now with God's grace,
70   and may He bring you to a place
where you'll be paid as you desire.
First of all, though, you should inquire
exactly where her house may be
before you leave the hostelry."
75   Then he set out, carefree and gay,
as soon as he'd been shown the way.
       He went straight on to her abode,
making no detour from his road,
but no one there was yet awake,
80   and so he crossed the road to take
a seat on a bench in plain sight
of the door, annoyed that despite
his lengthy vigil by the door
it stayed shut a long time before
85   the chambermaid rose in the end,
who usually couldn't spend
her morning hours just lying down,
but with the master out of town

que ses sires n'iert en la vile.
90 Quanque cil porpenssoit la guile
comment il porroit esploitier
de lui a la dame acointier,
la baissele esveillie fu,
son huis ovri, si fist du fu,
95 si vait son ostel arreer
tant qu'ele prist a regarder
celui qui devant l'us seoit,
qui en ses .ii. mains tornoioit
.i. blans ganz que il enformoit
100 & toz jors vers l'us regardoit;
durement s'en esmerveilla.
A tant la dame s'esveilla;
tant que fors de la chanbre oissi
si vit le vallet endroit li,
105 tres parmi l'us le vit seoir;
durement li plot a veoir
qu'il avoit les crins beaus & blons
(a merveille les avoit lons),
janbe sor autre iluec seoit—
110 mielz li plaist comme plus le voit.
 En son cuer a enmer le prist;
sa baïsse apele & li dist:
« Maroie, quar me di or voir
que cil est qui la voi seoir.
115 — Dame, foi que doi vos, ne sai.
Des hui matin que m'esveillai
le vi ge iluecques assis.
Ne sai por quoi tant i a sis.
Ge cuit que c'est .i. barestere.
120 — Maroie, par l'ame ton pere,
va si, li va tant demandant
que tu saiches qu'il vait querant
& por quoi iluec a tant sis. »

she had more time to take it easy.
90 So, while the man was keeping busy
by thinking up a likely scheme
to get her to agree to see 'im,
the servant rose and opened wide
the door and lit a fire inside
95 and started putting things in order,
when the man sitting outside caught her
attention, and she turned her glance
on him who's turning in his hands
a pair of white gloves, which he plays
100 with, holding their door in his gaze.
His presence was a big surprise.

Her mistress wasn't slow to rise
and leave her room. Then she, too, saw
the young man opposite her door,
105 easy to spot beyond the gate.
It pleased her much to contemplate
him, for he had a head of hair
amazingly long, blond, and fair,
his legs crossed, and the more she sees him,
110 the more she finds his manner pleasing.
Feeling her heart begin to stir,
she calls her maid and says to her,
"Seated outside I see a youth.
Who is he, Mary? Tell the truth."
115 "Lady, I've really no idea.
I first noticed him sitting there
when I woke earlier today.
What keeps him here, I couldn't say.
I doubt he's up to any good."
120 "On your father's soul, Mary, would
you go and ask, and so find out
why he's been lingering about
so long and what he's seeking here?"

Son cul a par l'oreille pris
125 Maroie devant & derriere,
si a passee la charriere;
sicom sa dame li commande,
au vallet vient, si li demande:
« Queus hom estes vos, beaus amis,
130 qui tote jor avez ci sis?
— Ge sui fouterres, bele suer,
que bone joie aiez au cuer.
— & bone joie vos doint Dieus,
beaus sire! Vos & vostre gieus
135 fussiez ore en une longaigne!
Molt me tornë a grant engaigne
que vos issi m'avez gabee! »
Par maltalent s'en est tornee,
s'a trespassee la charriere,
140 a sa dame revint arriere.
La dame la vit, si s'en rist:
« Maroie, fait ele, que dist
li vallez qui tant a la sis?
— Dame, ne me chalt de ses dis!
145 Ja est .i. gloz! .i. mal lechierre!
— Ne t'a mie fait bele chiere?
Quant si t'en revienz esmarie,
que dist il? Nel me celer mie.
— Ja me dit qu'il est .i. fouterre.
150 — Dit il ce, par l'ame ton pere?
— Oïl, dame, foi que vos doi.
— Tu me gabes, ge cuit, par foi!
— Non faz, dame, foi que doi vos.
— Maroie, alom i anbedous.
155 — Dame, alez i trestote soule;
il n'i a mie trop grant foule!
Ge n'ai cure de ses paroles;
trop sont anuieuses & foles.
— Maroie, ge i vois savoir.

So Mary gets her ass in gear
125 and doesn't stop until her feet
have carried her across the street,
and, just as her mistress desires,
approaches the youth and inquires,
"What kind of man are you, my friend,
130 to sit out here for hours on end?"
"By trade I am a fucker, miss,
so may your heart be filled with bliss."
"God grant you bliss as well, monsieur!
You ought to be thrown in a sewer,
135 and in with you, your way of joking!
It makes me angry to be spoken
to flippantly and to be mocked!"
    She turned her back upon him, shocked,
and, fuming, crossed the road and went
140 back to her by whom she'd been sent.
Her mistress looked at her and smiled
and said, "What did he answer, child,
that youth sitting across the way?"
"To hell with what he had to say!
145 He's scurrilous, foulmouthed, and crude!"
"What, Mary? Was the fellow rude?
Don't hide from me what he related
that brings you back so agitated."
"He says he's a fucker by trade."
150 "God bless us! Is that what he said?"
"Upon my oath, dear lady, yes."
"No way! You're kidding me, I'd guess."
"Lady, I'm not, upon my oath."
"Mary, we'll go and see him both."
155 "Lady, go see him by yourself.
He's free, for there's nobody else
around. For my part, I'll dispense
with his coarse words, devoid of sense."
"Mary, I'll see if it is so."

160   — En non Dieu, vos faites savoir!
     Ja en revenrez tote saige. »
         Cele qui ot le cuer volaige
     s'en va tot riant cele part,
     & cil ne fist pas le coart,
165   ainz se leva contre la dame,
     & cele, qui com joene feme
     ne se pooit tenir de rire
     quant el i vint, ne sot que dire,
     si que tote s'en vergoigna;
170   a chief de pose si parla:
     « Queus hom estes? » & il li dist:
     « Dame, donc ne le vos aprist
     la pucele qui ci fu ore?
     Volez que ge le die encore?
175   Ge sui fouterres a loier;
     se me volioiz alöer,
     ge cuit, si bien vos serviroie
     que vostre bon gré en avroie.
     — Alez, sire! Honiz soiez!
180   Bons estes, se vos ne piriez,
     qui la gent servez de tel guile!
     — [Dame, foi que je doi saint Gile],
     ge ai eü maint bel servise
     de servir dames en tel guise.
185   — Voire, d'aucunne sanz henor!
     & neporquant, ce est a jor
     ou en tasche que vos ovrez?
     Se vos ma pucele servez,
     .iiii. deniers de sa gaaigne
190   vos donra, se ele vos daigne.
     Tant avrez vos por lui servir
     se vos les volez deservir.
     — Dame, de la vostre besoigne
     penssez ainz que de ci m'esloigne,
195   quar ne vueil mais ci plus ester. »

160 "That's smart of you! In God's name, go!
You'll come back having learned your lesson."
        The lady's flighty heart was pressing
her on; she went there with a smile.
He didn't act ill-bred or vile,
165 but stood up out of deference,
and she, whose inexperience
could not conceal her merriment,
did not know what to say and went
red in the face when she came close.
170 She ventured after a long pause,
"What kind of man are you?" He said,
"Lady, then did your chambermaid
who was just here not let you know?
If you wish, I'll repeat it, though.
175 I am a fucker one can hire,
and I maintain, if you require
my services, I'll service you,
and you'll be thankful for them, too!"
"Come off it, sir! For shame, for shame!
180 I'm sure you're good. Why invite blame
by tricking people with your wiles?"
"I promise, lady, by Saint Giles,
I've well and often earned my pay
by serving women in this way."
185 "No doubt, but none of honest name!
But is it, tell me all the same,
per day or per job that you're paid?
If you'll service my chambermaid
and you're that good, she'll pay your fee
190 with fourpence from her salary.
That's what you'll get if she engages
you and if you can earn your wages."
"Lady, think whether you require
my labors before I retire
195 from here, for I've no wish to stay."

Lors s'en va sanz plus arrester,
& la dame le rehuscha:
« Mar i alez! Ça venez, ça!
Dites, foi que devez henor,
200 combien en vos done le jor.
— Dame, contre ce qu'elë est
me puet tote jor trover prest.
La laide me done sous .c.
por ce que ele l'aise sent,
205 & la bele me done mains.
— Par foi, vos n'estes pas vilains!
& conbien pranroiz vos de moi?
— Dame, fait il, foi que vos doi,
se ge ai .xx. sous & mon baig
210 & ge ai mon conroi de gaaing,
gel voldrai molt bien deservir,
quar ge sai bien & bel servir
une dame quant g'i met paine. »
A tant la dame o lui l'enmaine,
215 que plus lonc conte ne volt faire.
      Sa baiasse en ot grant contraire
quant o celui la voit venir;
tant dit, ne se pot atenir:
« Dieus, aïe! or avomes hoste!
220 Dahez ait il s'il ne vos oste
encui le mantel de cel col!
Par foi, ge le tenrai por fol
s'il n'i gaaigne son escot!
— Tais toi, si ne sone mais mot!
225 fait la dame. Ge te ferroie
si que sanglante te feroie!
Mais porchace, foi que doiz moi,
que nos aions .i. bon conroi
& que li bains soit eschauffez.
230 — Baig? fait ele. Por les mausfez
puis[se] ge mais hui baig [chaufer]!

He started then to walk away,
and she called after him and said,
"You come on back! Don't leave just yet!
Upon your honor, won't you say
200 how much it is you charge per day?"
"According to her person, lady,
will she who hires me find me ready:
a hundred shillings if she's plain,
since she's the one who stands to gain,
205 and pretty women pay me less."
"You're not exactly cheap, I guess!
And how much would you ask of me?"
"Lady, to tell you honestly,
for twenty shillings and a meal
210 along with a hot bath, I feel
I'll have been paid as I deserve,
for, when I mean to, I can serve
a woman with consummate skill."
    She bids him to come with her; she'll
215 waste no more time in bartering.
Her maid finds it disheartening
to see the two of them together
and says, at the end of her tether,
"God help us, here comes company!
220 I'll take him for a fool if he
can't steal the shirt right off your back!
Good luck to him, if he's the knack
to do his job and earn his keep!"
The lady says, "Not one word! Keep
225 quiet, or you will feel my blows
and end up with a bloody nose!
If you respect me, don't be slack
in fixing us a hearty snack,
and get a bath heated as well."
230 "A bath! May all the fiends in Hell
soak in the water that I draw!"

— Dame, ne fust por moi lasser
& por ce qu'il vos anuiast,
ceste pucele me loast.
235 Issi vers lui me deduiroie
que debonnaire la feroie
s'i la me laississez servir.
— Comment porrïez deservir
dont envers moi vostre loier?
240 — Dame, bien volez emploier
vostre avoir en marcheandise,
fait la garce, par seint Denise!
S'il me servoit a mon talent,
avoir porroit de mon argent
245 & du mien tost une grant part.
— Non fera, fole! Dieus l'en gart!
— Si ferai, s'il vos plaist, ma dame.
Ja n'i avra perte de l'ame!
Ge sai le mestier par usaige:
250 il n'a el mont oisel volaige,
moineaus ne colons, qui tant oevre
com ge faz quant ge sui en l'uevre.
— Sire, que vos done ma dame? »
Fait se il: « Bele, par saint Jame,
255 .xx. sous de bons deniers me done,
baig & conroi com a preudome.
— & vos conbien de moi prandrez?
— Par foi, grant solaz atendrez
hui cest jor de moi por .x. livres.
260 — Qu'avez vos dit? Estes vos yvres,
qui .x. livres me demandez?
Dites mains. — Se vos commandés,
.vi. livres soient. — Mais .iii., sire.
— Ge n'oseroie de mains dire;
265 .c. sous dorrez, fait il, au meins.
— Tendez donc ça, sire, voz mains,
si sera la paumee faite,

"It may be just to tire me or
because she has it in for you,
but this girl wants to hire me too,
235   lady. With her I'd gladly sport
and make her behave as she ought,
if you'll let me serve her in turn."
"And how do you propose to earn
what you've contracted for from me?"
240   The maid retorts, "By Saint Denis,
reserve the money in your pocket,
lady, for spending in the market!
If his performance gives me pleasure,
he can have a substantial measure
245   of what I've earned and what I own."
"He won't, you minx! Leave him alone!"
"I will, if you please, and I pledge
my sword won't lose its cutting edge.
I know this trade inside and out:
250   There's not a bird flitting about,
sparrow or dove, that through exertion
can equal me at my profession."
"Sir, how much will my mistress pay?"
"By Saint James, twenty shillings. They
255   must be laid out in ready cash
along with dinner and a wash."
"And for me what's your going rate?"
"In faith, for ten pounds you'll have great
satisfaction from me today."
260   "Are you drunk? How much did you say?
You ask me for ten pounds? What nerve!
Go lower." "If you want, I'll serve
your needs for six." "Let's make it three."
"I wouldn't dare decrease my fee.
265   Five pounds, and that's my minimum."
"Your hand upon it, mister. Come,
let's shake hands and call it a sale,

quar li marchiez molt bien me haite.
L'argent avrez ja en baillie. »
270 A son escrin en est saillie
ou li .c. sous nonbrez gisoient
qui des antan mis i estoient,
que de pieça aünez ot;
& sa dame s'en merveillot
275 quant fors de son escrin voit traire;
plus en ot joie que contraire
por ce que l'avoit ranposnee.
Par .ii. foiz l'a cil retornee
molt tost & molt isnelement,
280 & cele puis molt lieement
fist ce qu'an l'ostel ot a faire;
molt fu puis lie & debonnaire:
le baig chaufa, le mengier fist.
Quant le baig fu fait, si le mist
285 en une cuve enz en la chanbre,
& cil, a qui de riens ne manbre
fors de son preu & de son aise,
de quan qu'il onques puet s'aaise,
si entre el baig la dame o lui,
290 assez mengierent ambedui
& burent bon vin a plenté.
La dame ot bien sa volenté
de tot fors del deerain mes,
& cil, qui du mestier ert fres,
295 ne se volt a lui affroier
desi qu'il ot tot son loier,
.xx. sous, toz contez en sa main,
& quant cil en ot fait son plain,
de la cuve sailli lués fors,
300 a .i. drap essuie son cors,
o la dame couche en .i. lit;
molt plainement fist son delit
de la dame, une foiz sanz plus,

for I'm content to close the deal.
I'll pay you now what we've agreed."
270   　　She went to get a box where she'd
been saving up for some time past
one hundred shillings she'd amassed
over the years, penny by penny.
Her mistress, stunned to see so many
275   coins counted out of her maid's till,
felt pleasure rather than ill will
that Mary had answered her back.
He flipped her over on her back
and, quick as lightning, gave her double.
280   She gave her mistress no more trouble
and fulfilled every household function
contentedly, without compunction:
heated the bath, their meal prepared,
and when the bath was hot, she poured
285   a tub within the lady's chamber.
The fucker, being of a temper
to think only of earthly pleasure,
enjoyed the water in full measure.
The lady joined him for a soak;
290   in company the two partook
of choice wines and copious fare.
　　The lady got to have her share
of all she craved except dessert,
and he, fresh from work and alert,
295   refused to satisfy her wants
until his fee was in his hands,
twenty shillings, paid out in full.
When he'd eaten and bathed his fill,
he quickly stepped out of the tub
300   and took a cloth in hand to rub
his body dry; then with her he
got in bed and knew ecstasy,
but only once, and then he stopped

tantost *rest do lit* sailli sus.
305 Cil s'en entre el baig derechief,
mais cui qu'an soit ou bel ou grief,
a tant ez vos l'oste venu.
Lors croi que mal soit avenu!
     Marïon, lués que ele l'oit,
310 en la chanbre s'en va tot droit,
a sa dame vient, si li dist.
La dame l'ot, pas ne s'en rist,
ainz vient au baig au bacheler:
« Or tost, dit ele, du haster!
315 Mesire vient! Reponez vos!
     — Ce est donc autre que li cous?
     — C'est mes mariz. — Donc vait il bien!
     — Mais mal, fait el, por nule rien,
que por riens que el mont eüst
320 ne voldroie qu'il vos eüst
trové! Mais issiez molt tost fors!
     — Dame, foi que ge doi mon cors,
ge n'en istrai ore ne ore,
ainz me vueil ci deduire encore;
325 mais recouchiez en vostre lit,
s'alons faire nostre delit.
     — A mal eür! Que dites vos?
Vez ci ja mon seignor sor nos! »
A tant li sire en la chanbre entre,
330 & la dame, cui tuit li menbre
tranblent de hide & de paor,
ne dit .i. mot a son seignor,
ainz est fors de la chanbre issue,
& cil du baig ne se remue
335 mais, qu'il dist: « Bien viegnoiz, bel oste! »
Cil ne dit mot, qui sa cape oste;
quant le vit, si fu si pensis,
si dist: « Qui estes vos, amis,
qui en ma chanbre vos baigniez?

and from the bed directly hopped
305   and climbed right back into the bath.
Though some may cry and some may laugh,
who should come home then but the master?
Now I believe they'll meet disaster.
        Mary, soon as she hears him coming,
310   straight to her mistress comes a-running,
enters the room, and tells her news,
which certainly did not amuse
the lady. She goes to the tub
and tells the young man, "Hurry up!
315   The master's home! Conceal yourself!"
"The cuckold? Or somebody else?"
"My husband!" "A well-timed arrival!"
"But not," she says, "for our survival!
For all the world I couldn't bear
320   to have my husband find you here.
Get out right now and make a run for't!"
"Dear lady, as I love my comfort,
I'll get out later at my leisure;
for now I'll not cut short my pleasure.
325   Get back in bed now and lie down,
and later we can fool around."
"Like hell we can! Don't be so fatuous!
My husband is about to catch us!"
        Just then he comes into the chamber,
330   and his wife, whose every last member
shakes with the terror of the tomb,
seeing him enter, flees the room,
unable to utter a word,
while in the bathtub, undisturbed,
335   our hero says, "Welcome, good host!"
Dumbstruck, he takes his cloak off, most
befuddled and preoccupied
to see him there. "Say," he replied,
"who are you to bathe in my house?"

340　　　— Mais vos, qui ci ne me daigniez
　　　　respondre quant ge vos salu?—
　　　　quar ge sui cil qui a valu
　　　　plus as gentius dames du mont
　　　　que tuit cil qui el siecle sont,
345　　　quar ge sui un fouterres maistre—
　　　　ja mais si bon ne porra naistre!
　　　　.xx. sous doi ci gaaignier hui;
　　　　bien les i avrai saus encui
　　　　la dame qui m'a alöé,
350　　　quar bien la cuit servir a gré,
　　　　mais n'ai encor a li geü,
　　　　n'encore mon loier eü,
　　　　mais or est tens de comencier.
　　　　Molt tost la me faites coschier,
355　　　si irai faire mon revel.
　　　　— Amis, ge vos dirai tot el.
　　　　Desqu'ainsi est que löez fustes
　　　　ne vos avueques li geüstes,
　　　　por ce perdre ne devez rien,
360　　　por li vos paierai ge bien. »
　　　　Lors est cil fors du baig issuz,
　　　　autres .xx. sous a receüz;
　　　　or en porte [ ] double *loier*.
　　　　N'a cure de li convoier
365　　　la dame quant cil s'en ala.
　　　　Cil a Dieu commendez les a.
　　　　　　Cil qui .vii. livres enporta
　　　　son oste molt reconforta
　　　　quant il li monstra les deniers.
370　　　Toz dis, fu il toz costumiers
　　　　de servir dames en tel guise;
　　　　puis en reçust maint bel servise:
　　　　de povreté vint a richece,
　　　　& puis avint por sa pröece
375　　　qu'il quist de lui garir engien;

340 "What about you, who shut your mouth
and ignore my civility?
I'm a man whose ability
assures that I surpass in worth
for women's needs all men on earth,
345 a master fucker virtuoso,
compared with whom all men are so-so.
I've been engaged today for twenty
shillings. The lady will get plenty
in return now she's rented me:
350 I think I'll serve her to a tee.
I've not lain with her as contracted
nor has my fee yet been collected,
but it's high time that we began.
Put her to bed with me, my man,
355 and I'll commence my pleasure session."
"Friend, I've a counterproposition.
Since it appears you're under contract
but as of yet there's been no contact,
I'll see to it no money's lost
360 and buy her back from you at cost."
Then, stepping from the bathtub, he
received another one-pound fee,
a single job for double pay.
        When the young man went on his way,
365 the lady wouldn't see him off.
He wished good fortune to them both.
The seven pounds the young man had
made his innkeeper very glad
when he was shown the coins he'd earned.
370 Thus, in the end the young man turned
professional in women's service
and through his skill came to deserve his
quick rise to wealth from poverty.
Because of his audacity,
375 once only his wits saved the day;

nequedent il li chaï bien—
mais tel .c. meller s'en peüssent
qui en la fin honiz en fussent!—
mais Fortune, a qui il servi,
380 l'en dona ce qu'il deservi.
     L'en dit pieça: Qui va, il lesche,
     & qui toz jors se siet, il seche.

60. L'ESCUIRUEL

Ci vous vueil conter d'une fame
qui fu une molt riche dame;
de Röem fu, si com l'en conte,
& bien le nous dist & raconte
5   qu'ele avoit une fille bele
qui estoit molt gente pucele,
molt avenant & molt bien fete,
quar Nature l'avoit portrete
& si ot mis toute s'entente;
10   en former si bele jovente
avoit mis trestoute sa cure.
Ele estoit bele a desmesure;
son pere & sa mere l'amoient,
a *lor* pooir la chierissoient
15   plus que toz lor autres enfanz.
La pucele avoit .xv. anz.
     Sa mere forment le chastie
& dist: « Fille, ne soiez mie
ne trop parlant ne trop nonciere
20   ne de parler trop coustumiere,
quar a mal puet l'en atorner
fame quant l'en l'ot trop parler
autrement que el ne doit.
Por ce chascune se devroit

still, he came out of it okay.
(A hundred better men who earned
their bread this way would have been burned,
but Fortune, whom he served on earth,
380   made sure he got what he was worth.)
        The saying goes: Get out and use it!
Who sits around all day will lose it.

60. THE SQUIRREL

The story I want to relate
tells of a woman of estate,
a Rouennaise, by all accounts,
and likewise our story recounts
5   that the woman was also blessed
with a fair daughter of the best
breeding, comely and well proportioned.
Nature, who formed her, had apportioned
all of the graces one can find
10   in young girls and had set her mind
to lavish on her all her care.
Her beauty was beyond compare.
Her father's and her mother's love
was such that they put her above
15   their other children, truth be told.
        The girl was now fifteen years old.
Her mother lectured her and taught her
and said, "Don't let yourself, my daughter,
be too outspoken or loquacious,
20   nor, when you do speak, too audacious.
People won't readily forgive
a woman who's too talkative
and says things that are unbecoming,
and for this reason every woman

25   garder de parler folement,
         & une chose vous desfent
         sor toutes autres molt tres bien:
         que ja ne nommez cele rien
         qui cil homme portent pendant. »
30   Icele respont, qui ot tant
         escouté qu'il li anuiot
         quant el plus tere ne se pot:
         « Mere, dist ele, dites moi
         comment il a a non & qoi.
35   — Tais toi, fille! Je ne l'os dire.
         — Est ce la riens que a mon sire
         entre les janbes li pent, dame?
         — Tesiez, fille! Ja nule fame,
         s'ele n'est trop de male teche,
40   ne doit nommer cele peesche
         qui entre les janbes pendeille
         a ces hommes. — & quel merveille
         est ore de nommer peesche?
         Est ce ore ce dont l'en pesche?
45   — Taisiez, fille! vous estes fole.
         Ne dites pas cele parole;
         peesche n'a ele pas non.
         Ja nous fames ne le devon
         nommer en nis une maniere,
50   ne au devant ne au derriere.
         — Cele deable pendeloche,
         ma bele mere, est ce dont loche
         ou plonjon qui se set plongier
         & set nöer par le vivier
55   & par la fontaine mon pere?
         — Nenil, fille, ce dist la mere.
         — Que est ce dont? Dites le moi.
         — Bele fille, dirai le toi . . .
         — Oïl, foi que vous mi devez!
60   — . . .ja soit ce qu'il soit deveez,

25 ought to refrain from idle speech.
There's one thing more I want to teach
you most insistently of all:
Don't speak the word by which we call
that thing that hangs in a man's britches."
30 The girl says in reply—she itches
to have her say, these fine orations
having severely tried her patience—
"Mother," she answers, "tell me now
exactly what it's called and how."
35 "Be quiet, girl. I wouldn't dare."
"Is it that thing that's hanging there,
lady, between my father's legs?"
"Be quiet, girl! None but the dregs
of womankind who know no shame
40 would ever make so bold to name
that snippet which hangs dangling under
men's abdomens." "Is it a wonder
to speak aloud a word like *snippet*?
Tell me, do they go fishing with it?"
45 "Be quiet, girl! Don't be absurd
or utter such a wicked word!
A snippet isn't what it's called.
We women mustn't be so bold
as call it by its right name nor
50 refer to it by metaphor."
"That little hanging devil, mother,
is it some kind of fish or other?
Is it some kind of loon or duck
that likes to swim around and duck
55 its head in father's streams and ponds?"
"No, child, no," her mother responds.
"What is it, then? Don't keep it secret!"
"Since you insist, daughter, I'll speak it—"
"Yes, mother, tell me as I've bidden."
60 "—although to name it is forbidden.

& qui droit & reson le dit,
je te di bien que ce est vit. »
Quant la pucele ce oï,
si s'en rist & si s'esjoï:
65 « Vit! dist ele, Dieu merci, vit!
Vit dirai je, cui qu'il anuit!
Vit! Chetive!—vit dist mon pere,
vit dist ma suer, vit dist mon frere,
& vit dist nostre chanberiere,
70 & vit avant & vit arriere
nomme chascuns a son voloir.
Vous meïsme, mere, por voir,
dites vit, & je, toute lasse,
qu'ai forfet que vit ne nommaise?
75 Vit! me doinst Diez que je n'i faille! »
     Quant la mere ot que se travaille
en vain & que pas une bille
ne vaut quanqu'ele dit sa fille,
d'iluec s'en part, vait s'en plorant.
80   Demanois ez vous acorant
.i. vallet: Robins avoit non,
granz ert & de bele façon,
quar il ert niez a .i. prior;
de miches ot vescu maint jor,
85 & si manoit dedenz la vile;
de barat sot molt & de guile.
D'un leu secré ou il estoit
ot oï quanques dit avoit
la preude fame a la pucele
90 & tout ce que la damoisele
ot a sa mere respondu;
grant joie en ot & liez en fu.
Li pautoniers fu granz & gras,
si tint sa main desoz ses dras,
95 son vit commence a paumoier
tant qu'il l'avoit fet aroidier,

To name it rightly, just between us,
it properly is called a penis."
    As soon as the girl heard its right
name, she laughed loudly in delight.
65 "Penis!" she cried. "Penis, God bless it!
Like it or not, I shall express it!
Penis! My father and the other
children say penis. Sister, brother
say penis, and our chambermaid
70 says penis. Nobody's afraid
to say penis if they so choose.
You yourself, mother, even use
the penis word! What crime so heinous
have I done that I can't say penis?
75 Penis! Please God I'm not denied it!"
Her mother sees that she has chided
her all to no avail, that what
she tells her daughter counts for squat,
and goes away from her in tears.
80   Just then there suddenly appears
a young man. Robin was his name,
his manners gallant, large his frame,
raised on white bread and dainty buns,
one of the prior's siblings' sons,
85 and he resided in Rouen.
He was a master of the con.
He'd overheard them from a hiding
place how her mother had tried guiding
her daughter's moral education
90 and the effect of her oration
and how her daughter had responded,
and liked the way her answer sounded.
He was a big and strapping fellow.
He took his hand and slipped it below
95 his clothing and fondled his rod
until it was aroused and hard,

puis est venuz a la pucele
qui tant ert avenant & bele,
& dist: « Dieus vous saut, bele amie!
100   — Ha, Robert! Dieus vous beneïe!
Dites moi, se Dieus vous aït,
que vous tenez. » & il li dist:
« Dame, ce est .i. escuiruel.
Volez le vous? — Oïl, mon vuel
105   aus mains le tenisse je ore.
       — Amie, non ferez encore,
de ce parlez vous ore en vain,
mes tendez ença vostre main
tout souavet que nel bleciez.
110   S'il vous plest, si l'achatissiez. »
La pucele la main li tent,
& cil tout maintenant la prent,
se li a mis le vit el poing,
que de tel mes avoit besoing.
115   « Robin, fet ele, il est tout chaut.
       — Douce amie, se Dieus me saut,
il se leva or de son cruet.
       — Par les menbres dont il se muet,
en non Dé, quar il est toz vis,
120   voire! dist ele. Li chetis,
comme il tressaut & se remue! »
Ele avoit la coille veüe:
« Robin, fet ele, qu'est ce ci?
       — Bele, fet il, ce est son ni.
125   — Voire, fet el, je sent .i. oef.
       — Par foi, il le punst or tout nuef.
       — En non Dieu, .i. autre j'en sent.
       — Douce amie, que il n'en rent
nul mois de l'an que .ii. ensanble.
130   — Voire, fet ele, ce me sanble
que il est de molt bone orine.
A il a nule riens mecine?

and then insouciantly strolled
toward the fair fifteen-year-old.
He said, "Fair lass, God be with you!"
100   "Why, Robin! God be with you, too.
Tell me, as you hope for God's aid,
just what you're holding there." He said,
"A squirrel, lass. Do you aspire
to have your own?" "How I desire
105   to hold it in my hands and pet it!"
"No way, my lass, better forget it;
you speak of that to no avail.
Still, if you like, the beast's for sale.
Come, slip your hand beneath my shirt,
110   but gently, so he won't get hurt."
          The girl extends her hand; he reaches
out, takes and puts it in his breeches,
and nestles his dick in her fist.
Now, there's a treat it can't resist!
115   "Robin," she said, "he feels so warm!"
"Sweet lassie, God keep me from harm,
he just now climbed out of his niche."
"Just feel the little critter twitch!
In Jesus' name, he sure is cocky!"
120   she ventured. "How the poor unlucky
fellow jumps up and down and butts!"
Her eye had caught sight of his nuts.
"Robin," she says, "what is this here?"
He says, "Why, it's his nest, my dear."
125   "You're right! I feel an egg, I do!"
"He only laid it now. It's new."
"And here's another one," she says.
"Know, lassie, that he only lays
two eggs a month—no more, no less."
130   "Indeed," she says. "What's more, I'd guess
that he's of worthy ancestry.
Are they a potent remedy?"

— Oïl, voir, aus cöes enter
est bons, & aus plaies tenter,
135   & si garist de lent pissier.
    — Tant l'ai je, fet ele, plus chier.
Robin, amis, que menjue il?
Menjue il nois? — Par foi, oïl.
    — Ahi! lasse maleüree!
140   tant fis ore ier que forsenee
quant j'en menjai tout plain mon poing!
Molt les amaisse a cest besoing,
si s'en dignast a cest matin.
    — Ne t'en chaut, bele, dist Robin,
145   quar voir il les querra molt bien!
Ja mar vous en chaudra de rien.
    — & ou? — Par foi, en vostre ventre.
    — Je ne sai par ou il i entre.
    — Or ne t'en chaut, quar, par ma foi,
150   il en prendra molt bien conroi.
    — Par ou? Ja n'i entra il onques.
    — Par vostre con. — Or l'i met donques.
Se m'aït Dieus, j'en sui molt lie! »
    A tant Robins l'a enbracie,
155   si la gete soz soi enverse,
puis li lieve la cote perse,
la chemise & le peliçon,
son escuiruel li mist el con.
Li vallés ne fu pas vilains:
160   il commence a mouvoir des rains,
de retrere & de bien enpaindre—
ne se voloit il mie faindre!—
& cele, cui il molt plesoit,
en riant dist: « Que Dieus i soit,
165   sire escuiruel! or del cerchier!
Bones nois puissiez vous mengier!
Or cerchiez bien el plus parfont,
jusques iluec ou eles sont,

"Why, yes. They're good to reattach
a tail, and can be used to patch
135   a wound, and speed up urination."
"He's risen in my estimation
for that. Friend Robin, what's his feed?
Does he eat walnuts?" "Yes indeed."
"Oh, this is a catastrophe,
140   for yesterday unthinkingly
I ate a handful! Now they're gone,
and I won't see him nibble on
them! Would he take them from my fingers?"
"Don't be upset, my lass. The thing is,"
145   says Robin, "that he still can get
at those you ate. Don't be upset."
"Where are they?" "In your tummy, miss."
"I don't know where the entrance is."
"Don't worry about that, my lass.
150   He'll scurry up the straightest path."
"He never has. I can't think where
he'll go." "Through your cunt." "Put him there.
By God, how glad I am of this!"
        Then Robin gives the girl a kiss,
155   lays her beneath him on her back,
and lifts her dark blue overfrock,
her shift, and her other apparel,
and in her cunt he plants his squirrel.
The fellow is no uncouth novice.
160   He tilts his loins and rocks his pelvis,
pokes and withdraws and reinserts his
squirrel in the young lady's service,
while she, who loves to feel him do it,
calls gleefully, "By God, go to it,
165   my faithful squirrel! Go and hunt
for tasty nuts! Eat all you want!
So, happy hunting! Deeper! Harder!
By my head, go straight to the larder

869 ❧ THE FABLIAUX

quar, par la foi que doi ma teste,
170 molt a ci savoreuse beste!
Ainz mes tel escuiruel ne vi
ne de si bon parler n'oï,
quar il la gent mie ne mort;
il ne me blece mie fort.
175 Or del cerchier, biaus amis ch[iers]!
Certes jel vueil molt volent[iers]. »
En dementiers qu'ainsi parloit
la pucele & cil queroit
les nois, que de riens ne se faint,
180 tant a bouté & tant enpaint
que (ne sai par quele aventure—
je ne sai se ce fu nature)
prist mal au cuer a l'escuiruel,
si commence a plorer de *l'uel*,
185 & puis aprés a escopi
& a vonchié & a vomi.
Tant a vonchié, le fol, le glout,
que cele senti le degout
aval ses nages degouter.
190 « Esta! fet ele, ne bouter!
Ne ferir, Robin, ne ferir!
Tu as hurté de tel aïr
& tant feru & tant hurté
que .i. des oés est esquaté.
195 Ce poise moi, c'est granz domages—
l'aubun m'en cort par mi les nages! »
A cest mot s'est cil levez sus,
qu'il n'i avoit que fere plus,
joianz s'en va en son afere;
200 n'a mie failli a bien fere.
     Par cest fablel vueil enseignier
que tels cuide bien chastïer
sa fille de dire folie,

where all those walnuts are and treat your-
170 self royally, delicious creature!
I never heard of, never saw
a squirrel quite like this before,
for he is tame and doesn't bite,
the hurt he gives me very slight.
175 Go for the nuts, friend! Their removal
meets with my heartiest approval!"
         While she cheers him on and he puts
his squirrel in up to the nuts
in earnest, not toying or joking,
180 with all his prodding and his poking,
by some mischance the animal
(I'm not sure—was it natural?)
starts feeling queasy. By and by
his eye, filled with tears, starts to cry,
185 he's seized by a spasmodic hiccup,
and afterward begins to chuck up.
He vomited so much, the glutton,
that she felt running down her bottom
the trickle of the overflow.
190 "Stop pumping!" she implores him. "Whoa!
Stop pumping, Robin, stop your pumping!
You've gone about it with such thumping
and with such vigor beat and pushed
that now one of the eggs is squooshed.
195 What a great loss this is! Alas,
there's egg white running down my ass!"
         Robin then got back on his feet,
his business there at last complete,
and happily went on his way.
200 He'd had quite a successful day.
         My fabliau will demonstrate
that though a man may educate
his daughter to control her tongue,

& quant plus onques le chastie
205 tant le met l'en plus en la voie
de mal fere, se Dieus me voie.

61. LA DAMOISELE QUI N'OÏT
PARLER DE FOTRE QUI
N'AÜST MAL AU CUER

En iceste fable novele
vos conte d'une damoisele
qui molt par estoit orgoilleuse
& felonesse & desdaigneuse,
5   que par foi, je dirai tot outre,
ele n'oïst parler de foutre
ne de lecherie a nul fuer
que ele n'aüst mal au cuer
& trop en faisoit male chiere;
10   & ses peres l'avoit tant chiere
por ce que plus enfanz n'avoit
q'a son voloir trestot faisoit.
(Plus ert a li que ele a lui.)
Tuit sol estoient enbedui,
15   n'orent beasse ne sergent,
& si estoient riche gent.
& savez por quoi li prodom
n'avoit sergent en sa maison?
La damoisele n'avoit cure,
20   por ce qu'ele ert de tel nature,
que en nul sen ne sofrist mie
sergent qui nomast lecherie,
vit ne coille ne autre chose,
& por ce ses peres ne ose
25   avoir sergent un mois entier,

it only pushes her along
205   the road to sin, the more he tries,
       may I find favor in God's eyes.

61. THE MAIDEN WHO COULDN'T
ABIDE LEWD LANGUAGE

       Now here's a fabliau that's new
       and tells us of a maiden who
       was by her temperament so haughty,
       perverse and scornful, spoiled and naughty
5   that, on my oath, it was so shocking
       to her to hear folks talk of fucking
       or lewdness, she'd not tolerate it;
       she grew extremely aggravated
       and became physically ill.
10   Her father catered to her will;
       he doted on the girl like mad,
       she being the only child he had.
       (You'd almost think she was the parent.)
       They couldn't keep a maid or servant,
15   but lived together, just those two
       alone, though they were well-to-do.
       And do you know just what impeded
       his taking on the help he needed?
       The young lady had no intent,
20   because such was her temperament,
       of having household help so coarse,
       they'd even mention intercourse
       or cock or balls, et cetera,
       and her father, because of her,
25   did not dare keep one on for long.

s'an aüst il molt grant mestier
a ses blez batre & a vener
& a sa charrue mener
& a faire s'autre besoigne,
30   mais sergent a prandre resoigne
por sa fille que trop endure,
tant c'uns vallez par avanture
(qui molt savoit barat & guile)
herbergiez fu en cele vile,
35   qui aloit gueaignier son pain;
oï parler de ce vilain
& de sa fille qui aoit
les homes & cure n'avoit
ne de lor faiz ne de lor diz.
40   Icil vallez ot non Daviz,
si aloit toz seus par la terre
comme preuz, avanture querre.
Quant il sot veraie novele
de l'orgoilleuse damoisele
45   qui estoit de si mal endroit,
a la maison en vint tot droit
o ele estoit avoc son pere.
(O li n'avoit seror ne frere
ne clo ne droit ne mu ne sort.)
50   Li vilains estoit en la cort:
ses bestes atire & atorne,
& sa busche au soloil retorne;
de sa besoigne s'antremet.
A tant estes vos Daviet,
55   qui lo vilain a salüé,
si li a l'ostel demandé
por Deu & por saint Nicolas.
Li vilains ne l'escondist pas
ne otroier ne li par ose,
60   ainz li demande au chief de pose
qeus hom il est & de coi sert.

Nevertheless, his need was strong:
He'd wheat to thresh, stock to be fed,
a team of oxen to be led,
and all the other farmyard chores,
30 but he forgoes hired help because
of what his suffering daughter wants.
     At length it happened that by chance
a young man found lodgings in town,
a con man who went up and down,
35 working at random jobs. This charmer
soon came to hear about the farmer
and of his daughter, how she hated
men and how she repudiated
both what they did and what they said.
40 This young man, David, earned his bread
following Fortune all around
the world, a worthy vagabond.
Hearing men speak in every quarter
about the farmer's snooty daughter
45 and of her loathsome temperament,
the youth immediately went
to the house where they lived together
with no one else—not sister, brother,
healthy or mute or deaf or lame.
50 He found the farmer, when he came,
seeing to his beasts in the yard
and toting firewood, working hard
in the hot sun, doing his tasks.
Here's our friend Davy boy, who asks,
55 after he's said how do you do,
for God and Saint Nicholas, too,
if he could have a place to stay.
The farmer's not willing to say
he can nor give a flat denial,
60 but asks instead after a while
who he is and what work he does.

Daviez li dist en apert
que molt volantiers serviroit
.i. prodome s'il lo trovoit,
65   que bien set arer & semer
& bien batre & bien vaner
& tot ce que vallez doit faire.
« J'aüsse bien de toi afaire,
fait li vilains, par saint Alose,
70   ne fust sanz plus por une chose:
j'ai une fille donjereuse
qui vers homes est trop honteuse
qant parolent de lecherie.
Onques n'oi sergent en ma vie
75   qui longue me poïst durer,
que des que ma fille ot nomer
foutre, si li prant une gote
qui encontre lo cuer la bote
que de morir fait grant sanblant,
80   & por ce n'os avoir sergent,
biau frere, qu'il sont lecheor
& trop sont vilain parleor
que ma fille crainbroie perdre. »
Daviez prist sa boche a terdre,
85   & puis crache autresi & moche
com s'il aüst mangiee moche;
au vilain dist: « Ostez, biaus sire!
Si vilain mot ne devez dire!
Taisiez, por Deu l'esperitable,
90   que ce est li moz au deiable!
N'en parlez mais la o je soie—
por .c. livres je ne voldroie
veoir home qui en parlast
ne qui lecherie nomast,
95   que grant dolor au cuer me prant. »
Qant la fille au vilain [ ] antant
lo vassal qui dist tel raison,

Davy loudly proclaimed he was
a man ready to earn a wage
from any good man who'd engage
65   his services. He plowed, he planted,
threshed, winnowed . . . whatever was wanted
of him, he was prepared to do.
"I'm sure I could make use of you,"
the man replies, "by Saint Aloysius.
70   There's one thing, though: Hired help annoys us.
I have a domineering daughter,
whose temperament will not support a
man if he speaks of bedroom matters.
I've never had a servant—that is,
75   I never had one who could stay
here long before she'd hear him say
'fuck' and get so distressed, the smart
would rise and press against her heart
and she looked as if she would die.
80   I can't keep servants, sir. Here's why:
They're all a vulgar lot, who utter
the kind of words heard in the gutter
and leave my daughter in extremis."
Davy began to gag and grimace,
85   snorted repeatedly and spat
like choking on a fly or gnat.
"For shame, good gentleman!" he spluttered.
"A word like that must not be uttered!
Shun, as you would avoid the very
90   Devil, the Fiend's vocabulary,
for God's sake, when I am nearby!
Not for a hundred pounds would I
be with the kind of person who'd
mention or name anything lewd.
95   My heart aches at the very word."
        The farmer's daughter overheard
the man express this point of view.

si issi fors de la maison,
a son pere maintenant dit:

100 « Sire, fait el, se Deus m'aït,
cestui vallet retandroiz vos,
que il sera boens avoc nos.
Cist a trestote ma meniere.
Se vos m'amez ne tenez chiere,

105 retenez lo, gel vos commant.
     — Doce fille, a vostre talant, »
fait li vilains, qui molt ert beste.
Ensi retindrent a grant feste
Daviet, & molt l'orent chier.

110   Qant il fu ore de couchier,
li vilains sa fille en apele:
« Or me dites, ma damoisele,
o porra Daviez gesir?
     — Sire, s'il vos vient a plaisir,

115 il puet bien gesir avoc moi.
Molt me sanble de boene foi
& que en bon lou ait esté.
     — Ma fille, a vostre volanté
faites do tot », fait li prodon.

120 Pres do feu en mi la maison
se cocha li vilains dormir,
& Daviez s'ala gesir
en la chanbre o la damoisele,
qui molt ert avenanz & bele:

125 blanche ot la char com flor d'espine—
s'ele fust fille de raïne,
si fust ele bele a devise!
Daviez li a sa main mise
sor les memeletes tot droit

130 & demanda ce que estoit.
Cele dit: « Ce sont mes memeles,
qui molt par sont blanches & beles.
N'en i a nule orde ne sale. »

She left the house and hurried to
her father and made this request:
100 "Father," she says, "the Lord be blessed!
Do by all means employ this youth.
He'll fit right in with us, in truth,
so hire him. His nature conforms
to all our usages and norms,
105 so, if you love me, humor me."
"If you so wish it, let it be,"
the farmer says. (He's none too bright.)
    Much taken with him, they invite
Davy to stay and earn his keep.
110 When it comes time to go to sleep,
the farmer consults with his daughter.
"Now tell me, missy, where we ought to
set up a bed for Davy here."
"If you are willing, Father dear,
115 let's let him share my bed with me.
He seems a man of quality,
in all things worthy of our trust."
"Dear daughter, if you think that's best,"
the man said, "do as you desire."
120 In the main room beside the fire
the farmer lay down for the night,
and Davy and the girl went right
to bed together in her room.
She was so fair, a hawthorn bloom
125 was quite as white as was her skin;
were she the daughter of a queen,
her beauty would be no less rare.
Davy placed his hand on her bare
bosom and wanted to be told
130 exactly what those things were called.
The maiden answered him, "Why, they're
my breasts, so very white and fair,
in no way shameful or unclean."

& Daviez sa main avale
135   droit au pertuis desoz lo vantre
par o li viz el cors li entre,
si santi les paus qui cressoient;
soués & coiz encor estoient.
Bien taste tot o la main destre,
140   puis demande que ce puet estre.
« Par foi, fait ele, c'est mes prez,
Daviet, la ou vos tastez,
mais il n'est pas encor floriz.
— Par foi, dame, ce dit Daviz,
145   n'i a pas d'erbe encor planté . . .
& que est ce en mi cest pré,
cest fosse soeve & plaine?
— Ce est, fait ele, ma fontaine,
qui ne sort mie tot adés.
150   — & que est ce ici aprés
fait Daviez, en ceste engarde?
— C'est li cornerres qui la garde,
fait la pucele, por verté.
Se beste entroit dedanz mon pré
155   por boivre en la fontaine clere,
tantost cornerroit li cornerre
por faire li honte & peor.
— Ci a deiable corneor,
fait Daviez, & de put ordre,
160   qui ensi vialt les bestes mordre
por l'erbe qui ne soit gastee!
— Tu m'as ore bien portatee,
fait la pucele, Daviet. »
Tantost sor lui sa main remet,
165   qui n'estoit mal faite ne corte,
& dit qu'ele savra qu'il porte.
Lors li reprist a demander
& ses choses a detaster
tant qu'el l'a par lot vit saisi

Davy slides his hand down between
135   her legs below the abdomen,
the hole one puts one's penis in,
and felt the first hairs newly growing,
all soft and silky, barely showing.
Exploring with his right hand, he
140   again asks what that thing might be.
She tells him, "Davy, that's my pasture,
it truly is, where you have placed your
hand, but it's not much overgrown."
"I'd say it hasn't yet been sown,"
145   says David. "And here in the middle
of your fine meadow, what's this puddle,
this slippery-soft, ditchlike thing?"
"Davy," she answers, "it's my spring,
which right now isn't overflowing."
150   Then Davy asks her, "Are you going
to tell me what's ensconced down here?"
"Why, that's the bugler, Davy dear,"
the maiden says, "who's standing sentry.
If man or beast sought to gain entry
155   and try to drink from my clear spring,
the sentry would start trumpeting
and strike his heart with fear and shame."
"That scurvy bugler's much to blame,"
Davy observes, "for seeking strife
160   and heckling poor, harmless wildlife
just so it won't walk on the grass!"
"Now, Davy dear," replies the lass,
"you've given me a thorough feel."
She says, reaching for him, that she'll
165   use her long-fingered and unblemished
hand to find out how he is furnished,
and so she questions him and starts
to feel about his body parts,
and grasps him firmly by the prick

170 & demande: « Que est ici,
Daviet, si roide & si dur
que bien devroit percier .i. mur?
— Dame, fait il, c'est mes polains,
qui molt est & roides & sains,
175 mais il ne manja des ier main. »
Cele remest aval sa main,
si trove la coille velue;
les .ii. coillons taste & remue,
si redemande: « Daviet,
180 que est or ce en ce sachet?
fait ele. Sont ce .ii. luisiaus? »
Daviz fu de respondre isniaus:
« Dame, ce sont dui mareschal
qui ont a garder mon cheval
185 qant pest en autrui conpagnie.
Tot jorz sont en sa conpeignie;
de mon polain garder sont mestre.
— Davi, met lou en mon pré pestre,
ton biau polain, se Deus te gart! »
190 & cil s'an torne d'autre part,
sor lo paignil li met lo vit,
puis a a la pucele dit
qu'il ot tornee desoz soi:
« Dame, mes polains muert de soi;
195 molt en a aüe grant poine.
— Va si l'aboivre a ma fontaine,
fait cele. Mar avras peor!
— Dame, je dot lo corneor,
fait Daviz, que il n'en groçast
200 se li polains dedanz entrast. »
Cele respont: « S'il en dit mal,
bien lo batent li mereschal! »
Daviz respont: « Ce est bien dit. »
A tant li met el con lo vit,
205 si fait son boen & son talant

170 and asks him, "Davy, what's this thick
    and rigid thing, so hard and all
    that it could batter down a wall?"
    "Lady," he tells her, "that's my pony,
    who isn't listless, weak, and scrawny,
175 though he's not eaten for two days."
    She moves her hand still down a ways,
    finds two balls in a hairy scrotum,
    and moves her fingers all about 'em.
    "Do tell me, Davy," she goes on,
180 "are what I feel two balls of yarn
    that you are keeping in your sack?"
    David is quick to answer back,
    "Why, they're two stable hands, of course,
    whose business is to watch my horse
185 when grazing in another's field.
    They're experts, always there to shield
    him and stay close by when he strays."
    "Do put your pony out to graze
    here in my pasture, Davy, please."
190 He sidles up against her; she's
    right there; he presses up his penis
    against the maiden's mound of Venus,
    and rolling on top of her first, he
    says, "Lady, my pony's so thirsty,
195 he's parched and really suffering."
    "Go water him there in my spring,"
    she says. "No need to be afraid." He
    answers her, "But the bugler, lady!
    I fear the anger of your sentry
200 if we allow my pony entry."
    She answers him, "Your stable boys
    can beat him up if he makes noise."
    David replies, "Yes, I approve."
    He has his way and goes to shove
205 his cock up her cunt; his attacks

si qu'ele nel tient pas a lant,
que .iiii. foiz la retorna,
& se li cornierres groça,
si fu batuz de .ii. jumaus.
210   A icest mot faut li fabliaus.

62. LES .IV. SOHAIZ SAINT MARTIN

Un vilain ot en Normendie
dont bien est droiz que je vous die
.i. fablel merveilleus & cointe.
Toz jors avoit il a acointe
5   saint Martin, que toz jors nommoit
a ses oevres que il fesoit;
ja si liez ne dolenz ne fust
que saint Martins n'amenteüst.
Toz jors nommoit il saint Martin
10   Li vilains aloit un matin
en son labor si comme il seut;
saint Martin oublïer ne veut:
« Saint Martin! dist il, Or avant! » . . .
& sains Martins li vint devant.
15   « Vilains, fist il, tu m'as molt chier.
Ja ne voudras riene commencier
que toz jors au commencement
ne me nommes premierement.
Je t'en rendrai ja la deserte:
20   lesse ton travail & ta herte,
si t'en reva tout liement!
Je te di bien tout vraiement
ce qu'a .iiii. souhais diras
saches tu bien que tu l'avras,

redouble; she won't find him lax!
Four times in all he redirected
his siege. The trumpeter objected
and so got beaten by the twins,
210 and on that word this story ends.

62. SAINT MARTIN'S FOUR
WISHES

In Normandy there lived a peasant
of whom is told so quaint and pleasant
a fabliau that I've a notion
to tell you. Such was his devotion
5 to Saint Martin that he'd invoke
him in all things he undertook;
whether elated or depressed,
it was Saint Martin he addressed;
every day he called on Saint Martin.
10   The peasant set out on a certain
morning, as was his wont, to plow.
He'll not forget Saint Martin now.
"Saint Martin!" he cried out, "Geeyup!"
and that's when Saint Martin showed up.
15 "Peasant," he said, "you have been loyal
to me, and never start to toil,
no matter what your task may be,
without first calling upon me.
You have well earned my special favor.
20 Now leave your harrow, drop your labor,
and get you home with a light heart,
for I will truly do my part
and herewith promise I will grant
whatever four wishes you want,

25 mes garde toi au souhaidier—
  tu n'i avras ja recouvrier. »
  Li vilains l'en a encliné,
  puis s'en est arriere torné;
  en sa meson s'en va toz liez.
30   Il sera ja bien aresniez:
  sa fame, qui chauce les braies,
  li a dit: « Vilain, mal jor aies!
  Por qoi as tu ja lessié oevre—
  por le tens qui .i. poi se cuevre?
35 Il n'ert vespres jusque .vii. liues.
  Est ce por encressier tes giues?
  Paor avez n'aiez foraje?
  Onques n'amastes laborage;
  vous fetes molt volentiers feste.
40 A mal eür aiez vous beste
  quant vous n'en fetes vostre esploit!
  Vous en alastes orendroit—
  tost avez or jornee faite!
  —Tais toi, ma suer, ne te deshaite,
45 dist li vilains, quar riches sommes!
  Des or nous sont remez noz sommes
  & no travail, je le devin.
  Je ai encontré saint Martin,
  .iiii. souhais me dona ore;
50 nes ai pas souhaidiez encore
  tant que j'eüsse a toi parlé:
  selonc ce que m'avras löé
  souhaiderai tout maintenant—
  terre, richece, or & argent. »
55 Quant cele l'oï, si l'acole,
  si s'umelie de parole:
  « Sire, dist ele, dis tu voir?
  —Oïl, bien le porras savoir.
  —Ahi! fet ele, douz amis,
60 ja ai je en vous tout mon cuer mis

25 but use your wishes wisely, for
once they've been used you'll get no more."
        The peasant bowed low to the ground
in reverence, then turned around
and hurried home, walking on air.
30 There's trouble waiting for him there.
His wife, the one who wears the pants,
lit into him: "What evil chance
brings you home now, oaf? Did you quit
work 'cause it's clouded up a bit?
35 You've hours of daylight left for tilling.
Or is your paunch in need of filling?
Are you afraid you'll miss your chow?
You've never taken to the plow,
no—life for you is one big lark!
40 We may as well sell off the stock,
since you won't work them anyway!
See what you call a working day—
you're back when you have scarcely gone!"
"Don't be upset, my love, keep calm,"
45 the peasant said. "Our fortune's made!
Henceforth our burdens may be laid
aside, of that much I am certain,
because I met up with Saint Martin.
He gave me four wishes to use
50 as I thought best. I've yet to choose;
I meant first to consult with you,
and as you advise me to do,
I now intend to make my wishes
for gold and silver, land and riches."
55   When she heard this, the woman reached
to hug him and toned down her speech.
"Husband," she said, "can this be so?"
"Indeed yes, as you soon will know."
"My dearest, sweetest love," said she,
60 "my heart is yours eternally

de vous amer, de vus servir,
or le me devez bien merir.
Je vous demant, se il vous plaist,
que vous me donez .i. souhait—
65 vostre seront li autre troi,
& si serez lors bien de moi.
— Tais toi, dist il, ma bele suer!
Je ne le feroie a nul fuer,
que fames ont foles penssees;
70 tost demanderiez .iii. fusees
de chanvre, de laine ou de lin.
Bien me souvient de saint Martin,
qui me dist que bien me gardaisse
& que tel chose souhaidaisse
75 qui nous peüst avoir mestier.
Je les voudrai toz souhaidier,
& sachiez bien que je criembroie,
se le souhait vous otrioie,
que tel chose souhaidissiez
80 dont moi & vous empirissiez.
Ne connois pas bien voz amors?—
se deïssiez que fusse uns ours
ou asnes ou chievre ou jument,
jel seroie tout esraument.
85 Por ce si redout vostre otroi.
— Sire, dist ele, en moie foi
je vous afi de mes .ii. mains
que toz jors serez vous vilains.
Ja par moi n'avrez autre forme,
90 ja vous aim je plus que nul homme.
— Bele suer, dist il, or l'aiez.
Por Dieu, tel chose souhaidiez
ou moi & vous aiommes preu!
— Je demant, dist ele, en non Dieu
95 que vous soiez chargiez de vis:

to love and serve you hand and foot.
You should repay me good for good.
I ask you, please, to let me have
one of the wishes the saint gave.
65 You still will have the other three,
and you will have done right by me."
"Hush," he replied, "my darling wife!
I wouldn't, no, not on my life,
for women all have addled brains.
70 Why, you might ask to have three skeins
of hemp or wool or linen thread!
I remember Saint Martin said
that I should wisely use my wishes
and only wish for something such as
75 will benefit us evermore,
so I intend to use all four.
Know that I'm mortally afraid,
if I gave you one, that instead
you'd wish for something that might do
80 untold harm to both me and you.
If you should wish I was a bear
or jackass, or a goat or mare,
I would become one on the spot.
I know how much you love me: not.
85 That's why I fear to let you share
my wishes." "Sir," she said, "I swear
in good faith with both hands raised high,
you'll stay a peasant till you die.
I'll never wish you other than
90 you are, dearer than any man."
"My dear," he said, "let it be yours.
By God, when you wish, make a choice
by which you and I stand to gain!"
"I wish," she said, "that, in God's name,
95 there spring up penises galore

ne vous remaingnent oeil ne vis,
teste ne braz, piez ne costé,
ou par tout ne soit vit planté,
si ne soient ne mol ne doille,
100 ainz ait a chascun vit sa coille;
toz dis soient li vit tendu,
si sanblerez vilain cornu! »
        Quant ele ot souhaidié & dit,
du vilain saillirent li vit.
105 Li vit li saillent par le nez
& par la bouche de delez,
si ot vit lonc & vit quarrez,
vit gros, vit cort, vit reboulez,
vit corbe, vit agu, vit gros . . .

110 Sor le vilain n'ot si dur os
dont vit ne saillent merveillous.
Li vit li saillent des genous—
por Dieu, or entendez merveilles!—
li vit li saillent des oreilles,
115 & par devant en contremont
li sailli uns granz vis du front,
& par aval dusques aus piez
fu li vilains de vis chargiez;
molt par fu bien de vis vestuz
120 de toutes pars—fu bien cornuz.
Quant li vilains se vit si fait,
« Suer, dist il, ci a lait souhait!
Por qoi m'as tu si atorné?
J'amaisse mieus estre mort né
125 que seur moi eüsse tant vit—
onques mes nus hom tant n'en vit!
— Sire, dist el, je vous di bien
c'un seul vit ne me valoit rien:
sempres ert mol comme pelice,
130 mes or sui je de vis molt riche,

over your body, aft and fore!
On face, arms, sides, from head to foot,
may countless penises take root,
and let them not be limp or slack:
100   Let each be furnished with its sack,
and let them stand stiff and upright!
Now, won't you be a horny sight!"

       Then, as soon as the woman spoke,
hundreds of pricks began to poke
105   out all over. Penises grew
around his nose and his mouth, too.
Some pricks were thick, some oversized,
some long, some short, some circumcised,
curved pricks, straight pricks, pointed
                              and hardy . . .
110   every bone in the peasant's body
was miraculously endowed
and prickled, fully cocked and proud.
You've never heard wonders like these!
Pricks grow out of his ears, and he's
115   amidst his forehead, standing tall,
the most enormous prick of all,
and right down to his feet he's coated
with penises erect and bloated.
From toe to crown he was bedecked
120   with antlers, bloated and erect.
Weighed down by penis upon penis,
the peasant said, "This wish was heinous!
Why give me all this finery?
Better to be stillborn than be
125   with pricks so overgrown and cluttered!
Was ever any man so studded?"
"Husband," she said, "I'll tell you why.
Your one prick couldn't satisfy,
just hanging limply like a fox
130   stole, but now I've a wealth of cocks!

& s'avez encore autre preu,
que jamés ne serez en leu
ou vous doiez point de paiage.
J'ai esté au souhaidier sage;
135   vous ne devez estre irous:
il a molt bele beste en vous! »
Dist li preudom: « Ce poise moi.
Je souhaiderai aprés toi:
je souhaide, dist li preudom,
140   que tu aies autrestant con
com j'ai de vis par deseur moi.
Autrestant con aies seur toi! »
        Adonc fu ele bien connue,
qu'ele ot .ii. cons en la veüe,
145   .iiii. en ot ou front coste a coste,
& con devant & con d'encoste,
si ot con de mainte maniere,
& con devant & con derriere,
con tort, con droit & con chenu
150   & con sanz poil & con velu
& con pucel & con estrait
& con estroit & con bien fait
& con petit & con aorce
& con parfont & con seur boce
155   & con au chief & con aus piez.
Adonques fu li vilains liez!
« Sire, dist ele, qu'as tu fait?
Por qoi m'as doné tel souhait!
— Je te dirai, dist li bons hom.
160   Je n'avoie preu en .i. con
puis que tant vit me doniiez.
Bele suer, ne vous esmaiez,
que jamés ne vendroiz par rue
que vous ne soiez bien connue!
165   — Sire, dist el, or n'i a plus:

Your lot is likewise much improved
in that, whenever you are moved
to travel, you won't be assessed
tariffs or tolls. All for the best

135   I made my wish, so don't resent it.
There's not a creature half so splendid!"
The peasant said, "I'm not amused.
Three wishes more are yet unused.
I wish," the fellow said at once,

140   "that you had just as many cunts
on you as I have pricks on me.
May your cunts pop out rapidly!"
        At once the cunts start to arise.
A pair appears before her eyes,

145   four on her forehead in a row,
and cunts above, and cunts below,
and cunts behind, and cunts in front,
every variety of cunt—
bent cunts, straight cunts, cunts gray and hoary,

150   cunts without hair, cunts thick and furry,
and virgin cunts, narrow and tight,
wide, gaping cunts, and cunts made right,
cunts large and small, oval and round,
deep cunts, and cunts raised on a mound,

155   cunts on her head, cunts on her feet . . .
the peasant's joy is now complete.
"Husband, what have you done?" said she.
"Why have you wished this thing on me?"
The good man said, "One cunt won't do

160   for all the pricks I got from you.
Don't be alarmed, for your condition
will lead to widespread recognition.
When you go walking, you'll continue
to be known for all the cunt in you."

165   "Husband," she said, "what can I say?

nous avons .ii. souhais perdus;
Souhaidiez que vous vit n'aiez
ne je con. Ainsi le laiez,
s'en avrez .i. de remanant
170 & si serommes riche gent. »
& li vilains souhaide & dist
qu'ele n'ait con ne il n'ait vit.
Donques fu ele molt marie
quant de son con ne trova mie,
175 & li preudom, quant il revit
que il n'ot mie de son vit,
refu de l'autre part iriez.
« Sire, dist ele, souhaidiez
le quart souhait qu'encore avon
180 qu'aiez .i. vit & je .i. con,
si ert ausi comme devant
& si n'avrons perdu noiant. »
& li preudom resouhaida,
que ne perdi ne gaaigna,
185 que son vit li est revenuz
& ses souhais a il perduz.
        Par cest fablel pöez savoir
que cil ne fet mie savoir
qui mieus croit sa fame que lui:
190 sovent l'en vient honte & anui.

6⅗. LA SORISETE DES ESTOPES

Aprés vos cont d'un vilain sot
qui fame prist & rien ne sot
de nul deduit q'apartenist
a fame se il la tenist,
5 c'onques entremis ne s'en fu;
mais sa fame avoit ja seü

That makes two wishes thrown away,
and now you must use one to fix
us and remove these cunts and pricks.
You'll still have one left out of four,
170 and we'll be rich forevermore."
         The peasant wishes thereupon
that all their cunts and pricks were gone,
but she was anything but cheered
to find her cunt had disappeared,
175 and he, too, had an awful shock
to find himself without a cock.
Both of them were extremely wroth.
"Husband, it's time to make the fourth
wish we have left to us," said she;
180 "one prick for you, one cunt for me.
We'll return to our former state
no poorer off, at any rate."
He wished the wish that still remained;
and thus he neither lost nor gained:
185 he got his prick back at the cost
of the four wishes, which he lost.
         This fabliau clearly explains
that a man doesn't use his brains
when his wife's judgment sways his views.
190 Calamity often ensues.

6³. THE LITTLE RAG MOUSE

Next I'll tell of a stupid peasant
who took a wife, but of the pleasant
things that pertain to married life
which men can do who have a wife
5 he didn't know (he'd never tried),
but in those things men do his bride

tot ce que home sevent faire,
que, a la verité retraire,
li prestes son boen en faisoit
10 qant il voloit & li plaisoit
& que tant vint a icel jor
q'ele asenbla a son seignor.
Lors dist li prestes: « Doce amie,
je voil a vos, ne vos poist mie,
15 avoir a faire, s'il vos loist,
ainz que li vilains vos adoist. »
& cele dit: « Volantiers, sire,
que je ne vos os escondire,
mais venez tost & sanz demore
20 qant vos savroiz qu'il sera ore,
ainz que mes sires lo me face,
que perdre ne voil vostre grace.
Ensi fu enpris li afaire.

  Aprés ice ne tarda gaire
25 que li vilains s'ala cochier,
mais ele ne l'ot gaires chier
ne son deduit ne son solaz;
& il la prant entre ses braz,
si l'anbraça molt duremant,
30 que il nel sot faire autremant,
& l'a molt soz lui estandue,
& cele s'est molt desfandue
& dist: « Qu'est ce que volez faire?
— Je voil, fait il, vit avant traire;
35 si vos fotrai se j'onques puis,
se vostre con delivre truis.
— Mon con, fait ele enneslopas,
mon con ne troveroiz vos pas.
— O est il donc? Nel me celez.
40 — Sire, qant savoir lo volez
jel vos dirai o est, par m'ame:
muciez as piez do lit ma dame,

already had much expertise,
because, in fact, she used to please
the priest, who slept with her at will
10   and went on doing so until
the day she left her parents' house
and gave the man her marriage vows.
"My sweetest love," then said the priest,
"I'd like to be with you, at least
15   if you don't mind and will permit it,
before you let your husband get it,"
and she replied, "Most gladly, Father—
could I refuse you?—but I'd rather
you came by soon and didn't wait,
20   or you may find that it's too late
and he's already played his part.
I'd not lose my place in your heart."
Thus they arranged their little game.
      Not too long after the time came,
25   and when the peasant got in bed,
she wished it was her priest instead
and had no liking for his charms,
and when he took her in his arms
and hugged her hard with all his strength
30   and rolled on top of her full length
(for he had no experience),
she put up a valiant defense
and said, "What do you think you're doing?"
"To take my prick out and start screwing
35   you," says he, "as much as I want,
as soon as I can find your cunt."
"My cunt," she says, cutting him short,
"you will not find it where it ought
to be." "Then where? Don't keep it hidden."
40   "I'll tell you, husband, since you've bidden,
just where I put it. By my head,
I left it by my mother's bed

o jehui matin lo laissai.
— Par saint Martin, & je irai,
45 fait il, ançois que je ne l'aie. »
De l'aler plus ne se delaie,
ainz va querre lo con lo cors,
mais la vile, [o] estoit li bors
o sa fame avoit esté nee
50 loin d'iluec [fu] plus d'une lee.
Endemantres que li vilains
fu por lo con, li chapelains
s'ala couchier dedanz son lit
a grant joie & a grant delit
55 & fist qanque li plot a faire,
mais ne fait pas tot a retraire
com li vilains fu deceüz.
    Onques plus fous ne fu veüz!
Quant vint chiés la mere sa fame,
60 si li a dit: « Ma chiere dame,
vostre fille m'anvoie ça
por son con que ele muça,
ce dit, as piez de vostre lit. »
La dame pansa .i. petit
65 & en pansant s'aparcevoit
que sa fille lo decevoit
por faire aucune chose male.
A cest mot en la chambre avale
& trove .i. penier plain d'estopes:
70 « Qui q'an ait, fait ele, les copes,
cest panier li bailleroiz ci. »
Lors a cil lo panier saisi,
mais es estopes ot tornee
& bien s'i fu envelopee
75 une soriz, sanz nule dote.
Cele li baille, & il lo bote
tot maintenant desoz sa chape

this morning, neatly tucked away."
"I'll fetch it back without delay,"
45 he said, "sooner than go without,
by Saint Martin!" and he set out
to seek the body part she lacked,
but his wife's native town, in fact,
where her folks still resided, lay
50 well over a full league away.

    Now, while the peasant went to hunt
for and retrieve the woman's cunt,
the chaplain gladly took his place,
indulged himself in her embrace,
55 and did exactly what he'd meant . . .
But why expose the full extent
of how the man was cuckolded?

    Nobody weaker in the head
ever lived! At her mother's home
60 he said, "Good woman, I have come,
sent by your daughter, to retrieve
her cunt, which she left, I believe,
somewhere by the foot of your bed."
The woman got it in her head,
65 once she had thought a little while,
her child had sent him there by guile
and had some wickedness in mind,
so she went to her room to find
a basket filled with scraps of cloth.
70 "Someone's been careless, sure enough!
Here, give her this; it's what she wants."
He grabbed the basket from her hands.
(A little mouse had climbed inside
and made itself a place to hide
75 nestled among the rags, so goes it.)
She gives the basket, and he stows it
right then and there beneath his cape,

& au plus tost qu'il puet s'eschape
de li por revenir arriere,

80 &, qant il vint en la bruiere,
& dist une molt grant marvoille:
« Ne sai, fait il, se dort o voille
li cons ma fame, par saint Pol,
mais molt volantiers, par saint Vol,
85 lo fotisse ainz que je venisse
a l'ostel, se je ne cremisse
qu'il m'eschapast a mi *ces* voies...
& sel fotrai je totes voies
por savoir se c'est voirs o non
90 que l'an dit, que il a en con
molt docë & molt söef beste. »
Maintenant de son vit la teste
li lieve & fu droiz comme lance
& enz es estopes s'elance,
95 si commancë a parpillier,
& la soriz saut del penier,
si s'an torne par mi les prez.

Aprés est li vilains alez
grant aleüre & [a] grant pas,
100 si cuide qu'ele face en gas
& si dit: Deus! si bele beste!
Je cuit certes que de la teste
soit ele pas encor iree.
Si n'a gaires qu'ele fu nee—
105 je voi bien que molt est petite—
a Deu & a Saint Esperite
la commant & au Sauveor!
Je cuit certes qu'ele ait peor
de mon vit. Si ot el por voir,
110 par les iauz Deu, que le vit noir
& roige le musel devant.
Las! or me vois aparcevant

quick as he can makes his escape,
because he's anxious to be back in
bed.

80   While he's walking through the bracken,
he says what one would least expect.
"Is it asleep? or has it waked,
my wife's cunt? I'm not sure at all,
but I am eager, by Saint Paul,

85   to fuck it while I'm still out here
before I get home, though I fear
that it may try to run away.
So what? I'll fuck it anyway
to find out if they're true or not,

90   those things I've heard. They tell me twat
is a delicious, splendid thing."
By now his prick is pulsating,
its head reared up, straight as a lance.
He lets it poke out of his pants

95   and sniff around in the rag basket.
The mouse, alarmed (he didn't ask it),
comes leaping out, takes to its heels.

        The peasant chased it through the fields
at top speed and with giant strides,

100   thinking it's out of fun it hides
from him. "God! What a lovely critter!
I do believe my member did her
just now in for a nasty turn.
She looks like something newly born:

105   Just see how small she is, how tender!
To God the Father I commend her
and to the Son and Holy Ghost!
I do believe that she was most
afraid of my prick, which came smack

110   in front of her, God's eyes, all black,
with a red muzzle sticking out.
Alas! Now there's no room for doubt.

que ele en ot peor a certes.
Lasse, com recevré granz pertes

115 se ele muert! Sainte Marie!
Ele iert ja noiee & perie
en la fosse se ele i antre!
Ele en a moillié tot lo vantre
& tot lo dous & les costez.

120 Ostez, biau sire Deus, ostez!
Que ferai je se ele muert? »
Li vilains ses .ii. poinz detuert
por la sorriz qui braint & pipe:
qui li veïst faire la lipe

125 au vilain & tordre la jöe
manbrer li poïst de la möe
que li singes fait quant il rit.
Li vilains tot belemant dit:
« Biaus cons, doz cons, tost revenez!

130 Tote ma fiance tenez
que mais ne vos adeserai
devant que a l'ostel serai
& tant que vos avrai livré
a ma fame, si delivré

135 vos puis avoir de la rosee.
Faite en sera molt grant risee
s'an set qu'eschapez me soiez!
Ahi! vos seroiz ja noiez,
biaus cons, en la rosee grant!

140 Venez! si entrez en mon gant;
je vos metrai dedanz mon sain. »
Tot ensi se travaille en vain,
qu[e] il ne set tant apeler
que ele voille retorner,

145 ainz se pert en l'erbe menue.
Qant il voit que il l'a perdue,
si devient mornes & pansis.

She's terrified, most certainly.
What a loss it would be for me
115 if she died! Mary, holy Mother!
She will be drowned or else will smother
if she should stumble in a hole!
Now she's completely drenched, her whole
belly, both her sides, and her back. . . .
120 May the Lord help me now! Alack,
what shall I do if her cunt dies?"
The peasant wrings his hands and cries
for the poor mouse that squeals and pules;
to see the face the peasant pulls
125 and how he twists his jaw about,
you'd be reminded of the pout
a monkey makes when racked with laughter.
The peasant calls out softly after,
"Dear cunt, sweet cunt, return to me!
130 I give my word in surety
you'll not be touched, but left alone
until the two of us get home
and I can give you to my wife,
if only I may save your life
135 from the night dew, so damp and chill.
Folks will laugh heartily, they will,
if they learn how you wriggled free!
Good cunt, alas, then must it be
that you drown in the heavy dew?
140 Let my glove be a nest for you.
Come, and I'll place you in my breast."
In vain the peasant tries his best.
For all that he may plead and call,
the mouse won't come to him at all,
145 but disappears into the grass.
　　　When he sees what has come to pass,
his heart is sad and filled with pain.

Atant s'est a la voie mis,
n'aresta jusq'an sa maison,
150 tot sanz parole & sanz raison
s'estoit sor .i. banc deschauciez
(sachiez qu'il n'estoit mie liez),
& sa fame li dist: « Biau sire,
qu'est ce?—je ne vos oi mot dire.
155 Don n'iestes vos haitiez & sains?
— Je non, dame, » fait li vilains,
qui totes voies se deschauce
& despoille, & elle li hauce
la coverture & lieve en haut,
160 & li vilains joste li saut
& se coche trestoz envers,
ne ne dist ne que uns convers
cui li parlers est desfanduz,
ençois se gist toz estanduz.
165 Cele lo vit mu & taisant,
si li a dit demaintenant:
« Sire, donc n'avez vos mon con?
— Je non, dame, je non, je non!
Mar l'alasse je onques querre,
170 qu'il m'e[s]t la hors cheoiz a terre,
si est ja noiez en cez prez!
— Ha! fait ele, vos me gabez!
— Certes, dame, fait il, non faz. »
Ele lo prant entre ses braz:
175 « Sire, fait ele, ne vos chaille!
Il ot de vos peor sanz faille
por ce qu'il ne vos connoissoit,
& chose qui li desplaisoit,
au mien cuidier, li faisïez . . .
180 & se vos or lo tenoiez,
qu'an feroiez? Dites lo moi.
— Je lo foutroie, par ma foi,
& voir en l'oil li boteroie

He set off down the road again,
not stopping till he reached his house.
150   Not one word came out of his mouth,
and he sat down to take his shoes
off. (You can tell he has the blues.)
And his wife asks him, "Sir, what's wrong?
Why so silent? And such a long
155   face! Aren't you well? Don't you feel glad?"
"I'm not and don't," the peasant said,
taking his shoes off all the time,
and his clothes, too. So he can climb
in next to her, she lifts the cover,
160   and he gets in and just turns over
and lies facing the other way.
Just like a novice who can't say
a word unless given permission,
he lies there in a prone position.
165   She sees him silent and withdrawn,
and turns and asks him thereupon,
"Well, husband, don't you have my cunt?"
"Lady, I don't! I don't! I don't!
I'm sorry that I went to fetch it!
170   I dropped it out there, and the wretched
thing must have drowned there in the wet."
"You want to make a joke, I bet."
"Indeed, I don't, lady," says he.
      She hugs her husband soothingly
175   and says, "My dear, don't be put out.
It was afraid of you, no doubt,
and didn't know just who you were,
and you attempted, I infer,
to do something against its wish.
180   What if you had it now in reach?
What would you do? Do let me know."
"I'd fuck it hard, of course, and so
I would, and poke it in the eye

ensi que je lo creveroie
185 por lo coroz que il m'a fait. »
& ele li dist entresait:
« Sire, il est ja entre mes jambes,
mais ne vosisse por Estanpes
que il fust si mal atornez,
190 com il est en voz mains tornez
tot soavet & belement. »
& li vilains sa main i tant,
sel prant & dit: « Gel *tien* as mains!
— *Or* l'aplaigniez don tot as mains,
195 fait ele, qu'il ne vos estorde,
& n'aiez peor qu'il vos morde.
Tenez lo qu'il ne vos eschat. »
— Voire, fait il, por nostre chat,
fait li vilains, s'il l'ancontroit—
200 ja Deus a merci nel m'otroit
qu'il nel manjast, au mien cuidier! »
Lors lo commance a aplaignier,
si sant molt bien qu'il est moilliez:
« Ha las! encor est il soilliez
205 de la rosee o il chaï,
li vilains dit. Ahi, ahi,
con! vos m'avez hui corecié;
mais ja par moi n'iert grocié
de ce que il est arosez.
210 Or vos dormez & reposez,
que ne vos voil huimais grever—
las estes de core & d'aler. »
      Enseignier voil por ceste fable
que fame set plus que deiable,
215 & certeinement lo sachiez.
Les iauz enbedeus *me* sachiez
se *n'é* a esciänt dit voir!
Qant el viaut om[e] decevoir,
plus l'an deçoit & plus l'afole

and pop it good," was his reply,
185   "for all the anguish it has caused."
She answered him and never paused,
"Between my legs it's set up camp,
but, husband, not for all Étampes
would I wish it to be mistreated,
190   since it came back to you and heeded
your summons, docile, tame, and meek."
He reaches out his hand to seek
it, takes it, and says, "I can touch it!"
"With both your hands now gently brush it,"
195   she says, "so that it won't take flight.
Don't be afraid; it doesn't bite.
Hold it so it won't get away."
"Yes," says the peasant, "our cat may,
if it should catch it, just devour
200   the poor thing. God's eternal power
against this risk keep and protect it!"
Then he begins to stroke and pet it,
and he can feel that it's all wet.
"Alas, the tiny thing is yet
205   damp from when it fell in the dew,"
the peasant says. "Oh, naughty you,
cunt, for distressing me tonight!
But I won't scold it out of spite
for having got drenched to the bone.
210   Take your repose, sleep like a stone,
for I won't bother you again.
You've run around; you're all done in."

        From this exemplum may be gleaned
a woman knows more than the Fiend,
215   as you're aware, I have no doubt,
and you may pluck my two eyes out
if my words can't be justified.
When she wants a man mystified,
with just one word a woman can

220   tot solemant par sa parole
      que om ne feroit par angin.
      De ma fable faz tel defin
      que chascuns se gart de la söe
      qu'ele ne li face la cöe.

64. LE JUGEMENT DES CONS

      Cist fabliaus nous dist & raconte
      qu'il ot jadis desouz le conte
      de Blois .i. homme qui avoit
      .iii. filles, dont molt desirroit
5   qu'eles venissent a honor.
      Eles amoient par amor
      .i. bacheler molt bel & gent
      qui estoit de molt bone gent,
      mes il n'estoit mie molt riches,
10   & si n'estoit avers ne chiches.
      Toutes .iii. lor fet bon samblant:
      a chascune avoit couvenant
      que il les prendra a moillier;
      toutes .iii. l'orent forment chier.
15   Or vous dirai de lor afere.
         L'ainsnee ne se pot plus tere,
      ainz dist a sa suer qu'ele amoit
      .i. bacheler qui biaus estoit.
      L'autre respont: « Qui est il dont?
20   — C'est Robinés d'outre le pont.
      — Lasse! dist ele, mar fui nee
      quant ma suer est ainsi dervee
      qu'ele aime celui qui m'amoit!
      — La male passïons te loit!
25   dist la mainsnee. Il aime moi! »

220   trick us more than the best-laid plan
      of any man, however able.
      I say to finish up my fable:
      Let every man watch his wife close,
      or she will lead him by the nose!

64. TRIAL BY CUNT

      This fabliau gives an account
      about a subject of the Count
      of Blois in bygone days, who had
      three daughters and would have been glad
5   to see them rise to high estate.
      All three girls felt a passionate
      love for a handsome, fine young buck
      who came of respectable stock.
      Though not overly affluent,
10   he wasn't stingy, and he spent.
      All three enjoyed the man's attentions,
      and he'd told each that his intentions
      were to make her his lawful wife,
      and all three loved him more than life.
15   I'll tell you now what came about.
      The eldest let her secret out
      and told her sister heart and hand
      were promised to a fine young man.
      She answers, "So, who is your lover?"
20   "It's Robin from across the river."
      "Oh, woe is me," she said, "for it's
      clear that my sister's lost her wits
      and loves the man in love with me!"
      "May some atrocious malady,"
25   the youngest said, "throttle your life!

Ainsi furent en grant esfroi
trestoutes .iii. por .i. seul homme.
Estes vous venu le preudomme
qui peres est aus damoiseles,
30 & l'ainsnee des .iii. puceles
vint a son pere isnelement
& se li dist cortoisement:
« Peres, je me vueil marïer
se vous me voliiez doner
35 celui qui lonc tens m'a amee.
Trestoute en seroit honoree
nostre gent & nostre lignie.
— Fille, se Dieus me beneïe,
dist li peres. — Tu as grant tort,
40 voire! Ainçois me doinst Dieus la mort!
fet cele qu'aprés li fu nee.
De celui sui .iii. tans amee
de qui ele se vante & prise.
— Dont serai je arriere mise?
45 dist la mainsnee. Bien me vant
que il m'aime plus duremant
qu'il ne fet nule de vous .ii.. »
Li peres fu toz merveilleus
quant il les oï desresnier;
50 forment se prist a coroucier.
Dist li pere: « Ce ne puet estre!
Ne jugeroit ne clerc ne prestre
c'un homme eüssiez toutes .iii.
Mes ainçois que passe li mois
55 me serai de ce conseilliez. »
Celes dïent: « Or esploitiez,
quar nous voudrons par tens savoir
la quele le devra avoir. »
    Li preudom ala au moustier
60 por messe oïr; au reperier
encontra son frere germain,

It's me he loves!" Just see what strife
between three sisters for one man!
      The gentleman came home just then
who was the father of the three.
30   The eldest girl immediately
informed her father of her passion
in a modest and seemly fashion.
"I would, dear Father, gladly be
married if you will marry me
35   to one who has long been my suitor,
a well-born gentleman who'll suit your
standards and do our people honor."
"Child, I'll bestow my blessing on your
union," he said. "That's a mistake
40   for sure! I'd sooner that God take
my life!" the second-born exclaimed.
"I tell you that the man she's named
for me feels three times as much love!"
"Are my rights, then, to be brushed off?"
45   the youngest said. "You can be sure
the love he bears me is far truer
than his affection for you two."
The gentleman's amazement grew
the more he heard them carry on.
50   He lost his temper thereupon
and told them, "I won't have this, now!
What priest or cleric would allow
the three of you to marry one?
Sometime before a month has gone
55   by I will straighten out the matter."
They tell him, "The sooner the better!
We want you quickly to decide
which one of us will be his bride."
      The good man went to church to pray
60   and hear Mass sung, and on the way
back, as it happened, met his brother.

si l'avoit saisi par la main;
a conseil le tret d'une part.
« Frere, fet il, se Dieus me gart,
65 mes freres es, & conseillier
me dois se je en ai mestier.
— Voire, dist cil, que ce est drois.
— Frere, fet il, molt granz desrois
est avenuz en ma meson!
70 Mes filles sont en grant tençon:
eles aiment .i. bacheler
trestoutes .iii. Sanz demorer
chascune dist qu'ele l'avra. »
Dist lor oncles: « Bien i faudra
75 tele qui bien le cuide avoir
se puis esploitier par savoir. »
Li dui frere s'en vont ensanble
en la meson, si com moi sanble,
ou les .iii. puceles estoient
80 qui du vallet s'entremetoient.
Lor oncles les en apela:
« Nieces, dist il, or venez ça,
si me dites vostre errement. »
Les puceles tout esraument
85 sont devant lor oncle venues;
ne furent pas tesanz ne mues,
ainz parlerent molt hautement.
L'ainsnee tout premierement
li dist qu'ele avoit .i. ami
90 bel & cortois & molt joli,
& si le voudra espouser.
L'autre ne se volt plus celer,
ainz dist: « Tu mens, voir! Je l'avrai,
quar ainçois de toi l'acointai. »
95 La mainsnee ne set que dire;
plaine est de mautalent & d'ire;

So that he might speak with him further,
he drew him to one side a piece,
and said, "Brother, God grant me peace!
65 As brothers, when I face a crisis,
I need to know what your advice is."
The other answered, "As is right."
"You can't imagine what a fight
is raging in my domicile!
70 My girls refuse to reconcile,
for all three of them love the same
young man and each of them lays claim
to marry him soon as can be."
Their uncle said, "Leave that to me.
75 Though all are sure, some still will fail
to land him, if I can prevail."

      The two together, toward these ends,
ambled back to his residence.
It seems to me, waiting inside it
80 were the three girls by love divided.
Their uncle asked them to come near.
"Nieces," he called, "come over here
and let me know your situation."
The sisters without hesitation
85 upon their uncle's summons went
to him, not the least reticent,
but shouting as if fit to burst.
The eldest daughter spoke up first
and told him that she had a suitor,
90 no man was better bred or cuter,
and she would be the girl he wed.
Undaunted, the next sister said,
"I say you're lying! He'll be mine!
I've known him for a longer time."
95 The youngest doesn't say a thing,
but, filled with anger, takes a swing

prent .i. baston a ses .ii. mains,
sa suer en fiert par mi les rains
qu'a la terre la fet cheïr.

100   Lor oncles les va departir:
« Nieces, dist il, tenez en pais!
Li jugemenz sera ja fais
la quele le devra avoir,
& si avra de mon avoir:

105   .c. sous de tornois li donrai
& son ami li liverrai
cele qui mieus savra respondre
a ce que je voudrai despondre. »
Celes dïent communement:

110   « Nous l'otroions molt bonement.
Demandez; nous responderons.
— Volentiers », ce dist li preudons.
     Il apela de ses voisins
.iii. des plus mestres eschevins

115   por ce que jugaissent a droit
de ce que chascune diroit.
Premerain demanda l'ainsnee:
« Niece, n'i a mestier celee.
Qui est ainsnez, vous ou voz cons?

120   — Oncles, par Dieu & par ses nons,
mes cons si est, en bone foi,
se m'aït Dieus, ainsnez de moi:
il a la barbe, je n'en ai point.
Se je ai respondu a point,

125   si jugiez droit & lëauté! »
Li eschevin ont escouté
ce que la pucele avoit dit.
Dont vint l'autre sanz contredit.
Ses oncles la mist a reson:

130   « Or me dites de vostre con,
s'il est de vous ainsnez, ma niece.
— Oncles, dist ele, de grant piece

at her own sister, stick in hand,
striking her in the kidneys and
knocking her flat down on the floor.
100　Their uncle breaks them up before
more harm is done: "Now stop your fighting,
and I'll set my mind to deciding
to which of you he should belong
and furnish a dowry along
105　with him. A hundred Tournois sous
and husband go to the girl whose
good sense can find the best reply
to untangle the riddle I
will set for you." The girls agree:
110　"We'll go along with that, all three.
We'll answer you; just go ahead
and ask." "Okay," their uncle said.
　　　　　Among his neighbors he called three
who had the most authority
115　to sit in judgment and pronounce
which sister gave the best response.
He started with the eldest niece.
"Speak or forever hold your peace!
Who was born first, your cunt or you?"
120　"By all the saints and the one true
God, uncle, I swear in reply
that my cunt is older than I.
It has a beard, and I do not.
Now well and truly judge if what
125　I've answered you leaves room for doubt."
The worthy elders heard her out,
took note, and waited for the rest.
　　　　　The second came to pass the test.
Her uncle asked her, "To be blunt,
130　I want to know about your cunt.
Is it older than you are, niece?"
"Uncle," she answered, "if you please,

sui je ainsnee que mes cons,
que j'ai les denz & granz & lons,
135 & mes cons n'en a encor nus.
Or ne me contredie nus
Robin, se je le doi avoir. »
Or ont les .ii. dit lor savoir,
si apela l'en la mainsnee;
140 ses oncles l'a aresonee:
« Niece, fet il, or me direz
se voz cons est de vous ainsnez
ou estes ainsnee de lui.
— Oncles, dist ele, por nului
145 ne lerai que ne le vous die;
qui veut, si le tiegne a folie
Mes cons est plus jones de moi,
si vous dirai reson por qoi:
de la mamele sui sevree;
150 mes cons a la goule baee,
jones est, si veut aletier.
Or m'ose je bien afichier
que j'ai bone reson trovee.
L'ame de lui soit honoree
155 qui jugera ces moz a droit!
— Damoisele, par bon endroit
tel reson avez respondu.
Vous avez de trestout vaincu »,
li eschevin ce li ont dit,
160 puis li donent sanz contredit
celui qui lonc tens l'a amee.
    Or *vois* querant par la contree
se li jugemenz est bien fez.
Que Dieus vous pardoinst voz mesfez,
165 se vous i savez qu'amender,
je le vieng a vous demander.

I'm older, and by quite a bit.
As yet it has no teeth in it,
135 while I have teeth both sharp and long.
Let no one now tell me I'm wrong
to think that Robin will be mine."

      The first two have spoken their mind,
and now it's the turn of the last.
140 Her uncle called for her and asked,
"You need to let me know," he told her,
"dear niece, whether your cunt is older
than you are, or if it is younger."
"I'll not put off a second longer
145 my answer for anyone's sake
who may think haste is a mistake.
Uncle, my cunt's younger than I,
and I'll tell you the reason why.
While I have been weaned from the breast,
150 the mouth of my cunt gapes from thirst
and, at its young age, needs to suck.
Now I will boast that I have struck
on the best answer of them all,
and God's speed to the man who shall
155 render a wise and just decision!"
"For the verity and precision
of your answer, the court decides,
young lady, that you've won the prize,"
the worthy elders let her know,
160 and they proceeded to bestow
her hand on her devoted lover.

      I'm traveling the wide world over
to ask: "Was the right verdict given?"
and pray your sins may be forgiven.
165 If you'd amend this verdict, now
I call on you to tell me how.

Or entendez .i. petitet—
n'i ferai mie grant abet.

      Uns fevres manoit a Creeil
qui por batre le fer vermeil
5   quant l'avoit tret du feu ardant
avoit aloué .i. serjant
qui molt estoit preus & legiers.
Li vallés avoit non Gautiers;
molt ert deboneres & frans,
10   les rains larges, grailes les flans,
gros par espaules & espés,
& si portoit du premier mes
qu'il covient aus dames servir,
quar tel vit portoit, sanz mentir,
15   qui molt ert de bele feture,
quar toute i ot mise sa cure
Nature, qui formé l'avoit:
devers le retenant avoit
plain poing de gros & .ii. de lonc.
20   Ja li treus ne fust si bellonc,
por tant que dedenz le meïst,
qu'aussi roont ne le feïst
com s'il fust fez a droit conpas,
& des maillaus ne di je pas
25   qui li sont au cul atachié
qu'il ne soient fet & taillié
tel comme a tel ostil covient.
Toz jors en aguisant se tient
por retrere delivrement,
30   & fu rebraciez ensement
comme moines qui gete aus poires—
ce sont paroles toutes voires!—
rouges comme oingnon de Corbueil,

65. THE BLACKSMITH OF CREIL

If you'll just listen for a bit,
you'll not be sorry that you did.
      There was a smith who dwelt in Creil.
To help him beat the glowing steel
5   when he had pulled it from the fire,
he had a servant in his hire,
a talented and agile lad,
and Walter was the name he had.
He was agreeable and frank,
10   broad-backed and slender in the flank,
with shoulders muscular and thick,
and he was endowed with a prick,
the most colossal slab of meat
that's served to women as a treat,
15   God's honest truth, one shaped so fair
that Nature must have lavished care
to make it, and surpassed her craft,
around the bottom of the shaft
two palms in length, wide as a fist.
20   A hole, though shaped like an ellipse,
in which this well-hung stud had placed it
would look as if a compass traced it,
so very round would it become.
About his balls I'll not keep mum,
25   hanging between his ass and pizzle
like mallets sculpted with a chisel,
befitting such a master tool.
Ready for action, as a rule
on the qui vive his member stood,
30   its head uncovered, with its hood
thrown back, like monks who harvest pears
  (these words are true, your author swears!),
red as an onion grown in Spain,

& si avoit si ouvert l'ueil

35 por rendre grant plenté de seve
que l'en li peüst une feve
lonbarde tres par mi lancier
que ja n'en lessast son pissier—
de ce n'estuet il pas douter—

40 ne que une oue a gorgueter
s'ele eüst mengié .i. grain d'orge
li vallés qui maintient la forge
d'une part avoec son seignor.
Ne peüst pas trover meillor

45 en la vile de ce mestier.

Bien ot esté .i. an entier
avoec le fevre li vallés,
que de lui servir estoit pres.
.i. jor avint qu'il fu aroit

50 & que son vit fort li tendoit.
Ses sires le trova pissant
& vit qu'il ot .i. vit si grant,
de tel façon & de tel taille
com je vous ai conté sanz faille,

55 & penssa se sa fame set,
qui tel ostil mie ne het
comme Gautiers, lor serjant, porte,
ele voudroit mieus estre morte
qu'ele ne s'en feïst doner;

60 par tens la voudra esprover.
A sa fame vient, si a dit:
« Dame, fet il, se Dieus m'aït,
je ne vi onques si grant menbre
que je sace ne que moi menbre

65 comme a Gautiers, nostre serjanz,
quar se ce fust uns granz jaianz
si en a il assez par droit.
Merveille est quant il est aroit,
je le vous di tout sanz falose.

its one eye open wide to drain
35   off a great quantity of juice,
and you could toss inside and lose
a fava bean from Lombardy
and still not stop its flow of pee.
A grain of barley in her gullet
40   would no more gag a goose or pullet,
I'm sure, than the bean would engorge
the lad who stoked the blacksmith's forge
while his employer beat the irons.
Nowhere else throughout the environs
45   was any man so well equipped.

          A year or even more had slipped
by since the prompt and willing boy
had entered in the smith's employ.
One day it happened that his rod
50   had swollen up and become hard.
The smith found him taking a leak
and for the first time had a peek
at his gigantic, splendid tail
(which I've described in some detail),
55   and thought if only his wife, who
did not despise tools like that, knew
what size equipment Walter carried,
she'd sooner have been dead and buried
than not secure herself a share.
60   He meant to test her then and there.

          He goes up to his wife and says,
"Woman, as I hope for God's grace,
I've never seen a larger member,
as far as I know or remember,
65   than what our servant, Walter, sports.
Were he as big as Behemoth,
he'd not need one larger in size.
Don't think I'm just inventing lies;
erect, it floors imagination."

70 — Quar parlez a moi d'autre chose,
fet cele, cui sanble qu'el hee
ce dont ele est si enbrasee,
quar par la foi que je vous doi,
se plus en parlez devant moi,
75 je ne vous ameroie mie.
Tel honte ne tel vilonie
ne devroit nus preudom retrere! »
Li fevres ne s'en vout pas tere
de löer le vit au vallet;
80 plus que devant s'en entremet
& dist qu'en tel ostil ouvrer
ne sot mieus Nature esprover
qu'en rien que ele onques feïst.
« Dame, fet il, se Dieus m'aït,
85 onques mes hom de mere nez
ne fu de vit si racinez,
Dame! fet il, comme est Gautiers.
Je croi qu'il fout molt volentiers.
— Sire, fet ele, a moi que touche? »
90 qui bien savoit dire de bouche
le contrere de son corage.
(Mes molt bien pert a son visage,
que sovent color mue & change—
ja de sens ne fust si estrange
95 homme, qui garde s'en preïst,
qui bien ne seüst & veïst
que talent en ot fort & aspre:
une eure est plus blanche que nape,
autre eure plus rouge que feus.)
100 « Certes, molt estes anïeus
qui si parlez vilainement!
Je vous avoie bonement
proié que vous vous teüssiez—
bien tere vous en deüssiez.
105 — Ma dame, puis que il vous plest,

70   "Leave off this tasteless conversation,"
     she says—it seems she must abhor
     the thing that she's most burning for—
     "for, on my honor, be assured
     that if you say another word,
75   I'll hate you! Let the matter be.
     Such disgusting pornography
     is shameful for a man of breeding."
     The blacksmith goes right on repeating
     the young man's praises, waxes lyric
80   in superphallic panegyric
     and says in nothing that she's made
     is Nature's mastery displayed
     as clearly as in that man's rod.
     "Lady," he says, "so help me God,
85   no men on earth yet born of women
     have such a penis rooted in 'em
     as, Lord have mercy, Walter, who,
     unless I'm wrong, must love to screw."
     "And just how is that my concern?"
90   she asks, well knowing how to turn
     her words to hide what's in her breast;
     but her face shows her interest
     by changing hue in quick succession.
     No man could observe her expression,
95   however addled were his senses,
     and not see straight through her pretenses.
     So strong and biting her desire,
     one minute she's as red as fire,
     the next she's paler than a sheet.
100   "You're disagreeable indeed
     to go on with your gutter speech!
     How patiently did I beseech
     you to keep quiet on the topic!
     Now, don't you think it's time to stop it?"
105   "Well, if that's what you want, I guess

je m'en terai. » Atant se test.
       Or lais ceste parole ester.
« Dame, fet il, sanz arester
m'en irai a Saint Leu demain.
110   Prenez du feu, fetes a plain
Gautier nostre serjant ouvrer. »
Or fesoit sanblant de l'errer,
si s'est souz la forge repus.
La dame s'est levee sus
115   & prent du feu, porte a Gautier,
& cil commença a forgier,
qui molt fu sages & soutiz.
« Gautier, fet ele, tes ostiz,
est il ore tels que l'en dit
120   quant est aroit, se Dieus t'aït,
de la besoingne fere pres?
   — Tesiez, dame, fet li vallés,
qui grant honte a & grant vergoingne.
Parlez a moi d'autre besoingne;
125   de ce ne vous rendrai je conte.
   — Par Dieu, fet ele, rien ne monte,
quar il estuet que je le voie
or endroit sanz point de delaie,
par couvent que mon con verras.
130   Sez tu quel loier en avras?—
chemise & braies delïees
bien cousues & bien tailliees. »
Quant li vallés ot la promesse,
si trait le vit, dont une asnesse
135   peüst bien estre vertoillie;
cele qui estre en veut brochie
se descuevre jusqu'au nonbril.
« Gautier, fet ele, a ton ostil
fai mon con besier une foiz,
140   quar il est bien reson & droiz:

I'll say no more." No more he says.
     I, too, will let the matter lie.
The smith goes on, "Tomorrow I
must hurry off, wife, to Saint-Loup;
110 Walter will have plenty to do.
See the fire's lit, and keep him at it."
     Making them think he'd left, he squatted
and hid himself under the forge.
His wife got up and took a torch
115 and passed the fire on to young Walter,
who set to work and did not falter.
He was adept and no one's fool.
"Walter," she says, "about your tool,
can it be true, so help you God,
120 what people say—that when it's hard,
it's always ready for the task?"
The young man says, "Lady, don't ask,"
for he's self-conscious and ashamed.
"Say something else. On what you've named
125 I will not give you information."
"That will not change the situation,
by God," she says; "I'll have a look.
I mean to see it, and I'll brook
no delay. In return I'll show
130 my cunt to you. I'll have you know
you'll be repaid with shirt and britches
cut to your size, sewn with fine stitches."
Hearing her promise, he lays bare
a prick that might well cause a mare
135 to squirm if it were used to do 'er.
The woman, eager for the skewer,
lifts her skirt to her belly button.
"Walter," she says, "come here and put in
your tool, so it can kiss my cunt.
140 It's only right, for it's the wont

ne s'entrevirent onques mes,
si prendront l'un a l'autre pes. »
     Li vis fu roides comme pel;
si atasta s'il i ot sel
145 & si fu pres de hurter enz,
mes li fevres ne fu pas lenz:
de derrier la forge est saillis
& s'escria a molt hauz cris:
« Sire vassal, traiez ensus!
150 Par mon chief, vous n'en ferez plus
que fet avez, vostre merci!
Ne remaint pas n'en vous n'en li
que grant honte ne m'avez faite!
Vostre services ne me haite
155 ne ne me plest d'ore en avant.
Alez vous en! Jel vous commant
que vous n'entrez ja mes ceenz. »
Gautiers s'en part tristre & dolenz,
& la dame remest penssive,
160 & li sires a li estrive:
« Par Dieu, fet il, de grant ardure
vous venoit, & de grant luxure!
Vous ne le pöez pas noier
que vous voliez bien que Gautier
165 lessast les oevres de ses mains
por marteler desus voz rains.
Ja en avrez vo guerredon! »
Lors avoit pris .i. grant baston,
si la vous commence a paier
170 si que les os li fet ploier,
se li a tant de cops donez
qu'il est sor li trestoz lassez.
     Par cest example vueil moustrer
c'on doit ainçois le leu hüer
175 des bestes qu'il i soit venuz:
se li fevres se fust teüz

of strangers to exchange on meeting
a kiss of peace by way of greeting."
        His prick was stiffer than a shovel;
he rubbed it to make sure the devil
145 was seasoned. . . . Before he could shove
it in, the blacksmith made his move.
Out from behind the forge he loomed
and cried out in a voice that boomed,
"You arrant scoundrel, stop right there!
150 You'll do no more, by God, I swear,
than you have done already, thanks!
One moment more, you and this minx
would have defiled, defamed, disgraced
me! Henceforth I hold in distaste
155 the sundry services you do.
Get out! You're fired! I order you,
never again set foot in here!"
        A rueful Walter packs his gear,
and the smith's wife is melancholy;
160 her husband scolds her for her folly.
"By God," he says, "what great desire
consumed you, and what lustful fire!
You can no longer controvert
the fact—you wanted to subvert
165 Walter and make him leave his chores
to hammer on those loins of yours.
You'll get what's coming you, and quick!"
He'd laid his hands on a stout stick
and set out to give her her due,
170 and beat her body black-and-blue,
and gave the woman such a dusting
that he himself found it exhausting.
        My story gives sufficient proof
that one does well to holler wolf
175 before it decimates the herd.
If the smith hadn't said a word

que Gautiers eüst bouté enz,
la dame eüst fet ses talenz.
A cest mot finerons no conte.
180 Que Dieus nous gart trestoz de honte.

66. L'ANEL QUI FAISOIT LES VIZ GRANS ET ROIDES

Haiseaus redit c'uns hons estoit,
.i. merveilleus anel avoit:
tant com il l'avoit en son doit,
adés son membre li croissoit.
5   .i. jor chevauchoit une plaigne
tant qu'il trova une fonteine.
Descenduz est quant il la vit
& les la fonteine s'asist,
si lava ses meins & son vis,
10   & son anel qu'il a hors mis.
Quant il li plut, si s'en leva,
mes l'anel seur l'erbe oublia.
.I. esvesque par la passoit;
si tost com la fonteine voit,
15   il descent & trova l'anel.
Por ce que il le vit si bel,
en son doi l'a mis sanz atendre.
Le membre li commence a tendre
quant il i ot un peu esté.
20   *Ez* vos l'esvesque remonté;
a molt tres grant mesese estoit
du membre qui si li tendoit,
ne n'aloit pas sans plus tendant,
ençois aloit tor jors croissant.
25   Tant crut & va tant aloignant

before Walter had penetrated,
his wife's desire would have been sated.
So ends our little fabliau.
180 God save us all from shame and woe.

66. THE RING THAT
CONTROLLED ERECTIONS
by Haiseau

Haiseau has yet another thing
to tell. A man once owned a ring
which, when worn, by a magic spell
at once would make his manhood swell.
5 It happened one day that he rode
across a field where a stream flowed.
He got off his horse when he saw it,
strode to the bank and crouched before it,
and there he washed his hands and face.
10 He took the ring out in that place.
At length he got up and rode on,
but left the ring there on the lawn.
        A bishop soon came riding by.
As soon as the stream caught his eye,
15 he dismounted and found the ring,
and, enthralled by its glittering,
he picked it up and put it on.
His virile member thereupon
began to stiffen in due course.
20 The bishop, now back on his horse,
was disconcerted to detect
his penis had grown quite erect
and this growth didn't seem to end it,
for it grew ever more distended
25 and so enlarged, it burst the stitches

que ses braies vont deronpant.
Li evesque honteusement
montre s'aventure a sa gent,
mes nul n'i ot qui s'avertist
30 que ce li anel li feïst.
         Tant crut qu'il li traïne a terre.
Par conseil commanda a querre
home ou fame qui li aidast
& qui a point le ramenast.
35 Cil qui l'anel avoit perdu
ceste merveille a entendu,
a l'evesque est venuz tot droit,
si demanda qu'il li donroit
du sien si le poeit garir.
40 Cil qui avoit trop a soufrir
li dist: « Tot a vostre talent.
— J'avrai dont, fait il, par covent
vos .ii. aneaus tout au premiers
& .c. livres de vos deniers. »
45 Quant les aneaus furent fors tres,
li membres est tantost retrés.
Ainz que cil eüst ses .c. livres
fu li evesques tot delivres,
& cil marchié fu bien seanz,
50 comme chascun en fu joianz.

6⁊. DU COVOITEUS ET DE L'ENVIEUS

Seignor, aprés le fabloier
me vueil a voir dire apoier,
quar qui ne sait dire que fables
n'est mie conterres regnables
5 por a haute cort a servir

at the seams of the bishop's britches.
Ashamed, the bishop shows his servants
what hard luck mortifies and burdens
him, but they've no way of construing
30   this mischief is all the ring's doing.
       It grew till it dragged on the ground.
He sent his messengers around
to find someone who could advise
him how to bring it back to size.
35   The man who'd lost the ring got word
of what strange marvel had occurred,
and to the bishop straightaway
he went and asked how much he'd pay
him if he could effect a cure.
40   He said, unable to endure
such agony, "Just name your fee."
"Then I will ask you to agree
to give me those two rings you wear
and one hundred pounds as my share."
45   Without the rings on, his incessant
erection became detumescent.
Before the bishop paid his hundred
pounds to him, he was disencumbered,
and wasn't it a fair exchange
50   when each was glad to have the change?

67. MR. GREED AND MR. ENVY
by Jean Bodel

Now that I've told some fables, lords,
I'll turn my hand to truer words,
for one who can't tell something truer
is no suitable raconteur
5   to work at court, but must be able

s'il ne sait voir dire ou mentir,
mais cil qui du mestier est fers
doit bien par droit entre .ii. vers
conter de la tierce meüre.

10   Que ce fu veritez seüre
que dui conpaignon a .i. tans
furent bien a passé .c. ans
qui menoient mauvaise vie,
que li uns *ert* si pleins d'envie
15   que nul plus de lui a devise,
l'autre si plain de covoitise
que riens ne li pooit soufire.
Cil ert ainsi malvais ou pire,
que Covoitise si est tieus
20   qu'ele fait maint home honteus;
Covoitise preste a usures
& fait recouper les mesures
por covoitier d'avoir plus aise;
Envie si est plus malvaise
25   qu'ele va tot le mont coitant.
        Entre Envïeus & Covoitant
chevalchoient .i. jor ensanble,
s'aconsivirent, ce me sanble,
saint Martin en une champaigne.
30   Poi ot esté en lor compaigne
quant il les ot espermentez
de lor mauvaises volentez
qui es cuers lor erent plantees.
Lors truevent .ii. voies hantees,
35   ses departoit une chapele.
Saint Martin les homes apele
qui menoient malvais mestier:
« Seignor, fait il, a cest mostier
tornerai mon chemin a destre,
40   & de moi vos doit il melz estre.

to say what's true as well as fable,
for he who in his art takes pride
is bound to take care to provide
for every two lines one for teaching.
10   Now, it is true beyond impeaching
that there were once two comrades, though
it was some hundred years ago,
who both led lives of mortal sin.
As for the first, there's never been
15 anybody more envious,
and the other so covetous
that nothing satisfied his greed.
For sure, there's no more evil breed,
and many men have come to shame
20 all for the sin that bears the name
of Greed, who lends at cutthroat rates,
shortchanges, falsifies the weights,
in her attempt to swell her purse,
while Envy's faults are even worse,
25 which dun and infect every human.
        Greedy and Envious, these two men,
fell in with, while out for a ride
together in the countryside,
Saint Martin, so it seems to me.
30 He'd not been in their company
long, when he set about revealing,
by testing them, the evil feeling
and illwill rooted in their hearts.
Their road divided in two parts
35 beside a shrine. They reach it; then
Saint Martin calls upon these men
who were entrenched in wicked ways.
"Here at this chapel, sirs," he says,
"the path I take turns to the right.
40 God grant your meeting with me might

Ge sui saint Martin le preudon—
li uns de vos me ruist .i. don,
si avra lués que lui plaira,
& li autres qui se taira
45 en avra maintenant .ii. tanz. »
Lors se pensa li covoitanz
qu'il laira demander celui,
si en avra .ii. tanz de lui—
molt goulousent double gaaig.
50 « Demande, fait il, beaus conpaing,
seürement, que tu avras
quanque tu demander savras.
Soies larges de sohaidier.
Se de sohaiz te saiz aidier,
55 riches sera tote ta vie. »
Cil qui le cuer ot plain d'envie
ne demandera pas son vueil,
qu'il morroit d'envie & de duel
se cil en avoit plus de lui.
60 Ainsinc esturent anbedui
sanz demander une grant piece.
« Qu'atens tu, qu'il ne t'en meschiece?
fait cil qui avoit couvoitié.
G'en avrai tote la moitié
65 plus de toi, n'en avrai garant.
Demande, ou ge te batrai tant
que mielz ne fu asnes a pont!
—— Sire, li envïeus respont,
ge demanderai, ce sachiez,
70 ençois que vos mal me faciez;
mais se ge ruis argent n'avoir
vos en vorroiz .ii. tanz avoir,
mais n'en avrez riens se ge puis!
Saint Martin, dit il, ge vos ruis
75 que j'aie perdu .i. des elz

benefit you! I'm good Saint Martin,
and I'll grant one wish at our parting.
One of you will get on the spot
what he requests; he who does not
45   make a wish gets the same twofold."
        Greedy thinks it best that he hold
back and let his companion wish
and thus become two times as rich.
(Both of them lust for double pay.)
50   "Dear friend," he ventures, "wish away
with confidence, and your desire
will be fulfilled as you require!
Wish lavishly, and you shall have
all of the riches that you crave
55   your whole life long, if you are smart."
The man with envy in his heart
would sooner drop dead than request
a thing, consumed with envy lest
he end up with less than the other.
60   They both tried to wait out each other
and not wish as long as they could.
"Putting it off will do no good.
I mean to have," at long length said
the one of them who coveted,
65   "twice what you get. Don't dare deny me!
Ask, or else you'll be beaten by me
like the mule on the bridge that balks."
Thereon the envious man talks
and says, "I'll ask, if that prevents
70   your doing me such violence,
but be forewarned that I won't wish
for goods or coin to make you rich.
I'll see to it you get twice nil.
Saint Martin, cause me, if you will,
75   to lose an eye, and pay in kind

& mes conpainz en perde .ii.—
si sera doublement grevez. »
Tantost ot cil les elz crevez.
    Bien en fu tenuz li otroiz:
80 de .iiii. elz perdirent .iii.,
n'i conquistrent bien autre nule,
ainz fist l'un borgne, l'autre avugle,
sains Martins, & par lor sohait.
S'il perdirent, maldahez ait
85 de moie part cui en poise,
qu'il furent de male despoise.

68. BRUNAIN, LA VACHE
AU PRESTRE

D'un vilain cont & de sa fame
c'un jor de feste Nostre Dame
aloient ourer a l'yglise.
Li prestres devant le servise
5 vint a son proisne sermoner
& dist qu'il fesoit bon doner
por Dieu, qui reson entendoit,
que Dieus au double li rendoit
celui qui le fesoit de cuer.
10 « Os, fet li vilains, bele suer,
que noz prestres a en couvent:
qui por Dieu done a escïent,
que Dieus li fet mouteploier.
Mieus ne poons nous enploier
15 no vache, se bel te doit estre,
que por Deu le donons le prestre.
Ausi rent ele petit lait.

my friend twofold and strike him blind.
A double forfeit be his prize!"
      No sooner said, there go the eyes.
The saint kept his word faithfully:
80   out of four eyes, the two lost three.
So what have these two sinners won?
One has one eye, the other none.
Given the chance, they chose the worst.
As far as I'm concerned, accursed
85   be he who pities what it cost
them. It's their own fault that they lost!

68. BROWNIE,
THE PRIEST'S COW
by Jean Bodel

A peasant and his wife one day
went to the village church to pray
to celebrate Our Lady's feast.
Before he sang the Mass, the priest
5   stepped in front of the altar screen
and gave a sermon to explain
that he who gives to God does well,
for God will cause his gift to swell:
Who gives with a pure heart gets double.
10   The peasant said, "Hear what a noble
promise, wife, our priest just now made!
Give of your wealth to God, he said,
and He will make it multiply.
We'd not do better, though we try,
15   than offer to the priest our cow
for love of God, if you'll allow.
She's nearly dried up anyway."

— Sire, je vueil bien que il l'ait,
fet la dame, par tel reson. »
20 Atant s'en vienent en meson
que ne firent plus longue fable:
li vilains s'en entre en l'estable,
sa vache prent par le lïen,
presenter le vait au doien.

25   Li prestres ert sages & cointes.
« Biaus sire, fet il, a mains jointes,
por l'amor Dieu Blerain vous doing. »
Li lïen li a mis el poing,
si jure que plus n'a d'avoir.

30 « Amis, or as tu fet savoir,
fet li provoires, dans Constans,
qui a prendre bee toz tans.
Va t'en; bien as fet ton message.
Quar fussent or tuit ausi sage

35 mi parroiscien comme vous estes!
(S'averoie plenté de bestes!) »
Li vilains se part du provoire;
li prestres commanda en oirre
c'on face por aprivoisier

40 Blerain avoec Brunain lïer,
la seue grant vache demaine.
Li clers en lor jardin la maine,
lor vache trueve, ce me sanble,
an.ii. les acoupla ensanble,

45 a tant s'en torne, si les lesse.
      La vache le prestre s'abesse
por ce que voloit pasturer,
mes Blere nel vout endurer,
ainz sache le lïen si fors

50 du jardin la traïna fors,
tant l'a menee par ostez,
par chanevieres & par prez
qu'ele est reperie a son estre

"That sounds convincing, so she may
as well be his," replied his spouse.
20   No sooner had they reached their house,
without a word they set about
their plan. He went directly out
to the shed, took her by the lead
to give to the priest as agreed.
25   The priest had much ability.
"Father, in all humility,
for love of God I give you Blair."
He handed her into his care,
swearing he had no other wealth.
30 "Friend, you have done well by yourself,"
said Dom Constant, whose disposition
inclined toward gain and acquisition.
"You've done your errand; you may go.
Would that my parish all was so
35 obedient! (My faithful flock
would fill my barn and swell my stock.)"
        The peasant takes leave of the priest,
who quickly orders that the beast
be yoked together with his Brownie,
40 a good-sized cow, to help the scrawny
Blair adjust to the presbytery.
His clerk sets off, leading the wary
beast, takes their cow by the tether,
and ties the two of them together,
45 then leaves them standing in the pasture.
        The cow that belongs to the pastor,
wanting to graze, lowers her head,
but Blair won't let her browse. Instead,
she starts to tug, and pulls so hard on
50 the rope, she drags her from the garden,
and leads her over dale and hill,
through meadows, farms, and fields, until
at last she reaches her own byre,

avoeques la vache le prestre,
55 qui molt a mener li grevoit.
Li vilains garde, si le voit,
molt en a grant joie en son cuer:
« Ha! fet li vilains, bele suer,
voirement est Dieus bon doublere,
60 quar li & autre revient Blere:
une grant vache amaine brune!
Or en avons nous .ii. por une!
Petis sera nostre toitiaus! »
        Par example dist cis fabliaus
65 que fols est qui ne s'abandone:
cil a le bien cui Dieus le done,
non cil qui le muce & enfuet.
Nus hom mouteploier ne puet
sanz grant eür, c'est or del mains.
70 Par grant eür ot li vilains
.ii. vaches, & li prestres nule.
Tels cuide avancier qui recule.

69. LE PREUDOME QUI RESCOLT SON CONPERE DE NOIER

Il avint a .i. pescheor
qui en la mer aloit .i. jor
en .i. batel, tendi sa roi,
garda, si vit tres devant soi
5 .i. home molt pres de noier.
Cil fu molt preuz & molt legier:
sor ses piez salt, .i. croq a pris,
lieve, si fiert celui el vis
que par mi l'ueil li a fichié,
10 el batel l'a a soi saichié,
arriers s'en vait sanz plus atendre,

the priest's cow trotting along by 'er,
55 disgruntled and the worse for wear.
The peasant looks and sees them there;
his heart's about to overflow.
"Now, wife," he says, "we truly know
that God's adept dealing double.
60 Blair's coming back home as a couple,
bringing a cow. She's large and brown.
We had one; now that's two we own!
I think we'll need a bigger stable."
    Now for the moral of this fable.
65 Submit to God, renounce the self,
for he to whom God gives has wealth,
while he who hoards labors in vain.
Without luck none can count on gain
increasing. That's how things are now.
70 The peasant got a second cow,
for Fortune smiled. The priest has none.
He's often lost who thinks he's won.

69. THE MAN WHO SAVED HIS
BUDDY FROM DROWNING

This happened to a fisherman
one day on an occasion when
he'd taken his boat out to sea.
He cast his net and chanced to see
5 a stranger drowning in the surf.
He had agility and nerve,
and, jumping to his feet, he took
a hook and threw it, and it struck
him in the eye and there held fast.
10 He hauled him in, and then was fast
to steer his boat back to the shore—

totes ses roiz laissa atendre;
a son ostel l'en fist porter,
molt bien servir & honorer
15   tant que il fu toz respassez.
A lonc tens s'est cil porpenssez
que il avoit son oill perdu
& mal li estoit avenu:
« Cist vilains m'a mon ueil crevé,
20   & ge ne l'ai de riens grevé!
Ge m'en irai clamer de lui
por faire lui mal & enui. »
Torne, si se claime au maior,
& cil lor mest terme a .i. jor.
25   Endui atendirent le jor
tant que il vinrent a la cort.
Cil qui son hueil avoit perdu
conta avant, que raison fu:
« Seignor, fait il, ge sui plaintis
30   de cest preudome, qui tierz dis
me feri d'un croq par ostrage,
l'ueil me creva, s'en a[i] domaige.
Droit m'en faites, plus ne demant.
Ne sai ge que contasse avant. »
35   Cil lor respont sanz plus atendre:
« Seignor, ce ne puis ge deffendre
que ne li aie crevé l'ueil,
mais en aprés mostrer vos vueil
comment ce fu, se ge ai tort.
40   Cist hom fu en peril de mort
en la mer ou devoit noier.
Ge li aidai, nel quier noier;
d'un croq le feri qui ert mien,
mais tot ce fis ge por son bien:
45   ilueques li sauvai la vie.
Avant ne sai que ge vos die.
Droit me faites, por amor Dé! »

his nets could wait for one day more—
and brought him home with him, where he
was tended to honorably
15 until the fellow could recover.
        The one saved thought the matter over
for a long time, how it had cost
him dear and how his eye was lost.
"That wretch went and gouged out my eye,
20 and I'd done no harm to him! I
will take the man to court and sue him
and do my darnedest to undo him."
He went to see the magistrate
to plead his cause, who set a date
25 for the two to appear in court.
        They both showed up. The one who sought
redress for the gouged eye that he'd
lost was, as plaintiff, first to plead.
"I have a grievance, sire," said he,
30 "against this man, for recently
he struck me with a hook and gouged
my eye out, which is why I've lodged
complaint. I'm only asking for
what's right, and I need say no more."
35 The other speaks without delay
and says, "My lord, I can't gainsay
his claim: I did gouge out his eye,
but first I want to tell you why
and how it happened. The events
40 themselves attest my innocence.
My action rescued him from dying,
drowned in the sea. There's no denying
the fact I struck him with my hook,
but it was for his welfare. Look,
45 I saved the fellow's life that way,
for God's sake! What more need I say?
I'm only asking you for justice."

Cil s'esturent tuit esgaré
ensanble por jugier le droit,
50 quant .i. sot qu'an la cort avoit
lor a dit: « Qu'alez vos doutant?
Cil preudons qui conta avant
soit arrieres en la mer mis
la ou cil le feri el vis,
55 que se il s'en puet eschaper,
cil li doit son oeil amender.
C'est droiz jugemenz, ce me sanble. »
Lors s'escrïent trestuit ensanble:
« Molt as bien dit! Ja n'iert deffait
60 cil jugemenz. » Lors fu retrait.
Quant cil oï que il seroit
en la mer mis ou il estoit,
ou ot soffert le froit & l'onde,
il n'i entrast por tot le monde;
65 le preudome a quite clamé,
& si fu de plusors blasmé.

  Por ce vos di tot en apert
que son tens pert qui felon sert:
raembez de forches larron
70 quant il a fait sa mesprison,
jamés jor ne vos [...] savra gré.
A mauvais s'il li fait bonté,
tout oublie, riens ne l'en est,
ençois seroit volentiers prest
75 de faire li mal & anui
s'il venoit au desus de lui.

<pre>
        The subtlety of the case flusters
        the men assembled to decide.
50   A simpleton who was there cried
        aloud, "What makes you hesitate?
        Let the man who was first to state
        his case be thrown back in the sea
        right where his eye was gouged. If he
55   can get out of that situation,
        the other must pay compensation.
        It seems to me that judgment's fair."
        That suited everybody there:
        "Well said! Let no one override
60   this judgment." And they so decide.
        When the man heard that he would be
        once again cast into the sea
        to suffer in the icy waves,
        no way on earth he would; he caves
65   in and withdraws his wrongful claim,
        and quite a few think he's to blame.
        Let this teach you beyond a doubt
        never to help the wicked out.
        The gentle heart who rescues thieves
70   condemned to hang never receives
        their gratitude for what he does.
        Good deeds are lost on them, because
        they don't remember or don't care,
        and, what is worse, moreover, they're
75   the sort who'd repay right with wrong
        should the occasion come along.
</pre>

MY PROJECT OF translating the fabliaux spanned more than two decades, and more people helped and encouraged me than I can remember. Outstanding among them has been R. Howard Bloch, who read my earliest attempts and prodded me to do more . . . and more . . . and more. He used them in his classes and National Endowment for the Humanities (NEH) summer seminars, thus bringing my work to the attention of medieval scholars everywhere, whose valued input appears unacknowledged on almost every page. Were it not for Professor Bloch, this volume might never have seen the light of day.

I could not have undertaken so daunting a task were it not for my professors of Old French—Alice Colby-Hall, professor emerita at Cornell University, and the late Lionel J. Friedman and W. H. W. Field—who not only taught me to understand Old French but sensitized me to its nuances in such a way that the words on the page spoke to me in a familiar idiom. I owe a debt of gratitude to the late Gabriel Berns and to Joanna Bankier, who organized and led the 1989 NEH summer institute in literary translation, where I developed an interest in and respect for the translator's art and came to understand my personal objectives as a translator and how I might achieve them, however imperfectly. Nor would I have dared undertake so ambitious a project were it not for the support of the school at which I was employed, St. John's University, Collegeville, Minnesota, which approved and financed the sabbatical I used to write and research this book, provided funding when needed, and seconded my attendance at the NEH seminars and workshops that prepared me to do it.

I need to thank the Dutch publisher Koninklijke Van Gorcum BV for its generous permission to work with the diplomatic transcriptions contained in the *Nouveau Recueil Complet des Fabliaux* to create the critical edition on which I base my translations. I am likewise grateful to my editors at Norton/Liveright—Robert Weil, Carol Edwards, and William Menaker—for their tireless (and, to me, sometimes exhausting) attention to detail, ridding to a large extent the unavoidable inconsistencies due to my evolving aims and methods as the work progressed, and to my Old French proofreaders, Herman Koutouan and Adam Grant, who undertook the daunting task of checking every letter of every word of my texts against the transcriptions in the *NRCF*. My own lack of oversight is responsible for the flaws that must surely remain in both the English and Old French.

Many other people have contributed to this volume without realizing they were doing so. For example, those to whom I read my translations aloud to test their effectiveness for performance as the medieval *jongleurs* intended them—my sons, Matthew and Jonas, and my former students Patrick Seaman and Philip Bailey; F. R. P. Akehurst for helping me make sense of medieval customary law as laid out by Philippe de Beaumanoir; and the some three dozen teachers and scholars who have used the translations in their classes and cited them in articles, raising questions and making suggestions that prompted me to further refine what I had done, among whom I need to single out Peter Beidler, Regula Evitt, Ellen Friedrich, Jean Jost, Mary Leech, Janet Solberg, and Larrissa Tracy.

1. *The Cunt Made with a Spade*

I–7.   The anacoluthon draws attention to the connection between the Fall and the creation of woman.

17.   A husband could punish his wife by putting her on bread and water as well as beating her, or she might fast as a penance or as part of a regimen of mortification for her spiritual health.

24.   The bottommost protruding vertebra visible on the spine; the sacrum.

52.   Proverb.

4. *How the Priest Read the Passion Story*

4.   The account of the Passion from each of the four Gospels is read in turn during Holy Week, starting with Matthew on Palm Sunday. The text for Good Friday is John I8–I9.

8–9.   The priest's clerk would have put a straw in his copy of the Gospels to mark the place for the day's reading. Noomen speculates that a lost couplet must have informed the audience of his error, which seems likely. As it stands, *le* (9) lacks an antecedent.

I5.   The Lenten fast allowed for only one meal a day.

23–24.   The priest hits on Psalm II0, read at Sunday vespers (cf. 30), and does not even realize that this tome does not contain the Gospels.

24–25.   By *o* we may understand the rhyme sound the poet needs, the stressed pronoun (Latin *oc*) with *conconancie* used figuratively, or both.

51.   This priest does not know his Bible. Even if he had the right book, he would never reach the miracles of the darkness and ripping of the Temple veil, which appear in the other three Gospels but not in John.

5. The Priest and the Wolf

1.　The countryside around Chartres.

6. The Priest and Alison

8.　The Oise River flows southwest to join the Seine just west of Paris. Since the story takes place in a large town (398), Noomen suggests Creil or Pontoise.

16–19.　These lines set the scene for when the chaplain first (or perhaps repeatedly) catches sight of Marian, but the author only means to give a description of the girl and does not follow through, so the scene never actually occurs. The action begins on line 48.

28.　Noomen evidently does not accept Philippe Ménard's identification with the Saint-Cyr once located five kilometers from Creil at Cires-lès-Mello, and takes it as the name of a church, since no Saint-Cyr is today within walking distance of the Oise. However, this author chooses many names just for the rhyme (cf. 13–14, 33–34, 63–66, 127–28, etc.).

30.　A rhizome closely related to turmeric.

64–65.　Ardres lies one-third of the way from Calais to Saint-Omer, about forty-five kilometers to the southeast.

108.　The martyrs Gervais and Protais. The cathedral of Gisors, about halfway between Paris and Rouen and some thirty kilometers southwest of Beauvais, is dedicated to them.

175.　About sixty kilometers southeast of Paris.

188.　Not his source, but the author himself, Guillaume le Normand (see 4 and 439).

191.　The coinage then in circulation makes possible an approximate dating of the fabliau in the first quarter of the thirteenth century. As demonstrated by Urban T. Holmes ("Notes on the French Fabliaux," in *Middle Ages, Reformation, Volkskunde: Festschrifte for John G. Kunstmann* [Chapel Hill: University of North Carolina Press, 1959], pp. 39–44), the *esterlin* was an official currency from 1204 until 1266, while minting the *denier de Senlis* (193) came to an end in 1179 and the *parisis* was discontinued between 1223 and 1266.

202. Mahauld's name changes to Menhould at this point.

288–89. As I see it, this couplet explains why the priest takes no notice of what Hercelot is up to. Noomen places the table in front of Alison (ms. D regularly has *lui* for *li*), and takes 284–85 as superfluous information added for the rhyme, but if so, the information is also contradictory, for she cannot be both upstairs and near the table. In any case, by the table she would be in full sight of the priest.

↖. *The Crucified Priest*

2. A respected member of a prestigious profession, he is exempt from a number of civic duties and taxation on the materials of his trade. See Etienne Boileau, *Le Livre des métiers* (1897; reprinted, Geneva: Slatkine, 1980), p. 129; cited in Noomen.

12–13. That is, he would make a delivery at the same time. The *imagiers tailleurs* did not peddle their wares at the market; they worked on commission.

56. Noomen points out that according to the *Livre des métiers*, carvers of religious images were required to work by day in order to have sufficient light, a fact of which his wife might well remind him. Perhaps this interdiction gave her the idea of hiding her lover in the workshop.

𝟠. *The Priest Who Had a Mother Foisted on Him*

182. Most likely his parish church is dedicated to Saint-Cyr.

𝟡. *The Cunt Blessed by a Bishop*

201–2. The closing words of the blessing of ordination.

𝟙𝟘. *Brother Denise*

1. Proverb.

10–11. Cf. Luke 6.44.

15. Proverb.

33.	The Friars Minor, the mendicant order founded by Saint Francis of Assisi.
82.	Herod the Great, king of Judaea, who ordered the Slaughter of the Innocents, or perhaps his son, Herod Antipas, tetrarch of Galilee, who had John the Baptist beheaded and interrogated Jesus before the Crucifixion.
104–5.	That is, the boiling cauldron of Hell.
173–74.	A *trait* is both a halter and a liturgical chant.
204.	The site of a Franciscan abbey that housed a leprosarium.
211–12.	As a woman, Denise is neither ordained nor ordainable.
247.	The Franciscans were known as Cordeliers because they wore habits belted with rope.
284–85.	That is, he does not have to borrow the sum.
322.	A convent under royal protection between Paris and Saint-Denis.

11. *The Beaten Path*

8.	The meaning of the unattested Old French proverb ("who pays well may expect a good return") is clear.
17.	Athies is ten kilometers south of Pérrone.
25.	In the *Mélanges Chabaneau*, E. Langlois provides full texts of all passages that mention this game: *"Le jeu du Roi qui ne ment et le jeu du Roi et de la Reine,"* in *Romanische Forschungen*, vol. 23 (1907), pp. 163–73.
36.	That is, "if she had found him pleasing."
49–51.	It is impossible to tell whether this is an actual proverb or an aphorism the lady makes up on the spot, altering "the tree is known by its fruit" (Matthew 12.33) in order to more vividly suggest a beard.
77–78.	The knight counters her jibe with a well-known proverb: *Voie batue n'aquieut herbe* (Old French 78–79).
104–5.	Proverb.

12. *The Knight of the Red Robe*

2.	As Noomen suggests, most likely Dammartin-en-Goële, about ten kilometers northeast of Charles de Gaulle Airport and some twenty kilometers south of Senlis (25). Both the dialect of the fabliau and the

detailed geography point to its composition in eastern Ile-de-France.

3. July 4, the date the saint's relics were brought to Tours.

30. Mss. ACo specify that the robe is new instead of its color, evidently to eliminate the imperfect Picard-style rhyme *novele / vermeille*. However, the color plays too prominent a role in the story not to mention it here, and it is essential that we recognize it from the beginning as the red robe of the title and so associate both knights with the garment. *Escarlate* was woolen cloth of the highest quality and could be any color.

87. Poitiers: as no one can identify Pevier (Penier?), my translation follows ms. Ao.

164–65. Noomen cannot see how *a li servir* (Old French 163) fits the context, perhaps because he takes the husband as the sole butt of the humor. This must have troubled the copyists as well, since the other mss. merely say at this point, each in its own way, that he dressed hastily. *Servir* is, however, both the *lectio difficilior* and most to the point. Despite the lover's reputation for valor, he doesn't dare face the sedentary vavasor (though en route to their tryst he seemed not to care who saw him), and when he beats his hasty and ignoble retreat, the lady's service is the last thing on his mind (Old French 163–64).

271. Saint Ulrich, believed to protect people against rabies.

285–96. The mss. differ considerably. Noomen demonstrates that ms. C traces the most coherent pilgrimage route following a list of saints most appropriate to the vavasor's supposed affliction. The cult of Saint Loup, invoked to cure madness and epilepsy, was widespread throughout Flanders and northern France, with over half a dozen villages of that name within a hundred-kilometer radius of Dammartin. The shrine of Saint James the Major at Compostela, in Spain, was, along with Rome, the most popular pilgrimage site in Europe. His wife suggests he follow the example of the most dedicated pilgrims and make a detour through Asturia to visit the image of the Holy Savior in Oviedo. Finally, Saint Arnoul was the patron saint of cuckolds. (Molière, in *L'École de femmes*, takes the name

Arnolphe from this saint.) As Noomen points out, one of Arnoul's shrines lies directly on the husband's way between Saint-Leu and Orléans, the beginning of the pilgrimage road to Compostela. Ms. A, in which the husband suggests a batch of random saints, is equally funny in its own way.

299. As a special act of devotion, supplicants would cut a wick to their height and have a taper made, which they burned in honor of the saint.

313–18. The moral states the opposite of a proverb used as the conclusion of "The Peasant of Bailleul" ("There's nobody on earth as dense as / who trusts his wife more than his senses"). The morals to "The Fellow with a Dozen Wives" and "Saint Martin's Four Wishes" use different versions of the same proverb.

15. *The Stupid Knight*

7. A forested plateau in northern France and southeast Belgium.

8. A Belgian town on the Meuse, southeast of Brussels.

30. Ms. G says "seven times." Noomen finds one hundred excessive; I think seven is insufficient, and prefer the reading in ms. A. The story calls for exaggeration.

105. Aalst (Alost in French), west of Brussels, is the only town mentioned that's not in the immediate region. Another Aalst, close to Sint-Truiden, is not called Alost in French.

111. Identified by Livingston as Sint-Truiden, about forty kilometers north of Andenne.

144. Dinant is thirty kilometers southwest of Andenne.

151. Tongeren, a bit under twenty kilometers east of Saint-Trond.

199. As a liquid measure, the *sestier* equaled roughly two gallons.

264. This might be any of three towns in Occitan-speaking territory: Lessac, Laissac, or Lizac.

273. *Manefle* is a *hapax*, but the description of its use in the next lines suggests an awl.

308. Literally, they "drew the short straw."

316. Proverb.

14. *The Knight Who Made Cunts Talk*

19. Literally, its "little pocket."

56. Now called Descartes (formerly La Haie-Descartes), about fifty-five kilometers south of Tours.

77. Most knights owned at least two horses. The palfrey, more of a show horse, was not used in combat.

98. They can't afford to pay for lodgings in a castle.

298– Our manuscript largely reworks this passage as found in
320. the other mss. to play down the knight's moralizing and emphasizes their amusement.

491–93. Although the knight's horse and equipment are worth much less, the countess still stakes the full forty pounds against them.

601–2. In our manuscript only, no doubt originally a marginal notation not intended as part of the poem—the rhyme is imperfect and line 601 hypermetric. But the opportunity for a funny English couplet is too good to pass up.

15. *The Muleteer*

51–52. Some editors posit a missing line to rhyme with 51, others that the original ended at 50 and a copyist added it as an afterthought. I tend to think the latter, but I take advantage of the octosyllabic *explicit* to finish off the couplet, in spite of the imperfect rhyme.

16. *The Piece of Shit*

48–49. As Noomen points out, wax was a luxury item and its use regulated by sumptuary law. A peasant would not have had it in his home.

17. *Black Balls*

28. Any contestation of marriage fell under ecclesiastical authority (*The Coutumes de Beauvais of Philippe de Beaumanoir*, trans. F. R. P. Akehurst [Philadelphia: University of Pennsylvania Press, 1992], art. 313).

54–58. Inability to consummate a marriage was sufficient grounds for annulment.

90. A comic oxymoron in Old French, since a *hongre* is a gelding.

18. *The Peasant Doctor*

79–82. The closeness of these lines to 109–12 accounts for the copyist mistakenly inserting 111–12 between 82 and 83, giving us the same couplet twice.

145. The fourth century B.C.E. physician, author of the Hippocratic oath.

262. A castle town on the Loire, about sixty kilometers downriver from Tours.

366. A rhizome closely related to turmeric.

19. *Long Butthole Berengier*

11–12. The Lombards had a reputation for boasting as well as cowardice. The main character has both defects.

70. Nowhere else does he address his wife as *tu*. Noomen astutely suggests that the copyist misunderstood *seviaus* as two words ("if you wish").

296. Proverb.

20. *The Poor Peddler*

138. Saint Giles was the patron saint of paupers.

22. *The Knight Who Heard His Wife's Confession*

1. The Bessin is the region on the Cotentin Peninsula inland of the Normandy D-day beaches. Vire lies a bit to the south, about fifty-five kilometers due east of the Atlantic resort town of Granville.

125–26. Proverb.

176–77. In the Middle Ages, the Church did not distinguish between relationship by blood and by marriage in determining incest.

191–92. Previous commentators have attempted to explain this line in many ways, none very convincing, since they read *tortiau puant li gart*, which makes nonsense of the syntax of the next line. Noomen's suggestion that it is a set expression whose meaning eludes us and that Ligart is a proper name strikes me as convincing. He interprets it as a reference to her deceptions, I suspect it may have to do with her adultery and nymphomaniacal promiscuity.

264–73. The first couple of letters of each line have been lost because of a tear in the parchment. I follow Noomen's reconstruction, except for 265.

2₃. *Auberée, the Go-Between*

17. The region surrounding Beauvais, at the southern edge of Picardy.

87. In Lincolnshire, 130 kilometers north of London.

253. Proverb.

364. The line is ambiguous: *entre ens* may just refer to the bed.

433. The abbey basilica of Saint Cornelius, the principal church in Compiègne.

451. *Une toise* equals about two yards.

460. Presumably, we should imagine a Saint Andrew's cross, in the form of an *X*.

563. We should assign no special significance to his signing the cross at this point in the story. People routinely did so on leaving home.

647. The heel of the boot of Italy.

662. Three manuscripts append a moral saying that when a woman engages in illicit sex, another woman has usually led her astray.

2₄. *Thrice Around the Church*

18. Berry is the region surrounding the city of Bourges, about two hundred kilometers south of Paris.

30–31. Their "matter" (*besoingne*) is, of course, illicit sex.

42. That would make it just a little under a mile. Measures of distance varied by region.

44. A region some fifty to seventy kilometers northeast of Orléans.

136–37.　He intends to mark her publicly as an adulteress.

152–54.　By her own admission (144), now that she has told her husband about it, the hocus-pocus can no longer serve any purpose . . . except, of course, to facilitate further encounters with the priest.

25. *The Mourner Who Got Fucked at the Grave Site*

114–19.　This reads like a string of proverbs, but line 119 ("loves" and "hates") has no known close equivalent in Old French.

26. *The Three Girls*

3.　According to Noomen, Brilly has been absorbed into what is now the village of Vattetot-sous-Beaumont, about twenty kilometers northeast of Le Havre.

15.　A neigboring village, called Bernières since the seventeenth century. (Identified by Noomen.)

16.　These do not sound like knights' names.

25–26.　Rouen is over fifty kilometers away!

62.　This line "translates" an Old French expression whose meaning is unknown (*taillier chape*).

27. *The Girl Who Wanted to Fly*

105.　This translates an otherwise unattested Old French proverb ("Trouble comes to those who look for it").

28. *The Old Beggar Woman*

49.　"Notions": The ms. reads *mindokes*, the only occurrence of the word in Old French. Godefroy, the standard Old French dictionary, suggests "crutches" without giving a reason. She clearly does not need them.

50.　*Dokes* is dock (a medicinal plant).

54.　Olivier's sister and Roland's betrothed in *The Song of Roland*, or perhaps a lady described as beautiful in a *chanson de toile*.

61–62.　Yseult is Isolde. There are three Blancheflors: Tristan's mother, Percival's beloved, and the heroine of the romance *Floire et Blancheflor*.

79. A *vite* is a head ribbon or diadem, and can be used as a term of endearment, but a *vit* is a penis.

180. Literally, "I must have said it all" (in the sense of "That sums it up").

226–28. Proverb.

29. Walter and Marion

7. *Aproucha*, Noomen's emendation ("came close"), seems reasonable to me. Scholars take *apoucha* as a *hapax*, and have suggested a number of possible meanings.

30. Piggie

8. In fact, she does.

56. *Desfromantez* is a neologism. To my ear, "unwheated" does not have as comic an effect in English, where, because the language more readily allows this type of word-building, it lacks a learned ring, but translating the line calls for some kind of wordplay.

31. The Fellow with a Dozen Wives

2. The Lombards of northern Italy had a reputation as braggarts.

85–86. The rhyme requires *soient*, but the usual expresssion is *le diable y soit!*

135ff. In ms. I, the townspeople compel the wolf to marry a woman, who torments him so, he wastes away and loses his mind.

32. The Cleric Behind the Chest

7. A region in southern Belgium and northern France, just east of Douai.

11–15. Irony—a superfluous bit of discretion on Jean de Condé's part if he heard the story from someone else. He lets us know at the end (139–49) that this woman can take care of herself. If anyone, her husband needs someone to look out for his reputation.

59–60.   No one has proposed a satisfactory explanation of *un point loiié*, which most interpret as a gambling term, but *point* has many other uses. I agree with Noomen in seeing it as an adverbial expression, whatever it means. I admit my solution implies some pretty warped syntax. The gist of the line is clear enough.

137ff.   Closing the fabliau with the feigned discretion he used at the beginning, Jean has no trouble letting us know exactly what happened next—nothing!

💥 *Master Ham and Naggie, His Wife*

10.   *Chavestriaus* is a hapax.

32.   The *Alleluia*, chanted polyphonically as an extended melisma, required the singers' close attention to their parts.

174–75.   Ham has told Simon that he may give the signal, but Simon has not given it. Moreover, as appellant, Ham has the right to strike the first blow. Of course, they have both ignored all the other formalities, such as oaths.

177.   *Alemite* is a hapax.

300–3.   Opie breaks protocol by encouraging Naggie. During a trial by combat, "no one should be so bold as to say a word" (Beaumanoir, art. 1842).

323.   Noomen ingeniously proposes that Ham is alluding to the episode in *Le Charroi de Nîmes* (*laisse* 40) where the cart driven by Bertrand and bearing a vat hiding a batch of knights gets stuck in the mud.

324.   The well-known knight and minstrel, hero of his own cycle. Because of similarity between his name and *triste*, singing about him meant "lamentation."

💥 *The Gelded Lady*

24.   Proverb.

215–16.   Each of these lines is a proverb. Some editors punctuate them as authorial comment, not as the count's words. While the author comes through as a more forceful personality than any of his characters, he achieves this by the tone of his narration and seldom speaks *in propria persona* except in the prologue and epilogue.

241ff. The count pointedly accepts the father's wedding gifts after twice refusing to take anything from his wife. Also, in turning down a dowry, he underscores his wife's total dependence on him.

257–72. This passage is lacking in mss. De, which have instead:

> *que vos le lievre tost praignez,*
> *ou les chiés orendroit perdrez.*
> *Li levrier corent a eslés,*
> *nel porent consivir de pres;*
> *arriere s'en sont repairié*
> *& li sires lor a tranchié*
> *les chiés a l'espee tranchant.*
> *Lors a dit a son sor baucent. . . .*

While this moves the story along at a nicer pace, by killing dogs who have succeeded in catching the hare, the count makes a stronger statement. Also, it makes little sense for him to tell his horse not to stumble *again* if it hasn't already stumbled. More important, the transition to 273 is quite clumsy: "Then he said to his bay horse, says the count, 'Don't stumble again.'" I use mostly ms. C for my translation, because it reads the most smoothly, but 265–68 contain an obvious error, praising the lady's rosy complexion instead of having her flush with shock at her husband's brutality.

272. Some editors and translators have variously understood that the horse is ordered not to whinny, graze, or toss its head, although *cester* is, if uncommon, well attested, perhaps because a few mss. (including D) read *teste*, a *hapax*. All three are voluntary actions for which the count might have some justification in blaming the poor animal, while to kill it for stumbling makes him look far more imperious.

454. In all the mss., the count calls for both a knife and a razor, but no basin. When he emasculates the woman, however, he has a basin handy, but no knife. Noomen suggests replacing *costel* with *tonel*, a paleographically justifiable emendation.

495–500. These lines do not appear in mss. De, but clearly he pretends to cut out two testicles (cf. 451–52, 555–56,

565–66). The word is always plural, although *coille* (singular) can refer to the pair, and Old French 557 reads *.ii. coillons*. The copyist simply lost his place, since both 494 and 500 begin *Semblant fet* ("He pretends . . .").

55. *The Fisherman of Pont-sur-Seine*

2. About forty kilometers northwest of Troyes.

71–72. The verb *enosser* ("to choke on something") contains the word *os*, a more obscene term for penis than the wife will allow herself to utter.

123–24. Criminals were sometimes branded by having their ears cut off.

141–43. Noomen's translation ("Your wealth doesn't matter to me, only your misfortune"), the most straightforward grammatically and syntactically, probably reflects what the wife has in mind, but it overlooks the polysemy of her reply and shows her already admitting the importance she places on their sexual relationship. *Mauvestié* is ambiguous, and *rien* even more so: "I don't care about your thing; it's your wickedness" (or, despite the paradox, "I don't care about your thing, only your mishap"). We may even understand "I don't care a thing for you / your possessions" (*il ne me chaut rien de vostre*, the word order altered for the sake of rhyme). In short, she says more than she intends, as with *enosser*, still trying to hide her enjoyment of sex. Only later, when she learns that her husband still has his penis, will she bluntly admit it, unable to contain her joy.

151. As Noomen points out, the wife goes out the back so the neighbors won't know she's leaving her husband. Legally, if he cannot, in fact, fulfill his sexual obligations, she may have the marriage dissolved (see "Black Balls"), but she should not take back her dowry until she has done so.

154. *Toute cossee* (Old French 153) means "the pods were fully formed."

196–98. The author repeats the line to make sure everyone will catch the joke, which he has prepared from the beginning by giving an account of her dowry. *Beste* was a common (and not especially obscene) euphemism for penis.

199–200. These lines, which do not occur in ms. C, Noomen

sees as an anticlimactic addition to the pun on *beste*. On the contrary, it is the moment of the husband's vindication, for the naughty word *vit* has finally passed her lips. I use a euphemism, no less obscene, to underscore the pun (as does the author).

208.   King Arthur's nephew, the model knight (and, ironically, quite the ladies' man).

56. *The Donkey's Legacy*

29.   The Old French specifies "between Easter and Saint Remy's Day" (October 1), which marked the last day of the harvest, after which the abundance of wheat brought prices down. The priest can afford to sit tight throughout the growing season and sell his grain when the prices are highest.

56.   Proverb.

108.   Proverb.

112.   That is, he would prefer to avoid a trial if at all possible.

123.   Proverb.

133–36.   An elaborate piece of wordplay: The priest picks up on the bishop's word, *consoil*, by which he meant "deliberation," and repeats it three times with three different meanings, respectively, "advice/decision," "trial," and "private consultation," and concludes with a verb derived from it, "to come to terms."

150.   Literally, "in him I certainly had a good *escu*." *Escu* is both a shield (thus, figuratively, his helper) and a coin (meaning that the animal was profitable). His metaphor suggests in advance the bribe he will offer the bishop.

164.   Rutebeuf undercuts his earlier moralizing by feigning naïveté (as if he believed that the bishop rejoices that his error has made the priest a better person!) and reinforces his cynicism with a play on words. *Bontei* means "gift" as well as "goodness." This is the first time he has given anything to the bishop (cf. 90).

57. *The Peasant's Fart*

16–18.   Matthew 19.24.

50.   As pointed out in *NRCF*, this is the same proverb as Villon, *Ballade de proverbes*, 23: *Tant embrasse on que chiet*

la prise ("Clutching a thing too tightly makes you drop it"). Villon modifies it for the rhyme and the anaphora on *tant*. Rutebeuf replaces *cheoir* ("fall") with *chier* ("shit").

74–76. The opening lines of *Audigier*, a mock epic about bodily functions, identify Coccuce as a country ruled by Audigier's father where people stand waist-deep in shit. The episode Rutebeuf refers to does not take place there, however, and it is his bride-to-be, not Audigier, who defecates in his hat.

𝟹𝟾. *The Soul That Argued Its Way into Heaven*

35–39. Matthew 26.69–75; Mark 15.65–72; Luke 23.54–62; John 18.15–17, 25–27.

64–71. John 20.24–25.

92–93. John 7.58–8.1.

95–97. Acts 8.

98. Acts 9.3–6.

100–01. The peasant treats the blow dealt Saint Paul as the hand slap exchanged to close a deal.

159–60. John 10.27–28.

166ff. The last six lines read like five proverbs one after the other, as announced in 166, but as far as I can ascertain, only 169 and 172 are attested in Old French. 170 and 171 are commonplaces on a corrupt age.

𝟹𝟿. *The Crane*

5. The Basilica of Saint Mary Magdalene in Vézelay (Burgundy) was a starting point for the pilgrimage to Compostela.

59. The young man does not at first realize just how naïve the girl is.

64. One could also translate: "never yet a fuck or a prick." *Vit* means both "saw" and "penis" in Old French.

120–21. Proverb.

131ff. On their second encounter, the girl addresses him as *vous* and the young man says *tu* (he also now calls her *damoisele* instead of *dame*), reversing their usage at their first meeting. No one can assess with certainty the exact implications of the second-person pronoun in Old French, but obviously something has changed.

162. Proverb.

40. *The Peekaboo Priest*

84. Proverb.

41. *The Peasant of Bailleul*

3. France has a dozen towns or villages called Bailleul, ten of them within about sixty kilometers of Arras.

75. The penitential psalms are recited during the rite of extreme unction.

81. The priest rushes through the ritual without bothering to commend his soul to God.

115–16. Compare this proverb with "The Fellow with a Dozen Wives," 155–56, and "Saint Martin's Four Wishes," 188–90.

42. *The Priest and the Woman*

4. A hamlet about fifteen kilometers northeast of Étampes.

28. The door in the wall surrounding the courtyard, of course, since he will ride through it on horseback (line 56).

53–55. Her bathing explains the delay in unlocking the door.

156–57. The woman's comment may as well apply to his sexual prowess as to his failure to lift three people.

168. Proverb.

43. *Gombert*

This fabliau was Chaucer's source for "The Reeve's Tale."

69. He couldn't get it past the tip (line 28).

75–76. The author plays with two meanings of *s'umelie*: "one so begs / submits to the other. . . ."

44. *The Healer*

17. The author stresses the luxurious ostentation of his costume.

37. She simultaneously reveals to the "surgeon" what treatment she wants and hides it from her husband.

45. *The Butcher of Abbeville*

15. November 1.

16. Oisemont is a bit more than fifteen kilometers south of Abbeville.

31. A little over halfway between Oisemont and Abbeville. This could be the same Bailleul as in fabliau #41.

51. About seventy kilometers east of Paris.

72. As we shall see, the deacon is lying.

73–74. The deacon's obligations include providing hospitality for visiting Church dignitaries. Extending it to others is left to his discretion.

90. It is ironic that the deacon invokes Saint Peter when he refuses to let the butcher in his house.

305. *Jube domine*: Before the readings for the day, a junior cleric calls upon the celebrant to pronounce a benediction.

385. A German city on the Rhine.

448–49. The Abbey of Saint Cornille in Compiègne housed the winding sheet used for Christ's burial.

556. A diminutive of *cornu* ("horned").

46. *The Three Blind Men of Compiègne*

37. Proverb.

72. The region around Auxerre in northern Burgundy produced some of the most appreciated wines of the Middle Ages. Soissons was known for its white wine.

115. (*Mener*) *paticle* is a *hapax*. In his CFMA edition, Gougenheim suggests it must mean something like "make a racket," and Ménard proposes, among other possibilities, an association with the onomatopoetic *patac*.

252. Saint Giles was the patron saint of epileptics.

307–08. People invoked Saint Cornelius to cure mental illness.

Moreover, in Compiègne the scene would probably have taken place in the abbey church of Saint Cornelius.

ꝝ1. *The Three Women Who Found a Ring*

196. Proverb.

ꝝ8. *Boivin de Provins*

1. Ms. A consistently writes his name as two words: *Boi vin* ("Drink wine").

3. The city of Provins held fairs in May, September, and starting the last day of November.

71ff. A medieval audience, proficient in mental arithmetic from regular practice at the market, would have had little trouble following these calculations. If he sold one ox for thirty-nine sous and the other for nineteen and we deduct one sou for Gerald's commission, his profit should come to fifty-seven sous, which means Gerald has rooked him. He wants whoever overhears him to think him in possession of a considerable sum and an easy target.

90–91. This clumsy and repetitive couplet in the Old French between two lines on the same rhyme is most certainly a copyist's addition.

127. A mock peasant's name. There is a village called La Brosse in the environs of Provins, but *de la brouce* may just as well mean "from the sticks." Fouchier may imply digging or cutting hay (*fauchier*—the text contains many Picard dialectal features and often uses *au* and *ou* interchangeably).

160. Saint Julian is the patron of travelers and innkeepers.

162. About 120 kilometers southwest of Provins.

307. Saint Nicholas protects property from loss and theft!

ꝝ9. *The Good Woman of Orléans*

4. A city in Picardy, halfway between Beauvais and Arras.

265. The region around Auxerre, at the limits of Burgundy.

326. A fragment of a proverb: "You drink what you brew."

𝟓𝟎. *The Miller of Arleux*

> Enguerrant tells a good story, but the versification is weak. I use more imperfect rhymes here than in the other fabliaux to capture the effect of the Old French.

7. The mill at Arleux is ten kilometers south of Douai, the miller's house two kilometers farther down the road in Palluel.

18. Estrées is four kilometers northwest of Arleux.

22. Noomen takes the name *Sanson* as a place he cannot identify, but surely he comes from Palluel or Arleux. I would guess she uses his father's name to distinguish him from the many others named Jacques. (The ms., as always, has *ele*, but the pronoun regularly scans as a monosyllable throughout this text.)

85. Noomen explains that *batre* involves making the surface of the stone (which has worn smooth) ready for grinding and *lever* means adjusting the distance between the two millstones.

324. About five kilometers southeast of Palluel.

𝟓𝟏. *Jouglet*

3. Most likely the Montferrand of Clermont-Montferrand, in nearly the geographical center of modern France, although only a handful of fabliaux take place outside the *langue d'oïl*.

208–9. Proverb.

221. Noomen's solution. The ms. reads *males quiteles. Quitele* is a *hapax. Esquitele* is also unknown, but *esquiter* means "to shit."

245–46. Neither word at the rhyme is attested elsewhere. Since it is audible, *desverdellier* must refer to some sort of noise. Noomen's suggestion to take *borbeillier* as onomatopoeia seems right to me. *Barbouiller* ("to smear") would work later in the story, but not at this point.

313–14. The reference to his martyrdom indicates that this must be Saint Germain of Scotland, not the Saint Germain usually invoked in Old French texts.

351. Proverb.

390. July 25.

419–20. Proverb.

5 2. The Two Peasants

5. A village a few kilometers southeast of Douai.

6. The region around the Belgian border due north of Reims.

102. In the first *branche* of the *Roman de Renart*, the bear gets his muzzle caught in a tree trunk the woodcutter Lanfroi has wedged open.

137. *Sent* means "smells" as well as "feels."

141. *Mongiu* is the Saint Bernard Pass, between Italy and Switzerland.

162. No one has proposed a satisfactory explanation of *engite*. For want of anything better, I hazard the past participle of *engesir*, "to put to bed," in other words "lying in it," or perhaps we should read *en giste* in the sense of "she's made her bed."

168. The area south of Belgium between Douai and Valenciennes.

169. The society of wandering scholar-performers.

171. Two towns in the Ostrevant.

180. Idiomatically, *lembeaus* means "shenanigans," but its literal sense is "frippery." Le Leu thus suggests the wife has both supposedly literally soiled their sheets and actually done so in the figurative sense. *Molt vilain giu* (line 142) already points in that direction.

5 3. The Three Hunchbacks

7–8. Although the author claims not to know where the incident happened and only gives Douai as an example, the layout of the town indicates that the story probably does take place there.

113–15. A difficult passage. *Chaaliz* means "bed frame" and *escrins* "chests," but why should they move the furniture? Perhaps for warmth, but *charriier* could simply imply that they use it for storage. Its closeness to the hearth may explain the hunchbacks' death from overheating and/or suffocation.

241. Patron saint of Douai. At a public display of his relics in 1139, a nimbus appeared over the head of whoever touched them.

5 4. *The Portable Priest*

This fabliau is most commonly known as "The Sacristan Monk." "Le Prestre conporté" is the title given to another, and in my opinion, not nearly as good, fabliau with a similar plot.

23–24. The city of Provins held fairs in May, September, and starting the last day of November.

172. The Old French has "Nabugor," a fabulously wealthy emir of Babylonia in the *Roman d'Alexandre*.

336–37. That is, "May God turn His eyes from the person who would allow such a thing."

368. Proverb.

428. I translate thus because the prior thinks the sacristan has fallen asleep at his business, but as Noomen points out, as sacristan he was responsible for setting out the book open to the right place in advance of the reading of the epistle.

452–55. Murder because the sacristan would have been killed at night and people will believe it was premeditated (Beaumanoir, art. 825).

554. Saint Laud, not the Old Testament figure whose wife turned into a pillar of salt.

5 5. *Constant du Hamel*

3. There are two villages in Picardy called Le Hamel, about fifteen kilometers east and thirty kilometers southwest of Amiens. Since *hamel* means "hamlet," the name may simply indicate the hero's status.

90. Literally, "I'll keep throwing myself at her."

94. Proverb: loosely, "You can't argue with necessity."

201. Marriage between a child's godparents constituted incestuous adultery.

296–97. Constant protests he has been framed. The presence of the wheat in his home does not conclusively prove he himself stole it (Beaumanoir, art. 942).

371. Beaumanoir (art. 905) assesses compensation for stealing timber at only sixty sous (three pounds), but taking it at night would make it larceny.

897. Northern Holland.

951. That is, the money he had promised so they would let him off the hook.

57. *The Chaplain's Goose*

3. Noomen identifies Suevre as a river that once flowed into the Seine near what is now the southwest corner of Paris. The suburb of Sèvres still bears its name.
30–31. Proverb.
33–34. A proverb, but not Solomon's.
75. The line stands alone. The earliest editors postulated a missing line that rhymed with it. Noomen, because of its assonance with the next couplets, suggests three lines on the same rhyme. Perhaps we should delete it. The information is pertinent but not strictly necessary for the sense. The events make clear that he had a long time to wait.
106–7. Literally, "Now the priest can eat his goose and make his soup with different bread," an allusion to a proverb: "You can't make soup without bread."

59. *The Fucker*

36. Perhaps we should understand "who never spins" as her nickname. It implies that she is a fine and wealthy lady.
248. We might also understand "It's not as if your soul were at stake!" *L'ame* means "the soul" and *lame* means "blade."
381–82. A favorite fabliau proverb: "He who moves has fun; he who sits all the time dries up."

60. *The Squirrel*

41. *Peesche* (Old French 40) may be a *hapax*. The dictionaries see it as a derivative of *pechier* and cite it as an obscene euphemism, in the first case etymologically improbable, and in the second unjustified in the context of a girl who mischievously pretends innocence. Montaiglon-Raynaud gloss it as *pesque* ("scrap of cloth").
119. Wordplay on *vis/viz*. The line means both "He's very lively" and "He's one hundred percent penis."

125. Since squirrels make nests, common belief held that they also laid eggs.

133–34. Compare "The Girl Who Wanted to Fly," where the student "grafts a tail" onto the girl. The line also hints at cuckolding (*faire la coe*).

61. *The Maiden Who Couldn't Abide Lewd Language*

22–23. The author underscores and belittles the girl's prudery by a sudden incongruous switch from polite diction to the most vulgar words in the language. *Lecherie*, which she cannot countenance either, is a perfectly proper— in fact, an ecclesiastical—term.

56. Some traditions associated Saint Nicholas with travelers and hospitality.

62. *Saint Martin's Four Wishes*

57. The harridan cuts short her invective and for the space of this one line cajolingly addresses her husband using the intimate *tu*. She immediately switches back to *vous*, now a mark of deference. He generally uses *tu*. By the plural in line 70 he may mean "all you women," and perhaps 77–85 simply follow through. I cannot account for her use of *tu* in 157–58. Old French often does not bother distinguishing consistently between the two.

189–90. Proverbial.

63. *The Little Rag Mouse*

95. "Sniff around": *Parpillier* is a *hapax*. Montaiglon-Raynaud translate "ejaculate," which strikes me as premature.

65. *The Blacksmith of Creil*

3. A city on the Oise, on the southern border of Picardy, forty-five kilometers north of Paris.

33. The French says "a Corbeil onion." Corbeil could be any one of several French towns.

109. The closest Saint-Leu or Saint-Loup to Creil (there are some thirty of them in France) is Saint-Leu-d'Esserent, five kilometers downstream.

174–75. Proverbial.

6⁊. Mr. Greed and Mr. Envy

6. This could also mean "to speak the truth in a lie."

8–9. Proverb.

39. Saint Martin prepares to take leave of them, knowing that the sinners' road leads to the left, away from the path of righteousness.

68. Brownie, the Priest's Cow

3. August 15.

29. Ananias and his wife are struck dead for the same lie in the opening story of Acts 5.

66–67. Cf. the parable of the talents, Matthew 25.14–30. Noomen believes 66 must originally have read *qui*, but I am convinced the cynicism is intentional. The fabliau credits luck, not God, for the "miracle" of the two cows, and neither priest nor peasant takes the sermon in good faith.

72. Proverb.

69. The Man Who Saved His Buddy from Drowning

68. Proverb.

69–71. Proverb.

LIST OF *FABLIAUX* MANUSCRIPTS

A   Paris, Bibliothèque nationale, fr. 837
B   Berne, Bibilothèque de la Bourgeoisie, 354
C   Berlin, Deutsche Staatsbibliothek, Hamilton 257
D   Paris, Bibliothèque nationale, fr. 19152
E   Paris, Bibliothèque nationale, fr. 1593
F   Paris, Bibliothèque nationale, fr. 12603
G   Nottingham, University Library, Middleton L.M. 6
H   Paris, Bibliothèque nationale, fr. 2168
I   Paris, Bibliothèque nationale, fr. 25545
J   Paris, Bibliothèque nationale, fr. 1553
K   Paris, Bibliothèque nationale, fr. 2173
L   Paris, Bibliothèque nationale, fr. 1635
M   London, British Library, Harley 2253
O   Pavia, Biblioteca dell' Università, Aldini 219
P   Paris, Bibliothèque nationale, fr. 24432
Q   Paris, Bibliothèque nationale, fr. nouv. acq. 1104
R   Paris, Bibliothèque de l'Arsenal, 3524
S   Paris, Bibliothèque de l'Arsenal, 3525
T   Chantilly, Condé 475 (1578)
U   Turin, Biblioteca Nazionale, L. V. 32 (copy: Paris, Bibl. nat., fonds Moreau 1727)
V   Genève, Bibliothèque publique et universitaire, fr. 175bis
V^{bis} Lyon, Bibliothèque municipale, 5495
W   Paris, Bibliothèque nationale, fr. 1446
X   Paris, Bibliothèque nationale, fr. 12581
Y   London, British Library, Ass. 10289
Z   Oxford, Bodleian Library, Digby 86
a   Paris, Bibliothèque nationale, fr. 375
d   Paris, Bibliothèque nationale, fr. 14971
e   Paris, Bibliothèque de l'Arsenal, 3114
f   Chartres, Bibliothèque municipale, 620

g	Paris, Bibliothèque nationale, Rotschild 2800
i	Clermont-Ferrand, Archives du Puy-de-Dôme
j	Paris, Bibliothèque nationale, fr. 2188
k	Troyes, Paris, Bibliothèque municipale, 1511
l	Cologny, Bodmer 113
m	Le Mans, Bibliothèque municipale, 5495
n	Oudenaerde, Décanat 3
o	Oxford, Bodleian Library, Douce 111
p	Paris, Bibliothèque de l'Arsenal, 3527
q	Paris, Bibliothèque nationale, nouv. acq. fr.934
r	Turin, Biblioteca nazionale, 1639
s	Cheltenham, Philips 25970

BIBLIOGRAPHY

EDITIONS

Barbazan, Etienne, and Dominique M. Méon. *Fabliaux et contes des poëtes françois des XI, XII, XIII, XIV et XVᵉ siècles.* 4 vols. Paris, 1808–23; rpt., Geneva: Slatkine, 1975.

Faral, Edmond, and Julia Bastin. *Œuvres complètes de Rutebeuf.* Paris: Picard, 1969.

Levy, B. J. *Selected Fabliaux, edited from BN f. fr. 837, f. fr. 9152 and Berlin Hamilton 257,* with notes by C. E. Pickford. Kingston upon Hull, UK: University of Hull, 1978.

Livingston, Charles H. *Le Jongleur Gautier le Leu: étude sur les fabliaux.* Cambridge, MA: Harvard University Press, 1951.

Manfellotto, Annalisa Landolfi. *I 'fabliaux' de Jean de Condé. Edizione critica, con introduzione, note e glossario.* L'Aquila, Italy: Japadre, 1981.

Montaiglon, Anatole de, and Gaston Raynaud. *Recueil général et complet des fabliaux des XIIIᵉ et XIVᵉ siècles.* 6 vols. Paris: Librairie de Bibliophiles, 1872–90; rpt., Geneva: Slatkine, 1973.

Nardin, Pierre. *Jean Bodel. Fabliaux, nouvelle édition revue et augmentée.* Paris: Nizet, 1965.

Noomen, Willem, and Nico van den Bogaard. *Nouveau Recueil Complet des Fabliaux.* 10 vols. Assen, Netherlands: Van Gorcum, 1983–98.

Rychner, Jean. *Contribution à l'étude des fabliaux. Variantes, remaniements, dégradations,* vol. II: *Textes.* Neuchâtel, Geneva: University of Neuchâtel, 1960.

Zink, M. *Rutebeuf. Œuvres complètes.* Paris: Bordos, 1989.

CRITICISM

Beach, Charles Ray. *Treatment of Ecclesiastics in the French Fabliaux of the Middle Ages.* Modern Language Series, 34. Lexington: University Press of Kentucky, 1960.

Bédier, Joseph. *Les Fabliaux: Etudes de littérature populaire et d'histoire littéraire du moyen âge.* Paris, 1894; 6th ed., Paris: Champion, 1964.

Beyer, Jürgen. *Schwank und Moral: Untersuchungen zum altfranzösischen Fabliau und verwandten Formen.* Heidelberg, Germany: Carl Winter Universitätsverlag, 1969.

Blankenburg, Wilhelm. *Der Vilain in der Schilderung der altfranzösichen Fabliaux.* Greifswald, Germany: J. Abel, 1902.

Bloch, R. Howard. *The Scandal of the Fabliaux.* Chicago: University of Chicago Press, 1986.

Burns, E. Jane. *Bodytalk: When Women Speak in Old French Literature.* Philadelphia: University of Pennsylvania Press, 1993.

Cooke, Thomas D. *The Old French and Chaucerian Fabliaux: A Study of Their Comic Climax.* Columbia: University of Missouri Press, 1978.

Cooke, Thomas D., and Benjamin L. Honeycutt, eds. *The Humor of the Fabliaux: A Collection of Critical Essays.* Columbia: University of Missouri Press, 1974.

Crocker, Holly, ed. *Comic Provocations: Exposing the Corpus of Old French Fablaiux.* New York: Palgrave Macmillan, 2006.

Faral, Edmond. *Les Jongleurs en France au moyen âge.* Paris: Champion, 1910.

Gaunt, Simon. *Gender and Genre in Medieval French Literature.* Cambridge, UK: Cambridge University Press, 1995.

Gravdal, Kathryn. *Vilain and Courtois: Transgressive Parody in French Literature of the Twelfth and Thirteenth Centuries.* Lincoln: University of Nebraska Press, 1989.

Jordogne, Omer. *Le Fabliau et le lai narratif.* Turnhout, Belgium: Brepols, 1975.

Lacy, Norris J. *Reading Fabliaux.* New York and London: Garland Publishing, 1993.

Levy, Brian J. *The Comic Text: Patterns and Images in the Old French Fabliaux.* Amsterdam: Rodopi, 2000.

Lorcin, Marie-Thérèse. *Façons de sentir et de penser: les fabliaux français.* Paris: Champion, 1979.

Ménard, Philippe. *Les Fabliaux: contes à rire du moyen âge.* Paris: Presses Universitaires de France, 1983.

Merl, Hans-Dieter. *Untersuchungen zur Struktur, Stilistik und Syntax in den Fabliaux Jean Bodels.* Bern, Switzerland: Lang, 1972.

———. *Untersuchungen zur Struktur, Stilistik und Syntax in den Fabliaux Rutebeufs, Gautier Le Leus und Jean de Condés.* Bern, Switzerland: Lang, 1976.

Muscatine, Charles. *The Old French Fabliaux.* New Haven: Yale University Press, 1986.

Nykrog, Per. *Les Fabliaux: Etude d'histoire littéraire det de stylistique médiévale.* Copenhagen: Munksgaard, 1957; rpt., Geneva: Droz, 1973.

Perfetti, Lisa. *Women and Laughter in Medieval French Comic Literature.* Ann Arbor: University of Michigan Press, 2003.

Pfeffer, Peter. *Beiträge zur Kenntnis des altfranzösischen Volkslebens, meist auf Grund der Fabliaux.* 3 vols. Karlsruhe, Germany: Malsh & Vogel, 1898–1901.

Ribaud, Jacques. *Un Ménestrel du XIV siècle: Jean de Condé.* Geneva: Droz, 1969.

Ruggiers, Paul G., ed. *Versions of Medieval Comedy.* Norman: University of Oklahoma Press, 1977.

Rychner, Jean. *Contribution à l'étude des fabliaux. Variantes, remaniements, dégradations.* 2 vols. Geneva: Droz, 1960.

Stearns-Schenk, Mary Jane. *The Fabliaux: Tales of Wit and Deception.* Amsterdam and Philadelphia: John Benjamins, 1987.

Tiemann, H. *Die Entstehung der mittelalterlichen Novell in Frankreich.* Hamburg: Europa-Kolleg, 1961.

TRAINED IN ROMANCE PHILOLOGY with a specialization in Old French dialects, Nathaniel E. Dubin received his doctorate from the University of Washington. A Regents Professor Emeritus of modern and classical languages at St. John's University in Minnesota, he retired after thirty-seven years of teaching all levels of French language, literature, and civilization. During his tenure, he directed numerous study abroad programs in France and was also a regular instructor in the university's capstone ethics course.

For the past twenty years, Dubin has worked sporadically on his verse translations of, to date, some ten dozen Old French comic tales, most of them fabliaux, sixty-nine of which appear in this volume. This project resulted from a coming together of two summer programs sponsored by the National Endowment for the Humanities. The first, held in 1989 at the University of California, Santa Cruz, and devoted to literary translation, interested Dubin not as a translator but as a teacher of French who used literary translation as an exercise in his advanced stylistics course. The second, held three years later at the University of California, Berkeley, was R. Howard Bloch's seminar on the fabliaux, works with which Dubin had only a passing familiarity. Reading extensively in the genre for the first time, he sensed that one could "hear" the idiom of everyday speech behind the octosyllabic rhymed couplets. It was thus with an eye (and ear) to what he perceived as a new sound in Old French letters that Dubin undertook his translations.

The naturalness of fabliau style, as opposed to an elegant and sometimes stilted literary diction, is not just a matter of crude vocabulary; it affects the very syntax of the language and sounds more authentic than the flowery prose that was soon to make an appearance. The difference is immediately apparent if one compares the fabliaux and plays of authors like Jean Bodel and Rutebeuf with their other works. No doubt this is intentional. Where a fabliau seeks to parody courtly literature, as in "The Knight Who Made Cunts Talk," the literary idiom prevails, and the peasant's rhetoric in "The Soul That Argued Its Way into Heaven" is more literary than that of the saints.

Dubin makes his home in St. Cloud, Minnesota.

ABOUT THE INTRODUCER

R. HOWARD BLOCH is the Sterling Professor of French and chair of the Humanities Program at Yale University. He has written a number of works that make the Middle Ages less dark, more accessible, exciting, and vivid— *Medieval French Literature and Law, Etymologies and Genealogies, The Scandal of the Fabliaux, Medieval Misogyny and the Invention of Western Romantic Love, The Anonymous Marie de France, A Needle in the Right Hand of God.*

Nothing matches the fabliaux when it comes to bringing the medieval past alive. Bloch found himself laughing out loud, astonished by just how outrageous, wicked, and hilarious these depictions of everyday life in the twelfth and thirteenth centuries could be. When it comes to humor, the only human appetite to increase rather than to diminish with age, medieval poets are the equal of the ancient Greeks as well as the funniest of the moderns—Rabelais, Swift, Molière, Feydeau, Wodehouse, or Wilde. Bloch's natural desire as a teacher to share his experience with others was limited by a lack of translations as peppy and witty as the original Old French. The encounter with Nathaniel Dubin in a NEH summer seminar in the early 1990s was the beginning of the opening of a window upon medieval humor whose rich riotousness is now accessible to the English-speaking world.